P9-CCG-305

BECOMING AN
ACTIVE READER

A COMPLETE RESOURCE FOR READING AND WRITING

ERIC HENDERSON

OXFORD
UNIVERSITY PRESS

OXFORD
UNIVERSITY PRESS

Oxford University Press is a department of the University of Oxford.
It furthers the University's objective of excellence in research, scholarship,
and education by publishing worldwide. Oxford is a registered trade mark of
Oxford University Press in the UK and in certain other countries.

Published in Canada by
Oxford University Press
8 Sampson Mews, Suite 204,
Don Mills, Ontario M3C 0H5 Canada

www.oupcanada.com

Copyright © Oxford University Press Canada 2013

The moral rights of the author have been asserted

Database right Oxford University Press (maker)

All rights reserved. No part of this publication may be reproduced, stored in
a retrieval system, or transmitted, in any form or by any means, without the
prior permission in writing of Oxford University Press, or as expressly permitted
by law, by licence, or under terms agreed with the appropriate reprographics
rights organization. Enquiries concerning reproduction outside the scope of the
above should be sent to the Permissions Department at the address above
or through the following url: www.oupcanada.com/permission/permission_request.php

Every effort has been made to determine and contact copyright holders.
In the case of any omissions, the publisher will be pleased to make
suitable acknowledgement in future editions.

Library and Archives Canada Cataloguing in Publication
Henderson, Eric–
Becoming an active reader : a complete resource for reading
and writing / Eric Henderson.
Includes index.
ISBN 978-0-19-544750-7
1. English language--Rhetoric--Textbooks. 2. Academic writing--
Textbooks. 3. Report writing--Textbooks. 4. Reading comprehension--
Textbooks. 5. College readers. I. Title.

PE1408.H3854 2013   808'.042   C2012-907630-9

Cover image: leaf/Veer

This book is printed on permanent (acid-free) paper ∞.

Printed and bound in Canada

2 3 4 5 — 16 15 14 13

Contents

PART 2   READING

Chapter 6   Interacting with Texts   104

Chapter 7   Critical Thinking   113

READINGS

PART 3   HANDBOOK

Preface

Becoming an Active Reader is a multi-purpose textbook designed primarily for first-year college and university students in Canada. It is divided into a rhetoric and research guide (Part 1), a reader with 38 academic and non-academic readings (Part 2), and a writing handbook (Part 3). It is essential that today's textbook reflect the needs of both instructors and their students. *Becoming an Active Reader* aspires to this goal by its review of composition principles and practices in Chapter 1 and by the inclusion of common forms of first-year student writing; the summary, the rhetorical analysis, the argumentative essay, and the research paper are thoroughly discussed in Chapters 2–5. Points are amply illustrated by examples from student writing and excerpts from the readings in Part 2. *Becoming an Active Reader* is thus a practical, integrated text.

The stress on argument in Part 1 reflects a developing trend in composition pedagogy: the use of argument to introduce students to research. To this end, Chapter 4 features a student argumentative essay that employs research, with more specific information on research following in Chapter 5. Chapter 4 begins with the introduction of three models of argument before breaking down argument into various purposes, giving students a wider than usual frame of reference. Similarly, students are encouraged to think beyond Aristotle's three appeals—important as these are—in planning an argument.

Much of Part 2 (Chapters 6–10) focuses on areas neglected by traditional textbooks, which often present readings without concrete strategies for approaching and analyzing them. However, knowing the techniques and strategies of academic writers, as well as where important information is located, can make challenging essays more accessible and increase confidence (not to mention enjoyment) in the reading process—as well as promote class discussion.

Chapter 6 begins with general reading strategies and concludes with close reading techniques to ensure understanding of challenging material. Reinforcing the chapter on argument (Chapter 4), Chapter 7 helps students connect good argument with critical thinking. Too often, critical thinking remains an abstract concept as well-meaning instructors simply encourage students to exercise their critical thinking faculties, whatever that might mean. In this chapter, critical thinking is defined, then broken down through the use of concrete examples, exercises, and questions designed to engage students deeply and practically in the process of critical thinking.

In their academic careers, students will be exposed to various kinds of writing; through examples and clear explanation, Chapters 8–10 introduce students to the distinctive features of non-academic and academic prose. Whereas Chapter 8 orients the student by explaining basic similarities and differences, the two subsequent chapters identify features of both non-academic and academic writing discussing them within the context of the student's own writing aims and practices.

The readings in Part 2 introduce students to a variety of written discourse, including across-the-disciplines writing and different essay types, from personal and reflective essays to journalistic and academic essays, including scientific papers and review essays. Introductions to each section as well as each essay promote students' active reading and critical thinking skills at all stages of the reading and writing process. The 11 scholarly essays in Part 2 were chosen for their interest and accessibility—all are relatively short and discuss topics of interest to many students; they also illustrate key features discussed in Chapter 10.

Part 3 provides the basic resources for clear, grammatical writing. The stress falls on common, everyday errors, but more comprehensive information is also included (often in summary form, such as tables). Students are encouraged to analyze their own sentences rather than memorize a set of rules. For example, rather than dividing the section on punctuation into the comma, the colon, and the semi-colon followed by lists of rules and common errors, students learn to recognize specific contexts in their own writing and to approach "correctness" according to these contexts. In addition, the copious real-life examples from student writing are designed to help students see clear and correct prose as relevant to the various kinds of writing they do in college or university.

Of course, such comprehensiveness can be achieved only by some omissions. However, exhaustive information on citation styles can be found on college and university library websites, so only the most common formats appear in the research guide (Chapter 5); students can further test their knowledge of grammatical rules (Chapters 11–13) by accessing the companion website for this book or the many other online sources sponsored by educational institutions.

Highlights

Oxford University Press is delighted to introduce *Becoming an Active Reader*, an accessible, student-friendly approach to reading and writing effectively. With a guide to rhetoric and research, a reader, and a grammar handbook together in one volume, augmented by the following special features, students can be assured they have everything they need for success in their post-secondary classrooms and beyond at their fingertips.

Special-topic boxes offer checklists, FAQs, and review tools for quick reference.

Individual and collaborative exercises provide ample opportunity for practising skills.

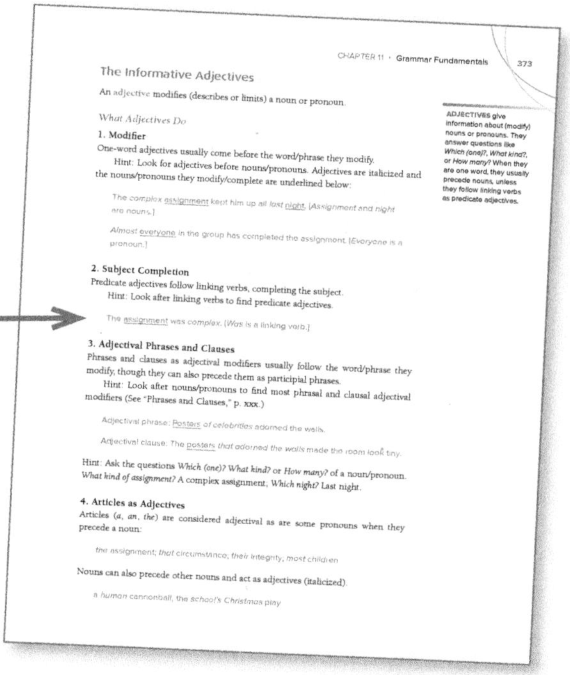
CHAPTER 11 · Grammar Fundamentals 373

The Informative Adjectives

An *adjective* modifies (describes or limits) a noun or pronoun.

What Adjectives Do

1. Modifier

One-word adjectives usually come before the word/phrase they modify.

Hint: Look for adjectives before nouns/pronouns. Adjectives are italicized and the nouns/pronouns they modify/complete are underlined below:

The complex assignment kept him up all last night. [Assignment and night are nouns.]

Almost everyone in the group has completed the assignment. [Everyone is a pronoun.]

2. Subject Completion

Predicate adjectives follow linking verbs, completing the subject.

Hint: Look after linking verbs to find predicate adjectives.

The assignment was *complex*. [Was is a linking verb.]

3. Adjectival Phrases and Clauses

Phrases and clauses as adjectival modifiers usually follow the word/phrase they modify, though they can also precede them as participial phrases.

Hint: Look after nouns/pronouns to find most phrasal and clausal adjectival modifiers (See "Phrases and Clauses," p. xxx.)

Adjectival phrase: Posters *of celebrities* adorned the walls.

Adjectival clause: The posters *that adorned the walls* made the room look tiny.

Hint: Ask the questions *Which (one)? What kind?* or *How many?* of a noun/pronoun. *What kind of assignment?* A complex assignment; *Which night?* Last night.

4. Articles as Adjectives

Articles (*a, an, the*) are considered adjectival as are some pronouns when they precede a noun:

the assignment; *that* circumstance; *their* integrity; *most* children

Nouns can also precede other nouns and act as adjectives (italicized).

a human cannonball, *the school's Christmas* play

ADJECTIVES give information about (modify) nouns or pronouns. They answer questions like *Which (one)?, What kind?,* or *How many?* When they are one word, they usually precede nouns, unless they follow linking verbs as predicate adjectives.

Part 3 hints
give useful prompts for remembering grammatical structures and functions.

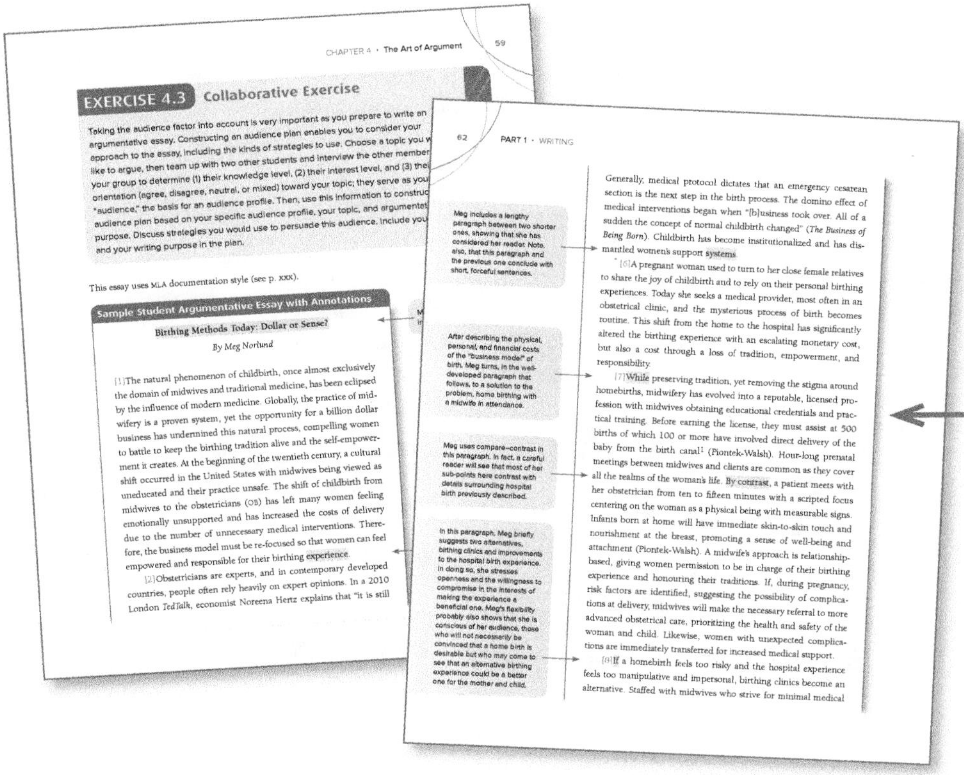
CHAPTER 4 · The Art of Argument 59

EXERCISE 4.3 Collaborative Exercise

Taking the audience factor into account is very important as you prepare to write an argumentative essay. Constructing an audience plan enables you to consider your approach to the essay, including the kinds of strategies to use. Choose a topic you w… like to argue, then team up with two other students and interview the other member… your group to determine (1) their knowledge level, (2) their interest level, and (3) thei… orientation (agree, disagree, neutral, or mixed) toward your topic; they serve as you… "audience," the basis for an audience profile. Then, use this information to construc… audience plan based on your specific audience profile, your topic, and argumentat… purpose. Discuss strategies you would use to persuade this audience. Include you… and your writing purpose in the plan.

This essay uses MLA documentation style (see p. xxx).

Sample Student Argumentative Essay with Annotations

Birthing Methods Today: Dollar or Sense?

By Meg Norlund

[1]The natural phenomenon of childbirth, once almost exclusively the domain of midwives and traditional medicine, has been eclipsed by the influence of modern medicine. Globally, the practice of midwifery is a proven system, yet the opportunity for a billion dollar business has undermined this natural process, compelling women to battle to keep the birthing tradition alive and the self-empowerment it creates. At the beginning of the twentieth century, a cultural shift occurred in the United States with midwives being viewed as uneducated and their practice unsafe. The shift of childbirth from midwives to the obstetricians (OB) has left many women feeling emotionally unsupported and has increased the costs of delivery due to the number of unnecessary medical interventions. Therefore, the business model must be re-focused so that women can feel empowered and responsible for their birthing experience.

[2]Obstetricians are experts, and in contemporary developed countries, people often rely heavily on expert opinions. In a 2010 London *TedTalk*, economist Noreena Hertz explains that "it is still

62 PART 1 · WRITING

Generally, medical protocol dictates that an emergency cesarean section is the next step in the birth process. The domino effect of medical interventions began when "[b]usiness took over. All of a sudden the concept of normal childbirth changed" (*The Business of Being Born*). Childbirth has become institutionalized and has dismantled women's support systems.

[6]A pregnant woman used to turn to her close female relatives to share the joy of childbirth and to rely on their personal birthing experiences. Today she seeks a medical provider, most often in an obstetrical clinic, and the mysterious process of birth becomes routine. This shift from the home to the hospital has significantly altered the birthing experience with an escalating monetary cost, but also a cost through a loss of tradition, empowerment, and responsibility.

[7]While preserving tradition, yet removing the stigma around homebirths, midwifery has evolved into a reputable, licensed profession with midwives obtaining educational credentials and practical training. Before earning the license, they must assist at 500 births of which 100 or more have involved direct delivery of the baby from the birth canal[1] (Piontek-Walsh). Hour-long prenatal meetings between midwives and clients are common as they cover all the realms of the woman's life. By contrast, a patient meets with her obstetrician from ten to fifteen minutes with a scripted focus centering on the woman as a physical being with measurable signs. Infants born at home will have immediate skin-to-skin touch and nourishment at the breast, promoting a sense of well-being and attachment (Piontek-Walsh). A midwife's approach is relationship-based, giving women permission to be in charge of their birthing experience and honouring their traditions. If, during pregnancy, risk factors are identified, suggesting the possibility of complications at delivery, midwives will make the necessary referral to more advanced obstetrical care, prioritizing the health and safety of the woman and child. Likewise, women with unexpected complications are immediately transferred for increased medical support.

[8]If a homebirth feels too risky and the hospital experience feels too manipulative and impersonal, birthing clinics become an alternative. Staffed with midwives who strive for minimal medical

Meg includes a lengthy paragraph between two shorter ones, showing that she has considered her reader. Note, also, that this paragraph and the previous one conclude with short, forceful sentences.

After describing the physical, personal, and financial costs of the "business model" of birth, Meg turns, in the well-developed paragraph that follows, to a solution to the problem, home birthing with a midwife in attendance.

Meg uses compare–contrast in this paragraph. In fact, a careful reader will see that most of her sub-points here contrast with details surrounding hospital birth previously described.

In this paragraph, Meg briefly suggests two alternatives, birthing clinics and improvements to the hospital birth experience. In doing so, she stresses openness and the willingness to compromise in the interests of making the experience a beneficial one. Meg's flexibility probably also shows that she is conscious of her audience, those who will not necessarily be convinced that a home birth is desirable but who may come to see that an alternative birthing experience could be a better one for the mother and child.

Annotated sample student essays
illustrate important techniques for good writing and rhetorical styles.

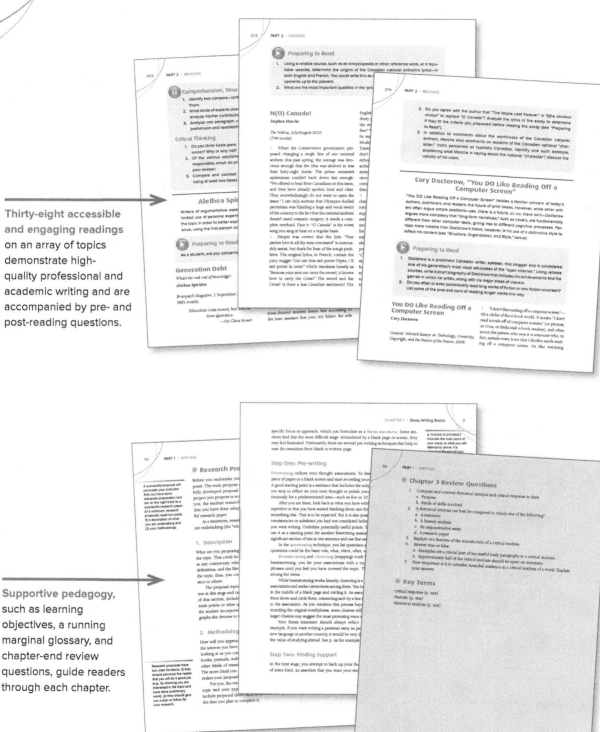

Thirty-eight accessible and engaging readings on an array of topics demonstrate high-quality professional and academic writing and are accompanied by pre- and post-reading questions.

Supportive pedagogy, such as learning objectives, a running marginal glossary, and chapter-end review questions, guide readers through each chapter.

Acknowledgements

As always, I wish to gratefully acknowledge the editorial staff at Oxford University Press Canada for their confidence in my work, as well as their enthusiasm and expertise in this, my fifth textbook with the Press. I would particularly like to thank Jodi Lewchuk for her excellent editorial guidance, as well as Leslie Saffrey for her constructive copyediting. Thanks also to reviewers Mark Feltham, Fanshawe College; Terry B. Jackson, College of New Caledonia; Matt Kavanaugh, Okanagan College; Teresa MacVicar, Conestoga College; Raj Mehta, Camosun College; Beth Ann Wiersma, Lambton College; and others who gave feedback anonymously, whose comments on both the proposal and draft manuscript helped to shape this first edition of *Becoming an Active Reader*.

For their generosity, I am indebted to the late Danielle Forster and to University of Victoria Research Librarian Scott Johnson, who updated the section on pages 73–80 originally written by Danielle. Feedback from many of my colleagues at the University of Victoria on *The Active Reader* provided an impetus for this book. I also acknowledge the many students who allowed their writing to be represented here.

Finally, I am grateful to my family for all manner of intellectual and creative stimulation, along with their support, love, and personal affirmation.

PART 1
WRITING

CHAPTER 1

Essay Writing Basics

In this chapter, you will learn:

◎ How to take a step-by-step approach to essay writing

◎ How to write an introduction with a strong thesis statement

◎ How to write unified, coherent, and developed paragraphs

◎ How to support your claim through evidence

◎ How to write a conclusion

Academic discourse can be thought of as a set of oral and written procedures used to generate and spread ideas within the academic community. Many of these ideas will be discussed outside the academic community by non-academics.

Academic discourse can be thought of as a set of oral and written procedures used to generate and spread ideas within the academic community. Most classes you take in college or university focus on written discourse: by writing down your thoughts, you are recording them to be analyzed by others (and, yes, usually graded).

This chapter focuses on the basic conventions of the student essay. Later chapters will consider more specific forms that student writing can take: summary, critical response, rhetorical analysis, argumentive essay, and research paper. Although there are many differences among these, in most cases they will draw on the elements discussed in this chapter.

An essay, like most projects, is written in stages. Although academic writing may emphasize revising and editing the rough draft or research more than you are used to, students approach academic writing knowing that it is a chronological process that usually begins with a broad topic.

◎ From Blank Page to Thesis

Using pre-writing techniques, you explore the topic, asking what you know and what you want to find out about it. The goal is to narrow the topic to express your specific focus or approach, which you formulate as a thesis statement. Some students find this the most difficult stage: intimidated by a blank page or screen, they may feel frustrated. Fortunately, there are several pre-writing techniques that help to ease the transition from blank to written page.

Step One: Pre-writing

Freewriting utilizes your thought associations. To freewrite, begin with a blank piece of paper or a blank screen and start recording your associations with a subject. A good starting point is a sentence that includes the subject you want to explore. Do not stop to reflect on your next thought or polish your writing: simply write continuously for a predetermined time—such as five or 10 minutes.

After you are done, look back at what you have written. You may find much of it repetitive or that you have started thinking about one thing and suddenly switched to something else. That is to be expected. But it is also possible that your writing reveals consistencies or subtleties you had not considered before or were not aware of when you were writing. Underline potentially useful points. You can take the best one and use it as a starting point for another freewriting session, or you could summarize a significant section of text in one sentence and use that sentence as a new starting point.

In the questioning technique, you list questions about the topic. Initially, these questions could be the basic *who, what, where, when, why, how.*

Brainstorming and clustering (mapping) work by generating associations. In brainstorming, you list your associations with a topic, writing down words and phrases until you feel you have covered the topic. Then you look for connections among the items.

While brainstorming works linearly, clustering is a spatial technique that generates associations and seeks connections among them. You begin by writing a word or phrase in the middle of a blank page and circling it. As associations occur to you, you write them down and circle them, connecting each by a line to the word/phrase that gave rise to the association. As you continue this process beyond the first words/phrases surrounding the original word/phrase, some clusters will become larger than others. The larger clusters may suggest the most promising ways to develop your topic.

Your thesis statement should always reflect your purpose in writing. For example, if you were writing a personal essay as part of your application to study a new language in another country, it would be very different from a research essay on the value of studying abroad. See p. 8 for examples of thesis statements.

Step Two: Finding Support

In the next stage, you attempt to back up your thesis. A thesis statement is a claim of some kind, an assertion that you want your reader to accept. This is where your

A **THESIS STATEMENT** includes the main point of your essay or what you will attempt to prove; it is placed at the end of your introduction.

FREEWRITING is a pre-writing technique in which you write on a subject without stopping to edit.

QUESTIONING is a pre-writing technique in which you list questions about the topic.

BRAINSTORMING is a pre-writing technique in which you list your associations with a subject in the order they occur to you.

CLUSTERING is a pre-writing technique that works spatially to generate associations with a subject and connections among them.

SUPPORT consists of evidence to help prove a claim.

support comes in. For example, although you could claim that the dog ate your homework, your instructor is not likely to take such a claim seriously. But if you produced your vet bill, the claim would have some support. If you were writing a critical analysis of a poem, the support would need to come from the poem itself (primary source). If you were writing a research paper, you would need to find out what other people have said or written about the topic as it relates to your thesis (secondary sources).

Your general claim (thesis statement) must be supported by more specific claims (main points), which, in turn, require support in the form of references to primary sources (English or history essay) or factual information such as statistics or secondary sources (research essay). If, during this stage, it becomes clear that you cannot support your thesis, consider adapting the thesis to be in line with the support you have found—or, you might have to come up with a new thesis.

Step Three: Organizing

When you have found enough support, you can begin thinking about how you will connect the general claim (thesis statement) to the specific claims (main points) and their support. With this in mind, you begin organizing claims and support in a logical and consistent way, one that clearly expresses the relationship between each claim and its support. One way to clarify these relationships is to construct an outline, a schematic representation of the essay and a plan you can use in the composing stage to keep yourself on track.

An **OUTLINE** is a linear or graphic representation of main points and sub-points, showing an essay's structure.

An outline can be a brief listing of your main points: a *scratch* or *sketch outline* is often used for an in-class or exam essay when you do not have much planning time. With a longer essay, an outline can include levels of sub-points (developments of main points) along with details and examples. The *formal outline* uses a number/letter scheme to represent the essay's complete structure. The conventional scheme goes like this:

I. First main point (topic sentence of paragraph)
   A. First sub-point (development of main point)
      1. First sub-sub-point (development of sub-point: detail or example)
      2. Second sub-sub-point
   B. Second sub-point
      1. First sub-sub-point
      2. Second sub-sub-point

This example represents a paragraph with a three-level outline—that is, one main point and two sub-points.

When you are considering your outline, especially if it is a formal outline, remember that it serves as the blueprint for the essay itself. Therefore, to construct a useful outline, you should ask questions like the following:

- How do the main points in my outline relate to my thesis statement?
- How do the sub-points relate to my main points?
- Do I have enough main points to support my thesis?
- Do I have enough sub-points (at least two) for each main point?
- Are there any points that seem either irrelevant or out of place? If the latter, where do they belong?
- What is the most effective order for my points? Are my points logically connected? What kinds of transitions would help connect them?
- Can points be expanded? Have I covered everything my reader would expect me to cover?

It's important that you consider your outline an "essay in the works," one that can be adapted as you proceed. Even the most polished and detailed outline can be changed if you find a better way to organize your ideas or new, important approaches to your topic.

Step Four: Composing

Making the commitment to the first draft is difficult for students and non-students alike. Approaching the composing stage should be similar to approaching the organizing stage: a significant step toward the final version in which second thoughts may surface. However, record your thoughts fully—imperfectly expressed as they may be. See below, pp. 7–18 for strategies for drafting the introduction, middle paragraphs, and conclusion.

Step Five: Revising and Editing

In composing the first, "rough" draft, your focus is on getting ideas down, explaining, clarifying, integrating, and ordering. During the revision stage, however, you should not expect to be just looking for minor errors. The word *revise* means to "see again."

One useful method is the "top-down" approach: consider large-scale issues before smaller-scale ones. Begin by taking a hard, objective look at your essay's purpose and audience, its structure, and its main points and their relation to your thesis. Review these areas as if you are seeing them for the first time. Waiting at least several hours after you have completed a rough draft before revising is sensible. Ask the kinds of questions you originally asked when you were creating an outline (see above, p. 3). Are you are satisfied with the results?

In the "top-down" approach to revision, you begin with large-scale concerns, such as essay organization, and finish by checking and rechecking grammar, spelling, and presentation, ensuring you allot plenty of time for all stages in the revising process.

Next, turn to individual paragraphs and check that each paragraph contains a main idea (claim) with ample support. Thoroughly check for correct grammar, clear expression, and concision. *Then*, it will be time to check for spelling errors and typos and ensuring that the essay conforms to the format your instructor requires.

Something that is **CONCISE** doesn't waste words.

Don't underestimate the importance of these end-stage activities. Try to see your essay through the eyes of your instructor. What often strikes a marker first are the very things you may have glossed over as your deadline approached: grammatical errors, lack of coherence, faulty word choice, poor or missing transitions, wordiness, typos, and mechanical errors that could easily have been fixed.

Though nothing replaces careful attention to every detail, Box 1.1 provides a checklist that will help you "re-see" your essay.

Box 1.1

Revising for Content and Structure

☐ Is the essay's purpose clear? Is it conveyed in the introduction, consistent throughout the middle paragraphs, and reinforced in the conclusion? (See pp. 7, 11, and 17.)

☐ Is it written for a specific audience? What would show a reader this (for example, level of language, voice or tone, kinds of evidence used, citation format)? (See p. 124.)

☐ Is the thesis statement in line with the focus of the essay and its main points? If not, consider adjusting the thesis—sometimes just changing a word or phrase will help. (See pp. 8–9.)

☐ Are all paragraphs adequately developed and focused on one main idea? Are they logically connected to your thesis? (See p. 11.)

☐ Are any paragraphs noticeably shorter or longer than others? If so, can you combine short paragraphs, ensuring a logical transition between them, or break up longer paragraphs, ensuring each can, in fact, stand on its own? (See p. 12.)

☐ Have different kinds of evidence been used for support? Does any part of the essay seem less well supported than other parts? (See p. 16.)

☐ Would an example, illustration, or analogy make an abstract point more concrete or a general point more specific? (See p. 16.)

☐ Is there a possibility a reader could misunderstand any part of the essay? If so, would this be owing to the complexity of a point or the way it is expressed? If your draft has been commented on/edited by a peer, pay particular attention to any

◎ Drafting the Essay

Virtually any essay you read is divided into an introduction, middle or body paragraphs, and a conclusion. Each part contributes in a unique way to the essay and requires a unique focus. The same is true for the essays you will be asked to write.

Writing an Introduction

The introduction is more than just a starting place. Its primary function is to inform the reader about the essay's purpose and topic and the writer's approach to the topic (usually through the thesis statement); sometimes, it also mentions the essay's main points. As well, the introduction may indicate the primary organizational pattern for the essay. In all these ways, the introduction previews what is forthcoming.

A good introduction is persuasive: it must sufficiently interest the reader, encouraging him or her to read on, perhaps by conveying the importance of the topic.

> The introduction previews the essay by announcing its purpose, topic, and thesis. A good introduction interests a reader and establishes the writer's credibility.

passages noted as unclear. If one reader has difficulty understanding it, others may too. (See p. 12.)

Editing for Grammar and Style

Give particular attention to

☐ Sentence structure (e.g., no sentence fragments) (See pp. 378–91.)

☐ Punctuation (See pp. 391–405.)

☐ Apostrophes (See p. 405.)

☐ Agreement (See pp. 410–19.)

☐ Pronoun consistency and reference (See pp. 419–21.)

☐ Misplaced and dangling modifiers (See pp. 425–29.)

☐ Parallelism (See p. 429.)

As well, good writers edit their prose to make it more clear, direct, and concise.

Mechanics

☐ Have all outside references been cited correctly? Have you used the documentation style preferred by your instructor or by your discipline? (See p. 89.)

☐ Have you met word length, essay/page format, and other specific requirements?

☐ Have you proofread the essay at least twice (once for content and flow, once for minor errors such as typos—breaking each word into syllables and reading syllabically throughout is the best way to catch minor errors)?

The introduction introduces not only the essay but also you, the writer; therefore you must come across as credible and reliable.

Student writers are often advised to write their introduction last, because they will not know precisely how the topic will develop until the body of the essay is written. On the other hand, many writers like to have a concrete starting point. If the latter describes you best, you should return to the introduction after you have completed drafting your middle paragraphs to ensure that it fits well with them.

The Thesis Statement

The Greek word **thesis** refers to the act of placing or setting down. A thesis statement sets down a generalization that is applicable to the entire essay. However, this generalization can take different forms depending on purpose and audience. Student and academic writers usually place the thesis statement in the introduction; journalistic writers often do not. (See pp. 150 and 133.)

The thesis announces the topic and includes a comment about the topic (*simple thesis statement*). The thesis statement may also include the major points to be discussed in the essay (*expanded thesis statement* or *essay plan*). The thesis statement usually embodies a **claim**, the nature of which depends on the essay's purpose. Typical argumentative claims are ones of *value* or *policy*. *Fact-based* claims are common in expository essays in the sciences and social sciences, while *interpretive* claims are used in many humanities essays in which the writer sets out to interpret one or more primary sources.

The following statements illustrate the different forms that a thesis can take:

Simple thesis statement from an expository student essay (fact-based claim): Social and economic pressures of the 21st century have given rise to what some experts are terming a new anxiety disorder, nomophobia, a fear of being without our cell phones and computers. (student writer Celeste Barnes-Crouse)

Expanded thesis statement from an argumentative student essay (policy claim): Decriminalizing prostitution in Canada would increase safety for Canadian sex workers; at the same time, tax payers would benefit from a decrease in health care and legal costs incurred by sex workers due to the inordinate stress and violence they experience at their jobs. (student writer Annika Benoit-Jansson)

Using an *expanded* thesis statement, as in the second thesis statement, puts your main points before the reader, which is often a strong way to begin an argumentative essay. This kind of thesis is also called an essay plan because it lays out the essay's organization, or plan.

A **THESIS** statement sets down a generalization that is applicable to the entire essay (simple thesis) or includes the essay's main points (expanded thesis, or essay plan).

A **CLAIM** is an assertion about the topic appearing in the thesis statement and topic sentences.

Thesis in the form of a question: Given the severity of the personal debt crisis in Canada, research into the extent and the reason for its occurrence is both timely and necessary. How far do our elevated levels of personal debt extend? How did we borrow ourselves to the brink of crisis? (student writer Sam Kerr)

Using a question as a thesis often creates interest and suggests a more open, or explorative approach to the topic. It may also help to create reader interest.

Creating Reader Interest

Although thinking about techniques to generate reader interest is especially import-ant when you are writing for a general audience, all readers need to be convinced at the outset that your essay is worth reading. The most traditional way to generate interest and persuade your reader of the topic's importance is to use a **logical open-ing**: to begin with a universal statement that becomes more specific and ends with the most specific claim, the thesis itself; this method is referred to as the inverted triangle method.

A **LOGICAL OPENING** is a technique for creating reader interest by beginning with a generalization and narrowing to the thesis.

One risk in this approach is that if you make the first sentence too broad or familiar, it might not interest the reader. Therefore, student writers are often encour-aged to use a **dramatic opening**, as non-academic writers often do (see Chapter 10 for examples). In the first example below, the writer uses a logical opening while in the second, the writer uses a dramatic approach. In both cases, however, the para-graph ends with a clear thesis statement (italicized).

A **DRAMATIC OPENING** is a technique for creating reader interest by beginning with a question, illustration, anecdote, quotation, description, or other attention-grabbing technique.

Logical: At the end of the 20th century, society was rocked by the creation of the Internet and the beginning of the digital age, giving rise to the era of instant communication with unlimited information and interaction. The first generation with access to this technology now makes up the world's student body, and it is becoming clear that conventional teaching techniques may not be effective with this group. As a result, today's educators have looked to this new technology, with many successful results. The next step in integrating technology is immersive interaction, such as the use of video games. Although challenges exist in their use, research has shown that, *if implemented properly, video games can be an effective supplement in teaching grade school and post-secondary students.* (student writer David Stephen)

Dramatic: What does it mean to say that one is a perfectionist? Does it mean that one does everything perfectly? In common language, the term "perfectionist" carries the connotation that the perfectionistic individual does everything perfectly, but according to perfectionism experts in social psychology, perfectionism is a term referring to a mentality, or set of cognitions, that are characteristic of certain people. According to Hollender (as cited in Slade & Owens, 1998), perfectionism refers to "the practice of demanding of oneself or others a higher quality of performance than is required by the situation" (p. 384). Although the name suggests to the layperson that perfectionism would be a desirable trait, this quality is in fact often unrecognized for its harmful effects on the lives of some people. *For these people, perfectionism is associated with mental illness and can contribute to problems in areas of life such as academic success and intimate relationships.* (student writer Erin Walker)

EXERCISE 1.1

In the following paragraphs:

a. Identify the method for creating interest.
b. Discuss how the writer establishes his or her credibility.
c. Identify the thesis statement and whether it is a simple thesis or an expanded one.

You can also pre-read "Rhetorical Patterns and Paragraph Development," p. 14, to determine the essay's main organizational method.

1. The North American Free Trade Agreement was a much-heralded accomplishment (NAFTA) when it was ratified in January 1994, eliminating most of the trade barriers between Canada, the United States, and Mexico. While some citizens feared that economic integration in the trilateral area would disrupt cultural independence, polls showed that most people believed free trade would be beneficial. When ratified, NAFTA became the world's largest free trade agreement (MacPherson 2054). The removal of restrictions on trade opened up vast new markets for the three countries, creating more competition among firms and growth opportunities for companies. However, despite NAFTA's potential to benefit consumers and workers alike, the legalities of the agreement have created many negative consequences. In particular, the adverse effects of the Agreement pose a threat to the average Canadian, Mexican, and American: poor labour conditions, agribusiness, and the unprecedented power of corporations are key issues resulting from NAFTA that must be renegotiated. (student writer Kourtney Lane)

2. As you dive into the beautiful, crystal-clear Pacific Ocean, you descend slowly among Hawaii's glorious underwater reefs. As you look around you, you see other divers in the cloudy water. But they are not admiring spectators; they are equipped with large syringes, nets, and crowbars. They are cyanide divers, engaging in the illegal practice of cyanide fishing. This practice does more than

(continued)

kill fish: it damages the environment, killing many species, destroying underwater reefs, and negatively affecting the economy worldwide. According to Charles Barber of the World Resources Institute, "this multimillion dollar industry is what drives many individuals to do some damaging acts and continue with such cruel practices" (39). Despite the millions of fish that are killed and the miles of underwater reef that end up looking like the aftermath of a category nine earthquake, thousands continue to cyanide fish every day, while governments do little to stop it. (student writer Ryan Campbell)

Writing Middle Paragraphs

The structure of middle paragraphs is often said to mirror that of the essay itself: each paragraph begins with a general statement that is supported by the sentences that follow. In its structure and function, the essay's thesis statement is equivalent to the topic sentence of a paragraph, which announces the main idea (topic) of that paragraph. This is a useful analogy because it stresses the importance of a predictable order for both essays and paragraphs, which helps a reader understand what is coming next.

A **TOPIC SENTENCE,** usually the first sentence, states the main idea in the paragraph.

When a writer uses a topic sentence to announce the central idea, the rest of the paragraph provides support, such as examples, reasons, statistical data, or other kinds of evidence. In some way, it illustrates, expands on, or reinforces the topic sentence. In the following paragraph, student writer Leslie Nelson expands on the main idea, first by explaining the function of talking therapies and then by dividing them into three different subcategories and explaining the function of each (the topic sentence is italicized):

Talking therapies—especially when combined with medication—are common to treatment of adolescent depression. There are several kinds of talking therapies, including cognitive and humanistic approaches, and family and group sessions. Each of these therapy types confronts depression in a different way, and each is useful to adolescent treatment. Cognitive therapies confront illogical thought patterns that accompany depression; humanistic therapies provide support to the patient, stressing unconditional acceptance. Group therapies, on the other hand, encourage depressed patients to talk about their feelings in a setting with other people who are undergoing treatment for similar problems. This therapy can inspire different coping strategies, and it allows people to realize that they are not alone in their problems.

Writing Strong Paragraphs

Effective paragraphs are unified, coherent, and well developed. A unified paragraph focuses on only one main idea; when you move to another main idea, you begin a new paragraph. If, however, a paragraph is long, you should consider dividing it into two paragraphs even if each contains the same idea. Look for the most logical place to make the division; for example, you could divide the paragraph where you begin an important sub-point.

A coherent paragraph is easy to follow. It is both clear and carefully arranged to place the emphasis where you want it. The term reader-based prose is used to suggest a focus on the concerns of the reader. In reader-based prose, the writer carefully designs the paragraph for a specific audience by using understandable and well-organized prose, stressing what is most important and omitting what is irrelevant, and clarifying the relationships among the points and sub-points. Like academic and non-academic writers, student writers can make their paragraphs easy to follow by considering the following points:

1. *Logical sentence order:* In logical sentence order, one sentence follows naturally from the preceding one, and there are no sentences out of order or off-topic (an off-topic sentence would not result in a unified paragraph); there are no gaps in thought that the reader has to try to fill.

2. *Organizational patterns:* You can order the paragraph according to a specific pattern (see "Rhetorical Patterns and Paragraph Development," pp. 14–16).

3. *Precise language:* When you consider what words to use, remember that it is not always a case of the right word versus the wrong word. Choose the *best word for the given context.* Whenever you use a word that is not part of your everyday vocabulary, you should confirm its meaning by looking it up in a dictionary to make sure you have used it correctly. A misused word could make the meaning of an entire sentence—even a paragraph—unclear.

4. *Appropriate adverbial transitions:* Transitional words and phrases enable you to convey precise relationships between one idea and the next.

5. *Selective rephrasing:* Being aware of the knowledge level of your audience helps you determine whether and when you should rephrase in order to clarify difficult concepts.

6. *Repetition of key words/phrases or the use of synonyms:* You can use repetition to emphasize important ideas. Of course, *needless* repetition should always be avoided.

UNITY is the principle of paragraph construction in which only one idea is developed throughout the paragraph.

COHERENCE is the principle of paragraph construction in which ideas are logically laid out with clear connections between them.

READER-BASED prose is clear, accessible writing designed for an intended reader.

7. *Parallel/balanced structures:* Employing parallel/balanced structures creates co-herence, in part, through the use of familiar word order. Balanced structures have a pleasing rhythm and thus may be more easily understood—and even remembered.

In the excerpt below, after defining the term *nanotechnology*, student writer Jeff Proctor makes effective use of transitions (in italics) to help explain a difficult con-cept to general readers. He uses a balanced structure in sentence 4 to make a com-parison understandable and repeats the key word *precision* at strategic points in the paragraph (the beginning, middle, and end); other words, too, can be considered near-synonyms for *precision* (synonyms and repetition are underlined):

[1]Nanotechnology will allow the construction of compounds at nanometre precision. [2]*Essentially*, this capability would allow scientists to form a substance one atom at a time and to put each atom exactly where it needs to be. [3]*Consequently*, any chemical structure that is stable under normal con-ditions could theoretically be produced. [4]In comparison to semiconductor lithography, which could be imagined as the formation of electrical circuits by joining large heaps of molecules, the techniques of nanotechnology could be imagined as the careful arrangement of molecules with a pair of tweezers. [5]With this incredible degree of precision, electrical circuits could be designed to be smaller than ever before. [6]*Currently*, each com-ponent in a computer is the size of thousands of atoms; *however*, if nano-technological processes were used to produce it, one component could be on the scale of several atoms. [7]This fact alone emphasizes the potential efficiency of next-generation computer circuits, for smaller components are closer together and, *thus*, able to communicate with each other in less time. [8]*Furthermore*, it could be guaranteed that products are reproducible and reliable as a result of the absolute precision of these formation processes.

Transitions in the paragraph above convey various relationships: *essentially* (transition of summary), *consequently, thus* (cause/effect), *currently* (time), *however* (contrast), *furthermore* (addition).

Striving for coherence throughout the writing process should not just enable a reader to follow you but also help you clarify your own train of thought as you write. Thus, it can be useful to consciously rephrase ideas and specific passages as you write. Without crossing out what you wrote, follow it with transitions like *in other words, in short, in summary, to reiterate, that is* and a paraphrase or expansion of the original. If your "second attempt" is clearer—and it often is—you can then consider crossing out the original to avoid needless repetition.

For information on reading challenging paragraphs, see Chapter 6 and Chapter 10, pp. 151–54.

Some common transitions include the following:

Transitions of limit or concession: admittedly, although, it is true that, naturally, of course, though

Transitions of cause and effect: accordingly, as a result, because, con-sequently, for this reason, if, otherwise, since, so, then, therefore, thus

Transitions of Illustration: after all, even, for example, for instance, indeed, in fact, in other words, of course, specifically, such as

Transitions of contrast or qualification: after all, although, but, by contrast, conversely, despite, even so, however, in spite of, instead, nevertheless, nonetheless, on the contrary, on the one hand . . . on the other hand, otherwise, rather (than), regardless, still, though, whereas, while, yet

Transitions of summary or conclusion: in conclusion, in effect, in short, in sum, (in summary), so, that is, thus

Rhetorical Patterns and Paragraph Development

RHETORICAL PATTERNS
are methods for organizing
and presenting information
in essays and paragraphs;
examples include cause
and effect, classification,
comparison and contrast,
cost-benefit analysis, and
definition.

Rhetorical patterns are systematic ways to organize and present information; they apply both to the essay itself and to individual paragraphs. All the claims you make in your essay—your general claim, or thesis, and your specific claims, usually made in your topic sentences—must be well supported or they will not be convincing. When drafting your essay, you should consider not just what kinds of evidence to use but how to organize it; thus, writers use specific patterns to organize and develop individual paragraphs, supporting the specific claims in the topic sentences. Part of an essay's success lies in choosing the most appropriate rhetorical pattern(s) to develop a particular claim.

Table 1.1   Organizational (Rhetorical) Patterns

Purpose	Rhetorical Pattern	Description/Explanation
To create an image or picture of something	Description	Uses images related to sight or the other senses to create immediacy and involve the reader; uses modifiers (adjectives and adverbs) to add detail; may systematically focus on a scene, using a logical method such as left to right, top to bottom, etc.
To tell a story	Narration	Relates an occurrence, usually in chronological order; stresses action through the use of strong verbs; provides anecdotes or brief narratives that introduce or illustrate a point
To show how something works or is done	Process analysis	Breaks down a (usually) complex process into a sequence of successive steps, making it more understandable; provides instructions or directions
To explain what something is	Definition	Explains the attributes or key features of something, usually in order to apply it in some way
To discuss similarities and/or differences	Comparison and contrast (sometimes referred to as Comparison, even if differences are focused on)	Systematically looks at the ways something is similar to or different from something else; can be organized by block method (all points of similarity and difference of Subject A, followed by all points relevant to Subject B) or point-by-point method (each point relevant to each subject discussed separately)
To show the way something changed/developed	Chronology	Uses time order to trace something, often from its beginning to the present day; can be applied to people, objects (like inventions), or situations
To particularize the general or concretize the abstract	Example	Gives particular instances of a larger category, enabling readers to better understand the larger category; gives immediacy and concreteness to what can seem otherwise broad or abstract
To analyze why something happened or a result/outcome	Cause and effect	Uses inductive methods to draw conclusions; works from causes to effects or from effects to causes; for example, to determine whether smoking leads to (causes) heart disease or to determine whether heart disease results from (is an effect of) smoking

(continued)

Table 1.1 *(continued)*

Purpose	Rhetorical Pattern	Description/Explanation
To account for or justify something	Reasons	Uses deductive methods that draw on one's knowledge or experience (which may ultimately be derived from inductive findings); for example, "you should not smoke because it often leads to heart disease" (reason derived via empirical evidence)
To analyze by dividing into subcategories	Classification/ division	Classification: groups items or ideas according to shared characteristics (e.g., types of bottled water: purified, mineral, sparkling). Division: separates large category into constituent parts (e.g., the essay into introduction, middle paragraphs, conclusion)
To look at two sides/ views of something	Cost–benefit analysis	Weighs the pros and cons of an issue, question, or action, usually to decide which is stronger; in argument, cost–benefit analysis is used to support a value or policy claim and/or refute an opposing claim
To identify a problem or solve/resolve it	Problem and solution	Analyzes or explains a problem or proposes a solution; may incorporate other methods, such as reasons, cause and effect, or cost–benefit analysis
To better understand something	Analogy	Shows how one subject is similar to another to clarify the nature or a feature of the first subject

Most topics can be developed by using one or more of the methods below. For example, if you were looking for ways to develop the topic "fighting in hockey," you could use description or narration to convey the excitement of a hockey brawl; conversely, you could use either method to convey it as an unseemly spectacle. You could use the process analysis pattern to depict the step-by-step procedures officials use to break up a fight, the chronological pattern to trace the history of rules governing fighting, or the pattern by example to call attention to notorious fighting incidents in recent years.

The examples below illustrate different rhetorical patterns that help develop individual paragraphs. In the first example, the writer breaks a broad category— vegetarians—into smaller ones, which are then briefly defined:

Classification and definition:
Vegans avoid all animal products for food, clothing or other purposes, while *lacto-ovo* vegetarians consume dairy produce and eggs, and *semi-* and *pesco*-vegetarians eat poultry and fish respectively. (Nick Fox and Katie Ward, "Health, Ethics and Environment: A Qualitative Study of Vegetarian Motivations," p. 187)

The next example breaks a process into successive stages (all stages of the process are given in the essay):

Process analysis:

To behave ethically is not a one-step process: Do the right thing. It is a sometimes arduous eight-step process. To behave ethically, you must:

1. Recognize that there is a situation that deserves to be noticed and reflected upon.
2. Define the situation as having an ethical component . . . (Robert J. Sternberg, "Slip-Sliding Away, Down the Ethical Slope," p. 241)

For examples of essays in this textbook that employ different rhetorical patterns, see "Classification by Essay Type and Organizational Pattern," located on the inside front cover of this textbook.

Kinds of Evidence

Although it is good to use various kinds of evidence in your essay, some are likely going to be more important than others. The choices you make depend on your purpose, audience, topic and claim, and the type of essay you are writing. For example, if you are writing a rhetorical analysis, it will focus on the essay you're analyzing as a primary source; if you are writing a research essay, your focus will likely be on secondary sources.

Common kinds of evidence may vary from discipline to discipline: humanities writing often uses direct quotation from primary sources; social sciences writing tends to focus on statistics, interviews, questionnaires, case studies, and interpersonal observation; the sciences rely on direct methods that involve experimentation.

Some kinds of evidence can be more authoritative than others. In fact-based writing, "hard" evidence—facts, statistics, and the findings of empirical research—provides the strongest support. Various kinds of "soft" evidence, such as expert opinion, examples, illustrations, and analogies, may also be important to help explain a concept but will likely be less important than "hard" evidence. Argumentative essays may use analogies, precedents, expert opinion, anecdotal evidence, and even, perhaps, personal experience. (See pp. 46–49 for kinds of evidence commonly used in argument.)

Issues of Credibility

Credibility factors include *knowledge*, *reliability*, and *fairness*. You exhibit your knowledge by appearing well informed about your topic and supporting each claim with solid and substantial evidence. You convey reliability in many ways:

- By using the accepted conventions of the discipline in which you are writing; this includes using the correct citation style, being aware of the specialized language of the discipline, and following format requirements, such as the use of an abstract and formal sections (science writing and report writing)
- By writing effectively and following the rules of grammar, punctuation, syntax, sentence structure, and spelling; writing efficiently, using words that express exactly what you want them to

Humanities writing often uses direct quotation from primary sources; social sciences writing tends to focus on statistics, interviews, questionnaires, case studies, and interpersonal observation; the sciences rely on direct methods that involve experimentation.

CREDIBILITY is essential for all writing: appearing credible involves showing knowledge as well as coming across as trustworthy and fair.

- By using credible and authoritative sources (research essays)
- By reasoning logically and avoiding logical fallacies (argumentative essays)

Although fairness applies particularly to argumentative essays, it can also be important in a research essay, for example, if you find sources whose findings contradict your claim or hypothesis; you will increase your credibility if you try to account for inconsistent results. In argument, you convey fairness in several ways:

- By using an objective voice and not showing bias
- By acknowledging and accurately representing the opposing view
- By looking for common ground
- By avoiding slanted language and emotional fallacies

Writing a Conclusion

Like an introduction, a **conclusion** can vary depending on the kind of essay and other factors. While a conclusion is always a vital part of an essay, it can perform different functions. The conclusion may refer back to the thesis statement, rephrasing it and reasserting its importance. It may also look ahead by considering a way that the thesis can be applied or the need for further research.

Although a conclusion may both look back to the thesis statement and look ahead to the thesis's implications, the stress often falls on one or the other. A circular conclusion primarily reminds the reader of your thesis and reinforces it. Even so, if you want to emphasize these functions, you should not repeat the thesis word for word, nor should you simply summarize what you have already said in your introduction. *You should draw attention to the significance of the body paragraphs in which you have developed your topic.*

A spiral conclusion looks beyond the thesis. In an argumentative essay, you may want to make an emotional or ethical appeal. Other spiral conclusion strategies include ending with a relevant anecdote or personal experience (informal essay) or a question that extends from your findings or that of the research you have used (expository essay). If you have focused on a problem, this may be the time to suggest solutions. If your topic is applicable to a relatively small number of people, you can suggest how it could be generalized to a larger group, one that would include the reader.

The paragraph on the next page uses the spiral pattern, though, like most conclusions, it also includes information from the introduction. However, in the second half of the conclusion, the writer considers the challenges and speculates on the future of video games as an educational tool. You can compare the conclusion to the introduction, above on page 9.

The last paragraph usually summarizes the thesis and/or main points in the body of the essay. A **CIRCULAR CONCLUSION** reinforces the thesis; a **SPIRAL CONCLUSION** suggests applications or further research.

Video games bring many benefits to educators, including, significantly, an increase in student academic achievement. However, there are financial and social challenges to meet if the use of video games is to be effectively implemented. The next step is the creation of a unified system that can be tested and modeled in schools across the globe; education also has its role to play in overcoming a prejudice against the use of this promising teaching tool. If the challenges can be met, it may be only a matter of time until games become a staple of our education. (Student writer David Stephen)

◎ Chapter 1 Review Questions

1. What are the five chronological stages of essay writing?
2. Choose one pre-writing method discussed on p. 3 and in your own words explain how it works (it might be good to choose a method that works well for you or one that you would like to try).
3. Explain the difference between editing and revising. Why are these important activities for the writer?
4. Name four functions of an introduction and three forms that a thesis statement could take.
5. When might a dramatic opening be a better choice than a logical opening?
6. a. What is the difference between unity and coherence in a paragraph?
   b. Rank the strategies for coherence in order of importance and explain why you have chosen the ones you did (see p. 12).
   c. Choose a paragraph from a piece of your own writing and suggest how you can make it more coherent.
7. Pick a topic other than hockey and suggest ways that you could use specific rhetorical patterns to develop that topic (see p. 14, above); give at least three examples of suitable patterns.
8. What could influence your decision to use mostly "hard" or mostly "soft" evidence in an essay?
9. What factors can influence your credibility as a writer?
10. Answer true or false:
    a. A circular conclusion repeats your thesis word for word.
    b. A spiral introduction is usually superior to a circular introduction.
    c. In a spiral introduction, you do not refer to your thesis.

◎ Key Terms

brainstorming (p. 3)

circular conclusion (p. 17)

claim (p. 8)

clustering (p. 3)

coherence (p. 12)

concision (p. 6)

conclusion (p. 17)

credibility (p. 16)

dramatic opening (p. 9)

freewriting (p. 3)

logical opening (p. 9)

outline (p. 4)

questioning (p. 3)

reader-based prose (p. 12)

rhetorical pattern (p. 14)

spiral conclusion (p. 17)

support (p. 4)

thesis (p. 8)

thesis statement (p. 3)

topic sentence (p. 11)

unity (p. 12)

CHAPTER 2

Writing Summaries

In this chapter, you will learn:

◎ What the different kinds of summaries are

◎ How stand-alone summaries are used

◎ How to use strategies for successful summarizing

Summaries are a major part of research-related writing. Research never occurs in a vacuum; it is a collaborative effort. Even the most original theories and innovative research must be placed within the context of what has been thought and written before. And that is often where summarization comes in.

◎ Times and Places for Summaries

> Summarization is a general term for representing the ideas of a writer in a condensed form, using your own words.

Summarization is a general term for representing the ideas of a writer in a condensed form, using your own words.

There are many occasions when you will be called on to represent the main ideas of a source:

- Writing a review of a book, movie, and the like. You typically summarize its plot or characters before you begin your analysis.
- Critiquing a text in order to argue for or against the author's position. You might begin by summarizing the author's arguments before replying with your own points.
- Writing a rhetorical analysis. You will likely briefly summarize a point before applying your critical thinking skills to it.
- Using sources in your research (see Chapter 5, p. 80).

The following are specialized summaries; their various functions are discussed below:

- Abstract
- Literature review
- Annotated bibliography

In many academic essays, a concentrated summary called an **abstract** precedes the essay, giving an overview of what follows. Unlike most other summaries, however, academic writers may include phrases used in the essay. Another form of summary is the **literature review**, in which the author, often in a phrase or sentence for each, summarizes the relevant studies in the field, before stating his or her own thesis or hypothesis.

Another special kind of summary is the **annotated bibliography**, an expanded bibliography that includes not only the information of standard bibliographies but also brief summaries of related works, including studies referred to in the text and other significant studies. Typically, each entry in the bibliography includes the main point, or thesis, of the work and a comment on what it contributes to the field as a whole—where it fits in. Annotated bibliographies may form appendices to book-length studies.

You may be assigned a more modest annotated bibliography as part of a research project or as an independent project. In either case, the purpose is to demonstrate your ability to research and summarize relevant works on a topic.

The following is an example of an entry in an annotated bibliography on the topic of decriminalizing Canadian prostitution laws. The student summarizes one of the studies she used in her research essay and provides a brief assessment of its value.

O'Doherty, T. (2011). Criminalization and off-street sex work in Canada. *Canadian Journal of Criminology and Criminal Justice, 53*(2), 217–245. doi:10.3138/cjccj.53.2.217

Using results from ten interviews with off-street sex workers, O'Doherty explores the impact of the current Criminal Code prostitution laws in Canada: she describes the resulting separation between police and sex workers: the lack of understanding of the laws among sex workers; and the physical health, mental health, legal and social implications. Though her sample size is small, O'Doherty incorporates external research to support her findings that the decriminalization of prostitution would positively impact sex workers; she also includes precautionary measures, such as the necessity of practicing sex workers input in the revision and creation of legislation.

—student writer Annika Benoit-Jansson

An **ABSTRACT** is a condensed summary used in empirical studies; it is placed before the study begins and includes its purpose, methods, and results. See chapter 10, p. 147.

A **LITERATURE REVIEW** is a condensed survey of articles on the topic arranged in a logical order usually ending with the article most relevant to the author's study. See chapter 10, p. 149.

An **ANNOTATED BIBLIOGRAPHY** is an expanded bibliography that includes not only the information of standard bibliographies but also brief summaries of related works.

Summarizing and Research

Summary is an important feature of scholarly discourse, whether practised by students or academics, because it enables writers to situate their own points relative to those of others. By presenting the main idea(s) of your sources and synthesizing them with your own ideas, you are developing and supporting your thesis. Writers of academic essays rely on this form of development to

- Support their own point
- Disagree with a relevant study
- Explain a concept or theory related to their topic
- Compare/contrast a study's findings with those of other studies

The amount of space you devote to a summary depends on how you want to use it and on its importance to your thesis. For a book or movie review, you want to provide enough plot to enable your reader to grasp what the work was about. If you are summarizing an author's position with which you disagree, you do not want to do more than briefly sketch the main arguments on the other side, unless your purpose in arguing is to reach a compromise. If one source is particularly important to your research essay, that summary should be longer than those of less important sources. Summaries, then, can range greatly in length as well as in purpose.

◎ The Stand-Alone Summary: The Précis

PRÉCIS is a term for a stand-alone summary. It is usually 20–25 per cent the length of the original.

A summary can also serve as an end in itself. A stand-alone summary, sometimes called a précis (meaning something precise), represents all the main points in a complete work or section(s) of a work. It follows the same order of points as the original but omits most sub-points and all detail. The specific guidelines that apply to stand-alone summaries do not apply to all types of summaries, but learning these guidelines and practising them is the best way to learn the exacting art of summary writing. The important skills required in précis writing include the following:

Stand-alone summaries help develop three main skills basic to reading and writing at the college and university level: comprehension, prioritizing, and concision skills.

Comprehension skills: Because a précis summary, like most summaries, requires you to change the wording of the original, you focus more closely on comprehension than if you quoted the words of the source directly: you have to be clear on content in order to write a successful summary.

Prioritizing skills (establishing a hierarchy of importance): Separating the main ideas from the less important ideas is a fundamental part of the reading process. When summarizing, you need to think about the importance of a point relative to other points, the importance of a sub-point relative to other sub-points, and so on, to know what to include in your summary. Including a less important sub-point and omitting a more important one would make your summary misrepresentative.

Concision skills: A crucial principle applies to précis writing: the more efficient your writing, the more content you can include and the more informed your reader will be. In addition, focusing on conciseness serves you well in any writing you do, making you a more disciplined writer.

Pointers for Précis Writing

When writing a précis-style summary, you should keep the following guidelines in mind:

1. Follow the exact order of the original. Begin with the thesis or first main point, not a generalization about the essay as a whole, such as why it was written.
2. Include only the most important points. Depending on space, you may include the most important sub-point(s)/developments.
3. Avoid detail. Do not include examples unless they are very important, in which case the writer will probably mention them more than once.
4. Avoid repetition. Although ideas stressed in the original should be also stressed in your summary, do not needlessly repeat.
5. Do not repeat the author's name or the work's title any more than necessary.
6. Do not analyze, interpret, or give your opinions.
7. Use your own words, keeping direct quotations to a minimum. If a brief passage cannot be easily paraphrased, you may quote it directly, but *ensure that you use quotation marks to show the reader that those exact words occur in the original.* Common everyday words from the original do not have to be placed in quotation marks unless they occur in a phrase of four words or more (the number of successive words requiring quotation marks can vary; check with your instructor).
8. Write efficiently. Rephrase the original concisely and check that you use no more words than you must; use basic words—nouns and verbs—with minimal modifiers—adjectives and adverbs. Use transitions to create a logical flow between one idea and the next.
9. Ensure that the verbs you use reflect the author's rhetorical purpose. For example, if the writer is arguing rather than explaining a point, use a verb that reflects this: The author *argues . . . claims . . . criticizes . . .* (argument); the author *states . . . explains . . . discusses . . .* (exposition).

For a summary, space is at a premium, so remember to be **SPACE** conscious. Be:

Specific
Precise
Accurate
Clear
Efficient

A How-To of Précis Writing

Reading to summarize means you should use the forms of selective reading appropriate for this activity. Begin by scanning the text to get its gist—its thesis—and to determine its structure—that is, how the author has divided the text. Box 2.1 provides checklists for two common methods of constructing a summary.

Box 2.1   Reading Strategies for Summarizing

Outline Method

☐ Identify main ideas by distinctive underlining such as double underlining. In *paragraphs*, pay attention to topic sentences. In *sentences*, look for independent clauses, which usually contain the main idea in the sentence.

☐ Identify the most important sub-points (developments) by single underlining. For information about using contextual cues, such as transitions and prompts to lead you to main ideas, see pp. 153–54.

☐ Prepare an outline with all main points and important sub-points. If you wish, indent sub-points as in a formal outline.

☐ Write your summary from the outline, using your own words as much as possible and adding transitions to create coherent prose. If the summary exceeds the allowable length, omit the least important sub-point(s). *This method is particularly useful for shorter summaries.*

Section Summary Method

☐ Prepare a section-by-section breakdown. Sections can be determined by headings or additional spacing between paragraphs. If there are none, try to determine where the writer has shifted focus or introduced a new concept.

☐ Summarize each section in your own words. Aim for one sentence for short sections, two sentences for mid-length sections, and two or three sentences for longer sections. As in the outline method, look for main ideas by trying to identify topic sentences. Pay attention to the opening paragraph of each section, where the main idea(s) in the section may be introduced.

☐ Combine your section sentences to write your summary, adding transitions to create coherent prose. If the summary exceeds the allowable length, omit the least important sub-point(s). *This method is particularly useful for longer summaries.*

Some Summary Writing Strategies

In addition to the guidelines discussed in Box 2.1, you might find the following summarization strategies helpful:

- Read through the essay at least twice before beginning to identify main points and important sub-points.
- If you find it difficult to identify what is important in a passage, ask whether or how it connects with or contributes to the thesis or controlling idea.
- You might find it easier to identify main ideas after you have first put parentheses around what you know are unimportant details and examples. For longer works, pay particular attention to the writer's own summaries, which may occur in the introduction, in the conclusion, or toward the end of long or complex sections.
- Remember that there is not necessarily a mechanical relationship between ideas and paragraphs. Not all paragraphs are equally important, and not all contain topic sentences. In much journalistic writing, for example, opening paragraphs may serve to attract the reader's interest; they may not contain a major point.

Outline to Summary: An Example

The following is a section from a book chapter. In the chapter (entitled "Bad Borgs?"), the author, Andy Clark, categorizes what he calls "spectres," possible threats to our autonomy posed by today's technology. Read the passage and consider strategies for summarization. The passage is 488 words; a 97-word summary would represent 20 per cent of the original, a typical length for a précis summary.

Overload

[1]One of the most fearsome spectres . . . is that of plain simple overload—the danger of slowly drowning in a sea of contact. As I write, I am painfully aware of the unread messages that will have arrived since I last logged in yesterday evening. By midday there will be around 60 new items, about 10 of which will require action. Ten more may be pure junk mail, easy to spot or filter, but it is the rest that are the real problem. These I read, only to discover they require no immediate thought or action. I call this e-stodge. It is filling without being necessary or nourishing, and there seems to be more of it every day.

[2]The root cause of e-stodge, Neil Gershenfeld has suggested, is a deep but unnoticed shift in the relative costs, in terms of time and effort, of *generating* messages and of *reading* them. Once upon a time, it cost much

more—again in terms of time and effort—to create and send a message than to read one. Now, the situation is reversed. It is terribly easy to forward a whole screed to someone else, or to copy a message to all and sundry, just in case they happen to have an opinion or feel they should have been consulted. The length of the message grows as more and more responses get cheaply incorporated. Other forms of overload abound. The incoming messages aren't all e-mail; there are phone calls (on mobile and land lines) and text messages, even the occasional physical letter. There is the constant availability, via the Google-enhanced web, of more information about just about everything at the click of a mouse.

[3]One cure for overload is, of course, simply to unplug. Several prominent academics have simply decided that "e-nough is e-nough" and have turned off their e-mail for good or else redirected it to assistants who sift, screen, and filter. Donald Knuth, a computer scientist who took this very step, quotes the novelist Umberto Eco, "I have reached an age where my main purpose is not to receive messages." Knuth himself asserts that "I have been a happy man since January 1, 1990, when I no longer had an e-mail address."

[4]We won't all be able to unplug or to avail ourselves of intelligent secretarial filters. A better solution, the one championed by Neil Gershenfeld, is to combine intelligent filtering software (to weed out junk mail) with a new kind of business etiquette. What we need is an etiquette that reflects the new cost/benefit ratio according to which the receiver is usually paying the heaviest price in the exchange. That means sparse messages, sent only when action is likely to be required and sent only to those who really need to know—a 007 principle for communication in a densely interconnected world. E-mail only what is absolutely necessary, keep it short, and send it to as few people as possible.

Clark, A. (2004). *Natural-born cyborgs: Minds, technologies, and the future of Human Intelligence.* New York: Oxford University Press, 176–177.

Preparing to Summarize

If you read the essay carefully, you will see that it is divided into two parts: the first two paragraphs describe a problem, while the last two present possible solutions. The summary, too, should be equally weighted. Unfamiliar words in this section might include *stodge* and *screed*: examples of informal diction, meaning, respectively, "something dull or stupid" and "a long piece of writing." Since the passage to be summarized is relatively short, it is best to use the outline method to focus on the main ideas and important developments. These might include the following:

Para. 1: *Main point* (topic sentence): "One of the most fearsome spectres . . . is that of plain simple overload—the danger of slowly drowning in a sea of contact."

Very important development: Email that creates the "real problem" is that which "require[s] no immediate thought or action. I call this e-stodge. It is filling without being necessary or nourishing, and there seems to be more of it every day."

Para. 2: *Main point* (topic sentence): "The root cause of e-stodge, Neil Gershenfeld has suggested, is a deep but unnoticed shift in the relative costs, in terms of time and effort, of *generating* messages and of *reading* them."

Sub-point 1: It is easy today to "forward a whole screed to someone else, or to copy a message to all and sundry."

Sub-point 2: In addition to email, "[o]ther forms of overload abound."

Para. 3: *Main point* (topic sentence): "One cure for overload is, of course, simply to unplug."

Sub-point: "Several prominent academics have simply decided that 'e-nough is e-nough' and have turned off their e-mail for good or else redirected it to assistants who sift, screen, and filter."

Para. 4: *Main point* (topic sentence): "A better solution, the one championed by Neil Gershenfeld, is to combine intelligent filtering software (to weed out junk mail) with a new kind of business etiquette."

Very important development: "E-mail only what is absolutely necessary, keep it short, and send it to as few people as possible."

Creating the Summary

What follows is a summary based on the outline above but using different words. Of course, there is more than one way to summarize this essay. To check its effectiveness, you can refer to the summarization pointers on page 23.

Summary of "Overload," by Andy Clark

Users of today's technology are in danger of being overwhelmed by unimportant email, which Clark calls "e-stodge." While creating messages used to take longer than reading them, today's problem results from the ease with which one can forward or copy an email to numberless contacts. Although it is possible to sever connection with email entirely or let subordinates handle the problem, Clark favours Neil Gershenfeld's solution, one that uses sophisticated spam filtering with "a new kind of business etiquette." Such a protocol requires that all emails be essential, concise, and carefully directed to a select few. [96 words]

◎ Chapter 2 Review Questions

1. Identify three different kinds of summaries and their main purposes.
2. Explain the importance of summarizing in the research process.
3. What three important skills are tested in a stand-alone (précis) summary? Why might these skills be crucial in other kinds of writing you do at college or university?
4. Answer true or false:
   a. A précis summary should begin with a generalization.
   b. A summary should be specific but avoid detail.
   c. A summary should include both your own words and direct quotations.
5. What steps can you take to ensure that your summary includes all the main points of the original?

◎ Key Terms

abstract (p. 21)

annotated bibliography (p. 21)

literature review (p. 21)

précis (p. 22)

Rhetorical Analysis

In this chapter, you will learn:

- ◎ What the differences are between a rhetorical analysis and a critical response

- ◎ How to organize a rhetorical analysis

- ◎ How to use questions to generate a rhetorical analysis

◎ Analyzing Texts

In-class and out-of-class assignments often require you to analyze an essay you have never seen before. To do so, you need to exercise your active reading skills, especially critical thinking. A rhetorical analysis, sometimes called a critical analysis, demonstrates your ability to analyze such elements as the writer's purpose, audience, and reasoning strategies. A critical response requires some of the same skills, as well as relating your observations and experiences to the topic of the essay you are responding to. In this chapter, we focus on the more objective critical analysis. However, Table 3.1 on p. 33 compares analyses and responses, and there is a brief student critical response on p. 37.

When you analyze a work, you break it down in order to examine its parts; thus, the rhetorical analysis assumes you are a knowledgeable reader familiar with how such texts are written and capable of evaluating the author's success in achieving his or her objectives. The main purposes of a rhetorical analysis are (1) to explain and (2) to evaluate/critique the text and the author's use of rhetorical strategies. An analysis needs to be planned carefully; for example, it is often a good idea to outline your points before beginning your draft.

Writing a rhetorical analysis makes you more conscious of the ways that texts written by academics and other professionals are put together, the kinds of strategies that can be used to make content clear and accessible, and successful (or

RHETORIC refers to the use of language to convince an audience. However, a rhetorical analysis usually involves more than looking at a writer's language.

A **RHETORICAL ANALYSIS** focuses on the text you have read. In a rhetorical analysis, you break down a work in order to examine its parts and the author's rhetorical strategies, using your critical thinking skills and your knowledge of texts themselves.

A **CRITICAL RESPONSE** focuses on your own opinions or observations about an issue raised in a text. Although a response is usually more informal than a rhetorical analysis, it should clearly demonstrate critical thinking.

unsuccessful) reasoning and argumentative strategies. In this sense, you critically analyze a text in order to see what works and what does not—and why. Honing your analytical abilities in this way helps you use the essays you analyze as models for your own writing.

◎ Rhetorical Analysis and Essay Type

Analysis of Literary Works

One kind of critical analysis, a literary analysis, applies to literary works. The literary analysis breaks down the elements of the text—in fiction, such elements include plot, character, setting, point of view, and language—showing how they relate to one another. Of course, such texts contain no thesis but rather themes, which can be inferred from the interconnections among these elements. Like other kinds of texts, literary texts can be analyzed according to their conventions, which vary by genre (poetry, drama, fiction, creative non-fiction) and by subgenre (lyric, dramatic, and narrative poetry, for example). Some non-fiction essays, like those on pp. 162, 211, and 337, can also be analyzed for their point of view, language, tone, and devices, like metaphors.

Analysis of Arguments

Argumentative claims are debatable—for example, one writer might claim that social media advocacy is a good thing, while another could argue it is not. Therefore, arguments make a good source for a rhetorical analysis. In a rhetorical analysis of an argumentative essay, you might question the validity of an author's premises or question the use of argument. A rhetorical analysis of an argumentative essay should focus on the hows and whys of the author's methods and strategies. *It should not be used as a forum for expressing your personal agreement or disagreement with the author's opinions but for evaluating the logic and effectiveness of the argument itself.*

> Premises underlie many kinds of thinking, especially deductive reasoning in which conclusions can be drawn from specific premises.

◎ Organizing a Rhetorical Analysis

The Introduction

A typical rhetorical analysis begins with an introduction that includes a generalization about the essay and/or the topic, such as its importance or relevance in today's world. It must also include a summary of the author's thesis. If a reader of your analysis isn't familiar with the source text, you should summarize the essay or at least give enough detail so that he or she will understand its essence. Summarization can be an important part of a rhetorical analysis, but rhetorical analyses are much more than simple summaries.

At the end of your introduction, include your thesis statement. The form of the thesis depends on the kind of text you are analyzing and your purpose. Essentially, though, it should address whether the text successfully fulfills its purpose and supports its own claims. If the essay is argumentative, your thesis might summarize the essay's strengths and weaknesses, concluding whether it is effective or not.

The Body Paragraphs

In the body paragraphs, your analysis should break down the most relevant features of the essay, attempting to explain how these features, such as the author's methods and rhetorical strategies, reflect his or her purpose, objectives, and audience. The aim is to explain and evaluate the how and the why of the source text: How does the author explore the subject, prove the claim, and support the main points? Why are those particular methods and strategies used and not other ones? What are the essay's strengths and weaknesses? How could the text be improved?

In any analysis, being specific is vital. Support all claims you make about a text by examples from the text, ensuring you include a citation for direct quotations and other specific points.

> In any analysis, being specific is vital. Support all claims you make about a text by examples from the text.

The Conclusion

In your conclusion, do not introduce new material. You could begin by referring to your thesis and answering the question of whether the essay was successful. A longer conclusion might summarize the essay's strengths and weaknesses, as discussed in the body paragraphs. One way to end is to comment on the essay's significance or influence, or suggest what can be learned from it.

Box 3.1   Preparing to Write a Rhetorical Analysis

The questions below, organized according to purpose, can form the basis of a rhetorical analysis. (Note also that many of the questions and activities that follow individual essays in this textbook are the kinds of questions you can ask of a text as you read it in order to analyze it.) The nature of the text itself and other factors help determine which questions of those below are the most relevant to your analysis; for example, the author of an article in an academic journal does not usually need to consider special strategies in order to create reader interest.

(continued)

Explaining

- [ ] When was the essay written, relative to similar studies in the field?
- [ ] Why was it written? Is it intended to inform, explain, persuade?
- [ ] For what kind of audience is it written? How do you know this?
- [ ] What do you know about the author? Does he/she appear to be an expert in his/her field or otherwise qualified to write on the topic? How is this apparent (if it is)?
- [ ] Is there an introduction? What is the writer's thesis or central question? What is the justification for the study? In what way(s) does the author propose to add to his/her field of knowledge? Is there an essay plan? How does the author convey essay structure?
- [ ] What are the essay's main points?
- [ ] What format does the essay follow? How does the text reflect the conventions of the discipline for which it was written? Does it follow these conventions exactly, or does it depart from them in any way?
- [ ] What kinds of evidence does the author use? Which are used most extensively?
- [ ] Is there a stress on either analysis or synthesis in the essay? (See pp. 127 and 130.) On both equally?
- [ ] What inferences are readers called on to make?
- [ ] How is the essay organized? Is there a primary rhetorical pattern? What other kinds of patterns are used?
- [ ] What level of language is used? Does the author include any particular stylistic features (e.g., analogies, metaphors, imagery, unusual/non-standard sentence structure)?
- [ ] Is there a conclusion? What is its primary purpose?

Evaluating/Critiquing

- [ ] In the introduction, does the author successfully prepare the reader for what is to follow?
- [ ] Does the author manage to create interest in the topic? How is this done? Would other strategies have worked better?
- [ ] Main points: Are they identifiable (in topic sentences, for example)? Are they well supported? Is supporting detail specific and relevant?
- [ ] If secondary sources are used, are there enough? Are most of them current references?
- [ ] What kinds of sources were used? Books? Journal articles? Websites? Other? Has the author published related works in the field of study?

(continued)

☐ What kinds of strategies and techniques does the author use to facilitate understanding? Are they effective? Are there other ways that organization or content could have been made clearer?

☐ Does the essay appear free of bias? Is the voice as objective as possible, given the argumentative stance? Has slanted language been avoided?

☐ Does the author appear reasonable? Has he/she used reason effectively, establishing a chain of logic throughout? Are there failures in logic (logical fallacies)?

☐ Does the author make the issue relevant to the reader? Does he/she appeal to the reader's values? Does he/she use other argumentative strategies?

☐ Does the author make emotional or ethical appeals? Are they extreme or manipulative? Are there any emotional fallacies? For more information on argumentative strategies, see chapter 4, "The Art of Argument."

☐ What makes the conclusion effective/ineffective?

Table 3.1   Main Features of Rhetorical Analyses and Critical Responses

Type of Assignment	Purpose	Style and Audience	Typical Activities/ Structure
Rhetorical analysis	To examine how a text is constructed and assess its importance or influence, or both; to better understand types of texts and arguments, their uses, and their effectiveness	Written in formal style and objective voice for readers knowledgeable about rhetorical practices and argumentative strategies	Focused reading; comprehension and critical thinking; analyzing and evaluating; stating main features of source text in thesis; breaking down text and its arguments to provide support for thesis; focusing on source text
Critical response	To explore your views on a topic and share them with others	Written in semi-formal style, perhaps from first-person point of view, for readers interested in the topic who might also have opinions and observations about it	Critical thinking; expressive and/or personal writing; stating your agreement/ disagreement in thesis; moving back and forth between text and your views and/or experiences

◎ Sample Rhetorical Analysis

The rhetorical analysis below, on Mark Edmundson's "Narcissus Regards a Book" (see p. 285), highlights some of the main features of the source text, using summary, explanation, and evaluation. The annotations refer to many of the points discussed above.

Sample Essay

A Critical Analysis of "Narcissus Regards a Book," by Mark Edmundson

Matt Gomez

In the first three sentences, Matt announces the topic and kind of essay. He summarizes its main point and explains the author's position or stance.

[1]"Narcissus Regards a Book," by Mark Edmundson, is a humanities-style essay that comments on popular media and the people who consume it. Edmundson portrays modern media as an institution geared to public taste, which began to stagnate when a previous generation of teachers and scholars failed to stress the value of classic literature. As a result, Edmundson contends that the "common readers" of today are ill-informed and too enamoured with their own personal tastes to explore literature that is influential or challenging. Published in *The Chronicle of Higher Education*, this essay is written for university faculty and administrators, and Edmundson's main points must be seen in this context. Despite some reckless generalizations and a somewhat elitist perspective, Edmundson's essay effectively asserts the argument that society is frozen by its own reflection.

Importantly, Matt stresses the relationship between Edmundson's essay and its intended audience. In his own thesis, Matt evaluates the author's success.

[2]Edmundson begins his essay by explaining "the common reader": someone who reads for amusement. In the average person's binary existence, consisting of work and play, reading is used as a way "to be diverted, assuaged, comforted, and tickled" (286) in between shifts and work weeks. Edmundson notes that in modern times "reading has largely become an unprofitable wing of the diversion industry" (286) that would disappoint the protesting youths from twenty years ago. The author then refers to a recollection of these youths, who questioned what they were being taught: "Students paraded through the campuses and through the quads, chanting variations on a theme. Hey, hey, ho, ho—they jingled—Western culture's got to go" (286). These students attracted attention from the media but were ultimately ignored by their professors. The essay places importance in the non-action of the students' educators, and then brings focus back to the present, where these students are now "working the levers of culture" (287). As arbiters of art and literature, they are "not comfortable with judgments of quality" (287) because they were not taught by the teachers who chose

to ignore their inquiries twenty years ago. This failure to "answer the question of value" (287) gave rise to the simple logic of what Edmundson calls "entertainment culture": "if it makes you feel good, it must be good" (287). According to the author, this way of thinking dictates the modern media, which now panders to the public's banal, self-affirming tastes. Edmundson concludes the essay by pointing out that there are common readers who forgo the entertainment culture; they "read in pursuit of influence" (288), and this quality, according to Edmundson, is "the desired thing."

[3]As Edmundson's essay was not scholarly, it did not require cited references. However, Edmundson's exposition sometimes slips into generalizations that feel too open-ended, even for a Humanities-style essay. For example, when Edmundson recounts the student protests, he fails to give the anecdote any grounding in specific time or place. Instead he uses vague terms: "the conservatives" referred to the tight-lipped professors, "the rebels" were the protesting students, and "the academy" represented the institution in question. By being overly general, Edmundson weakens an otherwise interesting example. Later, the author directly links the protests to the modern-day prevalence of entertainment culture: "The academy failed and continues to fail to answer the question of value, or even to echo the best of the existing answers. . . . So the arbiters of culture—our former students—went the logical way. They said, 'If it makes you feel good, it must be good'" (287). This connection presents a logical fallacy because Edmundson suggests that the lack of discourse between the students and teachers twenty years ago directly caused the phenomenon where trite, shallow literature is consumed by the masses. Edmundson expands with the example that "it seems that no one anymore has the wherewithal to say that reading a [Stephen] King novel is a major waste of time" (288). Harsh judgments aside, in reality Stephen King has been a novelist for over twenty years, finding commercial success well before the student protests. Furthermore, the prevalence of "bad literature" has been in existence since the times of Blake, Shakespeare and Chaucer; however, Edmundson chose to unfairly compare the seminal classics to the ephemerally popular pieces of literature that have yet to stand the test of time.

Throughout this summary paragraph, Matt combines his own words with significant words from his source. Doing so produces an efficient and highly readable paragraph and demonstrates his familiarity with the text he is summarizing.

In this sentence, which serves as a prompt for the paragraph's topic sentence, Matt shows his credibility by acknowledging that the source text is not scholarly and, therefore, does not include citations.

Matt carefully supports his point concerning the author's generalizations by analyzing an example of a generalization. However, his criticism is phrased in a positive way and does not seem an unfair attack: "Edmundson weakens an otherwise interesting example."

He continues this paragraph, which focuses on criticism mentioned in his thesis, by using two other key examples.

Matt uses square brackets to add information needed to make sense of the direct quotation (see p. 85). He finishes by suggesting Edmundson's elitist perspective, again referring to his own thesis.

In the topic sentence of his final body paragraph, Matt gives examples of the essay's strong points.

[4]Although Edmundson uses some ineffective argumentative techniques, he is quite successful in establishing credibility and a core message for his intended audience. For example, he establishes a credible voice through his writing style. Edmundson decides to discuss "the value of pure and simple literary pleasure" (287) by writing in a literary style, and he communicates his expertise on the subject by doing this. Also, Edmundson's negative tone when he describes the media is ultimately positive, given the context. The essay's attack on institutions that "no longer seek to shape taste" and readers that are "in love with [themselves]" (288) is not necessarily a scathing rebuke on local newsstands or today's housewives; it is a reminder to the teachers and administrators who read *The Chronicle of Higher Education* that the young influential minds of today, who read for more than pleasure, are "in [their] classrooms [and] before the pages of [their] poems and prose" (289), not to be ignored or belittled.

Matt's subtle reasoning and clear explanation demonstrate well-developed critical thinking skills.

[5]Even though some of his points are stronger than others, Marc Edmundson convincingly argues to his peers the importance of engaging students. If the essay's clarion call goes unheard, Edmundson predicts a dreary literary landscape that is as shallow and redundant as a reflecting pool.

Although Matt's conclusion could be considered too brief, it is made effective by the final image, recalling the metaphor of Narcissus.

◎ Sample Critical Response

In the following critical response, student writer Emily Tant draws on her observations about today's readers, using informal diction and referring to herself in the first person. Her response was part of an online forum in which students were asked to respond to one point from the essay. Many critical responses are more thorough and include a thesis, along with more supporting evidence.

Sample Essay

A Critical Response to "Narcissus Regards a Book," by Mark Edmundson

Emily Tant

[1]Although I found Marc Edmundson's view on society and its mindless choice of reading material slightly harsh, I have to admit that he makes valid points in his argument. People tend to read tabloids because it takes them out of their own lives, giving them a break from stress. They enjoy this kind of reading because they are not forced to critically analyze and assess anything. It is purely for entertainment. As Edmundson states, literature no longer seems to hold the prominent position that it used to. Instead of challenging our minds to question and learn from literature, many people in our fast-paced society would much rather kick back with a substance-less tabloid or light reading that will simply distract them for the time being.

[2]Mark Edmundson's "Narcissus Regards a Book" may frustrate and insult readers who love to indulge in their celebrity magazines, cheesy love novels, and propaganda, but he forces us to look at our reading choices with a critical eye. Many options and genres of reading exist today, and it is up to each individual to choose whether or not to read for entertainment or for academic and intellectual pursuits.

◎ Chapter 3 Review Questions

1. Compare and contrast rhetorical analysis and critical response in their
   a. Purpose
   b. Kinds of skills involved
2. A rhetorical analysis can best be compared to which one of the following?
   a. A summary
   b. A literary analysis
   c. An argumentative essay
   d. A research paper
3. Explain two features of the introduction of a critical analysis.
4. Answer true or false:
   a. Examples are a crucial part of successful body paragraphs in a critical analysis.
   b. Approximately half of the critical analysis should be spent on summary.
5. How important is it to consider intended audience in a critical analysis of a work? Explain your answer.

◎ Key Terms

critical response (p. 29)
rhetoric (p. 29)
rhetorical analysis (p. 29)

CHAPTER 4

The Art of Argument

In this chapter, you will learn:

- What the three different argumentative models are and how they are used

- What the goals of argument are

- What the different types of argumentative claims are

- How to use different kinds of evidence

- How to identify effective and ineffective uses of reason

- How to use strategies for effective arguments

- How to use rebuttal techniques

Classical argument had its origins among the ancient Greeks. The development of a scholar's rhetorical skills remained a vital part of Western education up to the end of the nineteenth century and beyond and was considered ideal vocational training. Specifically, the formal debate was thought to demonstrate life skills such as mental and verbal sharpness.

◎ Argument and Aristotle

Although **rhetoric** has taken on a range of meanings today, the Greek philosopher Aristotle (384–322 BCE) uses "rhetoric" to stress a speaker's choices available to persuade an **audience**. He believed that readers (or, more often listeners) would need to be persuaded—that showing knowledge alone was not enough. Aristotle identifies specific *topoi*, or strategies, that could help persuade an audience. Two such strategies are definition and comparison (see p. 55, below).

AUDIENCE Most writing is designed for a reader or readers. Being aware of potential readers, your audience, will help you decide what to include or not include or, in the case of argument, what strategies to use to help convince this audience.

RHETORIC concerns the structure and strategies of argumentation to persuade the members of a specific audience.

Aristotle divides arguments into three kinds: those founded on reason (**LOGOS**), on morality (**ETHOS**), and on emotion (**PATHOS**).

Aristotle's stress on knowing your audience and adapting your words accordingly remains a fundamental aspect of a successful argument.

Aristotle, who laid much of the groundwork for classical argument in his book *Rhetoric*, divides arguments into three kinds: those founded on reason (logos), on morality (ethos), and on emotion (pathos). Of the three, the most important appeal is to a reader's reason and logic. Ethical appeals play a major role, too, mostly in establishing the arguer's credibility and understanding of morality. Aristotle also stresses the connection between emotional appeals and knowledge of one's audience. He believes this consists not only of knowing the audience's "hearts" but also of understanding the causes of the different kinds of emotions and how they work. The stress on knowing your audience and adapting your words accordingly remains a fundamental aspect of a successful argument. Such knowledge can also be used in making emotional appeals, arousing the feelings of an audience in order to strengthen an argument.

Aristotle names and categorizes certain kinds of logical errors and, as he acknowledges in *Rhetoric*, realizes that faulty or distorted reasoning could seem convincing and even sway the uncritical reader; however, it does not produce a good argument. It fails not only the test of logic but also the test of fairness. (For more about fallacies in argument, see p. 51.)

◎ Two Modern Models of Argument: Rogers and Toulmin

Aristotle's model heavily influenced the development of rhetorical theory through to the twentieth century. But as modern arguers tried to make argument more relevant to real-life situations, two new approaches developed. First we will discuss the importance of Carl Rogers's ideas and then turn to a widely used approach today, that of Stephen Toulmin.

Carl Rogers's Approach to Argument

The approach of Carl Rogers emerges out of communication theory and involves "see[ing] the expressed idea and attitude from the other person's point of view." Rogerian strategies include framing your argument in terms that are acceptable to the other person. Rogers's approach, too, focuses on one's audience; it works best when your reader disagrees with you but is willing to listen.

In classical arguments, concerned mostly with victory, arguers may be encouraged to anticipate counterpoints in order to sharpen their *own* points, and not to genuinely engage with one's critics, as the Rogerian model invites. The Rogerian approach encourages establishing common ground—points of agreement—with your audience and discourages a "winner takes all" approach.

The Rogerian argument uses objective language, pointing out differences between the positions of the arguer and the reader, using strategies throughout that stress fairness and consciousness of the reader's position—for example, the arguer may make concessions as a way of showing the reader that compromise is possible (see p. 54).

Of course, most arguments are not *either* Aristotelian *or* Rogerian, but combine features of both: effective arguments may rely on Aristotle's logical, emotional, or ethical appeals and strategies yet include many features of the Rogers approach. For example, student writer Meg Norlund uses the Rogerian approach, stressing compromise and mutual respect, in the conclusion of her essay on the role of midwifery in the birth experience: "We now need to instill a willingness to have open and constructive dialogue between all birthing professionals" (see p. 64). (See also "Argumentative Strategies," p. 53.)

Stephen Toulmin's Approach to Argument

Stephen Toulmin's ideas are a direct response to the limitations of classical (Aristotelian) argument. The Toulmin model, based on the way lawyers present their cases before courts, was designed for many kinds of arguments, from complex written ones to casual oral ones. In particular, Toulmin realizes that claims alone aren't enough but must have a foundation, a means of linking the evidence to the claim: one can't simply argue in a vacuum. One of Toulmin's important contributions is the concept of the warrant, the basis or foundation of an argumentative claim.

The Role of Warrants in Argument

Strong arguments do not simply consist of an arguable claim and supporting evidence: there needs to be a link between claim and evidence, showing why the evidence is relevant to or supports the claim. Toulmin called this the **warrant**. If the warrant is obvious, it does not have to be announced. The following warrant is clear without being stated:

A **WARRANT** provides the foundation of a claim, linking the evidence to the claim being made.

> **Claim:** I have to buy a new watch.
>
> **Evidence:** My current watch says the same time as it did 30 minutes ago.
>
> **Warrant:** My watch is broken.

The evidence is sufficient support for the claim because the reader would infer the link ("My watch is broken"). On the other hand, if someone used the same claim and offered as evidence "I just bought a new outfit to attend a wedding," a reader or listener might ask what link existed between the evidence and the claim of having to buy a new watch. The speaker might then reply, "I could never show up at a wedding with an accessory that didn't match the rest of my outfit!" which would be an attempt to link the claim to the evidence—for most people, a less convincing one!

A warrant can arise from various sources, including physical laws, human laws, assumptions, premises, common knowledge, ethical principles, or, in the case of the fashionable wedding guest, above, aesthetic values. For an argument to be successful, the reader must agree with the warrant, whether stated or implied.

The underlying assumption of Bruce M. Hicks in "The Undiscovered Province" (p. 333) is based on an ethical principle: self-government for Aboriginals is an important goal for all Canadians as it would make Aboriginal representation a part of the Canadian democratic process. If readers didn't agree with the warrant, the author's claim regarding the creation of a province for Aboriginal peoples would likely be rejected.

> **Claim:** Create a new, eleventh province made up of Aboriginal lands.
>
> **Evidence:** Hicks presents several points to support his claim.
>
> **Warrant:** Aboriginal self-government is necessary for a fully functioning Canadian democracy.

Meg Norlund makes several claims in her essay about midwives (see p. 59). Her most important one is her assumption that the birth experience should be positive and deeply human. Again, if readers didn't accept this, they would be less likely to accept her claim and the supporting evidence.

Another aspect of Toulmin's argument is the need to qualify claims, to avoid absolute statements. A qualified general claim is more acceptable to a reader, who may simply reject a claim that is too broad. With or without a qualifier, though, a claim, says Toulmin, must have something behind it to justify it, to make it reasonable and acceptable to its audience. If arguers ask themselves "Why do I say so?"; "Why is this true/what makes it true?" they will be encouraged to consider the foundation for their claims, the warrant. Looking at *if* and *how* your claim is justified helps prevent the kind of reasoning that sees argument simply as stating your opinion—an oversimplified approach.

Table 4.1 summarizes the major features of the influential argumentative models of Aristotle, Rogers, and Toulmin.

If you ask, "Why do I say so?" "Why is this true/what makes it true?" you will be encouraged to reflect on the basis of your claim. Looking at *if* and *how* your claim is justified helps prevent the kind of reasoning that sees argument simply as stating your opinion.

Table 4.1   Summary of Major Features of Argumentative Models

Argumentative Model/Theory	Original Uses	Key Concepts/Terms	Uses in Argumentative Essays
Aristotle	Oratory/public Speaking	Logical, ethical, and emotional appeals, *topoi* (strategies)	Understanding inductive and deductive kinds of reasoning; using reason effectively; establishing authority and trustworthiness; appealing to audience emotions
Rogers	Psychology/ interpersonal communication	Common ground, consensus	Acknowledging opposing views; laying grounds for trust and acceptance; reaching consensus and mutual understanding
Toulmin	Law	Claim, warrant, data (support)	Providing foundation for/developing a claim to make it convincing; tying claim to support; qualifying claim to avoid generalizations

◎ Purposes for Arguing

From the above, it is evident that argument today cannot be simplified to an "us versus them" approach. Indeed, it can serve various purposes:

- To state or defend your point of view
- To seek to change a situation
- To critique a viewpoint, position, text, etc.
- To expose a problem or raise awareness of an issue
- To consolidate an opinion
- To reach a compromise

The most straightforward purpose for arguing is defending your point of view. By contrast, arguing to reach a compromise involves objectively analyzing both sides of the debate; it could be considered a more realistic approach than just defending your point of view. Thus, in her essay on a section of the Criminal Code that permits corporal punishment under "reasonable circumstances," student writer Danielle Gudgeon steers a middle ground between those who want the law upheld and those who want it abolished. Her middle position makes it likely that an audience on both sides will consider her points, making her argumentative goal more attainable:

Section 43 of the Criminal Code has a social utility for both teachers and parents, but it is an old law that must be amended to reflect society's progression. The addition of clear guidelines to the law regarding the severity of discipline and the use of objects as weapons will create a distinction between abuse and discipline. This will prevent subjectivity within the courts and discourage future abuse, while affording parents the option of disciplining their children.

In "Jazzwomen: The Forgotten Legacies," student writer Danica Long makes it evident in her thesis statement that she is arguing to draw attention to a neglected topic, to make her audience more aware of something:

> Where are all the classic female jazz musicians? In fact, they have excelled on every instrument, in every era, and in every style, yet they have been overlooked or underrated in the history of the jazz profession.

◎ Opinions versus Arguments

An *opinion* is not the same as a *fact*, which can be verified by observation or research; opinions are challengeable.

As you will see, you cannot "argue" a position on a topic that has no opposing view—in other words, that cannot be challenged. Yet, facts can be interpreted differently and used for different purposes. Facts, therefore, can be used to support the thesis of an argumentative essay. However, effective arguers are always clear about when they are using facts and when they are using opinion. In reading, use your critical thinking skills to ask if the writer always clearly separates facts from opinion. If not, he or she might be guilty of faulty reasoning (see p. 51).

Even though "facts" are not challengeable, the *interpretation of facts* may be. Interpreting facts to support your claim is an important strategy in argument. For example, the fact that just over 50 per cent of lung transplant recipients have a five-year survival rate could be used to support a claim that more resources should be allocated to boost this rate. The same statistic could be used to support a claim that fewer resources should be allocated to this procedure since the result is less promising than for other kinds of transplants in Canada. The way that the fact is used varies depending on the nature of the claim.

◎ Claims in Argument

We have been using the word *claim* in this chapter, rather than *thesis* or *point*. Claims are particularly appropriate to argument: a claim is an assertion that you actively attempt to prove through logic and various kinds of evidence in the body of the

---

An opinion is not the same as a fact, which can be verified by observation or research; opinions are challengeable.

A CLAIM is an assertion that you will attempt to prove through evidence. Claims occur in the thesis statement; many topic sentences also assert a claim about the topic of the paragraph.

essay. However, simply claiming something does not entitle you to it: you must convince people that the claim is valid, which is what you do when you argue effectively.

An argumentative claim is usually one of value or policy. In a value claim, you would argue that something is good or bad, right or wrong, fair or unfair, and so on. A policy claim advocates an action. In this sense, a policy claim goes further than the value claim on which it often rests. However, value claims can be used to make your audience consider something in a more positive light. For example, if you argue in favour of euthanasia to an audience of opponents you might not want to use a policy claim, one that focuses on changing laws. A value claim instead would focus on changing attitudes, getting the reader to see, as a first step, perhaps, that euthanasia relieves the suffering of a terminally ill patient. Value claims are used if you are critiquing a viewpoint or text (as book or movie reviews do), raising awareness, or trying to reach a compromise (i.e., to arrive at a middle ground).

> A **VALUE CLAIM** is an assertion about a topic that appeals to its ethical nature (e.g., good/bad or fair/unfair).
>
> A **POLICY CLAIM** is an assertion about a topic that proposes an action (e.g., to fix a problem or improve a situation).

Effective Argumentative Claims

In writing an academic argument, ensure that your claim is *arguable*, *specific*, and *realistic*.

Arguable Claims

It is difficult for facts themselves to serve as the basis of an argumentative claim, though they may be used to support that claim. For example, you could not easily argue against the fact that the closest star to Earth is 4.2 light years away. However, you could use this fact as evidence to support a policy claim, say, for allocating more financial resources to the space program.

In addition, a belief—for example, that God exists—is not arguable in a formal way, although you could argue the merits or interpretation of something within a given belief system, such as the meaning of a passage from the Quran or other religious text. Similarly, you could not logically argue that one religion is *better* than another since there are no clear and objective standards that reasonable members of your audience could agree on. *Arguable claims must be supported through objective evidence, not just opinion.*

> An arguable claim has an opposing viewpoint and has objective evidence to support it.

Where general agreement exists about a value, for example, the value of a safe environment or a healthy diet, you will find yourself arguing in a vacuum. You do not have a meaningful claim if your audience accepts an idea as obvious and not in need of proving. *If you cannot think of a strong opposing view to the one you want to argue, consider revising the topic so that it is arguable, or choose another topic.*

If, however, you are arguing to raise awareness, there may not be another "side." Even so, it is essential that you support your claim by objective evidence.

Specific Claims

A claim should not promise more than it is able to deliver. This applies particularly to claims that are too broad: "we need to change our attitude toward the environment"; "we need to do something about terrorism." On the other hand, if your claim relates to a problem that most people are not aware of, your argumentative purpose would be different—to draw attention to a problem—and it might be possible to argue a broad claim.

One way to narrow a general claim is to think about how it might apply to a subject you know something about. If you have come up with a broad topic, you can ask how it might affect people you know. For example, if you wanted to argue that the media promotes unhealthy weight loss in teenagers, a very big topic, and you were an athlete, you could consider what rules or procedures can lead to unhealthy weight loss in your sport. Many sports, such as rowing, have weight categories. In some provinces, the junior female lightweight category is 135 pounds and under. As a rower, you might be aware of unhealthy eating habits that rowers can develop seeking to remain in a lower weight category in order to be competitive. Your thesis statement might take this specific form: *To help prevent unhealthy and dangerous activities in young rowers, junior lightweight categories should be eliminated from provincial regattas.*

A broad claim can also be made more specific (and manageable) if you can apply it to a particular group. It might be unwise to apply an anti-smoking claim to Canada or even to an entire province since municipalities may have their own smoking bylaws; you might therefore restrict the focus to your city or even your campus. (See Chapter 1, p. 3, for more information about narrowing topics.)

> If a claim is too vague or general, it will be hard to support and to research. Narrow broad claims so that they are specific.

Realistic Claims

Some policy claims are unrealistic because they have little chance of being implemented. You may be able to come up with some points in favour of decriminalizing illegal substances to increase government revenues, but since such arguments would not take account of social conditions today, the claim would not be realistic. Unenforceable policy claims are also unrealistic.

Be careful not to use an exaggerated or weak claim as the basis for your argument—for example, that all cellphones should be banned in public places because they are distracting when they go off. A stronger argument would be for banning cellphone use in your classrooms because it distracts other students.

◎ Kinds of Evidence in an Argumentative Essay

Although an effective argument can be built around reasonable points with logical connections between them, specific kinds of evidence can strengthen a claim. Some are more common to argument than to exposition, but most can be used in both.

EXERCISE 4.1 Collaborative Exercise

In discussion groups, evaluate the five claims below, determining whether they would make good thesis statements for an argumentative essay. Are the claims arguable, specific, and realistic? If not, consider what changes would need to be made to make them arguable. Revise them accordingly.

1. The media has had a negative effect on the self-perceptions of young women.
2. In order to represent the interests of voters more accurately, give voters a wider selection of candidates, and provide a stronger voice for minority issues, the government should adopt the single transferable vote (STV) electoral model.
3. *Harry Potter and the Deathly Hallows Part 2* was the best of the Harry Potter movies.
4. Text messaging should be prohibited because it interferes with the ability to use correct English.
5. Internet dating services are an innovative, convenient, and affordable alternative to the singles scene.

Experts

Experts are directly involved in the issue you are arguing. You will usually use expert testimony to support your claim; however, the occasional use of experts with whom you disagree can make your argument more balanced. If you use experts who favour the other side, ensure you represent them accurately and fairly.

Examples and Illustrations

Using examples—specific instances or cases—can make a general claim more concrete and understandable, enabling the reader to relate to it. An illustration could take the form of an *anecdote* (a brief informal story) or other expanded example. In her essay "Generation Spend" (p. 199), Erica Alini begins by quoting a contestant on a reality TV show, using her as an example of the modern young consumer.

Anecdotal Evidence

Although anecdotal evidence is not "hard evidence," it can be convincing. Thus, if you are arguing that fighting in hockey should be banned but cannot find enough studies on this topic, you may seek the opinions of coaches or hockey players who

ANECDOTAL EVIDENCE is suggestive rather than conclusive; it is often based on reliable observation.

can comment on their own situations or others they have heard about. Sometimes, anecdotal evidence is combined with hard evidence to give a human dimension to which the reader can relate.

Precedents

A **PRECEDENT** is a specific example that refers to the way a situation was dealt with in the past in order to argue for its similar use in the present.

In law, a **precedent** is an important kind of example, a ruling that can apply to subsequent cases that involve similar facts or issues. To *set a precedent* means to establish a formal procedure for dealing with future cases. In argument, using a precedent—the way something was done in the past—can be particularly effective in policy claims. To use a precedent, you must show that

1.   The current situation (what you are arguing) is similar to that of the precedent
2.   Following the precedent will be beneficial

Of course, you can use a precedent as a negative example as well, showing that it has not produced benefits. For example, the authors of "Why We Should Allow Performance Enhancing Drugs in Sport" (p. 253) mention the negative effects produced by the prohibition of alcohol in the 1920s, including the rise in "black market" production. They then suggest that the prohibition of all performance-enhancing drugs could also have a negative effect.

Precedents can be used effectively in arguing controversial issues, such as decriminalizing marijuana or prostitution, providing universal access to post-secondary education, or justifying safe injection sites in urban areas.

Personal Experience

If you use personal experience, you should stress the ways that it has been a learning experience for you and, therefore, could be for the reader, too. Personal experience alone will not usually produce a good argument.

The occasional use of personal experience in argumentative essays can be a way to involve your reader. In some cases, it can also increase your credibility; for example, if you have worked with street people, you may be well qualified to argue a claim about homelessness.

Personal experience could be direct experience, observing something first-hand or reporting something that happened to a friend. However, simply announcing that you experienced something and benefited by it does not necessarily make your argument stronger; for example, saying that you enjoyed physical education classes in high school is not going to convince many people that it should be a required subject in schools.

If you use personal experience, you should stress the ways that it has been a learning experience for you. The following introduction serves as a compelling set-up for the carefully phrased value claim (italicized):

To most people, my brother, Terry, is just another face on a bus. For me, he is both the inspiration for this paper, and my brother and friend. When Terry was a child, he was diagnosed with autism, a disorder within the Autism Spectrum Disorders (ASDs). While all the other children were stuffing themselves with candy, Terry was "getting his fix" from hockey cards and statistics. At a very young age, he had memorized the statistics of all the major NHL players; for him, hockey was a form of escape. Terry is one of many in North America, where autism is one of the fastest growing but least known developmental disorders. A central question for parents and caregivers of autistic children is the type of education that offers the greatest benefits, an inclusive or exclusive one. Each system has its advantages and drawbacks, making this choice far from simple. However, *an inclusive educational system offers the best hope for those with the disorder to become well-adjusted individuals as well as contributing members of society.* (student writer Alex McLeod)

Facts, Statistics, and Scientific Studies

Policy claims often benefit from factual support. Make sure, however, that all factual data are accurate and clearly presented. Use the most current statistics from the most reliable sources. Referring to a fact, statistic, or study that is outdated can damage your credibility. Be wary of sources that do not reveal where the facts they cite come from or the methods used to obtain the statistical data (see pp. 80–82). Sources need to be acknowledged in your essay. (See "Documenting Your Sources," p. 88).

◎ Two Kinds of Reasoning

Two methods of reasoning are inductive and deductive reasoning. Knowing the differences between them will help you understand how a writer is using reason. Similarly, using one method—or, more likely both—will help you build a stronger argument.

In inductive reasoning, you arrive at a probable truth by observing and recording occurrences. Flaws in inductive reasoning can occur if (1) not enough observations have been made—that is, if there is not enough evidence to draw a conclusion, or (2) if the method for gathering the evidence is faulty.

Thus, researchers try to include as large a sample as possible within the population they draw from, making their findings more reliable. Similarly, researchers reveal the details of their experiment's methodology. They need to show that their evidence-gathering methods are unbiased.

INDUCTIVE REASONING relies on facts, details, and observations to form a conclusion.

DEDUCTIVE REASONING
is based on a
generalization, which
is applied to a specific
example or subset to
form a conclusion.

A **SYLLOGISM** is a logical
three-part structure that can
illustrate how deductive
conclusions are made.

While inductive reasoning works from detail to generalization, **deductive reasoning** begins with generalization, a major premise assumed to be true. A second premise, which is a subset or instance of the major premise, is then applied to the major premise. If both statements are true and logically related, the conclusion follows as true. The deductive reasoning method can be set up as a **syllogism**, a three-part structure that illustrates how deductive reasoning works in forming conclusions. Syllogisms have very complex applications in logic and mathematics. However, in its simple form, the syllogism can show the validity of a conclusion. The conclusion of the following is true because both premises are true and logically related:

> **Major premise:** All students who wish to apply for admission to the university must submit their grade transcripts.
>
> **Minor premise:** Saki wishes to apply for admission to the university.
>
> **Conclusion:** Saki must submit her grade transcripts.

Using Reason in Arguments

Whatever the purpose in arguing—whether to defend your view, expose a problem, or reach a compromise—getting the reader to agree with your premises is vital. It is also vital to make a neutral or hostile reader consider what you have to say; thus, it can be important to use specific strategies like concessions and appeals to common ground. Emotional and ethical appeals are useful argumentative strategies as well (see below p. 54). *But most successful arguments begin and end with your effective use of reason.*

However, reason can also be misused in arguments. Consider the following statements: the first illustrates the misuse of inductive reasoning because there is inadequate evidence to justify the conclusion; the second illustrates the misuse of deductive reasoning because a false premise has resulted in a faulty conclusion. Avoiding logical fallacies (failures in reasoning) in your own essays and pointing them out in the arguments of others makes your arguments stronger and more credible.

Avoiding logical fallacies
(failures in reasoning) in
your own essays and
pointing them out in the
arguments of others makes
your arguments stronger
and more credible.

> 1.   The premier broke a promise he made during his election campaign. He is a liar, and his word can no longer be trusted.

Should you distrust a politician because he broke one pre-election promise? If the premier broke several promises, there would be much stronger grounds for the conclusion. Thus, in most people's minds, there is not enough inductive evidence to prove the claim.

> 2.   Eduardo is the only one in our family who has a PhD. He's obviously the one who inherited all the brains.

Does having a PhD always indicate intelligence? Possessing an advanced degree could be partly a measure of intelligence; it could also indicate persistence, a fascination with a particular subject, a love of learning, inspiring teachers, an ambitious nature, strong financial and/or familial support, and so on.

Using your critical thinking skills will help you identify faulty arguments (see below and "Critical Thinking" in Chapter 7).

Failures in Reasoning

Just as we engage in different kinds of argument every day—from arguments over whose turn it is to clean up to arguments about sports, politics, or other topics we are passionate about—so we often make errors in our reasoning. The most common kind is rationalizing. Indeed, procrastination is a form of rationalizing in which you constantly make delays appear reasonable.

When you rationalize, you construct a framework for argument to hide the absence of one, substituting a convenient or unconvincing claim—for example, I can't babysit my young brother tonight because I have an important test tomorrow. Perhaps you did not intend to study much for the test—or you could easily study while babysitting your brother, an option you don't consider. The claim, then, masks the simple fact that you don't want to babysit.

Logical Fallacies

In writing, logical errors tend to be more subtle. They fall into several categories, termed **logical fallacies**. To argue effectively and to recognize weak arguments when you read them, it is not necessary to be able to categorize every failure in logic. Most errors are the result of sloppy or simplistic thinking—the failure to do justice to the complexity of an issue. Developing your critical thinking skills will make you alert to errors of logic. A few examples of faulty reasoning follow.

LOGICAL FALLACIES are categories of faulty reasoning.

Table 4.2   Ten Common Logical Fallacies

Term	Description	Examples
Certain consequences ("slippery slope")	A common fallacy (with other names) that insists that a result is inevitable based on an oversimplified cause–effect relationship	"If we legalize marijuana, other, more dangerous drugs are going to end up being legalized as well."
Circular argument	An argument based on an unproved assumption, as if it didn't need proving	"If *Sesame Street* was such a good show, where is the wave of geniuses out there?" The unproven assumption is that the program was designed to create geniuses instead of to stimulate children's interest in learning.

(continued)

Table 4.2   *(continued)*

Term	Description	Examples
Either/or (false dilemma)	Proposes only two possibilities, one supposedly better than the other	"I'm not a feminist; I'm a humanist." Here the arguer incorrectly suggests that the two are incompatible with the better choice being "humanist." Consider that notorious cry "you're either with me or against me," which takes the logical either/or fallacy and gives it a strong emotional thrust.
False analogy	Compares two things that are, in fact, not alike (while true analogies can provide support for a point, to draw a true analogy, there must be a real basis for comparison)	"Women taking part in combat roles in the army is like men getting pregnant: it isn't natural."
False cause (*post hoc*)	A cause–effect fallacy that asserts that simply because one event preceded another, there must be a cause–effect relationship between them	"I've lost two items in the last week, which is when our new roommate arrived. He must have stolen them." Here a conclusion is formed on the basis of a time relationship (i.e., the recent arrival of a roommate is judged cause for suspicion.) If one of the items was found in the roommate's room, such a conclusion would be more reasonable. A false cause assumes a connection without valid evidence.
Confirmation bias	Selects evidence solely on the basis that the results or argument matches one's own, ignoring contradictory results or arguments	"I found three sources who argue that 9/11 was really a U.S. government conspiracy; that should be enough to prove my thesis." Here the writer has looked for extreme arguments on one side of the issue and ignored contrary explanations. The best arguer looks at opposing views and is prepared to explain why they are inadequate.
Straw man	Misrepresents an opponent's main argument by putting a minor or simplified argument in its place, then attacks the minor argument	"My roommate doesn't go out drinking on Friday night. He doesn't know how to enjoy his life at college, and I'm going to enjoy mine!" The "straw man" is the roommate's decision not to go out drinking, which is then criticized. The roommate might have "fun" other ways or happily spend his or her Friday nights studying.
Hasty generalization	Uses too few examples or other evidence to support a conclusion (generalization)	"This is the coldest January in a long time. So much for the threat of global warming."
"It does not follow"	Suggests that there is a logical connection (such as cause–effect) between two unrelated areas	"I worked hard on this essay; I deserve at least a B+ ." Unfortunately, working hard at something does not guarantee success, even if it does make it more likely.
Red herring	A fallacy of irrelevance that attempts to distract or sidetrack the reader, often by using an ethical fallacy	"My honourable opponent's business went bankrupt. How can we trust him to run the country?"

Emotional and Ethical Fallacies

Fallacies may also make exaggerated or unfair appeals to a reader's emotions or sense of ethics. They are very different, then, from legitimate appeals to emotion. Similarly, using highly charged language often attempts to inflame, rather than inform and convince the reader.

Emotional and ethical fallacies are statements that appeal to a reader's emotions in a manipulative or unfair way, such as a partisan appeal, name-calling (*ad hominem*), guilt by association, or dogmatism (simply asserting something without offering proof—often, over and over). The *bandwagon* fallacy argues in favour of something because it has become popular:

> You have to buy the latest iPhone app. Everyone else has it.

The *ad hominem* fallacy directly attacks the arguer rather than the argument, while the *guilt by association* fallacy argues that something is unacceptable because a supposedly disreputable person or group favours it:

> How bad can whale hunting be when an extremist group like Greenpeace opposes it?

Effective arguers also avoid **slanted language**, negative language used to dismiss an opponent's claims. Simply characterizing an opponent as "ignorant" or "greedy" serves no constructive purpose. Of course, you may be able to show through unbiased evidence that the opponent has demonstrated these characteristics.

EMOTIONAL FALLACIES appeal to the emotions in a manipulative or unfair way, such as a partisan appeal, guilt by association, name-calling, or dogmatism.

SLANTED LANGUAGE is extreme or accusatory language; it will make an arguer seem biased.

◎ Argumentative Strategies

Although effective arguments depend heavily on the use of reasonable claims supported by convincing evidence, logic alone will not necessarily convince readers to change their minds or adopt the writer's point of view. Student writers should consider using the following strategies, depending on topic, purpose, and audience, to shape a logical and appealing argument, one that will make readers more responsive to the claim.

Although many of these strategies can be used at any point in the essay, 1–4 are often most effective when placed in the introduction or conclusion, while 5–7 are often used as supporting evidence in the body paragraphs.

1. *Dramatic introduction:* A dramatic introduction may enable the reader to relate to a human situation (see Chapter 1, p. 9). The introductory paragraph on page 49 illustrates a dramatic introduction to an essay on autism.

Establishing **COMMON GROUND** is an argumentative strategy in which you show readers that you share many of their values, making you appear open and approachable.

2. *Establishing common ground:* Getting your readers to see that you share many of their values enables you to come across as open and approachable. Although familiarity with your audience is important in knowing where your values and those of your audience intersect, you can assume that most readers will respond favourably to universal qualities like generosity, decency, security, and a healthy and peaceful environment. Rogerian arguments stress areas of agreement between arguer and audience.

Making **CONCESSIONS** is an argumentative strategy in which you concede or qualify a point, acknowledging its validity, in order to come across as fair and reasonable.

3. *Making concessions:* In granting concessions, you acknowledge the validity of an opposing point, demonstrating your fairness and willingness to accept other views, at least in part. After conceding a point, you should follow with a strong point of your own. In effect, you are giving some ground to get your reader to do the same. The concession can be made in a dependent clause and your own point in the independent clause that follows: "Although it is valid to say . . . [concession is made], the fact is. . . [your point]."

Concessions can be vital in cases in which there is strong opposition or in which you wish to reach a compromise. In his conclusion, Andrew D. Pinto (p. 268) acknowledges the "laudable humanitarian impulse" behind Haiti relief efforts following the 2010 earthquake before summarizing his key points.

Emotional and ethical appeals call forth the emotions and morals of your reader. They work best when they are subtle and not extreme.

4. *Emotional and ethical appeals:* While dramatic openings can be successful in many argumentative essays, the success of an opening that includes an appeal to emotion depends greatly on your audience. Beginning an essay on animal testing by describing a scene of caged animals at a slaughterhouse may alienate neutral readers. If you do use such an opening, you need to ensure that a typical reader will respond in the way you wish.

Emotional and ethical appeals, however, are commonly used in essay conclusions. They provide a final way that the audience can reflect on the topic. The following conclusion, from an essay about the riots in Vancouver after a Stanley Cup final game, includes both emotional and ethical appeals; the final two sentences also demonstrate the common ground strategy:

Wouldn't it be preferable to live in a society in which we actually *knew* our neighbours to begin with? To know and trust the people around us to act like responsible individuals? To enjoy a culture of mutual respect rather than suspicion, hyper-competition, and meaningless interaction mediated through our phones and iPads?

. . . There was a beautiful outpouring of love and support for our fair city this morning as hundreds of volunteers took to the streets to help clean up the terrible mess from last night. We do have the capacity to be kind, gentle, thoughtful individuals, and, hopefully, we can begin to repair the damage to our tarnished reputation. (Adrian Mack and Miranda Nelson, "Vancouver Hockey Riot is a Symptom of a Larger Problem," p. 210)

In the cases of neutral or opposing viewpoints, emotional and ethical appeals work best when they are subtle, not extreme.

5. *Definition:* Value claims often rely on definition (i.e., explaining what you mean by something). Carefully defining something may give it authority. Then, through the use of logic and various kinds of evidence, you can show that your claim is valid because it supports the definition. For example, the authors of "Why We Should Allow Performance Enhancing Drugs in Sport" use the definition of "the spirit of sport" to help them argue that making drugs available to athletes would not violate this definition (see p. 255).

6. *Comparisons:* Some topics have a compare–contrast component built into them; for example, arguing that it is better to live on campus than off campus or vice versa. For other topics, comparisons can provide strong support for a claim. Remember that comparisons require a valid basis. If you are arguing that professional athletes today are overpaid, comparing today's multi-million dollar salaries to the salaries of North American athletes in the 1920s would not be valid, owing to many factors, including inflationary ones and the additional income available today in endorsements. However, it could be valid to compare an average athlete's salary to the average salary of another working professional today, such as a doctor or lawyer.

    In his essay, "Does Peace Have a Chance?" (p. 237), John Horgan compares the numbers of those killed by armed conflict over several time periods, but carefully distinguishes between raw figures and percentages of total populations so that his comparisons are not misleading. (For a list of essays using comparison, see the inside front cover.)

7. *Appeal to reader interests:* When you appeal to the interests of your readers, you show how they might be affected by your claim. In a policy claim, it might consist of highlighting the practical advantages of adopting the policy or the disadvantages of not adopting it. For example, arguing for a costly social program may be a hard sell to those whose approval and support are vital, such as business leaders. Therefore, you could explain how the program could help them by preventing a bigger problem, such as increased health-care costs or taxes. If you know the values and motivations of your readers, you may be able to use this knowledge to make your points directly relevant to them.

When you appeal to the interests of your readers, you show how they might be affected by your claim.

A way to appeal to the interests of an undecided reader is to offer acceptable options. While not conceding your point, you show that you are flexible and open to alternatives. For example, student writer Meg Norlund discusses birthing clinics as an alternative to a home birth (see p. 62).

EXERCISE 4.2   Collaborative Exercise

Of course, arguments do not always take a verbal form; the image below, used by the Vancouver Humane Society shortly before the start of the 2012 Calgary Stampede, depends at least as much on its visual impact as its verbal one. Analyze the effectiveness of the argument. You could begin by looking at which of the strategies (above) are used and then considering questions like the following:

1. What are the strengths of the argument?
2. What are its weaknesses—e.g., fallacies?
3. How could audience affect the way the "message" is received?
4. Overall, does it satisfy the requirements of a successful argument as discussed in this chapter? Why or why not?

Just 3 months old

Would you abuse a baby to entertain a crowd?

BAN CALF ROPING
www.vancouverhumanesociety.bc.ca

Vancouver Humane Society

◎ Rebuttal Strategies

Since the existence of an opposing viewpoint is usually needed for an argumentative claim, you should refer to it directly in your essay—otherwise, it may appear that you are avoiding it. Although you may use concessions as part of your argument, you will mostly be concerned with refuting the competing claims. In your **rebuttal**, or *refutation*, you show the weaknesses or limitations of these claims.

Here are three general strategies to consider. Which one you use depends on the three factors that you need to take into account when planning your argumentative essay: your topic, purpose, and audience. There may be additional factors involved too, such as essay length.

> **REBUTTAL** is an argumentative strategy of raising opposing points in order to counter them with your own points.

Strategy 1: Acknowledgement

You may need to do no more than simply acknowledge the opposing view if the argument on the other side is straightforward or obvious. For example, this strategy would be a natural choice if the claim argued against the use of pesticides in lawn maintenance. The opposing view is obvious: lawn owners use pesticides to make their lawns look attractive. After acknowledging the competing claim, the writer would go on to raise strong points that counter this claim without necessarily referring to it again.

Occasionally, there may not be a recognizable opposing view to acknowledge. For example, if your argumentative purpose is to raise awareness of an important issue, as Paul Waldau does in "Animal Welfare and Conservation: An Essential Connection" (p. 173), there may be no clear view to refute. He is not refuting the goals of environmentalists but rather trying to get them to see the importance of animal welfare.

> Rebuttals can range from simply acknowledging the opposing viewpoint, to focusing on one or two main opposing points, to presenting a point-by-point critique. The rebuttal strategy you choose depends on your topic, your purpose in arguing, and your audience.

Strategy 2: Limited Rebuttal

In a limited rebuttal, you raise and respond to the major point(s) on the other side, then follow with your own points without responding to all the opposing points. This strategy may be appropriate if the strength of the opposing view depends on one or perhaps two major claims. You would not want to undermine your claim by raising and refuting less important issues unless you are trying to reach a compromise when both strengths and weaknesses might be considered. When you are analyzing the main argument on the other side, however, it is important to represent that position fairly.

Whether you adopt the limited rebuttal strategy can depend on your audience and purpose for arguing. For example, if your audience is not very knowledgeable about an issue, mentioning less important points on the other side might be counterproductive since the readers might not have been aware of them before you mentioned them.

Strategy 3: Full Rebuttal

There are two ways to organize a full rebuttal. You may raise competing claims and respond to them one at a time (*point-by-point rebuttal*). Although concessions could be involved, especially if your purpose is to arrive at a compromise, usually you point out the flaws in each before responding with your counterclaim.

Alternatively, you could summarize the competing claims before you present the support for your claim, right after your introduction or after your support, just before your conclusion (*block rebuttal*). Point-by-point rebuttals can be very effective if the competing claims of an argument are well known, as in the essay on the use of performance-enhancing drugs by athletes (p. 253), or if your readers strongly disagree with you. For example, since Bruce M. Hicks expects many to see his proposal of an "11th province" for Aboriginal peoples as radical or extreme, he carefully anticipates objections and responds to them separately (see p. 333).

If you are responding to a viewpoint in a specific text or if your argumentative purpose is to reach a compromise, you might also choose to use the point-by-point strategy. In the last instance, however, you would be attempting to reach out to the other side (or both sides), showing that you understand the points that define their position. This strategy would demonstrate your knowledge and fairness.

> The most thorough rebuttal is a full rebuttal in which you raise opposing views before countering them. In a limited rebuttal, you raise only the major claims on the other side, ignoring minor claims the reader may not be aware of.

◎ Organizing Your Argument

Before you begin an outline, you should decide on the order of your points. For most argumentative essays, this means choosing between two orders: the climax order or a mixed order. In the first, you begin with the weakest point and build toward the strongest; in the second, you could begin with a strong point—but not the strongest—follow with weaker points, and conclude with the strongest. It may not be advisable to begin with the weakest point if your audience opposes your claim, since an initial weak point may make your readers believe your entire argument is weak.

Other orders are also possible. For example, if you are arguing to reach a compromise, you might need to focus the first part of your essay on one side of the debate, the second part on the opposite side, and the third on your compromise solution. Whatever order you use, it should be identical to the order of points in your thesis statement.

Whichever refutation strategy you use, you should consider outlining the points on the other side before writing the essay—constructing a theoretical argument, as it were. In particular, consider how someone who disagreed with your claim might respond to your main points. This could reveal the strengths on the other side and any weaknesses in your own argument. More important, perhaps, it should serve to keep the opposing view in focus as you write, causing you to reflect carefully on what you are saying and how you say it.

> **CLIMAX ORDER** is the order of points that proceeds from the weakest to the strongest; other orders include inverse climax order and **MIXED ORDER**.

EXERCISE 4.3   Collaborative Exercise

Taking the audience factor into account is very important as you prepare to write an argumentative essay. Constructing an audience plan enables you to consider your approach to the essay, including the kinds of strategies to use. Choose a topic you would like to argue, then team up with two other students and interview the other members of your group to determine (1) their knowledge level, (2) their interest level, and (3) their orientation (agree, disagree, neutral, or mixed) toward your topic; they serve as your "audience," the basis for an audience profile. Then, use this information to construct an audience plan based on your specific audience profile, your topic, and argumentative purpose. Discuss strategies you would use to persuade this audience. Include your topic and your writing purpose in the plan.

This essay uses MLA documentation style (see p. 90).

Sample Student Argumentative Essay with Annotations

Birthing Methods Today: Dollar or Sense?

By Meg Norlund

[1]The natural phenomenon of childbirth, once almost exclusively the domain of midwives and traditional medicine, has been eclipsed by the influence of modern medicine. Globally, the practice of midwifery is a proven system, yet the opportunity for a billion dollar business has undermined this natural process, compelling women to battle to keep the birthing tradition alive and the self-empowerment it creates. At the beginning of the twentieth century, a cultural shift occurred in the United States with midwives being viewed as uneducated and their practice unsafe. The shift of childbirth from midwives to the obstetricians (OBs) has left many women feeling emotionally unsupported and has increased the costs of delivery due to the number of unnecessary medical interventions. Therefore, the business model must be re-focused so that women can feel empowered and responsible for their birthing experience.

[2]Obstetricians are experts, and in contemporary developed countries, people often rely heavily on expert opinions. In a 2010 London *TedTalk*, economist Noreena Hertz explains that "it is still

Meg uses a catchy title to interest the reader.

After briefly discussing the "cultural shift" in which natural childbirth gave way to "the business model," Meg follows with a clear policy claim (thesis) that highlights her most important point: self-empowerment.

experts we rely on the most, especially when the stakes are high and the decision really matters." In a 2009 study, Engelmann et al. attached adults to MRI scans while they listened to experts speak. The authors concluded that the "independent decision making part of the brain switched off," and the participants became agreeable to any advice the experts suggested (qtd. in Hertz). Relying only on expert advice can overwhelm a pregnant woman as she succumbs to every suggestion and subtle coercion because she believes it for the good of the baby. Obstetricians are part of a complex health–delivery system that considers pregnancy and birth like an illness with symptoms to be diagnosed and treated, as befits the medical model. Pregnant patients become statistics, a means to generate dollars based on services offered and provided. A more holistic view of childbirth that is client-centered and relationship-based is being replaced by a "conveyor belt approach to childbirth . . ." (Foster). Escalating malpractice insurance contributes to this change. The potential for a lawsuit and a large monetary settlement may direct some medical interventions as the obstetrician's need for risk-management skews his or her approach.

[3]Obviously, there is a vital, indeed an obligatory, role for medical interventions in defined high-risk pregnancy and deliveries. The problem is that many have filtered down into routine practice, adding to the profitability of the providers. Over the course of the last century, dependence on technology has cost obstetricians "hands-on ability" with pregnant or labouring women, according to Autumn Piontek-Walsh, a doula (labour coach) who has observed over 420 births and is currently a practising psychologist. Fetal heart monitors are used in most hospital births. Their readings are one of the main reasons for emergency cesareans; however, major studies reveal that the monitor results are not an indicator for surgery (Cassidy 121). One-third of all U.S. births in 2007 were delivered by cesarean section (Fillion 15), and today Canada follows closely with 30% (Dezil 58). It is assumed that not all these cesareans were medically necessary. While using this one procedure and its strip readings, the determination was made that vaginal delivery was a greater risk than a twenty-minute surgical procedure. However, the interruption of the mother and

---

Side annotations:

Meg has chosen to refer to the highly technical neurobiological study by Engelmann indirectly, using the phrase "qtd. in" as required by MLA style to refer to the source of her information.

In the first sentence of this paragraph, Meg makes a necessary concession. Note that this sentence acts as a prompt, directing us to the sentence that follows, which makes the point that medical interventions have become routine. See p. 152 for the use of prompts.

In these two sentences, Meg carefully distinguishes between her sources.

baby's first opportunity of touch, which "eases the transition from the womb to the world," can have adverse effects on an infant's first relationships (Dellinger).

[4] Today, women are many generations away from the common occurrence of homebirth. In addition, multi-media programming depicts natural childbirth as a terrifying, bloody and painful experience that requires intervention. Management of pain becomes the priority. This contemporary outlook causes many women to choose convenience over nature. Elective cesarean section deliveries are popular. Data obtained from the Center for Disease Control shows that, on average in the United States since 1992, a fetus is spending one week's less time in the womb. Loss in days of gestation can compromise a baby's lung and brain development, vision, and weight (Johnson). The modernization of childbirth is the new plastic surgery with unintended consequences.

[5] In addition, the cost of health care is exploding. Midwifery is "a means of keeping costs down . . . " (Cutlip). On average in Washington state, a midwife-assisted home birth costs $3,500 including post-partum care. In a hospital, the beginning fee is $10,000, which increases with each prescribed medical intervention (Piontek-Walsh). The home environment is a comfortable and familiar setting for the woman. Hospitals use dedicated wards to serve pregnant women where the constant flurry of activity and noise can create feelings of insignificance. She is a mere cog in a business cycle as "[h]ospitals have to get women in and women and babies out, to make room for the high volume of labouring women coming through the doors at any given day" (Curtis). The backside-baring hospital gown is reason enough to stay confined to the assigned bed, which reduces the walking and kneeling associated with speedier labours. Delayed dilation causes a woman to be labeled "slow to progress," and Pitocin is administered to artificially stimulate labour. This drug causes contractions to be longer and closer together, and subsequently a woman demands a pain-relieving epidural. The epidural slows down the labour, and more Pitocin may be administered. At this point, women connected to the fetal heart monitor will almost always get a reading that indicates that the fetus is in distress (*The Business of Being Born*).

In this unified paragraph, focusing on the technology of childbirth, Meg begins with a concession: interventions may, indeed, be needed in high-risk pregnancies. The problem, she says, arises when they become routine; thus, the first sentence is a prompt, directing the reader to the topic of the paragraph in sentence two. She then provides examples of excessive interventions. She ends her paragraph by mentioning a consequence of high-tech deliveries, the "adverse effects on an infant's first relationships," thus introducing a point that is further developed in the essay.

Meg includes a lengthy paragraph between two shorter ones, showing that she has considered her reader. Note, also, that this paragraph and the previous one conclude with short, forceful sentences.

After describing the physical, personal, and financial costs of the "business model" of birth, Meg turns, in the well-developed paragraph that follows, to a solution to the problem, home birthing with a midwife in attendance.

Meg uses compare–contrast in this paragraph. In fact, a careful reader will see that most of her sub-points here contrast with details surrounding hospital birth previously described.

In this paragraph, Meg briefly suggests two alternatives, birthing clinics and improvements to the hospital birth experience. In doing so, she stresses openness and the willingness to compromise in the interests of making the experience a beneficial one. Meg's flexibility probably also shows that she is conscious of her audience, those who will not necessarily be convinced that a home birth is desirable but who may come to see that an alternative birthing experience could be a better one for the mother and child.

Generally, medical protocol dictates that an emergency cesarean section is the next step in the birth process. The domino effect of medical interventions began when "[b]usiness took over. All of a sudden the concept of normal childbirth changed" (*The Business of Being Born*). Childbirth has become institutionalized and has dismantled women's support systems.

[6]A pregnant woman used to turn to her close female relatives to share the joy of childbirth and to rely on their personal birthing experiences. Today she seeks a medical provider, most often in an obstetrical clinic, and the mysterious process of birth becomes routine. This shift from the home to the hospital has significantly altered the birthing experience with an escalating monetary cost, but also a cost through a loss of tradition, empowerment, and responsibility.

[7]While preserving tradition, yet removing the stigma around homebirths, midwifery has evolved into a reputable, licensed profession with midwives obtaining educational credentials and practical training. Before earning the license, they must assist at 500 births of which 100 or more have involved direct delivery of the baby from the birth canal[1] (Piontek-Walsh). Hour-long prenatal meetings between midwives and clients are common as they cover all the realms of the woman's life. By contrast, a patient meets with her obstetrician from ten to fifteen minutes with a scripted focus centering on the woman as a physical being with measurable signs. Infants born at home will have immediate skin-to-skin touch and nourishment at the breast, promoting a sense of well-being and attachment (Piontek-Walsh). A midwife's approach is relationship-based, giving women permission to be in charge of their birthing experience and honouring their traditions. If, during pregnancy, risk factors are identified, suggesting the possibility of complications at delivery, midwives will make the necessary referral to more advanced obstetrical care, prioritizing the health and safety of the woman and child. Likewise, women with unexpected complications are immediately transferred for increased medical support.

[8]If a homebirth feels too risky and the hospital experience feels too manipulative and impersonal, birthing clinics become an alternative. Staffed with midwives who strive for minimal medical

interventions, birthing clinics honour the woman and her birthing plan, allowing her to feel in control of her delivery process, but with the comfort that a team of specialists is available. For the pregnant woman who decides to receive her prenatal care from an obstetrician and deliver in a hospital, it makes sense that the experience be made as positive as possible. While a reciprocal relationship is difficult to establish within the time allotted for each visit, speaking in common language as opposed to medical code would facilitate communication and build trust. The education and title that supports the OB can overpower a woman's personal birthing plan, but increased time with and consistency of the practitioner would lead to better understanding of a mother's birthing desires.

[9] The trend to increased medical interventions in low-risk births is reversible with more awareness about the safety of traditional birthing ways and the unjustifiable cost differential. Midwifery cuts the umbilical cord (IV lines) from the hospital and the disease model of birthing that is associated with elevated costs. Yet an atmosphere of professional misunderstanding exists whereby midwives often assume that obstetricians will not treat the birth as a personal process and obstetricians condemn the practice of homebirth midwifery as too risky. Marsden Wagner, an MD and former Director of the Women's and Children's Health, World Health Organization, describes these two polar views as "geographers who are trying to describe a country they have never been to because they are too afraid to go there" (*Business*). Education and awareness of the business of birth should allow obstetricians and midwives to come together to rethink and rekindle a more traditional birth experience.

Using the Rogerian model of argument in this paragraph (see p. 40), Meg stakes out the positions of the two sides and attempts to find a meaningful middle ground.

[10] In the United States, the increase in medical interventions and the litigious nature of its citizenry have sent traditional childbirth practices into near obscurity, leaving women vulnerable and disconnected from the anticipation and wonder of childbirth. Business models run hospital-patient care, and obstetricians negate the woman's story because of technology (Piontek-Walsh). Individuals need to be an equal partner in their own wellness experience and stop childbirth from being viewed as a disease that needs treatment. Tina Cassidy, author of *Birth*, drastically predicts that

Here Meg offers a provocative quotation but wisely puts the words in the mouth of another writer, and prefaces the quotation by the word "drastically." (The quotation also includes an analogy, a type of comparison; see p. 15.)

[11]"[g]iven the rate of technology, in one hundred years no one will be giving birth. We'll make children up from artificially conceived fetuses, all done technologically. What people don't realize today is the explosive advancement of technology that can override evolution. We override evolution to make better tomatoes. There's no reason we can't override evolution to make 'better humans.'" (26)

[12]In order to access technology wisely and not for convenience, a woman and her circle of support must be informed of all choices that are relevant and current, in common language, and coherent with her lifestyle. The medical model must change.

Having demonstrated her fairness in the previous paragraphs, Meg follows through with a strongly worded final body paragraph, ending with the short, emphatic statement, "The medical model must change."

[13]Each medical intervention has a cost factor, not only as a defined dollar cost, but also a cost in loss of experience. Childbirth is not a disease with compelling reasons to find a cure. It is a time-honoured tradition that gives women ownership of their bodies and self-efficacy. Obstetricians argue convincingly that in the cases of labour complications, hospitals have excelled. However, complications are the exception—not the norm. Cassidy states, "it is astonishing to me that we can touch the moon and predict the weather, map the human genetic code and clone animals, digitize a photograph and send it from Tokyo to Tehran with the touch of a button, but we can't figure out how to give birth in a way that is—simultaneously and consistently—safe, minimally painful, joyful, and close to nature's design" (8). Society has witnessed the rationale behind the transition from homebirth to hospital. We now need to instil a willingness to have open and constructive dialogue between all birthing professionals.

Meg has used a wide variety of sources in her essay, including a film, a book, and a video, along with newspaper, magazine, and journal articles. She also extensively used an interview with an expert in the field. In particular, the presence of academic sources enhances her credibility.

Note that Meg has correctly formatted her Works Cited page and been careful to precisely follow the requirements of the MLA documentation system as given in the seventh edition of *MLA Handbook for Writers of Research Papers*. See p. 90.

Note

1. The statistics apply to Washington state. Midwifery training in British Columbia is also extensive. See http://www.bcmidwives.com/node/50.

Works Cited

The Business of Being Born. Dir. Abby Epstein. Perf. Riki Lake. Amy Slolnick. New Line Home Entertainment, 2007. Film.

Cassidy, Tina. *Birth: The Surprising History of How We Are Born*. New York: Grove Press, 2006. Print.

Curtis, Beth Leianne. "Believe in Birth." *Natural Life.* 1 Jul. 2008: 44–46. *Academic Search Complete.* Web. 16 Nov. 2011.

Cutlip, Kimbra. "Midwifery Goes Mainstream As Hospitals Expand Options and Cut Costs." *Hospital Topics* 75.3 (1997): 17. *Academic Search Complete.* Web. 16 Nov. 2011.

Deziel, Shanda. "Don't Let Anyone Watch: One of the Fathers of the Natural Childbirth Movement Says Exhibitionist Births Are Dangerous." *Maclean's.* 28 Nov. 2011: 58. Print.

Dellinger, Juliana. "Infant Massage: Communicating Love Through Touch." *International Journal of Childbirth Education* 11.4 (1996): 34–37. *Academic Search Complete.* Web. 9 Nov. 2011.

Fillion, Kate. "On Labour, How Epidurals Changed Childbirth, and Why Women Don't Have to Push So Much." *Maclean's.* 3 Oct. 2011: 14–15. Print.

Foster, Sarah. "Why Women Need to Regain Control in Childbirth." *Northern Echo.* Newsquest Site Network. 16 Aug. 2005. Web. 9 Nov. 2011.

Hertz, Noreena. "How To Use Experts—and When Not To." *Ted Global.* London, November 2010. Web. 9 Nov. 2011.

Johnson, Nathanael California Watch. "Experts Warn of Health Risks with Early Births Study Finds Huge Increase in Number of Women Giving Birth Early for Nonmedical Reasons." *Press Democrat (Santa Rosa).* 28 Dec. 2010: A1. *Academic Search Complete.* Web. 17 Nov. 2011.

Piontek-Walsh, Autumn. Personal Interview. 12 Nov. 2011.

◎ Chapter 4 Review Questions

1. Describe two features applicable to argument that have been developed by each of the following:
   a. Aristotle
   b. Rogers
   c. Toulmin

2. Choosing two of the argumentative purposes listed on p. 43 and two topics, come up with a simple thesis statement for each that reflects the argumentative purpose.

3. Explain the differences between an opinion, a fact, and the interpretation of a fact.

4. a. Why might *claim* be a better word than *thesis* in argument?
   b. Identify two kinds of claims in argument.

5. What is needed for a valid claim (thesis) in an argumentative essay? What two other factors could affect the validity of your claim?

6. When might you choose to use the following in an argumentative essay?
   a. Anecdotal evidence
   b. Personal experience
7. What two steps are necessary to ensure that you use a precedent effectively?
8. The kind of reasoning that depends on the truth of a general statement is called _____ reasoning. The kind of reasoning that depends on observation and measurement is called _____ reasoning.
9. a. In your own words, define *logical fallacy*.
   b. For two of the logical fallacies discussed in Table 4.2 (pp. 51–52), come up with one example of your own that illustrates the fallacy.
10. How is an emotional or ethical fallacy different from an emotional or ethical appeal?
11. Write a sentence that contains an example of slanted language. Suggest two substitutes for the word or phrase that would result in a sentence without bias.
12. Answer true or false:
    a. Making a concession weakens your argument.
    b. When you appeal to reader interests, you try to get the reader interested enough to read on.
    c. Emotional and ethical appeals usually work best when they are not extreme or exaggerated.
13. What is a rebuttal and when is it needed in an argument? In which case(s) might it be unnecessary?
14. Explain the difference between a limited and a full rebuttal. When might a limited rebuttal be a better choice than a full rebuttal?
15. What does the order of points in an argument refer to?

◎ Key Terms

anecdotal evidence (p. 47)

audience (p. 39)

claim (p. 44)

climax order (p. 58)

common ground (p. 54)

concession (p. 54)

deductive reasoning (p. 50)

emotional and ethical fallacies (p. 53)

ethos (p. 40)

inductive reasoning (p. 49)

logical fallacies (p. 51)

logos (p. 40)

mixed order (p. 58)

pathos (p. 40)

policy claim (p. 45)

precedent (p. 48)

rebuttal (p. 57)

rhetoric (p. 39)

slanted language (p. 53)

syllogism (p. 50)

value claim (p. 45)

warrant (p. 41)

CHAPTER 5

Writing the Research Paper

In this chapter, you will learn:

- ◎ How to generate a thesis or research question
- ◎ How to write a research proposal
- ◎ How to use research strategies, including library resources and search techniques

- ◎ How to identify credible sources
- ◎ How to integrate sources into your writing
- ◎ How to cite sources using different documentation styles

Research essays call on a variety of reading and writing skills, many of which have been discussed in Chapters 1–4; others will be discussed in the remaining chapters. However, the fundamentals of research extend beyond these skills. In this chapter, we focus on

1. Locating sources in the modern library (pp. 73–80)
2. Assessing the reliability of sources, particularly those accessed electronically (pp. 80–82)
3. Integrating ideas and words smoothly and efficiently (pp. 82–86)
4. Giving credit to your sources (pp. 86–95)

But let us begin with an overview of the research process.

◎ Coming Up with a Topic

For many students, finding a topic is the first challenge to overcome. Here are some questions to consider if you need to come up with a topic from scratch:

- Where do your interests lie? You can consider hobbies, leisure pursuits, reading interests, extracurricular activities, and the like. Has a topic been discussed in another class that stimulated your interest? If so, this might be a good opportunity to explore it further.
- Is there something you have a unique perspective on? For example, Alex McLeod began his essay on autism and the education system after thinking about the school experience of his brother, who has autism (see p. 49). What would you like to learn more about? Curiosity is a good motivator. Writing a research essay is a good chance to satisfy that curiosity.
- What topic do you think readers might like to learn about? Thinking of *other* people's interests can guide you to a worthwhile topic. What topic could benefit society or a specific group in society (for example, students at your college/university or workplace)? Bethany Truman decided to write on relational bullying when she recalled how people around her reacted to hurtful words and gestures (see p. 71).
- Can you think of a new angle on an old topic? Neglected areas of older topics can be new opportunities for exploration or updating. Checking out "what's trending" and similar "hot" topics online can be useful at this early stage, though such topics may not have been well-researched yet.

◎ Preparing for Research

Research often begins after you have come up with a research question or a statement of a problem to be investigated. However, your question or thesis will likely not be clear until you have done some preliminary research.

Typically, this begins with narrowing a general topic. If you began with a topic like "energy sources in today's world," you will soon find that the topic is too large; the information available would overwhelm you. However, you can use any of the pre-writing strategies discussed on p. 3 to make the topic more manageable.

One way to narrow the topic of energy sources is to focus on alternatives to fossil fuels; for example, nuclear power, with its safety and environmental concerns, or thermo-mechanical energy, which is often considered a less viable long-term energy source. Most of this research must be done either in the library or online using your library's electronic resources.

Your reading will narrow the topic further. It could lead you to three specific energy sources: bio-diesel, solar energy, and hydrogen. However, if you wrote on all three sources in one essay, you would not be able to include much detail; you could not thoroughly explore the topic. These energy sources all offer a potential global solution to the energy crisis, but which offers the *best* potential based on what you

After completing preliminary (exploratory) research, you should be able to phrase your main idea or question as a thesis statement. Remember that a thesis or research question represents a solid starting point; it can change as you continue your research.

have read about them so far? Now focusing your research on comparing the costs and benefits of these three energy sources, you might decide that the most promising is hydrogen. After completing your preliminary research, you might come up with the following thesis:

> Current research into the development of alternative fuels provides hope for an oil and nuclear-free future, but of the different types of alternative fuels, hydrogen is the most promising because it satisfies the requirements for a long-term energy plan.

You could also phrase your thesis as a research question:

> Among the various alternative fuels being promoted today, does hydrogen live up to the claims of its advocates by being able to satisfy the requirements for a long-term energy plan?

Note that if you use a research question as a thesis, you do not answer your question yet; the answer(s) will be revealed as you explore the topic in your body paragraphs, and it will be summarized in your conclusion (see, for example, Bethany Truman's essay on p. 96). If your thesis is a statement, your conclusion will be part of the statement itself, as the thesis statement example above reveals (see, for example, Meg Norlund's argumentative essay on p. 59). Your instructor might have a preference for one or the other form.

Now, with a tentative thesis and organizational pattern (cost–benefit analysis in the case of the topic discussed above), you can conduct further research by turning to specific journals, especially peer-reviewed journals in which academics, scientists, and researchers publish their findings. This is where library search skills enter the picture. Knowing how the modern library works will save you a lot of time and help you find high-quality sources. By following the guidelines in "Research Resources for Today's Student," p. 73, you will be able to locate sources directly relevant to a topic like energy in peer-reviewed journals.

What if you can't find many academic sources during your preliminary research? It might be acceptable to use reliable non-academic sources, such as articles in newspapers, magazines, and websites. In fact, if your topic is very current, such sources may be the only ones available. Always be clear on what kinds of sources are permissible by checking the exact wording of the assignment, or ask your instructor for clarification.

As well as academic and non-academic sources, consider the potential value of questionnaires and surveys, along with interviews with experts or others directly involved in the field you are investigating.

If you use a research question as a thesis, your answer to the question will be revealed during your research and summarized in your conclusion; if you thesis is phrased as a statement, your conclusion will form part of the statement itself.

In **PEER-REVIEWED JOURNALS**, submissions are reviewed by experts before publication.

Always be clear on what kinds of sources are permissible by checking the exact wording of the assignment, or ask your instructor for clarification.

◎ Research Proposals

Before you undertake your major research, it is useful to write a research proposal. The main purpose of a proposal, whether for your instructor or the kind of fully developed proposal used in the workplace, is to convince a reader that the project you propose is worth doing and that you are the right person to do it. For you, the student researcher, a successful proposal will persuade your instructor that you have done adequate preparation and are on the right track to a successful research paper.

At a minimum, research proposals need two parts: (1) a description of what you are undertaking (the "what") and (2) your methodology (the "how").

1. Description

What are you proposing to do? Begin by providing background information about the topic. This could include what you already know or have recently learned, such as any controversy related to the topic, the kind of research being done, relevant definitions, and the like. You could also include your reason for wanting to explore the topic; thus, you could mention how you became interested in it or its importance to others.

The proposal represents a *probable* plan: your thesis and main points are tentative at this stage and can be revised as you learn more about your topic. At the end of this section, include your thesis/research question. You may also include your main points or other questions related to the topic. In the sample proposal below, the student incorporates some of her main points or questions into the two paragraphs she devotes to the description of her topic.

2. Methodology

How will you approach your topic and conduct research? Here you should include the sources you have found useful so far and the kinds of sources that you will be looking at as you continue your research. Be as specific as possible. Give names of books, journals, websites, and so on, along with article titles. If you are planning other kinds of research, such as interviews or questionnaires, mention them too. The more detail you provide, the more your reader will be convinced. Being specific makes your proposal credible.

For you, the researcher, the proposal serves as a plan to follow; it solidifies your topic and your approach to the topic in your own mind. A proposal may even include projected dates, such as the date you plan to begin your major research and the date you plan to complete it.

A successful proposal will persuade your instructor that you have done adequate preparation and are on the right track to a successful research paper. At a minimum, research proposals need two parts: (1) a description of what you are undertaking and (2) your methodology.

Research proposals have two main functions: (1) they should convince the reader that you will do a good job (e.g., by showing you are interested in the topic and have done preliminary work); (2) they should give you a plan to follow for your research.

◎ Sample Proposal

The sample research proposal below is by the writer of the essay on p. 96. While an outline represents your essay's structure, a proposal usually precedes the outline and has an exploratory function. Therefore, not all the points in the proposal below were included in the essay itself; furthermore, while the student's title suggests that she will look at both relational and physical aggression, she likely found this approach too broad, and she ended up discussing mostly relational bullying. (See her essay on p. 96.)

Sample Proposal

Research Proposal for "The Impacts of Relational Bullying on School-Age Children in Comparison to Physical Bullying"

By Bethany Truman

Description

[1]Bullying can come in many forms and affect people in different ways. While groups of girls tend to utilize "relational" bullying (that is, spreading rumours, gossiping about others behind their backs, verbal abuse, threats, etc.), boys usually implement more straightforward, obvious forms of physical aggression. Without doubt, both kinds of bullying can inflict serious harm on the victims, but is one ultimately more damaging than the other? With such differing impacts—damaged self-esteem versus a broken nose—it can be hard to determine. I chose the topic of relational bullying because it is something that has impacted both me and many people around me growing up. It has always struck me how words can sometimes be even more powerful than physical violence and how something as simple as a particular gesture or facial expression can be tremendously hurtful.

[2]Early in my essay, it will be important to clearly define the term "relational aggression," so readers have a clear idea of how it can be compared to more overt forms of physical aggression, such as hitting and kicking. I will focus on why this form of bullying attracts more girls than it does boys, as well as how it utilizes its "weapon of subtlety" to internalize self-doubt and insecurity in

(continued)

its victims. Since I will be analyzing the issue within a specific age group (school-age), I will look at possible motivations behind this form of bullying, primarily the attainment of social status. This essay will be organized using a cause-and-effect method, as it will describe various relational bullying tactics and their impacts.

[3]Central research question/thesis: What are the impacts of relational bullying compared to physical bullying, and what makes this more subtle version of aggression so powerful?

Methodology

[4]Most of the credible research in this field has taken place within the last two decades. My sources will consist of recent issues of peer-reviewed journals focused on the issue of relational aggression and its effects on school-age children. Using the library database, I have found several promising articles, including "It's 'Mean,' But What Does It Mean to Adolescents? Relational Aggression Described by Victims, Aggressors, and Their Peers," by Pronk and Zimmer-Gembeck; "Relational Aggression Among Students," by Young, Nelson, Hottle, and Warburton; and "Network Ties and Mean Lies: A Relational Approach to Relational Aggression," by Neal. Each of these articles explores the potential motives behind this form of bullying, the effects it has on targeted individuals, and possible sociological explanations as to why this method of bullying appeals more to some groups than others.

◎ Recording Important Information

Keeping methodical and accurate records during the research phase of the essay-writing process allows you to read material efficiently as well as save time (and your sanity) when you write your paper. You should record notes as you research, ensuring that they include the following information:

- A direct quotation, a summary, or a paraphrase of the writer's idea (if it is a direct quotation, make sure you put quotation marks around it)
- The complete name(s) of the author(s), ensuring correct spelling
- The complete name(s) of any editors or translators
- The complete name of the book, journal, magazine, newspaper, or website
- The title of the specific article, chapter, section, or webpage

- Full publication details, including date, edition, and translation (if appropriate)
- The name of the publisher and the company's location (including province or state) for books
- In the case of an article accessed electronically, the day you viewed the page and either the URL or the digital object identifier (DOI); the date of the site or its most recent update should also be recorded
- The call number of a library book or bound journal (to help you find it again if necessary)
- The page numbers you consulted, both those from which specific ideas came and the full page range of the work (or some other marker, such as section headings and paragraph numbers, for Internet documents without page numbers)

Organizing Research Notes

There are many ways to organize information from your research in order to use it later. The manual method is probably the most familiar to students: notecards, for example, are portable and practical. You can also record notes in a notebook or journal and use tabs to divide the book, using distinct subject headings. In addition, a number of software programs are designed to help with planning and organization. For example, RefWorks (www.refworks.com) is an Internet-based "citation manager" that allows you to import references from popular databases like Academic Search Complete, MLA Bibliography, and EconLit.

Others are databases, such as EndNote (www.endnote.com), Bibliographix (www.bibliographix.com), and Nota Bene (www.notabene.com). Tutorials are usually offered either on the program's website or through a college or university that has purchased licences for registered students. These programs offer many benefits, such as automatic formatting for a variety of citation methods.

◎ Research Resources for Today's Student

The 21st-century academic library can seem like an overwhelming mix of print and electronic resources, especially to the inexperienced researcher. In addition to the "traditional" materials found in the library's online catalogue, there are numerous other online resources available, including databases, e-journals, e-books and other digital formats and media. The sheer volume of information resources in today's academic library need not be intimidating. On the contrary, an effective research strategy enables you to take full advantage of the print and electronic information resources available to you. An effective strategy should include three important considerations:

1. Your *topic* or research question (see above, p. 69)
2. The *resources* that are most likely to contain information about your topic (p. 74)

A **DIGITAL OBJECT IDENTIFIER** (DOI) is a number-alphabet sequence often found on journal articles and begins with the number 10; it serves as a permanent link for digital material.

Keep your research notes, such as summaries and direct quotations, separate from your personal notes. Use a method that clearly distinguishes between the two; otherwise, you could end up plagiarizing by failing to attribute the idea or words of a source, thinking they were your own.

3.   The *search strategy* you will use to obtain information from those resources (p. 76)

When you understand how to choose a well-defined research topic, where to look for information on that topic, and how to construct an effective search in a catalogue or database, you will have the basic tools required for most research projects at the first-year level. As you become a more confident researcher, you can expand on these basic strategies by exploring more specialized resources and experimenting with advanced search methods. As choosing a research topic has been discussed above, we will focus below on choosing resources and coming up with effective search strategies.

Choosing Resources

Subject or Research Guides

When choosing your resources, it is logical to begin with general sources and let them guide you to more specific ones. Most academic libraries provide subject or research guides on the library website. These guides are prepared by subject librarians with specialized knowledge of the information resources for their particular subject areas. Many subject guides provide valuable information on reference resources like dictionaries, encyclopedias, biographies and bibliographies, call number ranges for the subject and select books, key databases, scholarly websites and primary source materials.

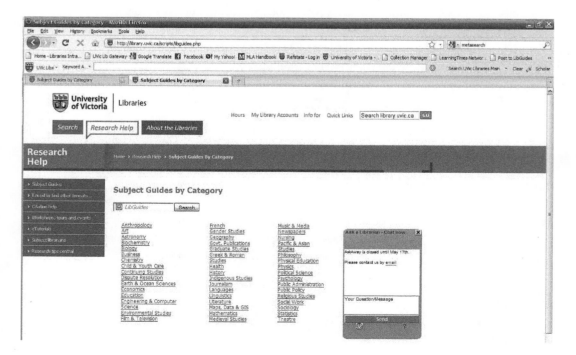

When you understand how to choose a well-defined research topic, where to look for information on that topic, and how to construct an effective search in a catalogue or database, you will have the basic tools required for most research projects at the first-year level.

The Library Catalogue

The library catalogue is an important tool for finding secondary print sources like books, encyclopedias, dictionaries, and journals in your library as well as any electronic versions of these materials that are available. Encyclopedias and dictionaries provide concise, general information on your topic and are often useful for helping you to narrow your focus by highlighting key issues and concepts. Reference sources may also provide suggestions for further research. Scholarly books relevant to your topic are also important sources for you to explore. As well as covering a subject in more depth than a journal article can, they often provide important historical, biographical, literary, or cultural context that may not be available in journal articles. Books also feature tables of contents that can help you to identify important aspects of the subject that you may want to explore further and bibliographies to help you locate other resources. E-books are especially useful for browsing tables of contents and bibliographies and for keyword searching within the full text of a book.

> Use your library's subject guides and catalogue to guide you to general sources, such as encyclopedias, dictionaries, and books where you will learn the key concepts relevant to your topic. They can also suggest more specific research sources.

Online Databases

Scholarly journal articles are a key secondary source for intensive research. Journal articles review what other scholars have said about your topic and often provide important supportive or alternative perspectives relevant to your thesis. Online databases and indexes are your main tools for finding journal articles in both print and online formats.

> Online databases and indexes are your main tools for finding journal articles in both print and online formats. Although books offer an in-depth approach, the most *current* research is usually found in academic journals.

Your library home page may provide a discovery tool such as Summon, or a metasearch tool such as MetaLib, for searching the databases. Summon is a new kind of library search engine with a Google-like interface that includes records for many kinds of sources including books, journal articles, newspaper articles, conference proceedings, dissertations, photos, and multimedia that is owned or subscribed to by the library. Results can be easily limited to scholarly sources and can be quickly narrowed by other facets including subject terms, publication date, and language.

MetaLib enables you to search for keywords for your topic within a predetermined set of general, multidisciplinary, or subject-specific databases. These systems retrieve relevant articles from each database in the set, and allow you to limit your search, save or export your results or link to the full text. This method is useful for quickly finding information on your topic or to identify the best databases for more in depth searching—usually those that return the most results.

Subject-specific Databases

Subject-specific databases are recommended for comprehensive searches on a topic. Most subject areas feature a "core" database that indexes the key journals for that discipline, such as ERIC for education, Sociological Abstracts for sociology, and the MLA International Bibliography for language and literature. It is important to get to know the core databases in your subject area. If your library has subject guides, these list the core databases or "best bets" for each subject. Most libraries also allow you to select databases by subject in addition to providing an A–Z list. This is

Modern libraries now offer options for accessing journal articles and other research sources, including library search engines and metasearch tools. They may also let you locate "core" databases which index journals most relevant to your discipline or field of research.

especially helpful if the database lists include information or abstract pages. These pages provide useful information on the kinds of resources indexed in the database, whether it includes full text, coverage dates available, whether it can be accessed remotely, and anything else pertinent to that particular database.

You should also consider the type of information you require. For example, it is unlikely that you will find complex data or statistical information unless you search a statistical database. Again, the subject guides, "databases by subject" lists, and the database abstract or information pages help you determine which databases include the type of information you need.

Bibliographic and Full Text Databases

Bibliographic databases or indexes contain a bibliographic record or citation for each item indexed in the database. The record usually includes the title, author and other publication information, article type and some subject headings or keywords. There may also be a brief summary of the article, called an abstract (see p. 147). Full text databases include the full text of the article or journal in HTML or PDF format along with the bibliographic record. Most bibliographic databases also enable you to connect to the full text, the library's online catalogue, and the interlibrary loan page through your library's link resolver system, so you may still be able to find the full text of the article even if you are not searching a "full text" database.

Search Strategies

Determining Keywords

Once you have chosen some relevant resources for your subject, the next step will be to identify the key concepts from your topic to use as keywords or search terms.

Once you have chosen some relevant resources for your subject, the next step is to identify the key concepts from your topic to use as keywords or search terms. For instance, if you want to search for information on risk factors associated with homelessness in youth, you will want to identify keywords that embody the concepts *risk factors, homelessness, youth*. Some risk factors might be *poverty, addiction, abuse*, etc. *Risk* or *factors* used as search terms would be far too broad and would not provide good search results. "*Risk factors*" combined as a single term would not find results unless the books or articles used this exact term as well.

Boolean Operators

The actual search process, to be effective, should employ some form of Boolean strategy. The most common Boolean operators, AND, OR, and NOT are used to combine, expand, or eliminate keywords in your search. For instance, AND combines the two different terms *homelessness* AND *youth*. A search conducted using AND also narrows your results compared to searching for each of the keywords separately because sources retrieved must include both terms.

The OR operator is used to expand your search results by including other concepts. These may be synonymous concepts or different aspects of a broader concept.

In this example, you might want to search for results that include the keywords *youth* OR *teens* OR *adolescents* which are synonymous concepts. Or you may want to search for *poverty* OR *abuse* OR *addiction* as different aspects of the risk factors concept. The NOT operator eliminates concepts you don't want to be included, such as *children*, if you don't want results that discuss young children. Use the NOT operator carefully, however, because you may eliminate an article that discusses both children and teens and therefore may be relevant to your topic.

Many databases now allow you to combine your keywords without using the Boolean operators at all. You simply enter your terms and choose the correct search mode. Using Basic Search in *Academic Search Complete* as an example, the search mode "Find all of my search terms" is equivalent to AND, and the search mode "Find any of my search terms" is equivalent to OR. Many other databases and catalogues now work in a similar manner, including Google Scholar.

> Boolean operators help you refine your search by defining relationships between different words or phrases. The most common Boolean operators are AND, OR, and NOT.

Truncation and Wildcards

Boolean search strategy is often used with truncation and/or wildcard symbols. Truncation symbols enable you to include all variants of a search term. Using the asterisk as the truncation symbol in *teen** ensures that your search results include all the terms: *teen*, *teens*, and *teenager*. Wildcards are used *within* a word, for instance in *colo#r* to search for an alternate spelling (*colour* and *color*) or *wom?n* to search for any unknown characters (*woman* and *women*). Most databases and catalogues use the asterisk (*) or a question mark (?) for the truncation or wildcard symbol. Some databases may also use the pound sign (#) or another symbol. If you are not sure what symbol to use, check the help menu. This is usually located in the upper right-hand corner of your screen. The help menu will also provide information on other advanced search strategies that can be used in that particular catalogue or database.

Basic or Advanced Search

Online catalogues and databases usually feature simple or basic search and advanced search options. The basic search field can be used to enter single terms, as described above, or more complex search statements using Boolean operators. However, to construct a search statement using Boolean strategy in a basic search field, you must use parentheses to separate the OR terms from the AND terms as indicated below. The database searches for the terms in parentheses first, then from left to right.

(Homeless* OR runaway*) AND (teen* OR adolescen* OR youth) AND (poverty OR abuse OR addict*)

Also, if you want to use a combined term such as *risk factors*, you must use quotation marks unless the field provides the option to search two or more words as a phrase.

The advanced search option is set up to allow you to insert your terms and then select AND, OR, or NOT to combine the fields and to add additional fields, if necessary. Advanced search also allows you to search for terms in various fields, such as *All Text*, *Author*, *Title*, *Subject Terms*, etc., or you can leave it on the default setting. By selecting a specific field, you limit the search for your term to that field alone. It is often best to try a search in the default field initially and then try other advanced strategies to refine your results, if necessary.

> The advanced search option is set up to allow you to insert your terms and then select AND, OR, or NOT to combine the fields and to add additional fields, if necessary. Advanced search also allows you to search for terms in various fields, such as *All Text, Author, Title, Subject Terms*, etc.

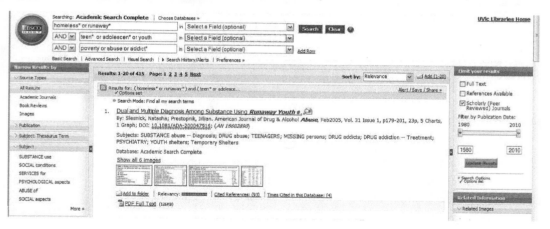

Subject Headings or Descriptors

Subject headings or descriptors are very useful for refining your search strategy. Subject headings have been applied to each bibliographic entry to describe what it is about. It is not always a keyword found in the article or abstract, although it may be. Some databases also enable you to search the subject *thesaurus* directly. This is a list of the specific subject terms used in that database. A thesaurus search can be useful to determine the best terms to use for your search initially, or if you have not had good results with your keyword searches. Subject headings within the results list are usually hyperlinked so that by clicking on the link, you narrow the results of the current search either to hits that all include that subject term or to all the records in the database with that subject term.

Another strategy is to take note of the subject headings for your most relevant hits in your initial keyword searches. Combining these terms again in the Subject Terms field will often return more relevant results. Most online library catalogues also provide subject headings that are hyperlinked to other resources with the same heading. Additionally, there may be a hyperlink for the call number that will direct you to other items in the immediate call number range. This enables you to easily "browse" the collection for other relevant materials.

Limiters

Another search strategy is using the limiters available to you in a particular database. This strategy is generally used to limit your results if there are too many or to limit to a particular date range, article type, format, or publication. One very useful limiter found in many databases is the scholarly or peer-reviewed limiter. Scholarly articles have been reviewed by a board or panel of scholars from the same discipline before being accepted for publication in academic journals. They are a more reliable source of information for your research than popular sources that are intended for a general audience. Some databases limit to scholarly sources automatically and return the results under a *peer-reviewed* link or tab. Academic Search Complete provides a *Scholarly (Peer Reviewed) Journals* check box to the right of your search results list, or you can check the *Scholarly (Peer Reviewed) Journals* box in the *Limit your results* field before you execute your search and the database will return only scholarly articles.

> Limiters can be used in advanced searches to narrow your results or restrict them to a specific date range, article type, format or publication.

Marking and Saving

Most databases and online catalogues provide a marking and saving feature. You can select your most relevant results, mark them by checking a box or adding them to a folder, and then choose from several options—usually print, email, save, or export. Export often includes an option to download or export to the bibliographic management software of your choice, such as RefWorks or EndNote. Some databases also allow you to create a personal account so that you can customize your preferences, save and retrieve your search history, organize your research in folders, or set up email alerts and RSS feeds. Again, the help menu for each database will provide information on all the special features available to account holders.

◎ Using Credible Sources

Although research sources accessed through your library are apt to be authoritative and reliable, some Internet sources may also be useful to flesh out your topic, especially if recent developments have occurred. In addition, if your topic is controversial, you may want to gauge popular opinions through the Internet.

The criteria below apply particularly to open-access resources, from Google Scholar to the range of commercial, governmental, and personal websites that anyone sitting in front of a computer screen can view. The way you use open-access resources, or if you use them at all in your research (your instructor may specify whether he or she considers them legitimate sources for your essay), depends on what kind of information you are looking for.

Are you looking for reliable information from an objective source that explains where its facts and figures come from (for example, Statistics Canada), or do you want to learn about a particular viewpoint? If the latter, it might be acceptable to use a website that advocates a position or supports a cause. If you were writing an essay on animal rights, you might want to access People for the Ethical Treatment of Animals (PETA) or Animal Rights Canada, since their position on animal rights is clear (although this does not guarantee that their information is always factual or accurate).

Not all websites, however, acknowledge their true stake in an issue, nor do all websites use quality control to ensure the accuracy of their content. Even seemingly reliable and objective websites, such as those affiliated with governments, may contain misleading or outdated information.

It may be necessary to re-evaluate your topic, choice of resources, or search strategy if your initial searches efforts are unsuccessful. This does not mean that your strategy is not a good one or has failed. However, it is important to start your library research early. This will allow you enough time to determine a manageable topic, explore as many resources as possible, refine your search strategy as necessary, and obtain any materials that are not readily available online or in your library.

Open-access resources are available to the public without charge and can normally be accessed without passwords or other safeguards.

Ask yourself why you want to use an open-access resource for your research. Are you looking for reliable information from an objective source that explains where its facts and figures come from, or do you want to learn about a particular viewpoint?

Reputable sources are usually associated with well-known organizations or acknowledged experts in their field.

Box 5.1   Assessing the Credibility of Sources

In determining whether to use a source in your research essay, bear in mind the 4 "Re's" of research sources: *re*putable, *re*liable, *re*cent, and *re*levant; the first two apply particularly to Internet sources.

Reputable

Reputable sources are usually associated with well-known organizations or acknowledged experts in their field. To determine reputation, ask

☐   What is the purpose of the website? Who are its sponsors?

(continued)

☐ Is the website associated with an official group/recognized organization?

☐ Are details available about the site's purpose, sponsors, or administration? This information can often be found in "About Us" or "Mission Statement."

Reliable

Information from reliable sources can be trusted as accurate and free of bias. To determine reliability, ask

☐ Can the information be relied on? Is it accurate? Where does it come from?

☐ Are sources given (names, dates)? Do they appear to be experts in their field?

☐ Are claims backed up by objective evidence?

☐ If opinion exists, is it clearly separated from fact? Are other points of view besides those of the author/organization represented? How are they treated?

☐ If you have doubts about accuracy, confirm the information through a second source that you know is reliable.

Information from reliable sources can be trusted as accurate and free of bias.

Recent

Although currency is more important to some topics than others, recent information is generally superior to older information. A site may be reputable but not current if its information is no longer valid. To determine currency, ask

☐ What is the date of the website or most recent update? How current does the information on the site appear to be?

☐ Remember that currency may be topic-relevant. In certain scientific and technological fields, information that is six months old might be outdated.

Recent sources are generally preferable to older ones, but there are exceptions, especially in the humanities.

Relevant

The information in relevant sources is directly related to your thesis and/or main points. To determine relevance, ask

☐ How is the information related to your essay? Does it directly support your thesis or one of your points?

☐ Does the source provide the best support for your claim? Are there other sources that address your topic more directly?

The information in relevant sources is directly related to your thesis and/or main points.

Other factors may also be important in determining the credibility of a website:

- How has statistical information been calculated (e.g., through censuses, surveys, questionnaires by reliable organizations)? How are statistical information and other factual data being used?
- Are there links to other sites? Do these sites appear reliable?
- Does content primarily consist of text, or do images and graphics dominate?
- Is the information on the website easy to access? Does it appear well organized? What specific resources are designed to enhance accessibility or ease of site navigation?

◎ Writing the Rough Draft: Integrating Sources

As you researched your topic, you decided on sources and how they would be used in your essay; that is, how they contributed to your thesis or helped answer your research question. During outlining, you decided on the best order for your points. As you compose, you will find yourself integrating these sources, combining the information and, in some cases, the exact words, with your own thoughts and words. Three main ways to integrate information are discussed below.

Summary and Paraphrase

When you SUMMARIZE, you include the main idea (or ideas) from a source, expressing it in your own words.

When you PARAPHRASE, you put someone else's ideas in your own words, keeping the length of the original.

When you summarize a source, you use your own words to express a main idea, discarding detail. You could summarize the main idea from a sentence, a paragraph, or an entire article. While a summary is selective, a paraphrase includes *all of the original in your own words*. Whereas a summary is an efficient method for synthesizing material, a paraphrased passage is about as long as the original. Because you include so much in a paraphrase, you must be careful to use different wording or you may unknowingly be plagiarizing. Changing the order of the original will also help you avoid plagiarism (see "Plagiarism," p. 86).

In the example below, a sentence from "The Impact of Pets on Human Health and Psychological Well-Being," p. 185, is summarized, then paraphrased.

Original: Our attitudes and behaviours toward and relationships with other species offer a unique window into many aspects of human nature. [20 words]

Summary: Our interactions with other species allow us to explore our own nature. [12 words]

Paraphrase: We can achieve striking insights into human nature by examining how we think about, act towards, and relate to other species. [21 words]

Direct Quotation

When you quote a source directly, you use exactly the same words as the original, putting quotation marks around them. However, while direct quotation is often essential in a literary analysis, summary or paraphrase is often the better choice for secondary sources. When you summarize or paraphrase, you concretely show your understanding of the material because you've put it in your own words.

> *Direct quotation unnecessary or inappropriate:* "Twelve percent of American teens are now battling anorexia nervosa and associated disorders, states a U.S. organization on eating disorders" (Gomez, 2001, p. 76).

Statistical detail does not need be quoted directly.

> *Paraphrase:* According to an American organization studying eating disorders, more than 10 per cent of U.S. adolescents are afflicted by an eating disorder like anorexia nervosa (Gomez, 2001, p. 76).

If facts can be easily put in your own words, prefer summary or paraphrase to direct quotation.

> *Direct quotation unnecessary:* "Beer and spirit producers tend to advertise in magazines with more young adult readers, men, and black people" (Nelson 40).

> *Paraphrase:* Young adults, males, and blacks are typical readers of magazines that contain advertisements for alcoholic beverages (Nelson 40).

You can use direct quotation if you want to define something or if the exact wording is otherwise important—for example, to lend authority to your point or if the wording of the source is significant:

> But how do we define our Canadian democracy? "The genius of a free and democratic people is manifested in its capacity and willingness to devise institutions and laws that secure fairness and equitable opportunities for citizens to influence democratic governance" (Royal Commission on Electoral Reform and Party Financing).

Using direct quotation is appropriate because the writer wants to stress the authority of the source.

When you quote a source directly, you use exactly the same words as the original, putting quotation marks around them.

When you summarize or paraphrase, you show the reader you've understood the material well enough to put it in your own words.

Combining Summary/Paraphrase with Direct Quotation

Combining summary or paraphrase with direct quotation is an efficient method of integrating sources.

Using summary or paraphrase with direct quotation can be an efficient method of integrating sources. In the example below, the writer includes a significant phrase that reveals discrimination against Asians in the first decade of the twentieth century in Canada.

> According to Sir Clifford Sifton, Prime Minister Wilfrid Laurier's interior minister, Canada was to be "a nation of good farmers," meaning Asian immigration was discouraged (Royal Commission 24).

Integrating Quotations

When you incorporate direct quotations into your essay, you must do so grammatically and smoothly. You must also provide enough context for the reader to grasp their significance.

When you incorporate direct quotations into your essay, you must do so grammatically and smoothly; you must also provide enough context for the reader to grasp their significance. The following shows a poorly integrated quotation and its well-integrated alternative:

> *Poorly integrated:* An unloving parent–child relationship can be characterized as "unaccepted, unacknowledged, or unloved" (Haworth-Hoeppner 216).

> *Well-integrated:* An unloving parent–child relationship exists when the child feels "unaccepted, unacknowledged, or unloved" (Haworth-Hoeppner 216).

Using Commas and Periods with Quotations

Do not automatically place a comma before a direct quotation (see p. 400) nor routinely precede the first word of the direct quotation by three dots. If the writer included punctuation, such as a comma or period, after the last word in the quoted material, do not include it.

Do not automatically place a comma *before* a direct quotation or precede the quotation by three dots (see p. 400):

> *Incorrect:* Cyberbullying can be defined as, ". . . the use of electronic communication technology as a means to threaten, harass, embarrass, or socially exclude" (Hinduja & Patchin, 2008, p. 5).

> *Correct:* Cyberbullying can be defined as "the use of electronic communication technology as a means to threaten, harass, embarrass, or socially exclude" (Hinduja & Patchin, 2008, p. 5).

If the writer included punctuation, such as a comma or period, *after* the last word in the quoted material you use, do not include it.

> *Incorrect:* Kate Moss's emphasis on thinness was "immediately condemned by campaigners," (Poulter).

> *Correct:* Kate Moss's emphasis on thinness was "immediately condemned by campaigners" (Poulter).

Making Changes to Direct Quotations

When you quote directly, you must take care to quote accurately; mistakes in direct quotations may look like carelessness and reduce your credibility. However, altering direct quotations is sometimes a good idea—or even essential.

Omitting Words

If you want to omit unneeded or distracting words from a direct quotation, you must show the reader what you have done by using ellipses, which means "omission."

> Indicate that you have left out words in a direct quotation by replacing the omitted word(s) by three or four spaced dots, or ELLIPSES. Of course, you should not leave out words if it changes the meaning of the quotation in any way.

If you omit one or more words in a single sentence, show this omission by using three spaced dots. However, if you leave out all the words *to the end of the sentence*—and if you leave out the following sentence(s) as well—add a fourth dot, which represents the period at the end of the sentence(s):

> *Original:* "In a multichannel era, each channel must sell not only its programs but the entire channel" (Gray 308).

If you wanted to leave out "not only its programs but" and include only the main idea, you must replace the words by three dots:

> Using three spaced dots in a direct quotation shows you have left out one or more words of the original and that the sentence continues after the third dot. Four spaced ELLIPSES shows you have left out all words to the end of the sentence.

> *Revised:* "In a multichannel era, each channel must sell . . . the entire channel" (Gray 308).

Adding and Changing Words

If you add to or change quoted material, you need to indicate this by using square brackets (properly called just brackets). Changes can be made for grammar, style, clarification, or explanation. The following examples from student essays illustrate some of the different reasons for using brackets to add or change words:

> BRACKETS are used to show a change or addition to a direct quotation or indicate parentheses inside parentheses.

> *Grammatical (change* is *to* as *to create a grammatical sentence):* Many people see "male sporting superiority [as] the 'natural' order of things" (Hargreaves, 1994, p. 6).

> *Stylistic (lowercase* s *to avoid a capital letter in the middle of a sentence):* A recent study found that "[s]urfing the Internet at work for pleasure actually increases our concentration levels" ("Researcher Says").

> *Clarification (to indicate a word added to original):* "With increasing frequency, the term [creativity] is used . . . in fields of endeavour as diverse as science, the arts, education, politics and business" (Prentice 146).

You can also use brackets to indicate a parenthesis inside a parenthetical statement:

> (I develop this more fully in an essay included in *Ignoring Nature*, ed. by Marc Bekoff [Chicago, IL: University of Chicago Press, forthcoming]).

Table 5.1 summarizes the main features of the integration methods discussed above. Note that whatever method you use, documentation is usually required. See Box 5.2, "Five Common Questions about Source Citation."

Table 5.1	Main Features of Integrating Research	
Method	**What It Includes**	**When and How to Use It**
Summary	Only main ideas or most important points; is in your words	When you want to refer to main idea in a paragraph, findings of a study, and similar uses; you can summarize as little as part of a sentence, as much as an entire article
Paraphrase	All of the original in your own words, with the structure changed if possible	When you want to refer to important material directly relevant to your point; paraphrases are used for small but significant passages
Direct quotation	Words and punctuation taken directly from the source; put in quotation marks	When material both is important to your point and is memorably phrased or difficult to paraphrase; must be integrated grammatically and smoothly, using brackets and ellipses as required
Combining method	Significant words from source with your own words (i.e., summary or paraphrase)	When you want to include only the most significant or memorable words, omitting the inessential; integrate words from the source grammatically and smoothly with your own prose, using brackets and ellipses as required

◎ Writing the Final Draft: Documenting Sources

Documenting sources serves several practical purposes: it enables a reader to sort your ideas from someone else's and makes it possible for a reader to access the source itself, either to ensure its accuracy or to focus on its content. Documentation formats (called documentation styles) enable scholars to communicate with other scholars—and also with student researchers, who must use correct documentation formats in their essays.

Plagiarism

Plagiarism is an extremely serious academic offence. Most students know that when they use another's exact words, they must acknowledge their source. But plagiarism encompasses more than this: you plagiarize if you in any way use material that is not your own—whether you quote directly, summarize, paraphrase, or refer to it in

DOCUMENTATION STYLE refers to guidelines for documenting sources put forth in style manuals and handbooks for researchers and other academic writers.

You **PLAGIARIZE** if you use any material that is not your own—whether you quote directly, summarize, paraphrase, or refer to it in passing in your essay—without acknowledging it. Finally, you plagiarize if you use the exact words of the source and do not put them in quotation marks or if you follow the structure of the original too closely.

passing in your essay—without acknowledging it. Finally, you plagiarize if you use the exact words of the source and do not put them in quotation marks, even if you acknowledge their source. You also risk plagiarizing if you follow the structure of the original too closely.

However, if a fact or idea is *common knowledge* (i.e., a typical reader probably knows it), you may not need to cite it. Further, if the fact or idea is *easily obtainable*, a citation may also be unnecessary. (You may be told a specific number of sources that satisfies the "easily obtainable" factor—often three.) If in doubt, make the citation.

The questions about source citation in Box 5.2 are often asked by first-year student researchers.

A good strategy for avoiding plagiarism (and consciously integrating the information) is to carefully study the passage you want to use; then, close the text and write the passage from memory completely in your own words. Finally, look at the passage again, ensuring that it is different in its structure as well as in its language—and that you have accurately restated the thought behind it.

Box 5.2 Five Common Questions about Source Citation

1. Do you need to cite information that you do not quote directly in your essay?

   Yes. Specific content requires a citation, whether you use direct quotation, paraphrase, or summary to integrate it into your essay. Even general information may require a citation.

2. If you already knew a fact and you encounter it in a secondary source, does it need to be cited?

   Probably. The issue isn't whether you know something but whether your reader would know it. If you are writing for an audience familiar with your topic, you may not need to cite "common knowledge"— that is, knowledge that all or almost all readers would be expected to know or which could be easily looked up.

3. Is it necessary to cite "popular" quotations, for example, the kind that appear in dictionaries of quotations? What about dictionary definitions?

   Yes, these kinds of quotations should be cited unless the quotation has entered everyday use. For example, the first quotation would probably not need a citation, though the second would—even though it's unlikely a reader would know either source:

(continued)

When the going gets tough, the tough get going. (Joan W. Donaldson)

Making your mark on the world is hard. If it were easy, everybody would do it. (Barack Obama)

Dictionary definitions should be cited.

4. If you provide a list of your sources on the final page of your essay, do you have to cite the sources within the essay itself?

    Yes. Most documentation methods require both *in-text and final-page citations.*

5. What can you do to guarantee that the question of plagiarism never arises in your essay?

    Follow the guidelines above, and for specific instances in which the guidelines don't provide the answer, don't hesitate to check with your instructor or another expert, such as a librarian.

Documenting Your Sources

As a general rule, you should ensure a reader will know what you have taken from outside sources and what are your own ideas, but do not repeat citations needlessly.

Knowing what to cite and citing accurately (see "Major Documentation Styles," below) are, of course, crucial; however, a third concern may arise as you integrate sources and acknowledge them during the composing and revising stages: unnecessary citations. Repetitive citations can clutter an essay, affecting ease of reading. They can also make you seem over-reliant on what other people have said.

As a general rule, you should ensure a reader will know what you have taken from outside sources and what are your own ideas, but do not repeat citations needlessly; for example, if you use the same source for two consecutive points with no other source intervening, you usually only include the page number in the second citation.

In the following body paragraph from an essay on creativity, student writer Taryn Burgar uses three sources to help develop the main idea; although the sources of her information are clear, she does not repeat unnecessary information. In particular, she does not repeat the name of the source if she has named the author(s) as part of the previous citation. Like the essay on p. 59, Taryn uses MLA documentation style; for an example of efficient citations in an essay that uses APA documentation style, see Bethany Truman's essay on p. 96 (see, in particular, paragraph 3, pp. 97–98).

Sample Student Body Paragraph with Annotations

The benefits of teaching students methods that improve their creativity can be seen in all the stages of the educational system. With pre-school and kindergarten children, imaginative activity assists in their growth into intellectually stimulated adults (Prentice 151–52). Such activity comes from play and the direct manipulation of materials and is often associated with creative endeavours, such as making new objects and artistic projects. Connecting physical material to ideas will resonate with young children as they have had less practice in understanding abstract concepts (154). Art should have a central focus in the elementary school curriculum as children are likely to develop an attachment to a specific type of art at this time in their lives. Even if they develop simply an appreciation for art, this will still allow for creative insights (De Backer et al. 63). Post-secondary education systems often focus on a class lecture format; however, Livingston argues that problem solving should become the driving pedagogy (59–60). Today's college students learn to be adept at research, which provides a playground for creative interaction, inquisition, and imagination. Focusing the last formal stage of education on "learning," instead of "teaching," encourages the next generation of teachers to perpetuate this creative cycle (59).

Taryn begins her paragraph with a topic sentence that announces the paragraph's main idea. By referring to "the stages of the educational system," a reader assumes she will develop the paragraph using the division method, where she applies the topic to different stages of a child's education.

In her first citation, Taryn gives the author's last name and the page numbers. Note that she drops the second (redundant) hundreds digit for the second number, as required by MLA style.

Taryn repeats the word *activity* to help link the previous sentence to the one that follows.

Because she includes only the page number, the reader assumes that the information comes from the previous source (Prentice).

Taryn needs to provide complete details because she is citing this material for the first time. A reader could turn to the Works Cited page and see that this source has five authors. The phrase "et al." following the first author's name is used for sources that have more than three authors.

The citation consists only of page numbers because the author's name has been given in a signal phrase (i.e., "Livingston argues").

Because the final point is taken from the same as the preceding source, the author's name is not repeated.

◎ Major Documentation Styles

There are three major documentation styles but many variants on these styles. The Modern Language Association (MLA) style is widely used in the humanities, including English literature. The American Psychological Association (APA) style is used in many social science disciplines and some science disciplines, as well as in education and business. Both are parenthetical styles, meaning that a brief citation including the author's name and page number (MLA) or name and publication year (APA) follows the reference in the text of an essay.

The *Chicago Manual of Style* (CMS), used in history and the arts, such as music, follows a number–note method. Superscript (raised) numbers are placed after the in-text references; they correspond to the numbers at the end of the document (endnotes) or at the foot of the page (footnotes) where full bibliographical information is given. All these styles also require an end-of-essay listing of sources alphabetically by last name.

In the parenthetical styles, there are two methods to integrate source material:

1. Give the name of the author(s) and (APA style) the publication year in a **signal phrase** (which includes the author's last name and a "signal verb," such as *states*, *explains*, or *argues*) *before* the information from the source. You do not repeat the author's name (MLA) or the author's name and year (APA) in the end citation:

> APA: **Pilon (2005)** explains that in strategic voting, people often have to compromise their vote to ensure an undesirable candidate does not win **(p. 14)**.

2. Give the name of the author, page number, and (APA style) publication year *after* the information from the source:

> MLA: In strategic voting, people often have to compromise their vote to ensure an undesirable candidate does not win **(Pilon 14)**.

In the number–note (Chicago) style, the number should be placed at the end of the relevant clause or sentence, after the comma or period:

> In strategic voting, people often have to compromise their vote to ensure an undesirable candidate does not win.[1]

Many of the main features of the MLA, APA, and number–note styles are given below. Examples of the most common bibliographic formats are then provided.

Electronic formats in all styles should include as much information as is available. If an author's name is not given, use the name of the organization or sponsoring group in its place. If there is no sponsor, use the work's title alphabetized by the first major word. MLA style requires you to include date of access for Internet citations; APA does not; with CMS, it is optional. Paragraph number or section heading can sometimes be used to identify location, if necessary, in the absence of standard page numbering. APA and CMS styles require you to use a digital object identifier (DOI) if it is available for journal articles.

MLA (Modern Language Association) Style

- MLA uses an "author/number" referencing format. The basic parenthetical format includes author's last name and page number with no punctuation in between. e.g., (Slotkin 75); (Rusel and Wilson 122). If a signal phrase is

---

SIGNAL PHRASES introduce a reference in a phrase that names the author(s) and usually includes a "signal verb" and, in APA style, year of publication.

used, only the page number is in parentheses. Block quotations should be used for important passages at least four typed lines long. They are indented 2.5 cm (1 inch) from the left margin and double spaced, and do not include quotation marks. The end period precedes the parenthetical citation.

- The final page, titled "Works Cited," alphabetically lists by author's last name all works used in the essay. Entries are double spaced with the first line flush left and successive lines indented 1.3 cm (half an inch). Each major word in a title begins with a capital letter. Names of books and journals are italicized, and the medium of publication is usually included at the end of the entry.

APA (American Psychological Association) Style

- APA uses an "author–year" referencing format. One basic format includes the author's last name and year of publication (references to the entire work). The other basic format also includes page number (direct quotations and paraphrases).
- Commas separate author's name from year and year from page number (if required); "p." or "pp." (for more than one page) precedes page number(s). e.g., (Huyer, 1997, p. 43); (Bryson & de Castell, 1998, pp. 542–544).
- If a signal phrase is used, the year follows the author's name in parentheses. If a page number is required, it is placed in parentheses after the reference.
- Works by the same author(s) from the same year are assigned different letters—e.g., 2004a, 2004b—in alphabetical order by title. They are listed in this order in "References."
- Block quotations should be used for important passages more than 40 words long. They are indented 1.3 cm (half an inch) from the left margin and double spaced, and do not include quotation marks. The end period precedes the parenthetical citation.
- The final page, titled "References," alphabetically lists by author's last name all works used in the essay; author's initials are used, not given names. Entries are double spaced with the first line flush left and successive lines are indented 1.3 cm (half an inch). In article and book titles, only the first letter of first words, first words following colons, and proper nouns, along with all letters in acronyms, are capitalized.

CMS (Chicago Manual of Style) Style

- CMS uses the "note" referencing format with numbered footnotes (at the bottom of the page) or endnotes (at the end of the text) corresponding to superscript numbers in the text of the essay. Each entry is single spaced with the first line indented 1.3 cm (half an inch) and successive lines flush left.

- If you are using Microsoft Word, use either "Insert" (Word 2003 and earlier) or "References" (2007 and later) to select automatic formatting and note placement.
- Full bibliographic details are given in the first reference, beginning with the author's first name(s), followed by last name, work's title, and (in parentheses) place of publication, publisher, date, and page number(s) (if needed):

> As is well known, the sociobiologist E.O. Wilson has entitled one of his books *Consilience*.[15]

The note would look like this:

> 15. Edward O. Wilson, *Consilience: The Unity of Knowledge* (New York: Alfred A. Knopf, 1998).

Successive notes are condensed forms of the first citation:

> 18. Wilson, *Consilience*, 55.

Consecutive references to the same work:

> 19. Ibid.

The page number would follow if different from the preceding note.

- Block quotations should be used for important passages at least four typed lines long. They are indented 1.3 cm (half an inch) from the left margin and double spaced, and do not include quotation marks. The end period precedes the parenthetical citation.
- On the final page, titled "Bibliography," entries are listed alphabetically by author's last name. Entries are single spaced with double spacing between them; the first line is flush left, and successive lines are indented 1.3 cm (half an inch).
- Include a DOI (Digital Object Identifier) if the journal lists one. A DOI is a permanent ID that, when appended to http://dx.doi.org/ in the address bar of an Internet browser, leads to the source. If no DOI is available, list a URL. Include an access date if one is required by your publisher or discipline. With websites, CMS recommends including an access date or a date the website was last modified.

Common Formats: Sample Citations

Book (one author)

MLA:

Westoll, Andrew. *The Chimps of Fauna Sanctuary*. Toronto: HarperCollins, 2011.
Print.

APA:

Embry, J. L. (1987). *Mormon polygamous families: Life in the principle*. Salt Lake City,
UT: University of Utah Press.

CMS:

Note:

   1. Michael Brown, *The Black Douglases: War and Lordship in Late Medieval
Scotland 1300–1455* (East Linton, Scotland: Tuckwell, 1998), 132.

Bibliography:

Brown, Michael. *The Black Douglases: War and Lordship in Late Medieval Scotland
1300–1455*. East Linton, Scotland: Tuckwell, 1998.

Book or Journal (multiple authors)

MLA:

Bolaria, B., Singh, and Peter S. Li. *Racial Oppression in Canada*. 2nd edn. Toronto:
Garamond Press, 1988. Print. [second author's name is not reversed]

More than three authors: The name of first author may be given, followed by a comma
and "et al."

APA:

Plester, B., Woods, C., & Bell, V. (2008). Txt msg n school literacy: Does texting
and knowledge of text abbreviations adversely affect children's literacy
attainment? *Literacy, 42*(3), 137–144. doi: 10.1111/j.1741-4369.2008.00489.x

All authors' names are reversed.

Two to seven authors: List all names.

More than seven authors: List the first six names followed by three points of ellipsis
(. . .) and the last author's name.

CMS:

Note:

   2. Bob Beal and Rod Macleod, *Prairie Fire: The 1885 North-West Rebellion*
(Edmonton: Hurtig Publishers, 1984), 104–07.

More than three authors: The name of first author is given, followed by "and others."

Bibliography:

Beal, Bob, and Rod Macleod. *Prairie Fire: The 1885 North-West Rebellion*. Edmonton: Hurtig Publishers, 1984.

More than three authors: All authors are listed (only the first author's name is reversed).

Selection in Edited Work

All entries give the page range; in-text citations give specific page(s) referenced.

MLA:

Wright, Austin M. "On Defining the Short Story: The Genre Question." *Short Story Theory at a Crossroads*. Ed. Susan Lohafer and Jo Ellyn Clarey. Baton Rouge: Louisiana State UP, 1989. 46–63. Print. [UP is the abbreviation for *University Press*]

APA:

Chesney-Lind, M. & Brown, M. (1999). Girls and violence: An overview. In D. Flannery & C. R. Huff (Eds.), *Youth violence: Prevention, intervention and social policy* (pp. 171–199). Washington, D.C.: American Psychiatric Press.

CMS:

Note:

3. Marcia K. Lieberman, "'Some Day My Prince Will Come': Female Acculturation through the Fairy Tale," in *Don't Bet on the Prince*, ed. Jack Zipes and Ingrid Svendsen (New York: Routledge, 1987), 185–200.

Bibliography:

Lieberman, Marcia K. "'Some Day My Prince Will Come': Female Acculturation through the Fairy Tale." In *Don't Bet on the Prince*, edited by Jack Zipes and Ingrid Svendsen, 185–200. New York: Routledge, 1987.

Journal Article

MLA:

Sugars, Cynthia. "Notes on a Mystic Hockey Puck: Death Paternity and National Identity in Wayne Johnston's *The Divine Ryans*." *Essays on Canadian Writing* 82.2 (2004): 151–72. Print.

Include both the volume and the issue number. For electronic articles in a database, include the database name in italics before "Web."

APA:

Cheung, C., Chiu, P., & Lee, M. (2001). Online social networks: Why do students use Facebook? *Computers in Human Behavior, 27,* 1337–1343. doi:10.1016/ j.chb.2010.07.028

The volume number is italicized; the issue number (required if each issue begins with page number "1") is not italicized. If available for print and electronic articles, include the DOI (digital object identifier) as the last item; it is not followed by a period. If there is no DOI, include the URL of the home page of the journal.

CMS:

Note:

     4. Robert Garner, "Political Ideologies and the Moral Status of Animals," *Journal of Political Ideologies* 8 (2003): 235.

For an electronic article, include the DOI as the last item if it is available, followed by a period for both a note and a bibliographic entry. If there is no DOI, include a URL. An access date is optional for an online article. The issue number is required following the volume number if each issue begins with page number "1" e.g., "8, no. 1 (2003)."

Bibliography:

Smith, John Maynard. "The Origin of Altruism." *Nature* 393 (1998): 639–40.

Internet Source

MLA:

"10 Things You Should Know About Climate Change." *Canada's Action on Climate Change.* Government of Canada, 16 Jan. 2012. Web. 6 Apr. 2012.

The first date is that of the article's publication on the website; next, the publication medium is given, followed by the access date. Use angled brackets (< >) to enclose .a website address if the source would be hard to find or read without it or if your instructor requires it.

APA:

Statistics Canada (2010, March 26). Gasoline and fuel oil, price by urban centre. Retrieved from www40.Statcan.ca/ 101/cst01/econ154a.htm.

CMS:

Note:

     5. "Record Household Debt Could Be Canada's Undoing, Economist Says," CBC News, accessed November 20, 2011, http://www.cbc.ca/fp/story/2011/07/26/ 5161723.html

Bibliography: Entries are listed alphabetically by first major word.

This essay uses APA documentation style.

Sample Student Expository Essay with Annotations

Relational Aggression: Patterns and Motives Underlying Bullying and Its Impact on Students

by Bethany Truman

[1]Aggression disguises itself in many different forms, some more obvious and blatantly physical, others more subtle and emotions-based. Most people have had experience with some form of aggression in their lifetime, most likely during their late childhood/early teenage years. Emotions-based, or relational aggression, a very common kind of bullying, is unique in its subtlety, its common motives, its prominence among girls as opposed to boys, and its impacts on both the aggressors and the victims. In what ways does relational aggression differ from physical aggression? How harmful is relational aggression when compared with physical violence, and what makes this more subtle version of aggression so powerful?

[2]Relational aggression, consisting of verbal abuse, gossip, rumour-spreading, and exclusion tactics, has the capacity to damage its victims just as thoroughly as some types of physical aggression (Archer & Coyne, 2005, p. 212). Although this form of bullying is subtle by nature, often resembling such passive aggressive behaviours as ignoring classmates in order to isolate and victimize them, it can occasionally manifest itself in more overt forms, such as verbal threats and outright name-calling (Radcliff & Joseph, 2011, p. 172). In its more subtle and manipulative form, relational aggression may not present itself as typical aggressive behaviour, thereby concealing itself from parents and educators. Unfortunately, this means that bullying of this form often gets overlooked in schools, as "overt physical violence is better understood, more readily observed, and more easily confronted" (Young, Nelson, Hottle, Warburton & Young, 2011, p. 25) than the subtle violence of relational aggression. Moreover, kids are often able to conceal their behaviours even more effectively by using nonverbal bullying tactics, such as eye-rolling, giving dirty looks, or turning their backs on individuals. Note-passing and cyber-bullying via email

Annotation (left margin): Although Bethany's introduction may be shorter than those in essays of comparable length, it succeeds in its purpose. She begins by making a general statement about aggression and becomes more specific in the next two sentences: in the second sentence, she mentions the age that people usually first experience aggression. It becomes obvious in the third sentence that she will be discussing "relational aggression, a very common kind of bullying." Her thesis is in the form of questions that her research will attempt to answer.

Annotation (left margin): Note Bethany's careful placement of her citation, showing exactly what information she got from her source and separating it from her own words.

and Facebook are also common methods employed by relational aggressors which can be exceptionally hard to detect (Pronk & Zimmer-Gembeck, 2009, p. 187). This covert form of aggression is predominant among students in middle school, possibly as a result of shifting adolescent relationships, a larger student body, and less monitoring by adults (Werner & Hill, 2010, p. 834).

[3]What, then, are the central motives behind these students' aggression towards their peers? According to Pronk and Zimmer-Gembeck (2009), there are three broad categories that explain the use of relationally aggressive behaviours: social dynamics, the emotional state of the aggressor, and characteristics of the victim. Included within social dynamics is the issue of social dominance, the most common reason for the use of relational bullying among students. Aggressive individuals see their manipulations of their peers as a necessity in order to climb the social ladder, become the centre of attention, and gain more friends (pp. 189–190). Werner and Hill (2010) agree with the notion that relational aggression is used primarily as a means to gain popularity and status, remarking that "strong associations between relational aggression and perceived popularity [indicate] that relational aggression is increasingly reinforced in the peer group with age, via benefits incurred from high status" (p. 827). Pronk and Zimmer-Gembeck describe how the internal emotional state of the aggressor, primarily that of jealousy, is another significant determining factor for the use of relational aggression among students. Aggressors often use relational bullying tactics in order to compensate for their own negative internal emotions, which at times serve to increase positive feelings about themselves. In addition to jealousy, anger and revenge were sometimes reported as motivating factors behind relational aggression (pp. 191–192). The final category described by Pronk and Zimmer-Gembeck is characteristics, both positive and negative, of the victim. Negative traits could include shyness, unattractiveness, boringness, or general submissiveness. Individuals possessing these traits often find themselves easy targets for relational bullying as they tend to be easily upset, and may be perceived as socially undesirable and therefore readily isolated. By contrast, individuals may be ostracized based on their own positive traits, such as popularity and

In this paragraph, which introduces readers to key characteristics of relational bullying, Bethany uses five different sources, effectively synthesizing with the help of transitions such as *unfortunately* and *moreover*, as well as subtle rephrasing (e.g., "This covert form of aggression," in the last sentence, refers to the examples in the previous sentence).

Bethany begins this body paragraph with a question. The next sentence announces the topic of the paragraph, showing that it will be developed by breaking a large subject into three smaller categories: division. What follows is a lengthy paragraph, which makes clear organization crucial.

Bethany cites the study before providing the information from the study. In this format, the study's year follows author names. The specific page is given when the reference is complete.

Bethany refers to several sources in this paragraph, giving author names *before* following with the information, thus clearly showing what comes from where.

If Bethany wished, she could have divided her long paragraph here, providing a clear transition from the previous material to what follows.

Note that in the APA documentation style, you do not repeat the year of the source if you have already given it in the same paragraph.

attractiveness; in this case, such individuals are targeted because they are seen as a threat to the aggressor and must be excluded so as to protect the social status of the aggressor. Finally, relational aggression is sometimes also used to create drama and excitement within a group of friends, alleviating boredom and contributing to the attention-seeking behaviours of the aggressor (p. 193).

[4]While the motives mentioned above apply to both boys and girls, there is a general tendency for boys to have a more central focus on social hierarchies and the attainment of power, whereas girls are more likely to focus primarily on the social isolation of the victim in order to feel important within their friendship group (Pronk & Zimmer-Gembeck, 2009, p. 180). Gender differences have also been noted in relation to the specific methods students use to relationally bully their peers. Boys tend to use more direct tactics, such as excluding individuals when picking sporting teams and teasing. Moreover, while they are more prone to becoming physically aggressive when they get angry with an individual, they are also more likely to forgive and forget more quickly than girls (p. 188). Girls, in addition to holding grudges, tend more towards giving dirty looks, gossiping behind people's backs, and maintaining a type of friendship exclusivity in which "three is a crowd" (p. 187). While girls often threaten physical violence when bullying other girls, they rarely follow through; boys, on the other hand, commonly use verbal and physical aggression concurrently (p. 186). Relational aggression often has exceedingly damaging impacts on girls as opposed to boys, as their relationships tend to have a greater emotional component; this causes their use of relational aggression with their peers to be much more prominent, whereas the same behaviours among boys are more likely to be overlooked (p. 196). According to Archer and Coyne (2005), girls rate relational aggression as more harmful than physical aggression, whereas boys generally believe that physical aggression has more damaging effects (p. 224).

[5]Relational bullying inflicts much of its damage by internalizing negative feelings of self-doubt and lowering self-esteem, resulting in a depletion of mental health and "other aspects of child and adolescent socio-emotional functioning" (Pronk & Zimmer-Gembeck, 2009, p. 176). As mentioned above, girls may

---

In this paragraph, Bethany summarizes a lot of material from page 193 of Pronk and Zimmer-Gembeck, including the page number after she finishes with this source.

This paragraph is developed through the compare and contrast organizational pattern. Note the various words and phrases showing differences: *While . . . , as opposed to, whereas.* Other transitions also guide the reader: *also, moreover, in addition to.*

Here Bethany may have made an unwise word choice. Can you think of a better word than *depletion*?

be particularly damaged by relational aggression since social status and friendship groups seem all important to them during adolescence. Girls who find themselves victims of relational bullying often respond with "self-destruction" strategies, such as smoking, doing drugs, or even committing suicide. In middle school, when relational bullying is most common, this form of aggression has many psychologically-damaging consequences, including high levels of depression, loneliness, anxiety, and peer rejection (Archer & Coyne, 2005, p. 224). Victims of relational aggression may also experience a lowered sense of self-worth, become more reluctant to initiate peer interactions for fear of rejection, and avoid social situations in general because of anxiety or fear of negative consequences (Young, et al., 2011, p. 25). Victims also report feeling more lethargic and impulsive when they are being relationally bullied, often describing how time seems to pass more slowly and life appears meaningless (Archer & Coyne, 2005, p. 224). The aggressors, too, experience consequences to their actions, such as "more negative life satisfaction, negative and unsatisfying relationships, and emotional instability over time" (Young, et al., 2011, p. 25). However, unlike the victims, the subtle nature of this form of aggression can work to the aggressors' advantage. Whereas outright physical aggression has been linked to risk factors such as unpopularity and lower academic performance, relational aggression has been related to being viewed as more attractive, being better at sports, and being regarded more favourably by teachers as assertive individuals; this suggests that those who use more obvious, direct forms of social manipulation end up being rejected, whereas those aggressors who are more subtle and keep their actions disguised can remain unnoticed and possibly even improve their social standing (Archer & Coyne, 2005, p. 225). Unfortunately, this means that such behaviour, especially when undetected, may be self-reinforcing, perpetuating the cycle by leading to more—and perhaps more intense—bullying.

[6]Relational aggression differs from physical aggression in many respects: it is the most common weapon of choice among middle school-aged students; the motives behind its use are very particular and centre mostly on social status; it predominates among girls and can inflict harsh consequences on its victims while

Bethany concludes her final body paragraph by considering the negative consequences of relational bullying, looking beyond her sources to briefly explore the long-term effects. This sentence, then, provides a link to the last two sentences of her conclusion in which she reiterates the importance of stopping the cycle of bullying.

simultaneously sheltering its aggressors and rewarding them with high social status. Furthermore, it has the capacity to be just as damaging as physical aggression by virtue of its subtlety. The covert nature of this form of aggression makes it exceptionally hard to detect, and therefore all the more effective at making its victims feel isolated and alone. It is of the utmost importance that parents and educators make an effort to identify the use of this form of bullying, and recognize that it can be just as harmful as physical aggression. It may be harder to see damaged self-esteem in comparison to a broken nose, but it is just as broken, and just as much in need of healing.

Note that Bethany has correctly formatted her References page and been careful to precisely follow the requirements of the APA documentation system as given in the sixth edition of *Publication Manual of the American Psychological Association*. See p. 91.

References

Archer, J., & Coyne, S. M. (2005). An integrated review of indirect, relational, and social aggression. *Personality and Social Psychology Review, 9*(3), 212–230. doi: 10.1207/s15327957pspr0903_2

Pronk, R. E., & Zimmer-Gembeck, M. J. (2009). It's "mean" but what does it mean to adolescents? Relational aggression described by victims, aggressors, and their peers. *Journal of Adolescent Research, 25*(2), 175–204. doi: 10.1177/0743558409350504

Radcliff, K. M., & Joseph, L. M. (2011). Girls just being girls? Mediating relational aggression and victimization. *Preventing School Failure: Alternative Education for Children and Youth, 55*(3), 171–179. doi:10.1080/1045988X.2010.520357

Werner, N. E., & Hill, L. G. (2010). Individual and peer group normative beliefs about relational aggression. *Child Development, 81*(3), 826–836. doi: 10.1111/j.1467-8624.2010.01436.x

Young, E. L., Nelson, D. A., Hottle, A. B., Warburton, B., & Young, B. K. (2011). Relational aggression among students. *Education Digest, 76*(7), 24–29. Retrieved from http://www.eddigest.com/

◎ Chapter 5 Review Questions

1. What are some strategies for coming up with a topic from scratch?
2. What does it mean to "narrow" a broad topic? Why is it necessary and how could you do it?
3. What is the difference between a thesis statement and a research question?
4. What is a peer-reviewed journal? Who would a typical reader be?

5. Choose the best statement among the following:
   a. Academic sources are always better than non-academic sources.
   b. Academic sources tend to be more reliable than non-academic sources.
   c. Research essays should always use a combination of academic and non-academic sources.
   d. No generalizations can be made about academic versus non-academic sources.
6. What are two functions of research proposals?
7. What three factors should you take into account before beginning your major research?
8. Answer true or false:
   a. You would typically use subject guides, dictionaries, and encyclopedias early in your research.
   b. The library catalogue includes only print sources contained within the library.
   c. Online databases are the best source for the most current research available.
   d. Using limiters in your searches produces more results than not using them.
9. The following questions apply to searches using your institution's databases:
   a. Why is it crucial that you choose your database carefully?
   b. Identify two ways that using an advanced search could make your results more precise.
   c. Name two Boolean operators and explain when you would use one and when the other.
   d. What are wildcard and truncation symbols used for?
10. Identify the 4 "Re's" of research and explain the importance of each.
11. Explain the differences between a summary and a paraphrase.
12. When should you use direct quotations and when should you avoid using them?
13. You can show the reader that you have omitted one or more words from a direct quotation by using _____. You can show the reader that you have made a change to a direct quotation by using _____.
14. Describe three writing situations that could result in plagiarism. When might it not be necessary to provide a citation for an outside source?
15. a. What are documentation styles?
    b. What is a "parenthetical style"?
    c. Define *signal phrase* and explain how the use of a signal phrase changes the form of the citation you would use (you can use APA or MLA style to illustrate this change).

◎ Key Terms

brackets (p. 85)

digital object identifier (p. 73)

documentation style (p. 86)

ellipses (p. 85)

paraphrase (p. 82)

peer-reviewed journals (p. 69)

plagiarize (p. 86)

signal phrases (p. 90)

summarize (p. 82)

PART 2
READING

CHAPTER 6

Interacting with Texts

In this chapter, you will learn:

- ◎ How to read actively and annotate what you read
- ◎ How to approach a text by considering your reading purpose and other pre-reading activities
- ◎ How to use specific strategies for understanding challenging texts

- ◎ How to determine meaning through word connotations
- ◎ How to determine meaning through context

Reading at the post-secondary level is not a passive process but an *interactive* one involving a relationship *between* you and the text you are reading (*inter-* is a prefix meaning "between").

The purpose of the author in writing, the audience the text was intended to reach, and the reason for reading it, all play a role in the way you interact with a text.

Reading at the post-secondary level is not a passive process but an *interactive* one involving a relationship *between* you and the text you are reading, which often changes as you read and apply critical thinking skills.

Each reader approaches a text in a different way: your ideas, beliefs, and specific knowledge about the topic reflect who you are and your unique experiences. You therefore interact with the text in a unique way.

In addition, the nature of the text itself, the purpose of the author in writing, the audience it was intended to reach, and the reason for reading play a role in the way you interact with it, as do the author's own ideas, beliefs, and background and the specific choices—in diction, style, and tone—that he or she makes.

However, all these factors do not necessarily come into play every time you read a text. For example, when you respond to a text, your own ideas, observations, and experience may well play a role; however, when you write a rhetorical analysis, you use objective standards to determine whether the essay is successful. (Rhetorical analysis and critical response were discussed in Chapter 3.)

Active reading refers to an approach to reading in which you take an active, rather than a passive role—first, by considering your purpose for reading. It also refers to reading at a more complex level than simply to understand what you are reading—though, of course, this is the crucial first step. It refers to the attitude of questioning, evaluating, and re-evaluating, using critical thinking skills. Finally, it means approaching a text as a learning experience and asking what it can teach you. Active reading, then, is a useful term because it suggests reading is an ongoing process that deepens and evolves over time.

ACTIVE READING refers to an approach to reading in which you take an active, rather than a passive role—first, by considering your purpose for reading.

Box 6.1   A Note on Annotation

When you make notes in the margins of an essay or in the text itself, you are taking a vital step towards active reading, following up on your pre-reading and reading(s) of the text (for more on pre-reading and reading academic essays, see Chapter 10).

Annotating can have many purposes: to identify main ideas, to help in comprehension—for example, by writing down the meaning of unfamiliar words—and to clarify your thoughts about the text. Importantly, annotating enables you to return to the text later and have your questions and responses fresh in your mind. When you annotate, you are *beginning your actual work on the assignment*, translating abstract ideas and impressions into concrete language, solidifying those ideas. What form the annotation takes depends on several factors, including your reading purpose.

Annotation (verb *annotate*): note that explains, expands, or comments on a written text. Annotation can refer to the comments themselves or to the process of making notes.

◎ Reading Purpose

There are many different reasons for reading a text—beyond the obvious one of satisfying a course requirement. Are you reading it to determine whether the essay is related to your topic? To identify the main ideas? To use the text as a secondary source in your essay? To write a critical response to the text? To write a rhetorical analysis? Knowing the answer to such questions affects your reading strategies, many of which are discussed in this and following chapters. The chart below outlines questions and strategies relevant to four major reading purposes.

Table 6.1   Summary of Reading Purposes

Reading Purpose	Questions to Ask	Strategies
To explore	What is it about? What kind of book or essay is it? Why was it written? How is it divided? What is the function of each section? How is it related to your topic?	Use general scan: scan title, abstract, and headings for content and writing purpose (see p. 107) Use target scan on introduction, looking for specific features (see p. 107) Note bibliographic information (title, author name[s], publication details)
To summarize (see Chapter 2)	What are the main ideas? How are they related to each other?	Use target scan to identify thesis, topic sentences, and important sub-points (see p. 107) (you can underline them) Use focused reading (see pp. 107–08) on main points in order to put them in your own words
To respond or analyze (see Chapter 3)	What is the writer's thesis? What are the main points? *Response:* Do you agree/disagree with the writer's points? *Analysis:* How is the text put together? What are its main features? What rhetorical strategies are used?	Use target scan to identify main points Use focused reading on points of agreement/disagreement and annotate these passages Use focused reading to identify conventions and other features of similar texts
To synthesize	How is the text related to my thesis? How does the text's thesis or findings relate to other theses/findings?	Use scan and focused reading to identify thesis, findings, and points relevant to your topic

◉ Selective Reading: Scanning and Focused Reading

SELECTIVE READING is planned, conscious reading in which you choose strategies that best reflect your reading purpose, what you are reading, and similar factors.

In selective reading, your reading strategy is determined by your pre-reading choices, which can depend on what you are reading (for example, an introduction, a book chapter, an academic essay, or a book review) and your purpose for reading, as discussed above. It is therefore very different from simply sitting down with a book or essay and closely reading every word from beginning to end. Unlike reading for pleasure, selective reading, then, is planned, conscious reading. Selective reading can be divided into scanning and close, focused reading.

Scanning

In a **general scan**, you read to get the gist of a text. You read rapidly, keeping an eye out for content markers, such as headings and places in which the author summarizes material (in experimental studies, this summary could include tables, graphs, and other visuals). You identify main ideas by locating topic sentences within major paragraphs but ignore examples and other detail.

In a specific scan, or **target scan**, you look for specific content. You might use this method if you are trying to determine whether a text is useful. After reading the work's title and abstract, you're not sure if you should spend more time on it. To investigate further, you target scan the entire text for specific content: you look for words and phrases related to your topic.

If you are looking for information in a book, you are likely able to locate it by referring to the **subject index** (or author index), a standard feature of most full-length reference and scholarly texts. These indexes, found at the back of a book, may give you many page references, so you may have to scan a number of pages in order to access the information you seek. If you are accessing a text online, you can use your browser's "Find" function under "Edit" to locate significant words or phrases in the text; or, in a library database, you can search by keywords.

Focused Reading

Because focused reading is time-consuming, you probably will have scanned the essay beforehand to find the most relevant portions of the text, which you then read in detail. Selective reading often involves both scanning and focused reading.

As the term **focused reading** implies, you read the text closely line by line and word by word. If you are writing a rhetorical analysis, you may look for rhetorical strategies, tone, or stylistic elements. You may also test the author's claims (premises) or question the conclusions he or she draws from the evidence. Many of the strategies for target scanning and focused reading are discussed in this chapter; critical thinking is discussed in Chapter 7.

In focused reading, you often concentrate on one or more short or medium-length passages and relate them to a main idea or to other sections of the text. For example, if you are writing an essay for a history class, you might concentrate on specific passages from a primary text, such as a historical document, say, The Indian Act (1876), in order to connect key ideas in the passage to a historical event or other historical element. The purpose of analyzing each specific passage is to support your thesis about the significance of the event.

However, before you proceed to analyze, summarize, or synthesize texts, as discussed in earlier chapters, you need to understand the text you are reading.

Scanning is a form of selective reading in which you look for features that will tell you more about the text, ignoring most detail. In a **GENERAL SCAN**, you try to get the essence of the work—for example, by looking at its title, abstract, and headings. A **TARGET SCAN** looks for specific content, such as a subject or keyword.

A **SUBJECT INDEX** is a list of important words in a text, ordered alphabetically and usually placed at the end of the text.

A *general scan* is helpful if you know you will be using the whole text, since it can give you an overview of content—for example, if you are going to summarize a work or refer to it often in your essay. A *target scan* is helpful if you want to assess the usefulness of a text; if you decide that it does contain relevant content, you can then apply another method of selective reading, such as focused reading.

In **FOCUSED READING**, you read the text closely line by line and word by word.

Writers of both academic and non-academic texts inevitably will use at least a few words whose meanings either seem different from your own sense of the word's meaning or are completely unfamiliar. The following pages focus on easing the reading burden by adopting a strategy of understanding words through their connotations and their context.

◎ Word Meanings

Connotations and Denotations

A reader needs to know *how* a writer is using each word before making assumptions about the meaning of a text. An individual word carries connotations, or implications, beyond those of its dictionary meanings, or denotations. Paying careful attention to context—the surrounding words—can help you determine a word's connotation and intended meaning. Sometimes dictionaries suggest a word's connotations, but you need to look at the passage itself to know exactly how it is being used. Dictionaries are often not the "final word" on meaning but necessary starting places.

A word can acquire different connotations through its use over time or within a specific group. In some cases, positive or negative values have become associated with the word. Many common words have several connotations. Consider, for example, the different implications of the words *slender, slim, lean, thin, skinny, underweight, scrawny,* and *emaciated,* which suggest a progression from positive (*graceful, athletic . . .*) to negative (*. . . weak, sickly*). Sometimes only context makes a word's connotation clear.

> While a word's **DENOTATION** is its dictionary meaning, words also carry **CONNOTATIONS**, which can be considered "shades" of meaning or associations (often determined by context).

EXERCISE 6.1　Collaborative Exercise

In groups, make a list of ten common adjectives. Then, for each word, come up with five words similar but not identical in meaning to the original word and use each in a sentence. The sentences should reveal the word's connotation, so ensure that you provide adequate context for each word's exact meaning in the sentence.

Determining Word Meanings through Context

Dictionaries are an indispensable part of the writing life whether you are a professional writer or a student writer. But while a good dictionary is part of the key to understanding challenging texts, it is not the only one.

To look up every unfamiliar word would be time-consuming and interrupt your reading, potentially reducing your understanding and retention of the material. Thankfully, you do not need to know the precise meaning of every word you read:

you need to know the exact meanings of the most important words but only approximate meanings for others.

Since relying *only* on a dictionary is both inefficient and unreliable, you should develop reading practices that minimize—not maximize—the use of a dictionary. Use a dictionary if you have to, but first try to determine meanings by using contextual clues.

Context Clues

Important nouns, verbs, adjectives, and adverbs are often revealed through context—the words around them. Writers may define difficult words or may use synonyms or rephrasing to make their meanings easy to grasp; such strategies are used if the author thinks the typical reader may not know them. On the other hand, authors may use an unfamiliar word in such a way that the meanings of the surrounding words clarify the meaning of the unfamiliar word. In the examples, below, the challenging word is italicized and the words that can help with meaning are underlined.

For clarification, terms may be explained or defined:

Here we focus on studies that measure accuracy using a *correlational* approach—that is, by comparing judgments by the self and others to a criterion. (Simine Vazire & Erika N. Carlson, "Others Sometimes Know Us Better Than We Know Ourselves," pp. 352–53)

Challenging words that are not explained can often be determined by the text immediately preceding or following. In the first example, below, the meaning of *enigma*, object of *solve*, can easily be inferred as something unknown, a puzzle. In the second example, the word following *edict* reveals that it must refer to some kind of order; it is stated that an emperor has made the order, so clearly an edict is an official order or proclamation:

These results help solve an *enigma* about whether playing "hard to get" increases one's attractiveness to others. (Erin R. Whitchurch, Timothy D. Wilson, & Daniel T. Gilbert, "'He Loves Me, He Loves Me Not. . .': Uncertainty Can Increase Romantic Attraction," p. 362)

In the year 213 BCE, the Chinese emperor Shih Huang-ti issued an *edict* ordering that all books in his realm should be destroyed. (Alberto Manguel, "Burning Mistry," p. 243)

If a writer uses examples, they can sometimes be used to infer the meaning of a previous word. In the following sentence, the author gives two examples of

Develop reading practices that minimize the use of a dictionary. Use a dictionary if you have to, but first try to determine meanings by utilizing contextual clues. Of course, a dictionary is always the best resource to check your spelling.

"travesties," according to seventeenth and eighteenth century thinking, in which undesirable role reversals are involved. (If you are not familiar with *gallants* or *breeches*, you might also guess them from context: since it can be inferred that *effeminate gallants* refers to "womanly" men, it can similarly be inferred that *women in breeches* refers to "manly" women—women (dressed) in breeches (pants):

> In the 17th and 18th centuries, bourgeois consumption qualified as "good," if it did not encourage *travesty*—men as effeminate *gallants*, for instance, or women in *breeches*. (Ulinka Rublack, "The Birth of Power Dressing," p. 282)

A reader can sometimes infer a word's meaning by using nearby information to clarify the word. In the following sentence, the writers suggest that an alternative to a *hypoxic air machine* is higher altitude training (where oxygen levels are low). The word *hypoxic* thus becomes clearer when the significance of this kind of training is considered:

> The cost of a *hypoxic* air machine and tent is about US$7000. Sending an athlete to a high altitude training location for several months may be even more expensive. (J. Savulescu, B. Foddy, & M. Clayton, "Why We Should Allow Performance Enhancing Drugs in Sport," p. 258)

Family Resemblances

If context does not help you determine a word's meaning, another strategy is to look for resemblances, recalling words that look similar and whose meanings you know. Many words in English come from Greek or Latin. A "family" of words may arise from the same Latin or Greek root. Thus, you may be able to infer the meaning of a new word by recalling a known word with the same word element. For example, you can easily see a family resemblance between the word *meritocracy* and the familiar word *merit*. You can take this a step further by looking at the second element and recalling that *meritocracy* and *democracy* contain a common element. In a *democracy*, the *people* determine who will govern them. In a *meritocracy*, then, *merit* determines who governs.

You may be able to infer the meaning of a new word by recalling a known word with the same word element.

Specialized Language

The strategies discussed above for understanding unfamiliar words apply to all kinds of writing. However, academic disciplines have their own specialized vocabularies that scholars use to communicate with each other. This type of language, known as **jargon**, is used by groups organized around a common purpose or activity. For example, in rowing, *to crab* is to lose an oar, while in medical jargon, *coding* means a patient is experiencing cardiac arrest.

JARGON is discipline- or subject-specific language used to communicate among members.

When you take courses in a particular discipline, like psychology, history, or exercise science, you begin to acquire its specialized vocabulary, which has developed along with the discipline itself. To learn about a subject is to simultaneously learn its language, in addition to the other conventions of the discipline.

Although some highly technical articles may use jargon that is beyond the reach of the student, both novice and more experienced readers can use the variety of discipline-specific dictionaries, encyclopedias, and research guides accessed through many libraries. For example, Oxford University Press publishes a series of subject dictionaries in art and architecture, the biological sciences, classical studies, computing, earth and environmental sciences, and many other disciplines.

EXERCISE 6.2

Using contextual or word resemblance clues, determine the meanings of the italicized words in the following passages, all of which are taken from readings in Part 2 of this book:

1. Although a *laudable* humanitarian impulse has driven relief efforts in Haiti, it alone is insufficient for the task of rebuilding the nation. (Andrew D. Pinto, "Denaturalizing 'Natural' Disasters: Haiti's Earthquake and the Humanitarian Impulse," p. 268)

2. In part because researchers employ so much *nuance* and strive to disclose all remaining sources of uncertainty, scientific evidence is highly susceptible to selective reading and misinterpretation. (Chris Mooney, "We Can't Handle the Truth: The Science of Why People Don't Believe Science," p. 321)

3. The predator *eclipsed* the scavenger, setting humankind on the fateful course of *ecocide*. (Richard Swift, "Predators and Scavengers," p. 172)

4. While initial motivation to adopt a vegetarian diet may thus be *divergent*, resulting in animosity between health and ethical vegetarians . . . , there may also be *convergence* among those who have adopted a vegetarian diet, possibly to provide further cognitive support for a difficult life choice. (Fox & Ward, "Health, Ethics and Environment," pp. 188–89)

5. With millions of young people out of work and looking for a way to put their skills to use, the potential for *burgeoning* movements to draw on the talents of those with suitable rage and creative skills presents limitless opportunities. . . . In past years Harper and the Conservatives have threatened artists' livelihoods with multi-million-dollar funding cuts. These moves were countered by massive *mobilizations* of artists and musicians across Canada." (Chris Webb, "Occupy Canada," pp. 291–92)

◎ Chapter 6 Review Questions

1. a. What factors could affect the way you interact with a text?

    b. In what ways does an "active reader" read a text?

2. Why is it important to annotate a text you read for class or for an assignment?

3. a. What is the difference between a general scan and a target scan?

    b. Identify one reading purpose for each of these strategies.

    c. What is focused reading and when should you use it?

4. Answer true or false:

    a. Context clues refer to determining a word's meaning by looking at the words around it.

    b. A word's connotations are its associations or shades of meaning.

    c. You should always use a dictionary to look up every word you're unsure of.

5. What is jargon? Give an example of jargon in an area that interests you (for example, a sport or activity you're familiar with, or a hobby).

◎ Key Terms

active reading (p. 105)

connotation (p. 108)

denotation (p. 108)

focused reading (p. 107)

general scan (p. 107)

jargon (p. 110)

selective reading (p. 106)

subject index (p. 107)

target scan (p. 107)

CHAPTER 7

Critical Thinking

In this chapter, you will learn:

◎ How to apply critical thinking skills to your reading

◎ How to use inference in critical thinking

◎ How to use critical thinking to develop an argument

◎ How to use critical thinking to respond to and analyze a text

As mentioned in the previous chapter, using your critical thinking skills will help you become a more active reader. But *critical thinking* doesn't mean merely thoughtful consideration of an author's ideas, though that is certainly one of its aims. Critical thinking covers a range of activities to use when approaching a challenging text.

Writing at the post-secondary level also requires readers to make inferences—to draw valid conclusions based on evidence. Reaching a conclusion could involve:

- Analyzing
- Questioning
- Recollecting
- Hypothesizing
- Evaluating
- Comparing
- Connecting
- Reconsidering
- Synthesizing
- Weighing the evidence
- Generalizing

If you look up the words *critical*, *critic*, and *criticism* in a dictionary, you will see that each word has several meanings. One meaning of *critical* is "negative, finding fault." However, the root of *critical* comes from a Greek word that means "to judge or discern, to weigh and evaluate evidence." It is this meaning that is implied in the term **critical thinking**.

CRITICAL THINKING can be defined as a series of logical mental processes, including evaluating and weighing the evidence, that lead to a conclusion.

Much of what we do today is done quickly. This is true not only of video games, text messages, Twitter, and email but also in business, where "instant" decisions are valued (especially if they turn out to be good decisions). However, because critical thinking involves many related activities, speed is not usually an asset. In fact, *since critical thinking is a process, the best way to succeed is to slow down, to be more deliberate in your thinking, so you can complete each stage of the process.*

◎ Inferences and Critical Thinking

We make an inference when we form a conclusion based on the evidence or ideas that a writer presents. Writers do not always openly state their conclusions but sometimes leave it to the readers to infer meaning. (Also, context clues can be used to infer the meaning of an unfamiliar word—see Chapter 6, "Word Meanings," p. 108).

Many research methods rely on inferences: astronomers, for example, study black holes by observing the behaviour of the matter that surrounds them. They know that before matter is swallowed up by a black hole, it is heated to extreme temperatures and it accelerates. In the process, X-rays are created, which escape the black hole and reveal its presence. Scientists cannot actually *see* black holes, but they can *infer* their existence through the emission of X-rays.

We practice critical thinking every day, inferring probable causes or consequences from what we observe—the evidence—and our interpretation of this evidence. For example, let's say you arrive at your workplace to see that all the staff are wearing red. After a pause, the wheels begin to turn (a sure sign you are thinking critically!): you realize it is Valentine's Day and that the email from your manager you ignored must have asked everyone to dress in red that day. You might further infer that it is not a good idea to ignore emails from your manager.

More than one inference might be possible in a given situation—an inference could be a *possible* conclusion, but not the *most probable* one. An inference that is more probable is usually a better one. However, an inference can also be incorrect; you might draw a hasty conclusion without thinking something through or if you had a bias (for example, if you prejudged someone based on first impressions). In reading, you might make an incorrect inference if you failed to read the instructions for an assignment or read them too quickly.

We receive messages today in many different forms—for example, visual ones, like a documentary film, a commercial, a photograph, or artwork; choices we make in our clothing may also give a message about ourselves, such as how we want others to see us. Using critical thinking to make correct inferences may be vital in certain situations, such as responding to visual clues that indicate someone isn't interested in what we're saying. As well, responding correctly or sensitively to a documentary film may increase our cultural awareness or change our beliefs

---

An **INFERENCE** is a conclusion based on what the evidence shows or points to, without the author stating that conclusion. More than one inference might be possible in a given situation, but the most *probable* one is said to be the *best* inference.

Inferences across the Disciplines:

Literary writers in the humanities don't announce the meanings, or themes, in their works but leave it to the reader to infer meaning by weighing the important elements in the work. It stands to reason that some readings are better than others because they take more into account of theme, character, and other elements.

Researchers in the sciences and social sciences make inferences based on their knowledge of phenomena or human behaviour and based on previous research. They also make inferences about the numerical data generated through an experiment; that is, they draw conclusions about their significance.

about a social or political issue, offering a learning opportunity we could otherwise miss.

Everyone has seen cartoons that, through humour or irony, draw attention to a controversial issue. What message does the cartoon below communicate to you?

a. Society is becoming obsessed with guns.
b. There are too many guns in Toronto.
c. Toronto is becoming a dangerous city due to the number of guns.
d. Guns are ruining Toronto's reputation.

© Graeme MacKay

Clearly, the best inference is not "a" because nothing is being said about society; the best inference here is a more specific one. Although the statements in "b" and "c" are possible inferences, critical thinking would likely lead you to "d" as the best, or most probable, conclusion. Even if you are unfamiliar with the expression "Toronto the Good," you likely realized that the message was not only about guns but also about what was happening to Toronto's "good" reputation as a result of gun-related crimes.

◉ Critical Thinking as a Process

Academic and non-academic writers ask questions about a topic and, using some of the activities listed above, come to a reasoned conclusion. For example, when Doug Saunders read that more people have cellphones than have access to a toilet, his immediate response was like most people's: it seemed ridiculous. But after evaluating, comparing, and weighing the evidence, Saunders concluded that a cellphone might be more useful than a toilet for people who are economically disadvantaged (see p. 313).

Making the best inference can help us adapt to an unfamiliar situation or enable us to take advantage of a learning opportunity.

In practice, critical thinking leads us to increasingly complex thoughts that evolve the more we think about the situation or text that triggered our original thought.

Similarly, academic studies often arise from a question about prior research or about a misperception. For example, Harold Herzog questions the common perception that pets provide physical and psychological benefits (p. 180).

Critical thinking, then, isn't simply a case of responding reflexively to a trigger, such as a situation or a statement in a text and concluding something about it. In practice, critical thinking leads us to increasingly complex thoughts that evolve the more we think about that situation or statement.

Breaking Down Critical Thinking: An Example

To better understand the process of critical thinking, consider the situation described by Dorothy Woodend in "Generation Velcro" (pp. 205–06):

> The other day I took my seven-year-old son Louis to buy some running shoes. "Pick something with Velcro," I said, as he trotted off to roam the racks.
>
> A clerk, hovering nearby, gave me a jaundiced look, "You know we get high school kids in here who have to buy Velcro because they never learned to tie their shoes. Every year their parents would just buy them Velcro because it was easier than making them learn how to tie laces."
>
> I stared at him and he went on.
>
> "The other day we had to special order a pair of shoes for this kid's high school graduation because he couldn't tie his laces, and he needed a pair of Velcro formal shoes."
>
> I put the shoes Louis had chosen back on the shelf, and picked out a pair of lace-up running shoes. It wasn't just that I'd been shamed into compliance by the salesman, but something Jane Jacobs had written about in her last book about the coming dark ages hit home. The loss of knowledge, she said, once vanished, is so difficult to regain—even if it's something as mundane as tying your shoes.

Woodend claims that she was not simply "shamed into compliance by the salesman," a reflexive response unconnected to critical thinking. Instead, various ways of thinking critically led her to a more complex perception. The process can be represented in three stages by a diagram (though we can't know for certain which activities Woodend did in the second stage):

Trigger   ⟶   clerk's comment about Velcro shoes

Activity   ⟶   connecting, recollecting, analyzing, generalizing . . .

Conclusion ⟶   inability to tie shoelaces related to loss of knowledge

Of course, to be convincing, Woodend must do more than simply state a conclusion and expect the reader (especially the critical thinker) to agree. She needs to present evidence to support her claim, as all arguers do. She refers to a newspaper article and a book by a professor of cognitive neuroscience who comments on the phenomenon of knowledge loss and its possible significance.

If her critical thinking ended here, her essay would only show one stage in the process of critical thinking (recall that critical thinking can best be defined as a *series* of logical mental processes that lead to a conclusion). However, later in her essay, she reconsiders the original situation that triggered her perception about the loss of knowledge and, by asking a question, reaches a second, more significant conclusion:

> Which brings me back to the question that has me tied up in shoe knots.
>
> If the lights start to go out sometime in the near future, and the Walmart closes its doors, who would really be useful? The answer changes, but basically it comes down to people who know how to do things, farmers, carpenters, doctors, people with a body of knowledge that can be applied directly, physically to the real world.

Trigger   ⟶   original conclusion seen in new light

Activity   ⟶   reconsidering, questioning, generalizing . . . other activities?

Conclusion   ⟶   Those with practical knowledge and skills will be badly needed in a future "dark age"

At an advanced level, critical thinking involves a chain of logic, a process that can lead you far beyond your original response or question (in the example, to Louis's inability to tie his shoes). In this way, the critical thinking process becomes a series of engagements with the situation and its larger significance, which increase in complexity or relevance to larger groups of people (in the example, Louis's inability eventually leads Woodend to think about her own parenting and that of her generation).

Does this mean that, as a reader, you shouldn't question the critical thinking processes of a writer? Not at all. In fact, conclusions can often be challenged, especially in an argument. For example, you could ask whether the writer sufficiently backs up the claims she makes or whether there is a flaw in her reasoning. You might think about the large gap between shoelace-tying ability and problems with coping during a dark age or, indeed, whether such a dark age is inevitable, as the writer seems to assume. Critically engaging with a writer who is critically engaged with his or her topic is a feature of critical thinking at the college and university level. In fact, this is what you do when you write a rhetorical analysis or a research paper (see Chapters 3 and 5).

Critically engaging with a writer who is critically engaged with his or her topic is a feature of critical thinking at the college and university level.

◉ Critical Situations for Critical Thinking

As we read a text, we may not even be aware that we are thinking critically until we automatically question a statement. A writer might make a claim that directly contradicts what our knowledge or common sense tells us—for example, that cats are more intelligent than humans. Another example might be a writer making a claim about a topic that experts have been debating for years—for example, that cats are smarter than dogs. Although you would probably just dismiss the first claim, the second claim would probably cause you to use critical thinking to evaluate the following:

- *The writer's credibility:* Who is the intended audience? Has the writer written for this audience? What shows you this? Who is the writer and what is his or her interest in their topic? Is the writer an expert? What kind? Is he or she a researcher into animal behaviour? A veterinarian? An animal trainer? Someone who has owned both dogs and cats? Someone who has owned dogs only? Could the writer have a bias? Are there examples of false reasoning? Has fact been carefully distinguished from opinion? Other factors also affect credibility (see "Support," below).

- *Nature of the claim (thesis):* Specific claims are stronger than general ones and often easier to prove. Since variability has been found among dog breeds, it would be difficult to generalize about the intelligence of *all* dogs.

- *Basis of the claim:* Some claims are more straightforward than others. A claim may depend on an underlying assumption, such as a definition. There are different ways to define and measure intelligence: physiologically (e.g., the weight of the brain in proportion to the weight of the body) and behaviourally (e.g., trainability, adaptability, independence). Those favouring a dog's intelligence may point to trainability as the intelligence factor, while advocates of cat intelligence may point to adaptability or independence. Both are valid criteria in an argument but could be challenged.

- *Method:* How does the writer attempt to prove the claim? Is the method appropriate? Intelligence can be measured. Therefore, a method that sought to measure intelligence scientifically would be more credible than one that relied on personal observation—especially since many pet-lovers are quite opinionated about their pets' intelligence and may not always separate fact from opinion. How many measurements were made? (More measurements will likely create more valid results than fewer ones.)

- *Support:* A credible writer needs to provide more than opinion to back up a claim. In critical thinking, you must evaluate the nature of the evidence and the way the writer uses it. Typical questions might include the following: What kind of evidence did the writer use? Has the writer relied too much on one kind of evidence or one source? How many sources were used? Were they current sources (recent studies may be more credible than older ones)? Did the writer provide relevant details from the source(s)? Did he or she ignore some sources (e.g., those that found dogs more intelligent than cats)?

- *Conclusion:* Conclusions result from the *incremental process of reading critically*. In arriving at a conclusion, you weigh the various factors involved in your analysis of the text. Obviously, some points are more important than others, and some evidence is more effective than other evidence. You might consider how weaker points affect the validity of the findings. Were there any gaps or inconsistencies in the use of reason? Was the writer's conclusion logically prepared for? Ultimately, your goal is to determine whether the accumulated weight of evidence supports the writer's claim.

EXERCISE 7.1

The specific statements in each passage below can lead to inferences either about the information presented or about the writer's attitude toward the subject. Choose the best (most probable) conclusion:

1. After missing the previous class, you are surprised to see your instructor enter the classroom and, without saying anything, take a seat in the back row. You ask the student beside you why she is not standing at the front preparing for class, but he just shrugs.

   a. The instructor has decided to take the day off from teaching.
   b. The instructor is just sitting down while she catches her breath.
   c. The instructor forgot to tell the class that there will be a guest speaker today.
   d. The instructor told the class there would be a guest speaker the next day, but the student beside you missed the previous class too.

2. Jen was hired as the manager of Cilantro due to her competence and high ethical standards. It was a stressful time because a new staff team had been hired to complete a company project. Jen, who was in charge of the project, was particularly annoyed when one of the team members told her they needed two more weeks to work on samples before they could begin production. After listening to team concerns, she left the room saying, "Well, if we keep going at this pace, we're not going to complete production in the projected three weeks." However, the following day, she submitted a report to her supervisors, indicating that the project was running smoothly.

    a.   She lied in the report to protect her job with the company.

    b.   She has decided to change her team and hire new members.

    c.   She found a solution to the problem and did not want to complain needlessly.

    d.   No inference is possible about the reason for Jen's statement.

3.   In your women's studies class, you have been asked to write a response on the ways that gender is shaped by socio-economic factors. When handing out the assignment page, your instructor says that she does not expect you to be an expert yourself but that your response must include the view of at least one expert on this topic.

    a.   Your instructor expects you to rely mostly on your own opinion.

    b.   Your instructor expects you to rely mostly on research sources.

    c.   Your instructor expects you to rely on your critical thinking skills.

    d.   You do not need to worry about the instructor's comment as the assignment page includes all the information you need to write a successful essay.

4.   It was Todd's roommate's turn to cook dinner, but when Todd got home, his roommate was glued to the TV and the kitchen looked untouched. "Wow! Something smells great," enthused Todd.

    a.   Todd has a poor sense of smell.

    b.   Todd is sarcastically voicing his displeasure.

    c.   Todd is trying to give his roommate a hint that he should start dinner.

    d.   No inference is possible.

5.   Lara works at the city's tourist centre, and she is often asked to recommend whale-watching tours. However, her boss has told her she should provide the relevant brochures and not make personal recommendations. She often tells tourists, "I've heard that Whales Galore is awesome, but I've heard a few good things about Spouting Off, too."

    a.   Lara favours Whales Galore over Spouting Off.

    b.   Lara favours Spouting Off over Whales Galore.

    c.   Lara is careful to praise both companies equally in order to satisfy her boss.

    d.   No inference is possible.

◎ Chapter 7 Review Questions

1. Which of the following activities is not usually associated with critical thinking?
   a. Questioning
   b. Comparing
   c. Memorizing
   d. Reconsidering
2. What meaning of the word *critical* is implied in the term *critical thinking*?
3. Define *inference* in your own words; give an example of an inference you made recently and what led you to this inference (it can be a correct or incorrect one).
4. Explain how inferences differ across the disciplines.
5. The best inference in a given situation is (choose one):
   a. The most probable one
   b. The least probable one
   c. The one most people accept as true
   d. The most recent one
6. Describe two situations which could result in an incorrect inference (they could be general or specific situations) and what would make them incorrect.
7. The situation that often begins the critical thinking process is called the
   _____.
8. In which of the following three assignments would critical thinking likely not play a major part?
   a. Rhetorical analysis
   b. Summary
   c. Research paper
9. What questions could you ask to determine whether a writer is credible?
10. Answer true or false:
    a. Specific claims are weaker than general claims.
    b. In drawing a conclusion, you should weigh all the evidence equally.

◎ Key Terms

critical thinking (p. 113)
inference (p. 114)

CHAPTER 8

An Introduction to Reading Texts

In this chapter, you will learn:

◎ How writers consider their audience

◎ How to identify two common kinds of writing, their formats and purposes

◎ How to distinguish between academic and non-academic texts

◎ How writers use analysis and synthesis in the writing process

Many tasks you undertake in your academic career will require you to read texts. Through careful reading, you can inform yourself on issues and views relevant to your world. Perhaps more important, by incorporating your reading experiences into your writing, you can inform others and shape the way they understand these issues.

Most writing, like other forms of communication, assumes the existence of an audience, a community of potential readers. Who are these readers? For researchers, they are other researchers, as well as decision makers who hope to make use of the research—from local school board members and administrators to national governments. For journalists, they are members of an interested public they hope to reach. Each writer is keenly aware of his or her audience and uses the most effective methods possible to reach this audience.

For student writers, the reader may be an instructor or, possibly, another student who will respond to your writing; however, learning to write for your audience prepares you for the community of readers that lies ahead.

Most texts, whether written, oral, or visual, are directed to an intended **AUDIENCE**—for writing, a group of readers. Each writer is keenly aware of his or her audience and uses the most effective methods possible to reach this audience.

◎ Kinds of Texts

For years you have been developing a variety of reading-related skills—whether you were conscious of them or not. The pages that follow are designed to help you extend and adapt these skills to new situations so you can become a more conscious and capable reader—and writer.

Although reading at the post-secondary level may be more diverse and challenging than you are used to, it helps to know that texts fall into one of two broad categories: (1) academic (usually research-oriented) texts written by experts for knowledgeable readers; and (2) non-academic texts written by non-experts for general, interested readers. In turn, these two categories can be subdivided (see p. 125).

The 38 readings in Part 2 reflect this division. Although non-academic texts are usually written for general readers, they often depend on outside sources, such as government publications or academic studies, even if they do not cite these sources.

In the two previous chapters, we discussed general reading and thinking strategies. In this and the following two chapters, we discuss specific characteristics of writing—non-academic and academic—that will help you read a wide variety of texts differing in their reading level, complexity, and conventions.

> For our purposes, texts can be divided into academic, written by experts for other experts, and non-academic, written often by non-experts for general readers.

◎ The Reading–Writing Connection

As a student, becoming one of a community of readers makes you part of a community of writers. One reason is that you will inevitably be asked to read something and respond to or analyze it, often in writing.

The more you think about your reading process, the better you will read, and the more you will think about what you read and ask appropriate questions. Having considered these questions, you will be prepared to write about what you have read. Usually, after you have written a rough draft, you read it over carefully and critically in order to make it reflect your purpose and make it understandable to your audience (i.e., you revise and edit it).

Most students know that the way they write on a friend's Facebook "wall" is very different in both content and style from the kind of writing they do for their instructor. Much of the writing we encounter online is too informal, subjective, or opinionated to serve as a model for academic writing. Similarly, as you will see in the examples of writing in this textbook, academic and non-academic writing have different purposes, and each is designed for different audiences (see "Purposes," below). In different ways, each can serve as a model for much of the writing you will do.

> The more you think about your reading process, the better you will read, and the more you will think about what you read.

◎ Academic versus Non-Academic Writing

Formats and Audience

It is usually not difficult to determine whether a piece of writing is intended for an academic or a non-academic audience. To begin with, you can consider *where* academic and non-academic writing is found. Someone who wanted a casual read might scan the magazine rack at the local store or a list of the top 10 bestsellers; he or she would not use a specialized database or seek out the publications of a university press. In short, experts and non-experts know where to find the material they're interested in.

Publishers design their covers with specific readers in mind. For example, a popular magazine displays a colourful photo or other graphic with, perhaps, a quotation to catch the reader's interest. Many academic journals include the titles of articles on their cover, stressing their knowledge-based approach.

Purposes

Academic and non-academic writing also differ in purpose. Articles in books and academic journals usually attempt to

- Interpret texts in new ways
- Generate new knowledge or confirm/disprove old knowledge
- Review related studies on a particular topic

In contrast, articles in magazines, newspapers, and other informal sources usually attempt to

- Inform
- Persuade
- Entertain

Of course, many non-academic articles combine these purposes in various ways—for example, to inform *and* entertain at the same time.

Figure 8.1 summarizes some of the different classifications of academic and non-academic writing, showing the formats, purposes, and audience of each. However, the categories are not always clear-cut; for example, some academic journals include material intended for a more general audience. (A periodical is a general term for the kind of publication that is issued periodically, at regular or semi-regular intervals.)

Academic writing is usually intended to interpret texts, generate new knowledge, or review knowledge about a topic for specialists. Non-academic writing is usually intended to inform, persuade, or entertain general readers.

A **PERIODICAL** is a general term for the kind of publication that is issued at regular intervals.

The line between the various kinds of periodicals, such as magazines, is often unclear, but there are major distinctions between them and academic journals. Although many different kinds of periodicals are represented in the selection of journalistic essays in Part 2, many could be considered "ideas" magazines in which professional writers, including some with academic affiliations, address compelling issues in today's world. The mandate of such magazines could be summed up by that of *Inroads*, a 20-year-old Canadian periodical that aims to publish "content [that] is well-researched but not academic."

> A **JOURNAL** is a kind of periodical designed for readers with specialized interests and knowledge containing original research, reviews, editorials—but little, if any, advertising; it may be issued in print and/or online format.

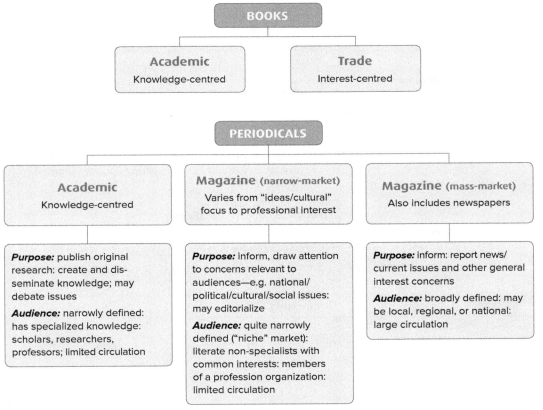

Figure 8.1   Published Texts Can Be Divided into Categories Depending on Their Purpose and Audience

Articles from mass-circulation magazines or newspapers are usually written for an audience with varied interests and knowledge levels; however, specific sections of newspapers and large-circulation magazines could be written for a narrower audience (e.g., the books section, which is part of the more general arts or lifestyles section, or the stock market quotations, part of the business section).

Other Differences

In addition to format, audience, and purpose, academic and non-academic writing differ in various ways, as shown in Table 8.1.

In this text, essays written mainly for an audience of scholars, researchers, and professors are referred to as *academic* or *scholarly essays*, whether they are in book or journal format, while essays written for an audience of non-specialists who share certain interests, beliefs, or ideologies are referred to as *non-academic* or *journalistic essays*.

Table 8.1   Academic versus Non-Academic Writing

	Non-academic	Academic
Structure	Varies; may be loosely structured	Tight and logical structure
Introduction	Dramatic introduction common; designed to attract attention	Dense; designed to give information
Thesis	May not be included in introduction	Found in the introduction
Paragraphs	May be short to maintain interest	Vary; tend to be well-developed
Argument/persuasion	Opinion may be evident throughout	Essays may offer recommendations but personal opinion minimized
Conclusion	May end with appeal or stress importance of topic; may be brief and informal	An important part of essay structure; may suggest further research directions
Style	Informal; may use *I, you*, etc.; contractions; occasional slang	Formal
Language	Geared to non-specialist; stimulates reader interest	Geared to specialist; conveys knowledge
Sentence structure	Sentence variety; more short and medium-length than long sentences; occasional use of fragments	Varies, but sentences may be long and complex

The following paragraphs from two essays in Part 2, one from a non-academic article and one from an academic article, differ in their language, style, and sentence structure:

The author begins with a sentence fragment: the list of four recognizable phrases quickly attracts the reader's attention.

A short sentence is followed by another fragment.

Asking a question directly involves the reader.

Colloquialisms, like *hyped-up*, are common in non-academic prose.

Non-academic: Selfish genes, survival of the fittest, competition, hawk and dove strategies. Like all theories, Darwinism has its own distinct vocabulary. So distinct, in fact, that we end up asking how else we can talk about evolution. After all, isn't competitive evolution the only possible context for explaining the biological facts? The drama implied by competition, war and selfishness passes unnoticed because people are used to this rather hyped-up way of talking even about current scientific beliefs. (Mary Midgley, "The Selfish Metaphor," p. 315)

Academic: If Iger's philosophy is one for the future of television, it is an industrial version of Raymond Williams's famous statement regarding television as *flow* between show-and-show, show-and-ad as "perhaps the defining characteristic of broadcasting, simultaneously as a technology and as a cultural form" (86). (Jonathan Gray, "'Coming Up Next': Promos in the Future of Television and Television Studies," p. 307)

> Authors of academic essays refer often to other researchers and theorists. Gray refers to two authors (the first was mentioned in the previous paragraph) and quotes directly from the second one.

◎ Breaking Down and Putting Together

Two important terms in almost all writing are analysis and synthesis. When you use your skills for **analysis**—from the verb *analyze*—you closely examine something. You analyze when you "break down" an essay or paragraph, an argument or point. Critical thinking involves the use of reason in breaking down ideas in order to reach a conclusion (see Chapter 7).

> The word *flow* is an example of jargon, or specialized vocabulary that other experts in the field would understand.

Different methods or patterns can be used to break something down—for example, you can look at causes and effects, pros and cons, or similarities and differences. A literary analysis could involve breaking down a poem's stanzas or a novel's narrative to study smaller units, such as metre (in a poem) or point of view (in a novel). There are many other methods as well (see Chapter 1, pp. 14–15).

> Although the sentence is 43 words long, it is not difficult to follow as the sentence structure is logical and joining words, such as *if*, *as*, *between*, and *and*, help the reader connect the thoughts.

Synthesis is the activity of "putting together" in order to reach a consensus or a conclusion. In a student research essay, you combine your own ideas with ideas/facts/findings from other sources; it is, therefore, sometimes called a synthesis essay. In a successful synthesis essay, the writer organizes sources logically, connects them to a central thesis, and clarifies the unique contribution of each source.

> Academic writers use citations to reveal their sources.

> When you **ANALYZE**, you break something down in order to look more closely at its parts. When you **SYNTHESIZE**, you put together in order to reach a conclusion.

◎ Chapter 8 Review Questions

1. The person or persons you are writing to is called your _____. Why is it important to be aware of this person/group before writing?
2. In your own words, explain the "reading–writing connection" and its importance to your development as a reader and writer.

3. Choose the one answer that doesn't apply: Academic writing usually attempts to
   a. Inform and entertain the reader
   b. Review research on a common topic
   c. Generate new knowledge
   d. Interpret a text in a new way

4. Choose three of the following five writing features and explain the difference(s) between academic and non-academic writing for each feature chosen:
   a. The introduction
   b. Paragraphs
   c. The conclusion
   d. Language
   e. Sentence structure

5. What are the differences between analysis and synthesis?

◎ Key Terms

analysis (p. 127)
audience (p. 122)
journal (p. 125)

periodical (p. 124)
synthesis (p. 127)

CHAPTER 9

Conventions of Non-Academic Writing

In this chapter, you will learn:

- ◎ How non-academic writers use analysis and synthesis

- ◎ How personal experience can be used in non-academic texts

- ◎ How to read and write different kinds of introductions, including introductions that create interest and introductions that state a thesis

- ◎ How to recognize features of language and style in non-academic texts

- ◎ How to understand the relationship between the journalistic and scholarly communities

◎ What Are Conventions?

Conventions (from the Latin for "come together") are practices that help direct the actions and thinking of specific groups of people. You can think of them as a set of instructions to help us communicate. For example, in formal letter writing, it is conventional to use a salutation like *Dear* before the name of the recipient; however, in emailing a friend, a more appropriate salutation might be *Hello* or *Hi*. Conventions depend on audience, along with other factors. Both academic and non-academic writing have their conventions, or "usual practices," which help direct the reader, organize the essay, and open up a channel of communication between writer and reader.

In this chapter, we consider "usual practices" of non-academic writing, including techniques you may use in your own writing. In Chapter 10, we turn to "usual practices" of academic writing. Studying the conventions of non-academic and academic writing will help you locate information and understand how it is being used, making you a better (and more confident) reader. Applying some of these

CONVENTIONS are practices that direct the actions and thinking of specific groups. You can consider them a set of instructions that help us communicate with one another.

conventions to your different writing assignments will also help you to be a better (and more confident) writer.

◎ Analysis or Synthesis?

Although non-academic essays, like student essays, usually combine analysis and synthesis, they can be divided into two main types:

1. Those whose main purpose is to analyze
2. Those whose main purpose is to synthesize

Non-academic writers may use both analysis and synthesis, but the stress is usually on one or the other. Essays seeking to persuade their readers, usually focus on analysis, while those seeking mainly to inform focus on synthesis.

Analysis

Some kinds of journalistic essays—those seeking to persuade readers—stress analysis over synthesis. Here, independence of *the writer's* opinion and ideas counts for more than evaluating and integrating what *others* have said. However, the writers of a persuasive essay may also synthesize the ideas and words of others if this makes the argument more convincing. In "Slip-Sliding Away, Down the Ethical Slope," p. 240, Robert J. Sternberg uses process analysis, breaking down ethical behaviour into eight steps, while Alberto Manguel in "Burning Mistry," p. 243, mostly analyzes causes and effects that led to an incident of book-burning (with some synthesis as well).

For more information on persuasive or argumentative essays, see Chapter 4.

Synthesis

Journalistic essays whose main purpose is to inform use synthesis more than analysis. This information comes from what others have discovered or said. Journalistic writers, then, often use other people's words and ideas, synthesizing them in an interesting and entertaining way for their audience. For example, Isabelle Groc in "Orca Encounters" (p. 158) uses mostly synthesis to "put together" the views of scientists and government officials who disagree on what should be done with solitary orcas who seek contact with humans. Similarly, Ken MacQueen and Martin Patriquin, in "Are We Ready to Subsidize Heroin?" (p. 327), synthesize the views of the supporters and opponents of safe injection sites.

Journalistic writers synthesize by using a combination of direct quotations, especially those that will make the greatest impact on the reader, and summary to explain complex material. Technical information is almost always simplified, or omitted if unimportant.

◎ Personal Experience in Non-Academic Writing

In contrast to most academic essays, human interest is often a focus in journalistic essays. Writers may interview those most directly affected by an event, as well as observers, often shaping the story around the emotions of those involved. On the other hand, sometimes the topic itself evokes the human interest factor, as Isabelle Groc's essay on sociable orcas, p. 158.

While academic writers seldom refer directly to themselves—except in the role of objective researchers—a common practice of non-academic writers is to "write themselves" into their essays, enabling their readers to relate to the writer's experience. For example, in "Generation Debt," p. 202, Alethea Spiridon begins by recalling her experience as a cash-strapped but job-hungry student, connecting with her audience of current or former students.

However, personal experience and observation may play a much larger role throughout the essay. For example, Madeline Sonik (p. 212) and Ian Brown (p. 248) write from their own experiences, whereas Andrew Irvine (p. 338) uses a personal experience to introduce his reflective essay on scientific progress. These types of essays are discussed in the next section.

> In contrast to academic writers, non-academic writers often use personal experience for various purposes, including the common ones of attracting the reader's interest and enabling the reader to relate to the author's experience.

Personal and Reflective Essays

Other non-academic essays tend to be literary or philosophical, rather than journalistic. The personal or expressive essay, creative non-fiction, the literary essay, and literary journalism are all terms that suggest the focus on elegant prose and thoughtful reflection. Their writers may use common fictional techniques, such as irony, imagery, dialogue, and metaphoric language. They may also use narration or description to render an incident or a scene.

Such essays tend to stress the writer's life or experience, but their ultimate purpose is to show us the large picture, to invite us to consider our own world in a new way. Although the distinctions between the many sub-forms are subtle, they can be divided into

> Successful personal and reflective essays are never self-indulgent: they use personal experience or observation as a means to reveal something of greater significance.

1. The personal essay, in which the writer's life experience is key
2. The reflective essay, in which the writer's observations and thoughts are key

It is important to remember that successful personal and reflective essays are never self-indulgent: they use personal experience or observation as a means to reveal something that goes beyond the personal.

The use of personal experience or observation in non-academic essays highlights a key difference between these and academic essays, which seldom include first-hand experience. If they do, it will usually be to provide support through "anec-dotal evidence" or to enhance writer credibility. For example, Harold Herzog states that his conclusions should not be taken "as a condemnation of pet keeping. Indeed, companion animals have always been a part of my own life. . . ." Making this state-ment clarifies the author's intentions by drawing a line between his life and his research subject, the contribution of pets to human health (see p. 184).

In addition to their use of analysis, synthesis, and personal experience, non-academic essays share other features, some of which may apply to the kinds of essays you will write.

> Academic essays, unlike non-academic ones, seldom use personal experience unless it is to directly provide support or increase credibility. Although non-academic ones sometimes do employ the first-person voice, it should have a specific purpose.

◎ Features of Non-Academic Writing

Non-academic writers use various conventions and strategies to create and maintain reader interest, beginning with the introduction. An interest-based introduction contrasts with the knowledge-based introduction in academic writing.

> Non-academic writers often try to directly engage their readers in their introductions. Interest-based introductions are less common in academic writing.

Interest-grabbing Introductions

Like the kinds of introductions you may be asked to write (see Chapter 1, p. 7), introductions in journalistic writing are designed to attract the attention of readers and draw them into the essay. There are many ways to interest readers. A typical method is to sketch a familiar scenario to which the reader can relate or one that is striking because it is unfamiliar. In a variant on this method, the writer makes a common observation or draws a familiar scene, only to use the reversal strategy to counter it.

Other common methods include the following:

- Narrating a personal experience or story that introduces the topic
- Describing a scene
- Using an example that represents a problem or issue central to the essay
- Narrating a brief anecdote
- Posing a provocative question
- Inserting a relevant quotation
- Citing a curious fact or making a challenging statement

Reversal: A sign at the [West Point War M]useum's entrance states, "Unquestionably, war-making is an aspect of human nature which will con-tinue as nations attempt to impose their will upon each other." Actually, this assertion is quite questionable. (John Horgan, "Does Peace Have a Chance?" p. 237.)

Narrating personal experience: In 1992, I was a high school graduate enrolled in studies at the University of Saskatchewan. Post-secondary education had never been a can-do for me—it was always a must-do. (Spiridon, "Generation Debt," p. 202.)

Narrating an anecdote and posing a question: You see your roommate at his computer, writing a paper. You notice him transferring text from an online document to the paper he is writing without attribution. . . . Is there a problem here? (Sternberg, "Slip-Sliding Away," p. 240.)

Quotation: Thich Nhat Hanh, the well-known Vietnamese Buddhist monk, is fond of suggesting that "there is no path to peace—peace *is* the path." (Paul Waldau, "Animal Welfare and Conservation: An Essential Connection," p. 174.)

Curious fact/challenging statement: About a third of the world's people have no toilet. (Saunders, "When a Cellphone Beats a Royal Flush," p. 313).

Using a Thesis

Thesis statements are less common in journalistic essays than in the kinds of essays that students are usually asked to write and in academic essays. The reason? A thesis statement is designed to inform the reader of the essay's content, its main point(s). In most interest-centred writing, announcing a thesis can work against the writer, deflecting the reader's interest where it is most needed, just before the body of the essay begins. In an essay you write, a thesis statement serves to inform the reader; in early drafts, it also ensures that you, the writer, are clear on your purpose and main point.

Instead of making a clear thesis statement, the journalistic writer may continue to draw out the reader's interest throughout the introduction, adding detail about the topic. Many successful journalistic essays contain no announced thesis or delay the thesis until later in the essay. Instead, the writer relies on rhetorical or literary devices to lead the reader on, using linguistic resources, evoking a distinct tone or mood, or seizing on a human connection.

In many cases, especially when literary techniques are used, it would be more precise to speak of a **theme** than of a thesis. You probably are familiar with themes from literary analysis. A theme, an overarching meaning or universal aspect, is seen through a work's basic elements, such as plot, setting, and characters in fiction, as well as literary devices such as images, diction, and figurative techniques like metaphors. A writer of this kind of essay does not "announce" a theme as you do a thesis; rather, a theme is evoked by recurrent patterns of these devices.

A thesis statement is designed to inform the reader of the essay's content, its main point(s). A thesis statement may be omitted in a non-academic essay in order to sustain interest in the topic.

The fact that a non-academic essay may not include a thesis statement in its introduction means that you need to read it differently and be open to the possibility that the thesis will be displaced (occur later in the essay) or indirect (not directly stated).

A **THEME** is an overarching meaning or universal aspect, seen through a work's basic elements, such as plot, setting, character, images, language, and figurative techniques.

Organization

Journalistic writing is organized logically, and the transitions from one point to another are clear through the use of organizational patterns common to all writing. For example, a writer could organize points chronologically (time order), beginning with the oldest and ending with the most recent. Journalistic writers often use description and narration to organize information, and all writing benefits from the use of examples to help explain abstract concepts. Paragraph organization tends to be looser than in academic writing, and paragraphs may be short.

Language

> All writers should know their audience well, and one way this knowledge is reflected is in the level of language that the writer uses.

In much non-academic writing, diction (word choice), serves the practical function of communicating complex information directly. The exception is literary writers who may use words that have more than one connotation (association); they may aim for richness, even ambiguity, through their language, rather than directness.

Language level is one of the main differences between academic and non-academic writing. Journalistic writers try to substitute common words for less common ones, especially technical terms or jargon. However, to describe journalistic writing as "simple" can be misleading. Writers of speciality or "interest" magazines may use words that only an educated audience would understand. All writers should know their audience well, and one way this knowledge is reflected is in the level of language that the writer uses.

> COLLOQUIAL, or conversational, LANGUAGE is a feature of some non-academic writing.

Although non-academic writing is not necessarily simple, it is sometimes colloquial and informal. For example, writers may use colloquial (conversational) language—even slang—and contractions are favoured as a space-saving device. As a general rule, you should not use colloquialisms or contractions in your own writing unless you are using dialogue in a narrative.

Tone

> TONE can be defined as the use of language to convey the writer's attitude toward the subject or the audience.

Writers can convey their attitude to their subject by their tone. One of the ways that you can infer a writer's tone—and what he or she is really saying—is by employing critical thinking skills and reading "between the lines," paying particular attention to the way language is being used. A writer could use a tone that is serious or solemn, light or comic, mocking or earnest, intimate, thoughtful, or ironic.

> In IRONY a second, or "deeper," meaning exists below the literal meaning, which contradicts the literal meaning.

Determining an author's tone will help you know how to respond to the essay itself. For example, if a writer uses an ironic tone, he or she is directing you beyond the literal surface meaning. In irony a second, or "deeper," meaning exists below the literal one, which contradicts or is inconsistent with the literal meaning. If you fail to pick up on an ironic tone, you may misread the essay, taking the surface meaning for the intended one. Irony can usually be detected through the writer's language or the subject matter, or both.

In the second half of the following sentence, language and subject matter convey the writer's irony or, perhaps, sarcasm:

"[The current government has] dragged its feet to renew and increase graphic labelling on cigarette packages—and thank goodness, because having to look at images of lung and oral cancers is just *such* a downer when you want a hit of nicotine." (Daniel Rosenfield et al., "Canadian Lifestyle Choices: A Public Health Failure," p. 219)

In sarcasm, a writer or speaker states something as its opposite.

EXERCISE 9.1

How would you define tone in the following passages? Identify specific features that reveal tone.

1. When humans experience others—again, it matters not whether these "others" are human or members of some other species—paradoxically this experience of getting beyond the self allows humans to become as *fully human* as we can be, that is, human in the context of a biologically rich world full of other interesting living beings. (Waldau, "Animal Welfare," p. 179.)

2. Because some information can't be avoided, [Mister and Missus Average Canadian] do know their systolic blood pressure is closing in on their bowling average of 220. They don't know, however, how that's been helped along by the food industry, which loves loading food up with salt, to make otherwise unpalatable cheap food taste good, prolong shelf life and keep the food industry rich. (Rosenfield et al., "Canadian Lifestyle Choices," p. 220.)

3. We raised him on our own for 10 years, and the experience almost shattered everything I valued—my family, my marriage, my healthy daughter's life, my finances, my friendships, life as I wanted to live it. There was no genetic test for his syndrome when he was born (there still isn't). For a long time, not a day went by when I didn't wish there'd been one. Today, I'm glad no test existed then—that I never had to decide, based on a piece of paper damp with my wife's blood, whether my strange and lonely boy ought to exist. (Ian Brown, "I'm Glad I Never Had to Decide Whether My Strange, Lonely Boy Ought to Exist," p. 249.)

Irony is often used in satire, a genre that mocks or criticizes institutions or commonly held attitudes. One way that satirists "tip off" their readers is through exaggeration. For example, in the thesis of the famous satire "A Modest Proposal"

SATIRE is a genre that mocks or criticizes institutions or commonly held attitudes.

(1729), Jonathan Swift proposes the sale of infants to Ireland's rich to be served up for dinner! The false thesis is so extreme that readers are able to see beneath the literal meaning and realize that Swift is actually attacking the callous attitude of the rich toward the poor. In his argument, he is really making really an indirect plea to Ireland's wealthy classes to help combat poverty, his "true" thesis.

Stylistic and Rhetorical Techniques

Repetition

A device of emphasis often used in non-academic writing is repetition. Of course, needless repetition wastes words, but occasionally, writers may repeat words or phrases to reinforce a point's significance. Repetition is a common device in argument: repeated ideas are more likely to be considered important and be remembered. For example, Mark Edmundson repeats clausal beginnings (italicized) to describe the mistrust of current editors and arts writers for the Western canon:

> *Though* the arts interest them, *though they read* this and *they read* that— there is one thing that makes them very nervous indeed about what they do. *They are not* comfortable with judgments of quality. *They are not* at ease with "the whole evaluation thing." (Mark Edmundson, "Narcissus Regards a Book," p. 287)

Sentence Length and Construction

Writers frequently vary the length and rhythm of their sentences. A succession of short sentences can create a dramatic effect, while longer, more flowing sentences can be used to expand on an idea. In periodic sentences, the writer builds towards the main idea, which is expressed at the end of the sentence. In cumulative sentences, the writer begins with the main idea and follows with words, phrases, or clauses that extend this idea.

In the examples below, note the different rhetorical effects created by these two sentence types, especially in the third, strongly cumulative sentence; the main idea is italicized in each example (the third sentence also contains examples of alliteration, the repetition of the identical sounds in *scarred* and *scored*, *bricks* and *bring*):

> **Moderately periodic:** In colleges and universities across the country, in individual blogs and in the public press, *readers expressed their outrage at both the burning and the banning.* (Manguel, "Burning Mistry," p. 244). The writer also uses repetition in this example.

In **PERIODIC SENTENCES**, the writer builds towards the main idea, which is expressed at the end of the sentence. In **CUMULATIVE SENTENCES**, the writer begins with the main idea and follows with words, phrases, or clauses that extend this idea.

Moderately cumulative: *There was general disdain of slovenly dress*, a strong theme, for example, in the writing of the Dominican priest Thomas Aquinas (1225–74), who thought that wives needed to look their best to keep their husbands faithful. (Rublack, "Power Dressing," p. 280)

Strongly cumulative: *When we are older we know this is the dream of a child*, that all hearts finally are bruised and scarred, scored and torn, repaired by time and will, patched by force of character, yet fragile and rickety forevermore, no matter how ferocious the defense and how many bricks you bring to the wall. (Brian Doyle, "Joyas Voladoras," p. 164)

The sentence above also demonstrates the use of parallel structures for rhetorical effect (the adjectival phrases beginning *bruised*, *scored*, *repaired*, and *patched* are parallel). Parallel structures contribute to the coherence of a paragraph, making it easier to follow; they also enhance the reading experience. For information about grammatical parallelism, see p. 429.

Space-Saving Techniques

Journalistic writers are trained to write concisely because space in newspapers and magazines (especially in print formats) is restrictive; in addition, loose, inefficient writing risks losing a reader's attention. The use of contractions is one example of a space-saving technique. Because efficiency is important in most prose, the two techniques below may find a place in your own writing.

Phrasal sentence openings: in phrasal openings, the sentence begins with a phrase that modifies a part of speech that follows. The adjectival phrases, modifying the noun (subject) *proponents*, are italicized below. (Note: if you use a phrasal opening, you must follow with the subject of the clause; see p. 396).

> *Buoyed with a Supreme Court decision* (and *armed with a raft of scientific evidence*), proponents of Insite and related harm reduction measures are poised to take the debate several steps further. . ." (MacQueen & Patriquin, "Are We Ready?," pp. 328–29).

A **PHRASE** is a group of words acting as a unit of speech. Thus, a group of words modifying a noun is an adjectival phrase while one modifying a verb is an adverbial phrase. For these and other kinds of phrases, see p. 379.

An **appositive** is a word or phrase that names, specifies, or explains the previous word or phrase; it is grammatically parallel to the preceding word or phrase. Although appositives are common in all writing, they are used routinely in articles designed for the mass market because they enable the writer to express information quickly. In the examples below, the sentences in 1 contain the same information as sentence 2, but in 2, the writer combines the information in 1 in an appositive (note the commas, in boldface, in the second sentence, separating the appositive from the main idea in the sentence):

An **APPOSITIVE** is a word or phrase that names, specifies, or explains the previous word or phrase. For more information, see p. 368.

1.   Toni Frohoff specializes in human–dolphin interactions. She is a wildlife behavioural biologist. She is based in Santa Barbara, California.

2.   Toni Frohoff, a wildlife behavioural biologist based in Santa Barbara, California, specializes in human–dolphin interactions. (Groc, "Orca Encounters," p. 159).

◎ Journalistic and Scholarly Writing: A Symbiotic Relationship

Although most traditional media—newspapers, magazines, and television—provide their readers and viewers with information about the news of the day, they also communicate new knowledge generated through research. Much of this knowledge is transmitted through print, in special sections or feature articles in newspapers or magazines, or through TV news features or specialized channels.

However, an increasing number of people get their daily news from the Internet. Internet search engines usually include in their general interest categories stories about scholarly research. For example, on a typical day, Google featured the following and other research-generated stories on its news home page:

- A recommendation by a US federal organization that would require automakers to design their cars so drivers could not text message or engage in any non-driving activity
- A study that helped explain the mass disappearance of honeybees
- Findings from medical research that showed a positive correlation between regular consumption of deli meats and incidence of pancreatic cancer
- The conclusions of a report, commissioned by the Canadian federal government, that examined wait lists for medical treatment

The connection between scholarly research and the popular press is affirmed through short articles that summarize the most significant findings for everyday readers.

Translating the complex findings of research into the language of everyday readers is often the work of media agencies: "wire services" like the Canadian Press, which locate significant studies and rewrite their findings for newspapers and other media. Academic articles are written for those with similar expertise and interest—their peers—while the popular press disseminates this knowledge, making it known to the very people whom it will most directly affect—for example, automobile drivers or those who may benefit from new medical discoveries. In this way, the connection between scholarly research and the reporting of this research to the public is reinforced every day.

EXERCISE 9.2

As described above, the role of the popular press is a vital one. However, a challenge for the journalist lies in translating the complexities of a study's findings into everyday language and writing an accurate story, in simplifying but not *over*simplifying. Three passages from online sources follow. Each reports on the same topic, the new guidelines for physical activity, which call for lowering the recommended hours of exercise for Canadians in order to encourage the most sedentary Canadians to exercise; the Canadian Society of Exercise Physiology (CSEP) made the recommendations to the Canadian government in 2011. Read the openings below and determine which is the most accurate; justify your answer. (Using your critical thinking skills, you should be able to explain your choice without seeing the CSEP report, which can be accessed at http://www.csep.ca/english/view.asp?x=804).

1. "Canadians are so inactive that even small amounts of exercise will make a difference in their risk for chronic disease, two fitness promotion groups said Wednesday. But they're still urging people to do more to get healthy and avoid illnesses like diabetes and heart disease."
2. "Canada is expected to take a 'less is more' approach with physical activity guidelines. The new fitness targets should make getting the recommended amount of exercise a little easier."
3. "It's OK, sit your butt back down on the couch. Canadians can get by with less exercise than previously thought, two national fitness groups say."

◎ Chapter 9 Review Questions

1. Analysis is often more important in non-academic essays whose main purpose is to _____. Synthesis is more important in non-academic essays whose main purpose is to _____.
2. Explain how personal experience can be used effectively in different types of non-academic writing.
3. a. What are some differences between personal/reflective essays and non-academic essays that do not rely on personal experience?
    b. Why might academic writers use personal experience?
4. What are some strategies that non-academic writers might use to get readers interested in their essays? Why are they less likely to be used by academic writers?

5. Answer true or false:
   a. Non-academic writers always include a thesis statement in an introduction.
   b. Writers who use literary techniques may include themes rather than a thesis.
6. Choose the best statement among the choices below:
   a. Non-academic writing is simple and unchallenging.
   b. Non-academic writing is of moderate difficulty.
   c. Non-academic writing uses mainly personal experience.
   d. Non-academic writing varies in difficulty depending on audience and other factors.
7. Define tone and give some examples of different kinds of tones. Why is it important that a reader be able to identify an ironic tone?
8. How could the device of repetition be successfully used in non-academic writing?
9. What is the difference between a periodic and a cumulative sentence?
10. Explain the interdependency of academic and non-academic writing. In your answer, discuss the ways that popular news outlets make use of the findings of academic researchers.

◎ Key Terms

appositive (p. 137)

colloquial language (p. 134)

convention (p. 129)

cumulative sentence (p. 136)

irony (p. 134)

periodic sentence (p. 136)

phrase (p. 137)

satire (p. 135)

theme (p. 133)

tone (p. 134)

CHAPTER 10

Conventions of Academic Writing

In this chapter, you will learn:

- ◎ How knowledge is defined across the disciplines

- ◎ How to tell a primary from a secondary source

- ◎ How to identify the features of voice and style in an academic essay

- ◎ How to use strategies to pre-read an academic essay

- ◎ How to identify important features of an academic introduction, including literature review and thesis

- ◎ How to recognize features of body paragraphs to retrieve information, including the use of topic sentences, prompts, and rhetorical patterns

- ◎ How to use transitions and other features to understand the relationship between ideas

Among the many writing and reading challenges that lie ahead, you will undoubtedly be asked to analyze researched and documented essays by experts who seek to advance knowledge in their discipline. In addition, you may be asked to include their findings in your own research paper.

◎ What Is Academic Writing?

For some people, *academic writing* is a euphemism for difficult or highly technical writing. However, successful academic writing is not intended to confuse but is designed for an audience familiar with a given discipline's conventions and modes of discourse, its central ideas and ways of presenting them.

Successful academic writing is not intended to confuse but is designed for an audience familiar with a given discipline's conventions and modes of discourse, its central ideas, and its ways of presenting them.

Like most other writing, academic writing has a distinct purpose, in this case, to advance knowledge in a discipline. It is also intended for a specific audience: knowledgeable and interested readers. Much academic writing is accessible to a wider audience than you might think; most of the "barriers" of academic discourse can be overcome by paying careful attention to its formal conventions.

Conventions are practices that direct the actions and thinking of specific groups. You can think of them as a set of instructions that help us communicate with one another. (See p. 129.)

Knowledge across the Disciplines

Although academic writing is generally written for knowledgeable readers, knowledge itself differs somewhat across the disciplines, as the following definitions suggest.

Humanities: The branch of knowledge concerned with examining the cultural tools that humans use to express and represent themselves. Humanities writing focuses on how ideas and values are used to interpret human experience, analyzing primary sources to draw conclusions about their literary themes, language, art and culture, historical significance, theoretical basis, or universality. Typical humanities disciplines are classical studies, history, linguistics, literature, modern languages, indigenous studies, philosophy, and religious studies, among others.

Social sciences: The branch of knowledge concerned with collective human behaviour and the systems (e.g., social, psychological, or political) humans create to study this behaviour. Social science disciplines include anthropology, economics, geography, political science, psychology, and sociology, among others.

Sciences: The branch of knowledge concerned with the study of natural phenomena using empirical methods to determine or validate their laws. The natural and applied sciences include biology, chemistry, engineering, environmental sciences, health sciences, mathematics, and many more.

◎ Audience: Who Reads Academic Writing?

PEER-REVIEWED (REFEREED) journals contain articles that have been reviewed by experts. These "peers" suggest whether the article meets the exacting standards in their discipline and may recommend that the article be published, published with revisions, or rejected.

It will come as no surprise that the largest audience for academic writing is scholars, people with knowledge about and interest in the subject. However, academic journals and many academic presses vary in their readership, from highly knowledgeable readers to those with a general knowledge.

The most reliable academic journals are peer-reviewed (refereed). As part of the editorial process, articles are read by experts in the field (peers), who decide whether an article should be published.

The aims of academic publications are well summarized by John Fraser, a columnist for *The Globe and Mail*:

> [T]he best academic publications extend our understanding of who we are in ways that trade publications and magazines and newspapers have largely abandoned. Canada's collective memory, our understanding of our social and economic conditions, aboriginal challenges to national complacency, the actual consequences of de-linking ourselves from the realities of our past . . . all find provocative and highly useful resonances from our academic publishers. (John Fraser. "Academic Publishers Teach Mainstream Ones a Lesson." *The Globe and Mail* 4 June 2005: F9)

◎ Features of Academic Writing

Some of the conventions of academic writing described below apply more to scholarly journal articles than books, but likely you will encounter more articles than books (other than textbooks) in your courses during the early years of your academic career.

Length and Complexity

Academic essays vary in length. Scientific studies may be as short as two or three pages; concise writing is a characteristic of such studies. Essays in some humanities disciplines, such as philosophy, history, and English, are often longer, focused on detailed analyses. Writers in the humanities explore new subtleties in and variations on texts and concepts long debated. In addition, writers in the humanities usually refer to primary sources, quoting often from these texts to support their points (see "Research Sources," below).

Length is often a function of the depth and detail expected in academic writing. Many science and social science essays use visual material, such as tables, graphs, and photos, to summarize results.

Research Sources

Academic writers rely on the writing of other scholars; however, this does not mean that all academic writing is concerned only with what has been written before in academic journals/books or delivered at academic conferences. Nor does academic writing consist mostly of summaries of other scholars' work. Thus, when you are asked to write a research paper, you too must do more than summarize your sources.

Most research, whether conducted by scholars or by scholars-in-training like yourself, involves analysis, which is often centred on first-hand or primary sources, *original material in a field of study.* Much research begins with primary source material; for example, it would be logical to study a literary work (primary source) before you looked at what other people had to say about it (secondary source). "Primary," then, means *first in order*, not necessarily first in importance. Secondary sources, by contrast, are *commentary on or interpretation of primary material.*

Kinds of primary sources vary from discipline to discipline. Here are a few examples from various disciplines:

- *Anthropology and archaeology:* Artifacts, fossils, original field notes, reports resulting from direct observations
- *Literature:* Poems, plays, novels, diaries/letters of writers
- *Fine arts:* Sheet music, recordings, photographs, sketches, paintings, sculpture, films
- *History:* Contemporary documents from the period being studied—e.g., newspaper accounts, letters, speeches, photographs, treaties, diaries, autobiographies
- *Natural sciences:* Data from experimentation, field/laboratory notes, original research reports
- *Sociology:* Interviews, questionnaires, surveys, the raw data from these sources

Of course, it is not just writers of scholarly articles who use research. Non-academic writers may interview experts, pore over archives, or read books. But a journalist, unlike a scholarly writer, does not usually provide a citation for the source, whether primary or secondary. *Documenting sources by using citations is a feature of academic writing.*

Voice and Style

The voice in an academic essay, especially in the sciences, is objective and analytical, detached from the subject of the experiment or the object of the analysis. An academic study often sets out to investigate a real-life problem, and its author may propose solutions to the problem at the end of the study. This may take the form of recommendations or suggestions for future research.

However, academic writing can be considered persuasive in that it seeks to convince its reader of the validity of the findings. And, of course, academic writers do have opinions and a stake in what they are investigating. Objectivity, then, refers to the degree of detachment that ensures the writer's conclusions are free of bias or faulty reasoning.

When you are asked to write a research paper, you must do more than summarize your sources. PRIMARY SOURCES are original, or first-hand, material in a field of study. SECONDARY SOURCES comment on, interpret, or analyze primary sources.

Academic writers do not usually stress their involvement in their research, especially if that involvement might make them seem biased.

To show their detachment and objectivity, academic writers may use passive constructions, in which the subject of the sentence is the receiver of the action, rather than the person or thing performing the action. Students are told to avoid the passive voice in their writing—with good reason, because an unnecessary passive construction often results in a weaker sentence. However, if the purpose is to de-emphasize the performer of the action, such as the researcher, or to stress the receiver of the action, such as that which is being studied, then a passive construction may be preferable. Note the difference between passive and active in the following example:

> **Active construction:** Researchers analyzed the data using the framework methodology for qualitative analysis.

Researchers is the active subject, but in this case, *data* (object of the verb) is more important than the generic subject, *researchers*; after all, the researchers (and most readers) are interested in what the data show, not the fact that the researchers analyzed them. By changing the construction of this sentence to the passive, the writer can replace an active but unimportant subject with a passive but more import-ant object. Note that in passive constructions, the active subject may not even be expressed. In the sentence below, the original, unimportant subject is shown by the use of brackets.

> **Passive construction:** Data were analysed [by the researchers] using the framework methodology for qualitative analysis. (Fox & Ward, "Health, Ethics and Environment," p. 190)

In an active construction, a writer might substitute *this study shows* or *the research confirmed*, emphasizing the study itself—not the researchers. The writer also takes care to use an appropriate verb with a subject like *this study* or *the research*. For example, it would be misleading and inaccurate to write *this study believes* or *the research has concluded* since studies and research don't believe or conclude; their authors do.

When the article has several authors, as often is the case in the sciences, the writers may refer to themselves in the first-person plural, *we*. Academic writers do not use the first person without a sound reason for doing so—for example, in order to be direct and concise.

In the following examples from readings in Part 2, the writers use the passive voice (italicized), direct phrasing (bolded) and/or the first-person (underlined) to help explain the purpose of their studies:

In a **PASSIVE CONSTRUCTION**, the subject of the sentence is the receiver of the action.

In addition to passive construction, science writers may also use constructions that stress the study rather than the author(s). However, for concision, they may sometimes refer to the first-person (e.g., *I*, *we*).

Some participants *were told* [by the researchers] that they were viewing the men who liked them the most, some *were told* that they were viewing the men who had given them average ratings, and some (in the uncertain condition) *were told* that they were viewing either the men who had liked them the most or the men who had given them average ratings. <u>We predicted</u> that participants in the uncertain condition would be most attracted to the men. (Whitchurch et al., "He Loves Me," p. 359)

The goal of this article is not to bring readers to despair of self-perceptions. (Vazire & Carlson, "Others Sometimes Know Us," p. 352)

Language

Compared to much literary writing, academic writing lacks ornamentation. Scientific writing, in particular, is direct, straightforward prose with few modifiers (adjectives and adverbs). Academic writers are also much less likely to use figurative language, such as metaphors, similes, personification, and the like, than are literary writers. They may, however, use analogies to help explain a point. For example, the authors of the essay on performance-enhancing drugs and sport draw an analogy between sport and classical music (see p. 255). An **analogy** is a systematic comparison between one item and another one that is similar in the point being discussed, but otherwise unlike the first one. An analogy can make the first item more easily understood.

An ANALOGY is a systematic comparison between one item and another one.

JARGON is discipline- or subject-specific language used to communicate among members.

Jargon and language level as well as other elements of style, such as complex sentence and paragraph structure, and intrusive documentation, can make academic writing hard to understand. Many of these obstacles can be overcome, though, by exposure to this kind of writing. Although inexperienced readers must read complex material more closely, more slowly, and more consciously than simpler material, new reading habits can be formed by adopting specific strategies, discussed below in "Finding Information in Academic Essays," and patiently practising them.

Fortunately, clarity is a major aim of academic writers, as for writers in general, and academic writers use deliberate techniques to make their writing clear and accessible.

◎ Finding Information in Academic Essays

Although it may be fine to "begin at the beginning" when you are idly browsing or reading for pleasure, preparing to read an academic essay can be broken into stages (for general strategies related to reading purpose, see Chapter 6, p. 106).

Stage 1: "Pre-reading" or Previewing Content

Strategy

Look closely at the title, the article's abstract (if present) and headings (if present) to determine the essay's subject and the writer's approach to the topic, along with organization and other important features.

Title

In contrast to the titles of non-academic articles, academic titles are often

- Lengthy and informative
- Divided into two parts with a colon separating them
- Composed of nouns, most relevant to the essay's content and/or method

The title of a scholarly article is designed to give the reader important information about content at a glance. This is helpful not only for experts, but also for students, because it enables them to scan the contents page of a journal to find potentially useful articles. Typically, key terms in the article appear in the title; thus, searching by "title" or "keyword" in an electronic database often yields useful entries.

Many titles include two parts separated by a colon. In this example from the *Journal of Clinical Child and Adolescent Psychology*, the first part summarizes the study's finding while the second part reveals the method: "School connectedness is an underemphasized parameter in adolescent mental health: Results of a community prediction study." If you check the titles of the academic essays included in this textbook, you can see that more than half use this structure.

> The title of a scholarly article is designed to give the reader important information about content at a glance. This is helpful not only for experts but also for student researchers because it enables them to gauge an article's potential usefulness by a scan of a journal issue's contents. Typically, key terms in the article appear in the title.

Abstract

Next, locate the abstract: it appears after the title, author names/affiliations and before the actual essay begins. It usually is labelled *Abstract* or *Summary* but sometimes has no label. An **abstract** is a condensed version of an article, giving a preview of content by focusing on the study's purpose, method, results, and conclusion. The abstract is usually written by the study's author(s) and is one paragraph long; sometimes, it includes brief headings.

> An **ABSTRACT** is a kind of summary or condensed version of an article. Abstracts precede most journal articles in the sciences and social sciences, giving a preview of content by focusing on the study's purpose, method, results, and conclusion.

Section Headings

Because of the complex organizational scheme of many academic essays, academic writers often announce upcoming content by using headings. (Non-academic writers may also use headings, especially if the essay is long.) There are two main types of headings, depending on the kind of essay: formal headings and content-focused or descriptive headings.

> **FORMAL HEADINGS** divide the experiment into stages; **DESCRIPTIVE HEADINGS** summarize section contents.

Empirical studies, such as experiments, use formal headings, which divide the essay into the experiment's stages:

1. The **Introduction** announces the topic and includes summaries of previous research; it ends with a hypothesis, research question, or statement of intent (essay plan).
2. The **Method(s)** explains how the experiment was conducted—for example, *who* took part, *how* it was designed, and *what* procedures were used.
3. The **Results** presents the raw data generated by the experiment, often with accompanying tables and figures.
4. The **Discussion** includes a summary of the results and relates them to similar studies; the section ends by suggesting directions for future research and, often, practical applications of the findings.

IMRAD stands for **i**ntroduction, **m**ethods, **r**esults, and **d**iscussion, the sections that compose an empirical study.

This structure can be abbreviated as IMRAD (introduction, methods, results, and discussion) and is found in most essays of this type—for examples, see pp. 186 and 357. If you are writing a scientific, engineering, or business report, you may be required to use formal markers to divide the major sections of your report.

In other kinds of academic studies, the markers serve a *descriptive function*, enabling readers to preview content. Descriptive section markers are one way that writers can clarify essay structure for their readers. Descriptive headings are especially useful in orienting the reader of a long academic essay or one that deals with complex material. Because the essays students write for class are usually much shorter, such markers are seldom necessary.

Such headings are usually brief, consisting of a key phrase that sums up the section. In "Delayed Transitions of Young Adults," p. 222, each heading summarizes the results discussed in that section: e.g., "Staying in school delays most transitions," "Women still leave home at a younger age than men," and the like.

In sum, examining the title, abstract, and headings can give you crucial information before you begin reading the essay in detail (see Chapter 6, "Selective Reading," p. 106) or if you need to quickly review it.

Stage 2: After "Pre-Reading"—Introductions in Academic Writing

Strategy

After pre-reading, look at the essay's introduction, identifying its main features. A scholarly introduction is usually designed to do most or all of the following:

1. Introduce the topic by providing background information and/or discussing the topic's importance

2. Situate the study in relation to work that has been done on the same topic
3. Justify the need for the study
4. Summarize the study's approach and/or content, lay out its structure, and, sometimes, include what the authors expect to find or the questions they hope to answer

These features are described in more detail below.

1. Introduce the Topic

Like virtually all essays, an academic essay begins with an introductory section. It may be titled "**Introduction**" or "Background," or have no heading, but its first purpose is to set the scene for the body of the essay by addressing the topic's significance or by introducing important concepts. Academic writers assume most of their readers are interested in and somewhat knowledgeable about the topic, so do not usually craft openings with a "hook" to draw readers in.

> Like most student essays, an academic essay usually begins by introducing the topic. This section may be called "**INTRODUCTION**" or "Background," or it may have no title of its own.

2. Situate the Study

An academic introduction often reviews previous studies on its topic. An experimental study usually includes this review in one section near the beginning of the essay. By including a literature review, the author demonstrates where his or her contribution fits in and how it furthers knowledge about the subject. Here, the writer summarizes the findings of scholars, often but not always in chronological order, and ends either with the most recent studies or those most closely related to the author's approach; see pp. 188 and 359 for examples.

Other essays, such as those designed *primarily to review* the available literature, focus on review throughout the essay, rather than just in the introduction; see pp. 180, 221, 340, and 349 for examples.

> **LITERATURE REVIEW** is the term for the section of the introduction that summarizes related studies on the topic. Some essays are devoted entirely to reviewing related studies rather than placing the review in one section of the essay.

3. Justify the Study

An academic essay, unlike a student essay, usually includes a justification; in other words, the author directly or indirectly states the reason for the study. While students generally write essays to become better planners, researchers, and writers (as well as to satisfy a course requirement and receive a grade, of course), academic authors need to convince their peers that their essays are worth reading. The justification answers questions like the following: Why was the study undertaken? Why is it important? What can I learn from it? What does it contribute to scholarship?

A typical justification for a study is a gap in knowledge—the absence of studies in an area of scholarship, according to the author.

> Academic writers usually justify their study in the introduction, either directly stating why it is needed or indirectly stressing its significance. A typical **JUSTIFICATION** is that there is a gap in knowledge, which the researcher will try to fill.

4. Summarize the Essay's Approach and/or Content

Student writers are familiar with the common practice of including a thesis state-ment in the introduction (see Chapter 1, "The Thesis Statement," p. 8). Like stu-dents, academic writers refer to the thesis near the end of the introduction, but the form that the thesis takes can vary. Two common forms are discussed below:

Thesis as Essay Plan

An essay plan is what it sounds like: an announcement of the essay's structure. It outlines the way the topic will be developed throughout the essay. The plan may be phrased directly through the first-person voice as in the following example: "In this paper, we report data that explore . . ." (p. 8). Students, however, may be discour-aged from using the first person in phrasing a thesis.

Thesis as Hypothesis

In experiments, the thesis may consist of a hypothesis, which is a prediction to be tested by the experiment. In the Discussion section, the researcher discusses the results of the experiment, beginning with whether the hypothesis is supported by the results.

The following excerpt from the introduction of an academic essay on bullying reveals most of the characteristics of an introduction discussed above.

> Bullying has been defined as negative actions—physical or verbal—that have hostile intent, are repeated over time, and involve a power differential between the bully and the victim (Olweus, 1993). Through the past 15 years of our research program on bullying, we have come to understand bullying as a relationship problem—because it is a form of aggression that unfolds in the context of a relationship in which one child asserts interpersonal power through aggression. The power that bullies hold over others can arise from their individ-ual characteristics, such as superior size, strength, or age (Olweus, 1993); and from knowledge of others' vulnerabilities (Sutton et al., 1999). The power in bullying can also arise from a position in a social group, either in terms of gen-erally high social status (Olweus, 1993) or by membership in a group of peers who support bullying (Salmivalli et al., 1997).
>
> In this paper, we examine bullying from a developmental perspective with a cross-sectional study from early through late adolescence. . . . Few studies examine the developmental pattern in the prevalence of bullying others beyond early adolescence . . . (Debra J. et al. [2006]. A developmental perspective on bullying. *Aggressive Behavior 32*, 376–384.)

An **ESSAY PLAN** includes the main points or main sections of the essay's development. It may use the first-person voice.

A **HYPOTHESIS** is a prediction or probable outcome of an experiment.

The essay begins directly as the writers introduce their topic by defining a key term.

In the second sentence, the authors become more specific, discussing their understanding of the true nature of bullying. They further establish credibility by mentioning their 15 years of research.

The authors begin their literature review in the first paragraph. In its entirety, the review demonstrates their knowledge and shows where their own study fits in.

The authors state the purpose of their essay. At the end of their introduction, they are more specific and detailed, phrasing their thesis as a series of hypotheses, or predictions about their subject (this excerpt does not include the end of the introduction).

The authors directly justify their essay, showing the gap in the scholarship that they will attempt to fill.

EXERCISE 10.1

Identify the key features of the introductions of two or three academic essays in this textbook (see the essays marked with "A" in the table of contents). In particular, show

    a.   Where and how the topic is introduced

    b.   The study's justification

    c.   The literature review (if applicable)

    d.   The thesis and the form it takes (see also Chapter 1, "The Thesis Statement," p. 8)

If one or more of these features is missing, try to determine why it was not needed.

Stage 3: Reading Body Paragraphs

The guidelines below will help you locate important information quickly in the body paragraphs of academic essays, enabling you to ignore less relevant information. (Of course, when you practise focused reading, p. 107, you will read more closely.) Although the advice given here applies mostly to academic writing, much of it can be applied to challenging texts in general—both academic and non-academic ones.

Sentence and paragraph length and complexity might make it hard for inexperienced readers to distinguish important from less important information. Thankfully, academic writers often use predictable paragraph construction. For example, they usually announce the paragraph's topic early in the paragraph; they may also use clear and recognizable patterns to organize their paragraphs.

By contrast, journalistic writing may be less structured, with topic sentences appearing later in the paragraph; some paragraphs do not contain topic sentences but may simply expand on the previous paragraph. Simple transitions, like *and* or *but*, may be preferred to precise transitions, like *in addition* or *in contrast*, showing the relationship between two ideas.

Using Structural Cues

Structural cues show how the paragraph is organized and where to find information.

Topic Sentences

Scanning paragraphs for important information is not just a mechanical process. A paragraph in academic texts may be full of detail; sentences may be long and complex. Therefore, it is helpful to know that important information often occurs in the topic sentence (see Chapter 1, "Writing Middle Paragraphs," p. 11). The topic sentence states the main idea of the paragraph and is usually the most general statement, which is developed by examples or analysis. Although the topic sentence is often the first sentence of the paragraph, a writer may build *toward* the central idea, in which case the topic sentence may be in the middle or even at the end of the paragraph.

Prompts

When the topic sentence is not the first sentence of the paragraph, the paragraph may contain a prompt, which directs the reader ahead to important information. Common prompts take the form of questions or statements that set up the paragraph but do not actually announce the main idea. A prompt can also appear at the end of a paragraph, setting up the paragraph that follows.

In the paragraph excerpt below, the writer begins by referring to the previous paragraph: the sentence acts as a prompt, leading the reader to find the topic sentence in the following sentence (italicized):

> In many cases, however, blind spots are not so innocent—they are the result of motivated cognitive processes. *One motive that has a strong influence on self-perception is the motive to maintain and enhance our self-worth* . . . (Vazire & Carlson, "Sometimes Others Know Us," p. 351).

A **PROMPT**, which can be as lengthy as a sentence or two, can help you locate important information.

Rhetorical Patterns

It is useful to scan first sentences of paragraphs not just because they may contain the main idea or a prompt but also because they may suggest each paragraph's development. Information can often be organized by specific rhetorical patterns; identifying these patterns makes the text easier to follow. For example, in the chronological method, the writer traces a development over time, usually from old to new. In process analysis, the stages of a process are broken down and analyzed (see Chapter 1, "Rhetorical Patterns and Paragraph Development," p. 14).

Specific content may be organized by **RHETORICAL PATTERNS**, ways of breaking down information for presentation. For example, compare–contrast, division, chronology, and cost–benefit analysis are rhetorical patterns. See p. 14.

Concluding Sentences

Much variety exists in paragraph conclusions. The last sentence of a body paragraph could provide further development. Or, it could summarize the paragraph's main idea; in this case, the sentence does not usually repeat this idea verbatim but connects it to the paragraph's development. In the short paragraph below, it is clear in the first (topic) sentence that the paragraph focuses on effects of television on language skills (cause–effect pattern). After the paragraph is developed by referring to research findings on short-term effects, it concludes by highlighting what the authors thought was significant in the findings.

> Since 1999, 3 studies have evaluated the effects of heavy television use on language development in children 8 to 16 months of age. In the short-term, children younger than 2 years who watch more television or videos have expressive language delays,[12,43,44] and children younger than 1 year

with heavy television viewing who are watching alone have a significantly higher chance of having a language delay.[44] Although the long-term effects on language skills remain unknown, the evidence of short-term effects is concerning. ("Media Use by Children Younger Than 2 Years." *Pediatrics* 128.5 [2011]: 1040–1045.)

Contextual Cues: Using Transitions and Repetition

Topic sentences, prompts, and rhetorical patterns are examples of structural cues since they help structure the paragraph, showing the reader where key information is located or how the information is organized. Writers use contextual cues to show the relationship between ideas and to stress words, phrases, and concepts that are critical in understanding the paragraph.

> Contextual cues show the relationship between ideas and stress words, phrases, and concepts critical in understanding the paragraph.

Transitions

Transitional words and phrases can indicate whether an idea is going to be expanded on or whether there will be a shift from one idea to another one. Transitions can occur between one paragraph and the next, between one sentence and the next, or between clauses within a sentence (see the annotated example below). Paying attention to transitions can help you break down an essay, a paragraph, or a sentence into smaller and more manageable units.

The following body paragraph illustrates use of transitions and other cues (the dots indicate words omitted in a direct quotation to save space):

> The first sentence, the topic sentence, clearly announces what the paragraph will be about.

There is nearly unanimous agreement among creativity researchers that a working definition of creativity must contain two facets, namely, originality and usefulness. . . . A review of the creativity literature further reveals the common agreement that creativity cannot be experienced or accessed—indeed, cannot truly exist, until and unless it is turned to some product, whether enduring or ephemeral. In other words, "originality per se is not sufficient—there would be no way to distinguish eccentric or schizophrenic thought from creative,"[11] or, as neatly explained by renowned psychologist Mihaly Csikszentmihalyi. . . . "Creative people, it seems, are original without being bizarre." (Lynn Helding, "Creativity in Crisis?" p. 295)

> The transition of expansion, *namely*, shows the reader that the writer will follow with specific detail.

> *Indeed* is a transition of emphasis, indicating that what follows will reinforce the previous idea.

> *In other words* is a transitional phrase that shows what follows will clarify and, perhaps, expand on the point in the previous sentence.

> The last sentence in the paragraph refers back to the topic sentence— in particular, the concept of originality. It does not merely repeat this sentence, however, but offers a new slant on the main idea, which was developed throughout the paragraph.

For more about the role of transitions in writing, see Chapter 1, "Writing Strong Paragraphs," p. 12.

Repetition

Writers can stress important words, phrases, and concepts throughout a paragraph by repeating them in strategic places or by using pronoun substitutes; similarly, synonyms enable a writer to emphasize a concept by using a word with the same meaning. Strategic repetition not only stresses important words but also makes the

Strategies for comprehension like those discussed in this section not only help you read texts but also should become part of your own writing process to enable your readers to follow your prose and understand your meaning. These kinds of strategies as they apply to your own writing have been discussed in Chapter 1, pp. 8–10.

paragraph more coherent and easier to follow. Repetition can help assert the importance of a key concept, like the one introduced in the first sentence below.

> How would *acknowledging actual histories* change the work of health professionals and humanitarian aid providers? Even in the initial response to a disaster, *it* would change how services are organized, who is leading the effort and who sets priorities. *Acknowledging actual histories* may have little impact on the technical details of the initial emergency response, but *it* may make a difference in how relief efforts are subsequently carried out. . . . *Actual histories* can help organizations to see how the best of intentions can undermine indigenous systems and societies. . . . (Pinto, "Denaturalizing 'Natural' Disasters," p. 267)

Balanced phrases in the paragraph above also contribute to comprehension: "how services are organized, who is leading the effort and who sets priorities." See Chapter 1, "Writing Strong Paragraphs," (p. 12) for strategies for making your own writing more coherent.

EXERCISE 10.2

Compare one body paragraph from an academic essay in this textbook (see the essays marked "A" in the table of contents) with one from a non-academic essay. You can refer to relevant features listed in Table 1.1 (pp. 14–15), along with others you find appropriate.

EXERCISE 10.3

Analyze the following paragraph, identifying comprehension strategies such as the topic sentence, prompts, rhetorical pattern, transitions, repetitions, and conclusion. All features may not be present.

There may thus be an exception to the reciprocity principle: People might like someone more when they are uncertain about how much that person likes them than when they are certain, as long as they have some initial attraction toward the person. Uncertainty causes people to think more about the person, we suggest, and, further, people might interpret these thoughts as a sign of liking via a self-perception effect (e.g., "I must like him if he keeps popping into my thoughts"; Bem, 1972). In short, people's uncertainty about how much another person likes them—such that they pick petals off a flower to try to find out whether that person loves them or loves them not—may increase their liking for that person. (Whitchurch et al., "He Loves Me," p. 359)

EXERCISE 10.4

Choose a body paragraph from one of the academic essays in this textbook and identify specific comprehension strategies (look for the essays marked with "A" in the table of contents).

◎ Chapter 10 Review Questions

1. Which best describes academic writing?
   a. Writing that is highly technical and inaccessible to non-experts
   b. Writing designed for those familiar with its conventions and knowledgeable about the subject
   c. Writing designed for experts and non-experts alike
2. How can knowledge be defined across the disciplines?
3. What accounts for the length of many academic essays?
4. How can the challenges of academic writing be overcome by the student reader?
5. Define primary sources and secondary sources and explain how they differ. Is one kind of source more important than the other?
6. Why do academic writers, especially in the sciences, use the passive voice? Illustrate the passive construction in a sentence of your own of at least eight words; then, rewrite the same sentence using the active construction.
7. a. In addition to passive constructions, how can academic writers convey objectivity?
   b. Why is it essential that they do so?
8. A systematic comparison between one item and another one is called an _____.
9. Choose the best answer: To find information efficiently in academic essays, you should first
   a. Adopt a "pre-reading" strategy and begin by looking at the title, abstract, and headings
   b. Start reading from the beginning, looking for important points
   c. Read the conclusion first, since the important information will be included there
   d. Focus on the first sentences of all paragraphs, since they will include the main ideas.
10. a. Identify two specific features of titles of academic essays.
    b. How do the titles of academic essays differ from those of non-academic essays?
11. Choose the best answer:
    a. An abstract serves as an introduction to the paragraph that follows
    b. An abstract serves as an overview or summary of the essay that follows
    c. An abstract is roughly 10 per cent of the length of the essay that follows
    d. All the above are true of abstracts
12. What are the two types of headings typically found in academic essays? What are their functions?

13. Identify the following features of an academic introduction and explain the importance of each:
    a. The literature review
    b. Justification
    c. Essay plan
    d. Hypothesis

14. Answer true or false:
    a. In academic writing, the topic sentence is usually not the first sentence.
    b. A prompt can direct you to the main idea, which usually follows directly.
    c. The concluding sentence of the paragraph should repeat the topic sentence in slightly different words.

15. Explain the importance of transitions and repetition in academic writing.

◎ Key Terms

abstract (p. 147)

analogy (p. 146)

descriptive heading (p. 147)

Discussion (p. 148)

essay plan (p. 150)

formal heading (p. 147)

hypothesis (p. 150)

IMRAD (p. 148)

Introduction (p. 148)

jargon (p. 146)

justification (p. 149)

literature review (p. 149)

Methods (p. 148)

passive construction (p. 145)

peer-reviewed (refereed) (p. 142)

primary sources (p. 144)

prompt (p. 152)

Results (p. 148)

rhetorical patterns (p. 152)

secondary sources (p. 144)

READINGS

Animal Issues

The domestication of animals began with the dog approximately 15,000 years ago. Since that time, the relationship between humans and other animals has become increasingly complex. Current opinions on many topics related to animals are often vocal and polarized. For example, in "Orca Encounters," the continuing presence of a sociable orca divides a community into starkly opposing factions. While its author mediates between the views of these camps, the author of "An Enviro's Case for Seal Hunt" argues from an environmentalist's perspective on what, for some, is a clear-cut, emotions-based issue.

Complexity is also seen in the growing field of animal law. In "Animal Welfare and Conservation: An Essential Connection," the author speaks directly to the shared concerns of animal rights activists and conservationists. The next two essays, "Joyas Voladoras" and "Predators and Scavengers," look at animals through metaphor and analogy, respectively, using many of the devices of literary fiction to reveal something new about ourselves and underscoring subtle links between the human animal and other animals.

The two academic essays that conclude this section focus on issues fundamental to many Canadians. "The Impact of Pets on Human Health and Psychological Well-Being: Fact, Fiction, or Hypothesis?" examines research to answer the question whether having pets provides physical and psychological benefits. Although pet owners, roughly 55 per cent of Canadians, greatly outnumber vegetarians, (less than 5 per cent), recent lifestyle recommendations have catapulted vegetarianism into the limelight. "Health, Ethics and Environment: A Qualitative Study of Vegetarian Motivations" analyzes the reasons why people become vegetarians.

Isabelle Groc, "Orca Encounters"

Like "Are We Ready to Subsidize Heroin?," p. 327, "Orca Encounters" brings together (synthesizes) various viewpoints in order to shed light on a controversial issue. Groc mediates between the opinions of experts and other interested parties, not expressing her opinion but, rather, trying to represent all views—and leaving it up to readers to draw their own conclusions. Authors of journalistic essays using synthesis apply various techniques to maintain reader interest while seamlessly integrating background information and a variety of viewpoints.

Preparing to Read

1. What does *anthropomorphize* mean (par. 31)?
   a. What are some of the benefits of the anthropomorphizing impulse for humans and other animals?
   b. What are some of the costs?
2. What kinds of responses to Luna's story were generated through the media? Summarize the content of at least three contemporary articles or websites about Luna.

Orca Encounters

Isabelle Groc

British Columbia Magazine, Fall 2010
(1682 words)

1 When the orca known as Luna died in British Columbia's waters, the world grieved. The gregarious orca orphan had won the hearts of whale lovers everywhere, with international media reporting on his antics about a year after his appearance at Nootka Sound in the summer of 2001. Visitors flocked to the community of Gold River on Vancouver Island's west coast to see the little killer whale snuggling up to docks and boats, rolling belly-up for friendly pats from people eager to touch a wild whale. Tragically, Luna's desire for close encounters with humans was the cause of his demise. In the spring of 2006, a tugboat propeller fatally slashed the young orca.

2 While many were deeply saddened, others were relieved, for the animal's curious behaviour posed a dilemma that remains unresolved today. Luna's whale-sized playfulness had damaged several boats, caused concerns for kayakers, and had put fisheries officers in the middle of a complicated conflict.

3 Animal-rights activists wanted to leave Luna alone. Some boat owners and fishermen wanted to be rid of him. First Nations people claimed he was the spirit of a recently deceased chief. Some business owners saw him as a godsend to Gold River's ailing resource-based economy. Scientists worried that Luna's habituation to humans would present an ongoing threat to people in small boats.

4 Luna was what researchers call a "solitary sociable"—an odontocete, or toothed whale, who seeks human contact after becoming separated from its family.

5 Toni Frohoff, a wildlife behavioural biologist based in Santa Barbara, California, specializes in human–dolphin interactions and travels the globe for her work. "As delightful as a human-cetacean bond can be, I believe it is our responsibility to look at the implications of that bond on them and put that first." She says it would be presumptive of us to believe that humans can satisfy all the social needs of whales, dolphins, and porpoises.

6 About 100 solitary sociables have been recorded worldwide, Frohoff says. Once considered an anomaly, solitaries seem to be growing in number, a possible sign that certain populations are fragmenting.

7 "Learning about the individuals who are remote and estranged from the population is increasingly critical to the species' survival," notes Frohoff, who visited Gold River to offer advice on the Luna case.

8   Killer whales are our largest dolphins. Adult males reach about 4500 kilograms in weight, and adult females about 2700 kilograms. Calves vary in birth weight, but up to 180 kilograms would be normal. Three distinct orca groups swim the seas off British Columbia. So-called "resident" orcas are salmon eaters that form family pods that stay together for life. Luna, officially named L98, was a member of the endangered resident L pod, today 39 members strong, commonly seen during summer in southcoast waters. No one knows how the two-year-old youngster was alienated from his family, but some researchers surmise that individual orcas are being forced to forage farther apart in their hunt for dwindling numbers of salmon.

9   "The more spread out you get, the more likely that a mom is not paying attention and a young one gets lost," explains Ken Balcomb, executive director of the Center for Whale Research on Washington's San Juan Island. He says Luna may have also just been adventurous, travelling around with his uncle, until out of range from their pod.

10   Regardless of the cause, orphaned orcas raise a critical question for those who manage interactions between people and wildlife. How much human help, if any, should we impose on wild animals in trouble?

11   So far, Luna is only the third documented orphaned orca in B.C. First was Miracle, a bullet-wounded female rescued from certain death in 1977 by a fisherman on Vancouver Island's east coast. The fisherman hand-fed her and stroked her skin, and the two formed a bond.

12   Angus Matthews, former manager of Victoria's Sealand of the Pacific, a Victoria-area attraction that closed in 1991, says the team there nursed the injured baby whale back to health. Unfortunately, Miracle later died after four years in captivity.

13   Six months after Luna appeared at Nootka Sound in 2001, Springer, or A73, a two-year-old female from the A4 pod, was found alone and unhealthy in Puget Sound, Washington, many kilometres from her family's foraging waters off B.C.'s central and north coasts. Like Luna, Springer showed a tendency to put herself at risk by interacting with boats in high-traffic areas. The scientific consensus was that she would not survive without human help.

14   In a rescue coordinated by the Vancouver Aquarium and other partners, she was captured in July 2002 and transported back to her pod in her home waters of Johnstone Strait, off northeast Vancouver Island. Today, Springer is healthy and regularly spotted in the company of her relatives.

15   Luna's story was more complex. He had been missing from the San Juan Islands area and, based on earlier observations, scientists speculated that he may have been swimming with a relative that later died. When Luna showed up in Nootka Sound, he appeared healthy and well fed. Officials at Canada's federal fisheries department hoped he would reunite naturally with his pod.

16   "The decision was made that it would be best to let nature take its course," says marine-mammal scientist John Ford of Fisheries and Oceans Canada. "There was no compelling reason to intervene and try to take him back to his group because we didn't know why he was on his own and he seemed to be doing fine."

17   Luna stayed on in Nootka Sound and increased the intensity and frequency of his interactions with people and boats—much to the delight of growing hordes of tourists. Fisheries officials attempted to keep Luna away from human contact by enforcing a law that prohibits people from disturbing marine mammals. But Luna, along with many people, ignored the law. He continued pushing boats around, touching

human hands, playing with hoses and boat fenders, and damaging vessels and floatplanes.

18 "Their daily existence is all about being in a group, and if they can't find a group of their own species, their instinct is that they form relationships with anything," says Lance Barrett-Lennard, marine-mammal scientist at the Vancouver Aquarium.

19 Fisheries and Oceans Canada staff contended that Luna was a danger to himself and to people, and, after a bidding process, determined that they would work with Vancouver Aquarium experts to relocate the whale to his pod's summer feeding waters off southern Vancouver Island. The local Mowachaht/Muchalaht First Nation objected to the plan, linking Luna's appearance to the death of former chief Ambrose Maquinna, who had told a friend he would come back as an orca. Others expressed suspicion that the move was a scheme to sell Luna to an aquarium.

20 In June 2004, a dramatic high-seas game of follow-the-leader unfolded in the choppy waters of Nootka Sound. Efforts by the would-be captors to entice Luna into a net pen were thwarted repeatedly by native paddlers, who sang and called out to the orca. The animal excitedly swam back and forth between the fisheries' launch and the paddlers' canoe, unsure of which boat to follow. Finally, after more than a week, fisheries staff abandoned the capture.

21 Less than two years later, Luna was killed. His tragic death left scientists, law enforcers, and animal lovers wondering what will happen when the next orphaned orca appears in our waters.

22 "These animals are so attracted to humans, and humans are so attracted to whales that when those whales are alone, the power of the attraction is magnified because they don't have their family with them," says Gil Hewlett, co-author of *Operation Orca*, a book that tells the stories of Luna and Springer. In Luna's case, even seasoned scientists were surprised.

23 "The level of social interactions escalated far beyond what we would have ever expected based on our experience with solitary animals. We didn't have any basis for ever thinking that he would have such a need for social interaction," observes Ford. "And the more Luna bonded with humans, the less likely it was for his successful reintroduction. Would he be interested in returning to his group?"

24 And, equally important, would the pod be willing to accept the estranged whale?

25 "What's in it for a pod of whales to accept a young one back?" says Barrett-Lennard, who recalls that Springer's group was initially reluctant to reunite with her. "What's the advantage? Not much."

26 Not all scientists agree. "I had no doubt that the social bonds that exist within family members, not just the parents, but brothers and sisters, uncles, would be sufficient to accept him back in the group," says Ken Balcomb, who has studied southern resident orcas for three decades. He believes that Luna's desire to interact with humans might have been managed to protect him from harm.

27 Balcomb suggests that one of the worst punishments imaginable for people is solitary confinement. "Deprivation is a terrible thing to do to a social animal. Why deprive him?"

28 "We are looking at some of the most social animals in the world who, in some cases, are finding themselves completely isolated without any others of their own kind," says Frohoff. "If we are not going to provide the companionship that they are seeking from us, we cannot in good conscience turn our backs on them and not try to come up with reasonable alternatives to human contact."

29   Filmmakers Suzanne Chisholm and Michael Parfit, who made the documentary *Saving Luna*, suggest that a program of managed interaction could have been established to dissuade Luna from dangerous or undesirable behaviour. But such a regimen would be difficult to sustain for a species that lives as long as humans do.

30   "There would have to be a long-term plan because once you go down that road, there is no turning back," says Ford.

31   Scientists increasingly agree now that any reunion of a wayward cetacean with its pod should happen quickly. But as to whether humans should intervene in nature, whether we can put aside our tendency to anthropomorphize animals like Luna in assessing their needs, are larger questions—ones sure to raise considerable debate when the next lone orca arrives at our shores.

❚❚ Comprehension

1.   Summarize the information in paragraphs 23–27 and show how the author synthesizes information here.

Structure, Organization, and Style

1.   Provide appropriate content headings for the essay; there should be four or five headings, including one for the introduction.
2.   Identify paragraphs whose main purpose is to provide background information, and explain why this information was necessary in each case.

Critical Thinking/Research

1.   What does the story of Springer (pars. 13–14) contribute to the essay?
2.   The issues raised in the essay often evoke readers' emotions. Did Groc successfully avoid arousing an emotional response? Was it desirable that she do so? Analyze the writer's attempt to look at the issues objectively and fairly.
3.   To what extent do you believe humans are responsible for the fate of Luna? Justify your answer by making specific references to the essay.

Brian Doyle, "Joyas Voladoras"

"Joyas Voladoras" is a literary essay that was originally published in *American Scholar*; in 2005; it was chosen for that year's *Best American Essays*. In addition to using highly figurative language, Doyle uses many other literary devices, such as anaphora (repetition of the first words of successive phrases, clauses, or sentences) and polysyndeton (repetition of conjunctions in a sentence), as well as juxtaposition (placing contrasting elements next to each other) to surprise the reader and evoke his or her sense of wonder.

Because Doyle's descriptive writing lies closer to literary than academic (or even journalistic) writing, it is more appropriate to talk about his theme than his thesis. However, as we do in both academic and literary works, we make inferences about what we are reading, using our critical thinking skills to make connections between images and ideas to understand the work's significance and effect on us.

Preparing to Read

Read the essay's first paragraph. What do you think the essay will be about?

Joyas Voladoras

Brian Doyle

American Scholar 2005
(also *Best American Essays* 2005)
(1025 words)

1   Consider the hummingbird for a long moment. A hummingbird's heart beats ten times a second. A hummingbird's heart is the size of a pencil eraser. A hummingbird's heart is a lot of the hummingbird. *Joyas voladoras*, flying jewels, the first white explorers in the Americas called them, and the white men had never seen such creatures, for hummingbirds came into the world only in the Americas, nowhere else in the universe, more than three hundred species of them whirring and zooming and nectaring in hummer time zones nine times removed from ours, their hearts hammering faster than we could clearly hear if we pressed our elephantine ears to their infinitesimal chests.

2   Each one visits a thousand flowers a day. They can dive at sixty miles an hour. They can fly backwards. They can fly more than five hundred miles without pausing to rest. But when they rest they come close to death: on frigid nights, or when they are starving, they retreat into torpor, their metabolic rate slowing to a fifteenth of their normal sleep rate, their hearts sludging nearly to a halt, barely beating, and if they are not soon warmed, if they do not soon find that which is sweet, their hearts grow cold, and they cease to be. Consider for a moment those hummingbirds who did not open their eyes again today, this very day, in the Americas: bearded helmetcrests and booted racket-tails, violet-tailed sylphs and violet-capped woodnymphs, crimson topazes and purple-crowned fairies, red-tailed comets and amethyst woodstars, rainbow-bearded thornbills and glittering-bellied emeralds, velvet-purple coronets and golden-bellied star-frontlets, fiery-tailed awlbills and Andean hillstars, spatuletails and pufflegs, each the most amazing thing you have never seen, each thunderous wild heart the size of an infant's fingernail, each mad heart silent, a brilliant music stilled.

3   Hummingbirds, like all flying birds but more so, have incredible enormous immense ferocious metabolisms. To drive those metabolisms they have race-car hearts that eat oxygen at an eye-popping rate. Their hearts are built of thinner, leaner fibers than ours. Their arteries are stiffer and more taut. They have more mitochondria in their heart muscles—anything to gulp more

oxygen. Their hearts are stripped to the skin for the war against gravity and inertia, the mad search for food, the insane idea of flight. The price of their ambition is a life closer to death; they suffer heart attacks and aneurysms and ruptures more than any other living creature. It's expensive to fly. You burn out. You fry the machine. You melt the engine. Every creature on earth has approximately two billion heartbeats to spend in a lifetime. You can spend them slowly, like a tortoise, and live to be two hundred years old, or you can spend them fast, like a hummingbird, and live to be two years old.

4   The biggest heart in the world is inside the blue whale. It weighs more than seven tons. It's as big as a room. It *is* a room, with four chambers. A child could walk around in it, head high, bending only to step through the valves. The valves are as big as the swinging doors in a saloon. This house of a heart drives a creature a hundred feet long. When this creature is born it is twenty feet long and weighs four tons. It is waaaaay bigger than your car. It drinks a hundred gallons of milk from its mama every day and gains two hundred pounds a day, and when it is seven or eight years old it endures an unimaginable puberty and then it essentially disappears from human ken, for next to nothing is known of the mating habits, travel patterns, diet, social life, language, social structure, diseases, spirituality, wars, stories, despairs, and arts of the blue whale. There are perhaps ten thousand blue whales in the world, living in every ocean on earth, and of the largest mammal who ever lived we know nearly nothing. But we know this: the animals with the largest hearts in the world generally travel in pairs, and their penetrating moaning cries, their piercing yearning tongue, can be heard underwater for miles and miles.

5   Mammals and birds have hearts with four chambers. Reptiles and turtles have hearts with three chambers. Fish have hearts with two chambers. Insects and mollusks have hearts with one chamber. Worms have hearts with one chamber, although they may have as many as eleven single-chambered hearts. Unicellular bacteria have no hearts at all; but even they have fluid eternally in motion, washing from one side of the cell to the other, swirling and whirling. No living being is without interior liquid motion. We all churn inside.

6   So much held in a heart in a lifetime. So much held in a heart in a day, an hour, a moment. We are utterly open with no one, in the end—not mother and father, not wife or husband, not lover, not child, not friend. We open windows to each but we live alone in the house of the heart. Perhaps we must. Perhaps we could not bear to be so naked, for fear of a constantly harrowed heart. When young we think there will come one person who will savor and sustain us always; when we are older we know this is the dream of a child, that all hearts finally are bruised and scarred, scored and torn, repaired by time and will, patched by force of character, yet fragile and rickety forevermore, no matter how ferocious the defense and how many bricks you bring to the wall. You can brick up your heart as stout and tight and hard and cold and impregnable as you possibly can and down it comes in an instant, felled by a woman's second glance, a child's apple breath, the shatter of glass in the road, the words *I have something to tell you*, a cat with a broken spine dragging itself into the forest to die, the brush of your mother's papery ancient hand in a thicket of your hair, the memory of your father's voice early in the morning echoing from the kitchen where he is making pancakes for his children.

Comprehension, Organization, and Style

1. What effect is created by the use of facts in paragraph 2?
2. Why does Doyle describe the hummingbird before the blue whale? Why might this be better than the other way around?
3. a. Show how paragraph 5 connects the paragraph that precedes it to the one that follows
   b. Paraphrase the last three sentences of this paragraph.
4. Analyze paragraph 1, 3, or 4 for its style. Among the features you could consider are diction (word choice); syntax (word order); sentence structure, length and/or variation; repetition; comparisons; non-literal language (e.g., similes and metaphors); imagery.

Critical Thinking

1. Show how Doyle uses one image—for example, the image of the heart—to encourage us to look behind facts and surface meanings for a deeper meaning or hidden truth.
2. What is the importance of the list in the last sentence? How are the items on the list connected to the rest of the essay?

Terry Glavin, "An Enviro's Case for Seal Hunt"

As its title suggests, "An Enviro's Case for Seal Hunt" is an opinion piece on a topic of long-standing controversy in Canada and the international community. The argument usually focuses on the way Atlantic seals are hunted and killed, whether humanely or inhumanely. Terry Glavin, however, takes a different—but no less controversial—approach, although he also touches on the issue of cruelty in paragraphs 8–9.

As in all arguments, readers should use their critical thinking skills to evaluate the author's use of reason. They should also ask: Is he fair and objective? Does he use argumentative strategies effectively? Is he credible?

Preparing to Read

Who is Terry Glavin? Use reliable sources to answer this question; include information on his publications and the kinds of topics he usually writes about.

An Enviro's Case for Seal Hunt

Terry Glavin

The Tyee, 7 March 2007
(1800 words)

1   I saw something the other day that made me sick to my stomach. It was in the February edition of *The Grocer*, a British retail-food magazine.

2   There was an article about a campaign that a group called Respect for Animals is waging to convince consumers to boycott Canadian seafood products. The magazine also carried two huge advertisements from the same outfit.

3   One of the ads consisted of a photograph of a masked man on an ice floe, and a seal lying prone at his feet. The man was brandishing a club with a spike on the end of it. The words *You Can Stop This* were superimposed upon the picture. The other advertisement proclaimed "Boycott Canadian Seafood & Save the Seals," with a picture of a can of Canadian salmon.

4   The Canadian fishing industry exports more than $100 million worth of products into Britain every year. The point of the campaign is to squeeze those sales until the industry begs our government to end the seal hunt.

5   Here's what makes me sick.

6   The Newfoundland seal hunt is transparently and demonstrably sustainable and humane. There are roughly half a million people in Newfoundland and Labrador, and nearly six million harp seals, which is almost three times as many seals as when I was a kid.

Free range seals

7   Roughly 6000 fishermen, mostly Newfoundlanders, but some are from Quebec and the Maritimes, take slightly more than 300,000 harp seals annually. The fishermen share more than $16 million from the hunt at a critical time of year when there's little in the way of fishing income to be had. The seals are harvested for their pelts and their fat, for a range of products, mostly for clothing and for Omega-3 vitamins.

8   The killing is about as clean as anything you're likely to find in an abattoir. Seals don't spend their lives cooped up in paddocks or feedlots. They live free, and in all but the rarest cases, the ones that die at the hands of a swiler (a sealer) die instantly. The hakapik (a spiked club) is an effective instrument.

9   Even so, most seals are first shot with rifles. The killing of nursing whitecoats was banned 20 years ago.

Exploiting empathy

10   Here's one of those obligatory disclosures: over the years, several environmental organizations—the Sierra Club, the David Suzuki Foundation, Greenpeace, etc.—have subsidized my preoccupation with things that move in the water by having me do research projects for them and so on. With that out of the way, I can now say, if it isn't obvious already, that it's the seal hunt's opponents who turn my stomach.

11   It's not just that anti-hunt crusades like this are especially foul in the way they dishonestly misrepresent facts. It's also that they dishonestly manipulate one of the most redeeming traits the human species has inherited from hundreds of thousands of years of natural selection and cultural evolution—our capacity to expand the embrace of our empathy to include other forms of life.

12   But far worse than all that, boycott campaigns like this muddy the important distinction between sustainability and sentiment, and between broadly co-ordinated acts of social responsibility and mere lifestyle choices. When

we fail to make these distinctions we undermine everything worthwhile that environmentalism has accomplished since it emerged in the early 1970s.

13   As citizens and consumers in free societies, we are burdened with the duty to make important decisions at the ballot box, in the work we do, and also in the marketplace. Boycotting Canadian seafood to try and stop the seal hunt is the consumer-choice equivalent of deciding to buy a tie-dyed shirt, move into a Volkswagen van and subsist solely on lentils and tofu.

Serious stakes

14   Just as the excesses of postmodernist relativism have enfeebled the left over the past quarter-century or so, a corrosive strain of fact-distorting, science-hating, Gaia-bothering obscurantism has enfeebled environmentalism.

15   It was there from the beginning, and it persists most noticeably in animal-rights crusades. It is the environmentalist equivalent of anti-evolution, rapture-seeking Christian zealotry. It has to be attacked wherever it rears its head. There's too much at stake to pretend we can be innocent bystanders here. This is a fight we all have to join.

16   Here's why.

17   The last time the planet was in the throes of an extinction spasm this cataclysmic was when the dinosaurs disappeared 65 million years ago. One in every four mammal species, one in eight bird species, one in nine plants, a third of all amphibians and half of all the surveyed fish species on earth are threatened with extinction.

18   When Greenpeace was born in Vancouver in 1971, the single greatest cause of species extinction was understood to be habitat loss. Now, the greatest threat to biological diversity is global warming. The last time the atmosphere was accumulating greenhouse gases this fast was 650,000 years ago. The prospects look exceedingly grim—broad-scale ecological disruption, crop failure and famine, desertification and the mass dislocation of some of the most heavily-populated regions of the world.

19   A key reason environmentalists found themselves so ill-prepared to convince the world to take global warming seriously was that their movement had been corrupted by precisely the same trippy sentiment-mongering that has animated the holy war against the Newfoundland seal hunt, which now turns its sights on Canadian fisheries products.

Where was Greenpeace?

20   When the founders of Greenpeace were being born, back in the 1950s, the world's fishing fleets were taking roughly 40 million tonnes of marine biomass from the world's oceans every year. By the 1980s, it was 80 million tonnes. Then the seas just stopped giving. Fully 90 per cent of all the big fish in the sea—the tunas, the marlins, the sharks, the swordfish—are now gone.

21   Of the many fisheries collapses that have occurred around the world in recent years, it is sadly ironic that the greatest single collapse occurred in the seas around Newfoundland, where the bulk of Canada's Atlantic seal hunt takes place. The Grand Banks cod fishery was the largest and oldest pelagic fishery in the history of the human experience.

22   The cod were mined from the sea by the same big-boat offshore fleets that had caused such devastation everywhere else. A way of life disappeared, and by the early 1990s, tens of thousands of workers were reduced to welfare. While all this was happening, what were environmentalists doing on the Newfoundland coast, in the country where Greenpeace was born, at a time when Greenpeace was at the height of its powers?

23   They were out cavorting with rich hippies and snuggling up to harp seal pups on the ice floes. They were meditating cross-legged in the snow and posing for the television cameras and demonizing the good people of Newfoundland, while the seas around them were being emptied of cod.

Rational agreements

24   When you go looking for the good that environmentalism has accomplished, you'll find it in such covenants as the United Nations Convention on Biological Diversity, the Montreal Protocol on ozone-depleting substances, and the Kyoto Accord. It's in the sustainability provisions of elaborately negotiated efforts such as the Brundtland Commission on the Environment and Development, and the UN Code of Conduct for Responsible Fishing.

25   The toughest global instrument to protect biodiversity is the Convention on the International Trade in Endangered Species. Fuzzy eco-drivel has already severely damaged CITES by forcing non-threatened species, such as North Atlantic minke whale, onto the CITES appendices. Now, in Germany and Belgium, animal-rights activists and their friends in the European Parliament are attempting to override CITES, and the European Union's own rules, with an outright ban on products from Canada's perfectly abundant harp seal population.

26   Similarly, seal-hunt opponents are dangerously undermining the historic victory that flowed from the Brundtland Commission. The commission established a commitment to sustainability as the key universal value to guide natural-resource harvesting policies for all the peoples of the world, regardless of their distinct cultural practices and sensibilities.

27   The whole point of sustainability is to ensure that people can exercise the rights and accept the responsibilities that come with sustainably harvesting the natural resources of the ecosystems within which they live. The harp seal hunt is a living embodiment of that principle. That's why environmentalists should not just give the boycott a pass, or stay neutral, but should actively support and defend the seal hunt.

28   The one consolation we can take from the recent hullabaloo is that it's faltering. Last year, when animal-rightists in the United States boasted that they'd convinced more than 200 restaurants and seafood retailers to boycott Canadian products to protest the hunt, it turned out that only a small minority were doing so. Most of them didn't even know they'd been listed as boycott-compliant.

29   Also, the European Commission, citing the absence of evidence to support contentions that the hunt is inhumane, has refused, for now, to enforce the European Parliament's proposed ban on seal products.

Contested council

30   But the consumer boycott campaign that's just begun in Britain is particularly insidious. Its aim is all Canadian fisheries products, and its targets are Tesco, Sainsbury's, Somerfield and other major retail chains that have already made a commitment to eventually carrying only those seafood products that have been certified by the Marine Stewardship Council.

31   The MSC standard remains hotly contested by responsible environmentalists, but its coveted "eco-label" holds out the hope of forcing improvements to fisheries-management policies around the world. In Canada, those improvements are increasingly driven by the fishermen

themselves, because they want the MSC label on their product.

32   British Columbia's halibut fishery was turned down once, and has since re-applied, because groundfish management has significantly improved—thanks in no small part to halibut fishermen. Other fishermen are now lobbying federal fisheries officials to improve stock-assessment research to give B.C.'s dogfish fishery a shot at the MSC label. British Columbia's sockeye salmon fisheries have just undergone an arduous certification examination, and a decision is imminent.

33   If the cuddliness of a particular species harvested in a particular country is allowed to become the factor that determines whether that country's products are considered environmentally acceptable, then everything we won at CITES

and in the Brundtland Commission is lost. If those are the kinds of choices we present to everyone from major retailers down to ordinary seafood consumers, then we'll have wasted all our efforts to marshal consumer power to force the sustainable use of the oceans.

34   It's long past time for conservationists to make a clean, clear, open and unequivocal break with crystal-gazing animal-rights eccentrics and all their camp followers. For them, the conservation of wild resources was always just a flag of convenience. They're dead ballast, so over the side with them.

35   On the question of the Atlantic harp seal harvest, there's only one defensible and honest position for a conservation-minded citizen to take.

36   Support the swilers.

Comprehension

1.   Summarize paragraph 27, which discusses the concept of sustainability.

Structure, Organization, and Style

1.   Identify Glavin's main points and comment on their order; was it the most effective order possible, in your view?
2.   Identify any analogies in paragraphs 13 and 15 and analyze their effectiveness.

Critical Thinking

1.   Show how Glavin arouses reader expectations in his first three paragraphs. Do you think this was a good strategy?
2.   What is the purpose of the author's "obligatory disclosure" in paragraph 10?
3.   Analyze the rhetorical effectiveness of the section "Where was Greenpeace?"; what does it contribute to the essay as a whole?
4.   Write a critical response or critical analysis, focusing on both the strengths and weaknesses (if any) of Glavin's argument. You could comment on argumentative strategies or any logical/emotional fallacies.

Richard Swift, "Predators and Scavengers"

This essay explores the interconnections between language, behaviour, and identity. *New Internationalist* promotes itself as concerned with world poverty and inequality.

Preparing to Read

1. How might the political viewpoint of a publication affect the way you read one of its articles?
2. What kinds of sources would you expect to find in an essay in *New Internationalist*?
3. What animals come to mind when you think of predators? Of scavengers?
   a. Explore your perception of each by freewriting for several minutes.
      OR
   b. Under the headings "Predator" and "Scavenger," list as many traits as you can about each.

Predators and Scavengers

Richard Swift

New Internationalist, July/August 2010
(1463 words)

1   The predator evokes ambivalent feelings in Western culture. We admire the lion, tiger, eagle, cougar and wolf for their strength and beauty, yet at the same time we fear them. Such big game predators are among the first to be targeted for extinction—we are also predators so it's a matter of "us or them."

2   We feel much less ambivalent about the scavenger—hyenas, vultures, crows, rats, coyotes and pigeons. These are creatures that feed off the remains of corpses or pick through the waste and leavings of both nature and humanity. Until recently, the valuable ecological niche filled by such scavengers was only recognized by a small group of biologists and naturalists. For most of us these are the lowest of the low. Bottom feeders. While we recognize (even glorify) the predator in ourselves, we are reluctant to acknowledge the scavenger side to our natures.

The predator ethos

3   It would not be too much of a stretch to say we live in a predator economy. US economist James Galbraith made this case recently. His theory of "economic predation" holds that "in a predatory regime, nothing is done for public reasons. Indeed, the men in charge do not recognize that 'public purposes' exist. They have friends and enemies, and as for the rest—we're the prey." In the latest unstable wave of predatory capitalism our savings and livelihoods did indeed prove to be prey to the manipulations of those who control capital. Yet there is still a sneaking admiration for the swashbuckling corporate shark (a Rupert Murdoch or a Conrad Black) that somehow escapes the way we think of the sexual predator. But these economic predators have a much bigger impact in destroying

hopes and lives than the occasional criminal deviant. It is they who set the tone for the predator ethos: eat as much as you can and don't worry about anyone else.

4   Hollywood and the computer game industry are the great glorifiers of militarized predatory behaviour—the *Predator vs Alien* series was a box-office smash for both. But this isn't just fantasy. The CIA's "predator drone" has perfected targeted killing from afar. Operatives in Langley, Virginia scour the hills of Northwest Pakistan or the tribal areas of Yemen looking for "high-value" targets. Peering through the drone's infrared camera they can then "neutralize" some tribal fundamentalist leader (and any family members who happen to be standing nearby). The CIA currently has some 200 predator drones, so many that there are sometimes turf fights between operators over who gets to vaporize a particular target. The estimated death count from these weapons hovers between 326 and 528 people.

5   Hollywood has little cultural ambivalence when it comes to scavengers. Take the spotted hyena portrayed in Disney's *The Lion King*—a wasteful coward on the fringes of decent animal society. Yet the hyena, with its close matrilineal family bonds, should be as worthy of human regard as any roaring tiger or soaring eagle.

6   Scavenger, when applied to humans, is either a form of metaphorical insult or a term of pity reserved for people forced to scavenge because of their hopeless situation. Those who rush to the sites of remote plane crashes to see what the pockets of the dead will yield are considered beneath contempt. Those who scavenge garbage dumps such as Manila's famous Payatas or Guatemala City's Basurero are thought of as the "lowest of the low." In Hindu and Japanese cultures "untouchables" who collect garbage, human waste or dead bodies are held in low regard for what are considered scavenger occupations.

When we were scavengers

7   In his work on human origins, the eco-anarchist writer Kirkpatrick Sale, in *After Eden: The Evolution of Human Domination*, combines a close analysis of the fossil record with a sharp sense of the ecological implications of our notion of progress and evolution. Sale holds that a kind of fall from grace occurred some 70,000 years ago with the rise of *Homo sapiens* and the eclipse of *Homo erectus*, one of our ancestors who had been around for about 1.8 million years. *Homo erectus* had a way of living very much based on a scavenger model and not that different from the few remaining hunter-gatherer peoples that exist today: the Penan of Borneo, for example, or various Amazonian tribal groups. *Homo erectus* was not entirely vegetarian—they scavenged meat and hunted small mammals and birds. But about 75 per cent of their diet came from gathering wild plants, nuts and berries. Sale believes that under pressure of climate change *Homo sapiens* eclipsed *erectus* and started to hunt in an organized way for big mammals, using metal spears and arrows. The alienation from (and the domination of) nature has not missed a beat since. Organized irrigation systems and surplus-based agriculture—examples of the first large-scale engineering of nature—were soon to follow. It wasn't long before slavery, warfare and empires grew out of these predator practices.

8   We *Homo sapiens* have proved ourselves predators *par excellence*. Like volcanoes and earthquakes, human beings have become a kind of uncontrollable force of nature. The costs of our predatory relationship with the environment continue to mount: climate degradation, rapidly depleting non-renewable resources, extinction of numerous other species, chemical poisoning of land, water and ourselves. Our alienation from nature now threatens the ecological basis of our

own existence as a species. Thus, the predator eclipsed the scavenger, setting humankind on the fateful course of ecocide.

9   Sale wants us to rethink our modern conceit about progress. *Homo sapiens* has been on the planet for nearly 70,000 years while our scavenger predecessors, *Homo erectus*, lasted 1.8 million. Given the current fruits of our progress one would be foolhardy indeed to think we could break their record. So, Sale asks, who is the evolutionary success story?

A scavenger revival

10   Sale hopes that there will be a revival of *erectus* sensibility and a more respectful way of living, in accord with a finite natural world. There are stirrings of at least a modest revival in the positive reputation of scavengers. The writer Carl Hiaasen has done his part by creating the character Skink, who appears in several of his best-selling detective series. Skink used to be the environmentalist governor of Florida until he was forced out of office by developers set on turning the state into one big theme park. Skink retreated into the depths of the Everglades, where he carries on a humorous guerrilla campaign against all environmental despoilers while surviving on a diet of road kill. On the other end of the spectrum is the more gentle approach to scavenging in Anneli Rufus's *Scavengers' Manifesto*, which has given birth to a quite circumspect code of scavenger ethics—"don't be a mooch" and "don't eat gross things." So modern scavenging covers a wide range of territory from dumpster diving to cruising second-hand and charity shops.

11   But maybe there is a wider interpretation of scavenging. The microcredit movement so beloved by development economics is frequently based on support for scavenger businesses. Find something, be it metal, wood, plastic, old electrical appliance, shell or stone. Reshape it. Remake it. Redesign it. And then sell it on as a product of utility or a thing of beauty.

12   As large portions of the world population become "surplus to requirement" for the dominant corporate economy, scavenging at least part-time is simply a matter of survival. The dumps of Majority World megacities are a source of livelihood for thousands. Manila's Payatas dump alone is said to provide income for 150,000 people. At least some are proud of their occupation, according to Teresa Jonoras, who works the dump. "Think about it. We don't have bosses. We live a free life. If I don't feel like going to work, I don't go to work. Here, your only concern is survival, your daily sustenance, and the dump can take care of that." Still it would be a mistake to lionize such employment, as it is often dangerous and poorly paid. Jonoras says on a good day she can make $3.

13   But it's not just in the Global South where this is happening. In almost every North American city, the night before garbage pickup is filled with the clatter of shopping trolleys as income-deprived scavengers systematically pick through the refuse looking for anything that might be sold. In Toronto, Ontario, a quick canvas of recycling scavengers indicates that a good night's take can yield about $50. One person's waste is another person's livelihood.

14   Perhaps our ambivalence about predators reflects our ambivalence about power—we admire the strong until we recognize ourselves as their prey. But if the world is to be saved by "reduce, recycle, reuse" it is the buried scavenger side of our natures that may just help us pull through.

Comprehension

1. Using context and/or reliable sources, briefly explain the significance of two of the following names from paragraph 3: James Galbraith, Rupert Murdoch, Conrad Black.
2. Summarize paragraph 5 in one sentence.

Structure and Organization

1. "Predators and Scavengers" uses the compare–contrast rhetorical pattern. Identify two consecutive paragraphs where this pattern is used and the basis of comparison in these paragraphs.
2. Identify Swift's most important source and explain what this source contributes to his thesis. (As a critical thinking question, evaluate the credibility and effectiveness of this source.)

Critical Thinking

1. Do you think Swift's examples of a "scavenger revival" are relevant and convincing? Why or why not? (You might have to do some research in order to answer this question.)
2. What is the author's perception of the fate of humanity? In his view, what would it take for humans to avert this fate?

Paul Waldau, "Animal Welfare and Conservation: An Essential Connection"

"Animal Welfare and Conservation: An Essential Connection" is a reflective essay that combines the author's experiences and a deliberate but rather unconventional use of argument—one whose purpose is to build bridges rather than score verbal victories. Thus, Waldau states at the end of paragraph 3: "I do hope to *invite* a wide range of readers into open-minded consideration of animal protection issues." Such a method is feasible, even desirable, given the typical reader of the online journal *Minding Nature*, a publication of the Centre for Humans and Nature (http://www.humansand nature.org/mission/our-vision/).

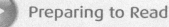

Preparing to Read

1. Access the above website in order to get a sense of a typical reader.
2. What does the term *animal rights* mean to you? Do you believe that animals should have some of the same rights as humans? Why or why not? (These questions could also be addressed in a group after you have read the essay.)

Animal Welfare and Conservation: An Essential Connection

Paul Waldau

Minding Nature, April 2011
(3090 words)

I

1　Thich Nhat Hanh, the well-known Vietnamese Buddhist monk, is fond of suggesting that "there is no path to peace—peace *is* the path." In this article, I pose a question that one likely encounters in a variety of forms if one walks the path of peace, which could also have been referred to by this Buddhist master as non-violence or *ahimsa* (non-harming). The specific form of the question I ask here is one, I suspect, that *every* reader of this journal will have heard at one time or another—what is the relevance of "animal rights" to the rich set of concerns we call out with words like "environmental," "conservation" and "ecological"?

2　This is a question that arises constantly in the "Animal Law" course I teach at Harvard Law School and in the "Religion and Animals" course I teach at Harvard Summer School. The question was constantly asked in the veterinary ethics courses and the "animals and public policy" graduate seminars I directed for a decade at Tufts University Cummings School of Veterinary Medicine. It also looms large in the minds of the students and scholars who today are enriching the burgeoning field of animals studies, such as the undergraduates and graduates whose concern for other-than-human animals drives the Anthrozoology programs now preoccupying me at Canisius College in Buffalo.

3　I do not claim that the particular answer to this question, adumbrated in this article, will convince every environmentally conscious person. Even the more extended, diverse arguments I make in the book from which a portion of this article is drawn, *Animal Rights: What Everyone Needs to Know*, may not convince everyone. I do hope to *invite* a wide range of readers into open-minded consideration of animal protection issues.

4　And I do believe that a serious discussion of "animal rights" and their relevance to environmental/conservation/ecological concerns is part of a peace-constituted path essential to human health and thriving. I suggest this because over the last decades, I have met countless leaders and rank-and-file animal protection people from all over the world whose lives are the richer for their work. Many of them today wonder what might open the minds and hearts of the environmentally-conscious who take joy in "minding nature" but, for some reason or another, shy away from noticing—or at least taking seriously—animal protection causes and complaints that people around the world group under the rubric "animal rights."

5   So what is the relationship of animal rights to environmental concerns? And what, indeed, do those in the environmental and conservation communities, as well as everyone else, need to know about animal rights? I contend that there are many reasons that individual humans, as members of a most powerful and dominant form of animal life on this shared Earth, *need* to know other animals' lives and realities. I also contend that the question of animal protection (a synonym for, but also a more generic term than, "animal rights") is deeply important for the environmental protection community. I rush to acknowledge that I am *fortunate* to know many conservationists and environmentalists (for example, the two law professors described in the anecdotes below) who are animal protectionists in every sense precisely because they *fully* grasp and support what I suggest in both this article and *Animal Rights*. But I also know, after decades of working on a range of causes and educational topics, that *at times* animal protection efforts and discussions have been marginalized, even excluded, by some people who are popularly called environmentalists or conservationists in ways that are not unlike how many other educators, scientists, veterinary administrators and religious leaders dismiss animal protection as sentimental or misguided in some way.

6   Though I feel on safe ground observing that tensions and unresolved issues remain, I relate here two anecdotes as a kind of "evidence" that such marginalization and dismissal are still significant factors today. At an annual animal law gathering at Harvard Law School in February 2011, a conservationist affiliated with a major midwestern American law school confided that his conservation colleagues on campus *oppose* establishing an animal law course at their university. Such opposition is troubling for many

reasons, but one is this—because two-thirds of the almost two hundred accredited American law schools and virtually all of the top-rated institutions *already* have such courses, proposals to offer an animal law course are hardly "radical" and controversial any longer. Further, *every one* of these courses of which I'm aware has been instituted because of *student demand*. What conceivably justifies this law professor's conservation colleagues opposing students seeking what they (the students) consider relevant education of a type already offered at a majority of similar institutions?

7   In an entirely separate conversation at that same conference, another faculty member at a major American law school lamented that even in the ecology-conscious Northwest of the United States there are conservationists known for aggressive challenges to power plant emissions of greenhouse gases who simply refuse to recognize the impact of greenhouse gas emissions from factory farming. What is tragic about this, of course, is that there are major reports, such as the 2006 report of the United Nations Food and Agriculture Organization entitled *Livestock's Long Shadow*, that reveal startlingly high figures for the emission of greenhouse gases from industrialized agriculture—in fact, as the FAO report indicated, the industrialized agriculture sector *out emits*, as it were, the *entire* transportation sector. Couple this with the tremendous pollution and social dislocation problems created by industrialized agriculture as described in a 2008 report published jointly by the Pew Charitable Trusts and the Johns Hopkins School of Public Health, and environmentalists and conservationists alike have reason to join active citizens in the animal movement in decrying factory farming.

8   Although I have friends who are fond of suggesting lightheartedly that "the plural of anecdote

is data," I do not claim that these two anecdotes fully represent what conservation-minded people think about animal law. In fact, such stories in no way exhaust the complex issues arising at the intersection of animal rights, on the one hand, and environmental concerns, on the other. But these two anecdotes do suggest that *today there still is tension* for some conservation-oriented citizens when it comes to the worldwide social movement that in so many circles goes under the rubric "animal rights."

9   Whatever name one gives this social movement, it has been marginalized for some time in important circles. A well-known early example in which a conservation-focused voice derided animal protection approaches is found in Baird Callicott's 1980 essay "Animal Liberation: A Triangular Affair." Callicott worked in this essay to distinguish what he clearly viewed as the superior qualities of "holistic environmental ethics" relative to the weaknesses and misguided features of the animal movement's concern for individuals. In animal protection circles, too, there are also well-known examples of reaction and dismissal going the other way, so to speak—one example is a comment by Tom Regan, who became a pre-eminent animal rights philosopher when he published *The Case for Animal Rights* in 1983. Regan suggested that those who advocate the interests or "rights" of *species* or the "good of the biotic community" are guilty of "environmental fascism" because they thereby override the "rights" of *individual* animals.

10   Importantly, each of these distinguished philosophers has since written much that indicates he recognizes the rhetorical overkill of these early claims. Puzzlingly, however, *the spirit of dismissal still moves some*, such that these cousin social movements have yet to walk arm-in-arm together. In effect, allowing relatively small differences to tyrannize the possibilities of these two major social movements working together is to miss the genius of each movement and thereby forego the obvious synergies these two movements can create when they work together. (I develop this more fully in an essay included in *Ignoring Nature*, ed. by Marc Bekoff [Chicago, IL: University of Chicago Press, forthcoming].)

11   Consider, in light of what follows, two possible conclusions. First, any claim to animal protection that does not foreground conservation and environmental insights, as well as consider the plight of human animals is a violation of the animal movement's spirit, internal values and logic (humans are, after all, animals, too). Second, any form of conservation or "environmentalism" that privileges *only* our own species (that is, privileges all and only members of the human species and no other animals at all) also violates the spirit, internal values and logic of the conservation and environmental movements, as well as that of science generally. Why? Because such positions are not merely *unscientific*, but also *anti-scientific*, for each repudiates the key tenet of the life sciences—that the animal kingdom includes both humans and other animals in the community of life and in shared ecosystems that are in every meaningful sense integrated and interdependent.

II

12   As I contemplated how to answer the question "What do people need to need to know about the important but controversial notion of animal rights?" I considered three things. First, I thought of the hundreds, perhaps thousands, of conversations on this topic that I have had with people in ordinary walks of life from all over the world. These have helped me appreciate the great variety of views on this topic.

13   Second, I thought about what I had learned during several decades of studying animal topics

in various educational contexts. I spent years in Oxford, England, studying the academic side of various issues, and I then spent a decade teaching in a veterinary school. At about the same time, I taught the subject of "animal law" at some of my country's best law schools. I also had the privilege of lecturing at dozens of universities and law schools as well as in public conferences, before thousands of people.

14   Third, I looked at hundreds of books, printed articles and Web sites that used the phrase "animal rights" because I wanted to see whether people were talking to—or past—one another.

15   Based on all of this background and research, I came to the conclusion that the following issues are the most important ones, and thus comprise "what everyone needs to know" about animal rights.

16   Animal rights is an ancient topic that recently has taken a special twist. The phrase "animal rights" has been, and still is, employed most often to describe *moral rights* and social values in favor of compassion and against cruelty. The modern twist is the emergence of conversations where the term means all of this *and more*, namely, the possibility of *legal rights* for some or all non-human animals. The latter are important protections, and today there is a very active debate over how often and to what extent our different human societies might put specific legal rights and other protections into place for specific animals.

17   This debate about "animal rights" as "specific legal rights" colors what many influential people say about the term, but this special and, I think, important sense of the term still remains secondary to the more generic meaning of "moral protections." "Animal rights" in the sense of moral rights is the larger and more fundamental issue, and specific legal rights for specific non-human individuals reflect but do not encompass all of animal rights as moral rights.

18   Second, the debate over animal rights often is polarized, but only in some circles. In those places where polarization impacts how people talk and hear one another as this issue is discussed, the advocates and activists at opposite ends of the long continuum of views continue to debate in ways that fuel even further polarization.

19   Third and most relevant to today's use of "animal rights," I found that many people do connect with each other when talking about animal rights. Further, many people recognize discussions about animal rights as being *pro-people*. This conclusion will seem counterintuitive to some, perhaps even an outright falsehood to others. But if you explore the debates over animal rights at length, you will notice that those who make the claim that animal rights can be pro-people argue their point in several different ways. Some argue this must be so because humans are "animals." Others argue that talk of animal rights affirms life, which of course has decidedly pro-human features. Still others argue that concerns to protect the living beings outside our own species honor *humans* in a special way by first affirming and then strengthening *our* ethical nature.

20   Lots of people also sense that the phrase "animal rights" is not a complicated phrase, but instead a phrase that easily and naturally means something very simple and basic along the lines of "protections for other living beings." Others think the phrase most truly means "we should listen to the voice of animals." Veterinary students often told me that "animal rights" is "a valuable term," but when they use it they risk condemnation by some classmates and, tragically, members of their veterinary school faculty and administration.

21   Many people feel "animal rights" has

undeniable appeal but that it is compromised whenever animal activists use violence on behalf of "the cause." Quite a few who mentioned violence commented on how rare such violence was, and then answered their own concerns by asking out loud, "Why let a few violent people control whether we use a term that describes a movement that was originally non-violent and today remains overwhelmingly so?"

22   Today, animal protection is a worldwide social movement. At times, active citizens in this movement challenge deeply cherished values and long-standing practices. Some other citizens react strongly to such challenges, which suggests that the risk of polarization is not going to disappear, no matter how effective any argument is at getting all of us to talk fairly, fully, and respectfully about the basic issue of our relationships with the life out beyond the species line.

23   What is most sorely needed is a willingness to recognize that the debate over "animal rights" is one in which fundamental values are being worked out. Without question, some people feel strongly that mere mention of the topic is a repudiation of humans and thus deeply immoral. But I found that many more people feel this kind of thinking focused solely on humans falls short of humans' ethical possibilities.

24   Thus, I think everyone needs to know how many people find multiple connections with the world in concerns for "animal rights." Because the phrase works for so many *not as a repudiation of humans* but as an affirmation of humans' special abilities to care about others—whether those "others" be human or other-than-human—the phrase opens doors to the rich, more-than-human world that is out beyond our species. For them, animal rights is a win-win situation, not an either/or matter.

25   Particularly revealing about those people who find the notion of animal rights to be a connecting, rather than a disconnecting, one is the range of connections affirmed by "animal rights." Of course, one set of connections is with other animals. As the English historian Marc Gold wrote in 1995, "The term animal rights is nothing more than a useful kind of shorthand for a movement based on the recognition that non-human animals live purposeful emotional lives and are as capable of suffering as humans. . . . kindness and tolerance for those different and weaker than ourselves are amongst the highest possible human aspirations." (Mark Gold, *Animal Rights: Extending the Circle of Compassion* [Oxford: Jon Carpenter, 1995, p. 73].)

26   *But the connections by no means stop there.* The phrase "animal rights" also connected people with "nature," "the environment," the local ecological world in and beyond their backyards, and, incredibly, *with other humans in a variety of ways*. Of great significance for the future, it seemed to me, was a pattern of children pushing their parents to consider "the animals."

27   These connections were not always called out explicitly. Yet even when these connections were only implicit, they were every bit as real, personal, and motivating. Both adults and children found animal rights to be one way to honor the world as—to use a phrase from the recently deceased visionary Thomas Berry—"a communion of subjects, not a collection of objects."

28   So one point is that *everyone needs to know* that polarization over animal rights need not be the dominant feature of the debate. Instead, the dominant feature of most discussions about animal rights is the common question, "What is the meaning of life?" My experience in exploring the animal rights debate has taught me that people ask this question because they feel emotionally committed to those around them. People recognize that daily actions, choices, and work can express human imagination and

our considerable ability to care, and they know that we thrive when we connect to some larger project that began before our own life and which will continue after it.

29 Ethical concerns for other living beings, whether human or not, provide such possibilities. Many people today understand "animal rights," however one defines it, to be a path of caring that leads to the fullest possible future. They have found that this form of life not only fosters virtues but in actual practice sustains the prospering of human imagination. My own experience is that in the class, as in life, inquiring beyond the species line prompts healthy, communicative forms of thinking and rationality, rather than the destructive, manipulative, instrumental forms of thinking so characteristic of selfishness and a small soul.

30 When humans experience others—again, it matters not whether these "others" are human or members of some other species—paradoxically, this experience of getting beyond the self allows humans to become as *fully human* as we can be, that is, human in the context of a biologically rich world full of other interesting living beings. As Viktor Frankl said in his influential *Man's Search for Meaning*, "self-actualization is possible only as a side-effect of self-transcendence." This is true not only for human individuals but also for the human species as a whole. This has in fact been the message of many religions, many ethical systems, and various wisdom traditions anchored in small-scale societies.

31 Through writing I came to understand that animal rights, as most people described it to me, is about connecting to the meaning of life.

III

32 A few words in conclusion—just as there is a surpassingly important insight driving the suggestion that there is no path to peace *because peace is the path*, so too one might suggest that environmental and animal protection concerns are not merely vehicles by which we get to a better, human-centered world—rather, they are themselves constitutive of a better whole and our larger and truest community.

 ## Comprehension

1. Summarize paragraph 11.
2. In one sentence each, define the two terms italicized in paragraph 16. Which is the more important term, according to the author. Why?

Structure, Organization, and Style

1. a. What is the purpose of paragraphs 2 and 3? What do they contribute to the essay?
    b. Who is the essay written for (paragraph 4)?
2. What two questions does Waldau set out to answer in the essay? In which paragraph does he begin to address the second of these questions?

Critical Thinking/Research

1. How does Waldau's language reflect his audience (see "Structure, Organization, and Style" question 1b)? Specifically, show how word choice and other linguistic resources encourage an "open-minded" approach to his topic.
2. What is the significance of quotation marks around "evidence" in paragraph 6? Analyze his use of anecdotes in paragraphs 6–7 to support his claim.
3. Analyze the effectiveness of Waldau's support for his main points. Questions you could answer include: What kinds of sources does he use and how does he use them? Are his points well developed? How does he show credibility?

Harold Herzog, "The Impact of Pets on Human Health and Psychological Well-Being: Fact, Fiction, or Hypothesis?"

"The Impact of Pets" illustrates the need for clear organization in academic review articles. Diverse studies on a topic need to be carefully categorized and logically connected to one another. Using critical thinking, the author begins by questioning the common perception that pets provide physical and psychological benefits for their owners. In his review, he underscores a vital principle: findings can be taken as reliable only if experimental results can be replicated.

Preparing to Read

Have you and/or your family owned a pet? Consider the pros and cons of pet ownership from your own perspective (you could freewrite on the topic).

The Impact of Pets on Human Health and Psychological Well-Being: Fact, Fiction, or Hypothesis?

Harold Herzog

Current Directions in Psychological Science,
August 2011
(2288 words)

Abstract

Because of extensive media coverage, it is now widely believed that pets enhance their owners' health, sense of psychological well-being, and longevity. But while some researchers have reported that positive effects accrue from interacting with animals, others have found that the health and happiness of pet owners is no better, and in some cases worse, than that of non–pet owners. I discuss some reasons why studies of the effects of pets on people have produced conflicting results, and I argue that the existence of a generalized "pet effect" on human mental and physical health is at present not a fact but an unsubstantiated hypothesis.

Keywords: pets, companion animals, health, psychological well-being, happiness

1   Many people are deeply attached to companion animals. In the United States, over two thirds of households include a pet, most of which are regarded by their owners as family members. Considering that the lifetime costs of owning a pet are about $8000 for a medium-sized dog and $10,000 for a cat (cats tend to live longer than dogs), devoting resources on a creature with whom you share no genes and who is unlikely to ever return the favor seems to make little evolutionary sense. Aside from the expense, there are other downsides to companion animals. In the United States, a person is 100 times more likely to be seriously injured or killed by a dog than by a venomous snake, and over 85,000 Americans are taken to emergency rooms each year because of falls caused by their pets. Further, people can contract a cornucopia of diseases from companion animals, including brucellosis, roundworm, skin mites, *E. coli*, salmonella, giardia, ringworms, and cat-scratch fever. And, pets are second only to late-night noise as a source of conflict between neighbors.

2   Although not culturally universal, pet keeping exists in most societies, and an array of theories have been offered to explain why people bring animals into their lives (Herzog, 2010). Among these are the misfiring of parental instincts, biophilia (a hypothetical biologically based love of nature), social contagion, the tendency for the middle class to emulate the customs of the rich, the need to dominate the natural world, social isolation in urban societies, and the desire to teach responsibility and kindness to children. While the reasons that pet keeping has become a widespread cultural phenomenon are unclear, it is evident that companion animals are vitally important in the lives of many people.

The "pet effect"

3   When asked what they specifically get from their relationships with pets, people typically mention companionship, having a play partner, and the need to love and care for another creature. But fueled by media reports and books with titles like *The Healing Power of Pets: Harnessing the Amazing Ability of Pets to Make and Keep People Happy and Healthy* (Becker, 2002), the public has come to accept as fact the idea that pets can also serve as substitutes for physicians and clinical psychologists. The idea that living with an animal can improve human health, psychological well-being, and longevity has been called the "pet effect" (Allen, 2003).

4   Most pet owners believe that their companion animals are good for them. Personal convictions, however, do not constitute scientific evidence. Claims about the medical and psychological benefits of living with animals need to be subjected to the same standards of evidence as a new drug, medical device, or form of psychotherapy. Over the past 30 years, hundreds of studies have examined the impact of pets on human health and happiness. Here I argue that, contrary to media reports, an examination of this body of literature indicates that the pet effect remains an uncorroborated hypothesis rather than an established fact. (Note that the main focus of this article is on the effects of pets on the physical and mental health of their owners, not the efficacy of animals as therapeutic agents for disorders such as autism and attention-deficit/hyperactivity disorder.)

The evidence that pets are good for people

5   The first demonstration of an association between pets and health was an early study of 92 heart-attack victims in which 28% of pet

owners survived for at least a year as compared to only 6% of non–pet owners (Friedmann, Katcher, Lynch, & Thomas, 1980). These findings generated a flurry of research on the positive impact of interacting with companion animals (see review by Wells, 2009a). For example, stroking dogs and cats, watching tropical fish in an aquarium, and even caressing a pet boa constrictor have been reported to reduce blood pressure and stress levels. The most convincing of these studies was a clinical trial in which hypertensive stockbrokers were randomly assigned to either pet or no-pet conditions. Six months later, when put in a stressful situation, subjects in the pet group showed lower increases in blood pressure than did those in the non-pet control condition (Allen, Shykoff, & Izzo, 2001). Researchers have also reported that psychological benefits accrue from living with animals. These include studies showing that pet owners have higher self-esteem, more positive moods, more ambition, greater life satisfaction, and lower levels of loneliness (El-Alayli, Lystad, Webb, Hollingsworth, & Ciolli, 2006).

6   Epidemiologists have also connected pet ownership to better health and well-being (see review by Headey & Grabka, 2011). For example, among 11,000 German and Australian adults, pet owners were in better physical condition than non-pet owners, and they made 15% fewer doctor visits, a potential savings of billions of dollars in national health expenditures. And an epidemiological study of Chinese women found that pet owners exercised more, slept better, felt more physically fit, and missed fewer days from work than women without pets. Further, these effects were particularly strong for individuals who reported that they were very closely attached to their pets.

Now the bad news

7   Pet owners are, of course, delighted to read about research that confirms the view that living with a dog or cat makes for a happier and longer life. But while the media abounds with stories extolling the health benefits of pets, studies in which pet ownership has been found to have no impact or even negative effects on human physical or mental health rarely make headlines. For instance, there was no media coverage of a recent study of 425 heart-attack victims that found pet owners were *more* likely than non–pet owners to die or suffer remissions within a year of suffering their heart attack (22% vs. 14%; Parker et al., 2010). Indeed, replication has been a persistent problem with research on the effects of pets on human health. Straatman, Hanson, Endenburg, and Mol (1997), for instance, found that performing a stressful task in the presence of a dog had no short-term effect on blood pressure. And a study of 1179 older adults found no differences in the blood pressure or risk of hypertension of pet and non–pet owners (Wright, Kritz-Silverstein, Morton, Wingard, & Barrett-Connor, 2007). (The pet owners in the study did, however, exercise less than non-owners and were more apt to be overweight.)

8   The impact of pets on psychological well-being has also been called into question. A Pew Research Center survey of 3000 Americans found no differences in the proportion of pet owners and nonowners who described themselves as "very happy" (in Herzog, 2010). Researchers in England administered the UCLA–Loneliness scale to people who were seeking a companion animal. When retested 6 months later, the individuals who had acquired pets were just as lonely as they were before they got their companion animal. In addition, they were no

happier than participants who had not gotten a pet (Gilbey, McNicholas, & Collis, 2007). Another recent study found that older adults who were highly attached to their dogs tended to be more depressed than individuals who were not as attached to their companion animals (Miltiades & Shearer, 2011).

9   Nor has pet ownership fared well in recent epidemiological studies. A study of 40,000 Swedes found that while pet owners were physically healthier than non–pet owners, they suffered more from psychological problems including anxiety, chronic tiredness, insomnia, and depression (Müllersdorf, Granström, Sahlqvist, & Tillgren, 2010). A Finnish study of 21,000 adults reported that pet owners were at increased risk for hypertension, high cholesterol, gastric ulcers, migraine headaches, depression, and panic attacks (Koivusilta & Ojanlatva, 2006). In an Australian study of 2551 elderly adults, dog ownership was associated with poorer physical health and with depression (Parslow, Jorm, Christensen, & Rodgers, 2005). Finally, in a longitudinal study of nearly 12,000 American adults, cat or dog ownership was unrelated to mortality rates (Gillum & Obisesan, 2010).

Reasons why pet-effect research is inconclusive

10   For many people, pets are profoundly pleasurable and a source of psychological support. The fact is, however, that empirical studies of the effects of pets on human health and well-being have produced a mishmash of conflicting results. While pets are undoubtedly good for some people, there is presently insufficient evidence to support the contention that, as a group, pet owners are healthier or happier or that they live longer than people who do not have companion animals in their lives. Why are the results of studies on the pet effect so inconsistent? Ioannidis (2005) argues that conflicting results and failures to replicate are especially prevalent in areas of science in which studies are characterized by small and homogeneous samples, a wide diversity of research designs, and small effect sizes. He also believes that research topics that are particularly "hot" are especially prone to replication problems. All of these criteria apply to research on the effects of pets on human health.

11   Design problems are common in studies of human–animal interactions. Meta-analyses enable scientists to look for patterns in the results of multiple studies on the same topic, but there have been no meta-analyses of studies of the effects of pets on owner happiness or health. However, for a meta-analysis in a related area (the effectiveness of animal-assisted therapy), Nimer and Lundahl (2007) had to comb through 250 studies to find 49 that met even minimal standards for methodological rigor.

12   There is also the problem of how to interpret differences between pet owners and nonowners. Most studies reporting positive effects of pets are not true experiments in which the subjects are randomly assigned to "pet" and "non-pet" groups. Rather, they involve correlational or quasiexperimental designs that compare people who choose to live with pets with people who do not. Hence, while it might be the case that pets *cause* their owners to be healthier and happier, it is equally possible that the causal arrow points the other direction—that people who are healthier, happier, and wealthier to begin with are more likely to have the energy and financial resources required to bring companion animals into their lives and to keep them for extended periods. (Of course, the caution against conflating correlation and causality also applies to studies in which pet

ownership has been found to be associated with poorer mental or physical health.)

13   In addition, many studies of human–animal interactions are based on self-reports of pet owners. While these can be useful, self-reports sometimes produce results that are at odds with more objective indices of health. For example, Wells (2009b) investigated the impact of acquiring a pet on individuals suffering from chronic fatigue syndrome. She found that while the pet owners in the study claimed their animals provided them with a host of psychological and physical benefits, their scores on standardized measures (the Chalder Fatigue Questionnaire, the General Health Questionnaire-12, and the Short-Form-37 Health Survey) indicated that they were just as tired, depressed, worried, and stressed as chronic fatigue sufferers who did not get a pet.

14   A problem called the "file drawer effect," which plagues many areas of research, also skews the scientific literature on human–animal relationships. This is the tendency for negative results to wind up in the researcher's filing cabinet rather than in the pages of a scientific journal. At a session at a 2009 conference on human–animal interactions, for example, one researcher reported that separation from their pets had no effect on the psychological adjustment of college students, another found that interacting with animals did not reduce depression in psychiatric nursing home residents, and a third found no differences in the loneliness of adult pet owners and nonowners. So far, none of these studies have appeared in print.

15   Finally, erroneous positive results are more common in areas of science in which researchers have vested interests— financial or otherwise— in a study's outcome. Researchers are often drawn to the study of human–animal relationships because they are pet lovers who are personally convinced of the healing powers of the human–animal bond. Hence, investigators in this field need to be particularly vigilant in designing studies that reduce the chances of unconsciously biasing research results. This can be especially problematic in studies on the impact of pets on human health in which it is often difficult or impossible to eliminate placebo effects via traditional methods such as single- and double-blind experimental and control groups.

Why psychologists should study human–animal relationships

16   In short, despite the growing body of research on the bonds between people and pets, the existence of a pet effect on human health and happiness remains a hypothesis in need of confirmation rather than an established fact. This conclusion should not be taken as a condemnation of pet keeping. Indeed, companion animals have always been part of my own life, and I understand the joys that come with living with members of other species. Nor am I arguing that behavioral scientists should avoid studying the impact of animals on human health and well-being. In fact, we need more rather than less research on this topic.

17   Rozin (2006) cogently observed that in their quest to explain general principles of behavior, psychologists have neglected huge domains of human life such as food, work, and religion. I would add our attitudes, behaviors, and relationships with other species to the list of topics that most people find fascinating but that psychologists have, for the most part, ignored. The study of our interactions with animals is interesting, important, and challenging.

Whether, and under what circumstances, pets make people happier and healthier is unclear. It is, however, clear that animals play a role in nearly every aspect of human psychological and cultural life. And our attitudes and behaviors toward and relationships with other species offer a unique window into many aspects of human nature.

Recommended Reading

Archer, J. (2011). Pet keeping: A case study in maladaptive behavior. In C.A. Salmon & T.K. Shackelford (Eds.), *The Oxford handbook of evolutionary family psychology* (pp. 281–296). New York, NY: Oxford University Press. Provides an overview of evolutionary theories of pet keeping.

Herzog, H. (2010). (See References). An accessible introduction to aspects of the psychology of human–animal interactions ranging from the effects of pets on human health and happiness to how people make moral decisions about the use of other species.

Knight, S., & Herzog, H. (Eds.). (2009). New perspectives on human–animal interactions: Theory, policy, and research [Special issue]. *Journal of Social Issues, 65.* Journal issue devoted to current research on aspects of human–animal relationships.

McCardle, P., McCune, S., Griffin, J.A., & Maholmes, V. (Eds.). (2011). *How animals affect us: Examining the influence of human–animal interaction on child development and human health.* Washington, DC: American Psychological Association. Edited volume focused on pets and child development but also including excellent reviews on the impact of animals on human health and well-being.

Declaration of Conflicting Interests The author declared no potential conflicts of interest with respect to the research, authorship, and/or publication of this article.

References

Allen, K. (2003). Are pets a healthy pleasure? The influence of pets on blood pressure. *Current Directions in Psychological Science, 12,* 236–239.

Allen, K., Shykoff, B.E., & Izzo, J.L. (2001). Pet ownership, but not ACE inhibitor therapy, blunts home blood pressure responses to mental stress. *Hypertension, 38,* 815–820.

Becker, M. (2002). *The healing power of pets: Harnessing the amazing ability of pets to make and keep people happy and healthy.* New York, NY: Hyperion Books.

El-Alayli, A., Lystad, A.L., Webb, S.R., Hollingsworth, S.L., & Ciolli, J. L. (2006). Reigning cats and dogs: A pet-enhancement bias and its link to pet attachment, pet–self similarity, self-enhancement, and well-being. *Basic and Applied Social Psychology, 28,* 131–143.

Friedmann, E., Katcher, A., Lynch, J., & Thomas, S. (1980). Animal companions and one-year survival of patients after discharge from a coronary care unit. *Public Health Reports, 95,* 307–312.

Gilbey, A., McNicholas, J., & Collis, G.M. (2007). A longitudinal test of the belief that companion animal ownership can help reduce loneliness. *Anthrozoös, 20,* 345–353.

Gillum, R.F., & Obisesan, T.O. (2010). Living with companion animals, physical activity and mortality in a US national cohort. *International Journal of Environmental Research and Public Health, 7,* 2452–2459.

Headey, B., & Grabka, M. (2011). Health correlates of pet ownership from national surveys. In P. McCardle, S. McCune, J.A. Griffin & V. Maholmes (Eds.), *How animals affect us: Examining the influence of human–animal interaction on child development and human health* (pp. 153–162). Washington, DC: American Psychological Association.

Herzog, H. (2010). *Some we love, some we hate, some we eat: Why it's so hard to think straight about animals.* New York, NY: Harper.

Ioannidis, J.P.A. (2005). Why most published research findings are false. *PLoS Medicine, 2,* 696–701.

Koivusilta, L.K., & Ojanlatva, A. (2006). To have or not to have a pet for better health? *PloS One, 1,* 1–9.

Miltiades, H., & Shearer, J. (2011). Attachment to pet dogs and depression in rural older adults. *Anthrozoös, 24,* 147–154.

Müllersdorf, M., Granström, F., Sahlqvist, L., & Tillgren, P. (2010). Aspects of health, physical/leisure activities, work and sociodemographics associated with pet ownership in Sweden. *Scandinavian Journal of Public Health, 38,* 53–63.

Nimer, J., & Lundahl, B. (2007). Animal-assisted therapy: A meta-analysis. *Anthrozoös, 20,* 225–238.

Parker, G., Gayed, A., Owen, C., Hyett, M., Hilton, T., & Heruc, G. (2010). Survival following an acute coronary syndrome: A pet theory put to the test. *Acta Psychiatrica Scandinavica, 121,* 65–70.

Parslow, R.A., Jorm, A.F., Christensen, H., & Rodgers, B. (2005). Pet ownership and health in older adults: Findings from a survey of 2,551 community-based Australians aged 60–64. *Gerontology, 51,* 40–47.

Rozin, P. (2006). Domain denigration and process preference in academic psychology. *Perspectives on Psychological Science, 1,* 365–376.

Straatman, I., Hanson, E.K.S., Endenburg, N., & Mol, J.A. (1997). The influence of a dog on male students during a stressor. *Anthrozoös, 10,* 191–197.

Wells, D.L. (2009a). The effects of animals on human health and well-being. *Journal of Social Issues, 65,* 523–543.

Wells, D.L. (2009b). Associations between pet ownership and self-reported health status in people suffering from chronic fatigue syndrome. *Journal of Alternative and Complementary Medicine, 15,* 407–413.

Wright, J.D., Kritz-Silverstein, D., Morton, D.J., Wingard, D.L., & Barrett-Connor, E. (2007). Pet ownership and blood pressure in old age. *Epidemiology, 18,* 613–617.

Comprehension

1. In your own words, explain the "file drawer effect" (par. 14).
2. Why does the author believe that more, rather than fewer, research studies on the effects of pets are needed?

Structure and Organization

1. Identify the bases of comparison in paragraphs 5–6 and 7–9. Why is it important that the same order of points is used in these two sections?
2. Identify two strategies for comprehension the writer uses in his article, referring to at least one specific example for each.

Critical Thinking

1. How does the author justify his study?
2. Of the reasons Herzog gives for the inconsistency of results in the section "Reasons why pet-effect research is inconclusive," which do you believe is the most important? Explain.

Nick Fox and Katie Ward, "Health, Ethics and Environment: A Qualitative Study of Vegetarian Motivations"

The study's authors use an experimental design to obtain qualitative results on their topic. In contrast to experimentation in which numbers are generated (*quantitative research*), the data from qualitative research take the form of individual responses generated by interviews, or unstructured or structured group discussions, such as focus groups or, in the case of this study, an online forum. The results are carefully recorded and systematically organized, often with the help of a reliable data analysis tool. Qualitative results have many benefits for researchers: the results often reveal the complexity of an issue and an understanding of its breadth, depth, or scope.

▶ Preparing to Read

1. Are you a vegetarian or have you ever considered becoming one? What was/would be the main reason for your decision to become one or not?
2. Do you believe vegetarianism is primarily a dietary choice or a lifestyle? Explain.

Health, Ethics and Environment: A Qualitative Study of Vegetarian Motivations

Nick Fox and Katie Ward

Research Report
Appetite, March-May 2008
(4966 words)

Abstract

This qualitative study explored the motivations of vegetarians by means of online ethnographic research with participants in an international message board. The researcher participated in discussions on the board, gathered responses to questions from 33 participants, and conducted follow-up e-mail interviews with 18 of these participants. Respondents were predominantly from the US, Canada and the UK. Seventy per cent were females, and ages ranged from 14 to 53, with a median of 26 years. Data were analysed using a thematic approach. While this research found that health and the ethical treatment of animals were the main motivators for participants' vegetarianism, participants reported a range of commitments to environmental concerns, although in only one case was environmentalism a primary motivator for becoming a vegetarian. The data indicate that vegetarians may follow a trajectory, in which initial motivations are augmented over time by other reasons for sustaining or further restricting their diet.

Introduction

1   Abstinence from the consumption of meat and animal products is an element of some religious practices including Buddhism and Seventh Day Adventism (Fraser, 2003). Others choose a secular vegetarianism, grounded in non-religious motivations (Whorton, 1994). The Vegetarian Society coined the term "vegetarian" in the mid-nineteenth century, and this is used to cover a range of dietary choices that avoid some or all foods with animal origins (Barr & Chapman, 2002; Hoek, Pieternel, Stafleu, & de Graaf, 2004). Vegans avoid all animal products for food, clothing or other purposes, while *lacto-ovo* vegetarians consume dairy produce and eggs, and *semi-* and *pesco-*vegetarians eat poultry and fish respectively (Phillips, 2005; Willetts, 1997).

2   Studies of vegetarians have identified a variety of non-religious motivations for adopting a meat-free diet (Beardsworth & Keil, 1992; Povey, Wellens, & Conners, 2001). Personal health and animal cruelty figure high on this list (Hoek et al., 2004, p. 266; Lea & Worsley, 2001, p. 127), while disgust or repugnance with eating flesh (Kenyon & Barker, 1998; Rozin, Markwith, & Stoess, 1997; Santos & Booth, 1996), association with patriarchy (Adams, 1990), food beliefs and peer or family influences (Lea & Worsley, 2001, p. 128) are also noted. Health vegetarians choose to avoid meat in order to derive certain health benefits or lose weight (Key, Appleby, & Rosell, 2006; Kim & Houser, 1999; Wilson, Weatherall,

& Butler, 2004), while ethical vegetarians consider meat avoidance as a moral imperative not to harm animals for food or other reasons (Fessler, Arguello, Mekdara, & Macias, 2003, p. 31; Whorton, 1994). Health concerns are also the major reason motivating individuals who are "partial vegetarians," who choose not to eat red meat, limit their consumption of flesh to fish, or select only organic products (American Dietetic Association, 2003; Bedford & Barr, 2005; Hoek et al., 2004, p. 266).

3   In addition to these commitments, vegetarianism has been linked to concerns with the environmental and ecological impact of meat (Gaard, 2002; Hoek et al., 2004, p. 265; Lindeman & Sirelius, 2001, p. 182). In the Kalof, Dietz, Stern, and Guagnano (1999) study of influences on vegetarianism, belief that a vegetarian diet was less harmful to the environment was the only factor significantly differentiating vegetarians and non-vegetarians, while beliefs concerning the health and animal welfare benefits of vegetarianism were non-significant. A range of commercial outlets now offer "health foods," "wholefoods" and most recently "organic foods" grown without additives, pesticides and artificial fertilisers that increase food productivity at the expense of the environment (Coveney, 2000, p. 141). Hoek et al. (2004) note the emergence of a "vegetarian-oriented consumerism" that addresses ethical and environmental concerns, while Allen Fox (1999) suggests that a vegetarian economy contributes to "ecosystem health" by reducing the impact on the environment and economies of pollution, intensive farming and land degradation by grazing, affecting both developed and less-developed countries. Awareness of their contribution to the future of the planet can also support good psychological health among vegetarians, according to Wilson et al. (2004).

4   Devine, Connors, Bisogni, and Sobal (1998) have described the feelings, strategies and actions in relation to food choices that people adopt over their life course as "trajectories" that demonstrate persistence and continuity as circumstances alter. These trajectories are underpinned by values that determine what foods are chosen (Sobal, Bisogni, Devine, & Jastran, 2006, p. 9). Jabs, Devine, and Sobal (1998) examined life-course trajectories and the impact of life events on vegetarians' food choices, finding different patterns of adoption among health and ethical vegetarians. Health vegetarians tended to make gradual "trial adoptions" of food choices, while "ethical vegetarians" made more sudden changes in their diet to support beliefs such as animal welfare, and create consistency in their lives (see also Hamilton, 1993). Both groups may graduate from semi- or ovo-lacto vegetarianism to a vegan diet over time.

5   Our research among vegetarian participants in an online forum (Fox & Ward, submitted for publication) has found a distinct fault-line between these two perspectives. Health vegetarians emphasised personal reasons for their diet above concern for animals, and were accused by some ethical vegetarians of being selfish and interested only in improving their own quality of life. Ethical vegetarians considered that their own practices were fundamentally altruistic, and involved personal sacrifice in order to prevent cruelty to animals. Lindeman and Sirelius (2001, p. 182) have suggested these perspectives have different ideological bases, with ethical vegetarianism broadly associated with humanistic commitments and health vegetarianism with conservative and normative values.

6   While initial motivation to adopt a vegetarian diet may thus be divergent, resulting in animosity between health and ethical vegetarians on occasions (Fox & Ward, submitted for publication),

there may also be convergence among those who have adopted a vegetarian diet, possibly to provide further cognitive support for a difficult life choice (Santos & Booth, 1996, p. 204), or as a consequence of exposure to other vegetarians' motivations, beliefs and practices (Bisogni, Connors, Devine, & Sobal, 2002). In this paper, we report data that explore this convergence, and specifically the emergence of environmentalist concerns among vegetarians whose motivations initially derived from personal health or animal welfare. We examine, by means of online ethnographic methods, vegetarians' own perspectives on how health, ethical and environmental beliefs motivate their food choices, to investigate the interactions between beliefs over health, animal cruelty and the environment, and how these may contribute to food choice trajectory.

Methods
Design and setting

7   The data reported here are drawn from "online ethnographic" research carried out in a web-based forum concerned with secular vegetarianism, which will be referred to here as the VegForum. The forum was selected because it attracted a high volume of users who posted regularly to the message boards, creating a lively website with a heavy flow of "traffic." The forum had a number of message boards, which included the provision of advice to new vegetarians, health, animal rights and ecology. Participants were an eclectic mix, from vegans who avoided all animal products for food or clothing, to those who ate dairy products or even fish. The language of communication was English, and participants were predominantly from North America, the UK and Australasia. Our research was largely confined to one discussion board that was intended to provide support to new vegetarians.

8   There is a growing body of research using Internet-mediated ethnographic methods, and there are various advantages and limitations. Internet interviewing is appropriate for sensitive subjects not amenable to face-to-face interviews (Illingworth, 2001), and Glaser, Dixit, and Green (2002, pp. 189–190) suggest that the anonymity of the Internet permits research into marginal groups for whom self-disclosure may have costs, and where participants may be suspicious of researchers and outsiders. The Internet provides a cost-effective way to access small or hard to find groups who interact in specialist fora (Illingworth, 2001; Nosek, Banaji, & Greenwald, 2002).

9   On the other hand, there are issues of validity in Internet-based research. Anonymity increases the potential for intentional or unintentional deception (Glaser et al., 2002, p. 191) and for identity manipulation (Hewson, Yule, Laurent, & Vogel, 2003, p. 115; Nosek et al., 2002, p. 172). Internet samples will underrepresent poor and minority groups (Nosek et al., 2002, p. 168). Hewson et al. (2003, p. 32) consider that this bias is disappearing with the rapid spread of Internet access, although research (Henning, 2005) indicates that Internet-based social networking is a predominantly youthful activity. Participants need access to hardware, skills in typing and motivation to participate in what can be lengthy online interviews (Chen & Hinton, 1999). Thomsen, Straubaar, and Bolyard (1998) suggest that multi-method triangulation using textual analysis, prolonged participant observation and qualitative interviews can provide valid and reliable data, and we have used this approach in past studies (Fox & Ward, 2006). In this study, observation of forum interactions, and active participation were triangulated with survey and online interview methods. As with most

qualitative approaches, we did not claim to be establishing a "representative" sample, but did apply a range of methods to gather data broadly and gain data saturation through follow-up questioning.

Data collection

10 All interviews were conducted by KW. To access the field of study, KW subscribed to the VegForum, announced her "presence," and explained that she was researching attitudes and beliefs among vegetarians. The research was carried out between August 2005 and February 2006 and consisted of three stages:

- 11 Participation in discussion within the VegForum. Permission was gained from participants to reproduce relevant posts from discussions.
- 12 KW posted a survey to one of the message boards within VegForum, to which there were 33 responses. Respondents were predominantly from the US and Canada, with some UK members. Seventy per cent were females, and ages ranged from 14 to 53, with a median of 26 years. The survey contained open-ended questions designed to elicit participants' motivations for vegetarianism, attitudes to meat-eating, health and animal welfare, and related lifestyle choices. Respondents were also asked for their age and nationality.
- 13 Respondents were invited to participate in online follow-up interviews, and 18 agreed to this. These were conducted using the VegForum's own messaging system. These were unstructured interviews based on cues in respondents' answers to the survey questions, to enable respondents to enlarge on their responses concerning their beliefs and attitudes, triggers and other factors that had

led them to become vegetarian, and the effects of being vegetarian on their lives.

Data analysis

14 Data were analysed using the framework methodology for qualitative analysis. This is an approach to analysis that is appropriate to deductive research that addresses pre-set aims and objectives (Pope, Zeibland, & Mays, 2000), and enables data to be systematically collated and displayed within a spreadsheet or other software package, in order to address specific topic areas. Collated data can then be indexed and key findings extracted. The topic areas then form the basis for the structure of the report, within which data extracts may be used to illustrate key findings from the ethnography. All data from the case study have been reported in the ethnographic past tense, participants have been fully anonymised, and spellings have been corrected to aid reading.

Results
Health and the vegetarian diet

15 Many participants in our study associated positive health and well-being with dietary choice. Diet was perceived as central to good health and longevity, with poor diet associated with lower levels of health and even specific diseases. Will argued that "nothing affects your mind and quality of life as much as nutrition" while Ruby suggested that "you can't expect your body to treat you right if you fill it full of crap all the time." Participants offered evidence for this link:

16 When eating a vegan diet my symptoms go away and I feel great. I never call myself a vegan or vegetarian. I tell people that I have food allergies and I have to eat like this for my health. I feel so much healthier when I eat vegan meals. (Mark)

17   Participants contrasted their current healthy diets with previous or childhood food intakes that they perceived as unhealthy. The change to vegetarian diet was associated directly with an improvement in health.

18   I was overweight as a kid, I ate junk food, no veggies, and did not drink water. All of my liquid came from sodas. . . . It was a long process to get out of that dietary sinkhole, and sometimes I am surprised that I did. Nowadays typical dinners for me are home-cooked with plenty of whole foods. I'm not 100% whole foods and I don't strive to be. I like white basmati rice way too much. But taken as a whole, my diet is full of fibre from other whole grain and legume sources. (Vinny)

19   Respondents reported a range of health issues that motivated them, from an effort to "cut down on my dairy for cholesterol reasons" or "to avoid high blood pressure and kidney stones."

20   My family has a history of breast/ovarian cancer and high cholesterol and I figured that eating the best possible diet of the most healthful foods (combined with exercise) would be the best thing I could do to prevent myself from developing these diseases as much as possible. Also most of my family is lactose-intolerant and though I didn't get sick when I ate dairy, I've noticed that when I don't eat it I feel better overall. (Lucy)

21   While health reasons were an initial motivator, they were also a justification for continuing a meat-free diet. Jane supported her ideological claims with personal experiences, which she suggested justified the decision.

22   If you want to live a longer life, then eating healthy is key. Eating unhealthy foods can really change your personality. When you switch to a healthy diet from an unhealthy diet you get this sudden spring in your step, so to speak. Every day that I wake up, I feel so much healthier and alive than I used to. It's so awesome to feel awake and alive.

Animal welfare and the vegetarian diet

23   The desire to avoid killing animals for human consumption was the other main reason offered for becoming vegetarian. At the heart of this perspective lies a view that animals should not be mistreated for human benefit. Not consuming meat was thus a sacrifice to be made by individuals as part of an ethical commitment.

24   I still use dairy and infertile egg sometimes because full veganism is hard for me. But the early death of male chickens and cattle is evidently a usual part of egg production—as a rule, they aren't needed where they are born. This, coupled with the bad conditions many laying hens are kept in, has driven me to almost completely eliminate those foods from my diet. (Tom)

25   Often a specific incident had been a trigger.

26   I went vegetarian after dissecting a chicken in seventh grade science class, and noticing that chickens were similar in build up to humans. I went vegan shortly after, because of animal rights, and because I felt that I was being hypocritical to be vegetarian in order to stop animal abuse, but still support it in other major ways. (Jane)

27   I became a lacto-ovo vegetarian when I was 13 years old, because I was sitting in my living room eating an Italian sub, and the thought came to me that an animal is not being honoured by sitting between two slices of bread. It made me so very sad that the reason that animal was

born was to die. Three months ago I adopted a vegan diet because I think too much about where things come from, and was tired of feeling grossed out every time I ate dairy or eggs. The guilt was too much. (Victoria)

28 While many health vegetarians offered experiential reasons for adopting and sustaining a meat-free diet, ethical vegetarians often cast their motivations within a philosophical, ideological or spiritual framework. Billy's commitment was initially to animal rights, before adopting vegetarianism.

29 I saw the "Meet Your Meat" video and began to research animal rights/ways vegetarianism can help the environment. I realized that I love animals dearly and couldn't call myself an animal rights supporter and eat meat. It seemed so contradictory. So, one day I just decided to become vegetarian.

30 For Cath, her ethical choices were associated with a perspective on her place in relation to the world and to her spirituality.

31 I try to grow as much of my own food and buy organic when I can because most farming practices are disrespectful to the Earth. I don't consume meat because it is disrespectful to the animals. I choose not to buy meat, leather, or eggs . . . because I believe that the torture and enslavement of feeling beings it is the ultimate form of disrespect to the creator.

32 Some of our ethical vegetarian respondents indicated that avoiding meat was not just a dietary choice, but a way of life.

33 Veg*ism [an abbreviation used on VegForum to cover both vegetarianism and veganism] is a

lifestyle for me, because instead of just trying to not eat animals, I try to live my life with the least harm to animals. I buy products not tested on animals or have animal products. I don't buy leather, silk, etc. It isn't just about what I eat, but how I live my life. (Ricki)

34 Being vegan I made the basic vegan changes, using products that I know have not been tested on animals, boycotting companies that do still test. I have also become more environmentally aware. . . . I'm not much of a dieting person, in fact I hate diets, I don't think of my veganism as a diet, it's more a lifestyle. (Millie)

35 Elsewhere we have differentiated these reasons for a vegetarian diet in terms of identity (Fox & Ward, submitted for publication). The focus within health vegetarianism is internal, addressing desires to sustain good health and avoid illness. For ethical vegetarians, by contrast, the focus is outward, towards other living creatures. Often for the latter, their own health and well-being came second to the welfare of other creatures, with strict vegans suffering poor health as a result of their diet (Fox & Ward, submitted for publication). This major difference led to conflict among the participants in the VegForum, with ethical vegetarians critical of perceived selfishness by health vegetarians.

36 Now, about health vegans. I certainly don't jump for joy just because "one less animal is killed." If people only care about themselves and their health, that shows they are selfish and egoistical. . . . I find their motivations for being vegan boring and selfish. There's nothing wrong with wanting to stay healthy. Obviously, that goes without saying. But there are lots and lots of healthy people who eat meat and/or fish every day of their lives and they live till they're 100. (Diana)

37 Stephen considered health vegetarians insufficiently radical, while Ruby saw ethical vegetarianism as superior to health vegetarianism, but still contributing to her over-arching objective of preventing harm to animals.

38 In any group, there are people who are going to play the "holier than thou" card. This includes veg*ns, of course. Some people believe the only "true path to veg*nism" is through the ethical abstaining of animal products. Then there are some who believe that any reduction in harm to animals is good, regardless of the reasons behind them. I personally would be happy if members of my family or my [boyfriend] gave up meat because it was better for their health . . . even if they didn't care about the animals. I can't quite put myself into the mindset of not caring about killing animals and eating their flesh, but obviously plenty of people can, whether they eat animals or not.

39 In our research we found surprisingly few respondents who genuinely straddled the two motivations of health and ethical commitments. However, in one specific area, environmental concerns, we did find common ground between those who identified either as health or ethical vegetarians.

Environmental commitments among vegetarians

40 Among our sample of 33 participants in the VegForum, only 1 respondent, 29 year old Canadian Simon, had become vegan for explicitly environmental motivations, in order to "do something to maintain the planet." At the same time as his adoption of a vegetarian diet, he also "went back to biking, walking, and trying not to travel by automobile." However, other respondents in the study whose initial

motivations were for health or ethical reasons, described a range of environmental commitments. Sometimes concern with the wider environment emerged directly from a perspective related to the impact of meat consumption for human or animal health.

41 I try and only eat organic egg and milk products, for the animal and human population health and well being. Non organic farming of animals are breeding grounds for antibiotic resistant bacteria and viruses, which can spread to humans. As well as not being very nice for the animal. I try and be environmentally friendly as I can. (Bryn)

42 The availability of organic foodstuffs that avoid the use of pesticides and artificial fertilisers provided a direct link to the dietary concerns for some health vegetarians.

43 I try to eat primarily organic. Being where I live the cost of organic food isn't really an issue. I try to eat as few processed foods as possible and eliminate added sugars. For the most part all of the above are working. (Will)

44 If I get the choice, I like to get organic vegetables, but it's not a high priority. I do try to be environmentally friendly—I recycle, try not to be wasteful. (June)

45 Tom started his vegetarian diet because of animal welfare. However, this broadened subsequently, linking environmental reasons for his diet to other ecological concerns.

46 I've found there are health and environmental benefits to vegetarianism, as well as lessened injury to animals. It's all good. I'm also environmentalist: I avoid wasting energy and making solid waste. I also make sure my diet is

healthy: I keep track of my intake of calories, trans and/or saturated fats, and refined carbohydrates.

47   Tim had been raised as a vegetarian, but said his move to veganism was a way to "do more for the environment. I just want to be as green as I can." Michael told us that his original motivation was "for health reasons, but now also for environmental reasons, as well as wanting to reduce animal suffering." For Andy, his reason for becoming vegetarian was

48   ethics, at first. I wanted others to stop dying so that I could eat. The environmental and health motivations followed.

49   For other respondents, the "alternative" lifestyle choices concerning diet co-existed with a range of other environmental behaviours. For example, Michael regarded vegetarianism as one amongst a number of "deviant" behaviours he had adopted.

50   I try and get organic food mostly and put a considerable amount of effort into being as environmentally friendly as possible: I recycle, try and cut down on waste, conserve energy, cycling instead of driving etc. Most of my friends think I'm weird because in addition to the above I also refuse to eat anything with E numbers or hydrogenated oils and also boycott animal-testing companies.

51   Environmentalism was part of the lifestyle choices of many of our respondents, who indicated a number of commitments including saving energy, using public transport, recycling, composting, tree-planting and picking up litter. Naomi commented that she was "the recycle queen, totally obsessed—reduce, reuse, recycle," while Babs had ". . . recycled for years, and

volunteer to pick up trash. I walk everywhere I can instead of driving." As noted earlier, Andy had become an ethical vegetarian but had subsequently linked this to environmental concerns and a variety of energy-reduction behaviours.

52   I tend to choose glass packaging over plastic for greater recyclability, though glass does consume more resources to transport. I telecommute, so I'm not burning gas sitting in rush hour traffic every day. I bought a less luxurious car than my previous one because it gets 50% better mileage. I keep my thermostat at 65 during the cold season and don't heat rooms that aren't used much, including my guest bedroom.

53   These data suggest that for both health and ethical vegetarians, environmental concerns had become important, even though they were not the initial motivation for their dietary choices. Particularly for vegan participants, both human and animal health became located within a nexus of efforts to lead a lifestyle that contributed positively to the environment. The "environmentally-friendly" aspects of vegetarianism also often linked implicitly with a range of other non-diet behaviours concerning environmental protection.

Discussion

54   Among the 33 respondents in this study, 2 distinct initial motivations for vegetarianism have been identified: personal health and animal welfare. Our qualitative study used purposive sampling, so we cannot generalise the proportions in these categories from our data. However, a recent straw poll of members of the VegForum concerning initial motivations indicated that out of 67 respondents, 45% had originally become vegetarian for ethical reasons, 27% for health reasons, 1% for environment reasons, and the

remainder for reasons including aesthetics (look, taste or smell of meat) and religion. Our data provide qualitative support for these trends. First, health is a significant motivator, both in terms of reducing symptoms of illness or discomfort, and as a preventive measure to avoid a range of minor and major illnesses. Second, ethical reasons concerning animal welfare motivate a further proportion of vegetarians, based both upon affective and philosophical reasons. Only one of our respondents (Simon) indicated environmentalism as a primary motivation.

55   Importantly, this study provides direct access to vegetarians' own descriptions of their routes into vegetarianism using qualitative responses to the original questions and the open-ended follow-up interviews. These data provide insights into how vegetarians think about their dietary choices and allow them to reflect on the reasoning that led them to their decisions. The lack of respondents citing environmental concerns as a primary motivation for vegetarianism, both in our data and in the VegForum straw poll helps refine findings from previous studies. For example, Kalof et al.'s (1999) quantitative study of 22 vegetarians found that belief that a vegetarian diet was better for the environment was the only significant variable predicting whether a respondent was vegetarian. Our data would suggest that these views concerning the environmental benefits of vegetarianism may be subsequent to, and a consequence of, a decision to avoid meat, rather than the cause of this dietary choice.

56   Our data also provide support to, and extend the notion of food choice trajectories developed by Devine et al. (1998) and discussed in relation to vegetarianism by Jabs et al. (1998). Our findings suggest that the trajectories that vegetarians follow show both continuity and development over time. Dietary choices may develop from eating organic food to partial vegetarianism, through ovo-lacto vegetarianism to veganism, and this was true for both health and ethical vegetarians in our study.

57   However, an initial health or ethical motivation may often be a starting point for a conceptual generalisation. Michael, a health vegetarian, subsequently adopted a wide range of environmentalist behaviours that had distanced him from his friends. Tom, on the other hand, began his trajectory as an ethical vegetarian but subsequently added health and the environment to his list of reasons. These subsequent commitments may be cognitive or affective strategies to bolster an initial decision, or may be a consequence of research or discussions with other vegetarians. In some instances, these build into a "lifestyle" in which behaviour is a manifestation of an underpinning philosophy that may encompass various "alternative" commitments within which vegetarianism is embedded. A number of our respondents (for example Naomi and Michael) self-consciously acknowledged that the totality of their beliefs and practices constituted a significant deviancy from mainstream behaviours.

58   Our findings indicate that an important element of the vegetarian trajectory is the incorporation into the practice and beliefs of respondents of a number of broader environmental commitments. While the non-representative nature of the sample precludes absolute assessments of what proportion of vegetarians hold such views, the data suggest these are not uncommon. For both ethical and health vegetarians, these commitments ranged from the use of organic food (which we may conjecture is at least in part motivated by health concerns) through to a variety of activities that contribute to an "environmentally-friendly" lifestyle. Some of these are not directly associated with diet or even with animal welfare, but appear to indicate a general concern for how human beings impact upon their environment. In this

context, vegetarianism may become part of a wider perspective in which humans are detrimentally affecting life on the planet: the dietary choice is one element of a wider concern to redress this negative impact. Although this environmentalism is not a primary motivator for vegetarianism, it may emerge as part of a generalisation of a narrower original focus, perhaps as a consequence of rationalisations of behaviour, as adoptees of a minority dietary choice seek additional reasons for their decision, or as they are exposed to the views of others within a vegetarian "community of practice" (Bisogni et al., 2002; Jabs et al., 1998). There may also be convergence between the "deviant" behaviour of avoiding meat (Kenyon & Barker, 1998; Lea & Worsley, 2001) and other lifestyle commitments including energy conservation and waste reduction, which have until recently been regarded as radical or alternative.

59   A qualitative study of this sort has some limitations in terms of its representativeness, and this is compounded by the sampling technique: the online forum is likely to over-represent younger vegetarians, and will not adequately sample non-English speakers. Nor is it possible to quantify proportions, for example, of health and ethical vegetarians that adopt behaviours in relation to environmental concerns. Quantitative research is required to establish whether there is a link between specific initial motivation and subsequent environment elaboration of motivations

and behaviours. Despite these limitations, the study identifies links between dietary choices and the wider commitments that people hold, and this finding suggests that research on dietary choice can benefit from exploring the related beliefs and behaviours of respondents.

60   We can conclude that motivations for vegetarianism are complex, following trajectories that broaden, both in terms of behaviours but also values, outlook or lifestyle. This finding refines Lindeman and Sirelius' (2001) argument that health and ethical vegetarians have dissimilar ideological underpinning. While this may be true to an extent (and our research confirms the divergences between these groups), many of the "health vegetarians" in our study also adopted ethical and environmental commitments subsequently. Convergence between these groups may thus be more common than indicated in previous studies, and suggests that not only do values and beliefs affect behaviour, as noted by previous researchers (Jabs et al., 1998; Kenyon & Barker, 1998; Lindeman & Sirelius, 2001; Willetts, 1997), but that behaviour may subsequently influence attitudes and beliefs, in turn leading to further behavioural changes. As environmental concerns become more pervasive in society, vegetarianism may become increasingly embedded within such commitments, even if environmentalism does not itself become a prime motivation for a meat-free diet.

References

Adams, C. J. (1990). *The sexual politics of meat: A feminist–vegetarian critical theory*, London: Continuum.

Allen Fox, M. (1999). The contribution of vegetarianism to ecosystem health. *Ecosystem Health, 5*, 70–74.

American Dietetic Association. (2003). Position of the American Dietetic Association and Dieticians of Canada: Vegetarian diets. *Journal of the American Dietetic Association, 103*, 748–765.

Barr, S., & Chapman, G. E. (2002). Perceptions and practices of self-defined current vegetarian, former vegetarian and non-vegetarian. *Journal of the American Dietetic Association, 102*, 354–360.

Beardsworth, A., & Keil, T. (1992). The vegetarian option: Varieties, conversions, motives, and careers. *Sociological Review, 40*, 251–293.

Bedford, J. L., & Barr, S. I. (2005). Diets and selected lifestyle practices of self defined adult vegetarians from a population-based sample suggest they are more "health conscious." *International Journal of Behavioral Nutrition and Physical Activity, 2,* 4–14.

Bisogni, C. A., Connors, M., Devine, C. M., & Sobal, J. (2002). Who we are and how we eat: A qualitative study of identities in food choice. *Journal of Nutrition Education and Behavior, 34,* 128–139.

Chen, P., & Hinton, S. M. (1999). Realtime interviewing using the World Wide Web. *Sociological Research Online, 4*(3). Retrieved from http://www.socresonline.org.uk/socresonline/4/3/ chen.html

Coveney, J. (2000). *Food, morals and meaning: The pleasure and anxiety of eating.* London: Routledge.

Devine, C. M., Connors, M., Bisogni, C. A., & Sobal, J. (1998). Life course influences on fruit and vegetable trajectories: Qualitative analysis of food choices. *Journal of Nutrition Education and Behavior, 30,* 361–370.

Fessler, D. M. T., Arguello, A, P., Mekdara, J. M., & Macias, R. (2003). Disgust sensitivity and meat consumption: A test of an emotivist account of moral vegetarianism. *Appetite, 41,* 312–341.

Fox, N. J., & Ward, K. (2006). Health identities: From expert patient to resisting consumer. *Health, 10,* 461–479.

Fox, N. J., & Ward, K. (submitted for publication). Vegetarianism, health and identity. *Social Science & Medicine.*

Fraser, G. E. (2003). *Diet, life expectancy and chronic disease.* Oxford: Oxford University Press.

Gaard, G. (2002). Vegetarian eco-feminism: A review essay. *Frontiers, 23,* 117–146.

Glaser, J., Dixit, J., & Green, D. P. (2002). Studying hate crime with the Internet: What makes racists advocate racial violence? *Journal of Social Issues, 58,* 177–193.

Hamilton, M. B. (1993). Wholefoods and healthfoods: Beliefs and attitudes. *Appetite, 20,* 223–228.

Henning, J. (2005). *Nothing old can stay.* Perseus Development Corporation. Retrieved from http://perseus.com/blogsurvey/blog/051223agerange.html

Hewson, C., Yule, P., Laurent, D., & Vogel, C. (2003). *Internet research methods.* London: Sage.

Hoek, A. C., Luning, P. A., Stafleu, A., & de Graaf, C. (2004). Food-related lifestyle and health of Dutch vegetarians, non-vegetarian consumers of meat substitutes, and meat consumers. *Appetite, 42,* 265–272.

Illingworth, N. (2001). The Internet matters: Exploring the use of the Internet as a research tool.

Sociological Research Online, 6(2). Retrieved from http://www.socresonline.org.uk/6/2/illingworth.html

Jabs, J., Devine, C., & Sobal, J. (1998). Model of the process of adopting diets: Health vegetarians and Ethical vegetarians. *Journal of Nutrition Education, 30,* 196–202.

Kalof, L., Dietz, T., Stern, P. C., & Guagnano, G. A. (1999). Social psychological and structural influences on vegetarian beliefs. *Rural Sociology, 64,* 500–511.

Kenyon, P. M., & Barker, M. E. (1998). Attitudes towards meat eating in vegetarians and non-vegetarian teenage girls in England—An ethnographic approach. *Appetite, 30,* 185–198.

Key, T., Appleby, P. N., & Rosell, M. S. (2006). Health effects of vegetarian and vegan diets. *Proceedings of the Nutrition Society, 65,* 35–41.

Kim, H. J., & Houser, R. F. (1999). Two small surveys, 25 years apart, investigating motivations of dietary choice in 2 groups of vegetarians in the Boston area. *Journal of the American Dietetic Association, 99,* 598–601.

Lea, E., & Worsley, A. (2001). Influences on meat consumption in Australia. *Appetite, 36,* 127–136.

Lindeman, M., & Sirelius, M. (2001). Food choice ideologies: The modern manifestations of normative and humanist views of the world. *Appetite, 37,* 175–184.

Nosek, B. A., Banaji, M. R., & Greenwald, A. G. (2002). E-research: Ethics, security, design, and control in psychological research on the Internet. *Journal of Social Issues, 58*(1), 161–176.

Phillips, F. (2005). Vegetarian nutrition. *Nutrition Bulletin, 30,* 132–197.

Pope, C., Zeibland, S. & Mays, N. (2000). Qualitative research in health care: Analysing qualitative data. *British Medical Journal, 320,* 114–116.

Povey, A., Wellens, B., & Conners, M. (2001). Attitudes towards following meat, vegetarian and vegan diets: An examination of the role of ambivalence. *Appetite, 37,* 15–26.

Rozin, P., Markwith, M., & Stoess, C. (1997). Moralization and becoming a vegetarian: The transformation of preferences into values and the recruitment of disgust. *Psychological Science, 8,* 67–73.

Santos, M. L. S., & Booth, D. (1996). Influences on meat avoidance among British students. *Appetite, 27,* 197–205.

Sobal, J., Bisogni, C. A., Devine, C. M., & Jastran, M. (2006). A conceptual model of food choice process over the life course. In R. Shepherd, & M. Raats

(Eds.), *The psychology of food choice* (pp. 1–18). Wallingford: CABI.

Thomsen, S. R., Straubaar, J. D., & Bolyard, D. M. (1998). Ethnomethodology and the study of online communities: Exploring the cyber streets. *Information Research, 4*(1). Retrieved from http://informationr.net.ezproxy.library.uvic.ca/ir/4–1/paper50.html

Whorton, J. (1994). Historical development of vegetarianism. *American Journal of Clinical Nutrition, 59,* 1103–1109.

Willetts, A. (1997). Bacon sandwiches got the better of me: Meat eating and vegetarianism in South East London. In P. Caplan (Ed.), *Food, health and identity* (pp. 111–130). London: Routledge.

Wilson, S. M., Weatherall, A., & Butler, C. (2004). A rhetorical approach to discussions about health and vegetarianism. *Journal of Health Psychology, 9,* 567–581.

Comprehension

1. What are the advantages of using "Internet-mediated methods"? (par. 8); what are the drawbacks (par. 9)? What step have the authors taken to help minimize the drawbacks for their study?

2. Summarize the last paragraph in the Results section (par. 53).

Structure and Organization

1. Which of the questions *who, what, why, when, where,* and *how* are addressed in the title and abstract?

2. Identify the topic of each paragraph in the literature review section of the Introduction.

3. In the Results section, how have the authors attempted to increase reader comprehension? Analyze their strategies and their success in achieving this objective.

4. Taking one paragraph from the Discussion section, explain how the authors synthesize the findings of their study with other sources—for example, other research studies.

Critical Thinking

1. An experimental study often includes a hypothesis at the end of the introduction. Why do you think the authors of this study did not do so?

2. Why might the qualitative method of interviews have been a good choice in order to explore subjects' motivations? What are some limitations of this method?

3. Compare one section of this study with one section of "He Loves Me, He Loves Me Not," (p. 358), a quantitative research study. Include at least two bases of comparison, such as length, use of sources, aids for comprehension, organization, etc. (Compare the Methods, Results, or Discussion sections, not the Introductions.)

Generational Perspectives

Although the term "generation gap" was popularized in the 1960s, it resonates in many different ways for today's formative generations, often referred to as "Gen(eration) X" and "Gen(eration) Y." "Generation Spend," an expository essay, and "Generation Debt," an argumentative essay, focus on economic realities, each proposing solutions to the current indebtedness of young Canadians. The author of "Generation Velcro," a member of Generation X, puts forth the provocative claim that the technological literacy of Generation Y comes with a high price, possibly its very survival. Controversial too is the thesis of the authors of "Vancouver Hockey Riot Is a Symptom of a Larger Problem"—that the response of some youths to the Vancouver Canucks 2011 Stanley Cup final game loss stems from feelings of hopelessness, the legacy of previous generations. The author of the personal essay "Flush" uses an unexpected image—the toilet—to "bridge" the generation gap, seamlessly and humorously juxtaposing past and present while touching on topics as diverse as censorship and genetic engineering.

Finally, the academic essays in this section examine generational choices and their consequences. The authors of the caustic editorial "Canadian Lifestyle Choices: A Public Health Failure" assert that the federal government's health policies have helped create an overweight, unhealthy generation of Canadians. "Delayed Transitions of Young Adults" uses current statistics to explain trends in 18–34-year-olds at key moments in their lives, such as leaving home and entering the work force, contrasting them with the choices of the previous generation and speculating on the reasons for the differences.

Erica Alini, "Generation Spend"

"Generation Spend" was part of a series that appeared in the business section of *Maclean's* magazine.

 Preparing to Read

1. If you are unfamiliar with the reality TV show *Til Debt Do Us Part*, do a search to determine the show's purpose and premise.
2. How would you describe your own spending and saving habits? How do they differ—if at all—from those of your friends and family? Are you concerned about your financial future? What circumstances might influence that concern?

Generation Spend

Erica Alini

Maclean's, 8 November 2010
(1161 words)

1   "If I want something I want it, no matter what," says Kezia, one of the protagonists of a new Slice TV series *Princess*, where *Til Debt Do Us Part* host Gail Vaz-Oxlade tries to put young, female serial shoppers through personal finance rehab. A makeup artist who normally makes "probably" around $30,000 a year, Kezia would shed up to $355 a month on her hairdo, and eat out "probably" four times a week. "I don't ever look at my credit card statements," the pretty (dyed) blond says, gazing dreamingly at the camera. "As soon as they come, I throw them away."

2   Twenty-five-year-old Kezia belongs to a new species of consumer whose capacity to spend will surpass that of the boomers sometime in the next decade. Variously referred to as Generation Y or Generation Next, they are loosely defined as the age group going from kids in their early teens to young adults. In the U.S., eight- to 24-year-olds are expected to spend $224 billion of their projected $348 billion annual income, according to Harris Interactive, a market research and consulting firm. Yet the percentage of those who have no savings at all is over 50 per cent. The stats in Canada are equally troubling. For young adults, the proportion between the ages of 25 and 34 who say they are impulsive spenders and can't save is 30 per cent, a figure very similar to the 31 per cent found among the so-called Generation X (or 35- to 49-year-olds), according to a recent study by the Royal Bank of Canada.

3   The recession was supposed to teach some important lessons about saving and living frugally, but Generation Y seems poised to fall into similar spending habits that left their parents with crippling debt. Whereas the financial crisis raised the national savings rate in the U.S. from a low of less than two per cent in 2007 to over eight per cent in mid-2009 (it is now at around five per cent), in Canada it edged up from 2.8 per cent on average three years ago to a still very modest 4.4 per cent overall this year. Despite this small effort to repair household balance sheets, four in 10 Canadians say they struggle to put a nickel in the piggy bank, according to RBC. It's an unsettling trend for those preaching financial good sense.

4   How then to raise a breed of conscientious spenders and good savers (if not by example)? Part of the answer, say experts, is coming from financial institutions trying to stage a digital catch-up to the marketing industry that has so effectively targeted young spenders. Most savings products, says Dilip Soman at the University of Toronto's Rotman School of Management, have "supremely boring advertising." On the other end of the spectrum of the battle for young wallets, however, are marketing firms with a sophisticated arsenal of advertising tools. Their methods range from social networking sites like Facebook and Twitter to guerrilla-style campaigns that use the power of peer pressure to encourage spending, (In one campaign for Neutrogena, for example, 4000 high school girls were recruited to work as "brand evangelizers," pitching the product to classmates and friends in exchange for prizes including concert tickets.)

5   Simple financial behaviours like saving, or making rational decisions about limited resources, must be embedded in a language young people understand—the same language that speaks to them about PlayStations and Coach

bags, say experts. A group of U.S. researchers has had good results, for instance, by having young people interact with digital, retirement-age avatars of themselves as they make hypothetical savings decisions. In one case study, the expression on the avatars' faces would display a smile or an unhappy grimace depending on the positive or negative impact of the savings decisions on the participants' future financial situation. In all cases, the study says, participants who interacted with their aged avatars showed a greater propensity to forgo the instant pleasure of spending for the delayed pleasure of having and using savings in the future.

6   Another way to go about this is finding "smart ways of leveraging social networking," says Alessandro Previtero at the University of Western Ontario's Richard Ivey School of Business. He says young people might find it easier to set and reach financial targets if they use something like StickK.com, a website designed by a team at Yale that helps people achieve their goals (from losing weight to quitting smoking) by, among other things, getting their friends involved. Much like friends on Facebook, supporters on StickK.com receive regular updates on status changes—in this case, a person's progress toward the stated goal. If constructive use of peer pressure helps people shed their extra pounds or their pack of cigarettes, it could also help them save, says Previtero.

7   And whether the lesson comes from social networking or old-fashioned parenting, teaching youngsters how to set financial goals is key, says Patricia Domingo, an investment retirement planner at RBC. She recalls setting up a savings account and a guaranteed investment certificate for a 15-year-old who made $8000 designing and selling a website. The parents, she said, sat

him face to face with the family financial adviser so he'd be forced to think about what he should do with the money.

8   Other healthy practices, says Greg Holohan, an investment executive at ScotiaMcLeod, include openly discussing family income, utility bills and even investment strategies with the kids; encouraging them to use their allowance or summer job money to pay for some of their needs; and refusing to pay for everything. A good strategy, he says, might also be to tell the young ones that they have to pay for part of their college and university costs, but then reward them afterwards by paying them back and giving them a tidy sum to start with as they enter the job market.

9   Deborah Beedie, an account executive in Dundas, Ont., thinks she got it right. "Our kids can probably tell you how much we make, what we have in terms of investments and what bills come up when," she says of sons Michael, 20, and Scott, 14. Whenever Scott gets his weekly allowance of $14 (one dollar per every year since he was born), he has to decide how much to put in one of three jars labelled "savings," "spending" and "other." Michael, a junior at Dalhousie University, had tuition, books and rent paid for, but must use summer job money to sustain his social life and contribute to food expenses. Apparently, he now has the grocery store mapped out according to product pricing and won't even go near the middle of the alley where, he says, the more expensive stuff is on display.

10   Whether it's trying to protect your kid from slick online marketing or the corner street dealer, says Beedie, all you can do is "have a value system that you can transmit"—leave the kids autonomy but know what they're up to, and hope for the best.

Comprehension, Structure, and Organization

1. Identify two compare–contrast paragraphs and summarize the content of one of them.
2. What kinds of experts does the writer focus on for support? Take one expert and analyze his/her contribution to the essay.
3. Analyze one paragraph, considering how the writer's strategies increase comprehension and readability.

Critical Thinking

1. Do you think Kezia (pars. 1–2) is a good representative of the Generation Y consumer? Why or why not?
2. Of the various solutions to make Generation Y consumers more financially responsible, which do you believe is the most promising? Give reasons to justify your answer.
3. Compare and contrast "Generation Spend" with "Generation Debt," below, using at least two bases of comparison.

Alethea Spiridon, "Generation Debt"

Writers of argumentative essays and, occasionally, of expository essays, may make limited use of personal experience. If the purpose is to reveal their involvement with the topic in order to better explain the issue or to enable readers to relate to the experience, using the first-person voice can be an effective argumentative strategy.

Preparing to Read

As a student, are you concerned about heavy debt after your graduation?

Generation Debt

What's the real cost of knowledge?

Alethea Spiridon

Briarpatch Magazine, 1 September 2009
(881 words)

> Education costs money, but then so
> does ignorance.
> —Sir Claus Moser

1   In 1992, I was a high school graduate enrolled in studies at the University of Saskatchewan. Post-secondary education had never been a can-do for me—it was always a must-do. My family was entrenched in middle-class mediocrity, my dad a high school teacher and my mother a stay-at-home mom. The only means of financing an education was through government-funded student loans, but according to the loan assessor that year, my father, the sole

breadwinner of the family, earned too much (at $45,000 per year) for me to qualify for assistance. He managed to fund that initial year; the next six years of study—four university, two college—were my responsibility. If I wanted the education I felt I needed to secure some kind of reasonable career and livelihood, I, like so many other students, would have to take on thousands of dollars in debt.

2   Education is increasingly thought to be for the good of the individual rather than for the greater good of society—a belief that has made it politically acceptable to place the bulk of education costs squarely on the shoulders of the students seeking that education. The cost of a year's tuition for a full-time Canadian undergraduate arts student has skyrocketed in recent years, from $1800, to $2400 in 1995, to $4700 in 2008—an increase of 260 per cent over the past 16 years. The result is increasing social stratification, as students from lower- and middle-class backgrounds, who can't pay up front, either take on long-term debt, if they qualify, or simply don't pursue further education.

3   The total Canada Student Loans debt surpassed $13 billion in January of this year, and continues rising at a rate of $1.2 million per day. These numbers don't include provincial student loans, bank loans, or credit card charges. The average cost of attending university, including tuition and living expenses, is now more than $12,000 per year. According to Statistics Canada, the average student debt for a Bachelor's degree is just shy of $25,000, and $15,000 for college. One in four student-loan-carrying graduates has reported difficulty in repaying their loans, with about 30 per cent defaulting on payments.

4   The consequences of such debt burdens on graduates' lives are significant, limiting their choices in all kinds of ways. Student loan obligations, according to Katherine Giroux-Bougard,

National Chairperson of the Canadian Federation of Students (CFS), reduce a new graduate's ability to "start a family, invest in other assets, buy a house, do career-building volunteer work, or take lower-paying jobs in their field to get a foot in the door." Other consequences of high student loan debt, Giroux-Bougard says, are "that some people will choose to not attend post-secondary education at all or will choose to not attend some programs."

5   When professional programs were deregulated in Ontario in 1998, explains Giroux-Bougard, many people from rural areas and low-income families were shut out. Statistics Canada reports that between 1995/1996 and 2001/2002, tuition fees rose by 168 per cent in dentistry, 132 per cent in medicine and 61 per cent in law, compared to a 34 per cent overall increase for all undergraduate programs in Canada. Many capable students from lower- and middle-income families are unable to consider such professions because they simply can't afford the tuition.

6   The Canada Student Grants Program, introduced in last year's federal budget, which was put forward in response to the outcry for more post-secondary financial support, is a victory for the CFS's "Grants NOT Loans" campaign. The Program provides needs-based bursaries throughout a student's years of studies (in monthly amounts of $250 for low-income students and $100 for middle-income students) to offset rising student debts.

7   Giroux-Bougard believes this is a good start. "The Federation has been calling for this for years. Canada is one of two countries in the world that does not have a program of grants. It is a first and important step for the government to take." Giroux-Bougard is now calling on the government to add more money to those grants and to the Canada Social Transfer payments to the provinces, thus reducing the share of

post-secondary costs borne directly by students. Government operating grants made up 80 per cent of university operating revenues in 1990. By 2007, that had fallen to 57 per cent.

8   I turned 35 in June and am only now nearing the retirement of my massive student debt of $73,000, of which roughly $21,000 is accumulated interest. According to the latest National Graduates Survey (2007), 56 per cent of graduates financed a post-secondary education by taking out loans.

9   Are post-secondary institutions merely selling high-priced degrees, diplomas and certificates to those who can afford them, or are these institutions serving a greater good by advancing knowledge and promoting creative and critical thinking? By placing the burden of paying for higher education on the student, our society is saying there is little social good or intrinsic value in an educated citizenry; it is the individual who benefits, not society as a whole. Therefore, the student pays.

10   Treating education like a luxury good impoverishes everyone. A society that recognizes the social value of an educated population should also recognize the public obligation to fund it. As Giroux-Bougard says, "Saddling a generation of students with billions in debt will have far-reaching implications for Canada's economy and socio-economic inequality."

Comprehension

1. What has the government done to support post-secondary students and what, according to Giroux-Bougard, should the government do to further decrease the financial burden of students?

2. Using a reliable source, summarize the aims of the Canadian Federation of Students (par. 4).

Structure and Organization

1. What is the reason for beginning the essay with the first-person perspective? Why does the writer return to this perspective in paragraph 8?

2. What kinds of evidence are used in the essay (see Chapter 1, "Kinds of Evidence," p. 16, and Chapter 4, "Kinds of Evidence in Argumentative Essays," pp. 46–49)? Briefly justify their use, analyzing what they contribute to the essay.

Critical Thinking

1. Whom do you believe Spiridon is writing to? In addition to the essay itself—its diction, tone, and rhetorical strategies, for example—consider where it is published: *Briarpatch* (http://briarpatchmagazine.com/about).

2. Compare and contrast "Generation Debt" with "Generation Spend," p. 200, using at least two bases of comparison.

Dorothy Woodend, "Generation Velcro"

"Generation Velcro" is an "opinion piece"; its author uses personal experience and other evidence to express a viewpoint. To use personal experience successfully when writing for an audience, the writer must generalize from the personal situation to one that is relevant to individual readers. Journalistic writers often begin with a "hook"—a technique to "catch" the reader's interest, such as asking a question or relating an anecdote. Having intrigued the reader, the author can apply the question or anecdote to universal issues like technological dependency and parental responsibility. In "Generation Velcro," Woodend skilfully employs an appealing style and occasional humour to highlight her serious concerns about today's youth.

However, the writer of an argument may sometimes oversimplify or otherwise not reveal all sides to an issue. The critical thinker should test assumptions and evaluate all the evidence when reading a journalistic essay—indeed, all essays in which argument is involved—before reaching a conclusion about the truth or validity of the argument.

▶ Preparing to Read

1. Do you believe that our society is too dependent on technology? Could you get by with less technology in your life? Using these questions as a prompt, freewrite for five minutes.
   OR
2. List the pros and cons of current technology in people's lives. Share your list with another student's and discuss one or two of the specific items on each list.

Generation Velcro

It's hell, but it builds character.
What will become of the children who
could not tie their shoes?

Dorothy Woodend

The Tyee, 21 November 2008
(1262 words)

1   The other day I took my seven-year-old son Louis to buy some running shoes. "Pick something with Velcro," I said, as he trotted off to roam the racks.

2   A clerk, hovering nearby, gave me a jaundiced look: "You know we get high school kids in here who have to buy Velcro because they never learned to tie their shoes. Every year their parents would just buy them Velcro because it was easier than making them learn how to tie laces."

3   I stared at him and he went on.

4   "The other day we had to special order a pair of shoes for this kid's high school graduation because he couldn't tie his laces, and he needed a pair of Velcro formal shoes."

5   I put the shoes Louis had chosen back on the shelf, and picked out a pair of lace-up

running shoes. It wasn't just that I'd been shamed into compliance by the salesman, but something Jane Jacobs had written about in her last book about the coming dark ages hit home. The loss of knowledge, she said, once vanished, is so difficult to regain—even if it's something as mundane as tying your shoes.

6   In case you think this episode is an isolated example, the other day I heard a youth worker, whose job it is to help teens at risk, say that almost none of them know how to tie their shoes. I'm sure this isn't a causal relationship—wear Velcro, go to jail—but it made me think. What else have we lost, or failed to pass along, to the generation of kids about to inherit an increasingly compromised planet?

7   Is this generation heading into a coming dark age with little more than the ability to update their Facebook statuses and watch Youtube, all with laces untied?

Failing memories

8   When I talk to my mother, ensconced on her farm in the Kootenays, about people quietly preparing for coming disaster, she says the first thing people in her neighbourhood say is "Well, my freezer is full." Then they metaphorically pat themselves on the back for having the forethought to freeze a supply of broccoli and peaches.

9   "But what happens if the power goes off?" I ask.

10   She shrugs and says, "The one thing I'm worried about is being able to get seeds." (In case you didn't know, Monsanto has been quietly buying up heritage seed companies for the past while.) Then she says, "I'm thinking about starting a farm school." I tell her it's not a bad idea.

11   In the *Vancouver Sun*, Meeru Dhalwala recently wrote a column about wanting to start a vegetable garden, but not having even the slightest notion of where to start. For those of us even just a generation removed from the family farm, already the loss of knowledge is enormous. I don't know how to butcher an animal, build a house or make my own soap, although my grandparents certainly did. To a lesser extent my mother still does. If I told my son to go outside, start a fire and cook himself some food, he wouldn't have the very first clue.

12   While this generation can text-message, download, update and surf online simultaneously, this constant deluge of information is in fact something of a mirage. Information is not knowledge, nor even close to wisdom. And it is actually getting harder to learn and remember things. In *The Overflowing Brain*, Torkel Klingberg, a professor of cognitive neuroscience at Sweden's Karolinska Institute writes, "If we do not focus our attention on something, we will not remember it." The inability to concentrate in a world of competing bits of information and constant multitasking have led to brains that can no longer keep up. Suddenly, I see why a podcaster has sought out my mother's repository of practical knowledge.

13   "We're counting on you, old lady," I tell her.

Is our society "self aware"?

14   In North America now, less than two per cent of people call themselves farmers and the median age of farmers in Canada is already pushing mid-50s. What happens when too many people who actually know stuff age and then buy the farm, as they say?

15   Which brings me back to the question that has me tied up in shoe knots.

16   If the lights start to go out sometime in the near future, and the Walmart closes its doors, who would really be useful? The answer changes, but basically it comes down to people who know how to do things—farmers, carpenters, doctors—people with a body of knowledge that can be applied directly, physically to the real world. It certainly won't be film critics or bond traders.

17   In *Dark Age Ahead*, Jane Jacobs writes that, "A society must be self-aware. Any culture that jettisons the values that have given it competence, adaptability and identity becomes weak and hollow."

18   James Kunstler shares Jacobs' dim view of the North American future, but he apparently has even less hope for the ability of the current population to do the work that needs doing. Kunstler writes often about the great tattooed, hedonistic, neo-Darwinian masses of Americans, who bear almost no resemblance to the hard-working, industrious people of the 1930s, who, when FDR announced his plans to turn the nation around, basically set to the task at hand.

19   I keep coming back to Kunstler's operatic outpourings of fury and despair, maybe because there is a bitter tang of something that isn't even approached in mainstream media. Kunstler opines that Americans in the 1930s and '40s bear little resemblance to the current crop, and if required to roll up their sleeves and dig ditches, they might not be up to task.

20   My grandfather came of age in the Great Depression. His mother died of cancer when he was seven years old, and he basically went to work at the age of 12. The same is true of my grandmother, who never made it past Grade 7 because she had to cook meals in the rooming house run by her mother. Their lives and their stories are unremarkable in some ways, in that they weren't all that unusual. They were born to work and they spent their entire lives doing just that, farming, day in and out, merely to survive. They were almost completely self-sufficient, both in food and in skills.

Life without Velcro

21   Louis, on the other hand, along with all of his Velcro-shod video game playing friends, has been kept safely inside since he was born. He is probably ill-prepared for the world if it becomes much more harsh. Am I, then, a failure? If your first impulse is always to protect your children, are you actually doing them a disservice? If suffering breeds character, does a complete lack of suffering foster utter helplessness?

22   This is why the public imagination was seized by the tragic story of 15-year-old Brandon Crisp, who ran away after a fight with his parents about video games. How could a young boy die so easily? Brandon discovered in the most terrible way that the real world bears little resemblance to a video game. It gets dark and cold, and if you fall out of a tree, you die.

23   Every day, while Louis struggles with his laces, wailing that he can't do it and I should do it for him, I say: "You need to learn to do this yourself; you can't depend on anyone to do it for you."

24   My own words echo oddly inside my brain, already assuming some larger meaning. It is as much my responsibility to teach him, as it is his to learn.

Structure, Organization, and Style

1. Identify Woodend's thesis, commenting on the specific form it takes.
2. Discuss Woodend's tone (attitude toward her subject, see p. 134), referring to specific passages.
3. Comment on Woodend's use of personal experience. You could consider its use in her introduction and conclusion and/or its use to support a point or provide a transition.

Critical Thinking/Research

1. Respond to or critically analyze one of the following statements from the essay:
   a. "The inability to concentrate in a world of competing bits of information and constant multitasking have led to brains that can no longer keep up" (par. 12)
   b. "If suffering breeds character, does a complete lack of suffering foster utter helplessness?" (par. 21).
2. Using reliable sources, discuss the significance of (a) Jane Jacobs (pars. 5 and 17) or (b) James Howard Kunstler (pars. 18–19) to Woodend's essay. Include a short biography that addresses Jacobs's or Kunstler's credibility and show how Woodend uses her or him to support her points.
3. Analyze Woodend's argument, considering argumentative strategies, use of evidence, and reasoning. Refer specifically to the text for support.

Adrian Mack and Miranda Nelson, "Vancouver Hockey Riot Is a Symptom of a Larger Problem"

This essay was published in *The Georgia Straight* the day after riots following the loss of the Vancouver Canucks in the final game of the 2011 Stanley Cup finals. The essay was one of many attempts of a shocked community to account for the behaviour of some of its citizens.

Billing itself as Canada's Largest Urban Weekly, *The Georgia Straight* focuses on social and cultural issues, often with a youth-oriented slant. Beginning as an "underground" newspaper, it has recently won several awards for its news and investigative features. Another essay on the same incident, " "Big Brother, *C'est Moi*," is on p. 246.

Preparing to Read

Using objective, reliable sources, summarize the events surrounding the riot and its aftermath.

Vancouver Hockey Riot Is a Symptom of a Larger Problem

Adrian Mack and Miranda Nelson

The Georgia Straight, 16 June 2011
(1172 words)

1   We've heard a lot of reasons (excuses?) batted around as to why last night's post-Cup riot happened. A very outraged man on the radio this morning blamed the whole thing on faulty parenting. Others look at the idiocy of city politicians for inviting 100,000 people into the downtown core, TransLink for ramping up service to a peninsula with limited escape routes, and the provincial order to close downtown liquor stores at 4 p.m., ensuring that those in attendance would be drunk before they even arrived. You can also look to the mainstream media for hyping up this series to unheard-of proportions and constantly reminding the populace of the infamous 1994 Stanley Cup riots.

2   But maybe what we have is just a sick culture. Maybe as a society, we've simply become borderline psychotic. You only need to ride a bus to see what an angry group of people we've become. We're rude, we're snotty, we don't talk or engage with each other. We've created the stupidest generation: a barely literate group of narcissists who don't know how to take care of themselves, but are like military-trained experts when it comes to tagging themselves in Facebook photos.

3   From all reports, there was a small group of young hooligans determined to riot and smash 'n' grab no matter what the outcome of the game was. Several sites have been set up to post pictures, Facebook screencaps, and video of morons proudly declaring their involvement in the violence. Should we be surprised? And doesn't it seem a little obvious that there was never going to be a good outcome, regardless of who won? At 4:30 p.m. the streets of the downtown core were already simmering with the dangerous and hair-trigger emotions of the mob, and all that emotion—good or bad—was going to be purged, somewhere, somehow. In the weeks leading up to the final, the magnitude of our bizarre, tribal attachment to a hockey team became more and more clear. And it exceeds far beyond a natural and healthy spirit of competitiveness or an appreciation of the beauty of the game itself. It's pathological. It's monstrously unhealthy. And it speaks to a monumental emptiness at the heart of our culture.

4   So, why are there so many hungry souls out there, ready and willing to bring chaos down on the so-called most liveable city on the planet? In reality, matters have only gotten much worse politically and economically since 1994, and Generation Y has been delivered into a beyond-callous world facing a perfect storm of crises. They know it. What does the future look like for the average 20 year old? It's a depressing, empty place where they can't get decent-paying (let alone secure) jobs or ever have a hope of owning property. Can you imagine how much more fearful and angry they would be if they fully comprehended the seriousness of peak oil?

5   And yet despite the terminal condition of a socio-economic superstructure hurtling towards the edge of a cliff while wondering if it even has enough gas to get there, the market rolls on, plundering the public coffers and starving the arts and education, producing a society that is spiritually malnourished but not sensitive enough to ask why. Meanwhile, we have dissonant messages relentlessly beamed into our heads: wealth is good, the poor have nobody but themselves to blame, personal devices make you happy, war is peace, "Save money, live better,"

Don Cherry deserves your attention and respect, and have some pride in your Canucks. Because what else have you got going for you?

6   The market practices institutional violence on every single one of us, every day, just by virtue of existing. It's not the game of hockey that's the problem; it's the capitalistic appropriation of our national pastime. It's the myriad of advertisers trotting out the "I am Canadian!" sentiments in order to sell products. It's the message we are force-fed that if we don't pay attention to the spectacle, we are somehow disenfranching ourselves. That's the way advertising has always worked: make people insecure about a fictional problem, and then sell them the fix.

7   This isn't to excuse the rioters, and we should remember and praise those who were there, and who resisted, and who did the right thing. There's a powerful clip on YouTube . . . of two men—one in a Canucks jersey, one not—trying to prevent assholes from smashing out the windows of the Bay downtown. They have some initial success, but then the non-jerseyed man pushes a rioter back and gets beaten for his efforts.

8   But we can't just blame a few "bad apples." This riot didn't happen on its own. Society as a whole ensured that it was the only outcome, starting with the assumption that our over-amped if not war-like passion for something as inconsequential as a hockey game is appropriate to begin with, let alone officially sanctioned. But hey, it's a . . . goldmine for advertisers and a hell of a vacuum to suck in a growing population of bored, distracted, disassociated, and quietly despairing Lower Mainlanders marinated in the hegemony of cheap sensation, and governed by institutions hostile to art, truth, and beauty. It's a problem that, as always, starts at the very top.

9   The wrong questions will inevitably get asked in the wake of all this, and the wrong solutions applied. Expect "tougher policing" and a ramped up culture of intolerance in a city that already turns a blind-eye to a tsunami of social ills. The VPD—which was quick to blame the violence on "criminals, anarchists, and thugs"—is encouraging anyone with high-resolution pictures to email them to the department, but is that really what we want to become? Yes, last night's violence was inexcusable and the offenders should be prosecuted, but the slope towards becoming a Big Brother-like society where we tattle on our neighbours is already slippery enough. Wouldn't it be preferable to live in a society in which we actually *knew* our neighbours to begin with? To know and trust the people around us to act like responsible individuals? To enjoy a culture of mutual respect rather than suspicion, hyper-competition, and meaningless interaction mediated through our phones and iPads? All we're doing right now is gawking at city-sanctioned spectacles—or plugging in our headphones so we can ignore each other.

10   There was a beautiful outpouring of love and support for our fair city this morning as hundreds of volunteers took to the streets to help clean up the terrible mess from last night. We do have the capacity to be kind, gentle, thoughtful individuals, and, hopefully, we can begin to repair the damage to our tarnished reputation. Unfortunately, there's no simple band-aid solution that will fix a sick society. The symptoms are clearly manifesting but, without facing up to the fact that there is an overarching problem, there is absolutely no chance for us to heal. But perhaps the first step towards solving this systemic problem is to acknowledge the fact that there is actually something wrong with us.

Comprehension

1. In your own words, explain the meaning of the following statement: "[A hockey game is] a . . . goldmine for advertisers and . . . a vacuum to suck in a growing population of bored, distracted, disassociated, and quietly despairing Lower Mainlanders marinated in the hegemony of cheap sensation, and governed by institutions hostile to art, truth, and beauty" (par. 8).

Structure, Organization, and Style

1. Comment on the authors' style and voice, paying particular attention to any possible biases and/or use of non-objective language.
2. Analyze the essay's final two paragraphs, showing whether they function as an effective conclusion to the authors' argument.

Critical Thinking/Research

1. Who or what do the authors ultimately blame for the riots? Discuss the accuracy and validity of their conclusions, referring to specific passages in the essay.
2. Respond to one of the following statements in the essay: "The market practices institutional violence on every single one of us, every day, just by virtue of existing" (par. 6); "[T]he terminal condition of [our] socio-economic superstructure . . . [has produced] a society that is spiritually malnourished but not sensitive enough to ask why" (par. 5).
3. Write a comparative rhetorical analysis of this essay and "Big Brother, *C'est Moi*," p. 246, ensuring that you use at least two bases of comparison.

Madeline Sonik, "Flush"

"Flush" is a personal essay, part of an essay collection that was nominated for two major non-fiction awards in 2011. Although it is ostensibly about the author's life, Sonik extends her vision beyond the personal to take in many larger issues relevant to her audience: like Ian Brown (see "I'm Glad I Never Had to Decide," p. 248), she enables us to question issues that affect us or those we know. Through juxtaposition, Sonik raises questions about technology, censorship, pollution, and generational stereotypes.

Although there are many differences between this essay and both journalistic and scholarly essays (beginning with its one-word title), there are also similarities; for example, like writers of scholarly and some journalistic essays, Sonik uses research. She seamlessly synthesizes facts and statistics with her personal narrative.

▶ **Preparing to Read**

Have you ever considered your life as a "story"? What would you include in such a story? What would you exclude? Why?

Flush

Madeline Sonik

Afflictions & Departures, 2011
(3980 words)

1   I arrived the year the toilet made its cinematic debut. Moments before the famous murder scene in Alfred Hitchcock's *Psycho*, Janet Leigh, the victim, flushes incriminating evidence down the loo. The first toilet to appear on the silver screen is strikingly white, and the flush strikingly loud. The appearance of this toilet is an indication of advancing times. Three years before, the commercial censors ban an episode of *Leave It to Beaver*, because a toilet bowl is shown. In 1960, I have not yet seen *Leave It to Beaver*, know nothing of June Cleaver's Princess dresses or her simple string of pearls. In the next few years, I will discover these things, but it will be decades before I understand the significance of the time into which I am born, this great evolutionary leap, this fundamental cultural turning point, and the way it will influence and shape my life. The year I am born is the year in which moving picture meets the appliance of moving bowel.

2   They say, "you can't go back," and although in 1960 I've never heard them say it, I already know my mother's uterus is out of reach to me, the pink, fleshy walls of her womb, the warm sack of fluid where I swam. I have been violently expelled from Eden, a wayfarer, a refugee, set in a cot, fed with a bottle, left to scream. And Janet Leigh flushes the toilet, and the flush sounds like death, like the first sound a baby hears when she enters the noisy, sordid world. But is the world any more sordid than it ever was? If only I had consulted my omniscience in those first few moments when I may have still been bound with heaven, perhaps I would have learned the reason I chose this moment to be born.

3   Fast forward 45 years: suffering from jet lag in England, unable to read or write, I switch on television. The program *No Angels* is playing. In the first 30 minutes, a drunken man shits his pants; a nurse has sex with a stranger in a car; and a young doctor experiences a premature ejaculation. In Canada, I have not watched TV for years, but I'm certain there's nothing comparable to this. Thirty-two years ago when I lived here, there was the lewd and bawdy *Benny Hill Show*, *George and Mildred*, and *Man About the House*. Having emigrated from North America, I was shocked by all of these programs with their blatant sexual and earthy content, though today I wouldn't even bat an eye if I saw them in Canada. Television "toilet humour" is what my father would have called it. And if he'd lived long enough to witness it, I imagine, he would have paid me, just as he had done with cigarette commercials, each time I switched such offending programs off.

4   It may be that Britain signals the shape of things to come for North American TV and cinema (Alfred Hitchcock was born in Leytonstone, London, after all), or it may be that all the continents of the world are on some kind of inevitable slippery slope. The censors refused to pass

Psycho, not because of the toilet, which was troubling enough, but because Janet Leigh's nipple was visible in the shower scene. Hitchcock didn't edit. He knew they wouldn't review the film again. He lingers in the bathroom, in a coming attraction teaser, gazing at the toilet, a master of suspense. When the white porcelain toilet flushes, the world changes. In Detroit, Michigan, in Crittenton General Hospital, there are women flushing toilets too. They have been routinely prepped and given enemas, some will soon be mothers for the first time; others, like my own, will have been through it all before. Obstetric ultrasound technology is in its infancy, so none of these women will know the sex of their children. The booties they have made and purchased are predominantly yellow. It will be six years before the foetal heart is "interrogated" and found to sound like "horses' hoofs when running" and another year before placental blood flow will be described as "rushing wind." It will be almost eight years before "the human eye pierces the 'black box' of the womb" and eighteen years before it's described this way in the foreword to an international ultrasound symposium proceeding. But in 1960, the human eye has long pierced the "idiot box." Ninety per cent of Americans have TV sets in their homes and watch programs like *Gunsmoke*, *My Three Sons* and, of course, *Alfred Hitchcock Presents*. In Britain, Granada TV launches *Coronation Street*. This will become the longest-running soap opera in the world and will remain the most popular show in England for over four decades.

5   Meanwhile, labouring women in North America are anaesthetized and sent into a haze of "twilight sleep"—these procedures numb their bodies, steal their minds and depress their infants. In 1960 it is better, simply, to forget—to accept amnesia with equanimity and afterwards be wheeled from delivery room to ward,

transferred to bed, and remain there, catheterised. Moving picture will not meet the appliance of moving bowel for the new mothers at Crittenton General, at least not yet, as ultrasonic foetus has still to make its real-time debut, and the paralysing drugs their bodies have absorbed will prevent anything resembling its natural functioning. When catheters are finally removed, these invalid mothers will still be bedridden. The only violent flush will be their crimson faces, as nurses slide bedpans under their sheets and encourage them to pee. Hitchcock once said, "The length of a film should be directly related to the endurance of the human bladder," but he said this not knowing the capacity of a mother's traumatized bladder to endure.

6   The portable television era began four years ago, and more than 500 television stations are broadcasting in the U.S., but few of these women have access to sets in the hospital. Instead, once they are mobile, they shuffle to the end of the long corridor, buy cigarettes from the dispensing machines, and painfully perch at the end of waiting room chairs to take in their favourite programs. These include soap operas like *The Edge of Night* and dramas like *Perry Mason*. Knowing the sex of their children now, friends and relatives have procured them appropriate coloured wool, so they can begin knitting gender-specific sweaters for their babies. They will speak to each other about their babies, gossip about other women, and drink prune juice by the gallon. They will watch commercials about *Spic and Span* and *Cheer*, and think about ways to get their homes, dishes, hair, husbands, laundry, children, pets and possessions really, really clean. Since the early 50's there has been an obsession with chemical cleanliness. Arrays of diverse cleansing products have mushroomed in the marketplace, and become increasingly specialized. For example, a farsighted company, knowing the toilet is

destined to come out of the water closet and need to be cleaned, has purchased *Ty-D-Bol* this year, but the famous little singing man in a boat, who serenades the goggled-eyed housewife from the bright blue tide waters, is only a glimmer in an ad man's eye. In 45 years, 70,000 new chemical compounds will have been dispersed into the world, and the *Ty-D-Bol* sailor moored, in spite of his popularity, and having nothing to do with water pollution. The toilet flushes, and the world changes. We have not yet begun to question the contents of what goes down the drain.

7   These new mothers at Crittenton General don't speculate. They smoke and chat about the here and now, about the nurseries they have assembled, about in-law problems. The environment consists only of hospital beds, tables and chairs, the pictures of babies on the walls. It is nine years before *Time* magazine runs its article on the chocolate-coloured Cuyahoga lake that has a history of spontaneous chemical combustion, and ten years before the first "Earth Day." In the future, historians will label this time "the gold rush" of nuclear reactors, when companies such as General Electric, Combustion Engineering, and Westinghouse are bursting to fill the world with the heat and light of nuclear fission, and almost everyone thinks it's a wonderful idea. Three Mile Island is nineteen years in the future, and no one in this hospital has ever even heard of the city of Chernobyl. But in England, there are still people who recall "the days of toxic darkness" when the combination of coal smoke and fog killed over 12,000. There are those who still reflect upon the creepy, insidious nature of this event that stole lives away, without anyone realizing until undertakers ran short of caskets and florists short on flowers.

8   But there is no shortage of flowers here: pink roses and carnations announce the birth of daughters; blue irises and delphiniums announce the birth of sons. Arthur Kornberg produced DNA in a test tube in 1957, but the genetic engineering of cut flowers is over three decades away, so all of these bouquets are destined to an early end. Blue carnations have not yet been developed, and although the smell is lovely, the dozen roses my father brings my mother have not yet been engineered to hold their scents.

9   Although I can't recall, I imagine my sleep is deep and dreamless when my father and his flowers arrive. When I open my eyes, I stare at the nursery ceiling, instead of looking into my mother's bewildered face. I imagine hearing the mid-western accents of the busy nurses, instead of my mother's British lilt. I imagine wondering, what the hell I'm doing here. *The Dick Van Dyke Show* is a year away, and the controversial episode in which Rob suspects he and Laura have been given someone else's child in the hospital will not be aired until 1963. Since DNA testing is still the jurisdiction of science fiction, there are no definitive ways to discover answers to questions of mix-ups, or unquestionable questions about paternity. It is still mother who knows best.

10   These new mothers are submissive in spite of the feminist movement, which is about to explode, and despite Betty Friedan, who is already thinking about "the problem that has no name." They will take the babies they are given, without question, and only later, when these babies reach adolescence, begin to ask themselves what went wrong. Haemorrhoids, episiotomies and paralysing drugs make the first bowel movements for these women a torturous experience, far more painful than the contractions of childbirth they cannot recall. The bathrooms in this hospital are small, box-like, cold. The toilets are clinical and high off the ground. Small, fat women like my mother teeter upon them. The room smells like a mixture of chemical

disinfectant and urine. If I were to make a film of my life now, I think I would begin it here: a tiny female child, cradled in her mother's arm, hovering over a hospital toilet.

11   "Drama is life with the dull bits left out," Hitchcock said, but it is more than the dull bits we extract. The General Principles of the Hays Code, which governed motion picture production from 1930 until the year of my birth, stated: "No picture shall be produced that will lower the moral standards of those who see it. Hence the sympathy of the audience should never be thrown to the side of crime, wrongdoing, evil or sin; Correct standards of life, subject only to the requirements of drama and entertainment, shall be presented; Law, natural or human, shall not be ridiculed, nor shall sympathy be created for its violation."

12   Forty-three years from the date the Hays Code is defunct, digital formatting will make it easy to create professional-looking movies on a computer. George Lucas will use digital cameras to film the last of the *Star Wars* movies, and a 32-year-old doorman, Jonathan Caouette, will use his "iMovie" program, spend just a little over $200, and produce an award-winning documentary about his troubled, down the toilet, past.

13   If I were to make a film of my life now, I wonder what I would include and what I would cut. Caouette included old videos of life with his mentally ill mother and his eccentric grandparents, of himself in foster care, in drag, in the persona of a battered woman, and as a young gay man throwing up in a toilet after receiving news of his mother's lithium overdose. What he does not include are videos of his son and of the woman he impregnated. He omitted these intentionally because they present aspects of his life out of keeping with its general trajectory.

14   There are years of my life, between the ages of 14 and 19, that haunt me from the cutting room floor. Like Caouette's omissions, these years are out of synch and do not follow a linear story line. They drop me in another continent; leave me in a cultural time warp, where only the toilet remains constant and true.

15   The spectre first appears in Cleveland. My five-year-old brother, four years my senior, pulls the channel selector off the television and flushes it down the toilet. The toilet is utterly blocked. My father, unwilling to pay a plumber, will fix it himself. Besides a wicked sense of humour, my father also possesses an eight-millimetre movie camera. He sets it up on a tripod to film this event. In years to come, we will sit in darkness watching my father shut off the water supply, siphon out the tank, remove the nuts that hold the bowl to the floor flange. We've heard the story a hundred times—seen it a hundred more—my father succeeds in removing the blockage. An expression of joy imbues his face. He sets the toilet down on the floor flange. As he moves to secure it, the film catches an alteration. We know what has occurred, though my father does not yet. We know that the toilet bowl has cracked and that the cost of replacing it will be significantly more than a plumber.

16   Four years after making this movie, my father is in debt, drinking hard liquor, and chain smoking. We travel to Chicago, to install an intercom system in our expensive, new house under construction. There are lines and vents of rough plumbing for three bathrooms, but the absence of toilets makes my bladder heavy. My father fiddles with hard square speakers and web-thin cords. I don't want to disturb him. I don't want to risk his rage. But he is not angry when I tell him. He places me on his shoulders, carries me to the dark stairless pit that opens into the basement and begins to descend a rickety ladder. Although I can't recall where I've seen it, I am thinking of Alfred Hitchcock's movie

Vertigo—or rather, the word "vertigo," which I learned as a result of seeing the film. It bombed in 1958 because, some say, it was too dark for the light-craving audiences of *Auntie Mame* and *Houseboat*. Hitchcock once said: "Give them pleasure—the same pleasure they have when they wake up from a nightmare." And that is exactly the kind of pleasure I am experiencing on my father's shoulders, the kind of pleasure that I have already experienced too much of in my life.

17   Although I am only seven, I already have trouble sleeping at night: I fear the dark, I fear spiders, I fear the invisible monsters lurking beneath my bed and the Princess lamp that once violently wobbled, for no apparent reason, on my bedside table. At home, I never fall asleep in bed, but always on a stair leading down into the living room, where my parents spend the evening fighting. As I teeter on my father's shoulders now, I think of my sleeping habits, and wonder how with such "vertigo" I have managed to survive. When my feet touch clay, my father directs me to a hole in the corner the construction workers made. I am humiliated, disgusted, incredulous. Only twice, so far, since I could use a toilet have I ever experienced not using one. Both times were bad.

18   Rewind to 1965. There I am, in the school ground, playing tag. I need a toilet, but the school doors are locked. I know I should go home, but my brothers aren't ready to leave, and I'm afraid to walk past the ravine alone. I continue playing, trying to forget the overwhelming pressure of my full bladder, hoping my mind can control this. No one is more surprised than me when I wet myself. The kids in the playground laugh. My brothers, mortified, escort me home. My mother gives me a bath and tries to assure me that no one at school will remember, but I know she is wrong. I make her promise to buy me a blond wig, sunglasses and a bright red sweater. I make her promise to re-enrol me in kindergarten as someone completely new. I will not calm down until she promises, and on Monday, when she does not buy me my disguise and insists I go to school exactly as I am, I know I will never completely trust her again.

19   Fast forward to 1966: our car breaks down on a highway. I go into the grassy field behind the car to pee. It is a hot summer day and we have been waiting for a tow truck for an eternity. I am embarrassed, but my parents assure me no one will see. Fast forward to the day after: my rear end is the colour of a Japanese sun and itches with a potency I have never known. I wonder what curse has befallen me, if I unintentionally touched my private parts while I was sleeping and brought this plague upon myself. I can't bring myself to speak of this, but when the blisters form and break, the pain drives me to my mother who, on examining my backside, summons our family doctor. He diagnosis my condition as poison ivy related. For the next week, I lie in my bed on my stomach, my ravaged naked bottom on display.

20   "You can't trust anyone over 30," Berkeley dissident Jack Weinberg told a reporter in 1964, and although I would not even hear this phrase until I was studying American history at The University of Western Ontario in 1981, something in the collective ethos had infected me. Both of my parents are over 30 when I'm born and they continue getting older. The white porcelain toilet flushes—or it doesn't. The world changes just the same.

21   My father's drinking keeps him out late, gets him in car accidents, fistfights, and finally an unemployment line. A month later, he gets a job as an Encyclopaedia Britannica salesman. This is the year Neil Armstrong lands on the moon. His small step is one giant leap for mankind, while my father's small step drags him around our

affluent neighbourhood. Nobody's hungry for knowledge. He can't give encyclopaedias away. It's 1969, *The Saturday Evening Post* stops its presses after 147 years, The Beatles record their last album, and Paul McCartney is rumoured dead. Charles Manson and his followers kill Sharon Tate, Nixon succeeds Johnson, and *The Brady Bunch* and *Sesame Street* make their network debuts.

22   On Christmas day, we move from our large, beautiful house to a small, shabby one in Windsor. My brothers share a bedroom and we all have to share one toilet. This would not be half so bad if my father did not have chronic constipation. He spends a large percentage of his time, when he's home, in the bathroom reading books on World War II. When he's not in the bathroom, he's in the basement, smoking and drinking and building a bar. There are no corporate rehabilitation programs, and although some health professionals view it as such, the vast majority do not consider alcoholism a disease. Every middle-class home has a wet bar. Cocktail hour begins at five. The only hope for a person like my father is to start a business of his own and to run it into the ground.

23   Fast forward to 1974. I am drunk and kneeling over a toilet at the Fire Side Inn restaurant at my father's funeral reception. Two hours earlier, my father was interred in the mausoleum at Green Lawn Cemetery, the same place his father was interred in 1961, and his mother will be interred in 1983. The year my father dies is three years after Dr. Denis Burkitt publishes the results of his study comparing diet and the incidence of colon cancer in North America and Africa, and brings the term "fibre" into common usage. It is three years after it has become stylish to eat bran cereals for breakfast and to bring raw broccoli and carrot sticks to parties as finger food. In years to come, there will be passionate debates about

the role of dietary fibre in cancer prevention, but right now, fibre seems to be a preventative panacea, and my father never liked eating high-fibre foods. It has not yet been postulated that cigarette smoking and alcohol increase the incidence of this cancer, nor that fat and lack of exercise are extremely unhealthy "lifestyle choices." In fact, the concept of "lifestyle choices" is new, and has not yet been exploited by weight loss businesses or dismissed by economists. In years to come, the colon will become the third most common site for cancer, and in 31 years, an estimated 104,950 new cases of colon cancer will be diagnosed in the United States alone.

24   But right now, as I lean over the toilet, I see my father. I am not thinking of his unhealthy lifestyle, or his bowel obsession, which began with his constipation several years ago. I am thinking of his split personality, his dichotomy, the kind, sober him and the mean drunk. I am projecting into the future and wondering how I will ever be able to reconcile the past. What kind of person was he? What was my experience of him? What will I choose to remember and what will I choose to flush away?

25   The year I am born, Jack Parr walks off the *Tonight Show* because the NBC censors edit out a segment in which he tells a joke about a toilet. The joke is innocuous—about travellers in England looking for a wayside chapel, and seeing a sign announcing "W.C." Parr doesn't even say the words "Water Closet." For weeks newspapers carry stories about this national controversy. Things will never be the same.

26   Fourteen years later some kind of amnesia falls over me. I awake in England, or at least partially awake. My mother, in her panic, has sold, given away or burned everything we owned in Windsor and has moved to England. She has had to make major decisions about what to take with her and what to leave behind. She has decided

that my father was a terrible bastard and that she's well rid of him. She has had to throw out her entire life in North America as bad business, to return to the place of her birth and the home of her brother and sister in-law. Because I am 14, she takes me with her. Everything is different here: the accents, the currency, the electrical outlets. In 1974 the school system in England is impenetrable to a North American high school student; there are no equivalencies, no opportunities of entry. One night, my aunt tells me she's found a job for me, and the next day, I begin working in a hotel as a chamber maid. I clean toilets every day of my life, toilet after toilet, for the next five years, until the white porcelain toilet flushes and I decide to make a final cut.

Structure, Organization, and Style

1. Sonik uses many literary devices in her essay. Discuss her use of two of the following: imagery, diction (word choice), figurative language, juxtaposition (placing contrastive elements next to each other).
2. Sonik does not use a conventional linear organization method. Comment on her organization and the way it relates to her theme, referring to specific passages.
3. Discuss Sonik's use of humour, referring to specific passages.

Critical Thinking

1. What do the quotations from Alfred Hitchcock contribute to her essay?
2. Analyze Sonik's use of (a) television or (b) the toilet as a metaphor or symbol that reveals the essay's underlying themes.
3. Discuss the ways that the author's examples from both her distant past and her more recent past illuminate the generational differences highlighted in the essay. How do they comment on or reveal aspects of social change?
4. Compare and contrast "Flush" with one of the journalistic essays in this textbook; or, compare and contrast "Flush" with either "Joyas Voladoras," p. 162, "I'm Glad I Never Had to Decide," p. 248, or "Is Scientific Progress Inevitable?", p. 338. Use at least two bases of comparison.

Daniel Rosenfield et al., "Canadian Lifestyle Choices: A Public Health Failure"

Although the *Canadian Medical Association Journal* publishes the results of research, it also publishes editorials in which professionals take a position on a topic of concern to its readers. However, the authors of "Canadian Lifestyle Choices" somewhat unusually utilize a satiric tone to make their argumentative points stand out. Satire criticizes institutions or commonly held beliefs through humour, ridicule, and irony. Writers who use satire to provoke changes have specific targets in mind, which are usually evident to a careful reader.

▶ Preparing to Read

1. After scanning the first sentences of the first few paragraphs, consider why the authors might have decided to use an ironic tone rather than present their points directly (in irony, two levels of meaning are evident, a surface meaning and a deeper one; see p. 134). What role might the topic, purpose, or audience have played in this decision? (You can also consider this question after you have read the entire essay.)

2. When you shop, do you pay attention to food labelling or to the nutritional content of your food? Would you pay more attention if it were more prominently displayed? How important do you believe this knowledge would be to a typical Canadian consumer?

Canadian Lifestyle Choices: A Public Health Failure

Daniel Rosenfield, Paul C. Hébert, Matthew B. Stanbrook, Noni MacDonald, Ken Flegel, and Jane Coutts

Canadian Medical Association Journal,
September 20, 2011
(695 words)

1   Recently, we caught up with Mister and Missus Average Canadian. Like classmates at our high school reunions (but Hey, not us of course!), they've changed a lot over the years, thanks in no small part to our federal government's health policies.

2   Back in the day, Mister Average Canadian was a lean, mean, hockey-playing machine who was pretty fit and healthy. The missus was an avid ringette player. In fact, they met at the arena. But 25 years on, they're fat, hypertensive, smoking, diabetic couch potatoes. Years of inaction by the federal government have helped shape the Canadians into people who can barely heft a hockey or ringette stick, let alone play a game.

3   The Canadians sleep easy (well, not quite, because of their obstructive sleep apnea) thanks to a government that lets the products they love onto the market unfettered. Their favourite diet,

high in trans fats and sodium, is not affected by regulation of the food industry, because the current government ignored calls from public health officials to ban trans fats and reduce salt and broke up the advisory panels that advocated for those changes.[1] It also dragged its feet to renew and increase graphic labelling on cigarette packages—and thank goodness, because having to look at images of lung and oral cancers is just *such* a downer when you want a hit of nicotine.[2]

4   The Canadians are something of an institution in their neighbourhood—and a growing one; two-thirds of their neighbours, like them, are overweight or obese.[3] It's the inevitable result of a steady diet of processed foods and meals at restaurants that rarely give nutritional information but love to serve up giant portions.

5   Through either convoluted or absent labelling, the Canadians are rarely aware of the nutritional content of their food, either in grocery stores or restaurants. Making healthy food choices can be difficult, and evidence shows that helpful, consumer-friendly labels on all consumer and restaurant food products can help people make healthy food choices.[4] Largely unaware of these benefits, the Canadians had no idea why groups such as the Canadian Institute for Health Information, Centre for Science in the

Public Interest and the Heart and Stroke Foundation called for mandatory food labelling.

6   Because some information can't be avoided, the Canadians do know their systolic blood pressure is closing in on their bowling average of 220. They don't know, however, how that's been helped along by the food industry, which loves loading food up with salt, to make otherwise unpalatable cheap food taste good, prolong shelf life and keep the food industry rich.[5] Also, like many tired parents, the Canadians just want happy children, and the billion-dollar junk-food industry helps by marketing its products to them, promising joy by the salty, sugary and fatty serving. That lets the Canadians give their children everything they missed when they were young—incidentally putting them on track to outdo their parents in obesity and hypertension. There's little fear of an interruption in that trajectory—their federal government had proposals for regulating sodium that would have saved health care costs and lengthened lives,[6] but decided the financial and flavour consequences were too high and instead disbanded Health Canada's Sodium Working Group.[7]

7   If the Canadians lived in the United Kingdom, their consumption of sodium and trans fats would be on its way down.[8] If they were from California, they would have access to proper food labelling, even in restaurants. If they were from Australia, their government would be introducing legislation to cover entire cigarette packages with generic warning labels. In short, their government would have already implemented some simple policies that have a substantial impact on the public's health.

8   In Canada, individual preference, industry influence and ideology all militate against evidence-based public health policy. This has created a population-health time bomb—which can and should be defused. As health professionals and role models, we must help our patients make healthy choices and do so ourselves. As health advocates, we need to put more energy into "nudging" governments into developing effective public health policies. The goal should be to make it easy for Canadians to improve their nutrition, make healthy choices and stay fit.

References

1. Trans Fat Task Force. *TRANSforming the food supply: report of the Trans Fat Task Force submitted to the Minister of Health.* Ottawa (ON): Health Canada; 2006.
2. Hammond D, Fong GT, McNeill A, et al. Effectiveness of cigarette warning labels in informing smokers about the risks of smoking: findings from the International Tobacco Control (ITC) Four Country Survey. *Tob Control* 2006;15(Suppl 3):iii19–25.
3. Data tables from the Canadian Community Health Survey (CCHS). Ottawa (ON): Statistics Canada; 2004. Available: www.statcan.gc.ca/pub/82-620-m/2005001/4053601-eng.htm (accessed 2011 Apr. 15).
4. Burton S, Creyer UH, Kees J, et al. Attacking the obesity epidemic: an examination of the potential health benefits of nutrition information provision in restaurants. *Am J Public Health* 2006;96:1669–75.
5. *Testimony of Bill Jeffery, LLB, National Coordinator Centre for Science in the Public Interest before the House of Commons Standing Committee on Health Hearing on Healthy Living February 3, 2011 in Ottawa* [technical brief]. Ottawa (ON): The Centre for Science in the Public Interest; 2011. Available: cspinet.org/canada/pdf/english.speakingnotes.cspi.pdf (accessed 2011 June 10).
6. Bibbins-Domingo K, Chertow GM, Coxson PG, et al. Projected effect of dietary salt reductions on future cardiovascular disease. *N Engl J Med* 2010;362:590–9.
7. Schmidt S. Sodium reduction panel disbanded. *Ottawa Citizen* 2011 Feb. 4. Available: www.ottawacitizen.com/health/Sodium+reduction+panel+disbanded/4220182/story.html (accessed 2011 Apr. 15).

8. Food Standard Agency. Agency publishes 2012 salt reduction targets. London (UK): The Agency; 2009. Available: www.food.gov.uk/news/press releases/2009/may/salttargets (accessed 2011 Apr. 15).

Competing interests: See www.cmaj.ca/site/misc/cmaj_staff.xhtml. None declared by Daniel Rosenfield and Jane Coutts.

Comprehension

1. Identify, then paraphrase, the thesis statement.

Structure, Organization, and Style

1. In paragraphs 6 and 7, identify the topic sentences.
2. Which paragraph uses compare–contrast? Comment on its placement and its effectiveness.
3. a. Give two examples of ironic statements in the essay.
   b. Give two examples of humour, such as exaggeration or word play.

Critical Thinking/Research

1. Who are the authors primarily criticizing in their essay? Refer to specific passages that show this.
2. Analyze the use of logical, emotional, and ethical appeals in the essay.

Warren Clark, "Delayed Transitions of Young Adults"

This article appeared in *Canadian Social Trends*, a periodical highlighting "social, economic, and demographic changes affecting the lives of Canadians." Published by Statistics Canada, *Canadian Social Trends* utilizes data from Canada's official census and from its many other surveys on specific subjects relevant to Canadians. Statistics Canada's reports have various practical uses for governments (see http://www.statcan.gc.ca/about-apercu/used-utiliser-eng.htm for more information).

"Delayed Transitions of Young Adults" uses the critical review format, combining the results of the recent national census with other reports, many but not all authored by Statistics Canada. Due to the extensive use of statistics, it is crucial that both the numerical data and their interpretation are presented clearly; therefore, as in all review articles, organization is vital.

▶ Preparing to Read

1. Interview a man and a woman who are about 30 years older than you (for example, your parents or an aunt and uncle) to determine at what age they were at each of the five transitions mentioned in paragraph 3. To fill out your profile, you could also use some of the categories from Table 1 of the article.
2. After reading the article, compare your results with those in the article.

Delayed Transitions of Young Adults

Warren Clark

Canadian Social Trends, 2008
(3424 words)

1   The transition to adulthood is often viewed as a period where young people move by stages into adult roles. The years after age 18 offer an opportunity for young people to become increasingly independent from their parents. During this period of transition, young people make a wide range of choices about where and with whom they live, how they will pursue their studies, what type of work they are interested in and whether or not they will get married and have children.

2   In recent years, social scientists have found that the transition to adulthood is taking longer to complete. Young people are living with their parents longer,[1] are more highly educated and attend school for more years than their parents did. The age at marriage has been rising, fertility rates have been falling and the age at which women have their first child has been increasing.[2]

3   This article explores the transitions that young people make on their way to adulthood. Using census data from 1971 to 2001, it documents how the timing of transitions has changed and been delayed. It profiles the young adult population aged 18 to 34 and examines the five transitions that many young people make on their way to adulthood: leaving school, leaving their parents' home, having full-year full-time work, entering conjugal relationships and having children.

Briefly: The young adult population

4   According to the 2001 Census, there were approximately 6.7 million young adults between the ages of 18 and 34 in private households. About 41% of them were under 25, which is that year when transitions to adulthood often occur most quickly. Young adults are also a highly heterogeneous group, reflecting the rapidly growing ethnic diversity of the Canadian population over the last 30 years: almost one in 5 is foreign-born, one in 6 is a member of a visible minority group (Table 1).

5   They are the most mobile group in the population—about one in four had moved in the year prior to the 2001 Census—as they actively seek out new education and employment opportunities and form their own households. They are also more likely to live in one of Canada's largest cities where education and job opportunities tend to be more abundant.

What you should know about this study

6   Typically the analysis of life course transitions uses longitudinal data where the same individuals are followed over a period of time. This article focuses on a comparative cohort analysis looking at four cohorts of young people aged 18 to 34 in private households from the 1971, 1981, 1991 and 2001 Censuses of Population. Five markers of the transition to adulthood are examined: leaving school, leaving home, working full-year full-time, finding a conjugal partner and having children.

7   These markers of adulthood are snapshots taken on the Census reference dates and do not represent completed or irreversible social changes: they simply record the state of transition young adults were in on those dates. If these young adults were questioned on other dates, they may have reversed direction in their transition to adulthood. For example, young adults who leave home at one point in time may return to live with their parents at a later date; those who no longer attend school may subsequently return; those who hold a full-time job may lose it or leave it. Some young people may combine school and work; others may test the labour market and then return to school. Some may begin their families before leaving school and entering the labour market, while others may wait to marry and have children until after they have established a career.[1] Nevertheless, these indicators reflect key entry points to adult status and are therefore still useful in understanding the transition to adulthood.

8   The five markers of adult transition are:

Left school—has not attended school, college or university either full-time or part-time during the nine-month period between September and May.

Left parental home—is not a child in an economic family or a never-married child in a census family.

Full-time full-year work—has worked full-time for at least 49 weeks during the last year.

Ever in a conjugal union—is married, widowed, separated or divorced (i.e., ever married) or is currently in a common-law relationship. In the text, this concept is referred to as "ever in a conjugal union."

Has children—has never-married children living in the same household.

---

[1] Rumbant, R.G. 2004. "Young adults in the United States: A Profile." The Network on Transitions to Adulthood. *Research Network Working Paper No. 4.* http://www.transad.pop.upenn.edu. Accessed 29 January 2007.

The pace of each transition is slower than in 1971

9   Age 18 is often viewed as one of the milestones passed on the way to adulthood. In Canada, eighteen is the legal age for voting. It is the age at which many young adults prepare to leave high school and explore other educational or work opportunities. At age 18, few have crossed any of the five traditional bridges to adulthood: leaving school, leaving home, steady full-time work, conjugal union and parenting.

Table 1   Today's young adults aged 18 to 34 differ substantially from those 30 years ago

	1971	1981	1991	2001
Number of young adults aged 18 to 34 living in private households (000s)	5,398	7,366	7,447	6,685
		percentage		
Age				
18 to 24	48	44	36	41
25 to 29	29	29	31	28
30 to 34	24	27	33	31
Years in Canada since immigrating				
Canadian-born	84	86	85	82
5 years or less	6	3	4	6
Over 5 years	10	11	9	11
Non-permanent resident	...	...	2	1
Visible minority	...	5	11	16
Highest level of schooling				
Less than high school graduation	33	31	24	18
High school diploma or some postsecondary	42[1]	33	35	34
Trades or college certificate or diploma	16[2]	24	27	28
University degree, certificate or diploma	9	12	14	20
Ever-married or currently common-law union	61	59	54	45
Has children in same household	44	39	35	29
Lives in one of the 3 largest census metropolitan areas	32	30	34	36
Montréal	14	12	12	12
Toronto	13	13	16	17
Vancouver	5	5	6	7

... not applicable

1. Includes people who had college certificate or diplomas other than trades or vocational programs as they were not identified in the 1971 Census.

2. Includes only apprenticeship, trades and other vocational certificates, diplomas and completions.

Source: Statistics Canada, Censuses of Population.

10   The number of transitions that a young adult has made is a rough indicator of their progress toward adulthood between ages 18 and 34. Using the markers set out in this article, that number can range from zero to five. Not surprisingly, on average, 18-year-olds have made fewer transitions to adulthood than 34-year-olds (Chart 1). But more importantly, young adults in 2001 had gone through fewer transitions than the 1971 cohort had when it was the same age.

11   On average, a 25-year-old in 2001 had gone through the same number of transitions as a 22-year-old in 1971 and a 30-year-old in 2001 had made the same number of transitions as a

Average number of transitions

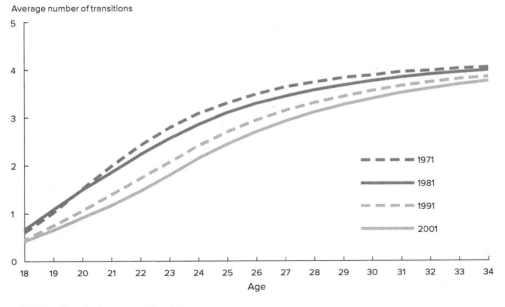

Source: Statistics Canada, Censuses of Population.

Chart 1 Young adults have made fewer transitions

25-year-old in 1971. This suggests that the path to adulthood is no longer as straight as it was back in 1971. In fact, you could say that the transitions of today's young adults are both delayed and elongated: delayed, because young adults take more time to complete their first major transition (leaving school), thus postponing all subsequent transitions; and elongated, because each subsequent transition takes longer to complete and stretches the process from their late teens to their early 30s (as shown by the much gentler slope of the line for the 2001 cohort in Chart 1). In contrast, the 1971 cohort packs more transitions into the years from their late teens to their mid-20s and fewer into their early 30s.

Women make transitions earlier than men

12 Women generally go through the major transitions to adulthood at a younger age than men. They are more likely to leave home, marry and have children at a younger age; on the other hand, men leave school earlier and have full-year full-time employment at a younger age. In 2001, at age 18, there is no difference in the average number of transitions that young women and men have made (each report 0.4). However, because women go through more changes earlier than men, the gender gap increases in the early to mid-20s. By the time they reach their 30s, the gap has closed (Chart 2).

13 This is quite different from the situation in 1971, when young women had made more transitions than men by age 18 and the gender gap had closed at age 27. This was a time before it was common for young women to receive a post-secondary education, and many women got a job, and most married and had children after leaving high school. Similarly, men of that era were more likely to be in a conjugal relationship and to have children, explaining why they matured faster than the 2001 cohort.

Average number of transitions

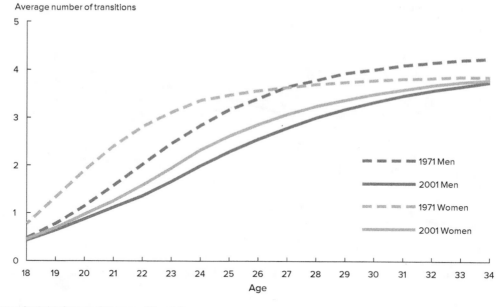

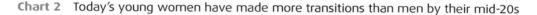

Source: Statistics Canada, Censuses of Population.

Chart 2 Today's young women have made more transitions than men by their mid-20s

Staying in school delays most transitions

14   The changing role of women in society has contributed to the remarkable progress women have made in their educational attainment over the last 30 years (Chart 3). No longer are they relegated to a narrow set of educational opportunities and career possibilities. The percentage of young women aged 30 to 34 who are university-educated has increased fourfold from 7% in 1971 to 29% in 2001. The proportion nearly doubled from 13% to 25% for young men over the same period. On many university campuses, women now outnumber men (although men still remain in the majority at the doctoral level).[3]

15   The result of these shifts in expectations and opportunities is that both women and men are finishing their education at later and later ages. In 1971, three-quarters of young adults had left

school by age 22 whereas only half had left by that age in 2001. Today's bachelor's recipients graduate at age 23, but they are much more likely than the previous generation to go on to a master's or doctoral program where the median age of graduation is 29 and 33, respectively.[4] Since most young people defer marriage and parenthood until they have completed their education, the extended period of schooling undertaken by today's young adults puts almost all other transitions to adulthood on "hold."

Women still leave home at a younger age than men

16   For many parents, an adult child leaving home is viewed as an indicator of successful transition to adulthood. However, it is taking longer to reach that stage; in 2001, for example, 60% of men and 73% of women aged 25 were

Gains in educational attainment . . .

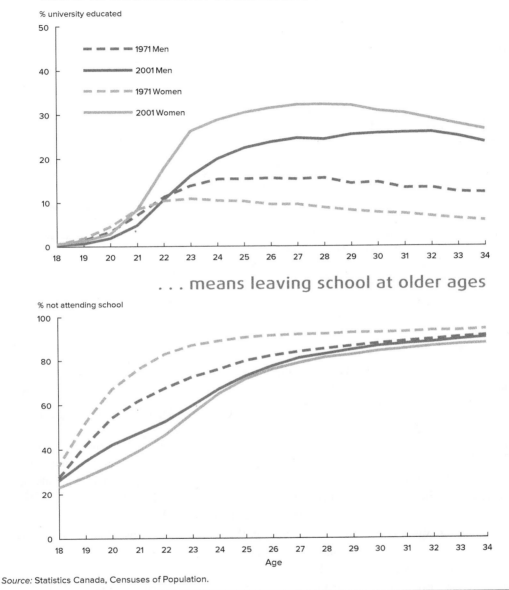

% university educated

Legend:
- 1971 Men
- 2001 Men
- 1971 Women
- 2001 Women

. . . means leaving school at older ages

% not attending school

Age

Source: Statistics Canada, Censuses of Population.

Chart 3   Gains in educational attainment . . . means leaving school at older ages

no longer living with their parents, compared with 78% of men and 89% of women aged 25 in 1971 (Chart 4). But most parents would also agree that living at home while attending school can make it easier and less expensive for young people to complete their education and obtain employment.[5] So more children delay their exit from the parental home until they complete

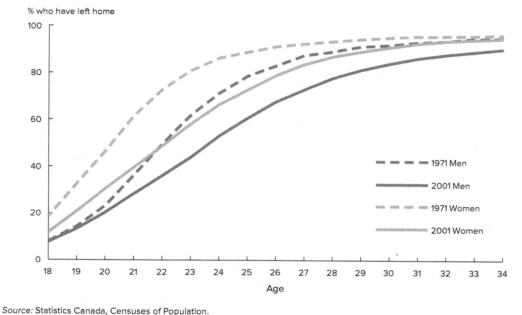

% who have left home

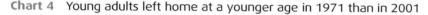

Source: Statistics Canada, Censuses of Population.

Chart 4   Young adults left home at a younger age in 1971 than in 2001

their studies and are able to be financially independent. However, not only are today's young adults leaving home at later ages than their parents' generation, but they are also more likely to be returning.[6]

17   In each generation, though, young women tend to leave home sooner than men. This gender difference reflects the fact that women enter into conjugal relationships at younger ages than men.

18   Once today's young adults do leave home, they are more likely to live alone. This is especially true for those with university education. Young men are also more likely than young women to live by themselves: the rate peaks at age 28 (13%) and remains fairly close to that peak until age 34. In contrast, the rate for women is highest at age 27 (9%) and then trails off. This suggests that, compared with the past, more young men have developed a bachelor lifestyle that lasts well into their thirties.

More women but fewer men make a transition to full-year full-time work

19   Compared with their counterparts in 1971, young men are less likely to be working full-time full-year while young women aged 24 and older are more likely to do so (Chart 5). This pattern clearly indicates that women today tend to stay in the labour market even after transitions such as having children.

20   Back in 1971, few mothers of pre-school children had full-year full-time work (9%), but by 2001, this proportion had tripled to 27%. Likewise mothers with older children also experienced increases in full-year full-time employment.[7] On the other hand, women without children reported little change over the period, with about one-third holding full-year full-time work in both years.

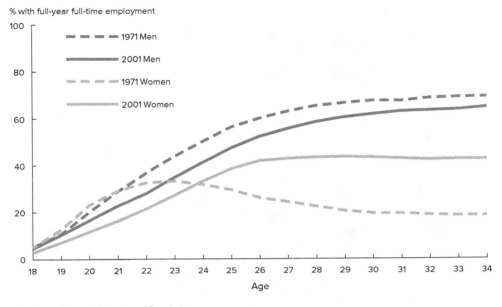

% with full-year full-time employment

- - - 1971 Men
——— 2001 Men
- - - 1971 Women
——— 2001 Women

Age

Source: Statistics Canada, Censuses of Population.

Chart 5   Young women are much more likely to have full-year full-time work now

Conjugal unions delayed

21   Dramatic changes have occurred in the living arrangements of young adults over the last 30 years. First, getting married and having children has become less common (Chart 6). Second, cohabitation and having children within a common-law union have become more popular, suggesting that for some, cohabitation may be a substitute marriage-like relationship where two partners share parenting, household chores, and resources. The third key trend is the increased popularity of remaining in the parental home (discussed earlier) and possibly leaving and returning to it several times.

22   The age at which people first marry has been edging up for both brides and grooms since the mid-1960s.[8] Just as they have taken longer to leave school, leave home and find permanent jobs, today's young adults have delayed entering into married or common-law relationships (Chart 7). In 1971, 65% of men and 80% of women were in or had been in a conjugal relationship by age 25; by 2001, these percentages had dropped by almost half to 34% and 49%, respectively.

23   Although the paths to adulthood have become more diverse over the last generation, the most common trajectory still seems to be from school completion, to work, to home-leaving and then to marriage or cohabitation.[9] With rising educational attainment extending the time needed to complete this first hurdle, it is not surprising that the formation of conjugal unions is delayed.

24   Census data show that young adults who leave school earlier are more likely to have a conjugal relationship at a younger age. In 2001, nearly half (49%) of 25-year-olds without a high school diploma had married or entered a common-law union compared with 32% of their university-educated peers. But even for people

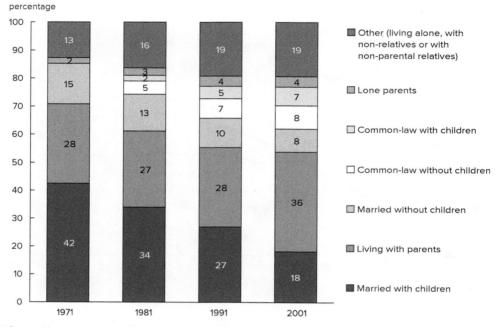

Note: Common-law unions were not identified in the 1971 Census.

Source: Statistics Canada, Censuses of Population.

Chart 6   Living arrangements of young adults have changed considerably

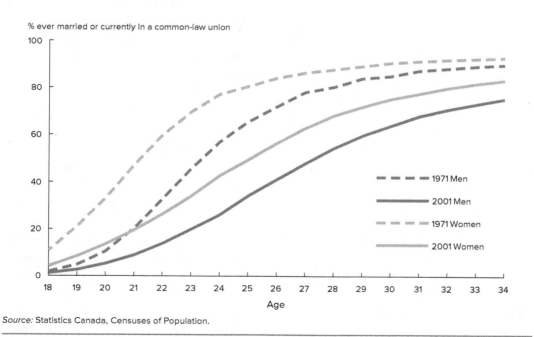

Source: Statistics Canada, Censuses of Population.

Chart 7   Conjugal unions are delayed for both women and men

with similar levels of education, young adults today are less likely to be in a couple than they were over 30 years ago.

25   More often than not, first unions are now cohabitations rather than marriages. According to the 2001 General Social Survey, in 2001, 63% of women aged 20 to 29 in their first union lived common-law.[10] Data from the Census show that common-law unions were most likely among young adults in their mid-20s (about 20%), but by age 34 only about 16% were cohabiting. The lower proportion of cohabitors in their early 30s may be because some people previously living together are now married or, given the greater instability of common-law relationships, more couples have separated.[11]

Most young adults now postpone parenthood

26   While the overall fertility rates in Canada for women under age 30 have dropped since the early 1970s, rates for women in their 30s have increased.[12] This delayed fertility is generally linked to women's increased education and labour force participation. Research has shown that women with high social status are more likely to complete their postsecondary education before motherhood, whereas women with lower social status tend to become mothers at younger ages and bypass postsecondary education, regular work and marriage.[13] The pursuit of higher education, career aspirations and the elusiveness of work-life balance may inhibit many women today from having children at the same age that their mothers did. (Chart 8).

27   However, although marrying and having children later allows many young people to pursue postsecondary education and to gain employment experience and security in a highly competitive labour market,[14] even those who have not gone beyond high school graduation have delayed childrearing.

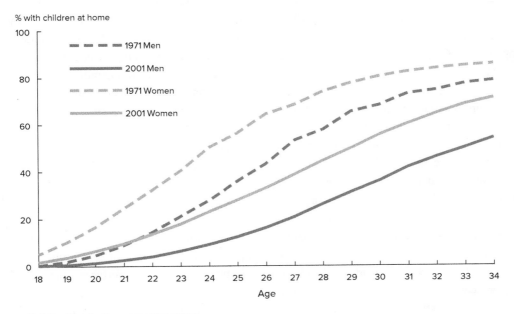

% with children at home

Source: Statistics Canada, Censuses of Population.

Chart 8   Today's young adults are less likely to have children

Why are transitions delayed?

28 Many social and economic factors have contributed to the delay in transitions to adulthood. Young adults today have a big incentive to continue their schooling beyond secondary completion for economic reasons. People with university degrees have significantly higher earnings and considerably lower unemployment rates than high school graduates. For example, since 1990, the number of jobs requiring a degree has doubled, while the number demanding high school education or less has shrunk.[15] Today, prolonged schooling is necessary to gain the skills and education needed in a technical and information-based economy.

29 But another important reason is that young people are increasingly expected to continue their schooling. For instance, 95% of parents with children under age 19 believe that education after high school is important or very important.[16] And over two-thirds of 15-year-olds intend to go on to university after completing their secondary studies, with many (39%) aspiring to more than one degree.[17]

30 Of course, a delayed exit from school has an impact on other transitions to adulthood. Although higher education enhances the chances of marriage, school enrolment impedes the first union formation, since most young people wait until they have finished university or college before they start thinking about marriage and parenthood. Tuition fees have been increasing more quickly than inflation since the early 1990s[18] and the amount students owe to government student loan programs has also been escalating.[19] The high cost of postsecondary education in many cases involves their continued reliance on their parents, so that young adults may not feel that they are sufficiently ready for marriage.[20]

31 Studies of labour market conditions of younger men in Canada show that their earnings have declined while the education premium that they had over their older counterparts has disappeared.[21] However, the decline in full-year full-time work for young men may equally reflect lower job quality as young men report having less pension plan coverage, lower unionization rates and increased earnings instability while pension coverage for young women has improved slightly.[22,23]

32 Today's young people face a labour market that earlier cohorts did not have to contend with: an increasing wage gap between newly hired employees and those with more experience; more temporary jobs for newly hired workers; and fewer male employees covered by registered pension plans, meaning that new hires are entirely responsible for saving for their own retirement without the backup of an employer-sponsored pension plan.[24]

33 Instability in employment is reflected in the much faster growth in part-time employment. The shift from full-time lifetime employment that many young adults entered 30 years ago to a work environment offering more part-time work with fewer benefits has contributed to insecurity, especially among young men, and is a contributing factor to delays in family formation.[25] Other researchers have found that union formation increasingly requires the earning power of both partners, so the labour market problems experienced by young men may reduce or delay the formation of unions.[26]

34 In addition, housing prices have risen more quickly than the income of young men and despite declines in mortgage interest rates, young men would still have to spend more of their income on mortgage payments in 2001 than they did in 1971.[27] This reinforces the increased need for two incomes in order to

own a home, adding to the economic insecurity young adults may feel.

35 Many young adults continue to live with their parents not just because of the financial burden of paying for their postsecondary education, but also because they may be unemployed or working in a low-paying precarious job. On the other hand, cultural factors may encourage continued co-residence with parents as generation gaps narrow and parents have developed more egalitarian relationships with their children.[28]

36 While the labour market has changed and the duration and cost of postsecondary education have increased, other social factors have also contributed to delayed transitions. Gender roles within marriage changed. As women became more educated, their earnings increased and they began to rely on their own earning capacity and less on their partner's to determine whether they should remain in the labour market after marrying and having children. In fact, with higher earnings, the care of children presented high opportunity costs to families, providing large incentives for women to return to the labour market after childbirth; consequently, women have seen strong increases in full-year full-time employment as their educational attainment rose. Back in 1971, women commonly entered the labour market after high school while remaining in their parents' home until a suitable marriage partner was found. By their mid-20s, many had married, had children and left the labour market to care for them.

Summary

37 In 1971, three-quarters of 22-year-olds had left school, nearly half were married and one in four had children. In contrast, in 2001, half of 22-year-olds were still in school, only one in five was in a conjugal union (usually common-law), and one in eleven had children. In 2001, young women led men in educational attainment and many more women had full-year full-time jobs than young women 30 years earlier.

38 Overall, the transition to adulthood is now delayed and elongated. It takes today's young adults longer to achieve their independence: they are leaving school later, staying longer in their parents' home, entering the labour market later, and postponing conjugal unions and childbearing.

39 Most 18- to 34-year-olds have passed through fewer adult transitions than people of the same age 30 years earlier. By age 34, however, today's women have made just as many transitions as 34-year-old women in 1971, although they are more likely to include full-year full-time work and less likely to include marriage and childbearing.

40 In contrast, men at age 34 have made fewer transitions than 30 years ago. This may be in part due to the economic changes that have made the labour market more dynamic. As a consequence, young men are less likely to have full-year full-time work than their fathers did 30 years earlier. Both men and women have upgraded their level of education in an effort to take advantage of the premium that university graduates enjoy in the labour market and this, by itself, has delayed other transitions to adulthood.

References

1. Beaupré, P., P. Turcotte and A. Milan. 2006. "When is junior moving out? Transitions from the parental home to independence." *Canadian Social Trends*, Winter 2006, No. 82, pp. 9–15; Boyd, M., D. Norris. 1999. "The crowded nest: Young adults at home." *Canadian Social Trends*, Spring 1999, No. 52, pp. 2–5.

2. Duchesne, D., F. Nault, H. Gilmour, R. Wilkins. 1999. *Vital Statistics Compendium 1996*, Statistics Canada, Catalogue No. 84–214, p.28.

3. Statistics Canada. 2007. CANSIM Table 477-0013 University enrolments, by registration status, program level, Classification of Instructional Programs, Primary Grouping (CIP_PG) and sex, annual (number). Accessed 18 April 2007.

4. Unpublished tables from the 2002 National Graduates Survey of 2000 Graduates.

5. Boyd and Norris (1999).

6. Beaupré, P., P. Turcotte, A. Milan. 2006. "Junior comes back home: Trends and predictors of returning to the parental home." *Canadian Social Trends*, Winter 2006, No. 82, pp. 28–34.

7. In 2001, 37% of young mothers with children 5 years of age or older had full-year full-time work compared with 19% in 1971.

8. Ram, B. 1990. "New trends in the family: Demographic facts and features." *Current Demographic Analysis*, Statistics Canada, Catalogue no. 91-535, p. 80; Duchesne et al (1999), p. 10.

9. Ravanera, Z.R., F. Rajulton, T.K. Burch. 2002 . "The early life courses of Canadian men: Analysis of timing and sequences of events." *Canadian Studies in Population*, Vol. 29, No. 2, pp. 293–312; Ravanera, Z.R., F. Rajulton, T.K. Burch. 2006. "Inequality and the life course: Differentials in trajectories and timing of transitions of Canadian women." *Population Studies Centre University of Western Ontario, Discussion Paper No. 06-03*. http://sociology.uwo.ca/popstudies/dp/dp06-3.pdf. Accessed 8 March 2007.

10. Statistics Canada, 2002. "Changing conjugal life in Canada." Statistics Canada, Catalogue no. 89-576-XIE.

11. Le Bourdais, C., G. Neill and P. Turcotte. 2000. "The changing face of conjugal relationships." *Canadian Social Trends*, Spring 2000, No. 56, pp. 14–17.

12. Statistics Canada. 2006. *Report on the demographic situation in Canada—2003 and 2004*. Edited by Alain Bélanger. Catalogue 91-209, p. 27.

13. Ravanera, Z., F. Rajulton. 2006. "Social status polarization in the timing and trajectories to motherhood." *Canadian Studies in Population*, Vol. 33, No. 2, pp. 179–207.

14. Lochhead, C. 2000. "The trend toward delayed first childbirth: Health and social implications." *ISUMA* Vol. 1, No. 2. http://wwwisuma.net/v01n02/lochhead/lochhead_.shtml. Accessed 19 April 2007.

15. Association of Universities and Colleges of Canada. 2007. "Trends in higher education: Volume 1. Enrolment." Ottawa., p. 31. http://www.aucc.ca/_pdf/english/publications/trends_2007_e.pdf. Accessed 1 May 2007.

16. Shipley, L., S. Ouellette, F. Cartwright. 2003. "Planning and preparation: First results of approaches to educational planning (SAEP) 2002." *Education, skills and learning research paper No. 10.* Statistics Canada, Catalogue no. 81-595, p. 7.

17. Human Resources and Skills Development Canada. 2004. "Aspirations of Canadian youth for higher education—Final report." *Learning Policy Directorate, Strategic Policy and Planning.* Catalogue SP-600-05-04E. http://www.hrsdc.gc.ca/en/cs/sp/hrsdc/lp/publications/2004-002631/sp-600-05-04.pdf. Accessed 29 May 2007.

18. Statistics Canada. 2006. "University tuition fees." *The Daily*, September 1, 2006.

19. Finnie, Ross. 2002. "Student loans: Borrowing and burden." *Education Quarterly Review*. Statistics Canada, Catalogue no. 81-003, Vol. 8, No. 4, pp. 28–42; Statistics Canada and Council of Ministers of Education, Canada. 2006. *Education indicators in Canada—Report of the Pan-Canadian Education Indicators Program 2005*. Statistics Canada, Catalogue no. 81-582. pp. 27–30, 107.

20. Blossfeld, H. 1995. *The new role of women: Family formation in modern societies.* Boulder: Westview Press.

21. Morissette, R. 1998. "The declining labour market status of young men." *Labour Markets, Social Institutions, and the Future of Canada's Children.* Edited by Miles Corak. Statistics Canada, Catalogue no. 89-553, pp. 31–50; Kapsalis, C., R. Morissette, G. Picot. 1999. "The returns to education, and the increasing wage gap between younger and older workers." *Analytical Studies Branch Research Paper Series.* Statistics Canada, Catalogue no. 11F0019MIE, No. 131.

22. Morissette, R., A. Johnson. 2005. "Are good jobs disappearing in Canada?" *Analytical Studies Branch Research Paper Series.* Statistics Canada, Catalogue no. 11F0019MIE, No. 239; Morissette, R., G. Schellenberg, A. Johnson. 2005. "Diverging trends in unionization." *Perspectives on Labour and Income.* Statistics Canada, Catalogue no. 75-001, April 2005, pp. 5–12; Morissette, R., Y. Ostrovsky. 2007. "Income instability of lone parents, singles and two-parent families in Canada, 1984 to 2004." *Analytical Studies Branch Research Paper Series.* Statistics Canada, Catalogue no. 11F0019, No. 297.

23. Morissette, R., Y. Ostrovsky. 2006. "Pension coverage and retirement savings of Canadian families, 1986 to 2003." *Analytical Studies Branch Research Paper Series.* Statistics Canada, Catalogue no. 11F0019, No. 286.

24. Morissette and Johnson (2005).

25. Fussell, E. 2002. "The transition to adulthood in aging societies." *Annals of the American Academy of Political and Social Science.* Vol. 580, pp. 16–39.

26. Goldscheider, F., D. Hogan, P. Turcotte. 2006. "The other partner: The changing role of good provider for men's union formation in industrialized countries." *Canadian Studies in Population*, Vol. 33, No. 1, pp. 25–48.

27. According to the 2001 Census, the median value of a dwelling was $134,000 while the 2000 median annual income of a young male adult with a full-year full-time job was $37,400. Hypothetically, a 75% mortgage on a median valued home would require him to spend 25% of his income on mortgage payments on a closed 5-year mortgage at market mortgage interest rates. In 1971, a young man working full-year full-time with a median income and buying a median-valued house would hypothetically have to spend 20% of his income on mortgage payments at the market interest rate.

28. Beaujot, R. 2004. "Delayed life transitions: Trends and implications." *Contemporary Family Trends.* Vanier Institute of the Family. http://www.vifamily.ca/library/cft/delayed_life.pdf. Accessed 16 March 2007.

ⅠⅠ Comprehension

1. In a paragraph, discuss the function of the box "What you should know about this study." What section does it correspond to in an experimental study? (See Chapter 10, "Section Headings," pp. 147–48)

2. Summarize in two to three sentences what is shown in one of charts 2, 3, 4, or 5, avoiding the same words as those in the text.

Structure and Organization

1. Analyze strategies that the author uses to present the wealth of information clearly to a reader. In addition to general strategies applicable to the entire article, consider those present in specific sections and/or paragraphs.

2. a. Identify one transition (word or phrase) of contrast in the section "Women make transitions earlier than men."

   b. Identify three other kinds of transitions (i.e., not ones of contrast) in the section "Why are transitions delayed?"

Critical Thinking

1. How does the section "Why are transitions delayed?" differ from the preceding sections? Discuss at least three differences and account for them.

2. What is the most important finding of this study, according to the author? Explain with reference to the text.

3. Write a pro versus con (cost–benefit) analysis essay or an argumentative essay focused on the need to stay in school versus the need to get a job, using at least two references from "Delayed Transitions of Young Adults."

III Modern Morality

For some, the idea of pure evil persists, but for most educated Westerners, the concepts of absolute evil or good are simplistic or irrelevant. With the breakdown of institutionalized beliefs, such as religious dogmas, and other hegemonies, evil, good, and moral issues have become relative rather than absolute issues. This is evident in the title of the first essay in the section, "Does Peace Have a Chance?" which challenges the common perception that war is inevitable. Similarly, the author of the second essay, "Slip-Sliding Away, Down the Ethical Slope," challenges our traditional way of thinking about dishonesty, which is summed up in his thesis that doing right is harder than doing wrong. Clearly, for the author of "Burning Mistry," as for most of us, book-burning is an expression of hatred and intolerance, yet the essay's target is not the act, per se, but the dubious morality of a government that refuses to condemn it.

While war, cheating, and even book-burning can be seen as age-old problems, "Big Brother, *C'est Moi*" explores a relatively recent, and (to the author) troubling, partnership between "citizen justice" and the new technology of social media. Technology, too, is the overarching subject of "I'm Glad I Never Had to Decide Whether My Strange, Lonely Boy Ought to Exist," a searchingly honest personal essay. Medical technology, such as genetic screening, brings many "trouble-free" promises. "But the answer is complicated," as the essay poignantly shows.

The intersection of ethics and technology is also implicit in "Why We Should Allow Performance Enhancing Drugs in Sport," an argumentative academic essay on an often debated and seemingly irresolvable topic. "Denaturalizing 'Natural' Disasters: Haiti's Earthquake and the Humanitarian Impulse," the second academic essay, acknowledges the human impulse to do good but asks whether, by itself, this enables us to solve the kinds of problems fostered by repressive colonial practices.

John Horgan, "Does Peace Have a Chance?"

In the journalistic essay "Does Peace Have a Chance?" John Horgan takes issue with a common perception concerning the aggressive tendencies of humans, questioning its logic primarily through the use of facts and statistics.

> ⏵ **Preparing to Read**
>
> 1. Who is John Horgan? Do an Internet search to answer this question.
> 2. Reflect on your own position in the debate. Do you believe that war and/or aggression is innate in humans? You could try to answer this question by brainstorming, dividing your ideas into two columns (yes and no); then, look back at your points and decide which are the strongest.

Does Peace Have a Chance?

John Horgan

Slate, 4 August 2009
(1191 words)

1   The West Point War Museum, right across the Hudson River from my home, offers a brisk tour of the history of weaponry, from Paleolithic stone axes to Fat Man, the atomic bomb dropped on Nagasaki in 1945. A sign at the museum's entrance states, "Unquestionably, war-making is an aspect of human nature which will continue as nations attempt to impose their will upon each other." Actually, this assertion is quite questionable. A recent decline in war casualties—especially compared to historical and even prehistorical rates—has some scholars wondering whether the era of international war may be ending.

2   Counting casualties is fraught with uncertainty; scholars' estimates vary according to how they define war and what sources they accept as reliable, among other factors. Nevertheless, a clear trend emerges from recent studies. Last year, 25,600 combatants and civilians were killed as a direct result of armed conflicts, according to the 2009 Yearbook of SIPRI, the Stockholm International Peace Research Institute, to be released Aug. 17. Two thirds of these deaths took place in just three trouble spots: Sri Lanka (8400), Afghanistan (4600), and Iraq (4000). In contrast, almost 500,000 people are killed each year in violent crimes and well over 1 million die in automobile accidents.

3   SIPRI's figure excludes deaths from "one-sided conflict," in which combatants deliberately kill unarmed civilians, and "indirect" deaths from war-related disease and famine. If these casualties are included, annual war-related deaths from 2004 to 2007 rise tenfold to 250,000 per year, according to "The Global Burden of Armed Violence," a 2008 report published by an international organization set up in the aftermath of the Geneva Declaration. Even this much higher number, the report states, is "remarkably low in comparison to historical figures."

4   For example, Milton Leitenberg of the University of Maryland's School for International and Security Studies has estimated that war and state-sponsored genocide in the first half of the 20th century killed as many as 190 million people, both directly and indirectly. That comes to an average of 3.8 million deaths per year. His analysis found that wars killed fewer than one-quarter of that total in the second half of the 20th century—40 million altogether, or 800,000 per year.

5   Even these staggering figures are low in comparison with prehistoric ones, if considered as a percentage of population. All the horrific wars and genocides of the 20th century accounted for less than 3 per cent of all deaths worldwide, according to one estimate. That is much less than the probable rate of violent death among our early ancestors.

6   The economist Samuel Bowles of the Santa Fe Institute recently analyzed dozens of archaeological and ethnographic studies of hunter-gatherer societies like the ones our ancestors are thought to have lived in for most of our prehistory. Warfare and other forms of violence led to 14 per cent of the deaths in these simple societies, Bowles concludes.

7   In his influential book *War Before Civilization*, the anthropologist Lawrence Keeley of the University of Illinois estimates that violence accounted for as many as 25 per cent of all deaths among early societies. Keeley includes not only hunter-gatherers but also tribal societies such as the Yanomamo in Amazonia and the Enga in New Guinea, which practice simple horticulture as well as hunting. These early people racked up such murderous totals with clubs, spears, and arrows rather than machine guns and bombs— and Keeley's stats don't even include indirect deaths from famine and disease.

8   Our prehistory seems to have grown more bellicose as time went on, however. According to anthropologist Brian Ferguson, there is little or no clear-cut evidence of lethal group aggression among any societies prior to 12,000 years ago. War emerged and rapidly spread over the next few thousand years among hunter-gatherers and other groups, particularly in regions where people abandoned a nomadic lifestyle for a more sedentary one and populations grew. War arose, according to this perspective, because of changing environmental and cultural conditions rather than because of "human nature," as the West Point War Museum suggests.

9   This view contradicts what many people believe about war. Since 2006, when I first started teaching a college course called "War and Human Nature," I've asked hundreds of students and other people whether humans will ever stop fighting wars. More than four in five— young and old, conservative and liberal, male and female—answer "No." Asked to explain this response, they often say that we have always fought wars, and we always will, because we are innately aggressive.

10   Of course, all human behavior ultimately stems from our biology. But the sudden emergence of war around 10,000 BCE and its recent decline suggest it's primarily a cultural phenomenon and one that culture is now helping us to overcome. There have been no international wars since the U.S. invasion of Iraq in 2003 and no wars between major industrialized powers since the end of World War II. Most conflicts now consist of guerilla wars, insurgencies, and terrorism—or what the political scientist John Mueller of Ohio State University calls the "remnants of war."

11   Mueller rejects biological explanations for this trend, noting in one paper that "testosterone levels seem to be as high as ever." At least part of the decline, he says, can be attributed to a surge in the number of democracies since World War II, from 20 to nearly 100 (depending on how democracy is defined). Since democracies rarely, if ever, wage war against each other, we may well see a continuing decline in the magnitude of armed conflict.

12   Harvard psychologist Steven Pinker identifies several other cultural factors contributing to the modern decline of violence, both between

and within states: First, the creation of stable states with effective legal systems and police forces has eliminated the endless feuding that plagued many tribal societies. Second, increased life expectancies make us less willing to risk our lives by engaging in violence. Third, as a result of globalization and communications, we have become increasingly interdependent on—and empathetic toward—others outside of our immediate "tribes."

13 If war is not inevitable, neither is peace. "This past year saw increasing threats to security, stability, and peace in nearly every corner of the globe," warns the SIPRI 2009 Yearbook. Global arms spending—especially by the United States, China, and Russia—has surged, and efforts to stem nuclear proliferation have stalled. An al-Qaeda operative could detonate a nuclear suitcase bomb in New York City tomorrow, reversing the recent trend in an instant. But the evidence of a decline in war-related deaths shows that we need not—and should not—accept war as an eternal scourge of the human condition.

14 In fact, this fatalistic view is wrong empirically and morally. Empirically, because war clearly stems less from some hard-wired "instinct" than from mutable cultural and environmental conditions; much can be done, and has been done, to reduce the risks it poses. Morally, because the belief that war will never end helps perpetuate it. The surer we are that the world is irredeemably violent, the more likely we are to support hawkish leaders and policies, making our belief self-fulfilling. Our first step toward ending war is to believe that we can end it.

Comprehension

1. To what does Horgan attribute the increase in group violence after 10,000 BCE?
2. Why does Horgan believe it would not affect his thesis if a single act of terrorism occurred tomorrow (par. 13)?

Structure and Organization

1. a. Explain Horgan's use of personal experience in his essay.
   b. Explain his use of compare–contrast. Do you believe he overuses personal experience or compare–contrast? Justify your answer.

Critical Thinking/Research

1. Why do you think Horgan does not address the opposing view other than simply acknowledging it in paragraphs 1 and 9?
2. Which paragraph do you believe is the most effective in the essay? Explain its effectiveness and the ways it strengthens the essay as a whole.

Robert J. Sternberg, "Slip-Sliding Away, Down the Ethical Slope"

The topic of student cheating has garnered a great deal of attention in recent years—not only in academic journals like *The Chronicle of Higher Education*, published for the college and university communities, but also in magazines and major newspapers. In his short argumentative essay, Sternberg challenges a common perception that underlies students' unethical behaviour.

▶ Preparing to Read

1. What do you believe causes students to cheat? Make a list of possible reasons that can result in unethical student behaviour.

2. Read the first two paragraphs of the essay and, in groups, discuss answers to the questions posed by the author.

Slip-Sliding Away, Down the Ethical Slope

Robert J. Sternberg

The Chronicle of Higher Education, 9 January 2011 (893 words)

1   "You see your roommate at his computer, writing a paper. You notice him transferring text from an online document to the paper he is writing without attribution. He changes a few words here and there so he cannot be accused of plagiarism. Is there a problem here? What, if anything, should you do?"

2   "Professor Johnson is known for not giving back exams because he uses pretty much the same questions from year to year. Your roommate comes back to your room with a big smile. A fraternity brother has managed to slip out a copy of last year's exam and has given it to him. Your roommate figures he can get an edge on this year's exam by studying last year's. 'Not my fault,' he says, 'that Professor Johnson reuses his test questions.' Is there a problem here? What, if anything, should you do?"

3   In presenting problems such as these to various student groups, I have been taken aback by the number of those who either do not see an ethical breach or, if they do, feel that it is minor or not of concern to them. It's a problem that goes much deeper than the occasional incident—we find cheating on the rise even before students get to college, and many cheaters are more concerned with getting caught than with actually committing the act.

4   When it comes to unethical behavior such as cheating, our society has, I believe, engaged in a fundamental misperception. It derives from our conviction that, through religious training or other ethical training—at home, for example—students have been brought up to know right from wrong and thus to behave ethically. The misperception is that it is easy to do the right thing, and that doing the wrong thing requires extra mental or other effort. In fact, the opposite is true: It is often hard to do the right thing, which is why there is cheating.

5   To behave ethically is not a one-step process: Do the right thing. It is a sometimes arduous eight-step process. To behave ethically, you must:

1. Recognize that there is a situation that deserves to be noticed and reflected upon.
2. Define the situation as having an ethical component.
3. Decide that the ethical component is important enough to deserve attention.
4. View the ethical component as relevant to you personally.
5. Ascertain what ethical rule applies to the situation.
6. Figure out how to apply the ethical rule.
7. Prepare for possible adverse consequences, such as retaliation, if you should act ethically.
8. Act.

6   All of those steps can be relatively difficult to execute, and, unfortunately, behaving ethically can be as challenging for parents as it is for students. Parents may cross the line by going from helping their children with homework, papers, science projects, and writing college-application essays to essentially doing the work. It is then little wonder that students reach college and hire others to do their work for them. This point came home in a *Chronicle Review* article, "The Shadow Scholar," by an individual who anonymously writes student papers for pay. Of course, it is not clear that professors are immune: Just as students are outsourcing the writing of papers, so are some professors now outsourcing the grading of papers. One wonders whether our society will eventually eliminate the middlemen—college students and faculty—and simply have the outsourced writers and the outsourced graders work together directly.

7   More realistically, educators need to stop assuming that ethical behavior is the normal course of action for a well-educated individual, and that cheating and other forms of unethical behavior are not the norm. Rather, they have to assume that behaving ethically is often challenging, as any fired whistle-blower can tell you.

8   Schools need to teach students the steps involved in ethical behavior and the challenges of executing them. And they need to do so with real-life case studies relevant to the students' lives. The steps toward ethical behavior are not ones that students can internalize by memorization, but only through active experiential learning with personally relevant examples.

9   There is a larger question our society must face: Have we abrogated what should be a fundamental responsibility of higher education? The financiers who helped to create the financial meltdown of 2008 were, for the most part, bright and well educated. Many were graduates of this country's finest colleges and universities. Is it possible that, in placing so much emphasis on grades and test scores, we are failing to select for and teach the qualities that will produce not just ethical individuals but also ethical leaders?

10   We have come, in large part, to use standardized-test scores and other objective measurements to provide opportunities to students who score well—opportunities that are much scarcer for others. But is it enough to look for such narrowly defined academic skills? Is it not time to search for and develop the wisdom and positive ethical skills that we need in order to steer this country *up* the slippery slope rather than *down*?

11   Once started on that slide, it is hard to stop before the crash at the bottom. Just ask any disgraced politician, executive, clergyman, or educator. While unethical behavior may start in schools with plagiarism or stolen exams, we know all too sadly, and all too well, that it doesn't end there.

Comprehension

1. Identify, then paraphrase, the author's thesis.
2. According to the author, how can schools best address the problem of unethical student behaviour?

Critical Thinking/Research

1. Is this essay just concerned about stopping students from cheating? What other, larger concerns does Sternberg raise? Do you believe they are important ones?
2. In groups, come up with a real-life scenario, like those that begin the essay, in which unethical behaviour might be involved and share them with other members of the class.
3. In the short term, what specific steps can be taken by instructors or administration to reduce the incidence of cheating at the post-secondary level?
4. Summarize the results of at least two studies that deal with problems of unethical student behaviour published in the last ten years; or, summarize at least two commentaries/editorials on the same topic, making sure the essays are from reliable sources.

Alberto Manguel, "Burning Mistry"

Many journalistic essays are inspired by specific events. Responding to the event, the writer may compare it to similar incidents and comment on its significance, moving from the particular to universal issues. Alberto Manguel begins "Burning Mistry" by referring to two incidents of book burning, one recent, one from the distant past, which leads into a discussion of the effects of censorship and the value of literature.

Preparing to Read

1. Who are Alberto Manguel and Rohinton Mistry? Using reliable sources, briefly summarize their careers as writers and their contributions to literature.
2. In an individual or group activity, come up with titles of books that have been considered too controversial or objectionable to be taught in schools or included in public libraries. What are the grounds for censoring literature? Are they justifiable in some instances? Why or why not?

Burning Mistry

Alberto Manguel

Geist, May 2011
(1093 words)

1   In one of the earliest instances of book burning we know (but certainly not the first), in the year 213 BCE, the Chinese emperor Shih Huang-ti issued an edict ordering that all the books in his realm should be destroyed. In one of the latest instances (but certainly not the last), in September 2010, Rohinton Mistry's *Such a Long Journey* was burned at the gates of Mumbai University by students belonging to the right-wing Shiv Sena party. Between the Chinese emperor's edict and the Mumbai students' action lie twenty-two centuries of books set on fire. If proof were needed of the essential power and value of literature, this long line of burning pages should suffice. Nothing less vigorously alive could elicit such fear.

2   Fear of what? we ask. Among other things, of the truth. Over half a century ago, Jorge Luis Borges suggested that one of the reasons for Huang-ti's action was the fact of his mother's adultery, which the emperor wished to erase from Chinese memory by erasing Chinese history itself. (Borges noted that his case was similar to that of a certain king of Judea who, wishing to kill one child, ordered that all children should be killed.) The burners of Mistry's novel complained that *Such a Long Journey* depicted right-wing politicians, and particularly the Shiv Sena party, in a less than flattering light, and assumed, like their remote Chinese ancestor, that by reducing the story to ashes they would eliminate the fact. No doubt somewhere, in the hundreds of thousands of pages that constituted the corpus of Chinese literature prior to the third century BCE, a mention might have been found of the emperor's mother's peccadillo, but if Huang-ti's reason was indeed to erase such a fact from public memory, his colossal task of destruction had the contrary effect, since the towering flames signalled, even to those quite uninterested in the affairs of the Chinese court, that there was something rotten in the Middle Kingdom.

3   The Shiv Sena students have now achieved much the same thing. As a keen reader of Mistry's books (having once written an afterword for a school edition of *Such a Long Journey*), I think I have a fair recollection of the events and characters in the novel. I must confess, however, that I had not paid particular attention to the presence in it of the Shiv Sena party, and had to go back to the book to refresh my memory. Yes, there is a mention (on page 298 of the first edition) of "dutiful Shiv Sena patrols and motley fascists who roamed city streets with stones at the ready, patriotically shattering windows that they deemed inadequately blacked-out." Mistry writes in a deceptively plain style, with great elegance and quiet humour, and his fiction is infused by a belief in what Robert Louis Stevenson called "the ultimate decency of things." But if I were to offer a selection of outstanding examples of Mistry's writing, I suspect the Shiv Sena passage would not be one of them: there are far subtler, stronger, deeper lines in the novel than this efficiently documentary one. (Here is one, for instance, describing what a father thinks of a hammer that belonged to his own father and that he hopes his son will one day inherit: "He will add his gloss to the wood.") However, now that the irate students have drawn my attention to the appearance of their grouplet in the book, the passage carries for me all the vigour of a political manifesto. We readers should always remember that it is often the censor who draws our attention to the hidden virtues of a text.

4   But there were two other consequences to the book burning that are, if not more outrageous than the act itself, then certainly as distressing. One was the response of the Mumbai University authorities. The other was the lack of response of the Canadian government.

5   In India, when the leader of the Shiv Sena students was interviewed by a television journalist, he said that Mistry was lucky to live in Canada: if he lived in Mumbai, they would burn him as well as his book. He then added that his group demanded the removal of *Such a Long Journey* (prescribed reading for years in the university's MA and BA courses) from the syllabus. After several days, the vice-chancellor of Mumbai University, Dr. Rajan Welukar, did as he was told. The decision, he said, was not his, but that of the outgoing Board of Studies who, with one foot on the stirrup, declared that *Such a Long Journey* should no longer be taught. Dr. Welukar responded, of course, in accordance to a time-honoured bureaucratic tradition, according to which, in such cases, the person responsible must always pass on the blame, preferably to someone departing or departed. Fortunately, India's readers reacted otherwise. In colleges and universities across the country, in individual blogs and in the public press, readers expressed their outrage at both the burning and the banning.

6   In Canada, where indignation is rarely expressed above a polite "Oh, you shouldn't," the response was more subdued. *The Globe and Mail* dutifully reported the incident, the *National Post* noted it briefly, CBC Radio mentioned it on an international program dealing with Canadian matters abroad, PEN Canada, the Writers' Trust and the Toronto Reference Library issued statements of protest, and Mistry's publisher sent out a stern press release. From the government of the True North, Strong and Free, came not a whisper. We must not forget that India has become a vital economic partner for Canada and it would not do to bring up anything that might upset business negotiations, whether in the electronic or the tourist trade. The silence of Harper's government should therefore not surprise us, nor that of the Honourable Michael Chan, Minister for Tourism and Culture of Ontario, Mistry's province: as the minister's title indicates, one industry takes precedence over the other.

7   However, for those with the long view, there is consolation in the fact that book burnings never quite succeed in their purpose. Huang-ti's determination to condemn to oblivion the three thousand years of books that preceded him failed, as these things always do. Today we can still read the sayings of Confucius and the parables of Chuang Tzu and the medical books of the Yellow Emperor, just as we will continue to read *Such a Long Journey*, to revisit its passionate pages or to discover what made it so powerful that a fanatical mob and a cowardly vice-chancellor believed that it merited the flames.

Comprehension

1. What does the author mean in the last sentence of paragraph 6 where he refers to Michael Chan's title?

2. According to Manguel, what is the ultimate effect of book burning?

Structure, Organization, and Style

1. Identify two examples of irony and explain what they contribute to the essay. (Writers employ irony through their use of language: irony reveals a second, deeper meaning under the literal surface; see p. 134).

Critical Thinking/Research

1. Manguel begins with a comparison, which is recalled elsewhere in the essay. Analyze its validity and effectiveness by referring to specific passages.

2. What is Manguel's purpose in comparing the passage of Mistry's prose on page 298 of his book to another passage in the same book (see paragraph 3)?

3. Discuss the ways that Manguel attempts to establish his credibility. Why is it essential that he does this?

Navneet Alang, "Big Brother, *C'est Moi*"

After riots in Vancouver following the defeat of the hometown Canucks in the Stanley Cup finals on 15 June 2011, the Vancouver police posted pictures of those possibly involved in criminal activity; many of these pictures were taken by citizens with video cameras, cellphones, and other social media tools. While many praised the impulse of "citizen justice," others, like Nanveet in the essay below, raised a flag of caution.

This essay appeared in *This Magazine* three months after the incidents it describes (see also "Vancouver Hockey Riot is a Symptom of a Larger Problem," p. 209).

Preparing to Read

What do the concepts "citizen justice" or "vigilante justice" mean to you? Is either of these concepts ever acceptable? Under what conditions? Freewrite on this topic for five minutes, using the prompt "To me, citizen justice is (un)acceptable . . . "; or discuss these or similar questions in groups in order to come up with a definition of "citizen justice."

Big Brother, *C'est Moi:* Vancouver's Post-Riot Web Vigilantes Can Be Tamed

Navneet Alang

This, September–October 2011
(832 words)

1   After the sheer surprise of Vancouver's Stanley Cup riots had dissipated, Canadian commentators tried to figure out what it all meant. Most beat their usual political drums—months later we're blaming the pinko anarchists, capitalist pigs, and beer companies for making their products so darn tasty and portable.

2   But this being 2011, many who broke windows with one hand held camera phones in the other. And as myriad pictures and videos of the event began to circulate, another worrying spectre emerged: social-media vigilantism. Images of those involved in violence and property damage spread quickly around the Web, often with the explicit intention of shaming, catching, and even punishing the perpetrators with acts of "citizen justice."

3   "We have seen Big Brother and he is us," portentously intoned social-media expert Alexandra Samuel to the *Globe and Mail.* And really, who could blame her? Anyone who has ever taken public transit or gone to a movie knows our fellow Canadians can't always be counted on to be fair, or even terribly nice. But if our mistakes and trespasses used to be judged by the mostly neutral bodies of the State, this new technology means we now run the risk of being tried and even convicted by the body politic.

4   This speaks to a phenomenon increasingly difficult to ignore, as centuries-long practices of law and social norms, whether privacy, ownership, knowledge, or even statecraft, are threatened by new technologies. These are worrying prospects to be sure, partly because they're just so new. But here's a radical idea: rather than throwing up our hands, or simply calling for the use of less technology, we need to spend time thinking about how we will reshape our legal and social institutions to deal with the inevitable change that is on its way. To protect the relative freedoms of liberal society, we need to build policing of technology right into our legal structures.

5   After all, it's not as if what we're experiencing now doesn't have some precedent. Take the telephone, for example. Though it was an incredible leap forward in communication, it also presented the rather sticky problem that your communication could be recorded and put to unintended ends. Similarly, having a point of communication in your home meant that people could contact you at any time, whether you happened to be eating dinner or not.

6   Our legal structures responded by enforcing laws about the conditions under which telephone calls could be made, recorded, and submitted for evidence in a legal trial. Maybe just as importantly, we also developed social strictures around the phone, including general rules about appropriate times for calling and the right way to answer. Like most social norms, some people follow them and some don't, but at least legally speaking, our rules around the telephone generally seem to work.

7   What we need, then, is a similarly measured response that institutes civic and legal codes for how surveillance technology can be used, whether that is encouraging social sanction for inappropriate use, or articulating under what circumstances public footage can be submitted for legal evidence. In the same vein, it would also mean the legal system has to deal with the dissemination of information for vigilante purposes, and ratchet up consequences for those who take the law into their own hands. It would involve

the tricky process of the law considering intent and context, but given the different degrees in murder charges and Canada's hate-crime laws, that kind of legal subtlety seems to make our system better, not worse.

8   Implementing these changes will take decades, not years, because the changes here are huge, involving how the State exercises its authority, but also how we as members of a society relate to one another. Yet the purpose of the legal system has always been to police out those two aspects of our lives. And rather than only decrying the downsides of mob mentality, the unfettered exchange of private information or the Web's detrimental impact on established business, we need to think about preserving the good in this new technology.

9   This is because there's another worry looming here too, and it also is about historical precedent. In the 19th century, the rise of printing technologies and cheap reading materials drastically altered how ideas were spread. The State responded by instituting literary study into the then-new school curriculum so that the young might "learn to read properly." Certainly, there were upsides: national cohesion, shared values, and proscriptions against anti-social behaviour. But it also meant that the radical element was contained and made safe, as youth were taught to think usefully, not dangerously.

10   We sit at the cusp of a similar moment in the history of information, and it's certainly true that it occasionally feels like a riot—out of control and of our very basest nature. The fitting response, then, is much like the delicate dance of riot-policing done right: a reaction that enforces some order on chaos, while still protecting the rights and privileges such acts are meant to restore.

Comprehension

1. Paraphrase the sentence that introduces the problem discussed in the essay; paraphrase the author's thesis.
2. What does the writer mean by his final sentence?

Structure, Organization, and Style

1. Although "Big Brother, *C'est Moi*" is a journalistic and not an academic essay, it is written for an educated audience. Referring directly to the text, discuss how the author's awareness of his audience influenced his word choice, sentence length and structure, and the like.

Critical Thinking/Research

1. Analyze Alang's use of the telephone as a precedent. (See p. 48 for a definition of precedent and its uses in argument.)
2. Analyze the effectiveness of Alang's argument; you could consider appeals to logic and ethics, along with other argumentative strategies.
3. Write a comparative rhetorical analysis of this essay and "Vancouver Hockey Riot is a Symptom of a Larger Problem," p. 209, ensuring that you use at least two bases of comparison.

Ian Brown, "I'm Glad I Never Had to Decide Whether My Strange, Lonely Boy Ought to Exist"

Ian Brown, a features writer with the *Globe and Mail,* has written a personal essay about his life with his severely disabled son. However, his essay is not *just* about him and his son. The best personal essays use a personal situation to enable a reader to relate to an experience and, usually, universalize an important issue—in this case, the ethics of genetic engineering. Although Brown also includes the words of members of the medical community, he keeps reminding the reader that he's involved—that the issue is complex and that it evokes deep feelings.

▶ Preparing to Read

1. What are some of the issues related to genetic testing? Genetic engineering? (For example, do you believe guidelines need to be put in place by governments?) You could approach this as a brainstorming or clustering activity (see p. 3).
2. To explore your own attitude toward these issues, freewrite for five to ten minutes, starting with a relevant prompt, such as "I believe that self-selecting your future child's physical traits is . . ."

I'm Glad I Never Had To Decide Whether My Strange, Lonely Boy Ought To Exist

Ian Brown

Globe and Mail, 27 August 2011
(2,316 words)

1   *New prenatal tests can check fetal DNA for everything from gender to serious medical conditions. But as the father of one disabled son asks, who has the right to decide which life isn't worth living?*

2   In the early years of my son's life, before I understood how far outside the norm his disabilities took us, I was always astonished to hear a parent say, "I wouldn't change my disabled child for anything."

3   My wife, Johanna—an exceptionally compassionate person, and a terrific mother—never made such statements.

4   "I hear parents of other handicapped kids saying all the time, 'I wouldn't change my child, I wouldn't trade him for anything,'" Johanna once said to me. We were lying on our backs in bed, talking in the night, which we did on the rare occasions Walker fell asleep. Talking into the darkness, you could say anything. "But I would. I would trade Walker, if I could push a button, for the most average child in the world, who got C's in school. I would trade him in an instant.

5   "I wouldn't trade him for my sake, for our sake. But I would trade him for his sake. I think Walker has a very, very hard life."

6   Trading him still isn't possible, but choosing him is getting closer. A new raft of ultra-accurate, at-home, fetal-DNA tests are flying off North American drugstore and Internet shelves these days, and a massive debate is close behind.

7   The DNA-testing industry (which is growing so fast that the U.S. Federal Drug Administration is investigating the tests) has no sooner offered us the opportunity to select the number and gender of the babies we can have—to say nothing of the chance to guarantee they are free of some debilitating syndrome—than doctors and bioethicists are up in arms, accusing medical researchers of promoting genetic cleansing.

8   These arguments come along every few years now. The more science lets us interfere in the beginnings of life, to engineer what kind of babies we can make, the more we seem to need to debate who we want to be as human beings. Maybe this should tell us something.

9   In my house, such debates always bring on an identity crisis. Walker suffers from CFC, an impossibly rare affliction (150 known cases, globally) caused by a completely random genetic mutation. He's 15 now, looks 10 and has the mind of a two-year-old. He always will.

10   He is an often charming and fantastic companion, but he can't speak, or live on his own (or even with us, anymore), or manage the toilet, or eat without a tube, or go for long without smashing his ears flat and ugly with his fists.

11   We raised him on our own for 10 years, and the experience almost shattered everything I valued—my family, my marriage, my healthy daughter's life, my finances, my friendships, life as I wanted to live it.

12   There was no genetic test for his syndrome when he was born (there still isn't). For a long time, not a day went by when I didn't wish there'd been one. Today, I'm glad no test existed then—that I never had to decide, based on a piece of paper damp with my wife's blood, whether my strange and lonely boy ought to exist.

13   Still, wouldn't he have been better off, thanks to a simple genetic test, not living his shadowy, pain-filled, so-called life? I understand the question. I understand the appeal of the DNA test, its trouble-free promise. But the answer is complicated.

14   Pregnant women can now self-administer a simple blood test as early as the seventh week of pregnancy, and know, with 95-per-cent accuracy, the gender of the child they will be having. This, in turn, gives them the opportunity to abort the fetus if it's not the gender they want. A set of fertility clinics in Los Angeles, New York and Mexico recently reported that 85 per cent of their clients wanted to select for sex (for purposes of "family balancing")—and that three-quarters of those clients came from overseas. (Some manufacturers of gender-testing kits refuse to sell them in India and China for that reason.)

15   The smorgasbord of genetic choices doesn't stop there. Women who use fertility drugs to have children now find a growing number of perinatologists willing to reduce healthy twins to a singleton in utero—purely for the convenience of the woman, as there is rarely any medical need today to perform the procedure.

16   And couples who buy donor eggs and sperm from commercial fertility clinics can now select for hair colour, ethnicity, temperament, athleticism and intellectual prowess—even for the length of the donor's eyelashes. If you think that's creepy, recall that at the beginning of the 20th century, cosmetic surgery was considered creepy too.

17   We do these things not just because we need to, but because we can. Ethics follow technology, not the other way around.

18   Of course, there are more humane and significant uses for the new tests. Duchenne muscular

dystrophy afflicts only boys, and a test can accurately identify the genders of potential candidates and evade the burden of a troubled life. Fetal-DNA researchers are reportedly close to marketing a cheap, accurate blood test for Down syndrome (which 800,000 people in North America live with); similar screens will soon identify even more serious genetic diseases in utero, such as cystic fibrosis (70,000 people worldwide) and sickle-cell anemia (20 per cent of the sub-Saharan population).

19 Geneticists even predict the imminent arrival of the holy grail of the medical testing business, "the $1000 genome"—the (fairly) cheap sequencing of all the most important exons (nucleic-acid sequences) in a fetus's DNA.

20 That will vastly expand would-be parents' understanding of the sicknesses their fetus is heir to (provided geneticists can figure out how to read the data—there are, after all, 4000 known single-gene diseases), and increase the odds they will take abortive action if a serious syndrome is revealed, thereby avoiding a great deal of pain and trouble and medical expense. Danish newspapers have predicted a Down-syndrome-free society by 2030.

21 Needless to say, there are a lot of people who find this revolution in genetic choice alarming and inhuman. Margaret Somerville, the well-known medical ethicist at McGill University, recently lambasted the prospect of widespread prenatal testing as a symptom of our diminished respect for human life. She called it nothing short of a "search and destroy" mission to wipe out disabled people.

22 But Dr. Somerville is an ethicist. The geneticists I know keep clear of the ethical debate. David Chitayat, a clinical pediatrician and geneticist at Toronto's Hospital for Sick Children, thinks Dr. Somerville is talking nonsense.

23 "We're not doing screening to eliminate Down syndrome," Dr. Chitayat explained rather testily the other day, when I phoned to see if he could help me sort out my complicated feelings. No amount of

screening, he points out, will eliminate the genes that cause Down syndrome. But he stoutly defends the right of parents to a choice in the matter.

24 In his view, the value of all life, even the life of the disabled, is counterweighed by the downside of any serious genetic syndrome—the physical toll it takes on the child and the family, the cataclysmic lack of government funding for lodging and care, and the isolation and parental guilt a serious syndrome causes.

25 "Dr. Somerville can do what she wants," he said, "but the decision to screen and to act is an individual decision. Let's say this is true—that severely disabled people teach us something. That is one thing. But to tell someone this is what they have to do because they cannot screen, that they have to have a disabled child? Does she know how many husbands leave when a disabled child is born into a family? Or what the impact is on other children? It's an individual decision in the context of the family about what is good and what's bad. The family decides."

26 "Would you have taken the test and had an abortion," I once asked my wife, "if there had been one?" It was his loneliness I couldn't bear, the boy's own sad sense of how different he was. Somehow he knew that.

27 "If there had been a test when I was pregnant that revealed what Walker's life would have been like, I would have had the abortion."

28 "But then you wouldn't have had Walker," I said.

29 Suddenly Johanna began to move around the kitchen a little faster. "You can't say that after I've known Walker—would I have done something to get rid of him? It's one thing to abort an anonymous fetus. It's another to murder Walker. A fetus wouldn't be Walker."

30 "What do you think the world would be like without people like Walker?" I asked. It was an obnoxious thing to ask. "Without kids

like him, I mean, kids who have real setbacks." Fetal-DNA testing makes this more and more of a possibility.

31 I'll always remember her answer. "A world where there are only masters of the universe would be like Sparta," she said. "It would not be a kind country. It would be a cruel place."

32 By then she was crying.

33 I suspect the reason we can't stop debating the value of genetic testing, despite its many virtues, is that we don't care to choose our fates.

34 Genetic control threatens what Harvard University political scientist Michael Sandel, in his book *The Case Against Perfection*, calls our "lively sense of the contingency of our gifts—our sense that none of us is wholly responsible for his or her success, [which] saves a meritocratic society from the smug assumption that that success is the crown of virtue."

35 We aren't really scared of the slick and dreamless future Dr. Somerville conjures out of her distaste for quasi-therapeutic abortion. We aren't even that afraid of what perfections we might attempt with genetic technology. We're afraid of what the new biotechnology will do to us—that its "stance of mastery and control," as Carl Elliott, a brilliant bioethicist in Minnesota, has written, "leaves insufficient cultural space for the alternate ways of living a human life."

36 I have no objection to genetic testing. If you can avoid it, I don't want your child to face the daunting, aimless future Walker may have, especially after his mother and I are gone.

37 But I have an objection if the results of those tests are the only measure you accept of what constitutes a valuable life. I object if you say that my son is a mistake, that we don't want more of him, and deny what he is: an exotic, living form of freedom; a way of being liberated from the grind of the survival of the fittest; free of all the orthodoxies by which we normals measure a "successful" life—the Harvard acceptance, the hot partner, the good job, the fit body, the millions.

38 Disability is by nature anti-establishment. It's the very lack of so-called normal expectations, the absence of the possibility that Walker and I can ever "achieve" much or even disappoint each other, that frees us from the established and the status quo, to be who we actually are with each other, rather than what society says we are supposed to be. A rare and often impossible form of love lies in that small hollow.

39 Genetic tests are a way to try to eliminate the imperfect, and all the pain and fear that comes with imperfection. (Especially our own.) But imperfection is not just pain and agony.

40 On his good days, Walker is proof of what the imperfect and the fragile have to offer—a reminder that there are many ways to be human, and that judgment is our least valuable human capacity.

41 In terms of physical human evolution, he is a mistake, an error. But he is peerless as a way of developing what Charles Darwin himself in *The Descent of Man* deemed the evolutionary advantages of "the social instincts . . . love, and the distinct emotion of sympathy."

42 I see him for three days every two weeks, now that he lives mostly in an assisted-living home. When he does come home, I try to take him for a walk down Bloor Street, the big city artery nearest our house, him in his chair and me on foot.

43 I lean down and push the chair with my elbows, so I can talk in the ear hole of his soft foam helmet. "Look, Walkie," I say, "look, the white micro-miniskirt is back this summer!" Or: "That Hungarian butcher has had that same side of meat hanging there for a year—let's never eat in there."

44 I say all sorts of things, whatever comes to view. I am pretty sure he understands none of it, rationally. But he knows we are having a Conversation, and he knows he is on one end of it. The wriggling, blasting laugh of pleasure our yakking

always gives him reminds me again and again how important it is to make that gesture—to engage another, to try to reach the Other, no matter how remote the likelihood of any return or result or reward.

45   It doesn't matter that Walker will never pass his genetic test. What matters is that I pass his test, that I had a chance to be a human being, a friend, a chatting buddy, a decent if doltish dad, and that I seized it.

46   I am ashamed to say I regret many things in my life. But I never regret those pointless but utterly unpredictable strolls, those strange, lifting afternoons on the hot city sidewalk with the test-failing boy. They're just one more way of measuring what we might be.

Comprehension

1. a. Explain the significance of the statement "Maybe this should tell us something." (par. 8)
    b. Explain the reason for quotation marks in paragraph 14.
    c. Explain the capitalization of "Conversation" and "Other" in paragraph 44.
2. Paraphrase one of the following two important paragraphs in the essay and summarize the other one: 37, 38.

Structure, Organization, and Style

1. Brown interweaves his personal perspective with facts and expert opinion. Taking one passage of at least three paragraphs, analyze his success. (Hint: the first or last paragraph should include a transition between personal perspective and facts/experts.)
2. How much of the essay would you consider the introduction? Analyze its effectiveness.

Critical Thinking/Research

1. Analyze Brown's writing style, commenting on its effectiveness. For example, you could consider sentence/paragraph length and variety, word choice, voice, tone, and other devices (see p. 129). (Remember that Brown is writing for readers of a national newspaper.)
2. Did the essay change your view about any aspect of genetic testing or engineering? Identify one passage that you considered particularly successful in support of his thesis and explain why you have chosen it.
3. To get a sense of the debate, use reliable sources, such as your library's database, to access two essays that argue one side or the other of an issue related to genetic testing—for example, "designer babies," fertility clinics, or embryo screening. Critically analyze the two essays, evaluating the strengths/weaknesses of their arguments.

J. Savulescu, B. Foddy, & M. Clayton, "Why We Should Allow Performance Enhancing Drugs in Sport"

Many academic essays are designed to answer a research question, test a hypothesis, or review current research. If appropriate, their authors might end by making recommendations. However, academic writers sometimes argue more directly that a particular action is correct or justified. Most effective arguments are based on tight logic and well-supported points, but academic arguments of this nature typically make extensive use of reliable studies for their support; the authors of "Why We Should Allow Performance Enhancing Drugs in Sport" provide 44 references in their essay, most from scholarly journals and official sporting groups.

This essay does not include a clearly stated thesis, though the title indicates what it is. In effect, the last two sentences of paragraph 6 make two points crucial to the essay's thesis and organization: (1) that the attempt to ban drugs from sport has failed and (2) that "an analytical argument" will explain the best course to take. The reader infers that much of the essay will present this "best course."

Preparing to Read

As a freewriting activity or in small groups, explore the following questions:

1. What do you know about the use of performance-enhancing drugs in sports?
2. What is your opinion about their use?
3. Should certain or all such drugs continue to be banned in all or some sports?
4. What are the main issues involved—e.g., excellence in performance, fairness, equality, health?

Why We Should Allow Performance Enhancing Drugs in Sport

J. Savulescu, B. Foddy, and M. Clayton

British Journal of Sports Medicine, December 2004 (4975 words)

1   In 490 BC the Persian Army landed on the plain of Marathon, 25 miles from Athens. The Athenians sent a messenger named Feidipides to Sparta to ask for help. He ran the 150 miles in two days. The Spartans were late. The Athenians attacked and, although outnumbered five to one, were victorious. Feidipides was sent to run back to Athens to report victory. On arrival, he screamed "We won" and dropped dead from exhaustion.

2   The marathon was run in the first modern Olympics in 1896, and in many ways the athletic ideal of modern athletes is inspired by the myth of the marathon. Their ideal is superhuman performance, at any cost.

Drugs in sport

3　The use of performance enhancing drugs in the modern Olympics is on record as early as the games of the third Olympiad, when Thomas Hicks won the marathon after receiving an injection of strychnine in the middle of the race.[1] The first official ban on "stimulating substances" by a sporting organisation was introduced by the International Amateur Athletic Federation in 1928.[2]

4　Using drugs to cheat in sport is not new, but it is becoming more effective. In 1976, the East German swimming team won 11 out of 13 Olympic events, and later sued the government for giving them anabolic steroids.[3] Yet despite the health risks, and despite the regulating bodies' attempts to eliminate drugs from sport, the use of illegal substances is widely known to be rife. It hardly raises an eyebrow now when some famous athlete fails a dope test.

5　In 1991, Vicky Rabinowicz interviewed small groups of athletes. She found that Olympic athletes, in general, believed that most successful athletes were using banned substances.[4]

6　Much of the writing on the use of drugs in sport is focused on this kind of anecdotal evidence. There is very little rigorous, objective evidence because the athletes are doing something that is taboo, illegal, and sometimes highly dangerous. The anecdotal picture tells us that our attempts to eliminate drugs from sport have failed. In the absence of good evidence, we need an analytical argument to determine what we should do.

Condemned to cheating?

7　We are far from the days of amateur sporting competition. Elite athletes can earn tens of millions of dollars every year in prize money alone, and millions more in sponsorships and endorsements. The lure of success is great. But the penalties for cheating are small. A six month or one year ban from competition is a small penalty to pay for further years of multimillion dollar success.

8　Drugs are much more effective today than they were in the days of strychnine and sheep's testicles. Studies involving the anabolic steroid androgen showed that, even in small doses much lower than those used by athletes, muscular strength could be improved by 5–20%.[5] Most athletes are also relatively unlikely to ever undergo testing. The International Amateur Athletic Federation estimates that only 10–15% of participating athletes are tested in each major competition.[6]

9　The enormous rewards for the winner, the effectiveness of the drugs, and the low rate of testing all combine to create a cheating "game" that is irresistible to athletes. Kjetil Haugen[7] investigated the suggestion that athletes face a kind of prisoner's dilemma regarding drugs. His game theoretic model shows that, unless the likelihood of athletes being caught doping was raised to unrealistically high levels, or the payoffs for winning were reduced to unrealistically low levels, athletes could all be predicted to cheat. The current situation for athletes ensures that this is likely, even though they are worse off as a whole if everyone takes drugs, than if nobody takes drugs.

10　Drugs such as erythropoietin (EPO) and growth hormone are natural chemicals in the body. As technology advances, drugs have become harder to detect because they mimic natural processes. In a few years, there will be many undetectable drugs. Haugen's analysis predicts the obvious: that when the risk of being caught is zero, athletes will all choose to cheat.

11　The recent Olympic games in Athens were the first to follow the introduction of a global anti-doping code. From the lead up to the games to the end of the competition, 3000 drug tests were carried out: 2600 urine tests and 400 blood tests for the endurance enhancing drug EPO.[8] From these, 23 athletes were found to have taken a banned substance—the most ever in an Olympic games.[9] Ten of the men's weightlifting competitors were excluded.

12 The goal of "cleaning" up the sport is unattainable. Further down the track the spectre of genetic enhancement looms dark and large.

The spirit of sport

13 So is cheating here to stay? Drugs are against the rules. But we define the rules of sport. If we made drugs legal and freely available, there would be no cheating.

14 The World Anti-Doping Agency code declares a drug illegal if it is performance enhancing, if it is a health risk, or if it violates the "spirit of sport."[10] They define this spirit as follows.[11]

> The spirit of sport is a celebration of the human spirit, body, and mind, and is characterised by the following values:
>
> - ethics, fair play and honesty
> - health
> - excellence in performance
> - character and education
> - fun and joy
> - teamwork
> - dedication and commitment
> - respect for rules and laws
> - respect for self and other participants
> - courage
> - community and solidarity

15 Would legal and freely available drugs violate this "spirit"? Would such a permissive rule be good for sport?

16 Human sport is different from sports involving other animals, such as horse or dog racing. The goal of a horse race is to find the fastest horse. Horses are lined up and flogged. The winner is the one with the best combination of biology, training, and rider. Basically, this is a test of biological potential. This was the old naturalistic Athenian vision of sport: find the strongest, fastest, or most skilled man.

17 Training aims to bring out this potential. Drugs that improve our natural potential are against the spirit of this model of sport. But this is not the only view of sport. Humans are not horses or dogs. We make choices and exercise our own judgment. We choose what kind of training to use and how to run our race. We can display courage, determination, and wisdom. We are not flogged by a jockey on our back but drive ourselves. It is this judgment that competitors exercise when they choose diet, training, and whether to take drugs. We can choose what kind of competitor to be, not just through training, but through biological manipulation. Human sport is different from animal sport because it is creative. Far from being against the spirit of sport, biological manipulation embodies the human spirit—the capacity to improve ourselves on the basis of reason and judgment. When we exercise our reason, we do what only humans do.

18 The result will be that the winner is not the person who was born with the best genetic potential to be strongest. Sport would be less of a genetic lottery. The winner will be the person with a combination of the genetic potential, training, psychology, and judgement. Olympic performance would be the result of human creativity and choice, not a very expensive horse race.

19 Classical musicians commonly use β blockers to control their stage fright. These drugs lower the heart rate and blood pressure, reducing

the physical effects of stress, and it has been shown that the quality of a musical performance is improved if the musician takes these drugs.[12] Although elite classical music is arguably as competitive as elite sport, and the rewards are similar, there is no stigma attached to the use of these drugs. We do not think less of the violinist or pianist who uses them. If the audience judges the performance to be improved with drugs, then the drugs are enabling the musician to express him or herself more effectively. The competition between elite musicians has rules— you cannot mime the violin to a backing CD. But there is no rule against the use of chemical enhancements.

20   Is classical music a good metaphor for elite sport? Sachin Tendulkar is known as the "Maestro from Mumbai." The Associated Press called Maria Sharapova's 2004 Wimbledon final a "virtuoso performance."[13] Jim Murray[14] wrote the following about Michael Jordan in 1996:

21   You go to see Michael Jordan play for the same reason you went to see Astaire dance, Olivier act or the sun set over Canada. It's art. It should be painted, not photographed.

22   It's not a game, it's a recital. He's not just a player, he's a virtuoso. Heifetz with a violin. Horowitz at the piano.

23   Indeed, it seems reasonable to suggest that the reasons we appreciate sport at its elite level have something to do with competition, but also a great deal to do with the appreciation of an extraordinary performance.

24   Clearly the application of this kind of creativity is limited by the rules of the sport. Riding a motorbike would not be a "creative" solution to winning the Tour de France, and there are good reasons for proscribing this in the rules. If motorbikes were allowed, it would still be a good sport, but it would no longer be a bicycle race.

25   We do not think that allowing cyclists to take EPO would turn the Tour de France into some kind of "drug race," any more than the various training methods available turn it into a "training race" or a "money race." Athletes train in different, creative ways, but ultimately they still ride similar bikes, on the same course. The skill of negotiating the steep winding descent will always be there.

Unfair?

26   People do well at sport as a result of the genetic lottery that happened to deal them a winning hand. Genetic tests are available to identify those with the greatest potential. If you have one version of the ACE gene, you will be better at long distance events. If you have another, you will be better at short distance events. Black Africans do better at short distance events because of biologically superior muscle type and bone structure. Sport discriminates against the genetically unfit. Sport is the province of the genetic elite (or freak).

27   The starkest example is the Finnish skier Eero Maentyranta. In 1964, he won three gold medals. Subsequently it was found he had a genetic mutation that meant he "naturally" had 40–50% more red blood cells than average.[15] Was it fair that he had significant advantage given to him by chance?

28   The ability to perform well in sporting events is determined by the ability to deliver oxygen to muscles. Oxygen is carried by red blood cells. The more red blood cells, the more oxygen you can carry. This in turn controls an athlete's performance in aerobic exercise. EPO is a natural hormone that stimulates red blood cell production, raising the packed cell volume (PCV)—the percentage of the blood comprised of red blood cells. EPO is produced in response to anaemia, haemorrhage, pregnancy, or living at

altitude. Athletes began injecting recombinant human EPO in the 1970s, and it was officially banned in 1985.[16]

29   At sea level, the average person has a PCV of 0.4–0.5. It naturally varies; 5% of people have a packed cell volume above 0.5,[17] and that of elite athletes is more likely to exceed 0.5, either because their high packed cell volume has led them to success in sport or because of their training.

30   Raising the PCV too high can cause health problems. The risk of harm rapidly rises as PCV gets above 50%. One study showed that in men whose PCV was 0.51 or more, risk of stroke was significantly raised (relative risk = 2.5), after adjustment for other causes of stroke.[19] At these levels, raised PCV combined with hypertension would cause a ninefold increase in stroke risk. In endurance sports, dehydration causes an athlete's blood to thicken, further raising blood viscosity and pressure.[20] What begins as a relatively low risk of stroke or heart attack can rise acutely during exercise.

31   In the early 1990s, after EPO doping gained popularity but before tests for its presence were available, several Dutch cyclists died in their sleep due to inexplicable cardiac arrest. This has been attributed to high levels of EPO doping.[21] The risks from raising an athlete's PCV too high are real and serious.

32   Use of EPO is endemic in cycling and many other sports. In 1998, the Festina team was expelled from the Tour de France after trainer Willy Voet was caught with 400 vials of performance enhancing drugs.[22] The following year, the World Anti-Doping Agency was established as a result of the scandal. However, EPO is extremely hard to detect and its use has continued. Italy's Olympic anti-doping director observed in 2003 that the amount of EPO sold in Italy outweighed the amount needed for sick people by a factor of six.[23]

33   In addition to trying to detect EPO directly, the International Cycling Union requires athletes to have a PCV no higher than 0.5. But 5% of people naturally have a PCV higher than 0.5. Athletes with a naturally high PCV cannot race unless doctors do a number of tests to show that their PCV is natural. Charles Wegelius was a British rider who was banned and then cleared in 2003. He had had his spleen removed in 1998 after an accident, and as the spleen removes red blood cells, its absence resulted in an increased PCV.[24]

34   There are other ways to increase the number of red blood cells that are legal. Altitude training can push the PCV to dangerous, even fatal, levels. More recently, hypoxic air machines have been used to simulate altitude training. The body responds by releasing natural EPO and growing more blood cells, so that it can absorb more oxygen with every breath. The Hypoxico promotional material quotes Tim Seaman, a US athlete, who claims that the hypoxic air tent has "given my blood the legal 'boost' that it needs to be competitive at the world level."[25]

35   There is one way to boost an athlete's number of red blood cells that is completely undetectable:[26] autologous blood doping. In this process, athletes remove some blood, and reinject it after their body has made new blood to replace it. This method was popular before recombinant human EPO became available.

36   There is no difference between elevating your blood count by altitude training, by using a hypoxic air machine, or by taking EPO. But the last is illegal. Some competitors have high PCVs and an advantage by luck. Some can afford hypoxic air machines. Is this fair? Nature is not fair. Ian Thorpe has enormous feet which give him an advantage that no other swimmer can get, no matter how much they exercise. Some gymnasts are more flexible, and some basketball players are seven feet tall. By allowing everyone

to take performance enhancing drugs, we level the playing field. We remove the effects of genetic inequality. Far from being unfair, allowing performance enhancement promotes equality.

Just for the rich?

37   Would this turn sport into a competition of expensive technology? Forget the romantic ancient Greek ideal. The Olympics is a business. In the four years before the Athens Olympics, Australia spent $547 million on sport funding,[27] with $13.8 million just to send the Olympic team to Athens.[28] With its highest ever funding, the Australian team brought home 17 gold medals, also its highest. On these figures, a gold medal costs about $32 million. Australia came 4th in the medal tally in Athens despite having the 52nd largest population. Neither the Australian multicultural genetic heritage nor the flat landscape and desert could have endowed Australians with any special advantage. They won because they spent more. Money buys success. They have already embraced strategies and technologies that are inaccessible to the poor.

38   Paradoxically, permitting drugs in sport could reduce economic discrimination. The cost of a hypoxic air machine and tent is about US$7000.[29] Sending an athlete to a high altitude training location for months may be even more expensive. This arguably puts legal methods for raising an athlete's PCV beyond the reach of poorer athletes. It is the illegal forms that level the playing field in this regard.

39   One popular form of recombinant human EPO is called Epogen. At the time of writing, the American chain Walgreens offers Epogen for US$86 for 6000 international units (IU). The maintenance dose of EPO is typically 20 IU per kg body weight, once a week.[30] An athlete who weighs 100 kg therefore needs 2000 IU a week, or 8600 IU a month. Epogen costs the athlete

about US$122 a month. Even if the Epogen treatment begins four years before an event, it is still cheaper than the hypoxic air machine. There are limits on how much haemoglobin an athlete can produce, however much EPO they inject, so there is a natural cap on the amount of money they can spend on this method.

40   Meanwhile, in 2000, the cost of an in-competition recombinant EPO test was about US$130 per sample.[31] This test is significantly more complex than a simple PCV test, which would not distinguish exogenous or endogenous EPO. If monetary inequalities are a real concern in sport, then the enormous sums required to test every athlete could instead be spent on grants to provide EPO to poorer athletes, and PCV tests to ensure that athletes have not thickened their blood to unsafe levels.

Unsafe?

41   Should there be any limits to drugs in sport?

42   There is one limit: safety. We do not want an Olympics in which people die before, during, or after competition. What matters is health and fitness to compete. Rather than testing for drugs, we should focus more on health and fitness to compete. Forget testing for EPO, monitor for PCV. We need to set a safe level of PCV. In the cycling world, that is 0.5. Anyone with a PCV above that level, whether through the use of drugs, training, or natural mutation, should be prevented from participating on safety grounds. If someone naturally has a PCV of 0.6 and is allowed to compete, then that risk is reasonable and everyone should be allowed to increase their PCV to 0.6. What matters is what is a safe concentration of growth hormone—not whether it is natural or artificial.

43   We need to take safety more seriously. In the 1960s, East German athletes underwent systematic government sanctioned prescription of anabolic steroids, and were awarded millions of

dollars in compensation in 2002. Some of the female athletes had been compelled to change their sex because of the large quantities of testosterone they had been given.[32]

44   We should permit drugs that are safe, and continue to ban and monitor drugs that are unsafe. There is another argument for this policy based on fairness: provided that a drug is safe, it is unfair to the honest athletes that they have to miss out on an advantage that the cheaters enjoy.

45   Taking EPO up to the safe level, say 0.5, is not a problem. This allows athletes to correct for natural inequality. There are, of course, some drugs that are harmful in themselves—for example, anabolic steroids. We should focus on detecting these because they are harmful not because they enhance performance.

46   Far from harming athletes, paradoxically, such a proposal may protect our athletes. There would be more rigorous and regular evaluation of an athlete's health and fitness to perform. Moreover, the current incentive is to develop undetectable drugs, with little concern for safety. If safe performance enhancement drugs were permitted, there would be greater pressure to develop safe drugs. Drugs would tend to become safer.

47   This is perhaps best illustrated by the case of American sailor Kevin Hall. Hall lost his testicles to cancer, meaning that he required testosterone injections to remain healthy. As testosterone is an anabolic steroid, he had to prove to four separate governing bodies that he was not using the substance to gain an advantage.[33] Any tests that we should be sensitive to the health of the athlete; to focus on the substances themselves is dogmatic.

48   Not only this, but health testing can help to mitigate the dangers inherent in sport.

49   For many athletes, sport is not safe enough without drugs. If they suffer from asthma, high blood pressure, or cardiac arrhythmia, sport places their bodies under unique stresses, which raise the likelihood of a chronic or catastrophic harm. For example, between 1985 and 1995, at least 121 US athletes collapsed and died directly after or during a training session or competition—most often because they had hypertrophic cardiomyopathy or heart malformations.[34] The relatively high incidence of sudden cardiac death in young athletes has prompted the American Heart Association to recommend that all athletes undergo cardiac screening before being allowed to train or compete.[35]

50   Sometimes, the treatments for these conditions will raise the performance of an athlete beyond that which they could attain normally. But safety should come first. If an archer requires β blockers to treat heart disease, we should not be concerned that this will give him or her an advantage over other archers. Or if an anemic cyclist wants to take EPO, we should be most concerned with the treatment of the anaemia.

51   If we are serious about safety in sport, we should also be prepared to discuss changes to the rules and equipment involved in sports which are themselves inherently dangerous. Formula One motor racing, once the most deadly of sports, has not seen a driver death in over six years, largely because of radical changes in the safety engineering of the tracks and the cars. Meanwhile, professional boxing remains inherently dangerous; David Rickman died during a bout in March 2004, even though he passed a physical examination the day before.[36]

Children

52   Linford Christie, who served a two year drug ban from athletics competition, said that athletics "is so corrupt now I wouldn't want my child doing it."[37] But apart from the moral harms to children in competing in a corrupt sport, should we withhold them from professional sport for medical reasons?

53 The case where the athletes are too young to be fully autonomous is different for two important reasons. Firstly, children are much less capable of rejecting training methods and treatments that their coach wishes to use. Secondly, we think it is worth protecting the range of future options open to a child.

54 There is a serious ethical problem with allowing children to make any kind of choice that substantially closes off their options for future lifestyles and career choices. If we do not consider children competent for the purposes of allowing them to make choices that cause them harm, then we should not allow them to decide to direct all of their time to professional gymnastics at age 10. The modifications such a choice can make to a child's upbringing are as serious, and potentially as harmful, as many of the available performance enhancing drugs. Children who enter elite sport miss large parts of the education and socialisation that their peers receive, and are submitted to intense psychological pressure at an age when they are ill equipped to deal with it.

55 We argue that it is clear that children, who are not empowered to refuse harmful drugs, should not be given them by their coaches or parents. But the same principles that make this point obvious should also make it obvious that these children should not be involved in elite competitive sport in the first place. However, if children are allowed to train as professional athletes, then they should be allowed to take the same drugs, provided that they are no more dangerous than their training is.

56 Haugen's model showed that one of the biggest problems in fighting drug use was that the size of the rewards for winning could never be overshadowed by the penalties for being caught. With this in mind, we can begin to protect children by banning them from professional sport.

Climate of cheating

57 If we compare the medical harms of the entire worldwide doping problem, they would have to be much less than the worldwide harms stemming from civilian illicit drug use. And yet, per drug user, the amount of money spent on combating drugs in sport outweighs the amount spent on combating civilian drug use by orders of magnitude.

58 We can fairly assume that if medical harms and adherence to law were the only reasons we felt compelled to eradicate doping, then the monetary value we placed on cleaning up sport should be the same, per drug user, as the monetary value we place on eradicating recreational drug use. And yet it is not.

59 Because of this, it should be obvious that it is not medical harms that we think are primarily at stake, but harm to sport as a whole, a purported violation of its spirit. It is a problem for the credibility of elite sport, if everyone is cheating.

60 If it is this climate of cheating that is our primary concern, then we should aim to draft sporting rules to which athletes are willing to adhere.

Prohibition

61 It is one thing to argue that banning performance enhancing drugs has not been successful, or even that it will never be successful. But it should also be noted that the prohibition of a substance that is already in demand carries its own intrinsic harms.

62 The Prohibition of Alcohol in America during the 1920s led to a change in drinking habits that actually increased consumption. Driven from public bars, people began to drink at home, where the alcohol was more readily available, and the incidence of deaths due to alcoholism rose or remained stable, while they

dropped widely around the world in countries without prohibition.[38] Furthermore, as the quality of the alcohol was unregulated, the incidence of death from poisoned alcohol rose fourfold in five years.[39]

63   Even when prohibition leads to a decrease in consumption, it often leads to the creation of a black market to supply the continuing demand, as it did in the Greenland study of alcohol rationing.[40] Black markets supply a product that is by definition unregulated, meaning that the use is unregulated and the safety of the product is questionable.

64   The direct risks from prohibiting performance enhancing drugs in sport are similar, but probably much more pronounced. Athletes currently administer performance enhancing substances in doses that are commensurate with the amount of performance gain they wish to attain, rather than the dose that can be considered "safe." The athletic elite have near unlimited funds and the goal of near unlimited performance, a framework that results in the use of extremely unsafe doses. If athletes are excluded when their bodies are unsafe for competition, this kind of direct consequence from prohibition would be reduced.

The problem of strict liability

65   Lord Coe, a dual Olympic champion, has defended the doctrine of "strict liability," as it is currently applied to athletes who use a banned substance:[41]

66   . . .The rule of strict liability—under which athletes have to be solely and legally responsible for what they consume—must remain supreme. We cannot, without blinding reason and cause, move one millimetre from strict liability—if we do, the battle to save sport is lost.

67   The best reason for adhering to this rule is that, if coaches were made responsible for drugs that they had given to their athletes, then the coach would be banned or fined, and the athlete could still win the event. In this situation, other athletes would still be forced to take drugs in order to be competitive, even though the "cheat" had been caught.

68   But the doctrine of strict liability makes victims of athletes such as those of the East German swim team, who are competing in good faith but have been forced to take drugs. It also seems dogmatically punitive for athletes like British skier Alain Baxter, who accidentally inhaled a banned stimulant when he used the American version of a Vicks decongestant inhaler, without realising that it differed from the British model.[42]

69   It seems that strict liability is unfair to athletes, but its absence is equally unfair. Our proposal solves this paradox—when we exclude athletes only on the basis of whether they are healthy enough to compete, the question of responsibility and liability becomes irrelevant. Accidental or unwitting consumption of a risky drug is still risky; the issue of good faith is irrelevant.

Alternative strategies

70   Michael Ashenden[43] proposes that we keep progressive logs of each athlete's PCV and hormone concentrations. Significant deviations from the expected value would require follow up testing. The Italian Cycling Federation decided in 2000 that all juniors would be tested to provide a baseline PCV and given a "Hematologic Passport."

71   Although this strategy is in many ways preferable to the prohibition of doping, it does nothing to correct the dangers facing an athlete who has an unsafe baseline PCV or testosterone concentration.

Test for health, not drugs

72 The welfare of the athlete must be our primary concern. If a drug does not expose an athlete to excessive risk, we should allow it even if it enhances performance. We have two choices: to vainly try to turn the clock back, or to rethink who we are and what sport is, and to make a new 21st century Olympics. Not a super-Olympics but a more human Olympics. Our crusade against drugs in sport has failed. Rather than fearing drugs in sport, we should embrace them.

73 In 1998, the president of the International Olympic Committee, Juan-Antonio Samaranch, suggested that athletes be allowed to use non-harmful performance enhancing drugs.[44] This view makes sense only if, by not using drugs, we are assured that athletes are not being harmed.

74 Performance enhancement is not against the spirit of sport; it is the spirit of sport. To choose to be better is to be human. Athletes should be given this choice. Their welfare should be paramount. But taking drugs is not necessarily cheating. The legalisation of drugs in sport may be fairer and safer.

References

1. House of Commons, Select Committee on Culture, Media and Sport. 2004. Seventh Report of Session 2003–2004, UK Parliament, HC 499-I.
2. House of Commons, Select Committee on Culture, Media and Sport. 2004. Seventh Report of Session 2003–2004, UK Parliament, HC 499-I.
3. Longman J. 2004. East German steroids' toll: "They killed Heidi," New York Times 2004 Jan 20, sect D: 1.
4. Rabinowicz V. Athletes and drugs: a separate pace? Psychol Today 1992;25:52–3.
5. Hartgens F, Kuipers H. Effects of androgenic-anabolic steroids in athletes. Sports Med 2004;34: 513–54.
6. IAAF, 2004. http://www.iaaf.org/antidoping/index.html.
7. Haugen KK. The performance-enhancing drug game. Journal of Sports Economics 2004;5:67–87.
8. Wilson S. Boxer Munyasia fails drug test in Athens: Associated Press, 2004 Aug 10.
9. Zinser L. With drug-tainted past, few track records fall. New York Times 2004 Aug 29, Late Edition, p. 1.
10. WADA. World Anti-Doping Agency Code, Montreal. World Anti-Doping Agency, 2003:16.
11. WADA. World Anti-Doping Agency Code, Montreal. World Anti-Doping Agency, 2003:3.
12. Brantigan CO, Brantigan TA, Joseph N. Effect of beta blockade and beta stimulation on stage fright. Am J Med 1982;72:88–94.
13. Wilson S. Sharapova beats Williams for title. Associated Press, 2004 Jul 3, 09:10am.
14. Murray J. It's basketball played on a higher plane. Los Angeles Times 1996 Feb 4 1996, sect C:1.
15. Booth F, Tseng B, Flick M, et al. Molecular and cellular adaptation of muscle in response to physical training. Acta Physiol Scand 1998;162:343–50.
16. Caitlin DH, Murray TH. Performance-enhancing drugs, fair competition, and olympic sport. JAMA 1996;276:231–7.
17. Fairbanks VF, Tefferi A. Normal ranges for packed cell volume and hemoglobin concentration in adults: relevance to 'apparent polycythemia,' Eur J Haemotol 2000;65:285–96.
18. Schumacher YO, Grathwohl D, Barturen JM, et al. Haemoglobin, haematocrit and red blood cell indices in elite cyclists. Are the control values for blood testing valid? Int J Sports Med 2000;21:380–5.
19. Wannamethee G, Perry U, Shaper AG. Haematocrit, hypertension and risk of stroke. J Intern Med 1994;235:163–8.
20. Catlin DH, Hatton CK. Use and abuse of anabolic and other drugs for athletic enhancement. Adv Intern Med 1991;36:399–424.
21. Cazzola M. A global strategy for prevention and detection of blood doping with erythropoietin and related drugs. Haematologica 2000;85:561–3.
22. BBC News 1998 23 Jul. http://news.bbc.co.uk/1/hi/special_report/1998/07/98/tour_de_france/138079.stm.
23. Toti G. "Doping fenomeno di massa. E' usato da 400mila italiani," Libera 2003 11 Nov, 17.
24. BBC Sport 2003 12 Feb. http://news.bbc.co.uk/go/pr/fr/-sport2/hi/other_sports/cycling/3258168.stm.
25. Hypoxico website. http://www.hypoxictent.com.
26. Browne A, LaChance V, Pipe A. The ethics of blood testing as an element of doping control in sport. Med Sci Sports Exerc 1999;31:497–501.

27. Australian Olympic Committee. AOC welcomes funding boost. http://www.olympics.com.au/defaultasp?pg=home&spg=display&articleid=943, 2001 Apr 24

28. Australian Olympic Committee. 2001–2003, Programs and funding guidelines for sports on the program for the 2004 Olympic Games in Athens (For the period 1 January 2001 to 31 December 2004). 9 March 2001. Updated 20 November 2003. http://www.olympics.com.au/cp7/c9/webi/externaldocument/00000954aay.pdf.

29. As of August 2004 from the Hypoxico website.

30. Russell G, Gore CJ, Ashenden MJ, *et al*. Effects of prolonged low doses of recombinant human erythropoietin during submaximal and maximal exercise. *Eur J Appl Physiol* 2002;86:442–9.

31. Abbott A. What price the Olympian ideal? *Nature* 2000 Sep;407:124–7.

32. Tufts A. Doped East German athletes to receive compensation. *BMJ* 2002;324:29.

33. Wilson B. Hall overcomes cancer, then red tape to reach Olympics. *Associated Press*, 2004 Aug 13.

34. Maron B, Shirani J, Liviu C, *et al*. Sudden death in young competitive athletes: clinical, demographic and pathological profiles. *JAMA* 1996;276:199–204.

35. Potera C. AHA panel outlines sudden death screening standards. *Phys Sportsmed* 1996;24:27.

36. Heath D. Local boxer dies two days after knockout. Jacksonville: *The Florida Times-Union*, 2004 Mar 30, sect E:1.

37. Coe S. Athletics: Christie out of order for corruption claims. *The Daily Telegraph*, 2001 Feb 13.

38. Warburton C. *The Economic results of prohibition*. New York: Columbia University Press, 1932:78–90.

39. Coffey TM. *The long thirst: prohibition in America, 1920–1933*. New York: WW Norton & Co, 1975:196–8.

40. Schechter EJ. Alcohol rationing and control systems in Greenland. *Contemp Drug Probl* 1986;18:587–620.

41. Coe S. We cannot move from strict liability rule. *The Daily Telegraph*, 2004 Feb 25.

42. Wilson S. British skier found guilty of doping, stripped of slalom bronze medal. London: The Associated Press State and Local Wire, 2002 Mar 21.

43. Ashenden M. A strategy to deter blood doping in sport. *Haematologica* 2002;87:225–34.

44. Downes S. Samaranch move stuns critics. *The Sunday Times* (London) 1999 Jan 31.

Comprehension

1. What are the two kinds of sports discussed in "The spirit of sport"? Briefly summarize their differences; paraphrase paragraph 18.

2. According to the authors, what single criterion should determine the use of performance-enhancing drugs by individual athletes?

Structure, Organization, and Style

1. Analyze the essay's introduction for its effectiveness.

2. Identify three different kinds of evidence used in the essay and discuss what each contributes to the authors' argument. Refer to specific passages.

Critical Thinking/Research

1. How important to the authors' argument is the definition of the "spirit of sport" (from the world Anti-Doping Agency code) mentioned in paragraph 14? Discuss its importance to the essay's development.

2. Explain why erythropoietin (EPO), introduced in paragraph 10, is a good drug to use as a key example in the essay.

3. a. Analyze one of the essay's main points for its effectiveness, explaining what it contributes to the essay as a whole.

   OR

   b. How well do the authors rebut the opposing viewpoint? Referring to at least two specific passages, analyze their rebuttal.

4. Using reliable research sources, summarize the controversy surrounding performance enhancing drugs as it emerged in either the 2008 or the 2012 Summer Olympics.

Andrew D. Pinto, "Denaturalizing 'Natural' Disasters: Haiti's Earthquake and the Humanitarian Impulse"

Academic writers often analyze issues of concern to readers, using formats similar to those of student essays. Like many such essays, "Denaturalizing 'Natural' Disasters" is cross-disciplinary: While the author is a physician specializing in community medicine, the essay touches on the disciplines of history, geography, economics, ethics, and political science. Pinto uses argumentative strategies to draw attention to a problem overlooked by governments and the mainstream media.

An increasing number of "open-access" journals, like *Open Medicine*, provide access to users without requiring passwords or charging fees. The *Open Medicine* website includes the journal's mission statement, along with the purpose of open-access journals.

Preparing to Read

Are you aware of the social and economic problems that have beset Haiti prior to the devastating 2010 earthquake? Using a reliable source, briefly summarize the facts surrounding the disaster and its aftermath.

Denaturalizing "Natural" Disasters: Haiti's Earthquake and the Humanitarian Impulse

Andrew D. Pinto

Open Medicine, November 2010
(2017 words)

1   On 12 January 2010, at 16:53 local time, Haiti experienced a catastrophic magnitude-7.0 earthquake 25 kilometres west of the capital, Port-au-Prince. The United Nations Office for the Coordination of Humanitarian Affairs estimates that more than 220,000 people died and 2.3 million were displaced.[1] This earthquake was more than twice as lethal as any previous of a similar magnitude in the last century.[2] In striking contrast, the magnitude-8.8 earthquake that struck Chile on 27 February 2010 resulted in fewer than 800 deaths, despite its higher magnitude.[3]

2   Why was Haiti's experience so different? Most commentators have pointed to physical factors, such as the shallow epicentre of the earthquake, its proximity to a major population centre, poor building construction and the lack of an adequate emergency response system.[2,4] These undoubtedly played a role in the extraordinarily high mortality rate. However, although many have noted Haiti's poverty and internal strife, only a few commentators have identified these as key determinants of the level of devastation caused by the earthquake.[5,6] Even fewer have suggested looking at the historical record or where Haiti stands in the current world order for an explanation.

3   What is considered "natural," in the context of disasters such as Haiti's, is seen as independent of human actions. Any analysis of such events must "denaturalize" them by examining the historic, political and economic contexts within which they occur.[7,8] Specifically, health professionals and policy-makers need to understand the unnatural determinants of the problems facing the country and how these affect any form of response. Without such an understanding, the humanitarian impulse informing international efforts to support Haiti's recovery and development may serve to merely reinforce the historic relationship between wealthy countries and Haiti and may fuel continued underdevelopment.

Foundations of a disaster

4   Knowledge of Haiti's history is integral to an informed understanding of the earthquake and its outcome. Only a brief review is possible here; more detailed accounts are available elsewhere.[9,10] Soon after Spanish colonizers led by Christopher Columbus arrived in 1492 on the island they christened Hispaniola—present day Haiti and the Dominican Republic—the annihilation of the island's indigenous peoples began.

Paul Farmer has argued that the triple assault of imported disease, malnutrition and maltreatment set a precedent for the subjugation of human life in Haiti at the hands of wealthy nations.[9] Plantations of sugar cane became fields of misery for tens of thousands of trafficked African slaves, while Spain and France reaped the profits.[11]

5   The French Revolution, which began in 1789, sparked a revolt of Haiti's middle class and an uprising of its slave majority. In 1804, Haiti became the second independent republic in the western hemisphere, after the United States. Further, it was the first example of slaves winning nationhood through their own resistance.[12]

6   In abolishing slavery and resisting colonial rule, Haiti was not easily tolerated by European powers or by the slave-owning United States. With its economy ruined by its revolutionary war, Haiti was forced to agree to unfair trading relationships with nations that refused to recognize its sovereignty. In 1825, France sent an armada to retake Haiti; the French invasion was averted only when the young nation agreed to pay 150 million francs as compensation for the loss of the slave trade. This indemnity was not paid off by Haiti until 1947.[10] Similar instances of gunboat diplomacy by the United States, Germany and Britain drained Haiti's national coffers throughout the 19th century.[9]

7   Foreign interference and political destabilization have continually undermined governance in Haiti. For example, the United States occupied Haiti from 1915 to 1934; although the Americans have claimed that their occupation improved Haitian economic and governance infrastructure,[13] contemporary accounts note that the presence of a military force enabled the passing of a constitution that permitted foreign ownership of land.[14] The US Marines also left behind a well-trained army that went on to rule

Haiti, installing and deposing leader after leader. "Papa Doc" Duvalier and his son "Baby Doc" would be the last and most horrific of these leaders, using *tonton macoutes* death squads to establish and entrench their rule between 1957 and 1986. Although foreign aid continued to flow to this regime, the national debt grew dramatically.[15] Historians agree that the Duvaliers were supported by the West throughout the Cold War, ostensibly to help fight against communism but also to support the interests of foreign companies who benefited from low-cost Haitian labour.[16]

8   Against significant odds, Jean-Bertrand Aristide was elected in the nation's first democratic elections in 1990, overwhelmingly supported by the poor and working class. His government was short lived, as his popular reforms threatened the status quo for Haiti's oligarchs and foreign interests. He was ousted in a coup after only eight months and sent into exile. After years of Aristide and his supporters lobbying the US government, and the intervention of numerous advocates, he was reinstated as president in 1994. He was re-elected in 2000, only to again be exiled during a coup in 2004. External forces played a role in both coups, leaving Haiti's political health tenuous ever since.[9,17,18]

The humanitarian impulse

9   With this historical background in mind, one can examine the response of the global community to the 2010 earthquake. Many individuals around the world generously donated funds, propelled by the humanitarian impulse, an innate, visceral urge to help fellow human beings who are suffering.[19] By November 14, over US$3.4 billion in donations poured into international aid agencies.[20] As with the 2004 Indian Ocean tsunami, the magnitude of the devastation and the natural aspect of the disaster led to a desire to help by the global community.

10   The immediate response by the international community succeeded in many ways. Many humanitarian non-governmental organizations (NGOs) and governmental development agencies should be given credit for what they accomplished in the face of enormous devastation. Numerous rescue attempts were mounted in the immediate aftermath, and emergency medical services were operational within hours of the earthquake. In the six months following the disaster more than 4.3 million families received food assistance and more than 900,000 vaccinations of children and adults were carried out. Over 1 million people received daily water rations, and thousands of latrines were built. As a result, no major epidemics have yet occurred in any of the camps for internally displaced persons,[21] although cholera has recently begun to spread throughout the country.

11   However, some aspects of the post-earthquake response have been problematic, reflecting the history of Haiti's relationship with external actors. Media coverage of the disaster and the response often played into the stereotype of Haiti as a cursed nation.[22] There was scant recognition of the legacy left by Haiti's colonial powers and of the role these nations were now playing in the relief effort. The US military assumed the leadership of the humanitarian response almost immediately. It began by coordinating flights at the request of the Haitian government, but its role soon extended to many aspects of the relief efforts. There were examples of medical supply flights being turned away in favour of military flights.[23] Some observers have argued that too great an emphasis was placed on security, at the expense of relief operations.[24] Others have noted a focus on the protection of private property, which may have detracted from efforts to ensure access to food and water for those in need.[25] Concern about the poor coordination of the response[26] has led

some commentators to take issue with the role of NGOs and with their agendas for participating in the relief efforts.[27,28] Finally, the focus on the immediate humanitarian response appears to have prevented a consideration of how the groundwork for future development could be best laid.[6]

12   At the time of publishing, the vast majority of those displaced are still living in tents or other temporary structures and over 95% of the rubble has yet to be cleared.[1] The provision of essential social services by the Haitian government, including accessible education, primary health care and a functioning police force and judiciary, is unlikely in the near future. Concerns about the trafficking of children and the sexual exploitation of women are growing.[29] Less than 10 per cent of the $5.3 billion pledged for Haiti at an international donors' conference in March 2010 has been provided.[30] Media attention has long since shifted away from Haiti, and no clear plan is evident for addressing the nation's long-term concerns, such as economic independence and a political environment free of foreign interference.

Humanitarianism based on actual histories

13   The humanitarian impulse is too often fitful and fragmented. Furthermore, the involvement of high-income countries in the root causes of the devastation caused by "natural" disasters in low-income countries is rarely examined. The political philosopher Thomas Pogge questions simplistic conceptions of injustice when they are seen primarily as issues of distribution.[31] He adds a relational element to the conception of justice. Investigations of relational justice seek to identify the causes of disparities, challenging us to look at the conditions and actions that have created them. In Pogge's reimagining of

justice, wealthy nations must address their role in creating the historic conditions that have led to the profound global economic disparities we see today. He calls on wealthy nations to recognize their complicity in the exploitation of human and natural resources, the degradation and oppression of good governance structures within poorer nations and to understand the consequences of their support for corrupt and illegitimate regimes.[32] These actual histories should replace the more palatable fictional histories that attempt to explain away wealthy nations' past contributions to the persistent poverty in the world.[33]

14   How would acknowledging actual histories change the work of health professionals and humanitarian aid providers? Even in the initial response to a disaster, it would change how services are organized, who is leading the effort, and who sets priorities. Acknowledging actual histories may have little impact on the technical details of the initial emergency response, but it may make a difference in how relief efforts are subsequently carried out, particularly in the long term. Some may argue that disasters on the scale of the Haitian earthquake wipe out the existing civil society leadership. However, even in such conditions, the affected communities can and should be involved from the start. Actual histories can help organizations to see how the best of intentions can undermine indigenous systems and societies and can help them to understand the difference between providing temporary charity and contributing to self-sustaining, just communities.[34,35]

15   Appeals for funds can be combined with educational initiatives to explain to policymakers and the public why an event has occurred and how it relates to social, economic and political forces. Resilience should be emphasized over victimhood. Such campaigns could also be linked to advocacy efforts; for example, calls for

economic justice could be supported[36] or efforts could be made to ensure that elections after a disaster are fair and free of foreign interference.

16 Acknowledging the actual histories that have led to Haiti's underdevelopment would require wealthy nations to probe their own political, social and economic involvement—through action or inaction—in Haiti's underdevelopment. This would also require companies and consumers to ask themselves how they have benefited from Haiti's underdevelopment. The answers to these questions need to meaningfully inform humanitarian efforts in Haiti for these efforts to address the root conditions that enabled an earthquake tó level Port-au-Prince.

Conclusion

17 Although a laudable humanitarian impulse has driven relief efforts in Haiti, it alone is insufficient for the task of rebuilding the nation. Any lasting efforts to improve life for Haiti's citizens must be informed by an understanding of the disaster's foundational causes. A humanitarian response based on actual histories could resemble the work of NGOs like Partners in Health, which has worked toward just, effective and sustainable humanitarianism in Haiti for years. Even better would be a response that explicitly supported Haitian organizations, civil society, and government institutions to lead the recovery effort.[37]

18 The analysis presented here is certainly applicable beyond Haiti. In numerous countries where humanitarians operate, respecting history and seeing the connection between historic actions and present conditions is essential. Ultimately, standing in solidarity means making a long-term commitment to transforming how we relate to Haiti and similar nations around the world.

References

1. United Nations Office for the Coordination of Humanitarian Affairs. *Haiti: 6 months after . . .* 2010. Available: http://www.reliefweb.int/rw/RWFiles2010. nsf/FilesByRWDocUnidFilename/SNAA-8AD4 A6-full_report.pdf/$File/full_report.pdf (accessed 2010 Nov 9).

2. Bilham R. Lessons from the Haiti earthquake. *Nature* 2010;463(7283):878–879.

3. Bajak F. Chile-Haiti earthquake comparison: Chile was more prepared. *The Huffington Post* 2010 Feb 27. Available: http:// www.huffingtonpost.com/ 2010/02/27/chile-haiti-earthquake-co_n_479705. html (accessed 2010 Nov 5).

4. Why Haiti's quake was so devastating. *CBC News* 2010 Jan 13. Available: http://www.cbc.ca/world/ story/2010/01/13/f-earthquake-devastation-comparison.html (accessed 2010 Nov 5).

5. Henley J. Haiti: a long descent to hell. *The Guardian* 2010 Jan 14. Available: http://www. guardian.co.uk/world/2010/jan/14/haiti-history-earthquake-disaster (accessed 2010 Nov 5).

6. Flegel K, Hebert PC. Helping Haiti. *CMAJ* 2010; 182(4):325.

7. Schrecker T. Denaturalizing scarcity: a strategy of enquiry for public-health ethics. *Bull World Health Organ* 2008;86(8):600–605.

8. Smith N. There's no such thing as a natural disaster. *Understanding Katrina: perspectives from the social sciences.* New York: Social Science Research Council. 2006 June 11. Available: http:// understandingkatrina.ssrc.org/Smith/ (accessed 2010 Nov 5).

9. Farmer P. *The uses of Haiti.* 2nd ed. Monroe (ME): Common Courage Press; 2003.

10. Hallward P. *Damming the flood: Haiti, Aristide, and the politics of containment.* London: Verso; 2007.

11. Mintz SW. Can Haiti change? *Foreign Aff* 1995;74 (1):73–86.

12. Prou ME. Haiti's condemnation: history and culture at the crossroads. *Lat Am Res Rev* 2005; 40(3):191–201.

13. Haggerty RA. Haiti: a country study. In: Metz HC, editor. *Dominican Republic and Haiti: Country studies.* Federal Research Division, Library of

Congress; 2001. Available: http://memory.loc.gov/frd/cs/httoc.html (accessed 2010 Nov 5).

14. Gruening E. The issue in Haiti. *Foreign Aff* 1993; 11(2):279–289.

15. Chatterjee P. Haiti's forgotten emergency. *Lancet* 2008;372 (9639):615–618.

16. Shamsie Y. Export processing zones: the purported glimmer in Haiti's development murk. *Rev Int Pol Econ* 2009;16(4):649–672.

17. Farmer P. Political violence and public health in Haiti. *N Engl J Med* 2004;350(15):1483–1486.

18. Dupuy A. Haiti election 2006: A pyrrhic victory for René Préval? *Lat Am Perspect* 2006;33(148): 132–141.

19. Sondorp E, Bornemisza O. Public health, emergencies and the humanitarian impulse. *Bull World Health Organ* 2005;83(3):163.

20. Financial Tracking Service. Table A: List of all commitments/contributions and pledges as of 14 November 2010. *Haiti—Earthquakes—January 2010*. New York: Office for the Coordination of Humanitarian Affairs; 2010. Available at: http://ocha.unog.ch/fts/reports/daily/ocha_R10_E15797_asof___1003150208. pdf (accessed 2010 Nov 14).

21. International Federation of Red Cross and Red Crescent Societies. *Haiti. From sustaining lives to sustainable solutions: the challenge of sanitation. Special report, six months on.* 2010. Available: http://www.ifrc.org/Docs/reports/199600-haiti-sanitation-report-july-2010-EN.pdf (accessed 2010 Nov 5).

22. British Broadcasting Corporation. White House calls Robertson's Haiti comment 'stupid.' 2010 Jan 15. Available: http://news.bbc.co.uk/2/hi/americas/8460520.stm (accessed 2010 Nov 7).

23. Médecins Sans Frontières—Canada. *Haiti: MSF cargo plane with full hospital and staff blocked from landing in Port-au- Prince.* 2010 Jan 17. Available: http://www.msf.ca/news-media/news/2010/02/haiti-msf-cargo-plane-with-full-hospital-and-staff-blocked-from-landing-in-port-au-prince/ (accessed 2010 Nov 7).

24. Associated Press. Haiti gets a penny of each U.S. aid dollar. *CBS News* 2010 Jan 27. Available: http://www.cbsnews.com/stories/2010/01/27/world/main6146903.shtml (accessed 2010 Nov 7).

25. Goodman A. With foreign aid still at a trickle, devastated Port-au-Prince General Hospital struggles to meet overwhelming need. *Democracy Now!* 2010 Jan 20. Available: http://www.democracynow.org/2010/1/20/devastated_port_au_prince_hospital_struggles (accessed 2010 Nov 7).

26. Lynch C. Top U.N. aid official critiques Haiti aid efforts in confidential email. *Foreign Policy* 2010 Feb 17. Available: http://turtlebay.foreignpolicy.com/posts/2010/02/17/top_un_aid_official_critiques_haiti_aid_efforts_in_confidential_email (accessed 2010 Nov 7).

27. Growth of aid and the decline of humanitarianism. *Lancet* 2010;375(9711):253.

28. Zoellick RB. How to rebuild Haiti. *Politico* 2010 Feb 1. Available: http://www.politico.com/news/stories/0110/32284.html (accessed 2010 Nov 7).

29. Gupta J, Agrawal A. Chronic aftershocks of an earthquake on the well-being of children in Haiti: violence, psychosocial health and slavery. *CMAJ* 2010 Aug 3. Available: http://www.cmaj.ca/cgi/rapidpdf/cmaj.100526v1 (accessed 2010 Nov 12).

30. Katz JM. Clinton: Donors still holding out on Haiti pledges. *The Boston Globe* 2010 Aug 6. Available: http://www.boston.com/news/world/latinamerica/articles/2010/08/06/clinton_donors_still_holding_out_on_haiti_pledges/ (accessed 2010 Nov 7).

31. Pogge T. Relational conceptions of justice: responsibilities for health outcomes. In: Anand S, Peter F, Sen A, editors. *Public health, ethics and equity.* Oxford (UK): Oxford University Press; 2004.

32. Pogge T. Real world justice. *J Ethics* 2005; 9(1–2):29–53.

33. Pogge T. World poverty and human rights. *Ethics Int Aff* 2005;19(1):1–7.

34. Yamin AE. Our place in the world: conceptualizing obligations beyond borders in human rights-based approaches to health. *Health Hum Rights* 2010; 12(1):3–14.

35. Ruger JP. Global health justice. *Public Health Ethics* 2009;2(3):261–275.

36. Willsher K. France urged to repay Haiti billions paid for its independence. *The Guardian* 2010 Aug 15. Available: http://www.guardian.co.uk/world/2010/aug/15/france-haiti-independence-debt (accessed 2010 Nov 7).

37. Schwartz D. The next challenge in Haiti. *CBC News* Available: www.cbc.ca/world/story/2010/03/26/f-haiti-rebuild.html (accessed 2010 Nov 7).

Comprehension

1. What is the significance of the quotation marks around *natural* in the title and in paragraph 3? What is the meaning of *denaturalize* and *unnatural* in the same paragraph? Why is it important to understand the precise way the author is using these words?

2. How does the author use the ideas of Thomas Pogge in paragraph 13? Paraphrase the last sentence in this paragraph.

Structure, Organization, and Style

1. In the introduction, identify the study's justification and the thesis statement.

2. Identify two different rhetorical patterns used in paragraphs 6 and 7; identify the main rhetorical pattern used in the section "Foundations of a disaster."

3. In the section "The humanitarian impulse," identify one paragraph in which the first sentence is the topic sentence; identify one paragraph that does not have a clear topic sentence.

Critical Thinking/Research

1. Do the last two paragraphs form a successful conclusion to Pinto's argument? Analyze their effectiveness, considering the role of any argumentative strategies discussed on pp. 53–56.

2. Using "Denaturalizing 'Natural' Disasters" and one other reliable source, such as a reference work like an encyclopedia, discuss the role of colonialism in Haiti's history from its independence to the present.

IV Contemporary Texts and Their Uses

Many people believe that texts are confined to written material, or perhaps can be expanded to include visual media like movies; but the contemporary sense of the word *text* embraces much more. For example, the way we present ourselves to others—the way we dress, speak, express ourselves through our body language, and even our behaviour—can be considered texts that are "read"—that is, interpreted by those around us. The essays in this section use both the traditional meaning of texts—printed texts—and the more modern meaning that has arisen as a result of cultural and media studies in the last two generations.

The author of "N(O) Canada" argues that our national anthem—a defining "text" for most Canadians—does not truly represent what Canada stands for. The next two essays address common practices of contemporary readers. In "Narcissus Regards a Book," the author blames a generation of teachers for what he terms the "narcissistic" motivations of readers today. The author of "You DO Like Reading Off a Computer Screen" asserts that, contrary to popular belief, computer screens are meant for reading and that reading computer text and reading print text are by no means incompatible. "The Birth of Power Dressing" explores the historical connections between fashion and membership in high-status groups. In addition to clothes and accessories as visual texts, other texts such as paintings and diaries are used to support the point that contemporary and Renaissance attitudes to clothing are strikingly similar. The author of "Occupy Canada" similarly refers to a variety of texts in arguing that movements like "Occupy Canada" can reap benefits from "creative types" working alongside the political leadership.

The author of the academic essay "Creativity in Crisis?" examines the concept of creativity, which lies behind text production, arguing, more specifically, that "texting" can inhibit creative practices. Although viewers often consider "promos" secondary to the texts they are designed to draw attention to, the author of "Coming Up Next: Promos in the Future of Television and Television Studies" argues that their functions are more complex and their influence more subtle than commonly believed.

Stephen Marche, "N(O) Canada!"

Many journalistic articles are occasioned by specific events or controversies. "N(O) Canada!" was written after a proposal to change one line from the English version of "O Canada" to make it gender inclusive was rejected by poll respondents.

Preparing to Read

1. Using a reliable source, such as an encyclopedia or other reference work, or a reputable website, determine the origins of the Canadian national anthem's lyrics—in both English and French. You could write this as a timeline, including all major developments up to the present.

2. What are the most important qualities in the lyrics of a national anthem today?

N(O) Canada!

Stephen Marche

The Walrus, July/August 2010
(749 words)

1   When the Conservative government proposed changing a single line of our national anthem this past spring, the outrage was ferocious enough that the idea was shelved in less than forty-eight hours. The prime minister's spokesman couldn't back down fast enough: "We offered to hear from Canadians on this issue, and they have already spoken loud and clear. They overwhelmingly do not want to open the issue." I can only surmise that Olympics-fuelled patriotism was blinding a large and vocal swath of the country to the fact that the national anthem doesn't need cosmetic surgery; it needs a complete overhaul. Face it: "O Canada" is the worst song you sing or hear on a regular basis.

2   Harper was correct that the lyric "True patriot love in all thy sons command" is inexcusably sexist, but that's the least of the song's problems. The original lyrics, in French, contain the juicy nugget "Car ton bras sait porter l'épée, / Il sait porter la croix!" which translates loosely as "Because your arm can carry the sword, it knows how to carry the Cross!" The sword and the Cross? Is there a less Canadian sentiment? The English version, which only took its current form thirty years ago, blunts the violence but sharpens the religion: "God keep our land glorious and free!" What we have is a national anthem that can't be sung full throatedly by Jews, Sikhs, Hindus, Muslims, or atheists. Granted, I live in downtown Toronto, but that's practically everyone I know. I don't think I'm being politically correct here, either. I'm being factually precise: our national anthem was written for a nation that no longer exists. There are reportedly a hundred thousand viewers for *Hockey Night in Canada* with Punjabi commentary; surely these people deserve a song they can sing without skipping lines.

3   I'm aware that it's a huge inconvenience to change a national anthem, especially when that nation is one as haunted by prevarication and suppressed conflict as Canada. But we have to make it a priority. I could forgive the lousy lyrics, and even the dumbed-down Mozart composed for them, if it weren't for the last note. It's a national disgrace, perfectly designed so only about a third of singers can actually reach it. In practice, whenever large crowds sing the song, "O Canada" ends in a wavering lack of conclusion. We can't even agree on a note! Worse, the failure often provokes laughter. There may be something appropriate about an exercise in Canadian nationalism that ends with a recognition of its ludicrousness, but we're singing this song

over the bodies of soldiers coming back from Afghanistan. It shouldn't be a complete joke.

4   The obvious choice for a replacement is "The Maple Leaf Forever," unofficial anthem for English Canada up until the '30s. Skip the opening stanza, which celebrates the conquest and subjugation of one of our founding nations by the other, and it might even be halfway decent:

> At Queenston Heights, and Lundy's Lane,
> Our brave fathers, side by side,
> For freedom, homes, and loved ones dear,
> Firmly stood, and nobly died;
> And those dear rights which they maintained,
> We swear to yield them never!
> Our watchword evermore shall be
> "The Maple Leaf forever!"

5   Civil rights, loving homes, and beating the Americans: surely we can all agree on that. The chorus would need some revision, with its mention of the Queen and Heaven, but there's definitely enough to work with. The melody has the requisite jauntiness, and the chorus is genuinely stirring.

6   But I have a better idea. There's a song that everyone in Canada already knows, one that excites the profoundest feelings of pride in the national psyche. I'm speaking, of course, about the ex–theme song for *Hockey Night in Canada*. No less a personage than Wayne Gretzky is on record as saying, "The greatest song in Canada is the theme song to *Hockey Night in Canada*, and to this day it still sends a shiver up my spine." CTV bought the tune in 2008 from the jingle writer who originally composed the piece in 1968. We simply have to nationalize it.

7   Imagine beginning every hockey game and school assembly with "Dunt-da-DUNT-da-dunt, dunt-da-DUNT-da-dunt, dunt-da-DUNT-da-dunt da-daaaaaa." As for the lyrics, I would like to suggest a simple message that is Canadian to the core and fits the melody perfectly: "Let's all get along." By this simple solution, we would instantly have the greatest, shortest national anthem in the world—something we could all feel good about fighting for.

Comprehension

1. Explain what Marche means by the following:
   a. "our national anthem was written for a nation that no longer exists" (par. 2)
   b. "I'm aware that it's a huge inconvenience to change a national anthem, especially when that nation is one as haunted by prevarication and suppressed conflict as Canada" (par. 3)

Structure and Organization

1. How many points does the author include? Which is the most important one in your opinion? Why?

Critical Thinking/Research

1. How could you describe the author's tone (attitude toward his subject matter)? Use specific language from the essay to illustrate your points. Do you believe such language strengthens or weakens his argument?

2. Do you agree with the author that "The Maple Leaf Forever" is "[t]he obvious choice" to replace "O Canada"? Analyze the lyrics in the essay to determine if they fit the criteria you proposed before reading the essay (see "Preparing to Read").

3. In addition to comments about the worthiness of the Canadian national anthem, Marche also comments on aspects of the Canadian national "character," traits perceived as typically Canadian. Identify one such example, explaining what Marche is saying about the national "character"; discuss the validity of his claim.

Cory Doctorow, "You DO Like Reading Off a Computer Screen"

"You DO Like Reading Off a Computer Screen" tackles a familiar concern of today's authors, publishers, and readers: the future of print books. However, while other writers often argue simple positions—yes, there is a future, or, no, there isn't—Doctorow argues more complexly that "long-form narratives," such as novels, are fundamentally different from other computer texts, giving rise to different cognitive processes. Perhaps more notable than Doctorow's thesis, however, is his use of a distinctive style to reflect his content (see "Structure, Organization, and Style," below).

Preparing to Read

1. Doctorow is a prominent Canadian writer, speaker, and blogger and is considered one of his generation's most vocal advocates of the "open Internet." Using reliable sources, write a short biography of Doctorow that includes his achievements and the genres in which he writes, along with his major areas of interest.

2. Do you often or even occasionally read long works of fiction or non-fiction onscreen? List some of the pros and cons of reading longer works this way.

You DO Like Reading Off a Computer Screen

Cory Doctorow

Content: Selected Essays on Technology, Creativity, Copyright, and the Future of the Future, 2008

1   "I don't like reading off a computer screen"—it's a cliché of the e-book world. It means "I don't read novels off computer screens" (or phones, or PDAs, or dedicated e-book readers), and often as not the person who says it is someone who, in fact, spends every hour that Cthulhu sends reading off a computer screen. It's like watching

someone shovel Mars Bars into his gob while telling you how much he hates chocolate.

2 But I know what you mean. You don't like reading long-form works off a computer screen. I understand perfectly—in the ten minutes since I typed the first word in the paragraph above, I've checked my mail, deleted two spams, checked an image-sharing community I like, downloaded a YouTube clip of Stephen Colbert complaining about the iPhone (pausing my MP3 player first), cleared out my RSS reader, and then returned to write this paragraph.

3 This is not an ideal environment in which to concentrate on long-form narrative (sorry, one sec, gotta blog this guy who's made cardboard furniture) (wait, the Colbert clip's done, gotta start the music up) (19 more RSS items). But that's not to say that it's not an *entertainment medium*—indeed, practically everything I do on the computer entertains the hell out of me. It's nearly all text-based, too. Basically, what I do on the computer is pleasure-reading. But it's a fundamentally more scattered, splintered kind of pleasure. Computers have their own cognitive style, and it's not much like the cognitive style invented with the first modern novel (one sec, let me google that and confirm it), *Don Quixote*, some 400 years ago.

4 The novel is an invention, one that was engendered by technological changes in information display, reproduction, and distribution. The cognitive style of the novel is different from the cognitive style of the legend. The cognitive style of the computer is different from the cognitive style of the novel.

5 Computers want you to do lots of things with them. Networked computers doubly so—they (another RSS item) have a million ways of asking for your attention, and just as many ways of rewarding it.

6 There's a persistent fantasy/nightmare in the publishing world of the advent of very sharp, very portable computer screens. In the fantasy version, this creates an infinite new market for electronic books, and we all get to sell the rights to our work all over again. In the nightmare version, this leads to runaway piracy, and no one ever gets to sell a novel again.

7 I think they're both wrong. The infinitely divisible copyright ignores the "decision cost" borne by users who have to decide, over and over again, whether they want to spend a millionth of a cent on a millionth of a word—no one buys newspapers by the paragraph, even though most of us only read a slim fraction of any given paper. A super-sharp, super-portable screen would be used to read all day long, but most of us won't spend most of our time reading anything recognizable as a book on them.

8 Take the record album. Everything about it is technologically pre-determined. The technology of the LP demanded artwork to differentiate one package from the next. The length was set by the groove density of the pressing plants and playback apparatus. The dynamic range likewise. These factors gave us the idea of the 40-to-60-minute package, split into two acts, with accompanying artwork. Musicians were encouraged to create works that would be enjoyed as a unitary whole for a protracted period—think of *Dark Side of the Moon*, or *Sgt. Pepper's*.

9 No one thinks about albums today. Music is now divisible to the single, as represented by an individual MP3, and then subdivisible into snippets like ringtones and samples. When recording artists demand that their works be considered as a whole—like when Radiohead insisted that the iTunes Music Store sell their whole album as a single, indivisible file that you would have to listen to all the way through—they sound like cranky throwbacks.

10 The idea of a 60-minute album is as weird in the Internet era as the idea of sitting through 15 hours of *Der Ring des Nibelungen* was 20 years ago. There are some anachronisms who love their long-form opera, but the real action is in

the more fluid stuff that can slither around on hot wax—and now the superfluid droplets of MP3s and samples. Opera survives, but it is a tiny sliver of a much bigger, looser music market. The future composts the past: old operas get mounted for living anachronisms; Andrew Lloyd Webber picks up the rest of the business.

11   Or look at digital video. We're watching more digital video, sooner, than anyone imagined. But we're watching it in three-minute chunks from YouTube. The video's got a pause button so you can stop it when the phone rings and a scrubber to go back and forth when you miss something while answering an IM.

12   And attention spans don't increase when you move from the PC to a handheld device. These things have less capacity for multitasking than real PCs, and the network connections are slower and more expensive. But they are fundamentally multitasking devices—you can always stop reading an e-book to play a hand of solitaire that is interrupted by a phone call—and their social context is that they are used in public places, with a million distractions. It is socially acceptable to interrupt someone who is looking at a PDA screen. By contrast, the TV room—a whole room for TV!—is a shrine where none may speak until the commercial airs.

13   The problem, then, isn't that screens aren't sharp enough to read novels off of. The problem is that novels aren't screeny enough to warrant protracted, regular reading on screens.

14   Electronic books are a wonderful adjunct to print books. It's great to have a couple of hundred novels in your pocket when the plane doesn't take off or the line is too long at the post office. It's cool to be able to search the text of a novel to find a beloved passage. It's excellent to use a novel socially, sending it to your friends, pasting it into your sig file.

15   But the numbers tell their own story—people who read off screens all day long buy lots of print books and read them primarily on paper. There are some who prefer an all-electronic existence (I'd like to be able to get rid of the objects after my first reading, but keep the e-books around for reference), but they're in a tiny minority.

16   There's a generation of web writers who produce "pleasure reading" on the web. Some are funny. Some are touching. Some are enraging. Most dwell in Sturgeon's 90th percentile and below. They're not writing novels. If they were, they wouldn't be web writers.

17   Mostly, we can read just enough of a free e-book to decide whether to buy it in hard copy—but not enough to substitute the e-book for the hard copy. Like practically everything in marketing and promotion, the trick is to find the form of the work that serves as enticement, not replacement.

18   Sorry, got to go—eight more e-mails.

Comprehension

1. Summarize paragraphs 6 and 7 in two sentences.

Structure, Organization, and Style

1. Doctorow uses several allusions in his essay. Using at least one reliable Internet source per allusion, briefly explain the significance of two of the following to the essay:
   a. Cthulhu (par. 1)
   b. Stephen Colbert (par. 2)

      c. Andrew Lloyd Webber (par. 10)

      d. "Sturgeon's 90th percentile" (par. 16).

2. a. Analyze Doctorow's style. Your analysis could include word choice, paragraph or sentence structure, voice, tone, and/or stylistic devices such as imagery.

   b. Explain how the author uses his writing style to reinforce his main points, referring specifically to the text.

3. Identify two examples of comparisons (they could involve similarities, differences, or both); explain what is being compared and the effectiveness of the comparison.

Critical Thinking/Research

1. What kind of reader was this essay written for? How do you know this? Refer to specific passages to support your claims.

2. Do you find Doctorow's argument convincing? Analyze its effectiveness, considering such factors as use of logic, kinds of evidence, and argumentative strategies and techniques. In your analysis, bear in mind his audience (see question 1).

3. Write a comparative analysis of this essay and another essay on the same or a similar topic (for example, the uses of today's technology). Essays on e-books versus print books can be found in many Canadian newspapers and magazines. Two recent examples include Robert Fulford, "Death of the Book: Long Live E-books," *National Post* (Apr. 26, 2011) and "The Book Will Survive," Andrew Irvine, *Ottawa Citizen* (May 20, 2011).

Ulinka Rublack, "The Birth of Power Dressing"

The articles in *History Today* are written by experts for a wide readership. Although they focus on scholarly subjects, they are not considered scholarly, as sources are not cited. Their main purpose is to make history relevant to non-specialists, utilizing a variety of techniques to enhance reader interest. For example, Rublack begins by narrating a personal experience and, in paragraph 3, ties it into the historical period she introduces in this and the following paragraph.

"The Birth of Power Dressing," like most humanities essays, uses primary (original) sources extensively for support—these include written texts like books and contemporary historical documents as well as visual ones, like paintings and other art.

▶ Preparing to Read

1. What are your associations with clothes—for example, school uniforms, consumerism, branding?

2. Do you think you and/or your friends pay too much attention to clothes? Why or why not?

The Birth of Power Dressing

Ulinka Rublack

History Today, January 2011
(3917 words)

Abstract

The article presents an examination of the history of clothing and fashion and explores how the Renaissance played an important, early role in creating fashion-conscious attitudes. It examines how the period provided individuals with an unprecedented access to textiles that created greater diversity in wardrobes and merchants extended markets bringing accessories such as hats, bags, gloves and hairpieces to new audiences. Additionally, technological developments in tailoring also contributed to ideas about being fashionable.

Dressing up

1   I shall never forget, while staying in Paris, the day a friend's husband returned home from a business trip. She and I were having coffee in a huge sunny living room overlooking the Seine. His key turned in the door. Next, a pair of beautiful, shiny black shoes flew down the corridor. Finally, the man himself appeared. "My feet are killing me!" he exclaimed. The shoes were by Gucci.

2   We might think that these are the modern follies of fashion, which now beset men as much as women. My friend certainly valued herself partly in terms of the wardrobe she had assembled and her accessories of bags, sunglasses, stilettoes and shoes. She had modest breast implants and a slim, sportive body. They were moving to Dubai. In her spare time when she was not looking after children, going shopping, walking the dog, or jogging, she would write poems and cry.

3   Yet neither my friend nor her husband would be much out of place in the middle of the 15th century. Remember men's long pointed Gothic shoes? In the Franconian village of Niklashausen at this time a wandering preacher drew large crowds and got men to cut off their shoulder-length hair and slash the long tips of their pointed shoes, which were seen as wasteful of leather. Learning to walk down stairs in them was a skill. Men and women in this period aspired to an elongated, delicate, slim silhouette. Very small people were considered deformed and were given the role of grotesque fools. Italian doctors already wrote books about cosmetic surgery.

4   When, how and why did looks become deeply embedded in how people felt about themselves and others? The Renaissance was a turning point. I use the term in its widest sense to describe a long period, from c. 1300 to 1600. After 1300 a much greater variety and quantity of goods was produced and consumed across the globe. Textiles, furnishings and items of apparel formed a key part of this unprecedented diffusion of objects and increased interaction with overseas worlds. Tailoring was transformed by new materials and innovative techniques in cutting and sewing, as well as the desire for a tighter fit to emphasise bodily form, particularly of men's clothing. Merchants expanded markets in courts and cities by making chic accessories such as hats, bags, gloves or hairpieces, ranging from beards to long braids. At the same time, new media and the spread of mirrors led to more people becoming interested in their self-image and into trying to imagine how they appeared to others; artists were depicting humans on an unprecedented scale, in the form of medals, portraits, woodcuts and genre scenes, and print circulated more

information about dress across the world, as the genre of "costume books" was born.

Dressed to thrill

5   These expanding consumer and visual worlds conditioned new ways of feeling. In July 1526 Matthäus Schwarz, a 29-year-old chief accountant for the mighty Fugger family of merchants from Augsburg, commissioned a naked image of himself as fashionably slim and precisely noted his waist measurements. He worried about gaining weight, which to him signalled ageing and diminished attractiveness. Over the course of his life, from his twenties to his old age, Schwarz commissioned 135 watercolour paintings showing his dressed self, which he eventually compiled into a remarkable album, the *Klaidungsbüchlein* (*Book of Clothes*), which is housed today in a small museum in Brunswick. From the many fascinating details the album reveals, we know that, while he was courting women, Schwarz carried heart-shaped leather bags in green, the colour of hope. The new material expression of these emotions, which were tied to appearances, heart-shaped bags for men, artificial braids for women or red silk stockings for young boys, may strike us as odd. Yet the messages they contained (of self-esteem, erotic appeal or social advancement and their effects, which ranged from delight in wonderful craftsmanship to concern that a look had not been achieved or that someone's appearance was deceiving) remain familiar to us today.

6   When cultures throw up new words, historians can be fairly sure that they have struck on new developments. The word "fashion" gained currency in different languages during the Renaissance. *Moda* was adapted from Latin into Italian to convey the idea of fashionable dressing as opposed to *costume*, which denoted more stable customs relating to dress. In 16th-century France, the word *mode* began to supersede the Old French expression *cointerie* to mean "in style." The French term was adapted in 17th-century German as *à la mode*. The English word "fashion" came from the Latin word for "making." It was first used c.1550 to refer to a temporary mode of dress in the physician Andrew Boorde's *Book of Knowledge*. Boorde depicted an almost naked Englishman on a woodcut, cheerily announcing: "Now I will wear I cannot tell what, all fashions be pleasant to me." Boorde thought that the English would never be role models for other nations if they assimilated other fashions. His book was also the first in Europe to include woodcut depictions of people in different dress from across Europe. Yet the new preoccupation with fashion reached beyond the continent. In 1570 the Chinese student Chen Yao wrote of how hairstyles, accessories and styles in his region of China changed "without warning. It's what they call fashion" (the word he used was *shiyang*, which literally translates as "the look of the moment").

7   Many people reacted with shock to these cultural transformations. Stability, or a return to old customs, signalled order, whereas change, and especially constant change, seemed threatening and corrupting. Moralists warned that there should be clear principles concerning who should wear what in terms of their profession and bodily needs in different climates. Once the right kind of clothing had been identified there would be no need ever to change. Elites naturally tried to preserve the signalling of high rank through fine clothing. Sumptuary laws, dating from Roman times and so called after the Latin word *sumptus*, meaning expense, had multiplied during the Renaissance. These sought to limit the amount of money wealthy people could

spend on apparel, so as to limit competitive spending. They also typically set out what kinds of materials and sometimes even colours each rank could wear. Like Andrew Boorde, many worried about the introduction of foreign styles. Moralists across Europe really believed that dress shaped people's mentalities, so that fine foreign clothing, for instance, would make a person more affected and licentious. Such commentators were concerned about the money that would be taken from one country to another and about people losing their virtuous, "national" customs of behaviour; the worst was when people mixed fashions from different cultures and thus became completely unidentifiable in any national, political or moral sense.

8   Alongside these reactions was the dawning realisation that clothing made one historical. Matthäus Schwarz was in his early teens when he started talking to old people about what they had worn in the past and began to make drawings of his own apparel. People began to be aware that future generations would look at them with a sense of historical distance and incredulity, simply on account of what they looked like. Rather than revering their ancestors, they might be laughing at their funny shoes. This uncomfortable realisation raised the question which underlies all cultural history: how were these changing customs to be explained?

9   One answer suggested by contemporaries, such as the Strasbourg-born poet and satirist Sebastian Brant (1457–1521), was that humans were like apes because they imitated others. Such a view was neither sophisticated nor uplifting. It presented two choices: either to join the apes and take part in the folly of human life or to turn rigidly moral and refuse the dance. The latter position was as ridiculous as the former because those opting out of fashion appeared archaic, particularly at a moment when beauty and inventions were highly esteemed. Cities such as Florence were praised for the beauty of their women and sumptuary laws were suspended, often for months, when important foreign dignitaries visited. People stored finery for such moments or forged links with those from whom they could borrow garments. Consequently, inventories that record the kind of clothing people possessed when they married or died often provide an incomplete account of the goods they had access to via networks of friends and family.

Colour and class

10   Lending and borrowing sustained much of early modern life, especially among poorer sections of society. Women in particular relied on such connections, because they were paid less than men or were engaged in unsalaried labour. At the same time unmarried women were expected to look attractive in their efforts to gain a partner, so sumptuary legislation sometimes made allowances for accessories they might wear. For example, a 1530 Imperial Police Ordinance permitted daughters and unmarried peasant women to wear hairbands of silk.

11   There was general disdain of slovenly dress, a strong theme, for example, in the writing of the Dominican priest Thomas Aquinas (1225–74), who thought that wives needed to look their best to keep their husbands faithful. New colours excited people, and since outfits were usually composed of many individual elements, such as detachable sleeves, those lower down the social scale might be able to afford one section in a fashionable colour, perhaps purchasing it second hand. Yellow, for example, became a fashionable colour at the beginning of the 16th century. Inventories from the Swiss city of Basel at this

time show that the colour was first adopted by wealthy men and women, but within a few years it became popular with prostitutes, journeymen, apprentices and maidservants, as well as minor officials and artisans. In 1512 the widow of the town piper in Basel is registered as owning a yellow bodice and her husband's yellow and green hose. By 1520 just about everyone in the city wore yellow and the colour appeared in many innovative combinations—yellow-brown, yellow-red, yellow-green, yellow-black.

12   Fashion gained favours for men and women alike. Matthäus Schwarz had three expensive outfits tailored for himself to please Archduke Ferdinand I of Austria, whom he met twice during the Imperial Diet of Augsburg of 1530, presided over by the archduke and his brother, the Holy Roman Emperor, Charles V. Members of the emperor's entourage were certain to write about how civilized or not a city appeared to be. Such diaries and travelogues were frequently published. Visitors were keen to see craft workshops and examples of urban ingenuity on display; they would dance, dine, be waited upon and bestow gifts. Few people wanted to seem "behind the times," especially since Italians had ingrained in European society the notion that a refined civilisation was a superior one. But what bearing did Schwarz's appearance have on the imperial party in 1530? Schwarz, who had slimmed in advance and had grown a beard like Ferdinand himself, used fashion to produce an image of himself which made the archduke like and trust him. In 1541 Schwarz himself received a particularly special reward from the emperor, whom he had also had a chance to impress in person; he was ennobled. Of course he had been loyal to the Catholic Habsburgs during the Reformation and had worked as head accountant for the firm that did most to finance them. Schwarz celebrated

this achievement and had himself depicted in a coat lined with marten skin, a fur which was restricted to the highest elites. Such fur was homogenously coloured dark brown and came in rectangular pieces measuring up to 60 centimetres. It materialised the rich man's garb in relation to that of the poor man, whose coat, in contrast, was likely to have been made of scraps of different furs.

13   What was new in the Renaissance is the dynamic ability of fashion to reach down the social scale. Schwarz was not an aristocrat, but a wine merchant's son. In the depictions he has left us (as well as the book of clothes he also commissioned two surviving oil paintings of himself) we see a burgher who knew how to create effective and lasting self images. Real life was less glamorous. In April 1538, at the age of 41, Schwarz married Barbara Mangolt, the not very exciting and not very young daughter of a local manager in the Fugger firm. In the picture of himself marking the occasion Schwarz is shown in his home from behind wearing a dark coat trimmed with green half-silken taffeta. The text accompanying the image reads simply: "20 February 1538 when I took a wife this coat . . . was made." After this he got fat, had a stroke and afterwards looked his age. Politics, too, did not work out the way he hoped because the Reformation made headway, and in the 1550s German trade entered a profound credit crisis. Schwarz left long gaps in between images of himself in his album. It was difficult to find a fitting end. When he had decided on his final image in September 1560, he could not help but look back at the paintings of himself in his prime to note, sardonically, that he looked so different now from then. Social expectation did not permit older people to be so playful with dress. Now his days in bright red were over and he wore mostly black and white.

14 Schwarz's extraordinary record of his clothes has wider meanings. It shows why it is too simplistic to treat fashion, as the French sociologist Gilles Lipovetsky does, as an engine of western modernity since the Middle Ages, in his view because it broke with tradition, encouraged self-determination, individual dignity and opinion-making. It did this in part, and importantly so, but not in uniform ways and not in the West alone. Clothes already formed an important part of what we might call people's "psychic landscapes." Wardrobes could become repositories of fantasies and insecurities, as well as reflecting expectations of what a person might look like and behave. These cultural arguments and tensions lie at the heart of our struggle to understand the Renaissance. People's interaction with material goods and visual media added further complexities to their lives. Images could sometimes be manipulated in highly controlled visual displays designed to achieve a specific response from large public audiences evoking, for example, divine magnificence at papal rituals. But they could also be used to explore more openly what was local, regional and foreign, to manage conflicting emotions, or to reflect ways in which an individual tried to appear to others.

New ideas of luxury

15 When we study the Renaissance, therefore, we need to trace the process by which increasing numbers of people outside courts became attached to material possessions and tried to work out how virtue and decorum might be maintained amid selfish, vain and competitive human tendencies. In southern and northern Europe this process was crucial to people's attempts to give meaning to life. Even English Puritans were able to acknowledge that possessions could be God's

temporal blessings as "ornaments and delights." Protestants, however, developed a particular notion of new, "justifiable luxury" as opposed to corrupt "old luxury." According to this view, "old luxury" was the preserve of a narrow elite trapped in a vicious circle of self-congratulation and greed, which cultivated extravagant, effeminate and over-sensuous tastes. Protestants saw examples of papal, oriental and monarchical splendour as excessive and guilty of creating a false world of fantastic illusion which overwhelmed onlookers and engendered envy even among elites. Furthermore, such manifestations of conspicuous consumption suggested an emotional style pertaining to uncontrollable passions rather than manageable emotion. "Old luxury" was perceived as doomed and, as in ancient Rome, set to lead to a republic's decline, as well as evincing the misery of human nature after the Fall.

16 "New luxury" could, by contrast, be declared virtuous. Together with the defence of new decencies, it could be identified with a republican spirit, public gain, gentility and politeness. This notion enshrined clear codes of honourable, often more frugal, consumption based on self examination of whether one needed something or was being over-indulgent.

17 In the 17th and 18th centuries, bourgeois consumption qualified as "good," if it did not encourage travesty—men as effeminate gallants, for instance, or women in breeches. In a rare miniature exploring sexual identities beyond the clear divisions of masculine and feminine so rigorously upheld by society, the Dutch artist Adriaen van der Venne depicts a vomiting cat next to an ordinary couple having fun by cross dressing. The cat symbolises sexuality, the act of vomiting a satire on the couple's subversive act. Bourgeois consumption was meant to establish

men as respectable heterosexuals, who would marry and take on public roles, women as distinctly feminine as well as destined for fidelity in marriage. The appearance of small flower patterns and pastel colours, meanwhile, created a softer, more delicate style, which took its cues from Persian designs and was an alternative to the hyper-masculinity of much of the 16th century, with its bold stripy patterns, daring slashes and frequently loud colours. Meanwhile, black, in its different shades, continued for some time as the international shade indicating sumptuous restraint for both sexes. New models of luxury consumption endorsed measured innovation and the notion of aesthetic pleasure to reinforce cultural competence. Sensations such as surprise and delight could be regarded as refined, because they were not linked to simple utility or physical pleasure. Necessity pointed to functional utility, whereas luxury suggested honourable decorum and progressive, though "polite," creativity. Such evaluations were connected to the notion that consumers should obtain a high degree of product information and an understanding of intricate cuts and constructions of clothing from artisans, shops and tradesmen, or books and magazines—hence the cultivation of taste based on knowledge and civil sociability rather than the kind that advertised conspicuous wealth. Bourgeois classes could positively cherish fashion as a forward-looking social tool. It could now be presented in a positive light as fuelling the wealth of nations and engendering emotional well-being.

French dressing

18 Molière's 1661 comedy *L'Ecole des Maris* (*The School for Husbands*) is a perfect example of the trend. This short, entertaining play was a pan-European success. It was not just performed, but published with plentiful captivating engravings. Its whole plot turns on two brothers who had totally different ideas about dress; each had been promised orphaned girls for marriage, if they looked after them. The younger brother, Sganarelle, wants his girl to dress in brown and grey wool and to remain indoors. Likewise, he himself only dresses functionally and traditionally. His older and more relaxed brother, Aristide, by contrast, considers social pleasures, such as the theatre and good company, as the meaning of life. To him, fine clothes are a further fount of pleasure that he acknowledges as a source of female self-esteem. As Aristide sees it, women feel well treated by men who provide money to clothe them nicely, making them feel honoured and happy. Hence, in Molière's play, commerce and sociability were presented overtly as guaranteeing female civility and emotional contentment.

19 Molière was writing during the reign of Louis XIV and thus did not advertise this life in any way as republican. Rather, it was linked to the notion of a good monarchy as opposed to a tyranny. Sganarelle exemplified tyranny in the way the household was run, which contemporaries thought of as a microcosm of the state. Tyranny was presented as resulting from a deep fear of rebellion; in the household this would be typified as adultery. For Sganarelle, the overly restrictive nature of his domestic regime resulted in him losing his woman to a fop. On the other hand, Molière gives Aristide's girl, Leonore, a voice to defend women's rights to enjoy dress and how these link to the values of a civilised society, which should encourage self regard, in contrast to the treatment of women by barbarous Turks. Leonore argues for women's liberty and against their subjection to men's will and suspicions. She speaks of trust enabling women's natural virtue to manifest itself:

20   Yes, all these stern precautions are inhuman.
Are we in Turkey, where they lock up women?
It's said that females are slaves or worse,
And that's why Turks are under Heaven's curse.
Our honour, Sir, is truly very frail
If we, to keep it, must be kept in jail . . .

21   All these constraints are vain and ludicrous:
The best course, always, is to trust in us.
It's dangerous, Sir, to underrate our gender.
Our honour likes to be its own defender.

The Renaissance watershed

22   Debates about fashion that started in the Renaissance did not end with Molière. The idea that the defence of decorous fashion was compatible with a good Christian existence evolved as did complex debates about clothing of the kind we are familiar with today. But the development of fashion in this period marks a historical watershed. How one dressed began to be seen as the right of an individual and this conviction helped gradually to erode sumptuary legislation. Interest in what one wore was increasingly informed by lure of what craftsmen were able to produce. Different kinds of half-silks, beautiful dyes and lovely patterned textiles seemed delightful to explore and purchase. Yet these choices could also cause confusion and cultural arguments. Women were worried about what colours would be considered seemly and students angered their mothers by asking for money for clothes. Family exchanges now included children bargaining with parents over what they might wear, while parents desperately sought to exercise control. Take the case of Paul Behaim, son of a Nuremberg merchant, who in 1574, aged 17, travelled to Italy with two friends. Having left unsettled debts in Leipzig, where he had been a student, he knew that he now needed to display to his widowed mother a more frugal attitude while simultaneously arguing his case. In his first letter home, he wrote:

23   Dear Mother . . . I have used the money from the sale (of a horse) to have the simplest coarse green clothing made for myself—a doublet with modest trim, pleatless hose (like those Gienger [the tutor] wears at home), and a hooded coat. . . . Lest you think things are cheap here, all this has cost me approximately 17 or 18 crowns, even though it was as plain and simple as it could be. I could not have been more amazed when I saw (that bill) than you will be when I send it to you.

24   In all these ways, then, clothing has changed the ways in which we feel and behave.
25   The Renaissance is in some ways a mirror which leads us back in time to disturb the notion that the world we live in was made in a modern age. Messages reflected in clothing about self-esteem, erotic appeal or social advancement of the wearer are all familiar to us today. Since they first surfaced, we have had to deal more intensely with clever marketing, as well as with questions about image and self-image and whether clothes wear us or we wear them. In short, dress has changed in history and it changes history.

Further Reading

Maria Hayward, *Dress at the Court of Henry VIII* (Maney, 2002)

Aileen Ribeiro, *Fashion and Fancy: Dress in the Art and Literature of Stuart England* (Yale University Press, 2005)

Margaret F. Rosenthal and Ann Rosalind Jones, ed. and trans., *Habiti Antichi et Moderni: The Clothing of the Renaissance World* (Thames & Hudson, 2008)

Evelyn Welch, *Shopping in the Renaissance: Consumer Cultures in Italy 1400–1600* (Yale University Press, 2005).

Comprehension

1. In your own words, explain Andrew Boorde's contribution to our understanding of clothing in the sixteenth century.
2. What were "sumptuary laws" (par. 7)? Explain the need for such laws in Europe.
3. Explain how religion and religious values came to play a role in shaping perception of material possessions in the Renaissance.

Structure, Organization, and Style

1. Discuss strategies that the author uses to make the topic relevant and interesting to a reader without a background in the history of clothing; refer to specific strategies and passages in the text.

Critical Thinking/Research

1. Analyze the importance Rublack gives to Matthäus Schwarz throughout her essay (he is first mentioned in paragraph 5).
2. Show how Rublack uses Molière's play *The School for Husbands* (par. 18) as "a perfect example of the trend" referred to in the previous paragraph.
3. Many of the references in Rublack's essay are to men. Does this surprise you? What accounts for this fact, do you think?
4. What similarities does the essay suggest between our perceptions of fashion today and those of the Renaissance? What differences are suggested?

Mark Edmundson, "Narcissus Regards a Book"

The writing life of college and university professors often focuses on their research, which is read by other researchers in the field. However, they may also write for a large group of readers, such as other teachers or those interested in education. As a teacher of English at the University of Virginia, Mark Edmundson is ideally suited to write an essay on the reading habits of the present and past generations. In "Narcissus Regards a Book," Edmundson argues that "serious" reading has become a lost art.

▶ Preparing to Read

1. Do a self-inventory of your current reading habits. Consider what books you have read recently.
   a. How much of your spare time is spent reading, and what kinds of reading do you find most satisfying?
   b. Do you read more or less than people around you?
   c. Do you find literary works a pleasure or a chore to read? Why?
2. What does it mean to be "narcissistic"? What is the myth of Narcissus?

Narcissus Regards a Book

Mark Edmundson

The Chronicle of Higher Education, January 2011 (2046 words)

1   Who is the common reader now? I do not think there is any way to evade a simple answer to this question. Common readers—which is to say the great majority of people who continue to read—read for one purpose and one purpose only. They read for pleasure. They read to be entertained. They read to be diverted, assuaged, comforted, and tickled. The evidence for this phenomenon is not far to seek. Check out the best-seller lists, even in the exalted *New York Times*. See what Oprah's reading. Glance at the Amazon top 100. Look around on the airplane. The common reader—by which I don't mean the figure evoked by Dr. Johnson and Virginia Woolf, but the person toting a book on the train or loading one into his iPad or Kindle—the contemporary common reader reads for pleasure, and easy pleasure at that. Reading, where it exists at all, has largely become an unprofitable wing of the diversion industry.

2   Life in America now is usually one of two things. Often it is work. People work hard indeed—often it takes two incomes to support a family, and few are the full-time professional jobs that require only 40 hours a week. And when life is not work, it is play. That's not hard to understand. People are tired, stressed, drained: They want to kick back a little. That something done in the rare off hours should be strenuous seems rather unfair. Robert Frost talked about making his vocation and his avocation one, and about his work being play for mortal stakes. For that sort of thing, assuming it was ever possible, there is no longer the time.

3   But it's not only the division of experience between hard labor and empty leisure that now makes reading for something like mortal stakes a very remote possibility. Not much more than 20 years ago, students paraded through the campuses and through the quads, chanting variations on a theme. Hey, hey, ho, ho—they jingled—Western culture's got to go. The marches and the chants and the general skepticism about something called the canon seemed to some an affront to all civilized values.

4   But maybe not. Maybe this was a moment of real inquiry on the kids' part. What was this thing called Western culture? Who created it? Who sanctioned it? Most important: What was so valuable about it? Why did it matter to study a poem by Blake, or ponder a Picasso, or comprehend the poetry latent in the religions of the world?

5   I'm not sure that teachers and scholars ever offered a good answer. The conservatives, protected by tenure, immersed in the minutiae of their fields, slammed the windows closed when the parade passed by. They went on with what they were doing. Those who concurred with the students bought mikes and drums and joined the march. They were much in demand in the news media—figures of great interest. The *Washington Post* was calling; the *Times* was on the other line. Was it true? Were the professors actually repudiating the works that they had purportedly been retained to preserve?

6   It was true—and there was more, the rebels yelled. They thought they would have the microphones in their hand all day and all of the night. They imagined that teaching Milton with an earring in one ear would never cease to fascinate the world.

7   But it did. The media—most inconstant of lovers—came and the media went, and the academy was left with its cultural authority in tatters. How could it be otherwise? The news outlets sell one thing above all else, and that is not so much the news as it is newness. What one buys when one buys a daily paper, what one purchases when one purchases a magazine, is the hypothesis that what is going on right now is amazing, unprecedented, stunning. Or at least worthy of intense concentration. What has happened in the past is of correspondingly less interest. In fact, it may be of barely any interest at all. Those who represented the claims of the past should never have imagined that the apostles of newness would give them a fair hearing, or a fair rendering, either.

8   Now the kids who were kids when the Western canon went on trial and received summary justice are working the levers of culture. They are the editors and the reviewers and the arts writers and the ones who interview the novelists and the poets (to the degree that anyone interviews the poets). Though the arts interest them, though they read this and they read that—there is one thing that makes them very nervous indeed about what they do. They are not comfortable with judgments of quality. They are not at ease with "the whole evaluation thing."

9   They may sense that Blake's *Songs of Innocence and Experience* are in some manner more valuable, more worth pondering, more worth preserving than *The Simpsons*. They may sense as much. But they do not have the terminology to explain why. They never heard the arguments. The professors who should have been providing the arguments when the No More Western Culture marches were going on never made a significant peep. They never quoted Matthew Arnold on the best that's been thought and said—that would have been embarrassing. They never quoted Emerson on the right use of reading—that might have been silly. (It's to inspire.) They never told their students how Wordsworth had saved Mill's life by restoring to him his ability to feel. They never showed why difficult pleasures might be superior to easy ones. They never even cited Wilde on the value of pure and simple literary pleasure.

10   The academy failed and continues to fail to answer the question of value, or even to echo the best of the existing answers. But entertainment culture suffers no such difficulty. Its rationale is simple, clear, potent: The products of the culture industry are good because they make you feel good. They produce immediate and readily perceptible pleasure. Beat that, Alfred Lord Tennyson. Touch it if you can, Emily Dickinson.

11   So the arbiters of culture—our former students—went the logical way. They said: If it makes you feel good, it must be good. If Stephen King and John Grisham bring pleasure, why then, let us applaud them. Let's give them awards.

Let's break down the walls of the old clubs and colleges and give them entry forthwith. The only really important question to pose about a novel by Stephen King, we now know, is whether it offers a vintage draught of the Stephen King experience. Does it deliver the spine-shaking chills of great King efforts past? Is the mayhem cranked to the desirable degree? Do homebody sadist and ordinary masochist get what they want and need from the product?

12   What's not asked in the review and the interview and the profile is whether a King book is worth writing or worth reading. It seems that no one anymore has the wherewithal to say that reading a King novel is a major waste of time. No chance. If people want to read it, if they get pleasure from it, then it must be good. What other standard is there?

13   Media no longer seek to shape taste. They do not try to educate the public. And this is so in part because no one seems to know what literary and cultural education would consist of. What does make a book great, anyway? And the media have another reason for not trying to shape taste: It pisses off the readers. They feel insulted, condescended to; they feel dumb. And no one will pay you for making him feel dumb. Public entertainment generally works in just the opposite way—by making the consumer feel like a genius. Even the most august publications and broadcasts no longer attempt to shape taste. They merely seek to reflect it. They hold the cultural mirror up to the reader—what the reader likes, the writer and the editor like. They hold the mirror up and the reader—what else can he do?— the reader falls in love. The common reader today is someone who has fallen in love, with himself.

14   Narcissus looks into the book review and finds it good. Narcissus peers into Amazon's top 100 and, lo, he feels the love. Nothing insults him; nothing pulls him away from that gorgeous smooth watery image below. The editor sells it to him cheap; the professor who might—coming on like the Miltonic voice does to Eve gazing lovingly on herself in the pool: "What thou seest / What there thou seest . . . is thyself," it says— the professor has other things to do.

15   The intervening voice in Milton (and in Ovid, Milton's original in this) is a source of influence. Is it possible that in the world now there are people who might suffer not from an anxiety that they might be influenced but rather from an anxiety that they might never be? Perhaps not everyone loves himself with complete conviction and full abandon. Maybe there remain those who look into the shimmering flattering glass of current culture and do not quite like what they see. Maybe life isn't working for them as well as it is supposed to be for all in this immeasurably rich and unprecedentedly free country.

16   Reading in pursuit of influence—that, I think, is the desired thing. It takes a strange mixture of humility and confidence to do as much. Suppose one feels anxious about not being influenced. To do so is to admit that one is imperfect, searching, unfinished. It's difficult to do when one is young, at least at present: Some of the oldest individuals I meet lately are under the age of 21. It is difficult to do when one is in middle age, for that is the time of commitments. One has a husband or a wife, a family and job—or, who knows, a career. Having second thoughts then looks like a form of weakness: It makes everyone around you insecure. One must stand steady, and sometimes one must pretend. And in old age—early or late—how can one still be a work in progress? That's the time, surely, to have assumed one's permanent form. That's the time

to have balanced accounts, gained traction, become the proper statue to commemorate one's proper life.

17 Of his attempts at works of art one writer observed: Finished? They are never finished. At a certain point someone comes and takes them away. (At a certain point, something comes and takes us away, whence we do not know.) We, too, are never truly finished. What Narcissus wanted was completion, wholeness; he wanted to be that image in the water and have done with it. There would be no more time, no more change, no more revision. To be willing to be influenced, even up to the last, is tantamount to declaring that we'll never be perfect, never see as gods see—even that we don't know who and what we are, or why (if for any reason) we are here, or where we'll go.

18 The desire to be influenced is always bound up with some measure of self-dislike, or at least with a dose of discontent. While the culture tells us to love ourselves as we are—or as we will be after we've acquired the proper products and services—the true common reader does not find himself adequate at all. He looks in the mirror of his own consciousness, and he is anything but pleased. That is not what he had in mind at all. That is not what she was dreaming of.

19 But where is this common reader—this impossible, possible man or woman who is both confident and humble, both ready to change and skeptical of all easy remedies?

20 In our classrooms, in our offices, before the pages of our prose and poems, watching and wondering and hoping to be brought, by our best ministrations and our love, into being.

Comprehension

1. a. Define "the common reader" as described in paragraph 1; how does this reader differ from the "true common reader" mentioned in paragraph 18? (*The Common Reader* was the name of a book comprising a series of essays about reading written by Virginia Woolf and published in 1925.)

    b. Why does this common reader need to be both "confident and humble"? (par. 19).

2. Explain the role of the media in the questioning of the canon 20 years ago, according to Edmundson.

Structure, Organization, and Style

1. Paraphrase the author's thesis and explain the reason for its placement.

2. Analyze the author's style, referring to at least two paragraphs in your answer. You could consider such features as paragraph/sentence length and variety, word choice, rhetorical devices, such as emphasis, and literary devices.

Critical Thinking

1. Who does Edmundson blame the most for the current practice of "narcissistic" reading habits? Support your answer by referring specifically to the text.

2. Choose one of the following statements by the author and write a response explaining your agreement or disagreement.
   a. "The products of the culture industry are good because they make you feel good. They produce immediate and readily perceptible pleasure" (par. 10).
   b. "Media no longer seek to shape taste. They do not try to educate the public" (par. 13).
   c. "To be willing to be influenced . . . is tantamount to declaring that we'll never be perfect, never see as gods see" (par. 17).

Chris Webb, "Occupy Canada"

The Occupy Movement began in New York in September 2011 as an attempt to imitate the public protests in Egypt, Tunisia, and other Middle East and African nations earlier in the year. The movement protested against social inequities and corporate privilege, popularizing the slogan "We are the 99 per cent," along with the "Occupy" label. In "Occupy Canada," the author argues that artists and other image makers are ideally positioned to give voice to the movement's aims.

Access *Canadian Dimension*, where "Occupy Canada" was published, in order to determine some of its goals and the profile of a typical reader.

▶ Preparing to Read

1. Using reliable sources, construct a timeline for the Occupy Movement in the United States and Canada.
2. What does the statement "We are the 99 per cent" refer to?
3. Were you aware of the Occupy Movement and its goals in 2011–2012? Do you believe mass public demonstrations, especially by youth, contribute positively to an ongoing dialogue about democracy? You could freewrite on this topic or discuss it in groups.

Occupy Canada

Chris Webb

Canadian Dimension, January/February 2012
(951 words)

1   The success of the Occupy movement in the U.S. is derived from the reclamation of public space, and the occupation of mental space through the production of cultural and political ephemera including political posters, videos, projections, memes, apps and publications. Political movements need all the elements of good theatre in order to grow and draw public support. They need heroes and drama, symbolism and foreshadowing, humour and tragedy. Artists, musicians and designers can provide movements with the figurative and symbolic tools they need

to voice their concerns in the public sphere. In France in 1968, for example, students occupied France's most prestigious art school and set up an ad hoc poster factory. Their posters expressed the frustration of alienated youth and the commodification of art and knowledge in capitalist society. This optic element of protest is crucial as it creates modes of collective identification, but it has notably been lacking in the Canadian Occupy movement. Why has the Occupy movement in Canada failed to attract significant artistic support and produced few cultural artifacts? With polls showing a majority of Canadians supportive of Occupy, why have Canadian artists been so reluctant to engage?

2   Artists in the U.S. quickly formed Occupy Musicians, Occupy Writers, Occupy Filmmakers and Occupy Comics in an effort to connect creative workers with grassroots occupiers. Aside from a flash appearance by Gordon Lightfoot at Occupy Toronto, celebrity sightings have been rare in Canada. Meanwhile, superstar philosophers and musicians have—for better or worse—flocked to Occupy Wall Street. This is not to suggest that Canadian artists are apolitical, but rather that the community suffers from a paradoxical lack of engagement with progressive political movements. There seems to be hesitancy on the part of established artists and literati to go beyond supporting causes like famine relief. As government art budgets shrink and art school students find themselves pulling lattes years after graduating, there is an urgent need for artists to confront the realities of creating art in an age of inequality and austerity. As Occupy evolves, it needs to find a niche for Canadian artists just as artists need to support this movement with their talent and creativity.

3   Posters, for example, can play a powerful role in unifying political demands and constructing the messages of a movement. They call for visual strategies and ways of thinking that promote modes of social and political identification. Some of the most successful political posters have had the simplest messages. Work for All; Hope; *Sí, se Puede*; Power to the People; Never Work. New technologies have made the production and sharing of design work far easier than before. In the days after Occupy Wall Street sprung up, groups of designers and programmers gathered in New York, San Francisco and Washington, DC to brainstorm various platforms to help the Occupy movement. Occupy Design emerged as a grassroots project to connect designers with demonstrators. The project's goal is "to create freely available visual tools around a common graphic language to unite the 99 per cent." Programmers have been working on a decentralized decision-making platform called Occupy Votes that could ease the consensus-making process in large general assemblies—a significant challenge for most Occupy encampments. Other programmers collaborated on an "I'm Getting Arrested" app to help those rounded up during evictions and raids. One of the most inspiring examples of cross collaboration between writers, designers and artists is the *Occupied Wall Street Journal*, one of the many unofficial newspapers of Occupy Wall Street.

4   What all these experiments point to is the incredible pool of untapped talent that movements so rarely take advantage of. With millions of young people out of work and looking for a way to put their skills to use, the potential for burgeoning movements to draw on the talents of those with suitable rage and creative skills presents limitless opportunities. Crowd sourcing and online fundraising tools hold great promise in giving back to artists and creative types who contribute to the movement. The materials produced by artists in support of the Occupy movement have been crucial in publicizing the

movement, but more importantly in giving it a relative coherence and framework despite its lack of concise political demands. Visually, political movements need to occupy a libidinal economy, a space of desires that is largely occupied by advertising and consumer-generated identities. It comes as no surprise that protestors have drawn on popular culture and media that commonly build these collective economies of desire. The famous Guy Fawkes mask, for example, comes from the graphic novel and film *V for Vendetta*. Many of the Occupy posters, from the striding women of "Occupy the Streets" to the zombie imagery of "Eat the Rich Before They Eat You," share the aesthetics of popular comic books, films and TV shows. The incredibly successful Internet meme that grew out of the UC Davis occupation (a portly cop casually pepper-spraying classical paintings and pop culture icons) is but one example of this potent collision of new media and history.

5   In past years, Harper and the Conservatives have threatened artists' livelihoods with multi-million-dollar funding cuts. These moves were countered by massive mobilizations of artists and musicians across Canada, but what has changed for artists since then? It remains difficult to secure grant funding and even more difficult to produce art as a full-time job. Artists and designers have suffered greatly due to the concentration of wealth and they stand to lose past gains in the coming age of austerity. As Occupy evolves, it will be crucial for artists to voice their own concerns within the movement and to assist it in building a visual and figurative framework to articulate visions of a better world.

Comprehension

1. a. Summarize the author's view of the roles that creative individuals can play in the Occupy Movement today

    b. In one or two sentences, explain the failure of the Canadian arts community to support the Movement, according to the author.

2. In your own words, paraphrase or define one of the following (par. 4):

    a. "libidinal economy"

    b. "collective economies of desire."

Structure, Organization, and Style

1. What kind of evidence does Webb primarily use to support his points (see Chapter 4, "Kinds of Evidence in an Argumentative Essay," pp. 46–49)? Referring to at least two examples, demonstrate the effectiveness of this means of support.

Critical Thinking

1. Why might the role of new media be especially important (par. 4) to the success of the movement?

2. Analyze Webb's argument, referring to specific strategies. In your analysis, consider Webb's audience and the way it might have affected his argumentative choices.

Lynn Helding, "Creativity in Crisis?"

Many essays are occasioned by a public incident, news story, or personal experience that reveals a new perspective on an important issue. Using critical thinking—and, in the case of an academic essay, current research as well—the author analyzes the topic and, often, ends by making recommendations. Like "Denaturalizing 'Natural' Disasters: Haiti's Earthquake and the Humanitarian Impulse" (p. 264), "Creativity in Crisis?" exemplifies a common pattern in argument in which a problem is analyzed and solutions are offered.

Preparing to Read

Are you aware that the concept of creativity has been widely explored by academic writers and theorists? Do you believe that the concept is relevant across disciplines or applicable only to specific disciplines, like those in the fine and performing arts? What does creativity mean to you?

1. a. Working in groups, come up with a definition of creativity that satisfies group members. Share the definition with other groups.

      OR

    b. In a freewriting session, reflect on/discuss the concept of creativity.

2. Using at least two reliable sources, explain the purpose and uses of the Torrance Tests of Creative Thinking (par. 3); briefly summarize its effectiveness as a measurement tool, according to your sources.

Creativity in Crisis?

Lynn Helding

Journal of Singing, 2011
(4546 words)

1   Hardly had the closing strains of "Auld lang syne" echoed off the Wasatch range at the 51st national NATS conference in Salt Lake City last July, than this urgent cover story appeared in *Newsweek* magazine:

2   The Creativity Crisis: For the first time, research shows that American creativity is declining. What went wrong—and how we can fix it.[1]

3   The cover itself was comprised of an American flag made of broken red, white, and blue crayons. These iconic symbols of childhood signaled the real focus population of the article, while the title, "Creativity in America," promised to reveal "the science of innovation" and "how to re-ignite our imaginations."[2] Alas, the article was less about creativity itself and more about testing for creativity (via the Torrance Tests of Creative Thinking), and a perceived lack of it among children. As a rule, I read all screeds decrying kids these days with a skeptical eye, but this caught my attention:

4   With intelligence, there is a phenomenon called the Flynn effect—each generation, scores go up about 10 points. Enriched environments are making kids smarter. With creativity, a reverse trend has just been identified and is being reported for the first time here: American creativity scores are falling.³

5   According to the authors, a Flynn effect could also be seen regarding creativity until 1990, when a precipitous drop in the creativity quotient (CQ) was noted. According to a leading researcher in the field, "It is the scores of younger children in America—from kindergarten through sixth grade—for whom the decline is most serious."⁴

6   Why the decline? The usual guilty culprits were trotted out: too much TV, too many video games, and the current assessment culture in American education ("teaching to the test"). Predictable, too, was that Bronson and Merryman's deliberately provocative article should spark critics, who simultaneously touted the creative benefits of digital technology, while ridiculing the very idea that an attribute as ethereal as creativity could actually be tested; after all, the article was about the decline in creativity scores, not creativity itself. The authors' suggestion that the "crisis" can be averted by teaching creativity in the classroom drew this outright guffaw:

7   What's the [authors'] recommendation for boosting America's impending underperformance? Why, put creativity classes in school curricula! . . . The same public schools producing students who underperform on standardized tests in math, science, writing and reading comprehension should be performing CPR—Creative Process Recovery—on America's schoolchildren? That doesn't even rise to the level of nonsense. . . . Please. America will truly have a "creativity crisis" when "creativity" becomes a required high school course.⁵

8   Considering how much attention this article has garnered, both for the authors and for the subject itself, "creativity" seems a subject worth considering for those of us who teach anything, but most especially for those of us engaged in the performing arts, an endeavor historically yoked to "creativity."

Creativity: An explosive field

9   It is important to begin by considering creativity as a *bona fide* field of scientific research. I myself have often dismissed "creativity" as a topic, simply because it seems all too familiar. Whether as a performing artist or village dweller, through direct engagement or exposure to the ubiquitous craft fairs and street festivals that attend the manufactured quaintness of the historic town in which I live, I feel fairly steeped in creativity. My earlier stint as the parent of two small children was a creative enterprise in itself, and that's not even counting the invention of car games, sewing of Halloween costumes, and hot-gluing of science fair projects on the dining room table. For many, the word "creativity" conjures up something homey and familiar, like doing crafts on a rainy afternoon. So it may be enlightening to learn that the serious study of creativity as a subject was itself a creative act, a linking of creativity with research "after centuries of being apart."⁶

10   The necessary first step in doing research was to have the concept of research in mind, which more or less required the invention of research. The next step was nearly as difficult but no less important. This was to believe that doing research on human nature—rather than merely speculating about it—was as important and as feasible as doing research on physical nature.⁷

11   Over its sixty-year growth as a field to the present time in which "the field can only be described as explosive,"[8] the worth of studying both the creative process and the consequences of that process to the advancement of knowledge has been undisputed. The growth in creativity studies has lately engendered a distinction between what researchers call "Big-C" creativity (big ideas that change the world, like Einstein's theory of relativity) and "little-c" creativity (the kind of projects that do-it-yourselfers shop for at Home Depot). The relatively recent introduction of "Positive Psychology"[9] into the mainstream has allowed for the serious study of such heretofore academically unworthy topics as emotion and happiness, and the respectful and humane consideration of "little-c" creativity as not only attainable for all, but essential to a well lived life, to liberty and, even, it turns out, to the pursuit of happiness.

The building blocks of creativity

12   There is nearly unanimous agreement among creativity researchers that a working definition of creativity must contain two facets, namely, originality and usefulness. "The ability to produce work that is both novel (i.e., original, unexpected) and appropriate (i.e., useful, adaptive concerning task constraints)."[10] A review of the creativity literature further reveals the common agreement that creativity cannot be experienced or assessed—indeed, cannot truly exist, until and unless it is turned to some product, whether enduring or ephemeral. In other words, "originality per se is not sufficient—there would be no way to distinguish eccentric or schizophrenic thought from creative,"[11] or, as neatly explained by renowned psychologist Mihaly Csikszentmihalyi in the monumental book, *Creativity: Flow and the Psychology of Discovery and Invention*, the critical difference is that "[n]ormal people are rarely original, but they are sometimes bizarre. Creative people, it seems, are original without being bizarre."[12]

13   The "Creative Cognition Approach," so named by psychologist Thomas Ward, holds that extraordinary creativity is not solely the province of geniuses, or what he calls "minds that operate according to principles that are fundamentally different than those associated with normative cognition."[13] Translation? You, too, can be creative!

14   It is this spirit of inclusiveness that sparked the assignation "little-c" to everyday creation and problem solving, and is expressed by Csikszentmihalyi in his bestselling books on "optimal experience," which he termed "flow."[14] All of Csikszentmihalyi's writing on the subject of "flow" includes meditations and tips on how to imbue the everyday, and even the mundane activities of life with creativity. To do so makes necessary tasks not only bearable in the moment, but repeatable to the extent that such tasks as washing dishes and taking out the trash demand repetition many times over. Still, Csikszentmihalyi's masterwork on the subject of creativity, the result of over thirty years of research, considers only the "Big-C" variety of creativity. The book is both fascinating and inspiring, especially the first-hand accounts of the lives of the ninety-one highly creative people who were gracious enough to participate in the study on which the book is based.

15   Indeed, a whole new field of research into "optimal experience" has produced a sea of research on what motivates us, and it is not, it turns out, the rewards and punishments of carrot-or-stick systems, but the opportunity to be deeply engaged in endeavor—in other words, creative. Since motivation and downright dogged determination are fundamental requirements for attaining even

minimal success in the performing arts, motivation deserves special consideration, so it is a topic to which I will return in a future column.

"The box"

16   Returning to cognition, creativity's two distinct cognitive pathways are, in order, *divergent thinking* and *convergent thinking*, or what psychologist Mark Runco termed "problem-finding" and "problem-solving."[15] In order to create something, a question or problem must first be sought, then identified. For some people, the problem to be grasped is apparent to the point of obviousness; for others, its absence incites a quest. Either way, "problem identification (just noticing that there is a problem at hand) and problem definition and redefinition (making a problem operational and workable),"[16] are the first steps in the creative process.

17   Creators in the divergent thinking phase are searching, flexible and able to "generate a great quantity of ideas."[17] This is the much balleyhooed "thinking outside the box," a concept that has been coopted by advertising firms to highlight products positioned on the vanguard of style, the implication being that those still stuck inside "the box" are pathetically out of fashion. This hackneyed term for the parameters of culture raises a compelling question: can creativity exist without the box? In other words, is creativity dependent upon resisting the parameters of culture, upon breaking free of the box to define a new set of parameters? Is creativity born only from struggle?

18   For the catch is, the seeker has to return to the box in order for his discovery to become relevant and valued. Once the questions or causes have been found, they are stowed like precious raw material and returned to a workshop, whether actual or of the mind, for fashioning into a useful product. This can be anything from an idea to an object, but in order to adhere to the working definition of creativity, it must retain its novelty while proving its worth within a cultural context. This is the moment of convergence, wherein the problem or idea is forged, through a messy combination of elimination (tossing out bad ideas) and plain hard work.

19   Tell anybody you're a sculptor and they'll say, "Oh, how exciting, how wonderful." And I tend to say, "What's so wonderful?" I mean, its like being a mason, or being a carpenter, half the time. But they don't wish to hear that because they really only imagine the first part, the exciting part. But, as Khrushchev once said, that doesn't fry pancakes, you see. That germ of an idea does not make a sculpture which stands up. It just sits there. So the next stage, of course, is the hard work. Can you really translate it into a piece of sculpture? Or will it be a wild thing which only seemed exciting while you were sitting in the studio alone? Will it look like something? Can you actually do it physically? Can you, personally, do it physically? What do you have by way of materials? So the second part is a lot of hard work. And sculpture is that, you see. It is the combination of wonderful, wild ideas and then a lot of hard work.[18]

20   Even though the preceding description of the creative process was given by a sculptor, as a singer, I found much in common with her description of her process, her concerns, and the reactions she provokes in nonartists. Upon seeing my office for the first time, an academic colleague of mine remarked, "How lucky you are to have a piano in your office!" (This same colleague also surmised that my job as music director of our college's biannual music theater production must be "fun.")

21   However it is completed, in mirth or in sweat, the product of hard work must adhere to

another hallmark of creativity that evinces itself at the final stage of the process, namely, its recognition as something of value by a wider community of experts, or what Csikszentmihalyi calls "social confirmation,"[19] and he, along with others, argues that this assessment of creative worth should be the province of experts in the field: scientists, artists, and intellectuals. Others argue that assessment by a select group of experts is an elitist usurpment of power, especially because the decision to deem an invention "creative" often has social and monetary implications. Extreme views on this subject erupt most noticeably over federal or state funded art. Recently, William Donohue, the spokesman for the Roman Catholic advocacy group Catholic League, objected so strenuously to the exhibit at the National Portrait Gallery called "Hide/Seek" that he called on Congress to eliminate all federal funding for the Smithsonian Institution.

22 "Why should the working class pay for the leisure of the elite when in fact one of the things the working class likes to do for leisure is to go to professional wrestling? And if I suggested that we should have federal funds for professional wrestling to lower the cost of the ticket, people would think I'm insane. I don't go to museums any more than most Americans do," Donohue said.[20]

23 (Before opening his mouth the speak, Donahue apparently neglected to check the facts on museum attendance; according to the American Association of Museums, "American museums average approximately 865 million visits per year, which translates to 2.3 million visits per day.")[21] As Csikszentmihalyi noted, noncreative people are rarely original, but they can be, sometimes, bizarre.

24 Some in the business community argue that the only voice that matters in judging the worth of a product is that of the consumers, who vote with their pocketbook by literally putting their money on a good idea.

25 In markets, creativity—and its value—is determined by consumers. The most creative industries such as fashion, music, video-games, software, and animated movies tend to have audiences and customers that think of themselves as creative. Customer openness to creativity—however defined—powerfully influences creative supply . . . My view is that creativity—like any meaningful exchange of value—is not declared but negotiated.[22]

26 But all agree that in creativity, context means everything; that, unlike the crashing tree in the classic physics conundrum, if no one besides the creator is there to experience it, let alone judge it, it is as if the creative act never occurred at all. On this point, Nobel prize winner George Stigler had this to say when interviewed for Csikszentmihalyi's creativity research:

27 I think you have to accept the judgment of others. Because if one were allowed to judge his own case, every one of us should have been President of the United States and received all the medals and so forth.[23]

28 And what happens to "the box"? If the product of creative endeavor is crowned with a capital C by social confirmation, then it is likely that the box itself is redesigned, setting a new cultural norm. This is an apt description of the significant inventions throughout human history that have transformed culture: the plow, the clock, the microscope, and the birth control pill, to name a few. But according to author Nicholas Carr, it is the group of inventions he dubbed the "intellectual

technologies" that has "the greatest and most last-ing power over what and how we think."[24]

Stupid and stupider: Google and the Internet

29   Carr's 2008 article, "Is Google Making Us Stupid?" received widespread attention, due in part to its provocative headline, but mostly to the search engine's ubiquitous reach in lives around the globe.[25] According to a study by its own engineers, Google processes over one bil-lion user-generated search requests per day—and that was in 2008.[26] There is every reason to believe that number is even higher three years later.

30   Carr reviewed the neuroscience literature in order to judge the impact of computers on our brains, and his conclusions are implicit in the title of his new book, *The Shallows: What the Internet is Doing to our Brains.*[27] He names soci-ety's wholesale embrace of new intellectual tech-nology an "intellectual ethic," that is, something previously limited to an elite band of inventors which then becomes available to the general population. Such propagation and wholesale acceptance ushers in "a set of assumptions about how the human mind works or should work."[28] Interestingly, he notes that the dissemination of an intellectual ethic is neither aimed for nor much noticed by its creators. (This rings espe-cially true in light of Google's tone deafness to repeated and legitimate charges of privacy viola-tions, as in this disdainful retort by Google CEO Eric Schmidt: "If you have something that you don't want anyone to know, maybe you shouldn't be doing it in the first place.")[29]

31   Heavily quoting from such masterworks in the neuroscience literature as Joseph LeDoux's *Synaptic Self,*[30] Carr notes that all intellectual tech-nologies literally change our brain tissue, and not always for the better. In a rejoinder to Stephen Johnson's now classic apologia of the new tech-nology, *Everything Bad is Good for You,* in which Johnson suggested that the constant stimulation provided by 24/7 connection to the Internet is more valuable to learning than the "chronic under stimulation" and isolation engendered by reading an old-fashioned book,[31] Carr writes: "When it comes to the firing of our neurons, it's a mistake to assume that more is better."[32]

32   Indeed, in my review of the creativity litera-ture, the component that revealed itself as the most important precondition for creativity was space: space in one's life, space in one's daily schedule to be sure, but most critically, space in the mind.

A space of one's own

33   The wonders of the digital age (and there are many) allow us to satisfy a fundament of our hardwiring, what scientists call *operant condi-tioning* and what researcher Jaak Panksepp dubbed the "seeking system."[33] Seeking is the original survival mechanism that stimulated our species' search instinct on the African savannah where humans first thrived. The seek-ing instinct was incentivized with a flood of feel-good dopamine, the hormone of reward, when food or mates were found. According to evolutionary biologists, not much has changed since we roamed that oft invoked plain from evolutionary literature. It is this seeking urge that compels us to surf the web and obsessively check our e-mail (even if we are at work and shouldn't), and more darkly, compels modern day scourges like gambling addiction and tex-ting while driving. Besides the obvious disasters that such compulsive behavior engenders, obsessive seeking packs our minds to the point of destroyed concentration, all on account of our famously feeble attention spans.

34 [We] lurch from site to site, if only because we constantly crave the fleeting pleasure of new information. But this isn't really the fault of the Internet. The online world has merely exposed the feebleness of human attention, which is so weak that even the most minor temptations are all but impossible to resist.[34]

35 Lest we believe that we are among the chosen (I can turn it off if I want to), Carr notes that "instrumentalism" (in this context, the belief that technological tools are "entirely subservient to the conscious wishes of their users") is the most widely held belief about technology, not due to its veracity but "because it's the view we would prefer to be true."[35]

36 While it is true that many tasks require focus and concentration, it has also been noted that too much concentration on a task—"trying too hard"—results in so-called "choking" and failure.[36] Indeed, research on "brainstorming," that is, the conscious effort to generate creative thought, demonstrates a similar effect.[37] Recent research into that most creative of musical enterprises, jazz improvisation, reveals that creativity flourishes when portions of the right hemisphere of the brain associated with creativity are allowed to ramble freely, unfettered by the self-monitoring and self-evaluation of the left hemisphere.[38] There is no reason to doubt that similar processes may be unleashed during creative voice practice.

37 Thus creativity does not require concentration in its generative, divergent phase, and indeed is probably choked by it. But it does need mental space. And space implies time. The experts are still debating whether or not digital technology destroys concentration, but no one who uses it can dispute the fact that it gobbles up big chunks of our time.

38 If Steven Johnson is right, what we receive in return for our connection to the net is intense mental stimulation, which he posits can only be as his book's title implied: "good for you." But all that mental stimulation doesn't just lodge benignly in the mind; it craves repetition and restimulation (recall the dopamine reward system), and in some, becomes a truly addictive cycle. With the real crisis being one of mental space, just imagine what a mind habituated to the constant overstimulation provided by a Smartphone does when confronted with the empty void of the practice room.

Texting: Cantus interruptus

39 Text messaging from cell phones, or "texting," is the current technology that provides the continuous stimulation and sense of being connected that have always been hallmarks of adolescence. It is a fair guess that within the NATS membership, the majority of voice students are adolescents and young adults, so we have more than just a passing interest in the texting habits of this population, which a recent Nielsen survey examined.

40 If it seems like American teens are texting all the time, it's probably because on average they're sending or receiving 3339 texts a month. That's more than six per every hour they're awake—an 8 per cent jump from last year . . . No one texts more than teens (age 13–17), especially teen females, who send and receive an average of 4050 texts per month. Teen males also outpace other male age groups, sending and receiving an average of 2539 texts. Young adults (age 18–24) come in a distant second, exchanging 1630 texts per month (a comparatively meager three texts per hour).[39]

41 Another recent study of the texting habits of college students, conducted by two psychology professors at Wilkes University, showed that among the 95% of students who responded to

the survey, all said they bring their cell phones to class every day. This is neither surprising nor disturbing. However, 91% of these respondents reported that they actually use their phones to text during class; almost half said their instructors don't notice, and 62% said that they should be allowed to text in class as long as they don't disturb others.[40] This attitude carries over to darkened movie theaters and concert halls, where the glare of cell phones is indeed disturbing to others; but perhaps not for long.

42   Recently, in separate but unabashed bids to engage young adults, both the Indianapolis Symphony and the New York Philharmonic invited audience members to choose the encore they most wanted to hear by text messaging their votes during the concert.[41] Even an opera company was so enthralled by cell phone "interactivity" that its director invited audience members to text their preferred pairing in the final scene of Mozart's *Così fan tutte*.

43   The opera ain't over until the audience texts. In a move purists will pray never comes to the Met, producers of the updated version of Mozart's fiancée-swapping classic "Così fan Tutte" . . . will ask patrons to use their cell phones to vote on who marries whom in the climactic wedding scene. "The cast will implement the favored ending," said a show rep, adding, "It's a rare opera when you are actually asked to turn your cell phones on."[42]

44   And the texting path is not just one-way. At a concert in the summer of 2009, the National Symphony Orchestra streamed program notes to the audience through the popular social networking and "micro-blogging" site "Twitter." Text message "tweets," created by conductor Emil de Cou, were sent in real time during a performance of Beethoven's "Pastoral" Symphony.

De Cou called the Twitter commentary, "an adult musical pop-up book written for first timers and concert veterans alike."[43]

45   Thus it is not a stretch at all to imagine voice students accessing, streaming, texting, and tweeting—almost anything but paying deep and sole attention during master classes, concerts, and practice sessions. Neuroscience research highlights the fact that the building of neural pathways in the brain—synaptic strengthening—is powerfully effective. We become what we practice, even if what we are practicing is inattention.

46   So I suggest one simple yet powerful way to counteract the "creativity crisis" in our sphere of influence: ban the use of cell phones during both lessons and practice. And it should be noted that "screen addiction" cuts across all categories of age, gender, and profession; teachers habitually hooked up to their iPhones contribute to the problem of scattered attention. (One wonders what would happen if students asked for discounts based on the number of interrupted lesson minutes that teachers spend fiddling with their cells to reschedule clients or texting their kids to do their homework.) Even if lesson interruptions seem as defensible to teachers as the right to text in class does to the Wilkes University survey students, the result is still quantities of lost time.

47   If you are like one University of Syracuse professor who finds texting during class "brazenly disrespectful," I would not suggest his solution (he walks out).[44] Better is a clear studio policy regarding cell phone use and then consistent enforcement of it. To be sure, it is easier to post a policy than to actually enforce it. But enforcement is a form of *feedback*, named as the second most critical component of motor learning (bested only by actual practice).[45]

48   The two main categories of *feedback* in the time domain are *delayed* and *immediate*, and if

students have the audacity to text while others are performing, a delayed response is not only useless to the offenders as learners, it is potentially damaging to the student performer. In my performance classes, "immediate feedback" translates to the immediate loss of the privilege of being there. The class is stopped and the offending texter is asked to leave. Why? In my book, texting in class is like sending notes in sixth grade; besides, their actions clearly signal a wish to be elsewhere. Student singers who won't summon the self-control to listen attentively must ask themselves who they think will listen to them when it is their turn to perform. The prospect of singing for an audience of bowed heads is deeply uninspiring.

49   Creating a "no text zone" in classes and lessons is relatively straightforward, but it is simply not possible to enforce in the practice room— but neither is it possible, in reality, to enforce in an automobile. Granted, the consequences of running one's vocal progress into the ditch are not as dire as if one's car lands there; the magnitude is different. But the effects are the same (ruined car/ruined concentration/ruined practice). And then there is what happens to creativity.

50   As the saying goes, "Nature abhors a vacuum;" space is filled, one way or another, but we can control the quality of what rushes in to fill that space. Lesson minutes protected from interruption are transformed into that dynamic arc of information exchange we know as teaching. Emptied chairs in performance classes soon fill with singers who want to participate completely. Cell phones switched to "off" (not "vibrate"— that doesn't count) allow neurons to form new synaptic connections—what Le Doux calls "synaptic plasticity"[46]—and what we call "learning."

51   If there really is a "creativity crisis" in America, I suggest that its primary source is a dearth of mental space, which is the fundamental necessity to creative thinking. As Carr discovered, in regard to neurons firing, more is not better. An empty head is a mind at once filled with one of the best resources imaginable in this harried age of information overload: the potential for creative thinking.

Notes

1. Po Bronson and Ashley Merryman, "Creativity in America," *Newsweek Magazine*, online version (July 10, 2010); http://www.newsweek.com/2010/07/10/the-creativity-crisis (accessed December 10, 2010).
2. Ibid.
3. Ibid., 2.
4. Ibid.
5. Michael Schrage, "The Creativity Crisis? What Creativity Crisis?" *Harvard Business Review*, online version (August 25, 2010); http://blogs.hbr.org/schrage/2010/08/the-most-important-thing-to.html (accessed December 10, 2010).
6. Mark A. Runco and Robert S. Albert, "Creativity Research," in James C. Kaufman and Robert J. Sternberg, eds., *The Cambridge Handbook of Creativity* (Cambridge: Cambridge University Press, 2010), 4.
7. Ibid.
8. Ibid., 5.
9. Martin Seligman and Mihaly Csikszentmihalyi, "Positive Psychology: An Introduction," *American Psychologist* 55, no. 1 (January 2000): 5–14.
10. Robert J. Sternberg and T. I. Lubart, "The Concept of Creativity: Prospects and Paradigms," in R. J. Sternberg, ed., *Handbook of Creativity* (Cambridge: Cambridge University Press, 1999), 3.
11. Gregory J. Feist, "The Function of Personality in Creativity," in Kaufman and Sternberg, 114.
12. Mihaly Csikszentmihalyi, *Creativity: Flow and the Psychology of Discovery and Invention* (New York: Harper & Row, 1996), 63.
13. Thomas Ward, "Cognition and Creativity," in Kaufman and Sternberg, 114.
14. Mihaly Csikszentmihalyi, *Flow: The Psychology of Optimal Experience* (New York: Harper & Row, 1990).
15. Mark Runco, "Creativity," *Annual Review of Psychology* 55, no. 1 (February 2004): 657–687.
16. Ibid., 675.

17. Csikszentmihalyi, *Creativity*, 60.

18. Ibid., 62.

19. Ibid., 25.

20. William Donahue interview on NPR: http://www.npr.org/2010/12/02/131748447/gay-portraiture-exhibit-sparks-funding-debate (accessed December 13, 2010).

21. American Association of Museums, http://www.aamus.org/aboutmuseums/abc.cfm (accessed December 13, 2010).

22. Schrage, 3.

23. Csikszentmihalyi, *Creativity*, 42.

24. Nicholas Carr, *The Shallows: What the Internet is Doing to our Brains* (New York: W.W. Norton, 2010), 45.

25. Carr, "Is Google Making Us Stupid?" *The Atlantic Monthly*, online version (July/August, 2008); http://www.theatlantic.com/magazine/archive/2008/07/is-google-making-us-stupid/6868/ (accessed December 13, 2010).

26. Jeffrey Dean and Sanjay Ghemawat, "MapReduce: Simplified Data-Processing on Large Clusters," *Communications of the Association for Computing Machinery* 51, no. 1 (January 2008): 107–113.

27. Carr, *The Shallows*.

28. Ibid., 45.

29. Cade Metz, "Google Chief: Only Miscreants Worry About Net Privacy," posted in *Music and Media*, December 7, 2009; GMThttp://www.theregister.co.uk/2009/12/07/schmidt_on_privacy/ (accessed December 10, 2010).

30. Joseph LeDoux, *Synaptic Self: How Our Brains Become Who We Are* (New York: Penguin Books, 2002).

31. Steven Johnson, *Everything Bad is Good For You* (New York: Penguin Group, 2005), 18–19.

32. Carr, *The Shallows*, 123.

33. See Jaak Panksepp, *Affective Neuroscience: The Foundations of Human and Animal Emotions* (New York: Oxford University Press, 2004).

34. Jonah Lehrer, "Our Cluttered Minds," *The New York Times* (June 3, 2010); http://www.nytimes.com/2010/06/06/books/review/Lehrer-t.html (accessed December 10, 2010).

35. Carr, *The Shallows*, 46.

36. See Lynn Helding, "Break a Leg! The Ironic Effect, Choking, and Other Mind Games," *Journal of Singing* 67, no. 2 (November/December 2010): 207–212.

37. Po Bronson and Ashley Merryman, "Forget Brainstorming," *Newsweek Magazine*, online version (July 12, 2010); http://www.newsweek.com/2010/07/12/forget-brainstorming (accessed December 10, 2010).

38. Charles Limb and Allen R. Braun, "Neural Substrates of Spontaneous Musical Performance: An fMRI Study of Jazz Improvisation," *PLoS ONE* (Public Library of Science) 3, no. 2, (February 2008), http://www.plosone.org/article/info:doi%2F10.1371%2Fjournal.pone.0001679.

39. U.S. Teen Mobile Report: "Calling Yesterday, Texting Today, Using Apps Tomorrow," *Nielsen Wire*, http://blog.nielsen.com/nielsenwire/online_mobile/u-s-teen-mobile-report-calling-yesterday-texting-today-using-apps-tomorrow, October 14, 2010 (accessed December 5, 2010).

40. "Wilkes University Professors Examine Use of Text Messaging in the College Classroom," http://www.wilkes.edu/pages/194.asp?item=61477 (accessed on December 5, 2010).

41. Stephanie Clifford, "Texting at a Symphony? Yes, but Only to Select an Encore," *The New York Times* (May 15, 2009); http://www.nytimes.com/2009/05/16/arts/music/16text.html (accessed December 5, 2010).

42. *The New York Post*, "The Opera Isn't Over Until the Audience Texts," March 27, 2009; http://www.nypost.com/seven/03272009/gossip/pagesix/the_end_of_opera_161471.htm (accessed December 5, 2010).

43. Dave Itzkoff, "A Different Tweet in Beethoven's Pastoral Symphony," *The New York Times* (July 23, 2009); http://arts-beat.blogs.nytimes.com/2009/07/23/a-different-tweet-in-beethovens-pastoral-symphony (accessed December 5, 2010).

44. "If You Text in Class, This Prof Will Leave," *Inside High Ed News* (April 2, 2008); http://www.insidehighered.com/news/2008/04/02/texting (accessed December 5, 2010).

45. Richard Schmidt and Timothy Lee, *Motor Control and Learning: A Behavioral Emphasis*, 4th ed. (Champaign, IL: Human Kinetics, 2005), 399.

46. LeDoux, 9.

Comprehension

1. In your own words, explain the difference between "Big-C" and "little-c" creativity (par. 11).

2. Explain what Helding means by *space* as she describes it in the section "A space of one's own."

Structure and Organization

1. Analyze the effectiveness of one of the essay's sections (not including the introduction or the final section), commenting on factors affecting its unity, coherence, and development (for example, use of evidence, rhetorical pattern, transitions, and the like).

Critical Thinking

1. Helding spends much of her introduction on readers' reaction to the *Newsweek* article. What is her purpose in doing so?

2. Are the ideas in the essay relevant to fields other than the performing arts? Support your answer by direct references to the text and through critical thinking.

3. a. Of the following experts referred to in the essay, choose two and analyze their importance in the section(s) in which they occur and to the essay as a whole:
   i. Mihaly Csikszentmihalyi
   ii. Mark Runco
   iii. Nicholas Carr
   iv. Stephen Johnson

   b. Which do you consider the most important to the essay? Why?

4. Analyze the author's argument in paragraphs 46–50. Does it satisfy the requirements of an effective argument?

Jonathan Gray, "'Coming Up Next': Promos in the Future of Television and Television Studies"

"Coming Up Next" is a humanities essay that interprets primary sources from a specific perspective; as is evident in the abstract, the sources that are analyzed in the pages that follow are promos for television shows. The author tries to persuade his audience that these kinds of texts are worth considering.

The concept of the "text" is crucial to an understanding of this essay and the author's approach to his subject. In the abstract, the word *text* and variants on this word—*contextualize* and *textuality*—are referred to. Obviously, by *texts*, the author means something more than books, articles, and other print formats. Come up with a definition of *text* that would include easily recognizable forms like books and movies but would also include advertisements (print or visual).

Preparing to Read

How much attention do you pay to promos of television shows, movies, or other media? What role do they play in your decision to watch or not watch a program or movie, or buy a product? Which are successful in attracting your interest and which are less successful?

1. Identify specific characteristics of successful and unsuccessful promos.
2. Discuss the questions above or similar questions in groups or freewrite on the topic of promos.

"Coming Up Next": Promos in the Future of Television and Television Studies

Jonathan Gray

Journal of Popular Film and Television, August 2010
(2709 words)

Abstract

This article argues for the importance of studying promos. First, it is noted that promos often begin the text, offering viewers their first understandings of and encounters with the text. Second, promos' role in creating notions of the channel as a whole and these notions' role in contextualizing our understanding of any given text are examined. Thus, while promos have often been regarded as annoying hype at worst, or as secondary and peripheral distractions at best, the article argues that they frequently make vital contributions to the production of television's textuality.

Keywords: channel idents, paratexts, promos, television, television studies, textuality

1   Campaigns to keep cancelled shows on the air have been commonplace in the world of television for many years. Increasingly, though, they are offset by the large number of people who have never even heard of many of the cancelled shows, let alone watched them. As much as our contemporary media environment is suffused with discussion of video "going viral," the sheer number of available channels on many televisions, mixed with formidable competition from a proliferation of other sources, has made a sterile, unheard-of existence the more regular state of affairs for many television shows. Or, posing as serious a problem for many shows' economic livelihoods is the increased incidence of viewers downloading their programs off iTunes, using online streaming episode players or BitTorrent, or buying the DVD, thereby forgoing the broadcast presentation of the shows and eluding the Nielsen ratings that keep said shows alive. In the face of such obstacles, only foolish, headstrong network executives would feel secure regarding their future advertising revenues, much less the future of their industry as they

know it. As such, promotion has become all the more important. Savvy showrunners and executives must now spend as much if not considerably more time and energy telling the world about their shows and bringing audiences to the network presentation of them as they must in creating the shows in the first place.

2   Amanda Lotz observes that the major American networks broadcast an estimated 30,000 promos a year, in the process forgoing approximately $4 billion worth of ad revenue (108–09). Rarely does a commercial break go by without at least one in-station promo. Stepping away from the television, though, we still experience promos aplenty. Public transit systems are often heavily populated by posters advertising television shows. Billboards along busy highways similarly announce the virtues of this or that show, online pop-up ads frequently accompany our e-mail, Facebook page, or other Web activities with flashy appeals to watch tonight, and online video-sharing sites such as YouTube are flush with trailers and promos. More innovative forms of promos exist, too; for instance, ABC covered beaches with messages in bottles advertising the castaway show *Lost* before it premiered and they circulated laundry bags to advertise the dirty laundry–peddling *Desperate Housewives*. When *Dexter* moved to England, it was accompanied by a Web site—www.icetruck.tv—that allowed people to send video postcards to friends (or foes?) that seemingly suggested that one of the show's feared serial killers was coming after them next. Many shows have long since learned the value of creating official Web sites that offer production details, clips, discussion forums, surrounding and background materials, and occasionally alternate reality games (ARGs) or other spaces of play for fans or would-be fans. Thus, *Heroes* has an online comic book; many television characters have their own blogs or MySpace or Facebook pages; and *The Office* invites viewers to become workers at the Dunder Mifflin paper company, personalizing their workspaces online. Meanwhile, late-night talk shows regularly host stars talking about their new shows, entertainment magazines and newspaper sections feature interviews that marketing teams have set up, and iTunes offers podcasts with additional information. The industry, in other words, is spending a lot of time, money, and labor to fill the mediascape with promos.

3   Amid such a situation, the promo campaign becomes an important entity for television scholars to examine. If we have proven slow to do so—and I believe we have—cultural critics' prevailing dislike of advertising is probably in large part responsible. Ads, after all, are seen as manipulative and as trying to get something out of us rather than to give something to us; they are seen as peddling stereotypes and as appealing to base instincts rather than addressing or even developing more noble instincts, and thus they are seen as more worthy of critique or scorn than of attention, much less engagement. Quite simply, too, when discussing television, television scholars have often operated as have the DVDs on which we study television, expunging the ads from a show's record as if they never existed. We have become quite skilled at ignoring ads *textually*, even if we will discuss them at length when examining the structure of the *industry*. How, then, might we start to think of promos differently in this, the age of the promo?

Where the text begins: Promos as frames

4   The key binaries that we must move beyond are those of art and promotion, text and ad, show and peripheral. What is an ad, after all, but an attempt to brand something, or, reworded, an attempt to create a text, a narrative for, and an

experience of something? To take the many Geico ads as an example: through using cavemen, a Cockney lizard, and a pile of money with eyes as "spokespeople," Geico aims to convince us that it is a personable, hip insurance company that, unlike the others, is kind of quirky, yet in a refreshing way. The simplicity of their ads, meanwhile, aims to suggest that all dealings with the company will be short, sweet, and simple. The ads create a brand identity for Geico, by way of creating a narrative of and an experience for Geico. However, shifting to promos for television shows, to create a narrative and an experience for a product that *is* a narrative and an experience will now contribute to that text. Cultural critics have long noted the at-times radical disconnect between brand and product—as most evident, for instance, when car ads consistently situate the action in vast expanses of nature to suggest environmental friendliness—and critics have rightfully been concerned about an ad's ability to take over the history, present, and experience of a product with branding (see, for instance, Jhally). With ads and promos for television shows, then, a similar situation exists, wherein the promo exerts strong *textual* pull over the show. Promos are "paratexts," as Gerard Genette called the material surrounding books such as covers, prefaces, and typeface choices—appended to the show without being considered a *bona fide* part of it, yet nevertheless working to create an idea of what that show is, means, and does. Promos quite frequently create a text.

5   This process begins with advance promos and buzz campaigns that hail a specific audience and that promise that audience a very particular set of pleasures, dictating what a text is while also creating a tone, mood, and sensibility for it. They might insist that a text is for men only, for instance, that it is for teens, that it is liberal, that it is post-ironic, that it is a dramedy, that it is just

like another beloved show, or so forth. They will introduce us to the cast in specific ways, privileging some over others, drawing on certain star intertexts while downplaying others, and inviting us to identify with some yet not others. And they will sample the world we are being invited to enter, aiming to give us our first interaction with it, yet a carefully framed and managed interaction at that. So, for example, when NBC began advertising its new show *Southland* in the spring of 2009, its ads suggested a gritty, realistic depiction of life in the Los Angeles Police Department. The ads regularly boasted how the show was from *ER*'s producers, thus laying claim to *ER*'s mantle of quality, realistic television. They prominently featured the show's star, Benjamin McKenzie, offering him as the viewer's surrogate on the show, at least while we, like McKenzie's rookie cop character, adjust to this crazy world. Meanwhile, a visit to the show's Web site reveals a quiz on LAPD radio codes and a short video on famous crimes in the real Los Angeles's history, both of which further aim to steep the show in realism, suggesting, respectively, that the show would offer specialist knowledge of LAPD life and that it would focus on Los Angeles as a character. Fans or viewers who then went on to watch the show would likely revise their understanding of the text and fill in the larger picture, but the promos still likely played a vital role in establishing the text and in creating initial expectations and the all-important intertextual and evaluative frames through which the viewer would make sense of the show. Advance promos are thus like the front covers and opening chapters of books, establishing the audience's initial contact with and first impressions of texts.

6   The importance of advance promos is best appreciated if we consider the situation of those who watch the promo yet decide not to watch the show. Clearly, such audiences have based

their decision not to watch on something, and that something is thus a form of text that is created largely by the promos and surrounding buzz. If, for instance, one decided not to watch *Southland* since it looked too somber and gritty, because one hated McKenzie on *The OC* and had no interest in a show centered on him, because it seemed too much of a boy's show, or for whatever other reason, one would have already created an image and a text of *Southland*. At this point, whether the promos were accurate in suggesting a somber and gritty, McKenzie-centered, boys-with-guns show is largely immaterial if that is a widespread image of *Southland* and if that is the text with which the public at large becomes familiar. For too long, we in television studies have considered the audience of a television show as limited to those who watch the show, but a show's public standing relies just as much on the opinions of those who have not watched the show, yet who have watched the promos, as on those who have seen the show.

The frame around the frames: Flow and channel idents

7   We must also be able to think beyond the level of the individual show, however, and when we do so, promos become even more important. In a multichannel era, each channel must sell not only its programs but the entire channel. At the 2008 International Radio and Television Society Foundation and Disney's Digital Media Summit that I attended in Burbank, Disney staffers continually repeated Disney president and CEO Bob Iger's instructions to them to think of themselves as selling not *shows* but the three central *brands* of Disney, ABC, and ESPN. Selling shows can backfire, since audiences can fall in love with a show yet buy it on DVD, download it via BitTorrent, or

otherwise avoid the broadcast presentation; if enough audiences do so, its resulting anemic Nielsen ratings may require cancellation. But if networks and cable channels can make viewers fans of the network or channel itself, and if, over and above love for any given show, fans identify with specific channels, such brand loyalty is likely to translate more easily into the kind of metrics on which the television industry relies. With the network or channel as the product for sale, however, on one hand, the shows become a form of promo themselves, and on the other hand, the industry must care all the more about audiences' images and understandings of texts they do not watch. *Southland* promos, as such, do not just send us messages about *Southland*—they also send us messages about NBC.

8   If Iger's philosophy is one for the future of television, it is an industrial version of Raymond Williams's famous statement regarding television as *flow* between show-and-show, show-and-ad, as "perhaps the defining characteristic of broadcasting, simultaneously as a technology and as a cultural form" (86). The "text" for sale is the entire channel. Although television studies need not, of course, follow this philosophy itself, we nevertheless find ourselves in the situation whereby we have often ignored promos, deeming them unimportant textually, yet now we find that the shows that we thought were important are themselves promos. In saying this, I do not mean to suggest that they have thus become devalued, but rather I mean to argue that television is full of promos, and it would be odd for textual studies to focus only on one set (namely, the programs).

9   We might also, therefore, pay renewed attention to channel idents and other promos for the network or channel itself. NBC, for example, is fond of channel idents involving some of its shows' more personable and likeable characters

or actors fooling around. *The Office*'s Pam and Jim will share a joke with the camera, *Heroes*'s Greg Grunberg and Masi Oka will goof around together, or *Chuck*'s titular character will address us directly. Such idents aim to create an intimate, friendly bond between the viewer and both the stars and the characters, while also branding NBC as a place for fresh comedy and for characters with whom we can identify. But what role do these idents play in the network's attempts to crawl out of the Nielsen basement? Television studies' focus on shows and the production, reception, and textual processes surrounding them may have blinded us to asking questions about the production, reception, and textuality of networks or channels as a whole. Promos, as I have argued, can best be thought of textually as frames, and thus closer attention to channel idents would equate to closer attention to the frames that surround television viewing. Such work promises to be all the more helpful in an era when many viewers have multiple choices of where they can watch their beloved shows, since their choice of venue on one hand may be greatly determined by the value added to that venue by branding, and on the other hand may subtly or profoundly change the experience and construction of the television text being watched. As the Mac/PC wars and accompanying ads suggest, viewers often care greatly (or are, at least, asked to care greatly) about interface, about the semiotics of their point of access to content, and about frames. Moreover, Derek Kompare has examined how cable channels use reruns to (re)brand their channel, and Lynn Spigel observes that the reruns are often reframed in the process (often becoming camp); both scholars' work, therefore, suggests that the textuality

and meanings of a channel and of a show are always contingent on one another. To understand a show textually, we may be required to study a channel textually.

Conclusion

10 To examine promos and channel idents more closely may also be a way to bridge an old divide in media studies, between studies of the audience, text, or industry. Often, undergraduate and graduate students are divided up into teams of audience, text, and industry scholars, as if in preparation for intramural sports competitions. The text and audience "teams" have usually enjoyed a healthy relationship, while the industry team has often operated by itself, a natural rival to both the text and audience scholars. Admittedly and refreshingly, though, many scholars have of late challenged these divisions, offering multiple models for a broader scholarship that takes audience, text, industry, and context into account. The closer study of promos could further contribute to this breaking down of barriers, since promos are intrinsically industrial entities, yet also, as I have argued, they are intrinsically textual. To study the promo is to study the logic by which the industry monetizes and publicizes its content *and* to study how texts work *and* to study how audiences work. While the industry funnels millions on millions of dollars into creating promos, while considerable creative care and energy is put into making many promos, and while audiences spend an increasing amount of time with promos—whether as trailers, ARGs, pop-up ads, or so forth—the nature of the business is shifting in a way that renders the promo profoundly important, for both popular and scholarly understandings of television.

Works Cited

Genette, Gerard. *Paratexts: Thresholds of Interpretation.* Trans. Jane E. Lewin. Cambridge: Cambridge UP, 1997. Print.

Jhally, Sut. *The Codes of Advertising: Fetishism and the Political Economy of Meaning in the Consumer Society.* New York: Routledge, 1987. Print.

Kompare, Derek. *Rerun Nation: How Repeats Invented American Television.* New York: Routledge, 2005. Print.

Lotz, Amanda. *The Television Will Be Revolutionized.* New York: NYU Press, 2007. Print.

Spigel, Lynn. "From the Dark Ages to the Golden Age: Women's Memories and Television Reruns." *Screen* 36.1 (1995): 16–33. Print.

Williams, Raymond. *Television: Technology and Cultural Form.* London: Fontana/Collins, 1974. Print.

Comprehension

1. Identify the essay's thesis and the form it takes. In view of the essay's purpose, why might this form be an appropriate one?

2. In your own words, define the following terms from paragraph 4: (a) *binaries*; (b) *paratexts*.

3. Why does the author believe that people who choose not to watch a television show might be just as important to the study of television as those who do watch? (par. 6)

Structure and Organization

1. a. What is the purpose of paragraph 2?

   b. What is the main method of development in this paragraph and how does it contribute to the introduction as a whole?

   c. Analyze paragraph organization, mentioning specific strategies that aid in comprehension.

Critical Thinking

1. Who is the intended audience of this article? Point to specific passages that show you this.

2. Analyze the author's credibility as it is established (or is not established) by specific passages in the essay.

3. Analyze the effectiveness of the conclusion, considering its purpose(s) and the way(s) it satisfies the requirements of successful academic conclusions.

V A Critical Thinking Casebook

Critical thinking (see Chapter 7) is integral to successful essays, but most of the essays in this section directly challenge assumptions we take for granted or explore unconventional arguments, encouraging readers to question what they read but to remain open to new viewpoints. The author of "Bullshit" argues that while seldom discussed, "bullshit" is endemic to our culture and secretly works to undermine it. After noting that more people currently own cellphones than have access to a toilet, the author of "When a Cellphone Beats a Royal Flush" explains why this is an entirely reasonable fact. For the author of "Is Scientific Progress Inevitable?" reflections on a trip to an archaeological site evoke insights into the relationship between scientific and social progress.

"The Selfish Metaphor" and "We Can't Handle the Truth: The Science of Why People Don't Believe Science" explore the cognitive bases of our thought processes as they are embedded in language and emotions, respectively. Both essays help explain why opinions can be hard to change. "Are We Ready to Subsidize Heroin?" is an expository essay that examines the two sides of the controversial debate about harm-reduction policies, while the author of "The Undiscovered Province" "modestly" proposes that Aboriginal self-government can best be achieved by creating a new province out of Aboriginal lands.

The first two academic essays in this section review research in the field to explain seemingly contradictory aspects of human nature. "How to Think, Say, or Do Precisely the Worst Thing for Any Occasion" accounts for counter-productive human behaviour, while "Others Sometimes Know Us Better Than We Know Ourselves" helps make sense of the paradoxical truth that we often misunderstand aspects of our own personalities. One of the purposes of academic essays is to test and potentially disprove previous research. Using an experiment, the authors of "'He Loves Me, He Loves Me Not . . . ': Uncertainty Can Increase Romantic Attraction" challenge the logical, but sometimes inaccurate, perception that we like people who we believe like us.

Robert Gibson, "Bullshit"

Non-academic writers often make extensive use of experts, such as researchers, teachers, or others actively involved in their field. Robert Gibson uses such an expert, Harry G. Frankfurt, an emeritus philosophy professor, to help organize his essay. Although not involved in research themselves, such writers serve a valuable function in spreading others' ideas to their readers while making their own contribution to the subject.

▶ Preparing to Read

This brief essay appeared in a Canadian online magazine aimed at readers with an interest in the environment. For more information, access the journal website and summarize the purpose of the journal, using information on or accessible from its main page.

What does the word *bullshit* mean to you? In one sentence, define *bullshit* using your own words; come up with two or three other words of similar meaning, considering some of the differences among them.

Bullshit

Robert Gibson

Alternatives Journal, January 2011
(637 words)

1   Back in 2005, Princeton University Press published an engaging essay by Harry G. Frankfurt, an emeritus professor of moral philosophy. The title of the little book, which spent many weeks on the *New York Times* bestseller list, was *On Bullshit*.

2   Frankfurt began his essay by observing that although bullshit is a particularly salient feature of our culture, it gets almost zero serious attention.

3   Bullshit is one of the many occupants of the space between truth and lies. Among the others are nonsense and codswallop, bunkum, hooey, humbug, bafflegab, chicanery and duplicity. Some are mean-spirited. Some are fun. Most are on the slope between highly irritating and largely harmless.

4   In this bunch, bullshit avoids attention because it is not obviously nasty and because it is too common and too easily accommodated to be immediately worrisome. Frankfurt says it is nevertheless deeply insidious because it undermines the expectation and practice of truthfulness.

5   Frankfurt defines bullshit as speech (or writing or even certain actions) that aims to influence perceptions and choices, but has no real concern for truth. The particulars of what is said may be true or untrue, but for the bullshitter that is irrelevant. Bullshit aims only to serve an immediate end—to puff up the reputation of the speaker and/or to promote a product or a position. That is all.

6   Advertising is mostly bullshit—intentional misrepresentation by exaggeration and omission. But so is much of what passes for debate these days. Even reasoned deliberation often takes the form of various stakeholders arguing one-sidedly for their favoured positions. The underlying model is decision making in an essentially adversarial forum where each player takes a stand and argues for it. Compromises may be made, alliances negotiated and agreements reached. It is even possible that some mutual learning and appreciation will emerge. But the focus is on winning, not understanding.

7   Environmentalists who claim to know for sure that we have only 10 years to save the planet are bullshitting. So are cornucopians who claim that technological progress will save us. Neither of them is seeking to present a well-founded summary of the full story. Their focus is persuasion, not truth. And in their world, the concept of truth fades.

8   Bullshit is not a recent invention. Over two millennia ago, Plato condemned rhetoric as manipulative oratory, and yet it continued to be

a focus of education until the 20th century. The old bullshit served established elites and the many conflicting versions of the One True Faith, enforced by burning heretics and enslaving unbelievers.

9   The old bullshit survives today in the intolerant fundamentalisms of overwhelmed people grasping for certainty. In a big, complex, diverse and dynamic world, the simple faiths of the Tea Parties and Talibans require massive ignorance. But the old bullshit is probably still less dangerous than the exaggerations and omissions of the post-modern bullshitters serving narrow interests. Their battles for influence based on swayed opinion threaten to bury the struggle for truthful communication, perhaps even truthful understanding.

10   More power, then, to the merry bands of bullshit exposers—the Yes Men, Adbusters and Ecobunkers—who have been busily poking spanners in the spinworks. More power as well to the independent scientists, non-aligned journalists and collaborative researchers who have been quietly delivering reliable reports on the state of life on our planet.

11   Most deserving of celebration, however, are the activists who refuse to stoop. There is nothing easier today than to step down into the trough and fight one-sided bullshit with other-sided bullshit. Maybe sometimes the green poop will prevail, but the smell remains and the substance is corrosive.

12   In his other short book, *On Truth*, Harry Frankfurt notes that establishing and sustaining an advanced culture is impossible if we are debilitated by error or ignorance. Bullshit is an agent of debilitation. The only viable response is to rise above it.

Comprehension

1. a. How is "bullshit" different from a lie? How is it similar, according to Frankfurt?
   b. What makes "bullshit" more dangerous than the other kinds of "untruths" mentioned in paragraph 3?
2. Using context, if possible, define the word *cornucopians* (par. 7); explain the phrase *spanners in the spinworks* (par. 10).
3. Summarize paragraph 11 in one sentence.

Structure and Organization

1. What organizational method (rhetorical pattern) is used in (a) paragraph 6; (b) 8; (c) 12?

Critical Thinking/Research

1. How does the term *rhetoric*, as used by Plato (par. 8), differ from other uses of this term today?
2. Recall one debate you have listened to—it could be a debate among your friends, in school, or on TV or the Internet. How did it resemble what is described in paragraphs 6–7? Was it different in any way?
3. Using a reliable source, such as a newspaper or magazine, access a review of Frankfurt's book *On Bullshit* and summarize the writer's opinions about the book.

Doug Saunders, "When a Cellphone Beats a Royal Flush"

In paragraph 2 of the essay that follows, *Globe and Mail* columnist Doug Saunders cites a surprising statistic concerning the number of cellphone users versus toilet users. While most people might respond by expressing shocked dismay, Saunders reasons that preferring a cellphone over a toilet might be a rational choice for those in developing countries. Using critical thinking, Saunders tries to account for the statistic.

Preparing to Read

Do you own a cellphone? If so, do you consider it a luxury or a necessity? Why?

When a Cellphone Beats a Royal Flush

Doug Saunders

The Globe and Mail, 26 March 2011
(752 words)

1 About a third of the world's people have no toilet. This is both unsanitary and inconvenient. In villages, it's often customary for the women to rise at 5 a.m. and pay a visit to the field, and the men to make their pilgrimage an hour later. In cities, there are open cesspits, fetid back alleys and plastic-bag "flying toilets."

2 Nowadays, it's increasingly familiar to see people composing text messages while engaging in such demeaning public activities. As we learned this week, 4.3 billion people have access to a toilet, and 4.6 billion people personally own a cellphone. This means there are 300 million people in the world, equivalent to the population of the United States, who have a cellphone in their pocket but no access to a toilet.

3 To many of us, this sounds absurd: A toilet is a basic necessity, whereas a mobile electronic device still seems like a frill or a minor luxury. People with family incomes below $2 a day shouldn't be buying $20 devices, should they?

4 That was certainly how it was taken when most people read those figures from World Water Day, which marks a worthy campaign to get proper sanitation to more people in poor countries.

5 But let's not discount cellphones for the very poor, or question their priorities. Why would someone want to have a cellphone before a toilet? I have met a good many people, on four continents, who have a stick of beeping silicon in their pocket but no slab of wet porcelain in their house, and while none are happy with the lack of sanitation, none would consider their phone to be anything less than vital.

6 There are a number of reasons why a cellphone is as important as a toilet, if not more so, for those at the bottom of the barrel:

7 Toilets are about sitting still, phones are about movement. A toilet in your house will prevent disease and bring dignity and value to life. But life for the very poor is about constant change and risk. Poor people have to move house much more

frequently than those with higher incomes; they have cash-flow problems and need to seize on ever-changing minuscule income opportunities.

8   They tend to make their livings from multiple sources—as economist Deepa Narayan has found, poor villagers manage by building "joint portfolios" of farming, small businesses and casual labour in the city, to hedge their risk across several platforms. As the four economists who wrote the recent study Portfolios of the Poor noted, the world's poorest people endure the "triple whammy" of "low incomes; irregularity and unpredictability; and a lack of tools."

9   Most of the world's poor now live in motion, with part of the family in the village and part on the margins of a city. There are more than 200 million Chinese families divided between village and city; they rely on instant mobile communications to avoid catastrophe and to find opportunities to escape their plight.

10   Poverty, in short, is vulnerable to sudden change. A phone at least provides a few more potential lifelines.

11   Phones can mean debt, but toilets can mean eviction. As anyone who's received a cellphone for Christmas knows, it's a gift that requires constant payments. In poor countries, cellphone use costs upward of $2 a month—so they can contribute to dangerous levels of indebtedness.

12   But they can also be ways out of debt. In Africa, small-hold farmers frequently use cellphone crop-information services such as Ghana's Esoko to locate buyers, get the best prices and find out what to plant based on futures markets—a useful service for a Western farmer but a lifesaver for a poor sub-Saharan one.

13   On the other hand, when an aid agency hooks up a toilet to your shack, there's the risk that your property value will be raised above the poor-family level: great if you own, but potentially tragic if you rent.

14   A phone won't stop your children from getting dysentery, but a toilet won't overthrow your dictatorship. Yes, the people of Eastern Europe managed to overthrow their autocrats in 1989 without cellphones. But they used very similar networks built on well-established connections. Among the new classes of the Middle East, the cellphone has become vital for communicating new opportunities—not just in income, but in politics.

15   Increasingly, it's the tool people are using for dramatic reform. It doesn't have the comforts of a toilet, but it can help you flush away that stinking mess.

Comprehension

1.   Explain what the author means in paragraph 12.

Structure, Organization, and Style

1.   What is the primary organizational method in the essay? Identify one paragraph that uses the cause–effect method and another that uses problem–solution.
2.   Discuss the author's use of humour in his essay.
3.   Give three examples of informal diction (words or phrases) in the essay. For each, provide a substitute that would be suitable for an academic essay.

Critical Thinking

1. Analyze the author's argument, commenting on any argumentative strategies and their effectiveness.
2. Think of a situation involving two alternatives and argue in support of the "least likely" alternative (for example, that a high-school education is more beneficial than a college or university education).

Mary Midgley, "The Selfish Metaphor"

This article, which appeared in the popular science magazine *New Scientist*, considers the role that metaphorical thinking can play in scientific thought. *New Scientist* is designed for readers interested in a wide variety of science-related topics. Access the magazine's website and scan recent articles in order to determine the kinds of articles published.

▶ Preparing to Read

1. What is a metaphor and how is it used in literary writing?
2. Have you ever considered how common metaphors can affect our perception?
3. Can you think of a metaphor that has an everyday use? For example, how is the Internet "web-like"?

The Selfish Metaphor

Mary Midgley

New Scientist, 29 January 2011
(1311 words)

Abstract

In this article the author discusses how metaphoric thinking has distorted perceptions on evolution. Evolutionary biologist Richard Dawkins mentions in the 30th anniversary of his book The Selfish Gene *that genes are actually cooperative instead of egoistic. It comments on the philosophy of individualism that rose out of the English civil war in the 17th century, and mentions that naturalist Charles Darwin hated the concept and rejected direct applications of natural selection to social policies.*

1 Selfish genes, survival of the fittest, competition, hawk and dove strategies. Like all theories, Darwinism has its own distinct vocabulary. So distinct, in fact, that we end up asking how else we can talk about evolution? After all, isn't competitive evolution the only possible context for explaining the biological facts? The drama implied by competition, war and selfishness passes unnoticed because people are used to this rather hyped-up way of talking even about current scientific beliefs.

2   The trouble with metaphors is that they don't just mirror scientific beliefs, but they also shape them. Our imagery is never just surface paint. It expresses, advertises and strengthens our preferred interpretations. It also usually carries unconscious bias from the age we live in— and this can be tricky to ditch no matter how faulty, unless we ask ourselves how and why things go wrong, and start to talk publicly about how we should understand metaphor.

3   Evolution has been the most glaring example of the thoughtless use of metaphor over the past 30 years, with the selfish/war metaphors dominating and defining the landscape so completely it becomes hard to admit there are other ways of conceiving it. In *How The Leopard Changed Its Spots*, biologist and complexity theorist Brian Goodwin suggested the kind of correction needed, remarking mildly that humans are "every bit as co-operative as we are competitive; as altruistic as we are selfish. These are not romantic yearnings and Utopian ideals; they arise from a rethinking of our nature that is emerging from the sciences of complexity." But that was in 1991—and few were listening.

4   From the merest glance at a wider context, it becomes clear that competition cannot be the ultimate human reality, still less (as philosopher Daniel Dennett argued) the central creative force behind the universe. Entities complex enough to compete cannot exist at all without much internal cooperation. To create cells, organelles must combine; to create armies, soldiers must organise. Even the evolutionary biologist Richard Dawkins pointed out on the 30th anniversary of publication of his iconic book, *The Selfish Gene*, that genes are actually cooperative rather than egoistic.

5   So why has this imagery become so prevalent? Because it expresses deep conflicts originating in 17th-century England which are still unresolved in the western world. The central clash is between communal and separatist views of human nature. It rose out of the English Civil War, which shifted the world picture from a feudal, communal pattern towards the more individualistic, pluralistic model we officially follow today. Ideals of personal allegiance, heroic warfare and the divine right of kings began to yield to civilian visions based on democracy, technology and commerce.

6   That individualistic, post civil-war world view has always been seen as scientific. This was largely because Newtonian physics viewed matter atomistically, as composed of hard, billiard-ball-like particles bouncing off each other in complex patterns—patterns which, under God, shaped that huge clock, the classical universe. Billiards, fashionable at the time, may have helped shape this view, while the vision of a vast, regular, unchanging cosmic machine was certainly reassuring.

7   The reality, however, was that society was changing unpredictably and would need other, very different kinds of metaphors and images— ones better able to reveal shifts and clashes of interest. To fill this need, philosopher Jean-Jacques Rousseau devised a kind of social atomism, along with the colourful individualistic metaphors it inspired and still inspires. Through this lens, people no longer appeared as parts of a machine: they were still atoms, but distinct, active, independent units.

8   But the philosopher Thomas Hobbes's claim that the natural state of humans was "a war of all against all" (put forward in a bid to stop people supporting misguided governments) accidentally launched a wider revolt against the notion of citizenship. The slogan made it possible to argue later that there is no such thing as society, that we owe one another nothing. This thought also inspired campaigns for admirable things

like easier divorce and universal suffrage and it is still strong today, even though physicists themselves no longer see their particles as radically disconnected.

9   In the 18th century, economists eagerly applied individualism to commerce, arguing that free competition always serves the general good. Its champions could thus believe they were being scientific while still acting as good citizens. And its emphasis on conflict reassured them they were still heroes, that bourgeois life had not corrupted their machismo. So atomistic thinking, originally drawn from physics, acquired a social meaning in economics and was then returned to science as ideas of competition began to dominate 19th-century biology. The resulting jumble of atomistic ontology, laissez-faire economics and warlike noises came together fully in the theories of 19th-century "social Darwinists" like Herbert Spencer.

10   Charles Darwin actually hated much of it, flatly rejecting the crude, direct application of natural selection to social policies. In *The Descent of Man* he insisted that humans are a deeply social species whose values cannot be derived from selfish calculation. Yet, as a man of his age, he still shared Spencer's obsessive belief in the creative force of competition. He ruled that natural selection was indeed the main cause of evolutionary changes, and—apart from sexual selection—he could not suggest any other possible source.

11   He was sure, however, that natural selection could not be their sole cause. He must be right: natural selection is only a filter and filters cannot be the sole cause of the coffee that comes from them. "Evolutionary coffee"—genuine new developments—could not emerge unless the range of selectables has somehow been shaped to make it possible. If that range were indefinite only randomness could follow, however much time elapsed.

12   Biologist D'Arcy Thompson pointed this out in *On Growth And Form* in 1917, noting the striking natural tendencies which contribute to evolution—the subtle, natural patterns such as Fibonacci spirals that shape all manner of organic forms, and the logic underlying patterns such as the arrangement of a creature's limbs. Thompson's work was little noted in the 20th-century's concentration on natural selection, but more recently biologists such as Brian Goodwin, Steven Rose and Simon Conway Morris have developed his work, showing how natural selection is supplemented by a kind of self-organisation within each species, which has its own logic.

13   Now the old metaphors of evolution need to give way to new ones founded on integrative thinking—reasoning based on systems thinking. This way, the work of evolution can be seen as intelligible and constructive, not as a gamble driven randomly by the forces of competition. And if non-competitive imagery is needed, systems biologist Denis Noble has a good go at it in *The Music of Life*, where he points out how natural development, not being a car, needs no single "driver" to direct it. Symphonies, he remarks, are not caused only by a single dominant instrument nor, indeed, solely by their composer. And developing organisms do not even need a composer: they grow, as wholes, out of vast and ancient systems which are themselves parts of nature.

14   Recognising the cultural origins of evolution's metaphors and that we are slowly, painfully, creating new ones takes the drama out of things, but it does mean we will learn how to think about metaphors and their philosophical underpinning. We will discover we need them to serve us as thinking tools, not to turn us into slaves of our own conceits.

Comprehension

1. Summarize paragraph 2 in a sentence.
2. Why does the author use the domain of 30 years in describing the use of the selfish metaphor?
3. Why does the English Civil War represent a turning point in the world view of the English, according to the author?
4. Of what use does Herbert Spencer make of the selfish metaphor? What is "social Darwinism"?

Structure and Organization

1. Identify two organizational methods (rhetorical patterns) used in paragraphs 5–9.

Critical Thinking

1. In addition to the selfish metaphor, identify one other metaphor used by the author and analyze its purpose and effectiveness.
2. Using a reliable source:
   a. Summarize in two or three sentences the contribution of one of the following figures in the history of ideas: Jean-Jacques Rousseau; Thomas Hobbes
   b. Explain in one or two sentences the importance of Rousseau and Hobbes to Midgley's essay.

Chris Mooney, "We Can't Handle the Truth: The Science of Why People Don't Believe Science"

"We Can't Handle the Truth" is a journalistic-style essay that reviews current scientific findings and presents them to the general reader. Such essays are written semi-formally or informally and use techniques to maintain the reader's interest. For example, this essay begins with a direct quotation that leads into an illustrative narrative. Language level is geared towards a non-specialist, and rephrasing is used to help with comprehension. Experimental results are interpreted, rather than simply presented unaided, to the reader. In addition, such an essay may not include a clear thesis at the end of its introduction; it may instead announce the topic and continue to rely on interest-based strategies to convey information in the body paragraphs.

> ▶ **Preparing to Read**
>
> 1.   "We Can't Handle the Truth" appeared in the magazine *Mother Jones.* Access the "About Us" section of the *Mother Jones* website; scan recent articles in order to determine the kinds of articles published as well as the magazine's readership.
>
> 2.   This essay focuses on the reluctance of most people to change their deeply held views in spite of factual evidence to the contrary. Explore this seeming paradox in light of your own experience: Do any of your friends or family hold opinions that are difficult to change in spite of reason or scientific evidence? What about your own opinions? How could your strongest opinions on a subject be changed?

We Can't Handle the Truth: The Science of Why People Don't Believe Science

Chris Mooney

Mother Jones, May–June 2011
(4312 words)

1   "A man with a conviction is a hard man to change. Tell him you disagree and he turns away. Show him facts or figures and he questions your sources. Appeal to logic and he fails to see your point." So wrote the celebrated Stanford University psychologist Leon Festinger in a passage that might have been referring to climate change denial—the persistent rejection, on the part of so many Americans today, of what we know about global warming and its human causes. But it was too early for that—this was the 1950s—and Festinger was actually describing a famous case study in psychology.

2   Festinger and several of his colleagues had infiltrated the Seekers, a small Chicago-area cult whose members thought they were communicating with aliens—including one, "Sananda," who they believed was the astral incarnation of Jesus Christ. The group was led by Dorothy Martin, a Dianetics devotee who transcribed the interstellar messages through automatic writing.

3   Through her, the aliens had given the precise date of an Earth-rending cataclysm: December 21, 1954. Some of Martin's followers quit their jobs and sold their property, expecting to be rescued by a flying saucer when the continent split asunder and a new sea swallowed much of the United States. The disciples even went so far as to remove brassieres and rip zippers out of their trousers—the metal, they believed, would pose a danger on the spacecraft.

4   Festinger and his team were with the cult when the prophecy failed. First, the "boys upstairs" (as the aliens were sometimes called) did not show up and rescue the Seekers. Then December 21 arrived without incident. It was the moment Festinger had been waiting for: How would people so emotionally invested in a belief system react, now that it had been soundly refuted?

5   At first, the group struggled for an explanation. But then rationalization set in. A new message arrived, announcing that they'd all been spared at the last minute. Festinger summarized the extraterrestrials' new pronouncement: "The

little group, sitting all night long, had spread so much light that God had saved the world from destruction." Their willingness to believe in the prophecy had saved Earth from the prophecy!

6   From that day forward, the Seekers, previously shy of the press and indifferent toward evangelizing, began to proselytize. "Their sense of urgency was enormous," wrote Festinger. The devastation of all they had believed had made them even more certain of their beliefs.

7   In the annals of denial, it doesn't get much more extreme than the Seekers. They lost their jobs, the press mocked them, and there were efforts to keep them away from impressionable young minds. But while Martin's space cult might lie on the far end of the spectrum of human self-delusion, there's plenty to go around. And since Festinger's day, an array of new discoveries in psychology and neuroscience has further demonstrated how our preexisting beliefs, far more than any new facts, can skew our thoughts and even color what we consider our most dispassionate and logical conclusions. This tendency toward so-called "motivated reasoning" helps explain why we find groups so polarized over matters where the evidence is so unequivocal: climate change, vaccines, "death panels," the birthplace and religion of the president, and much else. It would seem that expecting people to be convinced by the facts flies in the face of, you know, the facts.

8   The theory of motivated reasoning builds on a key insight of modern neuroscience: Reasoning is actually suffused with emotion (or what researchers often call "affect"). Not only are the two inseparable, but our positive or negative feelings about people, things, and ideas arise much more rapidly than our conscious thoughts, in a matter of milliseconds—fast enough to detect with an EEG device, but long before we're aware of it. That shouldn't be surprising: Evolution

required us to react very quickly to stimuli in our environment. It's a "basic human survival skill," explains political scientist Arthur Lupia of the University of Michigan. We push threatening information away; we pull friendly information close. We apply fight-or-flight reflexes not only to predators, but to data itself.

9   We're not driven only by emotions, of course—we also reason, deliberate. But reasoning comes later, works slower—and even then, it doesn't take place in an emotional vacuum. Rather, our quick-fire emotions can set us on a course of thinking that's highly biased, especially on topics we care a great deal about.

10   Consider a person who has heard about a scientific discovery that deeply challenges her belief in divine creation—a new hominid, say, that confirms our evolutionary origins. What happens next, explains political scientist Charles Taber of Stony Brook University, is a subconscious negative response to the new information—and that response, in turn, guides the type of memories and associations formed in the conscious mind. "They retrieve thoughts that are consistent with their previous beliefs," says Taber, "and that will lead them to build an argument and challenge what they're hearing."

11   In other words, when we think we're reasoning, we may instead be rationalizing. Or to use an analogy offered by University of Virginia psychologist Jonathan Haidt: We may think we're being scientists, but we're actually being lawyers. Our "reasoning" is a means to a predetermined end—winning our "case"—and is shot through with biases. They include "confirmation bias," in which we give greater heed to evidence and arguments that bolster our beliefs, and "disconfirmation bias," in which we expend disproportionate energy trying to debunk or refute views and arguments that we find uncongenial.

12   That's a lot of jargon, but we all understand these mechanisms when it comes to interpersonal relationships. If I don't want to believe that my spouse is being unfaithful, or that my child is a bully, I can go to great lengths to explain away behavior that seems obvious to everybody else—everybody who isn't too emotionally invested to accept it, anyway. That's not to suggest that we aren't also motivated to perceive the world accurately—we are. Or that we never change our minds—we do. It's just that we have other important goals besides accuracy—including identity affirmation and protecting one's sense of self—and often those make us highly resistant to changing our beliefs when the facts say we should.

13   Modern science originated from an attempt to weed out such subjective lapses—what that great 17th century theorist of the scientific method, Francis Bacon, dubbed the "idols of the mind." Even if individual researchers are prone to falling in love with their own theories, the broader processes of peer review and institutionalized skepticism are designed to ensure that, eventually, the best ideas prevail.

14   Our individual responses to the conclusions that science reaches, however, are quite another matter. Ironically, in part because researchers employ so much nuance and strive to disclose all remaining sources of uncertainty, scientific evidence is highly susceptible to selective reading and misinterpretation. Giving ideologues or partisans scientific data that's relevant to their beliefs is like unleashing them in the motivated-reasoning equivalent of a candy store.

15   Sure enough, a large number of psychological studies have shown that people respond to scientific or technical evidence in ways that justify their preexisting beliefs. In a classic 1979 experiment, pro- and anti-death penalty advocates were exposed to descriptions of two fake scientific studies: one supporting and one undermining the notion that capital punishment deters violent crime and, in particular, murder. They were also shown detailed methodological critiques of the fake studies—and in a scientific sense, neither study was stronger than the other. Yet in each case, advocates more heavily criticized the study whose conclusions disagreed with their own, while describing the study that was more ideologically congenial as more "convincing."

16   Since then, similar results have been found for how people respond to "evidence" about affirmative action, gun control, the accuracy of gay stereotypes, and much else. Even when study subjects are explicitly instructed to be unbiased and even-handed about the evidence, they often fail.

17   And it's not just that people twist or selectively read scientific evidence to support their preexisting views. According to research by Yale Law School professor Dan Kahan and his colleagues, people's deep-seated views about morality, and about the way society should be ordered, strongly predict whom they consider to be a legitimate scientific expert in the first place—and thus where they consider "scientific consensus" to lie on contested issues.

18   In Kahan's research, individuals are classified, based on their cultural values, as either "individualists" or "communitarians," and as either "hierarchical" or "egalitarian" in outlook. (Somewhat oversimplifying, you can think of hierarchical individualists as akin to conservative Republicans, and egalitarian communitarians as liberal Democrats.) In one study, subjects in the different groups were asked to help a close friend determine the risks associated with climate change, sequestering nuclear waste, or concealed carry laws: "The friend tells you that he or she is planning to read a book

about the issue but would like to get your opinion on whether the author seems like a knowledgeable and trustworthy expert." A subject was then presented with the resumé of a fake expert "depicted as a member of the National Academy of Sciences who had earned a Ph.D. in a pertinent field from one elite university and who was now on the faculty of another." The subject was then shown a book excerpt by that "expert," in which the risk of the issue at hand was portrayed as high or low, well-founded or speculative. The results were stark: When the scientist's position stated that global warming is real and human-caused, for instance, only 23 per cent of hierarchical individualists agreed the person was a "trustworthy and knowledgeable expert." Yet 88 per cent of egalitarian communitarians accepted the same scientist's expertise. Similar divides were observed on whether nuclear waste can be safely stored underground and whether letting people carry guns deters crime. (The alliances did not always hold. In another study, hierarchs and communitarians were in favor of laws that would compel the mentally ill to accept treatment, whereas individualists and egalitarians were opposed.)

19   In other words, people rejected the validity of a scientific source because its conclusion contradicted their deeply held views—and thus the relative risks inherent in each scenario. A hierarchal individualist finds it difficult to believe that the things he prizes (commerce, industry, a man's freedom to possess a gun to defend his family) could lead to outcomes deleterious to society, whereas egalitarian communitarians tend to think that the free market causes harm, that patriarchal families mess up kids, and that people can't handle their guns. The study subjects weren't "anti-science"—not in their own minds, anyway. It's just that "science" was whatever they wanted it to be. "We've come to

a misadventure, a bad situation where diverse citizens, who rely on diverse systems of cultural certification, are in conflict," says Kahan.

20   And that undercuts the standard notion that the way to persuade people is via evidence and argument. In fact, head-on attempts to persuade can sometimes trigger a backfire effect, where people not only fail to change their minds when confronted with the facts—they may hold their wrong views more tenaciously than ever.

21   Take, for instance, the question of whether Saddam Hussein possessed hidden weapons of mass destruction just before the US invasion of Iraq in 2003. When political scientists Brendan Nyhan and Jason Reifler showed subjects fake newspaper articles in which this was first suggested (in a 2004 quote from President Bush) and then refuted (with the findings of the Bush-commissioned Iraq Survey Group report, which found no evidence of active WMD programs in pre-invasion Iraq), they found that conservatives were more likely than before to believe the claim. (The researchers also tested how liberals responded when shown that Bush did not actually "ban" embryonic stem-cell research. Liberals weren't particularly amenable to persuasion, either, but no backfire effect was observed.)

22   Another study gives some inkling of what may be going through people's minds when they resist persuasion. Northwestern University sociologist Monica Prasad and her colleagues wanted to test whether they could dislodge the notion that Saddam Hussein and al-Qaeda were secretly collaborating among those most likely to believe it—Republican partisans from highly GOP-friendly counties. So the researchers set up a study in which they discussed the topic with some of these Republicans in person. They would cite the findings of the 9/11 Commission, as well as a statement in which George W. Bush himself denied his administration had "said the

9/11 attacks were orchestrated between Saddam and al-Qaeda."

23 As it turned out, not even Bush's own words could change the minds of these Bush voters—just 1 of the 49 partisans who originally believed the Iraq-al-Qaeda claim changed his or her mind. Far more common was resisting the correction in a variety of ways, either by coming up with counterarguments or by simply being unmovable:

> 24 Interviewer: [T]he September 11 Commission found no link between Saddam and 9/11, and this is what President Bush said. Do you have any comments on either of those?
>
> 25 Respondent: Well, I bet they say that the Commission didn't have any proof of it but I guess we still can have our opinions and feel that way even though they say that.

26 The same types of responses are already being documented on divisive topics facing the current administration. Take the "Ground Zero mosque." Using information from the political myth-busting site FactCheck.org, a team at Ohio State presented subjects with a detailed rebuttal to the claim that "Feisal Abdul Rauf, the Imam backing the proposed Islamic cultural center and mosque, is a terrorist-sympathizer." Yet among those who were aware of the rumor and believed it, fewer than a third changed their minds.

27 A key question—and one that's difficult to answer—is how "irrational" all this is. On the one hand, it doesn't make sense to discard an entire belief system, built up over a lifetime, because of some new snippet of information. "It is quite possible to say, 'I reached this pro-capital-punishment decision based on real information that I arrived at over my life,'" explains Stanford social psychologist Jon Krosnick. Indeed, there's a sense in which science denial could be considered keenly "rational." In certain conservative

communities, explains Yale's Kahan, "People who say, 'I think there's something to climate change,' that's going to mark them out as a certain kind of person, and their life is going to go less well."

28 This may help explain a curious pattern Nyhan and his colleagues found when they tried to test the fallacy that President Obama is a Muslim. When a nonwhite researcher was administering their study, research subjects were amenable to changing their minds about the president's religion and updating incorrect views. But when only white researchers were present, GOP survey subjects in particular were more likely to believe the Obama Muslim myth than before. The subjects were using "social desirabilily" to tailor their beliefs (or stated beliefs, anyway) to whoever was listening.

29 Which leads us to the media. When people grow polarized over a body of evidence, or a resolvable matter of fact, the cause may be some form of biased reasoning, but they could also be receiving skewed information to begin with—or a complicated combination of both. In the Ground Zero mosque case, for instance, a follow-up study showed that survey respondents who watched Fox News were more likely to believe the Rauf rumor and three related ones—and they believed them more strongly than non-Fox watchers.

30 Okay, so people gravitate toward information that confirms what they believe, and they select sources that deliver it. Same as it ever was, right? Maybe, but the problem is arguably growing more acute, given the way we now consume information through the Facebook links of friends, or tweets that lack nuance or context, or "narrowcast" and often highly ideological media that have relatively small, like-minded audiences. Those basic human survival skills of ours, says Michigan's Arthur Lupia, are "not well-adapted to our information age."

31 If you wanted to show how and why fact is ditched in favor of motivated reasoning, you could find no better test case than climate change. After all, it's an issue where you have highly technical information on one hand and very strong beliefs on the other. And sure enough, one key predictor of whether you accept the science of global warming is whether you're a Republican or a Democrat. The two groups have been growing more divided in their views about the topic, even as the science becomes more unequivocal.

32 So perhaps it should come as no surprise that more education doesn't budge Republican views. On the contrary: In a 2008 Pew survey, for instance, only 19 per cent of college-educated Republicans agreed that the planet is warming due to human actions, versus 31 per cent of non-college educated Republicans. In other words, a higher education correlated with an increased likelihood of denying the science on the issue. Meanwhile, among Democrats and independents, more education correlated with greater acceptance of the science.

33 Other studies have shown a similar effect: Republicans who think they understand the global warming issue best are least concerned about it; and among Republicans and those with higher levels of distrust of science in general, learning more about the issue doesn't increase one's concern about it. What's going on here? Well, according to Charles Taber and Milton Lodge of Stony Brook, one insidious aspect of motivated reasoning is that political sophisticates are prone to be more biased than those who know less about the issues. "People who have a dislike of some policy—for example, abortion—if they're unsophisticated they can just reject it out of hand," says Lodge. "But if they're sophisticated, they can go one step further and start coming up with counterarguments." These individuals are just as emotionally driven and biased as the rest of us, but they're able to generate more and better reasons to explain why they're right—and so their minds become harder to change.

34 That may be why the selectively quoted emails of Climategate were so quickly and easily seized upon by partisans as evidence of scandal. Cherry-picking is precisely the sort of behavior you would expect motivated reasoners to engage in to bolster their views—and whatever you may think about Climategate, the emails were a rich trove of new information upon which to impose one's ideology.

35 Climategate had a substantial impact on public opinion, according to Anthony Leiserowitz, director of the Yale Project on Climate Change Communication. It contributed to an overall drop in public concern about climate change and a significant loss of trust in scientists. But—as we should expect by now—these declines were concentrated among particular groups of Americans: Republicans, conservatives, and those with "individualistic" values. Liberals and those with "egalitarian" values didn't lose much trust in climate science or scientists at all. "In some ways, Climategate was like a Rorschach test," Leiserowitz says, "with different groups interpreting ambiguous facts in very different ways."

36 So is there a case study of science denial that largely occupies the political left? Yes: the claim that childhood vaccines are causing an epidemic of autism. Its most famous proponents are an environmentalist (Robert F. Kennedy Jr.) and numerous Hollywood celebrities (most notably Jenny McCarthy and Jim Carrey). *The Huffington Post* gives a very large megaphone to denialists. And Seth Mnookin, author of the new book *The Panic Virus*, notes that if you want to find vaccine deniers, all you need to do is go hang out at Whole Foods.

37 Vaccine denial has all the hallmarks of a belief system that's not amenable to refutation. Over the

past decade, the assertion that childhood vaccines are driving autism rates has been undermined by multiple epidemiological studies—as well as the simple fact that autism rates continue to rise, even though the alleged offending agent in vaccines (a mercury-based preservative called thimerosal) has long since been removed.

38   Yet the true believers persist—critiquing each new study that challenges their views, and even rallying to the defense of vaccine autism researcher Andrew Wakefield, after his 1998 *Lancet* paper—which originated the current vaccine scare—was retracted and he subsequently lost his license to practice medicine. But then, why should we be surprised? Vaccine deniers created their own partisan media, such as the website Age of Autism, that instantly blast out critiques and counterarguments whenever any new development casts further doubt on anti-vaccine views.

39   It all raises the question: Do left and right differ in any meaningful way when it comes to biases in processing information, or are we all equally susceptible?

40   There are some clear differences. Science denial today is considerably more prominent on the political right—once you survey climate and related environmental issues, anti-evolutionism, attacks on reproductive health science by the Christian right, and stem-cell and biomedical matters. More tellingly, anti-vaccine positions are virtually nonexistent among Democratic office-holders today—whereas anti-climate science views are becoming monolithic among Republican elected officials.

41   Some researchers have suggested that there are psychological differences between the left and the right that might impact responses to new information—that conservatives are more rigid and authoritarian, and liberals more tolerant of ambiguity. Psychologist John Jost of New York University has further argued that conservatives are "system justifiers": They engage in motivated reasoning to defend the status quo.

42   This is a contested area, however, because as soon as one tries to psychoanalyze inherent political differences, a battery of counterarguments emerges: What about dogmatic and militant communists? What about how the parties have differed through history? After all, the most canonical case of ideologically driven science denial is probably the rejection of genetics in the Soviet Union, where researchers disagreeing with the anti-Mendelian scientist (and Stalin stooge) Trofim Lysenko were executed, and genetics itself was denounced as a "bourgeois" science and officially banned.

43   The upshot: All we can currently bank on is the fact that we all have blinders in some situations. The question then becomes: What can be done to counteract human nature itself?.

44   Given the power of our prior beliefs to skew how we respond to new information, one thing is becoming clear: If you want someone to accept new evidence, make sure to present it to them in a context that doesn't trigger a defensive, emotional reaction.

45   This theory is gaining traction in part because of Kahan's work at Yale. In one study, he and his colleagues packaged the basic science of climate change into fake newspaper articles bearing two very different headlines—"Scientific Panel Recommends Anti-Pollution Solution to Global Warming" and "Scientific Panel Recommends Nuclear Solution to Global Warming"—and then tested how citizens with different values responded. Sure enough, the latter framing made hierarchical individualists much more open to accepting the fact that humans are causing global warming. Kahan infers that the effect occurred because the science had been written into an alternative narrative that appealed to their pro-industry worldview.

46 You can follow the logic to its conclusion: Conservatives are more likely to embrace climate science if it comes to them via a business or religious leader, who can set the issue in the context of different values than those from which environmentalists or scientists often argue. Doing so is, effectively, to signal a détente in what Kahan has called a "culture war of fact." In other words, paradoxically, you don't lead with the facts in order to convince. You lead with the values—so as to give the facts a fighting chance.

Comprehension

1. Using context, define the following in your own words: *motivated reasoning* (par. 7); *disconfirmation bias* (par. 11); *social desirability* (par. 28).

Structure, Organization, and Style

1. The author does not use section headings but, nonetheless, provides a clear structure for readers to follow. Come up with suitable content headings for the essay beginning with paragraph 8. Each heading should be a phrase (two or more words) that summarizes the content of that section. Use at least four headings.

2. Discuss strategies the author uses to help general readers understand his essay, referring to specific passages in the text (examples for comprehension include sentence and paragraph length and structure, use of transitions and repetition, word choice, organizational patterns, and the like).

3. Rewrite paragraph 30, using formal (academic) language and sentence structure. Include all the ideas from the original paragraph.

Critical Thinking/Research

1. Using reliable sources, summarize one of the following references in the essay, ensuring you explain the nature of the controversy involved: (a) "Climategate," paragraphs 31–35; (b) "Vaccine denial," paragraphs 36–38.

2. Do you believe the author fairly critiques both sides of the political spectrum in his essay? Analyze the author's fairness by referring to specific passages.

3. Although journalists often refer to academic studies, they do not provide bibliographical details about them, but may, instead, briefly summarize their findings and/or quote the study's author directly on their significance. Identify one such researcher in "We Can't Handle the Truth," and using a library database or online search engine, access one of the researcher's articles. (Hint: since the details are not given in Mooney's essay, a search by the researcher's name may yield useful results.)
   a. Summarize the article's findings.
   b. Briefly discuss its relevance to "We Can't Handle the Truth."

4. Drawing on paragraphs 44–46, choose a topic that has elicited strong opinions in the past. Then, come up with a statement or headline (par. 45) that frames the controversial issue so that it appeals to values of the person/group you are trying to convince. (This can be done collaboratively; group statements can then be shared with the class.)

Ken MacQueen and Martin Patriquin, "Are We Ready to Subsidize Heroin?"

"Are We Ready to Subsidize Heroin?" is a journalistic essay that represents two sides of a controversial issue, inspired, as many such essays are, by a significant news event: MacQueen and Patriquin wrote their essay after the Supreme Court of Canada ruled that Insite, the supervised injection clinic in Vancouver, could not be subject to drug possession laws. The authors interviewed both supporters and opponents of Insite. They synthesized their information to produce an expository essay that informs readers about the complexity of the issues involved.

Preparing to Read

Are you familiar with the controversy surrounding Insite since its establishment in 2003? Generally, what is your opinion about needle-exchange programs and safe-injection sites? What place should they have in today's society? You could freewrite on this topic or discuss it in groups.

Are We Ready to Subsidize Heroin?

Ken MacQueen and Martin Patriquin

Maclean's, 7 October 2011
(3050 words)

1   For the last 22 years, Cactus Montréal has doled out needles, crack pipes and other necessities of drug use to the city's addicts. North America's first needle exchange program had humble beginnings; it once provided its services from a cockroach-infested storefront on St-Dominique St., facing a particularly seedy section of Montreal's red-light district. Today, Cactus's headquarters are a monument to respectability. Its drop-in centre and needle exchange occupy a bright, glassed-in corner of an avant-garde building in downtown Montreal, across the street from a university pavilion. "A lively and warm place," as its website advertises, "where people of all stripes come to

get injection equipment, condoms, crack pipes, counselling and even to draw a picture or play an instrument."

2   Thanks to last week's landmark Supreme Court of Canada ruling directing the federal government to stop obstructing Vancouver's Insite supervised injection clinic, Cactus will soon be renovating once again. Cactus administrators, and those across the country who advocate harm reduction, a policy of mitigating the damage of drug use without requiring abstinence, interpret the ruling as essentially green-lighting supervised injection sites, albeit under strict conditions. By next spring, Cactus administrators hope to have an area where drug users will be able to inject drugs under the supervision of a medical professional. Many of Montreal's other needle exchange sites, as well as those in Quebec City, will likely follow suit in the coming year, if they meet the criteria the court established to win a federal exemption from drug possession laws.

3   You might say it's infectious. Supervised injection sites have the backing of several of the country's biggest health authorities, including those in Montreal and Vancouver. There are preliminary plans for another site in Vancouver, and possibly one in Victoria. Some advocates look ahead to a time when addicts might receive prescription heroin rather than street drugs. While many governments are reluctant to endorse giving addicts a place to shoot up, let alone the drugs to do so, every province has some sort of needle exchange program. Even Calgary gave out safer crack pipe kits for three years until health officials nixed the program over the summer.

4   For proponents, providing a clean, medically supervised place to imbibe drugs is simply a logical extension of a service already provided across the country. "The Supreme Court decision let us stop being hypocrites," Cactus community coordinator Jean-François Mary told Maclean's. "For 22 years, we gave people clean tools, then sent them out into the street. We were doing half the work. Now they'll be able to shoot up in complete safety."

5   For critics, this is tantamount to legitimizing an illegal activity and worse: providing government funding to support a destructive habit. "I'm disappointed," said Prime Minister Stephen Harper, who has made a war on crime and illegal drugs a central policy of his government. "The preference of this government in dealing with drug crime is obviously to prosecute those who sell drugs and create drug addiction in our population and in our youth," he told reporters in Quebec City after the ruling was announced. While he said the government will comply with the court's direction, he made clear he favours drug prevention and treatment. That is also the stance of REAL Women of Canada, a socially conservative family values organization that intervened in the Supreme Court hearing in opposition to Insite. "I think the drug traffickers in Vancouver are going to be the happiest people in Canada," says Gwen Landolt, both vice-president of REAL Women and president of the abstinence-based Drug Prevention Network of Canada. "The unhappiest will be the police because we know the crime rate will increase." (The Vancouver Police Department has supported Insite throughout much of its existence.)

6   Apart from the obvious rebuke of the Conservative government, which fought Insite over three years and in as many courts, the decision would seem to pave the way for a wholesale expansion of safe injection sites across the country. Buoyed with the Supreme Court decision (and armed with a raft of scientific evidence), proponents of Insite and related harm reduction

measures are poised to take the debate several steps further, and a quantum leap beyond the comfort zone of the current federal government, and perhaps even some health care advocates. They see supervised sites providing not only clean rigging and supervision, but the very drugs that go into users' veins.

7   "People need to understand that Insite is not the end of anything; it's the beginning of something," says Dr. Julio Montaner, director of the B.C. Centre for Excellence in HIV/AIDS, and an outspoken advocate of Insite because of its success in limiting the spread of the virus and other infections. "We demonstrated the benefits. The question now is how do we bring Insite to the people, and make it work for all British Columbians, for all Canadians?" He sees allowing public health nurses, perhaps even walk-in clinics or pharmacies in small or rural areas, to supervise drug consumption, in much the manner that HIV medication or methadone is delivered in B.C. now. He wants his badly addicted patients to be allowed to take drugs when they are hospitalized for infections or other ailments. Too often, they discharge themselves with disastrous results at the first sign of drug withdrawal, he says. And he and Insite staff favour providing addicts with pharmaceutical-grade drugs, perhaps paid for by provincial medical health plans. As it stands now, Insite clients feed the illegal drug trade and inject street drugs of often dangerous quality, says Montaner. Studies giving pharmaceutical grade heroin to addicts in Switzerland, Germany, Spain and the Netherlands proved it was more effective than the traditional heroin replacement drug methadone in stabilizing addicts, keeping them in treatment and away from crime.

8   The argument for providing medical heroin to users was further bolstered by a landmark Canadian study conducted in Vancouver and Montreal between 2005 and 2008. During that time, researchers with the North American Opiate Medication Initiative (NAOMI) oversaw the administration of nearly 90,000 injections of diacetylmorphine, the active ingredient in heroin, to 115 regular heroin users. The result: these users, chosen for their resistance to methadone, were 62 per cent more likely to remain in treatment. They also used drastically less heroin and committed fewer crimes, reported the New England Journal of Medicine in August 2009.

9   As successful as it was, NAOMI exceeded the limits of harm reduction in the eyes of at least two governments. It was funded and conducted in Canada largely because of what its authors called "financial and logistical barriers in the U.S." Researchers were forced to cut the scope of NAOMI's second phase after the Quebec government abruptly yanked its share of the funding in 2009. As a result, "The Study to Assess Longer-term Opioid Medication Effectiveness" (SALOME) is British Columbia's alone, and even there it is stalled. SALOME was slated to begin before the 2010 Olympics; to date, not one injection or oral dose of the morphine-derived drug Dilaudid has been administered.

10   The delay is at least partially due to public uneasiness at any large harm reduction initiative, which feeds the worst nightmares of conservative commentators and groups like REAL Women. So does the prospect that appointed judges can derail the policies of a democratically elected majority government. "You've got nine appointed people and not on the basis of law but the basis of ideology coming out with a decision that's going to affect all of Canada," says Landolt, a lawyer. "They've removed the discretion from the [health] minister. It's appalling, I mean, who are they to rewrite the law?"

11   Cognizant of those sorts of objections, most public health services are prone to move cautiously on establishing supervised injection sites. Many feel these sites are to 2011 as needle exchange programs were to the 1990s: beneficial, even crucial, institutions that should nevertheless be carefully sold to the public through persuasion and cold, hard science.

12   From the beginning of the trial program at Insite, and a smaller pioneering supervised injection site at the Dr. Peter Centre in Vancouver's west end for those with HIV/AIDS, the facilities have hosted a steady stream of political and health care delegations. "Just yesterday it was the city of Victoria," Maxine Davis, executive director of the Dr. Peter AIDS Foundation, told *Maclean's*. "They've been here a number of times." Other recent visitors include delegations from Kelowna and Prince George, B.C., Saskatoon, Toronto and Halifax, as well as from Russia, Georgia, Ukraine and Asia. At Insite it's a similar story. "I think almost every major urban centre in this country has at some point sent a delegation of various health policy experts, or community health care folks, or police, or RCMP officers," says Liz Evans, executive director of the Portland Hotel Community Services Society, which operates Insite.

13   With that level of interest, other communities and health authorities are likely to follow Vancouver's lead, now that the legalities have been sorted out. Proponents must prove a substantial need, and the potential to save lives, before the federal health minister would be compelled to issue an exemption from drug possession laws under the criteria dictated by the Supreme Court ruling. The judges also took into account Insite's backing by its neighbourhood, by police and by public health and political leadership.

14   Where Tony Clement, the Conservative health minister at the time, ran afoul of the Constitution, the judges said, was in arbitrarily refusing an exception for a program that was found to save lives. The risk of death or disease by withholding health services was deemed grossly disproportionate when compared against the benefit of an absolute ban on drug possession at the site. "In accordance with the Charter, the [Health] Minister must consider whether denying an exemption would cause deprivation of life and security of the person that are not in accordance with the principles of fundamental justice," said the unanimous ruling, written by Chief Justice Beverley McLachlin, who spent much of her career as a lawyer and judge in Vancouver. "Where, as here, a supervised injection site will decrease the risk of death and disease, and there is little or no evidence that it will have a negative impact on public safety, the Minister should generally grant an exemption."

15   Still, you won't see consumption rooms "spring up on every street corner," says Dr. Patricia Daly, chief medical health officer for Vancouver Coastal Health, which finances Insite's $3-million annual budget. "I think people will have to do their due diligence as we did here."

16   Even then it will be a tough political sell. Public health officials generally support evidenced-based harm reduction strategies, but without political, and therefore financial backing, any move toward supervised consumption is likely to go nowhere fast. In Ontario, days from a provincial election when the ruling was released, there was little political appetite for tossing a grenade like supervised injection sites into the debate. Liberal Premier Dalton McGuinty said there are no plans for such sites in Ontario. Toronto Mayor Rob Ford told reporters this spring he has long been opposed to supervised

injection sites. A study, approved in 2005, into whether Toronto and Ottawa would benefit from supervised drug consumption, may be released this fall, some 18 months after researchers first promised the results.

17 In Ottawa, Mayor Jim Watson said in a statement he does not back supervised injection sites. Watson, a former provincial Liberal minister of health promotion, said scarce public health resources should be spent on treatment centres.

18 Even in B.C., which has lived with the debate for more than a decade, municipal leaders have had a mixed reaction. Surrey Mayor Dianne Watts, who has led the fight to reclaim neighbourhoods plagued by drugs and crime, was lukewarm to the idea of a walk-in injection site, though the city has needle exchanges and detox facilities. "We don't have thousands of people in a Downtown Eastside," she told the *Vancouver Sun.* George Peary, mayor of Abbotsford, which has struggled to contain a drug-fuelled gang problem, said he considers the ruling a vindication for Insite. But he added that few cities share the scale of Vancouver's "horrific" problem.

19 The B.C. government, however, has been unwavering in its support for Insite and the Dr. Peter Centre. Health Minister Michael de Jong said the court rendered a "wise and humane ruling." Still, he said it's up to provincial health authorities to determine where or how similar programs might be expanded.

20 Victoria Mayor Dean Fortin, among those who had toured both Vancouver injection sites, says the court ruling removes a significant "impediment" to establishing a facility in the provincial capital. Fortin said a holistic program like the Dr. Peter Centre, which incorporates a small injection site into an array of health and social services, therapy and counselling, is one possible model. Victoria laid the groundwork with a feasibility study on drug consumption sites, and a mayor's task force, which also supported the concept. Now, "we can continue to do our work, only more stridently," Fortin said. "This is something we can move forward on as a community: how do you want to make this work?"

21 Mercifully, few cities have a concentration of injection drug use anywhere near the 5,000 estimated addicts in Vancouver's Downtown Eastside. Insite, which has supervised more than 1.8 million injections without a fatality since it opened in 2003, is already at capacity. It oversees an average 587 injections daily. It sits in one of the bleakest blocks in a tough neighbourhood, across from a row of long-abandoned buildings that were recently reduced to rubble, a visual improvement. Inside, the building is bright and airy. The 12 injection stalls are kept scrupulously clean, with new needles, water and antiseptic wipes laid out on a table in front of a mirror for each new client. Nurses attend to wounds, abscesses, vein and skin conditions. "You watch folks suffer and struggle so much on a day-to-day basis," says Evans, the executive director. "And they come in here and you realize this is the only square footage in the entire continent of North America that, when a person walks through that door, they're a human being and not a criminal."

22 Evans says there are plans to eventually add another such facility in the city. She also wants to expand the range of services far beyond supervised drug consumption to meet the complex needs of addicts. Lost sometimes in the rhetoric is that there are actually three floors to the Insite facility. The second story houses a small detox centre, which claims a 43 per cent completion rate among the more than 450 clients that have been admitted. The third floor offers transitional housing for those finished

detox. "This is just a tiny, tiny piece of what's needed, it really is just the beginning of a person's journey," Evans says.

23   In Quebec, where injection site proponents wholeheartedly approved of the Supreme Court decision, there is nevertheless little appetite to replicate the exact Insite model in downtown Montreal or Quebec City. Rather, a report from the province's health authority, expected later this year, will likely call for a more decentralized approach to supervised injection: small-scale injection sites scattered across the city, according to need. "Insite is located in a ghetto, and it serves a ridiculously huge number of users," says Gilles Beauregard, director of Spectre de Rue, one of eight needle exchanges in Montreal. "It is different in Montreal. We're in a neighbourhood that's gentrifying, and we need to be aware of the concerns of our neighbours." As for medical heroin, "it's very expensive," says Cactus president Louis Letellier de Saint-Just.

24   If Insite is less controversial in B.C., it helps to understand that it was born of desperation. In 1997, the Vancouver Richmond Health Board, as it was called then, declared a health emergency in Vancouver's Downtown Eastside in response to the level of overdose deaths and Third World levels of HIV, hepatitis C and other infections. More than 1200 people died in Vancouver of overdoses alone between 1990 and 2000. "We were in epidemic proportions, we were in hundreds of deaths," says Larry Campbell, the former RCMP drug squad member who was appointed chief coroner in 1996. "It was deeply disturbing when you start finding two people dead at a time, with the needles not even out of their arms," he says. Philip Owen, Vancouver's mayor at the time, was convinced that a four pillar approach to the disaster was necessary: one that incorporated prevention, treatment, enforcement, and harm reduction, including a supervised drug consumption facility. The idea so appalled members of his right-wing Non-Partisan Association that Owen was forced out. Campbell then successfully ran for mayor in 2002 on a commitment to establish Owen's safe injection site. Campbell, now a Liberal senator, saw his mayoral win as a mandate from a public desperate to end the carnage. "This is a compassionate, caring community. If you show them the proof, the evidence, they will react accordingly."

25   The day of the Supreme Court ruling, with the future of Insite hanging in the balance, volunteers held a pancake breakfast as a crowd of activists and addicts gathered in the early morning darkness to watch a live TV feed of the ruling from the court. There were tears and speeches as the ruling was celebrated. Delanie Supernault, 57, has been using Insite for six years. She said she couldn't imagine it closing, "now that we know what good it does." After a five-week detox on the second floor she weaned herself off crack cocaine, though she still injects opiates. You take your victories where you can.

26   As the 10 a.m. opening of Insite approached, the crowd of clients swelled even further. Many were jubilant. A few—a woman in a black leather coat who looked too young for the weight of her troubles, and others who looked too small for their clothes—were twitching and drug-sick and raging at the world.

27   It's a scene that would shock sensibilities in most any other city in Canada, yet in this neighbourhood it offered a strange kind of hope.

28   Inside the doorway to Insite, a First Nations man in an army surplus coat swept up the remnants of celebratory confetti before the crowd of clients surged in. "It's a good mess," he said, talking about the glitter on the floor or maybe bigger things. "A good mess."

Comprehension

1. In your own words, define (a) harm reduction policy; (b) supervised injection site.
2. a. Paraphrase paragraph 4.
   b. Summarize paragraph 5.

Structure and Organization

1. Explain the authors' use of parentheses in paragraphs 5, 6, and 8.
2. Provide brief content headings for the essay, summarizing in a phrase what each section is about (use four or five headings, not including the introduction).
3. Focusing on one section of the essay (see question 2 above), discuss the organizational strategies the authors use to make this section easy to follow.

Critical Thinking/Research

1. In paragraph 6, the authors state, "[The Supreme Court] decision would seem to pave the way for a wholesale expansion of safe injection sites across the country." Analyze the remainder of the article to determine the validity of this statement. Specifically, what points are raised that might throw doubt on the statement?
2. The need for solid evidence in support of supervised injection facilities is stressed in the article (see, e.g., pars. 11, 16, and 24). Using your library's electronic database or similar reliable resource, access two studies on Insite's success rate. Summarize their findings in one paragraph each; in a third paragraph, compare their results, noting similarities and any differences or inconsistencies.

Bruce M. Hicks, "The Undiscovered Province"

In journalistic essays, where writers do not usually cite their sources, credibility of the writer is crucial. Scan the essay to determine Hicks's credibility. Then, using a reliable website, determine the writer's credentials, such as his background, vocation, and publishing history.

Preparing to Read

1. What do you know about the Idle No More protest movement in Canada? Are you interested in, or concerned about, issues related to Aboriginal self-government and cultural autonomy?
2. Should these issues be of concern to all Canadians? You could discuss this in groups or freewrite about it using for your prompt: "Canadians should (not) be concerned about Aboriginal self-government . . ."

The Undiscovered Province

Bruce M. Hicks

This, January/February 2010
(1205 words)

1   The Royal Proclamation of 1763 included a clause prohibiting British colonists from purchasing "Lands of the Indians," so as not to commit more of the "Frauds and Abuses" that characterized colonial takeovers of Aboriginal territory. To my reading, this measure was intended to make clear to the English colonists that Aboriginal Peoples enjoyed equal status. As we know, that's not quite how it worked out.

2   In 1987, after the premiers met at Meech Lake and agreed to open the Constitution, I posed to several prominent people involved in the process that the easiest way to respect that commitment, and to lessen the offense of their putting Quebec before Aboriginals, would be to create an 11th province out of the remaining Aboriginal and territorial lands. Twenty-two years later, First Nations are still fighting to get even a modicum of self-government.

3   When Canada was patriating the Constitution in 1982, Aboriginal leaders were able to create enough domestic and international pressure on the federal and provincial governments that the first ministers committed to making the next round of constitutional change about Aboriginal issues. They even enshrined in the Constitution a requirement for first ministers to have one, and then two more meetings with Aboriginal leaders.

4   But the election of the Progressive Conservative party under Brian Mulroney in Ottawa, and the defeat of the separatist Parti Québécois in Quebec at the hands of the Liberals under Robert Bourassa, suddenly moved the now infamous "Quebec round" ahead of Aboriginal people. While the constitutional requirement of first ministers' meetings with Aboriginal leaders to amend the Constitution was met, it seems with hindsight that these meetings were simply pro forma, as Bourassa and Mulroney already had plans for the Meech Lake Constitutional Accord.

5   The accord failed, in part, due to a single Aboriginal member of the Manitoba legislature named Elijah Harper who refused to give unanimous consent so it could be adopted by the Manitoba legislature by the Mulroney government's declared deadline for ratification: June 23, 1990.

6   A year later, the Mulroney government appointed a Royal Commission on Aboriginal Peoples. Among its recommendations were a list of powers that Aboriginal nations needed to protect their language, religion, culture, and heritage.

7   The underlying concepts are similar to the powers that the Fathers of Confederation from Lower Canada had identified as necessary for the preservation of the francophone language, religion, culture, and heritage. Letting provincial governments have the powers necessary to protect language, culture, and religion was the key to Confederation and then the innovation of federalism was chosen for the new Dominion of Canada. Even though Canada was based on this idea of division of powers to allow for regional cultural autonomy, the federal and provincial governments have rejected similar devolution of powers to Aboriginal communities or provincehood for the Northern territories. The federal and provincial governments claim the population is too few and too dispersed to manage all these powers. And, of course, small provinces and Quebec do not want to start adding multiple provinces, beginning with three in the North, as their own relative influence would diminish.

8   But what about one province for all Aboriginal Peoples?

9   Aboriginal lands, including the three Northern territories, are legally held in reserve on

behalf of Aboriginal Peoples. The federal government acts as trustee over the land, and this creates a rather distasteful paternalistic dimension to Aboriginal–Non-Aboriginal relations. What if our government simply takes all this land held in reserve and returns it to Aboriginals? Make all that land the 11th province of Canada.

10   The structure of government for this new province is unimportant and frankly not the business of the people who don't live on this land. The constitutional change would be simpler than one would imagine. It would not require the unanimous consent of the provinces. According to the Constitution Act, 1982, the agreement of only seven provinces, representing the majority of the population, is needed for the federal parliament to create a new province. But it also states that this is "notwithstanding any other law or practice," and for the federal parliament to take all remaining Aboriginal land and designate it the "final" province, given constitutionally

entrenched treaty rights and federal jurisdiction over "Indians, and land reserved for Indians," it may even be possible to do part of the change without provincial consent.

11   This change does not even have to significantly alter the existing structures of Aboriginal communities—unless, of course, they decide to alter them on their own once they have obtained provincehood. In many of the current provinces there are three levels of government managing provincial powers, namely the provincial government, regional governments and municipal governments. So, for example, the Government of Nunavut could continue as a regional government within the new Aboriginal province and the Sambaa K'e Dene Band could continue to operate similar to a municipal government, with authority delegated from the Aboriginal province. As the Aboriginal province would have all of the powers that Aboriginals have identified as central to the preservation of their languages,

CP PHOTO/POOL

Nunavut Commissioner Helen Mamayaok (L) and Canadian Governor General Roméo Leblanc look on as the Nunavut flag is unveiled in a ceremony in the arctic town of Iqaluit, April 1, 1999. On that day the territory of Nunavut came into being.

religions, and cultures, it can delegate powers as needed locally or act provincially as expedient.

12   With the exception of the creation of a provincial government, this is pretty close to the position the federal government has been taking vis-à-vis territorial governments and local band councils. The big change will be that in the future, instead of Aboriginals demanding from the federal government the right to handle their own affairs, they would be dealing with their own provincial government—a government they elect and that is accountable to them.

13   For those concerned about corruption within band councils, their own provincial government would regulate these matters and being concerned about how monies transferred to the local governments are handled, it would undoubtedly do so more effectively than the federal government, and without the racism or paternalistic interference. Equalization payments to the province would replace the now direct transfer to Aboriginals and their band councils, thus eliminating the demoralizing stigma of dependency. What is more, some of the Aboriginal land held in reserve is resource-rich, providing an independent source of revenue.

14   Critics of nationalism most strongly reject the idea of a province based on ethnicity. But based on its territory and its land base, the new 11th province would not be exclusively Aboriginal. Many non-Aboriginals live on these lands and within the broader Aboriginal grouping there are First Nations, Inuit, and Métis, subdivided by hundreds of individual Aboriginal nations. This would be a civic nation like Quebec, and a province like any other, though the provincial leadership will likely be Aboriginal.

15   This largely Aboriginal province will be bigger in territory, richer in resources, and competitive in population size to the average Canadian province. It can negotiate with the more influential provinces, where many of its off-reserve citizens live or work, namely Alberta, B.C., Quebec, and Ontario. And, like the other civic nation of Quebec, its premier, by virtue of representing a cultural group that is in the minority across Canada, would have a powerful voice at the table of first ministers.

16   With provincehood would come an increase in Aboriginal members in the Senate and House of Commons. Aboriginal Peoples would finally be truly engaged in Canada's political process and this is essential for full citizenship and equality.

Comprehension

1. In one sentence, paraphrase Hicks's proposal as it is presented in paragraph 9.
2. In which paragraphs does Hicks address the views of opponents? Summarize one of these paragraphs.

Structure and Organization

1. Before discussing the practical implications of his proposal, Hicks refers to several historical/political events:
   a. What is the purpose of his timeline (pars. 1–6)?
   b. Taking one such event, analyze its importance to the essay as a whole and the writer's thesis.

Critical Thinking/Research

1. Using a reliable source, summarize the significance of two of the following:
    a. Patriation of the Constitution, 1982
    b. The Meech Lake Constitutional Accord
    c. Elijah Harper
2. What is the function of the comparisons between Quebec-related issues and Aboriginal issues? Analyze the validity of these comparisons in the essay.
3. Analyze the persuasiveness of Hicks's argument. You could consider such factors as order and effectiveness of points, kinds and organization of evidence, essay structure, specific argumentative strategies and/or fallacies.

Andrew Irvine, "Is Scientific Progress Inevitable?"

"Is Scientific Progress Inevitable?" is an essay in the book *In the Agora: The Public Face of Canadian Philosophy*, co-edited by Andrew Irvine, in which Canadian writers discuss the intersections between philosophy and current topics, such as the limits of scientific advancement. The Agora was a marketplace in ancient Athens where people discussed important topics of the day; the essays in *In the Agora* are intended for a similar purpose.

Irvine uses personal experience in his essay to help him introduce his topic; he has not, unlike Ian Brown, p. 248, or Madeline Sonik, p. 212, written a personal essay but a reflective one.

Preparing to Read

1. Using reliable sources, investigate the concept of medicine wheels. In your own words, explain what they are, why they might have been erected, and how they were once used.
2. Do you believe that the progress of science is inevitable? Why or why not?

Is Scientific Progress Inevitable?

Andrew Irvine

In the Agora: The Public Face of Canadian Philosophy, 2006
(1175 words)

1   When my daughter was nine, I took her to see an aboriginal medicine wheel in rural Saskatchewan. Built between 1500 and 4500 years ago, some 150 of these stone structures are still scattered throughout the Canadian prairies and the American Midwest. Most are found within 200 kilometres of the confluence of the Red Deer and South Saskatchewan Rivers. Many have spokes like a wagon wheel. Others have series of concentric circles. Some are in the shape of turtles or people.

2   The medicine wheel we visited rests atop the rolling Moose Mountains, a two-and-a-half-hour drive southeast of Regina. Constructed by the Plains Indians, it consists of a central stone cairn and five stone spokes laid out at various angles from the cairn. At the end of each spoke is a smaller cairn. An elliptical ring of stones, approximately sixty-two by fifty feet, surrounds the central cairn.

3   It is difficult to take children much younger than nine or ten to this wheel since they need to be able to control a horse to reach it. You also need permission from the Pheasant Rump Reserve and a guide to show you the way.

4   Once you reach the site, it's easy to be impressed. For one thing, the view is tremendous. As *everyone* knows, Saskatchewan is flat. This means that from a good rise of land there is nothing between you and the horizon. Just as on the ocean, on a clear day the only thing blocking your view is the curvature of the earth. Also, it's a rare thing in North America to come face to face with any man-made object as old as England's Stonehenge or Egypt's pyramids. The mere fact that some of these structures have stood undisturbed for thousands of years is enough to remind you of the shortness of your own life and the fragility of human existence.

5   Another thing of which we are reminded is the fragility of science. We often think of science as something inescapably linked to progress, and of progress as continually marching forward. We assume that there is something inevitable about the increase of knowledge and the benefits this knowledge brings. Yet nothing could be further from the truth. The advancement of knowledge in general—and of scientific knowledge in particular—is much more like a Saskatchewan wheat field than a solid rock structure: without appropriate care and nurturing, it could very easily shrivel up and die.

6   This point was brought home as we looked at the Moose Mountain medicine wheel. It is likely that there is no single explanation as to why these stone structures were built. Some may have been built to commemorate the dead; others as ceremonial sites to help communities observe important occasions; and yet others simply as landmarks on an otherwise barren prairie. Whatever their original purpose, there is no denying that all of the sites have had important spiritual connections to Native communities, both past and present.

7   But some of the wheels may also have been built with a more scientific purpose in mind. Two structures in particular, the Moose Mountain medicine wheel and the larger but similar Bighorn wheel in Wyoming, more than 700 kilometres away, have spokes marking several important astronomical sightings. The two wheels have so many similarities that one archeologist has commented that they could have been built from the same set of plans.

8   Perhaps most striking, the longest spoke in both wheels lines up directly with the point of

sunrise at the summer solstice. As every ancient people could observe throughout the year, sunrise and sunset shift along the horizon. As spring comes closer, the sunrise moves farther north each morning. This continues until 21 June, the summer solstice, when the sun's northern motion stops. Six months later the winter solstice marks the end of the sun's opposite motion southward along the horizon. Other small cairns mark the positions of three of the northern hemisphere's brightest stars: Aldebaran in the constellation Taurus, Rigel in Orion, and Sirius in Canis Major.

9   Today, the alignments between the cairns and these various astronomical sightings are off by a few degrees, but if corrections are made for how the stars have shifted over the centuries since the cairns were built, the alignments become nearly perfect.

10   The importance of the astronomical sciences to many ancient cultures has been well documented. It's not at all improbable that this knowledge would also have been important to the Plains Indians. Whenever we speak of a "blue moon" or the "dog days of summer" we are reflecting the significance the night sky had to ancient cultures. On the prairies, the summer solstice was marked by important ceremonies such as the sun dance; it would also have helped regulate the nomadic movements of a people with no written calendar. It is also interesting that many medicine wheels have spokes or cairns that point to other, similar structures fifteen, thirty, even seventy kilometres away.

11   Today, the astronomical knowledge underlying these structures has been all but lost to the original inhabitants of the plains. Even so, this knowledge was once of great importance to aboriginal communities, as evidenced by the fact that even today they recognize and celebrate these monuments as sacred sites.

12   Just as importantly, these monuments remind us that scientific knowledge is not inevitable, that it can just as easily decline as advance. They tell us that scientific progress is linked in complex, unpredictable ways to social progress, and vice versa.

13   When I think about these issues, I'm reminded of the words of the philosopher Sidney Hook. As he neared the end of his life, having witnessed the social and political turbulence of almost the entire twentieth century, he was convinced that nothing about human existence is inevitable. As he put it,

14   Looking back on a life longer than I ever expected . . . I am confident that one of my strongest beliefs will remain unaltered. This is the overwhelming conviction that what has happened need not necessarily have happened. The great events of our time, or of any time, good or bad, victories or disasters, need not have occurred. I am not saying that anything *could* have happened at any time. We do not live in a magical world or one of absolute chance. . . . Yet the more closely we explore the tangled web of causation of any historical event, the more likely it is that we will conclude that it didn't have to be.

15   In other words, there is no guarantee that social progress will continue unabated or that scientific knowledge will continue to increase. Unless we continue to nurture what is important, to look for ways to improve what we already have, life has no guarantees.

16   We know that science has the potential to alleviate hunger, disease, and even war. But without the will to protect these accomplishments and the desire to improve on them, life will remain unpredictable. Scientific knowledge remains a rare and valuable commodity in the history of the world, and this is as true today as it was thousands of years ago.

Comprehension

1. Summarize paragraphs 12 and 15, which discuss the nature of scientific knowledge.

Structure, Organization, and Style

1. How does the author connect the scene he witnesses at the top of the Moose Mountains with his perceptions about science and scientific knowledge (pars. 4–6)?

2. How does Irvine use language, imagery, and/or style to evoke his experience at the Moose Mountain medicine wheel?

Critical Thinking/Research

1. Who was Sidney Hook and why might he be an appropriate source for Irvine (pars. 13–15)?

2. Write a critical response, using one of the following statements as a prompt:

   a. "We assume that there is something inevitable about the increase of [scientific] knowledge and the benefits this knowledge brings. Yet nothing could be further from the truth" (par. 5)

   b. "We know that science has the potential to alleviate hunger, disease, and even war. But without the will to protect these accomplishments and the desire to improve on them, life will remain unpredictable" (par. 16)

3. Write an analytical/reflective essay about a specific incident or observation, such as one involving the natural world, that led you to reflect on its larger significance or a universal truth. You can begin, as Irvine does, with narration or description.

Daniel M. Wegner, "How to Think, Say, or Do Precisely the Worst Thing for Any Occasion"

The author of this essay uses the format of the critical review to explore a puzzling, apparently contradictory, aspect of human behaviour. Although the essay appeared in the respected peer-reviewed journal *Science*, it was not written for highly trained experts but for those with a general knowledge of and interest in science. Readers could infer by the work's title, its abstract, and the first paragraphs that it was not an experimental study.

> ▶ **Preparing to Read**
>
> Have you ever said or done the precise thing you did not want to do? How did you respond at the time (for example, upbraid yourself, laugh it off)? Freewrite for five to ten minutes about this time, trying to recall your reaction. If appropriate, this could be a group or class exercise in which individuals shared their experiences.

How to Think, Say, or Do Precisely the Worst Thing for Any Occasion

Daniel M. Wegner

Science, 3 July 2009
(3085 words)

In slapstick comedy, the worst thing that could happen usually does: The person with a sore toe manages to stub it, sometimes twice. Such errors also arise in daily life, and research traces the tendency to do precisely the worst thing to ironic processes of mental control. These monitoring processes keep us watchful for errors of thought, speech, and action and enable us to avoid the worst thing in most situations, but they also increase the likelihood of such errors when we attempt to exert control under mental load (stress, time pressure, or distraction). Ironic errors in attention and memory occur with identifiable brain activity and prompt recurrent unwanted thoughts; attraction to forbidden desires; expression of objectionable social prejudices; production of movement errors; and rebounds of negative experiences such as anxiety, pain, and depression. Such ironies can be overcome when effective control strategies are deployed and mental load is minimized.

1   There are many kinds of errors. We can fall short, overreach, or skitter off the edge, of course, but we can also miss by a mile, take our eyes off the prize, throw the baby out with the bath water—and otherwise foul up in a disturbingly wide variety of ways. Standing out in this assortment of would-be wreckage, though, is one kind of error that is special: the precisely counter-intentional error. This is when we manage to do the worst possible thing, the blunder so outrageous that we think about it in advance and resolve not to let it happen.

2   And then it does. We see a rut coming up in the road ahead and proceed to steer our bike right into it. We make a mental note not to mention a sore point in conversation and then cringe in horror as we blurt out exactly that thing. We carefully cradle the glass of red wine as we cross the room, all the while thinking "don't spill," and then juggle it onto the carpet under the gaze of our host. Normally, our vigilance for such pitfalls helps us avoid them. We steer away from ruts, squelch improper comments, and protect carpets from spills by virtue of our sensitivity to error. Knowing the worst that could happen is essential for control. But sometimes this sensitivity backfires, becoming part of a perverse psychological process that makes the worst occur.

3   Observers of human psychology have suggested that the mind can indeed generate just such ironic errors. Edgar Allan Poe called this unfortunate feature of mind the "imp of the perverse" (1). Sigmund Freud dubbed it the

"counter will" (2). William James said too that "automatic activity in the nerves often runs most counter to the selective pressure of consciousness" (3). Charles Baudouin pronounced it the "law of reversed effort" (4), and Charles Darwin joined in to proclaim "How unconsciously many habitual actions are performed, indeed not rarely in direct opposition to our conscious will!" (5). Hieronymus Bosch illustrated this human preoccupation with the worst, depicting a world in which error, sin, and ruin are the usual consequence of human endeavor (Fig. 1).

Intentions and ironies: Best and worst

4   Do we do the worst thing more often than other things? Fortunately for the proprietors of china shops, we do not. However, accumulating evidence on ironic processes of mental control (6) reveals conditions under which people commit precisely counterintentional errors. The prototypical error of this kind occurs when people are asked to keep a thought out of mind (e.g., "don't think about a white bear"). The thought often comes back. When asked to signal any return of that thought, people may indicate that it comes back about once per minute (7)—often to echo for yet longer periods (8) and, at the extreme, to return for days (9, 10). Some people are better at such thought suppression than others (11, 12), of course, and some try more than others (13), but keeping a thought out of mind remains a challenge for most of us even when we have only arbitrarily tried to suppress it.

5   Why would thought suppression be so hard? It does seem paradoxical: We try to put out of mind what we are thinking now, while still remembering at some level not to think of it later. The ironic process theory (6) suggests that we achieve this trick through two mental

Fig. 1   This detail from *The Last Judgment* by Hieronymus Bosch illustrates the artist's apocalyptic vision of some of the worst that humans can think, say, or do.
Hieronymus Bosch (c.1450–1516) Erich Lessing / Art Resource, NY

processes: The first is a conscious, effortful process aimed at creating the desired mental state. The person engaged in suppressing white bear thoughts, for example, might peruse the room or otherwise cast about for something, anything, that is not a white bear. Filling the mind with other things, after all, achieves "not thinking of a white bear."

6   As these distracters enter consciousness, though, a small part of the mind remains strangely alert to the white bear, searching for indications of this thought in service of ushering it away with more distractions. Ironic process theory proposes that this second component of suppression is an ironic monitoring process, an unconscious search for the very mental state that is unwanted. The conscious search for distractions and the unconscious search for the unwanted thought work together to achieve suppression—the conscious search doing the work and the unconscious search checking for errors.

7   The control system underlying conscious mental control is unique, however, in that its monitoring process can also produce errors. When distractions, stressors, or other mental loads interfere with conscious attempts at self-distraction, they leave unchecked the ironic monitor to sensitize us to exactly what we do not want. This is not a passive monitor, like those often assumed in control system theories, but rather is an active unconscious search for errors that subtly and consistently increases their likelihood via processes of cognitive priming (14). For example, when people are asked not to think about a target word while under pressure to respond quickly in a word association task, they become inclined to offer precisely that forbidden target word (15). Indeed, with time pressure people more often blurt out a word while suppressing it than when they are specifically asked to concentrate on it.

8   Fortunately, the ironic return of suppressed thoughts is not inevitable, or we would be plagued by every thought we had ever tried to put out of mind. We can stop thinking of things quite successfully when we have time to devote to the project and become absorbed in our self-distractions. The ironic rebound of suppressed thoughts after suppression is mainly evident when people abandon the attempt to suppress or are encouraged to revisit the suppressed thought (16, 17). The ironic return of suppressed thoughts during suppression is found only sporadically when people are simply reporting their thoughts but is readily observed with measures of thought that are sensitive to automatic, uncontrollable indications of the thought (18).

9   For example, when people are asked to name the colors in which words are displayed and encounter a word they have been asked not to think about, they name the word's color more slowly—apparently because their attention is rapidly drawn to the word's meaning and so interferes with color-naming (15, 19). Such automatic attention to suppressed thoughts surfaces in color-naming when people are under mental load (such as holding a five-digit number in mind) and can be found as an effect of load in many paradigms (20, 21). Color-naming research reveals, though, that ironic monitoring processes are not limited only to suppression; they also occur during intentional concentration. People intentionally concentrating on particular words under load show slowed color-naming for words that are not concentration targets because these nontargets now pop more easily to mind (19). Perhaps this is why concentrating under pressure, such as during last-minute studying, seems to accentuate the clarity of every stray noise within earshot.

10   The ironic monitoring process also influences memory. Memories we try to forget can be more easily remembered because of the ironic

results of our efforts, but they do this mainly when mental loads undermine conscious attempts to avoid the memories (22, 23). People attempting to forget many items at once can do so with some success (24, 25), perhaps because monitoring multiple control projects dilutes ironic monitoring effects (26). Functional magnetic resonance imaging studies show a similar disparity in brain activity: People trying to forget many targets show a suite of changes in brain activity associated with forgetting (27), whereas those trying not to think of a single target show specific monitoring-related activity of the anterior cingulate and dorsolateral prefrontal cortex (28, 29). The brain regions subserving ironic and intentional processes are differentiable when people do targeted mental control tasks.

Taboos and faux pas: Worst thoughts and utterances

11   Ironic lapses of mental control often appear when we attempt to be socially desirable, as when we try to keep our minds out of the gutter. People instructed to stop thinking of sex, for example, show greater arousal (as gauged by finger skin conductance) than do those asked to stop thinking about a neutral topic. Indeed, levels of arousal are inflated during the suppression of sex thoughts to the same degree that they inflate during attempts to concentrate on such thoughts (8). In research on sexual arousal per se, male participants instructed to inhibit erections as they watched erotic films found it harder than they had hoped, so to speak—particularly if they imbibed a mental load in the form of a couple of alcoholic drinks (30). Ironic effects also may underlie the tendency of homophobic males to show exaggerated sexual arousal to homoerotic pictures (31).

12   The causal role of forbidden desires in ironic effects is clear in experimental research on the effects of imposed secrecy (32). People randomly paired to play "footsie" under the table in a laboratory study reported greater subsequent attraction to their assigned partner when they had been asked to keep their contact secret from others at the table, and survey respondents revealed similar effects of tainted love: a greater desire for past romantic partners with whom relationships had first started in secret (33). This desire seems to arise as an ironic emotional effect of suppression: People who are asked not to think about a specific old flame show greater psychophysiological arousal than do others when later allowed to think about that relationship (34).

13   Like forbidden romance, other occasions for social deception are a fertile source of ironic effects. People admonished to keep an item private in conversation, for example, become more likely to mention it; speakers asked to keep a target hidden from an addressee more often leaked its identity by making inadvertent reference to it—for example, describing the target in Fig. 2 as a "small triangle" and thereby revealing that the occluded object was a larger one (35). Interviewees with eating disorders who role-played not having a disorder for the interviewer also showed ironic effects. During the interview, they reported intrusive thoughts of eating and revealed preoccupation with the topic by rating the interviewer, too, as the likely victim of an eating disorder (36).

14   Another challenge for mental control is keeping a lid on our social prejudices. There is substantial evidence that racism, sexism, homophobia, and other prejudices can be expressed automatically after all, even when we try to control them (37, 38). But the ironic process theory holds that unconscious urges to express such

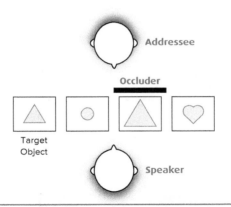

Fig. 2 Speaker who is asked to describe the mutually visible target becomes more likely to mention a clue to the hidden target that is irrelevant to the addressee (e.g., saying "small triangle" rather than "triangle") when instructed to conceal the identity of the target from the addressee. [Adapted from (35)]

prejudices will be especially insistent when we try to control them under load. This possibility was initially documented in research that asked British participants to suppress their stereotypes of skinheads (white supremacists) and found that such stereotypes then rebounded—even leading experimental participants to sit far away from a skinhead in a waiting room (39). Ironic effects have since surfaced showing that expressions of prejudice against racial, ethnic, national, and gender groups are often prompted by attempts to be "politically correct" under mental load (40–42). The desire to be fair and unprejudiced, exercised in haste or distraction, can engender surprising levels of bias and prejudice.

Yips and worries: Worst movements and emotions

15 Pressures to avoid the worst are not always a matter of doing what is socially desirable—they can arise in attempts to achieve self-imposed goals as well. The desire to succeed at a task defines the worst thing that could happen in that situation as failure at this task. So, when people grasp a string with a weight attached and try to keep this pendulum from swinging in one direction, they often find that the pendulum swings in just the way they hope to avoid (43). And, as predicted by ironic process theory, the pendulum is even more likely to swing in the unwanted direction when its holder is distracted by counting backward from 1000 by threes (Fig. 3).

16 Sports psychologists and coaches are familiar with ironic movement errors, counterintentional movements induced by the very desire to prevent them. Former major league baseball players Chuck Knoblauch, Steve Blass, and Rick Ankiel were famed for sporadic wild throws as well as for the desire to avoid them, Ankiel even calling his chronic error "the Creature" (44). In golf putting, the ironic tendency has a name (the "yips"), and golfers who are instructed to avoid a particular error (e.g., "don't overshoot") indeed make it more often when under load (43, 45). Eye-tracking cameras reveal that soccer players who are instructed to avoid kicking a penalty shot to a particular part of the goal more often direct their gaze to the very area to be avoided (46). Perhaps the common sensation we get as we look over a precipice—that we are teetering toward

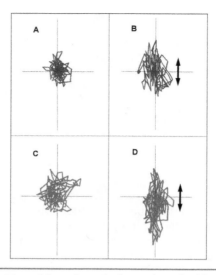

Fig. 3 Sample tracings of 30-s videos from below a handheld pendulum on a string when pendulum holder is asked to (A) hold it steady, (B) keep it from swinging parallel to the arrow, (C) hold it steady while counting backward from 1000 by threes, or (D) keep it from swinging parallel to the arrow while counting backward from 1000 by threes. [Figure based on data from (43).]

the edge—is an accurate perception of our subtle ironic movements. (It may be best when poised at the brink, by the way, not to count backward from 1000 by threes.)

17 Worries and fears are also fertile ground for ironic effects. Unwanted emotions associated with thoughts not only provide a reason to avoid those thoughts but also prompt an unwanted emotional punch when the thoughts return. Emotions we put out of mind are experienced with unusual intensity when the emotional thoughts recur after suppression (19, 34, 47). Depressed mood is especially recalcitrant, recurring after suppression when reminders, negative events, or increased mental loads are encountered (48). And when anxious thoughts are suppressed under mental load, their return can rekindle anxiety with particular vigor (49).

18 Worry about falling asleep yields similar ironic effects: People urged to fall asleep as quickly as possible, but who are also given a mental load (in the form of Sousa march music), are particularly likely then to have trouble sleeping (50). The common observation that dreams center on unpleasant and emotionally disturbing topics makes sense in this light: When people are instructed to suppress thoughts of neutral or emotional topics before sleep, they report more frequent dreaming about those topics (51–53). If we spontaneously choose to avoid unpleasant or worrisome thoughts in daytime, it makes sense that such thoughts would then populate our dreams.

19 Puzzling ironies arise too in response to pain. Usually, people exposed to painful stimulation report higher levels of felt pain when they direct their attention toward the pain. However, suppression of laboratory-induced pain can result in some ironic effects, including ironic increments in suppressed pain and ironic decrements in attended pain (54–56). Such effects are unreliable and have not been examined under

variations in mental load, so conclusions are not yet clear (57, 58). Caution should also be exercised in considering ironic effects of thinking about death. People suppress thoughts of death spontaneously or use strategies other than direct suppression, so ironic effects of suppressing thoughts of one's own death are not always evident (59). Research on such effects is complicated when natural attempts people make to gain mental control obscure the effects of experimental manipulations of control striving.

Putting the worst behind us

20 The ubiquity of ironic effects suggests we should consider it something of a treat when we control ourselves successfully. According to ironic process theory, however, successful control is likely to be far more prevalent than ironic error because people often use effective strategies for control and deploy them under conditions that are not mentally loading. Ironic effects are often small, and the experimental production of ironic errors often depends on the introduction of artificial loads, time pressures, or other means of magnifying ironic effects. Even such amplifiers of ironic error may be overcome, however, in certain individuals with talents for mental control. People who are susceptible to hypnotic suggestion, for example, and who are given suggestions to control thoughts show heightened mental control without ironic effects (60, 61).

21 The rest of us, however, who go through life without special talent for mental control, sometimes must turn to other tactics to overcome ironic error. Strategies people use to relax excessive striving for control, for example, show promise in reducing the severity of ironic effects. Potentially effective strategies include accepting symptoms rather than attempting to control them (62) and disclosing problems rather than keeping them secret (63). Therapies devised for improving mental control—or for helping people to relax it—remain largely untested, however, and there are enough ambiguities surrounding the translation of laboratory research into effective treatments that recommendations for clinical practice at this time are premature. Current research indicates only that, under certain conditions, we may be better able to avoid the worst in what we think, do, or say by avoiding the avoiding. Failing that, our best option is to orchestrate our circumstances so as to minimize mental load when mental control is needed.

References and Notes

1. E. A. Poe, "The imp of the perverse," *Graham's Lady's and Gentleman's Magazine* (July 1845), vol. 28, pp. 1–3.
2. S. Freud, in *The Standard Edition of the Complete Psychological Works of Sigmund Freud*, J. Strachey, Ed. (Hogarth, London, 1950), vol. 1, pp. 115–128.
3. W. James, *Mind* 4, 1 (1879).
4. C. Baudoin, *Suggestion and Autosuggestion* (Dodd, Mead, New York, 1921).
5. C. Darwin, *On the Origin of Species by Means of Natural Selection* (Broadview, Peterborough, Canada, 2003).
6. D. M. Wegner, *Psychol. Rev.* 101, 34 (1994).
7. D. M. Wegner, D. J. Schneider, S. Carter, T. White, *J. Pers. Soc. Psychol.* 53, 5 (1987).
8. D. M. Wegner, J. W. Shortt, A. W. Blake, M. S. Page, *J. Pers. Soc. Psychol.* 58, 409 (1990).
9. H. Trinder, P. M. Salkovskis, *Behav. Res. Ther.* 32, 833 (1994).
10. P. Muris, H. Merckelbach, R. Horselenberg, *Behav. Res. Ther.* 34, 501 (1996).
11. R. D. V. Nixon, J. Flood, K. Jackson, *Pers. Individ. Dif.* 42, 677 (2007).
12. D. F. Tolin, J. S. Abramowitz, A. Przeworski, E. B. Foa, *Behav. Res. Ther.* 40, 1255 (2002).
13. D. M. Wegner, S. Zanakos, *J. Pers.* 62, 615 (1994).
14. E. T. Higgins, in *Unintended Thought*, J. S. Uleman, J. A. Bargh, Eds. (Guilford, New York, 1999), pp. 75–123.

15. D. M. Wegner, R. E. Erber, *J. Pers. Soc. Psychol.* 63, 903 (1992).

16. J. S. Abramowitz, D. F. Tolin, G. P. Street, *Clin. Psychol. Rev.* 21, 683 (2001).

17. E. Rassin, H. Merckelbach, P. Muris, *Clin. Psychol. Rev.* 20, 973 (2000).

18. D. M. Wegner, in *Advances in Experimental Social Psychology*, M. Zanna, Ed. (Academic Press, San Diego, CA, 1992), vol. 25, pp. 193–225.

19. D. M. Wegner, R. E. Erber, S. Zanakos, *J. Pers. Soc. Psychol.* 65, 1093 (1993).

20. A. C. Page, V. Locke, M. Trio, *J. Pers. Soc. Psychol.* 88, 421 (2005).

21. L. S. Newman, K. J. Duff, R. F. Baumeister, *J. Pers. Soc. Psychol.* 72, 980 (1997).

22. C. N. Macrae, G. V. Bodenhausen, A. B. Milne, R. L. Ford, *J. Pers. Soc. Psychol.* 72, 709 (1997).

23. S. Najmi, D. M. Wegner, *Conscious. Cogn.* 17, 114 (2008).

24. M. C. Anderson, C. Green, *Nature* 410, 366 (2001).

25. D. M. Wegner, F. Quillian, C. E. Houston, *J. Pers. Soc. Psychol.* 71, 680 (1996).

26. R. M. Wenzlaff, D. E. Bates, *Pers. Soc. Psychol. Bull.* 26, 1200 (2000).

27. M. C. Anderson et al., *Science* 303, 232 (2004).

28. J. P. Mitchell et al., *Psychol. Sci.* 18, 292 (2007).

29. C. L. Wyland, W. M. Kelley, C. N. Macrae, H. L. Gordon, T. F. Heatherton, *Neuropsychologia* 41, 1863 (2003).

30. H. B. Rubin, D. R. Henson, *Psychopharmacology (Berlin)* 47, 123 (1976).

31. H. E. Adams, L. W. Wright Jr., B. A. Lohr, *J. Abnorm. Psychol.* 105, 440 (1996).

32. J. D. Lane, D. M. Wegner, *J. Pers. Soc. Psychol.* 69, 237 (1995).

33. D. M. Wegner, J. D. Lane, S. Dimitri, *J. Pers. Soc. Psychol.* 66, 287 (1994).

34. D. M. Wegner, D. B. Gold, *J. Pers. Soc. Psychol.* 68, 782 (1995).

35. L. W. Lane, M. Groisman, V. S. Ferreira, *Psychol. Sci.* 17, 273 (2006).

36. L. Smart, D. M. Wegner, *J. Pers. Soc. Psychol.* 77, 474 (1999).

37. A. G. Greenwald, M. R. Banaji, *Psychol. Rev.* 102, 4 (1995).

38. J. A. Bargh, in *Dual Process Theories in Social Psychology*, S. Chaiken, Y. Trope, Eds. (Guilford, New York, 1999), pp. 361–382.

39. C. N. Macrae, G. V. Bodenhausen, A. B. Milne, J. Jetten, *J. Pers. Soc. Psychol.* 67, 808 (1994).

40. M. J. Monteith, J. W. Sherman, P. G. Devine, *Pers. Soc. Psychol. Rev.* 2, 63 (1998).

41. A. D. Galinsky, G. B. Moskowitz, *J. Exp. Soc. Psychol.* 43, 833 (2007).

42. C. N. Macrae, G. V. Bodenhausen, *Annu. Rev. Psychol.* 51, 93 (2000).

43. D. M. Wegner, M. Ansfield, D. Pilloff, *Psychol. Sci.* 9, 196 (1998).

44. J. Merron, "Ankiel can't seem to conquer 'The Creature'" (2003), http://assets.espn.go.com/mlb/s/2003/0615/ 1568307.html.

45. D. L. Beilock, J. A. Afremow, A. L. Rabe, T. H. Carr, *J. Sport Exerc. Psychol.* 23, 200 (2001).

46. F. C. Bakker, R. R. D. Oudejans, O. Binsch, J. Van der Kamp, *Int. J. Sport Psychol.* 37, 265 (2006).

47. E. H. W. Koster, E. Rassin, G. Crombez, G. W. B. Naring, *Behav. Res. Ther.* 41, 1113 (2003).

48. C. G. Beevers, R. M. Wenzlaff, A. M. Hayes, W. D. Scott, *Clin. Psychol. Sci. Pract.* 6, 133 (1999).

49. D. M. Wegner, A. Broome, S. J. Blumberg, *Behav. Res. Ther.* 35, 11 (1997).

50. M. E. Ansfield, D. M. Wegner, R. Bowser, *Behav. Res. Ther.* 34, 523 (1996).

51. D. M. Wegner, R. M. Wenzlaff, M. Kozak, *Psychol. Sci.* 15, 232 (2004).

52. F. Taylor, R. A. Bryant, *Behav. Res. Ther.* 45, 163 (2007).

53. R. E. Schmidt, G. H. E. Gendolla, *Conscious. Cogn.* 17, 714 (2008).

54. D. Cioffi, J. Holloway, *J. Pers. Soc. Psychol.* 64, 274 (1993).

55. L. Goubert, G. Crombez, C. Eccleston, J. Devulder, *Pain* 110, 220 (2004).

56. J. D. Eastwood, P. Gaskovski, K. S. Bowers, *Int. J. Clin. Exp. Hypn.* 46, 77 (1998).

57. A. G. Harvey, B. McGuire, *Behav. Res. Ther.* 38, 1117 (2000).

58. A. I. Masedo, M. R. Esteve, *Behav. Res. Ther.* 45, 199 (2007).

59. J. Arndt, J. Greenberg, S. Solomon, T. Pyszczynski, L. Simon, *J. Pers. Soc. Psychol.* 73, 5 (1997).

60. B. J. King, J. R. Council, *Int. J. Clin. Exp. Hypn.* 46, 295 (1998).

61. R. A. Bryant, S. Wimalaweera, *Int. J. Clin. Exp. Hypn.* 54, 488 (2006).

62. P. Bach, S. C. Hayes, *J. Consult. Clin. Psychol.* 70, 1129 (2002).

63. J. W. Pennebaker, *Psychol. Sci.* 8, 162 (1997).

64. Thanks to K. Gray, A. Heberlein, A. Jenkins, A. Knickman, K. Koh, and T. Wegner for helpful comments. This work was supported by National Institute for Mental Health grant MH 49127.

Comprehension

1. a. In your own words, define the following: *counterintentional errors* (pars. 1 and 4); *ironic process theory* (pars. 5 and 6).

    b. Find a synonym or near-synonym for *counterintentional error* in the introductory section.

2. Define *mental load* (par. 9, etc.) and explain the importance of this concept in Wegner's essay.

3. Summarize one paragraph from "Taboos and faux pas: Worst thoughts and utterances."

Structure and Organization

1. Consider the range of examples in paragraph 3. What disciplines are referred to in this paragraph, and what is its main function?

2. Discuss the ways that the author attracts our interest in his essay as well as the strategies he uses to maintain it throughout. Refer to specific passages.

3. Discuss strategies used to make information understandable to a reader with minimal knowledge of science or psychology (i.e., an educated non-specialist). Refer to specific passages.

Critical Thinking

1. Who appears to be the most important researcher in this field (pars. 1–5)?

2. a. Does Wegner consider counterintentional errors a major problem in most people's lives?

    b. Can these errors be overcome by most people? Explain why or why not.

Simine Vazire and Erika N. Carlson, "Others Sometimes Know Us Better Than We Know Ourselves"

This article is a critical review that evaluates the current state of knowledge on a topic of interest. Such essays use analysis and synthesis in order to determine how much has been done and how much research needs to be done, concluding with suggestions for practical applications.

Because these kinds of academic essays deal with interrelated research areas, differing methodologies, and (usually) a large number of studies, organization is crucial to their success. In this case, the authors use questions as headings to suggest specific subtopics while providing a coherent structure for each section (see "Structure and Organization," question 1).

Preparing to Read

1. Have you ever thought about how well you know yourself, or whether others' opinions about you might be more accurate than your own perceptions? Write down five positive or neutral personality traits that best describe you; then, have a close friend or family member write down five positive or neutral traits he/she believes describe you. Compare the results.

2. If you have ever taken personality tests like the "Big Five" or the Myers-Briggs Type Indicator (versions may be available online from reliable websites), compare the test results with your own perceptions. Can you account for any differences in test results and your own beliefs about yourself?

Others Sometimes Know Us Better Than We Know Ourselves

Simine Vazire and Erika N. Carlson

Current Directions in Psychological Science,
April 2011
(2562 words)

Abstract

Most people believe that they know themselves better than anyone else knows them. However, a complete picture of what a person is like requires both the person's own perspective and the perspective of others who know him or her well. People's perceptions of their own personalities, while largely accurate, contain important omissions. Some of these blind spots are likely due to a simple lack of information, whereas others are due to motivated distortions in our self-perceptions. Perhaps for these reasons, others can perceive some aspects of personality better than the self can. This is especially true for traits that are very desirable or undesirable, when motivational factors are most likely to distort self-perceptions. Therefore, much can be learned about a person's personality from how he or she is seen by others. Future research should examine how people can tap into others' knowledge to improve self-knowledge.

Keywords: self-knowledge, accuracy, peer reports, personality, meta-perception, self-insight

> "Do we understand each other?"
> Gracie wants to know. . . .
> "Better than we understand ourselves,"
> I tell her.
> —*Straight Man*, Richard Russo, p. 106

1   Who knows you best? Most of us have the powerful intuition that we know ourselves better than others know us (Pronin, Kruger, Savitsky, & Ross, 2001). Indeed, there are several good reasons to think that we are the best judge of ourselves: We have privileged knowledge about our own histories, our thoughts and feelings, and our private behaviors. Yet, we all know people who seem to be deluded about themselves—which raises the uncomfortable possibility that we, too, might be so deluded.

2   When it comes to our own personalities, there is increasing evidence that our blind spots are substantial. Moreover, others can sometimes see things about our personalities that we cannot. The aim of this paper is to review the latest

evidence concerning the accuracy of self- and other-perceptions of personality and show that a complete picture of what a person is like requires both the person's own perspective and the perspective of others who know him or her well. This conclusion has implications for researchers and practitioners who rely on self-reports and for people who want to get to know others—or themselves.

How could we not know?

3   The first step in establishing that others know things about our personality that we do not is to show that there are gaps in our self-knowledge. Why do we sometimes misperceive our own personality? Some blind spots may be due to a simple lack of information. We have all experienced the supervisor who, unbeknownst to him, has a persistent frown when listening intently and, as a result, is a lot more intimidating than he realizes. A simple dose of feedback could bring his self-perception in line with his behavior (or even better, bring his behavior in line with his self-perception). Blind spots can also be due to having too much information—we have access to so many of our thoughts, feelings, and behaviors that we often have a hard time mentally aggregating this evidence and noticing patterns (Sande, Goethals, & Radloff, 1988). For example, most of us can probably think of many times when we have acted friendly or unfriendly, making it difficult to know how friendly we are in general. In other words, it is difficult for us to see the forest for the trees.

4   In many cases, however, blind spots are not so innocent—they are the result of motivated cognitive processes. One motive that has a strong influence on self-perception is the motive to maintain and enhance our self-worth (Sedikides & Gregg, 2008). There is a great deal of research documenting the lengths people will go to in order to maintain a positive view of themselves, leading to flawed self-assessment (Dunning, 2005). While our desire to protect our sense of self-worth influences our self-perception, it is not clear that these biases are always in the positive direction. Indeed, there are important individual differences in self-enhancement (Paulhus, 1998) and some people seek to confirm their overly negative self-views (Swann, 1997). What is beyond doubt is that self-perception is not simply an objective, neutral process. Motivated cognition influences and distorts self-perception in a multitude of ways that help to create and maintain blind spots in self-knowledge. As a result, we cannot judge our own personality as dispassionately as we might a stranger's.

5   One vivid example of blind spots in self-knowledge comes from research on the discrepancies between people's explicit and implicit perceptions of their own personality. Implicit personality is typically measured by tapping into people's automatic associations between themselves and specific traits or behaviors. The logic behind these measures is that people form automatic or implicit associations (e.g., between the concepts "me" and "assertive") based on their previous patterns of behavior. Thus, the traits that people automatically associate with themselves in implicit tests may predict behavior above and beyond the traits they consciously endorse in explicit measures of personality. Indeed, this is exactly what has been found. In one study, people's implicit self-views of their personality predicted their behavior even after controlling for what could be predicted from their explicit self-views (Back, Schmukle, & Egloff, 2009). This pattern was strongest for extraversion and neuroticism, traits that are non-evaluative and that people are typically willing to report honestly, which suggests that people have implicit knowledge about their pattern of behaviors that they cannot report on explicitly.

6   Are these implicit blind spots merely an efficient way to process information—it may be easier to form implicit associations than to constantly update our explicit self-views—or are they the result of motivated cognition? If processing self-knowledge implicitly were merely a matter of efficiency, we should be able to increase the congruence between our explicit and implicit self-views simply by focusing our attention on the behavioral manifestations of our implicit personality. Contrary to this prediction, participants who watched themselves on video did not bring their explicit self-views more in line with their implicit personality, despite the fact that strangers who watched the same videos were able to detect the implicit aspects of the targets' personalities (Hofmann, Gschwendner, & Schmitt, 2009). Thus, it seems that our motives sometimes lead us to ignore aspects of our personality that others can detect. As a result, our conscious self-perceptions provide a valuable but incomplete perspective on our personality.

How do they know?

7   The second step in establishing that others may know things about our personality that we do not is to show that others are adept at detecting personality. As it turns out, many aspects of personality are remarkably transparent to others, even when we are not intentionally broadcasting them. For example, many traits can be judged accurately from people's physical appearance, their Facebook profiles, or a brief interaction (Kenny & West, 2008). This evidence suggests that our day-to-day behavior is infused with traces of our personality and that others make good use of these cues when inferring our personality (Mehl, Gosling, & Pennebaker, 2006). In addition, we (intentionally and unintentionally) broadcast our personality in our living spaces, music collections, and online habitats (Gosling,

2008). In other words, others have plenty of fodder for detecting our personality, while we see ourselves through the distorted lens of our own motives, biases, wishes, and fears.

8   Of course, not all others are created equal—the relationship between the judge and the target matters. While too much intimacy can lead to the same biases that distort self-perceptions (e.g., one's self-worth can be threatened as much by the knowledge that one's spouse is incompetent as it is by the thought of one's own incompetence), closeness is usually associated with greater accuracy (see Biesanz, West, & Millevoi, 2007, for a thorough review). Moreover, the better we get along with others, the more accurately they can infer our thoughts and feelings (Thomas & Fletcher, 2003). Overall, across all types and levels of acquaintance that have been examined, people form remarkably accurate impressions of one another.

9   These findings show that we are astute judges of each others' personalities, likely due to the importance of interpersonal perception for our social species. As a result, other people—especially those who spend a lot of time around us and who we open up to—almost inevitably become experts on our personality. This conclusion should cast serious doubt on the long-standing assumption among researchers that we necessarily know our own personality better than others know us. It seems likely that, at least for some aspects of personality, others might be in a better position to see us clearly than we are.

Who knows what?

10   The goal of this article is not to bring readers to despair of self-perceptions. Rather, the goal is to make the case that others sometimes see aspects of our personality that we are blind to. Perhaps the most important evidence is the body of research that directly compares the accuracy of self- and other-perceptions of personality. Here we focus on

studies that measure accuracy using a correlational approach—that is, by comparing judgments by the self and others to a criterion. The available evidence suggests that self- and other-perceptions are roughly equally good at predicting behavior in a laboratory (e.g., behavior in a group discussion; Kolar, Funder, & Colvin, 1996; Vazire, 2010), predicting real-world behavior (e.g., behavior when out with friends; Vazire & Mehl, 2008), and predicting outcomes (e.g., discharge from the military; Fiedler, Oltmanns, & Turkheimer, 2004). However, the overall equality in levels of accuracy obscures a more interesting pattern: Self- and other-ratings of a person's personality do not simply provide redundant information. Instead, they capture different aspects.

11 Vazire (2010) recently proposed the self–other knowledge asymmetry (SOKA) model to map out the aspects of personality that are known uniquely to the self or uniquely to others. According to this model, the differences between what we know about ourselves and what others know about us are not random but are driven by differences between the information available to the self and others and motivational biases that differentially affect perceptions of the self and others (Andersen, Glassman, & Gold, 1998).

12 Specifically, Vazire (2010) proposed that the self has better information than others do for judging internal traits—traits defined primarily by thoughts and feelings, such as being anxious or optimistic—but that others have better information than the self for judging external traits—traits defined primarily by overt behavior, such as being boisterous or charming. In addition, Vazire argued that self-perception on highly evaluative traits (e.g., being rude, being intelligent) is severely distorted by biases. As a result, self-ratings on evaluative traits often do not track our actual standing on those traits (but instead might track individual differences in self-esteem or narcissism). In contrast,

when perceiving others on highly evaluative traits, we are able to form impressions that are mostly accurate (assuming we have enough information). This is not to say that others see us more harshly than we see ourselves. In fact, there is evidence that close others may in fact have more positive impressions of us than we do, but that their perceptions are nevertheless more accurate. This can happen if people who have the most positive ratings from their friends also tend to actually have the most positive personalities (even if nobody's personality is quite as delightful as their friends portray it). In this case, friends' ratings would be overly positive in an absolute sense, but more accurate in their rank order, and thus friends' ratings would be a very good predictor of actual behavior (e.g., those whose friends say they are the most friendly are likely to behave the friendliest).

13 To test these hypotheses, Vazire (2010) compared self- and friend-ratings of personality to how people behaved in videotaped laboratory exercises and how they performed on intelligence and creativity tests. Consistent with Vazire's first hypothesis, self-ratings of internal, neutral traits (e.g., anxiety, self-esteem) were better than friends' ratings at predicting behavior (Fig. 1). Consistent with her second hypothesis, friends' ratings of evaluative traits (e.g., intelligence, creativity) were better than self-ratings at predicting performance in these domains.

14 Consistent with the SOKA model, other research has shown that close others are often better than the self at predicting very desirable or undesirable outcomes, such as college GPA, relationship dissolution, and coronary disease. Together, these findings suggest that those who know us well sometimes see things that we do not see in ourselves, particularly when it comes to aspects of our personality that are observable to others and that we care a lot about (and thus cannot see objectively).

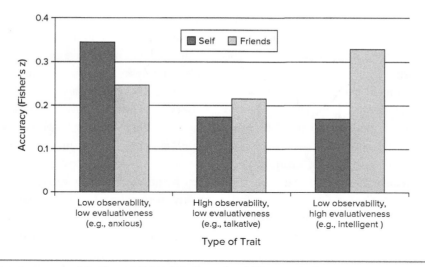

Figure 1   Accuracy of Self- and Friend-Ratings for Different Traits

Average accuracy scores (transformed to Fisher's z-scores for purposes of comparison) for self- and friend-ratings of personality traits that are less observable and less evaluative (left), more observable and less evaluative (middle), and less observable and more evaluative (right). Adapted from Vazire (2010).

What do we do now?

15   The appropriate conclusion from the empirical literatures seems to be that to know people's personalities, we need to know both how they see themselves and how they are seen by others who know them well. The fact that self-perception is an important part of personality is not new; the novel finding is that others also know a lot about us that we don't know. How can we tap into others' knowledge to improve our self-knowledge? Direct, honest feedback might be very useful, but it is rare, and probably for good reason. A more realistic strategy is to take the perspective of others when perceiving our own personality (i.e., meta-perception). Research suggests that although we overestimate the degree to which others share our perception of ourselves, we are able to detect the impression we make on others, even when meeting someone for the first time (Carlson, Furr, & Vazire, 2010). We also seem to know how we are seen differently by people who know us in different contexts (e.g., parents versus friends;

Carlson & Furr, 2009). In short, it seems that we have some awareness of how others see us, but we do not always make use of this information when judging our own personality. Thus, we may be able to improve our self-knowledge by placing more weight on our impressions of how others see us—particularly, as Vazire's (2010) research suggests, when it comes to observable, evaluative traits (e.g., funny, charming).

16   Finally, introspection has historically attracted a great deal of attention as a route to self-knowledge. Unfortunately, recent research shows that many aspects of ourselves are hidden from conscious awareness, limiting the effectiveness of introspection in the pursuit of self-knowledge (Wilson, 2009). Perhaps a more promising avenue for increasing self-knowledge is to reduce the self-protective motives (e.g., defensiveness) that prevent us from seeing ourselves objectively. Recent work suggests that self-affirmation reduces defensive responding and makes us more open to negative information about ourselves (Critcher, Dunning, & Armor, 2010).

Along the same lines, training in mindfulness meditation (i.e., nonjudgmental attention to one's current experience) improves people's emotion-regulation skills, memory, and attention and can improve their ability to differentiate between their transient emotional experiences and their global dispositions (Williams, 2010). Thus, these techniques may reduce the two major obstacles to self-knowledge: lack of information and motivational biases.

17 In short, little is known about successful routes to improving self-knowledge. Clearly, much remains to be learned about how we can know ourselves better. What is now evident, however, is that, as a fortune cookie admonishes, "There are lessons to be learned by listening to others."

Acknowledgments

We thank Krystle Disney, John Doris, Sam Gosling, Sanjay Srivastava, and Tim Wilson for their helpful suggestions concerning this article.

Declaration of Conflicting Interests

The authors declared that they had no conflicts of interest with respect to their authorship or the publication of this article.

Recommended Reading

Dunning, D., Heath, C., & Suls, J.M. (2004). Flawed self-assessment: Implications for health, education, and the workplace. *Psychological Science in the Public Interest, 5*, 69–106. A comprehensive, highly accessible review of the practical implications of biases in self-assessment.

Oltmanns, T.F., Gleason, M.E.J., Klonsky, E.D., & Turkheimer, E. (2005). Meta-perception for pathological personality traits: Do we know when others think that we are difficult? *Consciousness and Cognition: An International Journal, 14*, 739–751. A study that illustrates the importance of self-knowledge for personality disorders.

Vazire, S., & Carlson, E.N. (2010). Self-knowledge of personality: Do people know themselves? *Social and Personality Psychology Compass.* An accessible review of the latest evidence regarding the accuracy of self-perceptions of personality, with a more thorough reference list than is provided in the current paper.

Wilson, T.D., & Dunn, E.W. (2004). Self-knowledge: Its limits, value, and potential for improvement. *Annual Review of Psychology, 55*, 493–518. A comprehensive and thorough review of research and theory on self-knowledge.

References

Andersen, S.M., Glassman, N.S., & Gold, D.A. (1998). Mental representations of the self, significant others, and nonsignificant others: Structure and processing of private and public aspects. *Journal of Personality and Social Psychology, 75*, 845–861.

Back, M.D., Schmukle, S.C., & Egloff, B. (2009). Predicting actual behavior from the explicit and implicit self-concept of personality. *Journal of Personality and Social Psychology, 97*, 533–548.

Biesanz, J.C., West, S.G., & Millevoi, A. (2007). What do you learn about someone over time? The relationship between length of acquaintance and consensus and self-other agreement in judgments of personality. *Journal of Personality and Social Psychology, 92*, 119–135.

Carlson, E.N., & Furr, R.M. (2009). Evidence of differential metaaccuracy: People understand the different impressions they make. *Psychological Science, 20*, 1033–1039.

Carlson, E.N., Furr, R.M., & Vazire, S. (2010). Do we know the first impressions we make? Evidence for idiographic meta-accuracy and calibration of first impressions. *Social Psychological and Personality Science, 1*, 94–98.

Critcher, C.R., Dunning, D., & Armor, D.A. (2010). When self-affirmations reduce defensiveness: Timing is key. *Personality and Social Psychology Bulletin, 36*, 947–959.

Dunning, D. (2005). *Self-insight: Roadblocks and detours on the path to knowing thyself.* New York, NY: Psychology Press.

Fiedler, E.R., Oltmanns, T.F., & Turkheimer, E. (2004). Traits associated with personality disorders and adjustment to military life: Predictive validity of self and peer reports. *Military Medicine, 169*, 207–211.

Gosling, S.D. (2008). *Snoop: What your stuff says about you*. New York, NY: Basic Books.

Hofmann, W., Gschwendner, T., & Schmitt, M. (2009). The road to the unconscious self not taken: Discrepancies between self- and observer-inferences about implicit dispositions from nonverbal behavioral cues. *European Journal of Personality*, 23, 343–366.

Kenny, D.A., & West, T.V. (2008). Zero-acquaintance: Definitions, statistical model, findings, and process. In N. Ambady & J.J. Skowronski (Eds.), *First impressions* (pp. 129–146). New York, NY: Guilford Press.

Kolar, D.W., Funder, D.C., & Colvin, C.R. (1996). Comparing the accuracy of personality judgments by the self and knowledgeable others. *Journal of Personality*, 64, 311–337.

Mehl, M.R., Gosling, S.D., & Pennebaker, J.W. (2006). Personality in its natural habitat: Manifestations and implicit folk theories of personality in daily life. *Journal of Personality and Social Psychology*, 90, 862–877.

Paulhus, D.L. (1998). Interpersonal and intrapsychic adaptiveness of trait self-enhancement: A mixed blessing? *Journal of Personality and Social Psychology*, 74, 1197–1208.

Pronin, E., Kruger, J., Savitsky, K., & Ross, L. (2001). You don't know me, but I know you: The illusion of asymmetric insight. *Journal of Personality and Social Psychology*, 81, 639–656.

Russo, R. (1988). *Straight man*. New York, NY: Vintage.

Sande, G.N., Goethals, G.R., & Radloff, C.E. (1988). Perceiving one's own traits and others': The multi-faceted self. *Journal of Personality and Social Psychology*, 54, 13–20.

Sedikides, C., & Gregg, A.P. (2008). Self-enhancement: Food for thought. *Perspectives on Psychological Science*, 3, 102–116.

Swann, W.B., Jr. (1997). The trouble with change: Self-verification and allegiance to the self. *Psychological Science*, 8, 177–180.

Thomas, G., & Fletcher, G.J.O. (2003). Mind-reading accuracy in intimate relationships: Assessing the roles of the relationship, the target, and the judge. *Journal of Personality and Social Psychology*, 85, 1079–1094.

Vazire, S. (2010). Who knows what about a person? The self–other knowledge asymmetry (SOKA) model. *Journal of Personality and Social Psychology*, 98, 281–300.

Vazire, S., & Mehl, M.R. (2008). Knowing me, knowing you: The accuracy and unique predictive validity of self-ratings and other-ratings of daily behavior. *Journal of Personality and Social Psychology*, 95, 1202–1216.

Williams, J.M. (2010). Mindfulness and psychological process. *Emotion*, 10, 1–7.

Wilson, T.D. (2009). Know thyself. *Perspectives on Psychological Science*, 4, 384–389.

Language and Comprehension

1. Identify specific words or phrases in the first three paragraphs that show this essay is intended for a wider audience than researchers in perceptual psychology.

2. Define *implicit personality* (par. 5) and briefly explain its importance to personality researchers.

3. Explain:
   a. How Vazire tested her hypotheses that the self is a better judge of internal traits but not as good a judge of external traits of the individual
   b. The results of the testing (pars. 12–13).

Structure and Organization

1. Analyze the organizational strategies used in the section "How Do They Know?" to increase comprehension. (You can consider paragraph structure and development; strategies for coherence, such as repetition, transitions, and word choice; and use of sources.)
2. In your own words, explain the importance of the graph on p. 354.

Critical Thinking

1. Why is direct feedback rarely used to help us understand our own personalities (par. 15)?
2. After reading the concluding section, "What Do We Do Now?" do you think the authors are optimistic about the opportunities that exist for gaining self-knowledge? Explain your answer by referring to at least three specific points in this section.

Erin R. Whitchurch, Timothy D. Wilson, & Daniel T. Gilbert, "'He Loves Me, He Loves Me Not . . .': Uncertainty Can Increase Romantic Attraction"

This scholarly essay presents the findings of an experiment designed to explore an aspect of human relationships—using the medium of Facebook. Articles based on lab experiments usually adhere to a very specific structure: they are divided into introductory, methods, results, and discussion sections (abbreviated as IMRAD). (See "Health, Ethics and Environment: A Qualitative Study of Vegetarian Motivations," p. 187, which uses the same structure). Each section has a specific function; for example, in the Results section, the researchers present the numerical data, usually with the help of tables or charts. In the Discussion section, they summarize their results and suggest how their findings can be used.

The article's abstract takes the reader through the stages of the experiment, beginning by defining an important term; it includes brief mention of the study's method before summarizing its results and conclusions.

> ▶ Preparing to Read
>
> Read the first three paragraphs of the essay, noting their organization and layout.
> 1. Was the meaning of the paragraphs clear?
> 2. Were ideas logically developed?
> 3. Why might clarity and accessibility of information be important in essays like this one?

"He Loves Me, He Loves Me Not . . . ": Uncertainty Can Increase Romantic Attraction

Erin R. Whitchurch, Timothy D. Wilson, and Daniel T. Gilbert

Psychological Science, February 2011
(2783 words)

Abstract

This research qualifies a social psychological truism: that people like others who like them (the reciprocity principle). College women viewed the Facebook profiles of four male students who had previously seen their profiles. They were told that the men (a) liked them a lot, (b) liked them only an average amount, or (c) liked them either a lot or an average amount (uncertain condition). Comparison of the first two conditions yielded results consistent with the reciprocity principle. Participants were more attracted to men who liked them a lot than to men who liked them an average amount. Results for the uncertain condition, however, were consistent with research on the pleasures of uncertainty. Participants in the uncertain condition were most attracted to the men—even more attracted than were participants who were told that the men liked them a lot. Uncertain participants reported thinking about the men the most, and this increased their attraction toward the men.

Keywords: uncertainty, sense making, interpersonal attraction, reciprocity

1   Substantial research shows that people like others who like them—which is known as the reciprocity principle (Aronson & Worchel, 1966; Gouldner, 1960; Kenny, 1994; Luo & Zhang, 2009). It is rewarding to be liked by others, and these social rewards generate positive feelings. Further, people assume that those who like them have benevolent intentions and will treat them well (Montoya & Insko, 2008). Thus, if we want to know how much Sarah likes Bob, a good predictor is how much she thinks Bob likes her.

2   But what if Sarah is not sure how much Bob likes her? He seems interested, but in the words of a popular book and movie, maybe he is "just not that into" her (Behrendt & Tuccillo, 2009). How much will Sarah like Bob under this condition of uncertainty? Research on reciprocity suggests that she should like him less than if she were certain that he liked her, because the less certain she is, the fewer social rewards she should experience and the less sure she can be that he has good intentions toward her. In other words, according to the reciprocity principle, Sarah should like Bob more when she is certain that he likes her than when she believes he might not.

3   Recent research on the pleasures of uncertainty, however, suggests otherwise. Under some

circumstances, uncertainty about the nature of a positive event can produce more positive affect than certainty about the nature of that event (Bar-Anan, Wilson, & Gilbert, 2009; Kurtz, Wilson, & Gilbert, 2007; Lee & Qiu, 2009; Wilson, Centerbar, Kermer, & Gilbert, 2005). When people are certain that a positive event has occurred, they begin to adapt to it, primarily by reaching an understanding of what the event means and why it occurred (Wilson & Gilbert, 2008). Thus, whereas people may be very pleased that someone likes them, once they are certain of this fact they construct explanations as to why, and as a result the news loses some of its force.

4   In contrast, when people are uncertain about an important outcome, they can hardly think about anything else. They think about such an event but do not yet adapt to it, because they do not know which outcome to make sense of and explain. The affective consequences of such uncertainty depend on the valence of the thoughts people have about the potential outcomes. Often these thoughts are negative, because one of the possible outcomes is undesired and people's attention is drawn to that possibility (e.g., "the biopsy might show that I have cancer"). In such a case, uncertainty will lead to an increase in negative affect. Sometimes, however, the potential outcomes are positive or neutral, such as the possibility that a new, attractive acquaintance is very fond of us (positive) or has no special impression of us (neutral).

5   There may thus be an exception to the reciprocity principle: People might like someone more when they are uncertain about how much that person likes them than when they are certain, as long as they have some initial attraction toward the person. Uncertainty causes people to think more about the person, we suggest, and, further, people might interpret these thoughts as a sign of liking via a self-perception effect (e.g., "I must like

him if he keeps popping into my thoughts"; Bem, 1972). In short, people's uncertainty about how much another person likes them—such that they pick petals off a flower to try to find out whether that person loves them or loves them not—may increase their liking for that person.

6   Prior studies of the pleasures of uncertainty have examined the effects of uncertainty about such things as the source of a gift, and the dependent measure in prior studies was overall mood, not interpersonal attraction (e.g., Kurtz et al., 2007). We are unaware of any studies that have examined the effects of uncertainty on interpersonal attraction.[1] In the present study, female college students learned that male college students at other universities had looked at Facebook profiles of several college women, including the participants' profiles, and had rated how much they liked each woman. Participants then looked at the profiles of four of the men. Some participants were told that they were viewing the men who had liked them the most, some were told that they were viewing the men who had given them average ratings, and some (in the uncertain condition) were told that they were viewing either the men who had liked them the most or the men who had given them average ratings. We predicted that participants in the uncertain condition would be most attracted to the men.

Method
Participants

7   Participants were 47 female undergraduates at the University of Virginia who participated in return for partial course credit.

Procedure

8   Participants signed up at least 48 hours in advance of their session, with the understanding that their Facebook profiles would be viewed by

students at other universities. When participants arrived for the experimental session, the experimenter explained that the study was exploring the effectiveness of Facebook as an online dating website and that several male students from two collaborating universities had viewed the Facebook profiles of approximately 15 to 20 female college students, including the participant's, and had rated the degree to which they thought they would get along with each woman if they got to know her better. Each participant was told that she would see the Facebook profiles of four of the men. In the liked-best condition, participants learned that they had been randomly assigned to see the four men who had given them the highest ratings (e.g., "of all the people who saw your profile, these are the four who thought they would like you the best"). In the average-liking condition, participants learned that they had been randomly assigned to see the four men who had given them average ratings (e.g., "of all the people who saw your profile, these four did not rate you as the highest or the lowest; they are people who liked you about average"). In the uncertain condition, participants read:

9   For reasons of experimental control neither you nor the experimenter knows the condition you have been randomly assigned to. The profiles you will see might be the participants who saw your profile and liked you the most. Or, the profiles you see might be the participants who saw your profile and gave you an average rating.

10 Participants then examined four fictitious Facebook profiles that convincingly portrayed likeable, attractive male college students (two Caucasian, one African American, and one Asian), ostensibly from the University of Michigan and the University of California, Los Angeles. Next, participants completed several filler tasks and dependent measures.

11 *Time 1 mood.* After completing a filler task, participants rated the degree to which the adjectives *positive*, *pleased*, *disappointed*, and *sad* described how they felt at that moment. Ratings were made on 21-point dot scales (1 = *not at all*, 21 = *extremely*).

12 *Attraction to the male students.* After completing additional filler tasks, participants rated each man according to how much they liked him, how much they wanted to work with him on a class project, and how similar they were to him (1 = *not at all*, 8 = *extremely*); how much they would be interested in him as a casual acquaintance and as a friend (1 = *not at all*, 10 = *extremely*); and how much they would be interested in him as "someone I would hook up with" and as "a potential boyfriend/girlfriend" (1 = *not at all*, 10 = *extremely*). A factor analysis revealed that all of these items except interest in the man as a casual acquaintance had a loading of at least .40 on a primary liking factor. We therefore averaged the standardized ratings of all items except the casual-acquaintance item to form an attraction index (α = .86).

13 *Time 2 mood.* After rating their attraction to the men, participants rated their mood again on the same measures that they had received earlier.

14 *Reported thoughts.* Finally, participants rated the extent to which thoughts about the men had "popped into their head" during the previous 15 min (1 = *not at all*, 9 = *extremely often*) and then were thoroughly debriefed.

Results
Attraction

15 An analysis of variance revealed a significant effect of condition on participants' attraction toward the men, $F(2, 44)$ = 15.06, $p < .001$ η^2 = .41. As Table 1 shows, participants in the liked-best condition were more attracted to

the men than were participants in the average-liking condition, $t(44) = 3.52$, $p = .001$. This finding replicates the reciprocity effect. As predicted, participants in the uncertain condition were most attracted to the men—even more attracted than were participants in the liked-best condition, $t(44) = 2.07$, $p = .04$. In other words, women were more attracted to men whose liking for them was uncertain than to men who they knew liked them the best.

Reported thoughts

16 As predicted, participants in the uncertain condition reported having thought about the men the most, followed by participants in the average-liking condition and then participants in the liked-best condition (see Table 1). Although the overall effect of condition was not significant, $F(2, 43) = 2.14$, $p = .13$, $\eta^2 = .09$, participants in the uncertain condition reported thinking significantly more about the men than did participants in the liked-best condition, as predicted, $t(43) = 1.99$, $p = .05$.

Mediation

17 In a mediation analysis, we compared participants in the uncertain condition (dummy code = 1) with participants in the liked-best condition (dummy code = 0). Condition significantly predicted participants' frequency of thought about the men, $b = 1.51$ ($SE = 0.70$), $p = .04$, and frequency of thought marginally predicted participants' level of attraction (controlling for condition), $b = 0.09$ ($SE = 0.05$), $p = .10$. These results are consistent with our hypothesis that the effect of uncertainty on attraction would be mediated by frequency of thought about the men. However, because a bootstrapping analysis revealed that the 95% confidence interval for the indirect effect ([-.03, .40]) did not quite exclude zero, the evidence for mediation is tentative (Shrout & Bolger, 2002).

Mood

18 We averaged responses to the four mood items after reverse scoring the two negative items (Time 1 $\alpha = .86$, Time 2 $\alpha = .84$). A 3 (condition; between subjects) × 2 (time; within subjects) analysis of variance revealed a main effect of condition, $F(2, 44) = 3.86$, $p = .03$, $\eta^2 = .15$. Participants were in a better mood in the liked-best condition than in the average-liking condition, $t(44) = 2.70$, $p = .01$ (see Table 1). Participants were in an even better mood in the uncertain condition, though the difference between the uncertain and like-best conditions was not significant, $t(44) = 0.92$, $p = .36$.

Table 1 Mean Attraction to the Men, Frequency of Thought About the Men, and Mood by Condition

Measure	Condition		
	Uncertain	Liked best	Average liking
Attraction	0.57 (0.44)	0.12 (0.60)	−0.62 (0.71)
Reported thoughts	5.07 (2.17)	3.56 (1.67)	4.63 (2.34)
Mood, Time 1	16.64 (3.62)	16.09 (2.04)	13.55 (4.25)
Mood, Time 2	16.89 (2.97)	15.24 (3.11)	13.40 (4.41)

Note: Standard deviations are in parentheses. The attraction index is the average of the standard scores of six items. The mood index is the average of ratings of two positive adjectives and two (reverse-scored) negative adjectives. Higher numbers reflect greater attraction to the men in the profiles, more frequent thought about the men, and more positive moods.

Discussion

19   This study replicated the effects of reciprocity on attraction: Participants liked the men more when they believed the men liked them a lot than when they believed the men liked them only an average amount. As predicted, however, participants in the uncertain condition were most attracted to the men. Put differently, women were more attracted to men when there was only a 50% chance that the men liked them the best than when there was a 100% chance that the men liked them the best. Also as predicted, women in the uncertain condition reported thinking about the men more than did women in the like-best condition.

20   These results help solve an enigma about whether "playing hard to get" increases one's attractiveness to others. Numerous popular books advise people not to display their affections too openly to a potential romantic partner and to instead appear choosy and selective. Social psychological research, however, has not confirmed this advice. Walster, Walster, Piliavin, and Schmidt (1973), for example, found evidence only for a "selectively hard to get" hypothesis: Men were most attracted to a potential date who expressed interest in them but not other people, and were less attracted to a woman who was "uniformly hard to get" (she was unenthusiastic about dating anyone) or a woman who was "uniformly easy to get" (she was enthusiastic about dating several men).

21   A form of playing hard to get that has not been tested, however, is keeping the person guessing about how one feels about him or her without communicating anything about how interested one is in other people. Ours is the first study to manipulate uncertainty in the absence of any information about choosiness, and by so doing has confirmed a new version of the playing-hard-to-get hypothesis: People who create uncertainty about how much they like someone can increase that person's interest in them.

22   We should note some limitations of the present research. First, the participants rated the men on the basis of a small amount of information, and it is unclear whether people's uncertainty about how much someone likes them would continue to increase attraction once they meet the person and begin a relationship. However, many people meet online these days, and this study simulated the kind of information people often get about potential dating partners. Uncertainty at the very beginning of this process appears to confer some benefits.

23   Second, we included only female participants. Previous research has not found gender differences in the pleasure of uncertainty (e.g., Wilson et al., 2005), but this is the first study examining the effects of uncertainty on interpersonal attraction, and it is possible that there are gender differences in this domain.

24   Finally, we did not replicate previous studies that found that participants who were uncertain about a positive outcome were in a significantly better mood than participants who were certain (e.g., Wilson et al., 2005). However, our results were in the same direction, and it is notable that participants in the uncertain condition were in at least as good a mood as participants in the liked-best condition, given that there was only a 50% chance that the former participants had seen the men who liked them the best. Uncertainty increased attraction and had no deleterious effect on people's mood.

25   Clearly, the determinants of interpersonal attraction are complex, and there is no simple formula people can use to get someone to like them. When people first meet, however, it may be that popular dating advice is correct: Keeping people in the dark about how much we like them will increase how much they think about us and will pique their interest.

Declaration of Conflicting Interests The authors declared that they had no conflicts of interest with respect to their authorship or the publication of this article.

Note

1. Norton, Frost, and Ariely (2007) found that the more information people had about another person, the less they liked him or her, but this effect was mediated by participants' perception of their similarity to the person and not by uncertainty about how much the person liked them. Eastwick and Finkel (2008) found that increasing attachment anxiety toward someone increased attraction to that person. It is possible that perceived uncertainty about reciprocity contributed to the effect.

References

Aronson, E., & Worchel, P. (1966). Similarity versus liking as determinants of interpersonal attractiveness. *Psychonomic Science, 5,* 157–158.

Bar-Anan, Y., Wilson, T.D., & Gilbert, D.T. (2009). The feeling of uncertainty intensifies affective reactions. *Emotion, 9,* 123–127.

Behrendt, G., & Tuccillo, L. (2009). *He's just not that into you: The no-excuses truth to understanding guys.* New York, NY: Gallery.

Bem, D.J. (1972). Self-perception theory. In L. Berkowitz (Ed.), *Advances in experimental social psychology* (Vol. 6, pp. 1–62). New York, NY: Academic Press.

Eastwick, P.W., & Finkel, E.J. (2008). The attachment system in fledgling relationships: An activating role for attachment anxiety. *Journal of Personality and Social Psychology, 95,* 628–647.

Gouldner, A.W. (1960). The norm of reciprocity: A preliminary statement. *American Sociological Review, 25,* 161–178.

Kenny, D.A. (1994). *Interpersonal perception.* New York, NY: Guilford Press.

Kurtz, J.L., Wilson, T.D., & Gilbert, D.T. (2007). Quantity versus uncertainty: When winning one gift is better than winning two. *Journal of Experimental Social Psychology, 43,* 979–985.

Lee, Y., & Qiu, C. (2009). When uncertainty brings pleasure: The role of prospect imageability and mental imagery. *Journal of Consumer Research, 36,* 624–633.

Luo, S., & Zhang, G. (2009). What leads to romantic attraction: Similarity, reciprocity, security, or beauty? Evidence from a speed-dating study. *Journal of Personality, 77,* 933–964.

Montoya, R.M., & Insko, C.A. (2008). Toward a more complete understanding of the reciprocity of liking effect. *European Journal of Social Psychology, 38,* 477–498.

Norton, M.I., Frost, J.H., & Ariely, D. (2007). Less is more: The lure of ambiguity, or why familiarity breeds contempt. *Journal of Personality and Social Psychology, 92,* 97–105.

Shrout, P.E., & Bolger, N. (2002). Mediation in experimental and nonexperimental studies: New procedures and recommendations. *Psychological Methods, 7,* 422–445.

Walster, E., Walster, W., Piliavin, J., & Schmidt, L. (1973). "Playing hard to get": Understanding an elusive phenomenon. *Journal of Personality and Social Psychology, 26,* 113–121.

Wilson, T.D., Centerbar, D.B., Kermer, D.A., & Gilbert, D.T. (2005). The pleasures of uncertainty: Prolonging positive moods in ways people do not anticipate. *Journal of Personality and Social Psychology, 88,* 5–21.

Wilson, T.D., & Gilbert, D.T. (2008). Explaining away: A model of affective adaptation. *Perspectives on Psychological Science, 3,* 370–386.

Comprehension, Structure, and Organization

1. Summarize the contrastive explanations given in paragraphs 1–3; include the topic or main idea in each paragraph.
2. a. In the Introduction, how do the authors justify their study?
   b. Paraphrase the authors' hypothesis (prediction).
3. In a short paragraph, summarize the results shown in Table 1 (you can also use the information in the text of the Results section).

Critical Thinking

1. Referring to the Discussion section, to what extent does this study confirm the results of previous experiments? What unique findings does this study contribute to the subject of attraction?
2. Does the mention of limitations of the study (par. 22) weaken or strengthen its results? Explain.
3. Referring to one of the gaps or limitations of the current study, come up with a hypothesis that could be used in a future study in this subject area.

PART 3
HANDBOOK

CHAPTER 11

Grammar Fundamentals

In the academic world, as in the professional world, good grammar is a given. The benefits of good grammar are twofold: for the writer, grammar and punctuation rules help make your writing clearer and communication with your audience easier. Academic and professional readers expect to read grammatical, well-punctuated prose. Even if they can't always explain *why* a sentence is wrong, they may still need to stop and reread an ungrammatical sentence. If they do this too often, they may give up reading or begin to question your content. By contrast, grammatical writing enhances your credibility.

In addition, becoming more conscious of grammatical writing will help make you a better writer by focusing your attention on words, phrases, and sentences—in other words, on the building blocks of prose. People don't read in paragraphs; they read by processing words, phrases, and sentences first. Focusing on grammar and other sentence-level concerns can help you communicate your intended meaning to your intended audience.

EXERCISE 11.1 Grammar Preview

Most of the following sentences contain a grammatical or punctuation error. Identify and/or explain the errors. Then write out the complete paragraph. The answers can be found on p. 435.

1. Obsession over one's weight is a common practice in todays society.
2. The desire to be thin and the need to possess the perfect body overshadows everything else.
3. Advertisements that feature skinny models help fuel this desire; promoting unhealthy expectations for young women.
4. Expectations that can't be met by the average woman, who weighs 140 pounds.
5. By contrast, the average model weighs less than 120 pounds, and is almost 6 feet tall.
6. Body consciousness begins early, it can even be seen in young girls following exposure to Barbie dolls.
7. At age 13 50 per cent of girls exposed to Barbie dolls don't like the way they look.
8. Increasing by age 18 to more than 80 per cent.
9. If we change our cultural ideals, young girls will begin to see themselves as "normal."
10. With a positive self-image, young women will be better able to succeed socially, academically, and in their chosen vocation.

◎ The Parts of Speech and Their Functions

In the following sections, we introduce the parts of speech and their functions. We then turn to the larger units in a sentence—phrases and clauses—before discussing sentence errors.

The parts of speech can be compared to members of an organization. Each has both a "job title" and a "job description." They are called by their name (title), but what they do (job description) in the organization (sentence) helps determine the organization's success (i.e., whether it is a grammatical sentence).

Here, then, is the profile of the sentence with its seven principal members. Examples and hints for identifying the parts of speech are given.

The Take-Charge Nouns

Nouns name people, places, things, qualities, or conditions. A proper noun begins with a capital letter; a common noun does not. You can often identify common nouns, like the singular common noun *singer*, by the fact you can put an article (*a, an, the*) in front of them: *a/the singer*.

NOUNS name people, places, things, qualities, or conditions.

What Nouns Do

1. Subject of Verb

A noun acts as a **subject** of the verb if it performs the verb's action. (We speak of subjects performing the action of a verb, but many verbs convey a state or condition rather than an action.) See "The Busy Verbs," below. The noun subject is italicized and the verb is underlined below:

> *Lady Gaga*, a world renowned singer, sometimes <u>consults</u> astrologers.

Hint: A subject usually precedes a verb. (See p. 411 for exceptions.)

The **SUBJECT** performs the verb's action.

2. Object of Verb

A noun acts as an **object** of the verb (direct object) if it receives the verb's action. The noun object is italicized and the verb is underlined below:

> Lady Gaga, a world renowned singer, sometimes <u>consults</u> *astrologers*.

Hint: An object usually follows a verb.

The **OBJECT** receives the verb's action.

3. Object of Preposition

A noun can act as an **object of a preposition** (indirect object). The indirect object is italicized and the preposition is underlined below:

> Lady Gaga, a world renowned singer, sometimes consults astrologers <u>before</u> a *tour*.

Hint: An indirect object may follow the direct object, if there is one, and is usually preceded by a preposition.

The **OBJECT OF A PREPOSITION** is the indirect object of the verb.

4. Appositive

A noun can act as an **appositive**, naming or rephrasing a preceding noun or noun phrase. The appositive is italicized and the preceding noun is underlined below:

> <u>Lady Gaga</u>, *a world renowned singer*, sometimes consults astrologers.

Hint: An appositive follows a noun or noun phrase.

An **APPOSITIVE** names or rephrases a preceding noun or noun phrase.

5. Subject Complement

A noun acts as a **subject complement** if it completes the subject after a linking verb. The subject complement is italicized and the linking verb is underlined below:

> Lady Gaga <u>is</u> a world renowned *singer*.

A **SUBJECT COMPLEMENT** completes the subject after a linking verb.

Hint: Look for subject complements—nouns or adjectives—after verbs like *is*, *are*, *was*, and *were*.

In the examples below, the noun subject is bolded, the object is italicized, the object of a preposition is underlined, the appositive is in caps, and the subjective complement is bolded and italicized.

> The overly eager **student** in the front <u>row</u> always raises his *hand* unnecessarily.

> **Montréal**, the CAPITAL OF QUEBEC, was once the largest *city* in <u>Canada</u>, but **Toronto** now has 1.7 million more *people*.

The Understudy Pronouns

The pronoun usually takes the place of a noun (called the antecedent) in a sentence.

Personal pronouns refer to people and sometimes animals (e.g., *I*, *you*, *he*, *she*, *we*, *they*) or things, places, etc. (e.g., *it*, *they*). In the possessive case, they can function as adjectives (see "The Informative Adjectives," below). The pronouns are bolded and the antecedents are italicized below:

> *Beth* trained in *yoga* for three months, but **she** gave **it** up to pursue a martial arts diploma.

Relative pronouns relate what follows to a preceding noun or pronoun (antecedent); the complete grammatical unit, including the relative pronoun and what follows (which will be at least a verb), is called a relative clause, a type of dependent clause (see p. 381). Relative pronouns include *who*, *which*, *that*, *whose*, and a few others. The relative clause is italicized, the relative pronoun is bolded, and the antecedent is underlined below:

> The "Now Hiring" <u>sign</u> ***that*** *appeared at 8 am* was taken down by 8:30.

Interrogative pronouns introduce questions and include *how*, *what*, *which*, *when*, *why*, *who*, *whose*, and *where*. Interrogative pronouns are italicized below:

> *Whose* turn it is to cook dinner tonight? *When* will it be ready?

Demonstrative pronouns (*this*, *that*, *these*, *those*) point to nouns; they can function as adjectives when they precede nouns. Demonstrative pronouns are italicized below:

> *This* is the easiest path to take to get us home. *That* path will get us lost.

Nouns, which name people, places, and things, can act as subjects, objects (of verbs and prepositions), appositives, and subject complements.

Most **PRONOUNS** replace nouns. Personal pronouns refer to people, places, and things. Relative pronouns refer back to a previous noun/pronoun. Interrogative pronouns introduce questions. Indefinite pronouns refer to non-specified groups. Other pronouns include demonstrative, intensive, reflexive, and reciprocal.

PERSONAL PRONOUNS refer to people and sometimes animals, things, or places.

RELATIVE PRONOUNS relate what follows to a preceding noun or pronoun.

INTERROGATIVE PRONOUNS introduce questions.

DEMONSTRATIVE PRONOUNS point to nouns.

INDEFINITE PRONOUNS
refer to non-specified
individuals or groups.

Indefinite pronouns refer to non-specified individuals or groups. Most indefinite pronouns are singular and do not have antecedents; in fact, they may act as antecedents for personal pronouns.

Common singular indefinite pronouns include words ending in -one, -body, and -thing, such as *everyone, anybody*, and *something*, along with *each, either, much, neither, none, nothing*, and *one*.

The indefinite pronoun is italicized, the personal pronouns underlined below:

If *anyone* saw any suspicious activity, he or she should contact the supervisor.

For agreement problems involving indefinite pronouns, see pp. 416–17.

Intensive, reflexive, and *reciprocal* pronouns are other kinds of pronouns, showing different kinds of relationships with their noun/pronoun antecedent.

I *myself* met the visitor's plane. [Intensive pronoun, emphasizes subject, *I*]

I embarrassed *myself* when I forgot the visitor's name. [Reflexive pronoun, names receiver of action, which is the same as the doer of the action, *I*]

The visitor and I looked at *each other* a few seconds before laughing. [Reciprocal pronoun, refers to separate parts of a plural antecedent—*visitor and I*. Use *one another* if the antecedent refers to more than two.]

What Pronouns Do

Most pronouns have the same jobs as nouns in the sentence (see "The Take-Charge Nouns," pp. 367–69 above). In this example, the pronoun subjects are bolded, the object of the verb (direct object) is italicized, the object of the preposition (indirect object) is underlined, and the possessive form of the personal pronoun is in caps:

He promised to leave after her so that **he** could follow *her* in HIS car.

The Busy Verbs

The **VERB** conveys (1) an
action or (2) state of being,
or (3) combines with a main
verb to express conditions
like possibility or a complex
temporal (time-related)
action.

The verb conveys (1) an action or (2) state of being, or (3) combines with a main verb to express conditions like possibility or a complex temporal (time-related) action.

A subject noun or pronoun paired with a verb makes up the basic form for a sentence. If a "sentence" lacks either a subject noun/pronoun or a verb that shows what the subject is doing (its action) or the state of the subject, it could be an incomplete sentence. (See "Sentence Fragments: Errors of Incompletion," p. 383.)

What Verbs Do

1. Action Verb

An action verb conveys an action (physical: e.g., *jumps*, *smiles*, *takes*—or mental/emotional: e.g., *thinks*, *expects*, *hopes*). An action verb can be followed by an object (direct or indirect) or be modified by adverbs (see "The Versatile Adverbs," p. 374). The verb is italicized, the direct object is bolded, and the adverb modifiers are underlined below:

> The overly eager student in the front row <u>always</u> *raises* his **hand**
> <u>unnecessarily</u>.

An **ACTION VERB** conveys an action.

2. Linking Verb

A linking verb links the subject to the predicate noun/pronoun or adjective that completes the subject (e.g., *be*, *act*, *appear*, *become*, *feel*, *look*, *seem*, along with verbs referring to the senses—*smell*, *sound*, *taste*). Forms of *be* include *am*, *is*, *are*, *was*, *were*, *being*, and *been*. Linking verbs are followed by subject complements, predicate nouns or adjectives, not objects, and they are not modified by adverbs. The linking verbs are italicized, the predicate nouns are bolded, and the predicate adjective is underlined below:

> Freestyle skier Jennifer Heil *became* the top Canadian female **athlete** of
> 2011. She said it *was* an **honour** and *appeared* <u>delighted</u> by the award.

A **LINKING VERB** links the subject to the predicate.

The predicate is the part of the sentence that contains at least a verb that states something about the subject—for example, what it is doing.

Action verbs can be modified by adverbs. Linking verbs are completed by predicate nouns or predicate adjectives.

Most of the verbs listed above can also be used as action verbs, depending on context, but forms of *to be* are always linking verbs.

Hint: Learn the various forms of the verb *to be* so you can recognize a common linking verb.

3. Helping Verb

A helping (auxiliary) verb combines with the main verb (action or linking) to express a condition such as time, necessity, probability, and other relationships. For more about helping verbs and verb tense, see the inside back cover of this textbook. Helping verbs are italicized and the main verbs are bolded below:

> She often *will be* **playing** video games when she *should be* **studying**.

A **HELPING (AUXILIARY) VERB** combines with the main verb to express a condition such as time, necessity, probability, and other relationships.

Hint: The helping verb precedes the main verb in a sentence.

Box 11.1 Verb Impersonators

Verbals are formed from complete verbs, but do not act as verbs in a sentence. They are "impersonators" because they can be mistaken for verbs. The *-ing* form of the verb (called the present participle) combines with a helping verb to make a complete verb form. The past participle (*-en*, *-ed*) can also form a verbal:

Complete verb forms: am hoping, is running, will be competing, has eaten

However, *hoping*, *running*, *competing*, and *eaten* when used alone are incomplete verb forms and cannot combine with subjects to make grammatical statements: *I hoping*, *she running*, *they competing*, and *we eaten* don't make sense.

But *-ing* and other incomplete verb forms do have their uses in sentences as nouns, adjectives, and adverbs, as illustrated below.

Participles usually end in *-ing*, *-ed*, *-en*, or *-t* and act as adjectives or adverbs (see "The Informative Adjectives" below). Participles used as adjectives are underlined:

The <u>Running</u> Man is a novel <u>written</u> by Stephen King.

Gerunds end in *-ing* and act as nouns. Gerunds are underlined:

<u>Running</u> in the morning is healthier than <u>drinking</u> coffee.

Infinitives include *to* along with the base verb form and act as nouns, adjectives, or adverbs. A noun infinitive is italicized and an infinitive used as an adverb underlined below:

He hoped *to run* this morning. She drank two cups of coffee <u>to wake up</u>.

Hint: Do not confuse an infinitive with a prepositional phrase beginning with *to*. The infinitive is italicized and the prepositional phrase is underlined below:

She put her coffee in a thermos *to keep* it warm; it was good <u>to the last drop</u>.

Verbals often combine with other words to form phrases, which can act as nouns, adjectives, or adverbs in the sentence. See "Phrases," p. 379.

Incomplete verb forms, or verbals, can be used as nouns, adjectives, and adverbs. They shouldn't be mistaken for complete verb forms.

PARTICIPLES usually end in *-ing*, *-ed*, *-en*, or *-t* and act as adjectives or adverbs.

GERUNDS end in *-ing* and act as nouns.

INFINITIVES include *to* along with the base verb form and act as nouns, adjectives, or adverbs.

The Informative Adjectives

An **adjective** modifies (describes or limits) a noun or pronoun.

What Adjectives Do

1. Modifier

One-word adjectives usually come before the word/phrase they modify.

> Hint: Look for adjectives before nouns/pronouns. Adjectives are italicized and the nouns/pronouns they modify/complete are underlined below:

> The *complex* assignment kept him up all *last* night. [*Assignment* and *night* are nouns.]

> *Almost* everyone in the group has completed the assignment. [*Everyone* is a pronoun.]

Hint: Ask the questions *Which (one)? What kind?* or *How many?* of a noun/pronoun. *What kind of assignment?* A complex assignment; *Which night?* Last night.

2. Subject Completion

Predicate adjectives follow linking verbs, completing the subject.

> Hint: Look after linking verbs to find predicate adjectives.

> The assignment was *complex*. [*Was* is a linking verb.]

3. Adjectival Phrases and Clauses

Phrases and clauses as adjectival modifiers usually follow the word/phrase they modify, though they can also precede them as participial phrases.

> Hint: Look after nouns/pronouns to find most phrasal and clausal adjectival modifiers (See "Phrases and Clauses," p. 379.)

> Adjectival phrase: Posters *of celebrities* adorned the walls.

> Adjectival clause: The posters *that adorned the walls* made the room look tiny.

4. Articles as Adjectives

Articles (*a, an, the*) are considered adjectival as are some pronouns when they precede a noun:

> *the* assignment; *that* circumstance; *their* integrity; *most* children

Nouns can also precede other nouns and act as adjectives (italicized).

> a *human* cannonball, the *school's Christmas* play

ADJECTIVES give information about (modify) nouns or pronouns. They answer questions like *Which (one)?*, *What kind?*, or *How many?* When they are one word, they usually precede nouns, unless they follow linking verbs as predicate adjectives.

The Versatile Adverbs

An **adverb** modifies a verb, an adjective, or another adverb. It can also modify a complete sentence.

Hint: Adverbs tend to be more moveable than adjectives, so the best way to identify them is by asking the questions *How? When? Where? How much?* or *To what degree?*

· Hint: Most (but not all) adverbs end in *-ly*.

ADVERBS give information about verbs, adjectives, and other adverbs. They answer questions like *How?, When?, Where?, How much?,* or *To what degree?*

What Adverbs Do

1. Verb Modifier

Adverbs most often modify verbs. The adverb, answering the question *How?*, is italicized and the verb it modifies is underlined below:

Hockey has <u>changed</u> *greatly* over its 100-year existence.

2. Adjective Modifier

Adverbs often modify adjectives. Below, the italicized adverb modifies the underlined adjective (answers *To what degree?*); the adjective *entertaining* modifies the noun *sport*:

It is still a *very* <u>entertaining</u> sport in spite of these changes.

3. Adverb Modifier

Adverbs can modify other adverbs. Below, the italicized adverb modifies the underlined adverb by answering the question *To what degree?* (The underlined adverb modifies the verb by answering the question *When?*):

It remains watched *more* <u>often</u> by Canadians than any other sport.

4. Sentence Modifier

An adverb can modify a complete sentence. Below, the adverb *however* modifies the sentence. *Today*, an adverb, modifies *believe*, a verb (answers *When?*):

· *However*, <u>some fans today believe fighting undermines the sport's integrity.</u>

Adverbs like *however*, above, can be recruited to act as joiners (see "The Workhorse Conjunctions," p. 375). When they are used to join parts of a sentence, they are punctuated differently than when they act as ordinary adverbs.

The Overlooked Prepositions

A preposition is a small word that often refers to place or time and which is followed by a noun/pronoun object. Thus, prepositions introduce prepositional phrases (see "Phrases," p. 379).

A **PREPOSITION**, which often refers to place or time, joins the noun/pronoun that follows to the rest of the sentence.

What Prepositions Do

Prepositions join the noun/pronoun to the rest of the sentence, helping it modify another part of speech.

Hint: A preposition is usually followed by a noun/pronoun object. The prepositions are italicized, the objects underlined below:

> You will find the game *on top of* the Xbox *beside* the television.

Hint: To help you recognize prepositions, it's a good idea to become familiar with the most common ones (bolded) among those below. Prepositions can be more than one word (e.g., *on top of* in the sentence above).

about	**at**	down	near	over	under
above	**before**	**during**	next (to)	past	until
across	behind	except	**of**	regarding	up
after	below	**for**	off	since	upon
against	beside(s)	**from**	**on**	than	**with**
along	**between**	**in**	onto	**through**	within
among	beyond	inside	opposite	throughout	without
around	**by**	**into**	out	**to**	
as	despite	**like**	outside (of)	toward(s)	

The Workhorse Conjunctions

Like prepositions, conjunctions are joiners. They fulfill all the other joining functions in the sentence.

CONJUNCTIONS join words, phrases, or clauses in a sentence. **COORDINATING CONJUNCTIONS** join *equal* grammatical units.

What Conjunctions Do

1. Coordinating Conjunction

Coordinating conjunctions join *equal* grammatical units, such as noun to noun, verb to verb, and independent clause to independent clause (see "Clauses," p. 381). The coordinating conjunctions are italicized and the words they join are underlined:

> Video games have evolved <u>rapidly</u> *yet* <u>controversially</u>, often resembling horror films in their crude <u>language</u> *and* gory <u>images</u>.

Yet joins two adverbs; *and* joins two nouns.

> <u>Parents try to protect their children from violent content</u>, *but* <u>graphic content seems everywhere.</u>

But joins two independent clauses, or sentence equivalents.

Hint: Memorize the seven coordinating conjunctions, whose first letters spell out FANBOYS: *for, and, nor, but, or, yet, so.*

2. Subordinating Conjunction

Subordinating conjunctions join *unequal* grammatical units, specifically dependent to independent clauses (see "Clauses," p. 381), showing how they are related. The subordinating conjunction is italicized, and the dependent clause is underlined; the remainder of the sentence is the independent clause.

> She was the first in her family to get her degree, *though* <u>she was 68 years old</u>.

Note that the subordinating conjunction introduces the dependent clause and is part of it.

Hint: Although there are too many subordinating conjunctions to memorize, learn to recognize the bolded ones below. (Relative pronouns are also included as they, too, introduce dependent clauses; they are discussed on p. 382.)

after	because	in case	**though**	**where**	who
although	**before**	in order that	**unless**	**whereas**	whoever
as	even though	once	**until**	wherever	whom
as if	ever since	rather than	what	**whether**	whose
as long as	how	**since**	whatever	which	why
as soon as	**if**	so that	**when**	whichever	
as though	if only	**that**	whenever	**while**	

3. Adverbial Conjunction

Adverbial conjunctions are adverbs (see "The Versatile Adverbs," p. 374) used to connect two independent clauses. When an adverb is used this way, a semicolon precedes the adverbial conjunction and a comma follows it. The adverbial conjunction is italicized, and the independent clause it introduces and joins to the first is underlined.

SUBORDINATING CONJUNCTIONS join *unequal* grammatical units.

ADVERBIAL CONJUNCTIONS are adverbs used to connect two independent clauses.

Adverbs have many uses in a sentence; *however*, <u>they must be punctuated with care.</u>

Hint: Since many one-word adverbs and transitional phrases can be used to connect two independent clauses, the best way to identify them is to look at how they are being used. If an independent clause precedes *and* follows the adverb, it is probably an adverbial conjunction and should be preceded by a semicolon. See "Clauses," p. 381 and "2. Semicolon (;)," p. 392.

Here are some adverbial conjunctions and transitional phrases. The bolded are commonly used:

accordingly	hence	meanwhile	still
afterward	**however**	**moreover**	subsequently
also	if not	namely	that is
as a result	**in addition**	**nevertheless**	**then**
besides	**in fact**	next	**therefore**
certainly	in the meantime	**nonetheless**	**thus**
consequently	indeed	on the contrary	undoubtedly
finally	instead	on the other hand	
for example	later	otherwise	
further(more)	likewise	similarly	

4. Correlative Conjunction

Correlative conjunctions are paired conjunctions (e.g., *either . . . or*, *neither . . . nor*, *both . . . and*, *not only . . . but also*). See p. 430.

> **CORRELATIVE CONJUNCTIONS** are paired conjunctions.

EXERCISE 11.2

Identify the parts of speech (noun, pronoun, verb, adjective, adverb, preposition, conjunction) in the following sentences. A sample sentence has been done for you.

Hint: (1) separate the subject from the predicate; (2) identify nouns/pronouns and verbs; (3) look to see if these words are modified by adjectives or adverbs; (4) identify joiners (prepositions and conjunctions). Not all the sentences contain all seven parts of speech.

Researchers once thought that chocolate had little nutritional value.

1. Researchers |once thought that chocolate |had little nutritional value.
2. Nouns: *researchers, chocolate*; verbs: *thought, had*
3. Adjective: *nutritional*; adverbs: *once, little*
4. Joiner (conjunction): *that*

(continued)

1. The judge announced her decision yesterday.
2. Hockey is certainly a very aggressive sport.
3. The puppies romped happily under the mother's watchful eye.
4. Most people in North America now access their news on the Internet.
5. They attended the rally during class time after the professor gave his permission.

◎ Sentences

As we have seen, above, the parts of speech can have various roles within a sentence—from small ones, like prepositions that join a noun/pronoun to the sentence, to larger ones, like adverbial conjunctions that join two "sentences" (independent clauses). We now turn to the sentence itself and to units larger than single words. These are the phrases and clauses that make up sentences.

What Is a Sentence?

A **SENTENCE** can be defined grammatically as a group of words that contains a subject and a predicate and that needs nothing else to complete it.

A sentence expresses a completed idea, or thought. On the other hand, an incomplete sentence, or sentence fragment, *sounds* incomplete. However, sound is not the best way to identify a fragment. A sentence can be defined grammatically as a group of words that contains a subject and a predicate and that needs nothing else to complete it.

Subject

The subject of a simple sentence is the noun or pronoun that states who or what is acting: the actor. Most, but not all, subjects precede the verb. A simple subject consists only of the main noun/pronoun. A complete subject contains not only the main noun/pronoun but also any modifiers of that word.

A **SIMPLE SUBJECT** consists only of the main noun/pronoun. A **COMPLETE SUBJECT** contains not only the main noun/pronoun but also any modifiers of that word.

The *moon* shines brightly.

The simple subject is *moon*.

The subject of a simple sentence is the noun or pronoun that states who or what is acting. The **PREDICATE** tells you what the subject is doing or shows you the state or condition of the subject.

The full moon seen through the telescope was extremely bright.

The complete subject is *The full moon seen through the telescope*.

Predicate

The predicate tells you what the subject is doing or shows you the state or condition of the subject. A **simple predicate** consists only of the main verb; a **complete predicate** includes other words, such as modifiers, direct or indirect objects, and the like.

In the first example under "Subject," above, the complete predicate tells you that the moon *shines brightly* (an action). In the second example, the complete predicate tells you that the moon *was extremely bright* (a state).

In an imperative sentence, the subject is *you*. Although it may not actually be in the sentence, it is understood to be there acting as the subject.

> Shine! = (You) shine!

An imperative sentence issues an order or direction and is a complete sentence—other grammatical sentences must have at least two words. (For more on incomplete sentences, or sentence fragments, see p. 383.)

Phrases and Clauses

Phrases and clauses are grammatical units that are larger than single words. One type of clause, an independent clause, is equivalent to a complete sentence. Phrases and clauses have various functions in the sentence.

Phrases

A phrase is a group of two or more words that lacks a subject and a predicate. Among the functions of phrases *within* sentences, they could act as a subject or a predicate in a complete sentence or could modify a noun or verb.

1. Prepositional Phrases

A prepositional phrase begins with a preposition and can act adjectivally (as an adjective modifying a noun/pronoun) or adverbially (as an adverb modifying a verb In the sentence below, the line separates subject from predicate. Prepositional phrases are italicized below, and arrows show the words they modify:

| A clerk ◄—— *with a jovial smile* | I directed me | *to the second room* ◄—— *on the right.* |
| Noun   adjectival phrase | verb | adverbial phrase   adjectival phrase |

In the sentence above, *A clerk with a jovial smile* is a noun phrase, the subject of the sentence.

> A clerk with a jovial smile = complete subject, noun
>
> *clerk* = simple subject, noun
>
> *with a jovial smile* = prepositional phrase, adjective modifies *clerk*, noun
>
> *with* = preposition, introduces phrase
>
> *jovial* = adjective, modifies *smile*, noun
>
> *smile* = object of preposition, *with*

Sidebar:

An **IMPERATIVE SENTENCE** issues an order or direction and is a complete sentences even if it consists of only one word, a verb.

Make sure that the subject of a clause makes sense with the verb. In the following sentence, the verb, *believes*, shouldn't be used with the non-animate subject, *justice system*.

Mismatched subject–verb: The *Canadian justice system believes* citizens should be accountable for our actions.

Matching subject–verb: A basic principle of the Canadian justice system is that *citizens should be accountable* for their actions.

A **PHRASE** is a group of two or more words that lacks a subject and a predicate.

A **PREPOSITIONAL PHRASE** begins with a preposition and can act adjectivally or adverbially.

A verb phrase consists of a main verb and any helping verbs:

> It *has been raining* hard since Tuesday.

Has been is a helping verb form; *raining* is the present participle of the verb *rain*, the main verb.

Verbals (see above, p. 372) can combine with other words, such as objects or modifiers, to function as adjectives, nouns, and adverbs in a sentence. There are three types of verbal phrases.

Verbals (see above, p. 372)

2. Participle (Adjective) Phrases

Participle phrases are formed from present (*-ing*) or past (*-ed, -en, -t*) participles of verbs. As adjectives, they modify nouns or pronouns. The participial phrases are italicized and the pronouns are underlined below:

> *Satiated after a full meal*, <u>he</u> yawned and fell asleep. *Dreaming of more
> food*, <u>he</u> awoke suddenly.

When you use a participial phrase, make sure that the noun/pronoun that it is intended to modify is in the sentence.

> **Dangling modifier error:** Satiated after a full meal, sleep suddenly arrived.

Satiated after a full meal mistakenly modifies the noun *sleep*, making it appear that sleep was satiated. (To fix this kind of error, see p. 427, "Dangling Modifiers.")

(To fix this kind of error, see p. 427, "Dangling Modifiers.")

3. Gerund (Noun) Phrases

Gerund (noun) phrases are formed from present (*-ing*) participles of verbs and function as nouns; for example, as subjects or objects. While other nouns are modified by adjectives, adverbs can form part of a gerund phrase. The gerund (noun) is italicized and the gerund phrase subject is underlined below:

> <u>*Jogging* briskly</u> was part of her daily routine.

Jogging briskly is the complete subject; *briskly* is an adverb modifying the gerund (answers the question *how?*).

4. Infinitive (Noun, Adjective, or Adverb) Phrases

Infinitive phrases are formed by putting *to* before the base verb form. The infinitive phrase is italicized below:

> She planned *to lose weight*.

To lose weight acts as the noun object of the verb *planned*. (Like most objects, it follows the verb.)

A VERB PHRASE consists of a main verb and any helping verbs.

PARTICIPLE PHRASES are formed from present or past participles of verbs.

GERUND (NOUN) PHRASES are formed from present participles of verbs and function as nouns.

INFINITIVES include *to* along with the base verb form and act as nouns, adjectives, or adverbs.

EXERCISE 11.3

Identify the underlined words as prepositional, noun, verb, or verbal (participial, gerund, infinitive) phrases. If applicable, identify the word(s) they modify or their function. A sample sentence has been done for you.

<u>The death penalty</u>	<u>exists today</u>	<u>in 58 countries</u>	<u>across the globe.</u>
noun phrase (subject)		prep. phrase (adverbial, modifies verb *exists*)	prep. phrase (adjectival, modifies noun *countries*)

1. <u>Reintroduced in 1976</u>, the death penalty remains hotly debated <u>in the US.</u>
2. Approximately 3,000 inmates currently reside <u>on death row.</u>
3. Most countries, however, <u>have abolished</u> the death penalty.
4. <u>Having murderers pay for crimes with their own lives</u> is considered barbaric by many people.
5. At this time, Canada has no plans <u>to bring back</u> capital punishment.

Clauses

A clause is a group of words that, unlike a phrase, contains a subject and a predicate. An independent clause can stand on its own as a complete sentence and needs no other words to complete it; although a dependent clause contains a subject and a predicate, it cannot stand on its own as it does not express a complete thought.

What is the main idea in the following sentence?

> Although an eighteenth-century novel was on the course, it had fewer than 300 pages.

> *Although an eighteenth-century novel was on the course*? Or, *It had fewer than 300 pages*?

Answer: *It had fewer than 300 pages* expresses a complete thought, though it is shorter than the word group that precedes it.

> A clause is a group of words that contains a subject and a predicate. An **INDEPENDENT CLAUSE** is equivalent to a complete sentence. A **DEPENDENT CLAUSE** contains a subject and a predicate but does not express a complete thought.

The point is that the sentence is grammatically complete with a subject (the pronoun *it* and a main verb, *had*). On the other hand, *Although an eighteenth-century novel was on the course* hints at an upcoming contrast. But more information is needed—specifically, the second part of the contrast. In fact, you could write several endings to a sentence that began this way:

Although an eighteenth-century novel was on the course, I decided not to take it.

. . . , four twentieth-century novels were on it too.

. . . , it had fewer than 300 pages.

An independent clause, such as *it had fewer than 300 pages*, can stand alone or complete a sentence that begins (or ends) with a dependent clause.

A dependent clause indicates a specific relationship with the independent clause. The subordinating conjunction *although*, in the example above, begins the dependent clause and shows a contrastive relationship with the independent clause or main idea.

Another kind of dependent clause begins with a relative pronoun (see p. 369) rather than a subordinating conjunction. A relative clause, which usually begins with *that*, *which*, *who*, *whom*, or *whose*, follows a noun/pronoun and modifies it. The relative pronoun is bolded, the relative (dependent) clause is underlined, and the noun that the clause modifies is in caps below:

VIRGINIA WOOLF, **who** wrote *Mrs Dalloway*, is a twentieth-century writer on the course.

The NOVEL, **which** recalls the memories of a middle-aged woman, explores societal ills in post-World War I England.

In the two examples, above, a dependent clause interrupts the independent clause.

A **RELATIVE CLAUSE** follows a noun or pronoun and modifies it.

See p. 376 for a list of common subordinating conjunctions.

EXERCISE 11.4

Underline independent clauses, put parentheses around dependent clauses, and circle the subordinating conjunction or relative pronoun. A sample sentence has been done for you.

The end of the transatlantic slave trade came in 1807 ((when) importing slaves was finally banned in the US).

1. While drug testing has become more common, athletes are still taking drugs.
2. The battle against cancer will continue until a cure is found.
3. When Nelson Mandela became South Africa's president, a more democratic era began.

(continued)

4. The game "Baggataway," which was played by many Aboriginal tribes, intrigued British colonizers.

5. Although 8,000 women belong to the Canadian Armed Forces today, only a few are members of the combat force.

Sentence Fragments: Errors of Incompletion

The two definitions of the sentence given below can be used to ensure that you always write in complete sentences and do not use incomplete sentences, or sentence fragments, in formal writing.

1. A sentence is a group of words that includes a subject and a predicate and that needs nothing else to complete it.

2. A sentence is a group of words that expresses a complete thought.

Sentence fragments fail to satisfy these two requirements. They either (1) lack a subject or a predicate or both subject and predicate, or (2) consist of a dependent clause by itself without an independent clause. Consequently, they do not express a complete thought.

Fragment Type 1: Lacks Subject, Predicate, or Both
Example 1
A noun subject by itself is an example of a fragment, whether it is a simple subject or a complete one with added detail.

> The moon.

> The full moon.

> The full moon whose beams glittered eerily on the still lake.

To make any of these word groups into a complete sentence, you would need to add a verb so that the moon is doing something or a state about the moon is revealed. The subject is italicized and the predicate (verb) is underlined in the examples below. A line separates simple subject from simple predicate.

> The *moon* | <u>rose</u>. [action]

> The full *moon* | <u>looked</u> within reaching distance. [state]

> The full *moon* whose beams glittered eerily on the still lake | <u>recalled</u> a long-forgotten memory. [action]

> A **SENTENCE FRAGMENT** is a phrase or clause that lacks a subject, a predicate, or both.

> You can use these two definitions of a sentence to help avoid incomplete sentences, or sentence fragments:
> 1. A sentence is a group of words that includes a subject and a predicate and that needs nothing else to complete it.
> 2. A sentence is a group of words that expresses a complete thought.

Note that in the last example there is a verb connected to the subject *moon* while in the original version, the verb *glittered* described (modified) *beams*, not *moon*.

All the sentences are now complete as they have a subject *and* a predicate; they also express a complete thought.

Example 2

A sentence must include both a subject and a *predicate that consists of a complete verb form.*

> I experienced an odd desire. Looking at the full moon.

Looking is an incomplete verb form. What follows *desire*, then, is a fragment. To turn it into a complete sentence, you would need to add a helping verb plus a subject.

> I experienced an odd desire. *I was looking* at the full moon at the time.

More efficiently, add the phrase *looking at the full moon* to the previous sentence:

> I experienced an odd desire as I was looking at the full moon.
>
> OR
>
> Looking at the full moon, I experienced an odd desire.

Example 3

A noun in a group of words doesn't always indicate that a subject is present.

> At a *position* near the *Ocean* of *Storms* on the *surface* of the *moon.*

Although there are five nouns (italicized) here, they are all preceded by prepositions (underlined) and are objects of prepositions, not subjects. A subject and a predicate need to be added to make this a grammatical sentence.

> *I was looking* at a position near the Ocean of Storms on the surface of the moon.

> At a position near the Ocean of Storms on the surface of the moon *was a gigantic crater.*

Fragment Type 2: Dependent Clause Fragment

This kind of fragment contains a subject and predicate but does not express a complete thought. It begins with a subordinating conjunction or relative pronoun. In the first sentence below, the subordinating conjunction is italicized; in the second sentence, the relative pronoun is italicized.

> Looking at the full moon, I experienced an odd desire. *As* a howl came to my lips.

> Looking at the full moon, I experienced an odd desire. *Which* found expression as a howl.

To fix dependent clause fragments, simply join the dependent clauses, which give less important information, to the independent clauses, which express the main idea.

> Looking at the full moon, I experienced an odd desire as a howl came to my lips.

> Looking at the full moon, I experienced an odd desire, which found expression as a howl.

A dependent clause fragment contains a subject and predicate but does not express a complete thought. It begins with a subordinating conjunction or relative pronoun and needs to be completed by an independent clause.

EXERCISE 11.5

Turn the sentence fragments below into grammatical sentences that contain a subject and a predicate, and express a complete thought. A sample sentence has been done for you.

> Being careful not to write a sentence fragment.
>
> I am being careful not to write a sentence fragment.
>
> OR
>
> Being careful not to write a sentence fragment can make you a better writer.

1. Although a sewage plant would fix the city's waste problem.
2. A novel about a boy who loses his parents to a disaster at sea.
3. The goalie lost his stick in the mad scramble. Which led to the winning goal.
4. Many people today are obsessed with the Internet. Whether they connect with friends on Facebook or watch videos on YouTube.
5. The relationship between adolescent boys and girls affects nearly everything in their lives. From clothing choices to self-esteem.

Errors of Joining

Incorrectly joined sentences, like incomplete sentences, are difficult to read. The rules for using commas, semicolons, and colons in Chapter 12 (pp. 391–402) will familiarize you with methods for connecting your sentences. This section focuses on two errors in sentence combining, the run-on sentence (or "fused sentence"), and the comma splice (or "comma fault").

Run-On Sentences

In a run-on sentence, the writer follows the first sentence (independent clause) with the second sentence (independent clause) without any punctuation in between. It is left up to the reader to figure out where the first ends and the second begins.

> Macs come with iPhoto, Photobooth, and iMovie these add-ons are useful to today's consumer.

The simplest way to fix a run-on sentence is to put a period after the first independent clause and follow with the second independent clause as a new sentence.

> Macs come with iPhoto, Photobooth, and iMovie. These add-ons are useful to today's consumer.

However, you can also join independent clauses by using a coordinating conjunction preceded by a comma or, in some cases, by using a semicolon:

> Macs come with iPhoto, Photobooth, and iMovie, and these add-ons are useful to today's consumer.

> Macs come with iPhoto, Photobooth, and iMovie; these add-ons are useful to today's consumer.

Comma Splices

Commas are used in various ways *within* sentences, rather than to join two complete sentences. However, as you will see, *a comma + a coordinating conjunction can be used to join two sentences* (independent clauses). Learning to identify independent clauses will make it easier to avoid comma splices.

How many independent clauses do the following sentences contain?

1. Having tried to shut down his computer for several minutes, the frustrated student finally had to resort to unplugging the power source.
2. The frustrated student tried to shut down his computer for several minutes, he finally had to resort to unplugging the power source.

Sidebar notes:

In a run-on sentence, the writer follows the first sentence (independent clause) with the second sentence (independent clause) without any punctuation in between.

The coordinating conjunctions are *for, and, nor, but, or, yet, so* (FANBOYS).

A comma splice is the incorrect use of a comma alone to join two independent clauses.

Answer: Sentence (1) contains one independent clause, or subject–verb unit: *the frustrated student finally had to resort to unplugging the power source.* There is no subject or complete verb form in the preceding word group, a participial phrase. Sentence (2) contains two independent clauses, or subject–verb units, which are incorrectly joined by only a comma. The subject of the first is *the frustrated student;* the subject of the sentence is *he.*

As is the case with run-on sentences, above, the simplest way to fix a comma splice is to make the two independent clauses into simple sentences:

The frustrated student tried to shut down his computer for several *minutes.* *He* finally had to resort to unplugging the power source.

However, a coordinating conjunction preceded by a comma would probably be better in this case because "but" clarifies the link between the clauses:

The frustrated student tried to shut down his computer for several *minutes,* *but* he finally had to resort to unplugging the power source.

See Chapter 12, "Joining Independent Clauses" (p. 391) for other ways to fix the problem.

Hint: Many comma splices occur when the second independent clause ("sentence") begins with a pronoun, such as *he, she, it,* or *they.* Pronouns often look less important than nouns, but both nouns and pronouns can act as grammatical subjects.

EXERCISE 11.6

Identify the sentence error (fragment, run-on sentence, or comma splice). Correct it by adding punctuation if it is an error of joining; if it is a fragment, add information to turn it into a grammatical sentence. A sample sentence has been done for you.

Multiculturalism connects youth with one another, it provides them with a meeting place, a common ground. [comma splice]

Multiculturalism connects youth with one another. It provides them with a meeting place, a common ground.

Multiculturalism connects youth with one another, for it provides them with a meeting place, a common ground.

(continued)

1. Massive Multiplayer Online Role-Playing Games (MMORPGs) are the last frontier in escape gaming they literally take you into another world.
2. Women from Afghanistan who share the Muslim religion.
3. We can no longer turn our backs to what is happening in the north, it is time to take action.
4. Modern technology has resulted in astonishing benefits for our communities. Though it has created many new problems as well.
5. It has been more than 40 years since the last pandemic, another one is clearly overdue.

EXERCISE 11.7

Correct any fragments, run-on sentences, and comma splices in the following paragraph (all these errors may not be present).

The life of Aboriginals in Canada has undergone many disruptions. Since the arrival of Europeans in the early 1400s. The introduction of guns greatly affected their lifestyle, it also affected their trades with Europeans. Along with this new lifestyle came diseases and alcohol, these brought on problems that were unknown before the arrival of Europeans. In 1869, John Wesley Powell introduced the concept of "reservations." Which he intended to serve as a "school of industry and a home for [those] unfortunate people." This concept was designed to assimilate the Natives of Canada. Teaching them English and the values of White society.

◎ Chapter 11 Review Questions

1. What are the benefits of learning correct grammar and punctuation?
2. a. Name the seven parts of speech.
   b. Briefly explain one way that can help you identify
      i. A noun acting as a subject
      ii. A noun acting as an object of a verb
      iii. A noun acting as an object of a preposition
3. Most pronouns replace _____. The class of pronoun that refers to people and things is called a _____ pronoun; the class of pronoun that refers to non-specified individuals or groups is called an _____ pronoun.
4. Answer true or false:

a. *Has eaten* is an example of a complete verb form.

b. A verbal is one kind of complete verb form.

c. A verbal can act as a noun in a sentence.

5. Summarize the grammatical functions of adverbs and adjectives.

6. Which of the following words is *not* a conjunction?

a. because

b. when

c. and

d. between

7. Give two definitions of a sentence and explain which is more useful for a student of grammar.

8. Explain the difference between

a. A phrase and a clause

b. An independent and a dependent clause

9. Identify two kinds of fragments and make up sentence fragments that illustrate the two kinds; then turn the fragments into complete sentences.

10. a. Define a run-on sentence and illustrate by making one up; turn it into a complete, correctly punctuated sentence or two sentences.

b. Define a comma splice and illustrate by making one up; turn it into a complete, correctly punctuated sentence or two sentences.

◎ Key Terms

action verb (p. 371)

adjective (p. 373)

adverb (p. 374)

adverbial conjunction (p. 376)

appositive (p. 368)

complete predicate (p. 378)

complete subject (p. 378)

conjunction (p. 375)

correlative conjunction (p. 377)

coordinating conjunction (p. 375)

demonstrative pronoun (p. 369)

dependent clause (p. 381)

gerund (p. 372)

gerund (noun) phrase (p. 380)

helping (auxiliary) verb (p. 371)

imperative sentence (p. 379)

indefinite pronoun (p. 370)

independent clause (p. 381)

infinitive (p. 372)

infinitive (noun, adjective, adverb) phrases (p. 380)

interrogative pronoun (p. 369)

linking verb (p. 371)

noun (p. 367)

object (p. 368)

object of a preposition (p. 368)

participle (p. 372)

participle (adjective) phrase (p. 380)

personal pronoun (p. 369)

phrase (p. 379)

predicate (p. 378)

preposition (p. 375)

prepositional phrase (p. 379)

Punctuation and Apostrophes

In this chapter, you will learn:

◎ How to use correct punctuation to join two ideas (independent clauses)

◎ How to use commas, semicolons, and colons correctly with a series

◎ How to use commas after an introductory word, phrase or clause when an independent clause follows

◎ How to use commas with parenthetical (non-essential) information

◎ How to use correct punctuation with quotations

◎ How to use commas with adjectives, dates, addresses, and numbers

◎ How to use apostrophes to indicate relationships like possession and to show letters left out in contractions

The choice of using a comma, semicolon, or colon may depend on whether you are writing informally, for example, for a student newspaper or a blog, or formally, for your English instructor or an admissions committee.

The rules below apply especially to formal writing, but they are applicable to almost all kinds of writing. For clearer understanding, we will deal with the rules for joining complete sentences before discussing the rules for separating elements within a sentence. Punctuation rules are summarized on p. 402.

◎ Joining Independent Clauses

Independent clauses are the equivalent of simple sentences: they contain a subject–predicate unit. When two simple sentences are grammatically joined, they produce a compound sentence.

A **SIMPLE SENTENCE** is equivalent to an independent clause.
A **COMPOUND SENTENCE** consists of two independent clauses joined by a comma and coordinating conjunction, a semicolon, or a colon.

1. Comma + Coordinating Conjunction (cc)

To create a compound sentence from two independent clauses or simple sentences, you can use a coordinating conjunction to join the independent clauses, making sure you precede the joining word by a comma:

> **Simple sentence A:** The first smartphone, made by IBM, was known as Simon.

> **Simple sentence B:** It was demonstrated at a computer industry trade show in 1992.

Sentences joined by a coordinating conjunction preceded by comma: A, cc B

> The first smartphone, made by IBM, was known as Simon, *and* it was demonstrated at a computer industry trade show in 1992.

Do not use a comma before a coordinating conjunction if it is joining only two words or phrases. In the example below, *and* is joining two verbs, *made* and *known*. There is only one independent clause with a compound predicate (that is, two verbs making up the predicate):

> The first smartphone *was made* by IBM and *was known* as Simon.

The coordinating conjunctions are *for, and, nor, but, or, yet,* and *so*; their first letters spell out FANBOYS.

Use a comma with a coordinating conjunction to join two independent clauses, not two nouns, verbs, adjectives, and the like.

2. Semicolon (;)

You may use a semicolon instead of a comma + coordinating conjunction if you want to stress that the ideas in the clauses are closely related. For example, the second clause could expand on the first or add information; it could also express a contrast with the first one: A; B

> The first smartphone, made by IBM, was known as Simon; it was demonstrated at a computer industry trade show in 1992. [adds information]

> Smartphones were originally created to benefit modern businesses; the main use of smartphones today is social interaction. [contrast]

3. Semicolon (;) + Adverbial Conjunction (ac)

Adverbial conjunctions are ordinary adverbs, such as *however, therefore, moreover,* and *thus,* along with transitional phrases, such as *for example, in addition,* and *in fact,* that can join independent clauses. They indicate a specific relationship between the clauses. A comma usually follows the adverbial conjunction: A; ac, B

> Smartphone apps can be created for almost anything; for example, one man created an app that triggered a mini-fridge to shoot a beverage can at the operator.

When these kinds of adverbs occur within clauses, rather than as joiners, they are enclosed by commas (see p. 397). Failing to recognize their two distinct roles in a sentence is responsible for a common writing error.

Hint: If an independent clause precedes *and* follows the adverb, it is probably an adverbial conjunction and needs to be preceded by a semicolon and followed by a comma.

> Use a semicolon to join two independent clauses if you need to use a word other than a coordinating conjunction. Adverbs like *however*, *therefore*, *moreover*, and *thus* are examples of common joiners. *For example*, *in addition*, and *in fact* are common transitional phrases used as joiners. Usually, you should follow the joining word/phrase by a comma. For a list of common adverbial conjunctions and transitional phrases, see p. 377.

4. Colon (:)

A colon can be used to join independent clauses if the second clause (the one after the colon) answers or explains the reason for the statement in the first clause. This rule is not quite the same as the rule for using a semicolon alone to join independent clauses (compare "Semicolon," above): A: B

> A colon can be used to join independent clauses if the second clause answers or explains the reason for the statement in the first clause.

> There appears to be one disadvantage of smartphones: they can create a dependency, or even an addiction, in some users.

EXERCISE 12.1

Consider the rules for joining independent clauses, and decide which would be the best in each instance. Write out the complete sentence and include the most suitable joining word if you do not choose to use only a semicolon or colon (do not use *and* unless it is the only conjunction that makes the sentence make sense). A list of coordinating conjunctions is on p. 392; a list of common conjunctive adverbs is on p. 377. A sample sentence has been done for you.

> The number of single-parent families is increasing.
>
> Many people today believe that a child needs two parents.
>
> **Answer 1:** The number of single-parent families is increasing, but many people today believe that a child needs two parents.
>
> **Answer 2:** The number of single-parent families is increasing; however, many people today believe that a child needs two parents.

(continued)

1. As more air is blown into a balloon, its volume increases. Its surface area also increases.
2. The language of music is universal. People everywhere connect with others through some form of music.
3. Most homeless people who live on the street carry some cash in their pockets. They are more vulnerable to street crime.
4. Global warming and the depletion of our resources are major problems. They are preventable ones.
5. Caffeine affects the central nervous system. Its effects include heightened awareness, decreased reaction time, and improved coordination.

◎ Punctuation within Sentences (Internal Punctuation)

To punctuate within sentences, you will probably use commas most of the time; however, sometimes a semicolon or colon is the best choice or, occasionally, parentheses or dashes. The punctuation rules are discussed under four rule categories below: (1) a series, (2) sentence introductions, (3) non-essential information, and (4) miscellaneous, including adjectives, dates, addresses, and direct quotations.

Items in a Series (three or more items)

Use commas to separate simple items (three or more) in a series whether they are nouns, adjectives, predicates, independent clauses, or other parallel items:

> Studies show that bullying is a learned behaviour in primary, middle, and secondary schools.

Use commas to separate three or more items in a series.

Omission of Comma before and

In informal writing, you can often omit the comma before the coordinating conjunction *and*, (as in the example above). But if the second or third element contains a coordinating conjunction, as in the italicized element in the example below, the comma should be included, even in informal writing:

> Contrary to common belief, the victim of cyberbullying is often competent, *popular, and even admired*, and high-functioning.

Parallel Elements

When you make a list in formal prose, all the elements should be the same part of speech and have the same grammatical function; that way, the elements will be parallel (see p. 429 for more information about parallel structure):

List not parallel: Cyberbullying is relentless, public, and it is usually anonymous. [two adjectives and one independent clause]

List parallel: Cyberbullying is relentless, public, and, usually, anonymous. [three adjectives]

Serial Semicolon

If one or more of the elements in the list contain commas, separate each item by a semicolon rather than a comma.

Bullying is traditionally divided into verbal bullying, marked by taunts, threats, and teasing; physical bullying, such as shoving, pushing, and theft; and relational bullying, involving gossip, excluding, and spreading rumours.

> If one or more of the elements in the list contain commas, separate each item by a semicolon rather than a comma.

Colon to Set Up a List

A colon can set up a list if it follows an independent clause. Do not insert a colon before a list if the thought is incomplete:

Incorrect: Cyberbullying has distinct characteristics from those of traditional bullying including: a distinct set of victims, a different environment, and an enhanced sexual component.

Correct: Cyberbullying has distinct characteristics from those of traditional bullying: a distinct set of victims, a different environment, and an enhanced sexual component.

Also correct: Cyberbullying has distinct characteristics from those of traditional bullying, including the following: a distinct set of victims, a different environment, and an enhanced sexual component.

When you use a colon or a semicolon with a list, your sentence should end after the last item in the list. Do not continue the sentence after the list:

Incorrect: Cyberbullying has distinct characteristics from those of traditional bullying: a distinct set of victims, a different environment, and an enhanced sexual component, and should not be thought of as just another kind of bullying.

Correct: Cyberbullying has distinct characteristics from those of traditional bullying: a distinct set of victims, a different environment, and an enhanced sexual component. It should not be thought of as just another kind of bullying.

Sentence Introductions

An introductory word, phrase, or dependent clause should be separated by a comma from the independent clause that follows. Exceptions can be made for brief introductions, especially referring to time or place (e.g., *On Tuesdays* . . . ; *In Toronto* . . .). However, in formal writing it is a good idea to make a habit of using a comma after an introduction when an independent clause (main idea) follows.

> **One word introduction:** *Ultimately*, students will not reach their full learning potential if the educational system fails to emphasize creativity.

> **Phrasal introduction:** *Through the use of a rigid structure*, the education system tends to stress conformity, not creativity.

> **Dependent clause introduction:** *When curriculum designers choose to stress factual knowledge above everything else*, the freedom to explore options is threatened.

A sentence that includes both an independent clause and a dependent clause is called a complex sentence. For how to punctuate a sentence that begins with an independent clause and ends with a dependent clause, see pp. 398–99.

Non-essential Information

In the process of writing, writers often add detail or emphasis, qualify a point, or suggest a contrast. When this information does not affect the basic meaning of the sentence or clause, it is called non-essential, or parenthetical, information.

Non-essential elements, whether words, phrases, or clauses, are sometimes referred to as parenthetical because, much like the information inside parentheses, they are a word or word group set off from the main or essential part of the sentence.

Separating non-essential from essential information is often important for the reader's understanding: it assists the reading process. Non-essential information can be studied by dividing it into four subcategories: (A) adverbs and transitional phrases that interrupt sentence flow, (B) appositives, (C) adjectival relative clauses, and (D) concluding phrases and clauses.

Sidebar:

An introductory word, phrase, or dependent clause should be separated by a comma from the independent clause that follows.

A **COMPLEX SENTENCE** is made up of an independent and one or more dependent clauses. A **COMPOUND-COMPLEX SENTENCE** contains two independent clauses (the "compound" part) and at least one dependent clauses (the "complex" part).

Example of a compound-complex sentence (the compound part is bolded, the complex part italicized):

When curriculum designers choose to stress factual knowledge above everything else, **the freedom to explore options is threatened, and students may become apathetic about their studies**.

Information that does not affect the basic meaning of the sentence or clause is called **NON-ESSENTIAL**, or **PARENTHETICAL**, **INFORMATION**. Commas are used to separate this information from the more important information.

Use two commas for a non-essential element unless it occurs at the end of the sentence before the period, in which case you will use one comma before the non-essential element.

A. Adverbs and Transitional Phrases

Adverbs and transitional phrases that interrupt sentence flow should be set off by commas in formal writing. These words may emphasize, qualify, or contrast with preceding words.

> **Emphasis:** The act of dropping the gloves is, *undoubtedly*, a sign that a hockey fight is imminent.

> **Qualification:** Not all fans, *however*, are in favour of fighting.

> **Contrast:** Many "enforcers" today fight just for the sake of fighting, *not for passion*, some fans believe.

Adverbs and transitional phrases that interrupt sentence flow should be set off by commas in formal writing.

B. Appositives

Appositives are nouns and noun phrases that are grammatically parallel to preceding nouns or noun phrases. They do not modify the noun, but name or restate it. Thus, they do not contain essential information, and as non-essential elements, they are set off by two commas.

> Last year, Leonard Katz, *acting chairman of the CRTC*, announced that broadcasters could no longer air loud advertising.

An appositive consists of a noun or noun phrase that follows and is parallel to a preceding noun/noun phrase, which it renames. Two commas set off the appositive from the rest of the sentence.

What follows the proper noun *Leonard Katz* names him by giving his position. It can be taken out of the sentence without affecting the main idea; it gives additional information.

Nouns can modify other nouns as adjectives. Be careful not to place two commas around nouns acting as adjectives.

> **Incorrect commas:** Last year, acting chairman of the CRTC, Leonard Katz, announced that broadcasters could no longer air loud advertising.

> **Correct:** Last year, *acting chairman of the CRTC* Leonard Katz announced that broadcasters could no longer air loud advertising.

If you try to take *Leonard Katz* out of the sentence, you can see that it is essential information: *Last year, acting chairman of the CRTC announced that broadcasters could no longer air loud advertising* doesn't make sense. (The only comma in the sentence separates the introductory phrase *Last year* from the rest of the sentence.)

C. Adjectival Clauses

An adjectival (relative) clause modifies the preceding noun/pronoun (see p. 373) and begins with a relative pronoun, such as *who*, *which*, or *that*. Depending on the writer's intent, it can give additional information or essential information and is punctuated accordingly. In the following example, additional (non-essential) information is given in a clause (italicized):

(see p. 373)

> Louis Riel, *who stood up to the Canadian government of John A. Macdonald*, remains a hero to many today.

The main idea is that Riel is a hero to many; the description of Riel given in the adjectival clause, though it adds detail, is not essential to the sentence's meaning.

Sometimes, the parenthetical information could be a phrase rather than a clause. In the following sentence, a phrase gives non-essential information:

> Louis Riel, *having stood up to the Canadian government of John A. Macdonald*, remains a hero to many today.

Having stood up to the Canadian government of John A. Macdonald is a participial phrase modifying *Louis Riel*.

When a clause provides essential information, no comma should be used:

> A person who stands up for his or her beliefs is often considered a hero.

Who stands up for his or her beliefs is needed or the sentence will state vaguely, "A person is often considered a hero."

Hint: To test for non-essential material, whether words, phrases, or clauses, try taking the material out of the sentence. Is the essential meaning unchanged? Is it clear to the reader who or what you are describing? If so, put commas before and after the non-essential material.

Remember that *two commas* are normally required with non-essential material.

D. Concluding Words, Phrases, and Clauses

You should precede a concluding word, phrase, or clause with a comma if it is considered a non-essential element in the sentence. However, if it completes the thought expressed in the independent clause that precedes it, do not use a comma.

> **Non-essential phrase:** The forests provide humans with numerous services and resources, *from lumber for our homes to the oxygen we breathe.* (David Suzuki Foundation, http://www.davidsuzuki.org/issues/wildlife-habitat/)

Sidebar notes:

If adjectival (relative) clauses beginning with *who*, *which*, *that*, and the like give non-essential information, use commas around the adjectival clause.

Use a comma before a concluding word, phrase, or clause if it is considered a non-essential element in the sentence. However, if it completes the thought from the independent clause, you do not use a comma.

The main idea is complete before the comma; the concluding phrase gives examples of services and resources.

> **Non-essential dependent clause:** Quebec, Ontario, and BC have made the most progress in combating climate change, *whereas Alberta and Saskatchewan rank at the bottom of the list.*

The main idea is complete before the comma. Often, the subordinating conjunctions *although*, *though*, *even though*, *whereas*, and sometimes *while* are preceded by a comma when they introduce a concluding dependent clause because they suggest a contrast with the main idea rather than a continuation of it.

A dependent clause beginning with *although*, *though*, *even though*, and *whereas* is usually separated from the preceding independent clause by a comma. In most cases, however, the dependent clause conclusion is not preceded by a comma.

> **Essential dependent clause:** According to the David Suzuki Foundation, Canada as a whole is making progress on climate change *because the provinces have stepped in with new initiatives.*

The concluding dependent clause completes the thought begun in the preceding independent clause.

EXERCISE 12.2

Add commas where necessary to indicate non-essential (parenthetical) material. A sample sentence has been done for you.

> Classmates may avoid students with low social status who may then feel depressed increasing their chances of being bullied.
>
> Classmates may avoid students with low social status, who may then feel depressed, increasing their chances of being bullied. [*who may then feel depressed* is a relative clause modifying *students*—non-essential info; *increasing their chances of being bullied*—non-essential concluding phrase]

1. Every year, more diesel-powered cars are being announced whereas only a few were produced in the past.
2. After the 1976 Olympics an economic disaster for taxpayers Canadians looked forward to the 2010 Olympics.
3. Young women who believe they can look like the skinny models in advertising will likely continue with their unhealthy eating patterns.
4. Penicillin an antibiotic crucial in treating bacterial infection was possible due to the biodiversity of plants.
5. Researchers are uncertain whether the link between media and aggression is a causal one.

◎ Miscellaneous Uses of the Comma

Direct Quotation

Punctuating a direct quotation depends on how the quotation is integrated into your sentence. If the source is named before the quotation, a comma follows the verb; if the source is named after, a comma follows the quotation, separating it from the source:

> Hicks states, "As we know, that's not how it turned out" (334).

> "As we know, that's not how it turned out," Hicks states (334).

Do not put a comma before a direct quotation if the word *that* precedes it or if, otherwise, grammar does not require a comma:

> Joan Petersilia argues that "imprisonment has reached often counterproductive levels" (2).

> Brand recognition is an advertising strategy that builds "social or emotional associations with products or brands" (Connor 1483).

As mentioned, a colon may precede a direct quotation if the thought is completely expressed before the colon (see "Colon to Set Up a List," p. 395).

Adjectives

Coordinate adjectives precede a noun and modify it individually; they are separated by two commas. However, non-coordinate adjectives together modify the noun and cannot be separated; commas are not used with non-coordinate adjectives.

One test of whether adjectives are coordinate is to put the word *and* between the adjectives. If you can't do this without changing the meaning, the adjectives are non-coordinate, and a comma should not be used:

> **Coordinate:** The animal that could best portray Canadian values is the powerful, *resourceful* polar bear. [powerful *and* resourceful polar bear: coordinate]

> **Non-coordinate:** Polar bears often swim in search of *new hunting* grounds or *alternative food* sources. [new *and* hunting grounds? alternative *and* food sources? non-coordinate]

If the source is named before the quotation, a comma follows the verb; if the source is named after, a comma follows the quotation, separating it from the source. Do not precede a direct quotation by a comma unless grammar requires it.

COORDINATE ADJECTIVES precede a noun and modify it individually. If two or more adjectives precede a noun and modify it individually, use commas between the adjectives. If the adjectives together modify the noun and cannot be separated, they are **NON-COORDINATE**; do not use commas.

Dates, Addresses, and Numbers

Dates

Commas are conventionally used with month, day, and year when the elements occur in that order; when the date begins with the day or when the day is left out, commas are not used:

> May 12, 2013, will be her fiftieth birthday; her younger daughter will celebrate her twenty-fifth birthday in November 2013.
>
> BUT
>
> 12 May 2013

Addresses

Commas are conventionally used between elements of addresses. If the sentence continues, a comma is included after the name of the province or state:

> The leader of the opposition resides at Stornoway, 541 Acadia Avenue, Ottawa, Ontario, which was built in 1914.

Numbers

A comma is conventionally used in numbers of four or more digits, separating them into groups of three: *45,000 visitors*; *$1,330,000*. In the metric system, spaces replace commas.

◎ Other Punctuation: Question Marks, Dashes, and Parentheses

Question Marks

Use a question mark at the end of an interrogative sentence:

> Do laws concerning Muslim veils restrict women's rights?

If a direct quotation ends in a question or exclamation mark, include it inside the second quotation mark, but if you continue your sentence, do not include a comma even if a rule appears to require it.

> "Do laws concerning Muslim veils restrict women's rights?" asked the group's spokesperson.

The question mark replaces a comma, which would normally be required.

Table 12.1   Summary of Major Punctuation Rules

Mark	Rule	Description of Rule
,	Independent clauses	Use a comma before a coordinating conjunction that joins two independent clauses.
	Series	Use commas to separate items in a series, whether words, phrases, or clauses.
	Introductions	Use a comma after an introduction, whether a word, phrase, or dependent clause, when followed by an independent clause.
	Non-essential elements: relative clauses	Use commas around relative clauses, which often begin with who, which, or that, when they give non-essential information.
	Non-essential elements: appositives	Use commas around appositives, nouns or noun phrases that give non-essential information.
	Non-essential elements: interrupters	Use commas around adverbial interrupters or other parenthetical elements when they give non-essential information.
	Essential elements	Do not use commas if the word, phrase, or relative clause is essential to meaning.
	Coordinate adjectives	Use a comma to separate coordinate adjectives before a noun; coordinate adjectives separately modify the noun.
	Direct quotations	Use a comma before a direct quotation if the preceding or following phrase includes the author's name and a verb; do not use a comma if to do so will make an ungrammatical sentence.
	Dates, addresses, and numbers	Use a comma if convention requires it (see p. 401).
;	Independent clauses	Use a semicolon in place of a comma and coordinating conjunction between independent clauses to stress that the clauses are closely related.
	Adverbial conjunctions	Use a semicolon before an adverbial conjunction or transitional phrase when it joins two independent clauses; follow the joiner with a comma.
	Series with commas in one or more elements	Use a semicolon to join items in a series if at least one of the items contains commas.
:	Quotations and lists	Use a colon to set up a direct quotation or list if the thought is complete before the colon. Other methods exist for setting up a direct quotation or list.
	Independent clauses	Use a colon between independent clauses if the second clause answers or explains the reason for the statement in the first independent clause. The thought should be complete before the colon. Note: What follows a colon could be just a word or phrase if it answers a question implied in the independent clause preceding the colon.

Dashes and Parentheses

Use two dashes, or one dash if at the end of a sentence, to set off important or dramatic words or phrases. While dashes emphasize something, parentheses deemphasize. Placing words in parentheses shows the reader that the material is not important enough to be included in the main part of the sentence. Too many dashes or parentheses should be avoided as they could distract your reader.

> Many women who wear a burqa do so as a personal choice—not as a religious duty.

> A woman wearing a veil in France could face a fine of 150 Euros (C$195).

Do not put a comma before a parenthesis; if punctuation is required after the parentheses, ensure it goes outside the closing parenthesis unless what is in parentheses is a complete sentence by itself—not part of a sentence.

In parenthetical citation styles, parentheses enclose brief information about a source; see pp. 89–91:

> Supporters of the veil suggest they can "offer women protection and a safe haven" (Leane 1053).

Use two dashes, or one dash if at the end of a sentence, to set off important or dramatic words or phrases. Use parentheses to show that the material is not important enough to be included in the main part of the sentence.

EXERCISE 12.3

There are 20 marks of underlining in the two paragraphs below. Identify the rule, summarized in the chart above and/or discussed in the preceding pages, that accounts for the mark of punctuation or for the absence of punctuation.

Selah's Vegan Moment

Selah wanted to be cool and healthy, so she thought she would make a New Year's resolution to go vegan. She knew that beans, tofu, and nuts were high-protein options for vegans. Unfortunately, Selah was allergic to nuts; they made her violently ill. She had tried tofu, which consists of mashed soya beans, and found it had a rubbery, mushy texture. She liked beans well enough, but not every day!

She knew several people who were vegans. For example, there was her ex-roommate, Ruth; her boyfriend, Bal; and her best friend, Frieda. They were all healthy people; however, were they cool? Ruth had once exclaimed, "tie-dyed shirts are awesome!" and Bal wore white knee socks with his sandals. Frieda was the least cool of all: she once invited Selah to the movie Vampires from Outer Space—and was on the edge of her seat (literally) the whole time. After she had weighed all these factors to her satisfaction, Selah sighed regretfully and ordered out for pepperoni pizza with extra cheese.

EXERCISE 12.4

Add commas as necessary in the sentences below. There is more than one punctuation rule to be applied in some sentences. A sample sentence has been done for you.

Small amounts of cocaine may cause hyperactivity elevated blood pressure and heart rate and increased sexual interest but large amounts can cause violent unpredictable behaviour.

Small amounts of cocaine may cause hyperactivity, (1) elevated blood pressure and heart rate, (2) and increased sexual interest, (3) but large amounts can cause violent, (4) unpredictable behaviour.

(1) Separates items in list; (2) separates items in list; (3) separates two independent clauses joined by coordinating conjunction; (4) separates coordinate adjectives

1. Brain development occurs rapidly at young ages and this development can be affected by music.
2. The first video game *Tennis for Two* was created in 1958.
3. Some instructors treat sites that rate professors as a learning opportunity whereas others think such websites should be banned.
4. To relieve stress explore the world and have fun students should take a break after high school.
5. Some studies suggest that exposure to modern media contributes to low self-esteem in young girls and increases the odds of developing an eating disorder.
6. It was predicted that the movie "The King's Speech" would win the Oscar for Best Picture and it did.
7. Textese a hybrid of spoken and written English is the language of text messaging a recent global phenomenon.
8. On July 19 2005 the same-sex marriage law in Canada was passed but many Christians remained opposed to this law.
9. He always wanted to write a popular critically acclaimed novel; she always wanted to write "the great Canadian novel."
10. Alcohol affects every part of the body and the brain such as the circulatory nervous and gastrointestinal systems.

◎ Apostrophes

Apostrophes have two main uses: (1) in formal and informal writing, they are used to indicate possession and other relationships between two nouns or an indefinite pronoun and a noun; (2) in informal writing, they are used in contractions to show one or more letters omitted.

APOSTROPHES are used to indicate possession and other relationships between two nouns or an indefinite pronoun and a noun, and to show the omission of one or more letters in contractions.

1. Apostrophe Showing Possession and Other Relationships

Use an apostrophe for

> **Ownership:** The neighbour's property [the property belongs to the neighbour]

> **Authorship:** Margaret Atwood's poem [the poem was written by Margaret Atwood]

> **Duration:** Two days' extension [an extension that lasts two days]

> **Similar relationships:** The professor's classes [the classes are taught by the professor]

Many indefinite pronouns also require an apostrophe when followed by a noun if the relationship between them is one of ownership or the like. However, personal pronoun forms do not include apostrophes:

> **Indefinite pronoun examples:** *everyone's* beliefs, *somebody's* laptop, *one's* motive [the beliefs of everyone, the laptop of someone, the motive of one]

> **Personal pronoun forms:** hers, theirs; NOT her's, their's

When nouns and pronouns form the possessive and are placed before nouns, they function adjectivally.

Hint: If you have trouble knowing whether something you have written requires an apostrophe, try inverting the two "nouns" and placing *of* or *of the* in between the rearranged words:

> **If you've written:** *the neighbours property. . .*

> **Rearranged:** the property *of the* neighbour

> **Corrected:** the neighbour's property

The same can be done with an indefinite pronoun and a noun (see "Indefinite Pronoun Subject," p. 413):

If you've written: *ones motive . . .*

Rearranged: the motive *of* one

Corrected: *one's motive*

Forming the Possessive

1. For singular nouns, add *'s*
2. For plural nouns that end in *-s* or an "s" sound, add an apostrophe after the *s*:

the city's businesses [the businesses of the city]

BUT

the cities' businesses [the businesses of the cities—more than one city]

Hint: After determining whether the possessive applies to a noun, ask whether the affected noun refers to one or more than one. If it is a singular noun, add *'s*; if it is plural, add *'* after the *s*.

A few common plural nouns don't end in *-s* and are treated like singular nouns in forming the possessive:

people's choice, women's sports, men's team, children's toys

If two nouns equally own or partake in something, use an apostrophe with the second noun only:

Jake and Jeff's presentation [Jake and Jeff gave the same presentation]

BUT

Leat's and Layne's presentations [Leat and Layne gave separate presentations]

If a singular proper noun ends in s, such as a person's last name, the rule states that you add *'s* to make it possessive. However, if the last name is at least two syllables, you will sometimes see only an apostrophe added:

Mr. Burns's lackey; Mr. Smithers's boss [correct]; Mr. Smithers' boss [also correct]

Margin notes:

To form the possessive in singular nouns, add *'s*; in plural nouns ending in *-s*, add an apostrophe after the *s*.

A few plural nouns don't end in *-s* and are treated like singular nouns in forming the possessive.

If two nouns equally own or partake in something, use an apostrophe with the second noun only.

Hint: Do not use an apostrophe with a simple plural or with the third-person singular verb form:

Incorrect: There are several backpack's at the front of the room.

Correct: She is looking through the *backpack's* contents to find her calculator. [contents of the backpack]

Incorrect: She look's happy: she must have found her calculator.

Correct: She *looks* happy: she must have found her calculator.

Occasionally, an apostrophe can be used with the plural of a word if the context requires it:

He received two B's on his transcript; The '60s were a time of youth revolt.

2. Apostrophe for Contractions

An apostrophe is used to show a letter omitted as, for example, in the following contractions:

don't = do not   isn't = isn't   couldn't = could not
it's = it is   who's = who is

> An apostrophe is used to show a letter omitted. Contractions are not often used in academic writing.

Hint: Do not confuse the contraction *it's* or *who's* with the possessive forms *its* and *whose*. If you're uncertain whether the spelling is correct, try substituting *it is* or *who is* in the sentence. If the sentence makes sense, use an apostrophe as required for contractions:

If you've written: Its sad to see the parrot without its mate.

Try: Its [it is?] sad to see the parrot without its [it is?] mate.

Corrected: *It's* sad to see the parrot without *its* mate.

Note: Contractions are avoided in much formal writing.

EXERCISE 12.5

Add apostrophes where needed in the sentences below; also, add *s* if required. A sample sentence has been done for you.

> Among the premiers promises is his pledge to stimulate the middle-class earning power.
>
> Among the premier's promises is his pledge to stimulate the middle-class's earning power.

1. Childrens playground games today often involve acting the role of contemporary superheroes.
2. A students grade point average can affect an employers hiring decision.
3. The medias obsession with celebrities lives contributes to todays obesity epidemic.
4. Two reasons for pet overpopulation today include societys lack of awareness and pet owners refusal to have their pets neutered.
5. Music is part of most peoples day, whether its classical or jazz, rock, or heavy metal.

◎ Chapter 12 Review Questions

1. What is a compound sentence? Make up two examples of compound sentences, using different joiners in each case. Punctuate correctly.
2. a. When could you use a semicolon to join two independent clauses (simple sentences)? Give two rules.
   b. When could you use a colon to join two independent clauses? Give one rule.
3. What is a complex sentence? Give an example, ensuring that your sentence has the right number of subject–predicate units. Punctuate correctly.
4. Answer true or false:
   a. You should always use a comma to separate two items if they are joined by *and*.
   b. You can always omit the last comma before the "and" for a series of three items.
   c. You should use semicolons to separate three items if at least one of the items contains commas.

5. Explain the rule for using a colon to set up an independent clause.

6. What is parenthetical information? How can you determine whether information in a sentence is parenthetical?

7. When would it be correct to use commas around the words *however, therefore, furthermore,* and the like? When would it be correct to precede these same words by a semicolon?

8. Nouns and noun phrases that are parallel to preceding nouns and noun phrases are called _____. They identify or rename the previous noun/phrase and are set off by _____ (number) commas.

9. Explain the rule that determines whether you use commas around relative (adjectival) clauses.

10. Choose the correct statement:
    a. You precede a direct quotation by a comma.
    b. You place a comma after a direct quotation if the name of the source follows.
    c. You usually place a comma after "that" if a direct quotation follows.
    d. None of these statements are true.

11. Should you normally use a comma when you begin a sentence with a dependent clause and follow with an independent clause? Should you use one when you begin with an independent clause and conclude with a dependent clause?

12. What are coordinate adjectives? What is the punctuation rule for coordinate adjectives?

13. What are the two main uses of apostrophes?

14. a. What are the rules for using the apostrophe to show possession in singular and plural nouns?
    b. Name four plural nouns that form the possessive like singular nouns.

15. When would you use an apostrophe with the word *its*?

◎ Key Terms

apostrophe (p. 405)

complex sentence (p. 396)

compound sentence (p. 391)

coordinate adjectives (p. 400)

non-coordinate adjectives (p. 400)

non-essential (parenthetical) information (p. 396)

simple sentence (p. 391)

Agreement, Pronoun, Modifier, and Parallelism Errors

In this chapter, you will learn:

- ◉ How to apply the rules for subject–verb and pronoun–antecedent agreement

- ◉ How to use gender inclusive pronouns

- ◉ How to identify and correct pronoun reference, consistency, and case errors

- ◉ How to identify and correct modifier errors

- ◉ Why parallel structure is important and how to fix parallelism errors

Logic and consistency require that a verb in the present tense agrees in number with its subject and that a pronoun agrees in number with the noun it replaces. Although you will probably not need to stop and think about agreement in every sentence you write, the guidelines below are useful in situations where agreement is not straightforward.

The two sections that follow, on subject–verb agreement and pronoun–antecedent agreement, focus on the most common agreement problems. A more comprehensive chart summarizing subject–verb agreement is on p. 413.

◉ Subject–Verb Agreement

The singular third-person form of the verb (*he*, *she*, *it*) ends in *-s* in the present tense. Plural forms of verbs do not.

Checking for subject–verb agreement involves three steps: (1) finding the subject, (2) using the guidelines below and on p. 413 to determine if the subject is singular or plural; (3) using the corresponding singular (usually ends in *-s* in the third person) or plural form (usually does not end in *-s*) of the verb.

Finding the Subject

Most subjects precede their verbs and can easily be found, even if the sentence begins with another noun:

> In most sentences, the *subject* comes before the verb.

Subject is the noun subject and *comes* is the verb. The singular form of *come*—ending in *-s*—agrees with the singular *subject*. (*Sentences* is not the subject; it is the object of the preposition *in*.)

> However, there *are* <u>situations</u> where the subject follows the verb.

In the sentence above, the subject, *situations* (underlined), comes after the verb, *are*. The plural form, *are*, agrees with the plural subject, *situations*.

Hint: If a sentence or clause begins with *there is/are*, *there has been/have been*, *there will be*, *here is/are*, and similar forms of *there/here is/are*, find the subject, which will be after the verb, to determine whether the verb should be singular or plural.

In some question constructions and the delayed subject construction, the subject also follows the verb. The verb is italicized and the subject is underlined below:

> **Question:** *Is* the <u>student</u> with the computer in the back row paying attention?

> **Delayed subject:** Surrounded by empty desks *sits* the <u>student</u> in the back row.

Hint: Restructure the sentence so that the subject comes first:

> **Change question to statement:** The <u>student</u> with the computer in the back row *is* (not) paying attention.

> **Change to usual word order:** The <u>student</u> in the back row *sits* surrounded by empty desks.

In some **QUESTION CONSTRUCTIONS** and the **DELAYED SUBJECT CONSTRUCTION**, the verb is placed before the subject.

A subject can follow a verb when (1) the sentence/clause begins with *there is/are*, *here is/are*, and variants of these; (2) when it is structured as a question; and (3) when the delayed subject structure is used.

Intervening Nouns

Many problems in subject–verb agreement result from nouns and pronouns that come between the subject and the verb, obscuring the true subject. Ensure that the verb agrees with the true subject, not with an object of a preposition.

Be careful that the verb agrees with the true subject, not with nouns or pronouns that come between the subject and the verb.

Hint: To help you find the subject, put parentheses around prepositional phrases that come between the subject and the verb:

If you've written: A coalition of organizations, students, and unions oppose the college's planned development.

Identify true subject: A *coalition* (of organizations, students, and unions) *oppose* the college's planned development.

Corrected: A *coalition* of organizations, students, and unions *opposes* the college's planned development.

Rules for Compound Subjects

When a subject is composed of two nouns, two pronouns, or a noun and a pronoun, it is called a **compound subject**. The rule for agreement depends on the word or phrase that joins the two parts of the subject.

> **A COMPOUND SUBJECT** is composed of two nouns, two pronouns, or a noun and a pronoun. The rule for agreement depends on the word or phrase that joins the two parts of the subject.

1. Nouns/pronouns joined by *and* make up a plural subject, requiring a plural verb form unless they are parts of one idea that can't be separated, as in the second sentence below, or if they are preceded by *each* or *every*, as in the third sentence:

   The tortoise *and* the hare *are* taking part in this year's fabled Aesop's Run.

   When asked for a pre-race comment, the tortoise predicted, "*slow and steady wins* the race."

   Each mammal, bird, and reptile *was* asked who would win.

2. A compound subject in which the nouns/pronouns are joined by *or, nor, neither . . . nor,* or *either . . . or* could be singular or plural depending on the second noun/pronoun—the one closest to the verb. If it is singular, the verb form will be singular; if it is plural, the verb will be plural:

   Neither the hare *nor* the other *animals expect* the tortoise to win, according to the odds-makers.

3. A compound subject in which the nouns/pronouns are joined by phrases like *along with, alongside, as well as, combined with, in addition to, together with,* and the like is singular if the first noun/pronoun is singular and plural if it is plural.

   "A full *meal along with* two naps *has* caused the hare to lag far behind the tortoise with only one metre left to go," the crow cawed.

Indefinite Pronoun Subject

Since most indefinite pronouns are considered singular (see p. 370) when they function as subjects, the verb should also be singular. The indefinite pronoun is italicized and the verb is underlined below:

> *Everyone* taking the practice quizzes <u>is</u> going to get one bonus mark per quiz, but *no one* <u>is</u> allowed more than ten bonus marks.

Some indefinite pronouns, however, are always plural, and a few can be singular or plural depending on context.

> *Several* of the textbooks *have* been left in the classroom.

Table 13.1 can be used for quick reference for checking subject–verb agreement. It includes the major rules discussed above as well as other rules that will arise occasionally in your writing.

Common singular **INDEFINITE PRONOUNS** include words ending in -one, -body, and -thing, such as *everyone, anybody,* and *something,* along with *each, either, much, neither, none, nothing,* and *one.*

Table 13.1 Quick Reference Chart for Checking Subject–Verb Agreement	
Rule Category	**Rule States:**
Subject–verb agreement	Verb agrees with its subject in number whether that subject precedes or follows verb
Compound subject joined by *and*	Plural verb form unless compound refers to one concept
Compound subject joined by *or, nor, either . . . or, neither . . . nor*	Verb agrees with second noun/pronoun
Compound subject joined by *as well as, in addition to,* and similar phrases	Verb agrees with first (main) noun/pronoun
Indefinite pronoun as subject	Verb is singular if pronoun is singular
Collective noun subject: refers to a class or group of individuals (e.g., *audience, board, class, committee, couple, crowd, faculty, family, government, group, jury, mob, team*)	Verb is singular unless stress is on individuals within the group rather than group as a unit: The *class is* listening to the speaker (class as unit); the *class are* giving their presentations (class as individual members)
Portions and fractions plus *of* (e.g., *all, a lot, a number, any, a variety, half, more, most, much, none, number, part, plenty, some, the majority/minority + of*)	Verb number depends on the noun/pronoun that completes the *of* phrase: Only *part of the garden was* destroyed by aphids, but *all of the azaleas were* obliterated. The phrase *the number of* requires a singular verb form.
Subjects referring to distance, time, money, weight, and mass	Verb is singular if required by context: *Three kilometres* ahead *is* where the trail ends; *45 minutes is* about how long it will take us to get there.

(continued)

Table 13.1   *(continued)*

Rule Category	Rule States:
Singular nouns ending in *s* (e.g., *athletics, economics, gymnastics, mathematics, news, the Philippines, physics, politics, statistics, the United States*)	Some nouns that end in *s* refer to a single concept and, thus, take a singular verb form: *The Philippines is* the third-largest English-speaking country. Some of these nouns take a plural verb form if they refer to a plural concept or set of properties, rather than a single concept: The *politics* of the twenty-first century *are* radically different from those of earlier centuries. Books and other titles and names of businesses that end in *s* are considered singular: *Starbucks is* opening a new store.
Relative clauses	The verb in a clause that begins with a relative pronoun like *who, which, that,* or *whose* agrees with the noun/pronoun that the pronoun refers to: The *person who is* standing looks familiar. *The only one of* . . . will require a singular verb form while *one of* . . . will require the plural form: She is *the only one of* the people who *is* standing. She is *one of* the people who *are* standing.
Gerunds as subjects; gerunds are formed from present participles of verbs and end in *-ing*.	Gerunds as subjects are singular and require singular verb forms: *Understanding* grammar rules *is* not too difficult if you know the principles behind them.

EXERCISE 13.1

Choose the correct form of the verb in each sentence. A sample sentence has been done for you.

> The cost of "big box" stores (exceeds/exceed) their benefits to local economies.
>
> The cost of "big box" stores exceeds their benefits to local economies. [*Exceeds* agrees with its subject, *cost*.]

1. Truly, arts and culture (is/are) valuable to most Canadians today.
2. Small class sizes and a low student population (means/mean) few opportunities to meet new people.
3. Several decades of experimental data (has/have) shown that violent video games can cause aggression and hostility.

(continued)

4. One-half of the participants in each group (has/have) been asked to complete a questionnaire.
5. The shortcuts that are common in instant messaging (is/are) creeping into young children's vocabulary.
6. With shipping and oil drilling (comes/come) the risk of oil spills.
7. The immediate economic benefit of genetically modified foods (is/are) clearly visible.
8. Overindulging in alcohol and drugs often (leads/lead) to unsafe sex.
9. In the past, there (has/have) been larger amounts of trans-fat consumed in North America than in Southern Europe and Asia.
10. The regular practice of yoga in addition to a healthy diet (inhibits/inhibit) cell deterioration, according to one study.

◎ Pronoun–Antecedent Agreement

The antecedent of the pronoun is the noun or pronoun it replaces. Many problems in pronoun–antecedent agreement occur when the antecedent is (1) a compound (see "Rules for Compound Subjects," p. 412),(2) a collective noun, (3) an indefinite pronoun, or (4) a generic singular noun. In (1) and (2), you can be guided by the similar rules for subject–verb agreement as discussed on pp. 410 and 412.

> The antecedent of the pronoun is the noun or pronoun it replaces.

Finding the Antecedent

Checking for possible agreement errors begins with identifying the pronoun antecedent, usually a noun or indefinite pronoun, just as the first step in subject–verb agreement is identifying the subject.

Hint: To ensure you have correctly identified an antecedent, try substituting the antecedent (italicized) for the pronouns (underlined) that replace it in the sentence below:

> The *shrub* looks unhealthy, and it [the shrub] is shedding its [the shrub's] leaves.

Note that pronoun–antecedent agreement includes adjectives, like *its*, above, that are formed from pronouns.

Main Problems in Pronoun–Antecedent Agreement

1. Compound Antecedent

If the elements of the compound antecedent are joined by *and*, the pronoun will usually be plural, but if the elements are joined by *or* or *nor*, the pronoun will agree with the second element (the one closest to the pronoun).

The professor *and* the students are looking for *their* classroom.

Neither the professor *nor the students* found *their* classroom.

Note that if the nouns *professor* and *students* are reversed, the result would be a somewhat awkward sentence:

Neither the students nor the *professor* found *her* classroom.

The rule provides consistency, but writers should also be conscious of sound and sense and be ready to revise if necessary.

2. Collective Noun Antecedent

Collective nouns refer to groups of people, usually acting collectively. When these nouns act as antecedents, the pronoun is singular unless the stress is on individuals within the group; then, the pronoun is plural. If in doubt, use the singular form of the pronoun.

The *committee* issued *its* recommendations to the government last week. [It acted as a unit.]

After failing to reach a consensus, the *committee* will meet with *their* constituents to gather more input. [The stress is on individual members.]

COLLECTIVE NOUNS refer to groups of people, usually acting collectively. When these nouns act as antecedents, the pronoun is singular unless the stress is on individuals within the group; then, the pronoun is plural.

Avoid the practice of using a singular verb along with a plural pronoun with nouns like *government* or names of businesses that represent a single entity. Both verb and pronoun forms should be singular.

Incorrect: Fort McMurray, Alberta, *has* experienced an increase in *their* population since the development of the Athabasca Oil Sands project. [A singular verb and plural pronoun are awkwardly used with the singular subject/antecedent, *Fort McMurray*.]

Correct: Fort McMurray, Alberta, *has* experienced an increase in *its* population since the development of the Athabasca Oil Sands project. [A singular verb and singular pronoun are used with the singular subject/antecedent, *Fort McMurray*.]

3. Indefinite Pronoun Antecedent

Most indefinite pronouns are singular and, along with nouns, can act as antecedents for pronouns, which should be singular to match the antecedent. You can often tell by context whether an indefinite pronoun is singular or plural. You will then use the appropriate pronoun form:

> *Each* of the alligators *is* sunning *itself* on the rock by my brother's foot.

> *Both* of the alligators *are* sunning *themselves* on the rock by my brother's foot.

However, indefinite pronouns that are always singular can cause problems when they need to be replaced by third-person singular pronouns.

> **Incorrect:** To set a good example, *everybody* on the safety committee has been told to clean up *their* work area.

The antecedent, *Everybody*, is singular; the pronoun that replaces it, *their*, is plural. (*Their* is the possessive form of the pronoun *they*. Agreement applies to these possessive forms as well as to the subjective and objective forms—for example, *they* and *them*).

Indefinite pronouns refer to non-specific individuals without regard to gender. For example, *everyone* usually includes both genders. However, the third-person pronouns *he*, *she*, *him*, *his*, and *her* specify gender. The following sentence is therefore grammatically correct but does not reflect the gender-neutral goal of most texts:

> **Not gender neutral:** To set a good example, *everybody* on the safety committee has been told to clean up *his* work area.

The antecedent, *everybody*, is singular and does not specify gender; *his* is also singular but specifies gender. If the committee were composed of males only, the statement would be both grammatical and precise. However, if there were at least one female on the committee, the statement would be imprecise and reflect sexist usage.

Hint: If you need to use an indefinite pronoun as an antecedent, ensure that the pronoun that follows matches the antecedent in number and reflects gender-neutral, or unbiased, usage.

> **If you've written:** To set a good example, everybody on the safety committee has been told to clean up their work area.

> **Match for grammar and gender:** To set a good example, *everybody* on the safety committee has been told to clean up *their* [ungrammatical] *his* [gender biased] work area.

> **Corrected:** To set a good example, *everybody* on the safety committee has been told to clean up *his or her* work area.

Indefinite pronouns refer to non-specific individuals without regard to gender. When they are replaced by personal pronouns, these pronouns should be singular as well as gender neutral.

The practice of using a plural pronoun, like *their*, with a singular indefinite pronoun antecedent is becoming more acceptable in some contexts—but not in academic writing.

4. Generic Singular Noun Antecedent

When used in the singular as antecedents, generic singular nouns should be followed by singular pronouns and should reflect gender-neutral usage.

Generic nouns refer to non-specific individuals. When used in the singular as antecedents, they should be followed by singular pronouns.

> **Incorrect:** The candidate should read their exam instructions carefully.

> **Correct:** The *candidate* should read *his or her* exam instructions carefully.

If the *him* or *her* substitution seems otherwise awkward, consider (1) making the singular antecedent plural or (2) omitting the pronoun and revising the sentence.

Hint: If the *him or her* substitution seems awkward, consider (1) making the singular antecedent plural or (2) omitting the pronoun and revising the sentence:

> **Correct with a plural antecedent:** *Candidates* should read *their* exam instructions carefully.

> **Sentence revised:** *Candidates* should read *the* exam instructions carefully.

Another example:

> **Incorrect:** To prevent bullying, a parent should ensure their child has a friendly adult they can approach.

The antecedent *parent* is singular, but *their*, the pronoun replacing *parent*, is plural; the antecedent *child* is singular, but the pronoun replacing *child* is plural.

> **Sentence revised:** To prevent bullying, a parent should ensure the child has a friendly adult who can be approached.

The sentence can also be revised by pluralizing the antecedents, *parent* and *child*.

EXERCISE 13.2

Correct any errors in pronoun–antecedent agreement or sexist usage. A sample sentence has been done for you.

If a predator lacks a food source, they will often try to adapt by changing their main food source.

If *a predator* lacks a food source, *it* will often try to adapt by changing *its* main food source.

(continued)

1. Anyone can increase their self-confidence greatly by participating in physical activity.
2. The ad hoc committee on gender equity will be submitting its interim report on April 30.
3. Copy protection is often ignored as it inconveniences the consumer and makes them allies of those who pirate music.
4. In laparoscopic surgery, the surgeon operates through small insertions using information he receives from a camera inside the patient.
5. When people don't express their anger, feelings of frustration can build up until it is released in an unhealthy way.

◎ Pronoun Reference, Consistency, and Case

Care needs to be taken with pronouns, as errors can occur in pronoun reference, consistency, and case. Each of these areas is discussed below.

Pronoun Reference

Problems with pronoun reference arise when the pronoun's antecedent is unclear or absent. Pronouns replace specific nouns/pronouns, and a reader should always know what antecedent is intended.

> Pronoun *reference* errors can occur when the noun/pronoun to which the pronoun *refers* (its antecedent) is unclear or absent.

Ambiguous Reference

The reader of the following sentence may be unable to tell the antecedent of *it*:

> The committee issued its recommendations to the government, but *it* has decided that they need revisions.

Clearly, *they* refers to *recommendations*, but is *committee* or *government* the antecedent of *it*? Both singular nouns could serve as grammatical antecedents. In the case of ambiguous antecedents, you can replace the pronoun by the intended noun or, to avoid repetition, revise the sentence:

> **Pronoun replaced:** The committee issued its recommendations to *the government*, but *the government* has decided that they need revisions.

> **Sentence revised:** The committee issued its recommendations to *the government*, *which* has decided that they need revisions.

In the second sentence, *government* is the grammatical antecedent of the relative pronoun *which*.

Broad or Vague Antecedent

Another problem with pronoun reference occurs when the antecedent refers to a concept or group of words rather than a specific noun/pronoun. What is the antecedent of *which* in the following sentence?

> Back in the 1930s, goalies did not have face protection, *which* was a safety hazard.

Although the grammatical antecedent of *which* appears to be *face protection*, the sense indicates that *not* having face protection is the hazard. Sentences where the pronouns *which*, *this*, *that*, or *it* replaces more than a one-word antecedent often need to be rewritten:

> **Revised:** Back in the 1930s, the absence of face protection for goalies was a safety hazard.

Missing (Implied) Antecedent

Be wary of sentence openings that lack grammatical antecedents. In the following sentence, the author's name cannot be the antecedent of *he* because it is in the possessive (i.e., adjectival) form (underlined):

> **Incorrect:** In <u>Michael McKinley's</u> *Hockey: A People's History*, he discusses the origin of Canada's national game.

> **Revised:** In *Hockey: A People's History*, Michael McKinley discusses the origin of Canada's national game.
>
> OR
>
> **Alternative revision:** In Michael McKinley's *Hockey: A People's History*, the origin of Canada's national game is discussed.

In the following sentence, what does the pronoun *it* refer to?

> By teaching today's youth safe and healthy approaches to sexuality, *it* will elevate their self-esteem.

It appears to refer back to *teaching*. However, *teaching* is not a subject but the object of the prepositional phrase *by teaching*. Avoid beginning a sentence with prepositions like *at*, *by*, *for*, *in*, *on*, or *with* where the object of the preposition serves as an antecedent of a pronoun like *it*.

> **Revised:** Teaching today's youth safe and healthy approaches to sexuality will elevate their self-esteem.

Teaching is now the subject, and no pronoun is needed.

Pronoun Consistency

The principle behind pronoun consistency is simple: Do not unnecessarily change the person of a pronoun. Table 13.2 shows the singular and plural for each person of pronouns. Do not needlessly shift between pronouns in different rows.

Table 13.2	Person of Singular and Plural Pronouns	
Pronoun person	Singular	Plural
First person	I, me, my	we, us, our
Second person	you, your	you, your
Third person	he, she, it, his, her, its	they, them, their

> **Unnecessary pronoun shift:** Whether music is coming from *your* own headset or blasting from *your* neighbour's house, *we* have all experienced music in *our* lives.

> **Corrected:** Whether music is coming from *our* own headset or blasting from *our* neighbour's house, *we* have all experience music in *our* lives.

Similarly, do not unnecessarily shift from a noun (it can be considered third person) to a first- or second-person pronoun:

> **Unnecessary shift of noun to second-person pronoun:** If *students* can learn effective time management, *your* stress levels will be greatly reduced.

> **Corrected:** If *students* can learn effective time management, *their* stress levels will be greatly reduced.

If your readers are students whom you wish to address informally, the following would be acceptable:

> **Informal address:** If *you* can learn effective time management, *your* stress levels will be greatly reduced.

Pronoun Case

The personal pronouns *I/me, we/us, he/him, she/her,* and *they/them,* along with the relative and interrogative pronouns *who/whom* and *whoever/whomever,* use the form that reflects their grammatical function in the sentence or clause. In order to use the correct pronoun form, or case, you may have to first determine the pronoun's function.

Do not unnecessarily change the person of a pronoun—for example, from *you* to *he* or from *us* to *them*.

First-person pronouns refer to the one *doing the speaking*; second-person pronouns refer to the one *spoken to*; third-person pronouns refer to the ones *spoken about*.

Pronoun case is the form the pronoun takes that shows its function in the sentence or clause. Only a few pronouns change their form to reflect their function.

Personal Pronoun Forms

For the personal pronouns *I/me, we/us, they/them,* etc.:

1. If the pronoun is the subject of the verb or subject complement after a linking verb, use the subjective forms (see Table 13.3, column 2).
2. If the pronoun is the object of the verb or object of a preposition, use the objective forms (see Table 13.3, column 3).

For the possessive forms of the personal pronoun, see column 4 of Table 13.3.

Table 13.3 shows pronoun person by function. Note that the second-person pronoun does not change its form depending on whether it is a subject or an object.

Table 13.3   Pronoun Person by Function

1	2	3	4
Pronoun person	Subjective singular/plural	Objective singular/plural	Possessive singular/plural
First person	I/we	me/us	my/our
Second person	you	you	your
Third person	he, she, it/they	him, her, it/them	his, her, its/their

Note the spelling of the possessive singular pronoun *its*—without an apostrophe.

For example:

> *She* asked *them* about *him* and *his* new job.
>
> *She* = subject
>
> *them* = object of verb
>
> *him* = object of preposition
>
> *his* = possessive pronoun (adjective)

A common pronoun case error occurs with compounds in which both elements are pronouns or one is a noun and the other a pronoun.

With two pronouns: Omit one of the pronouns, leaving the one you are in doubt about. It should then be easier to see which form is correct.

If you've written: You and me can work on the grammar project together.

Omit you: *Me* [??] can work on the grammar project . . .

Corrected: *You and I* can work on the grammar project together. [subject of verb]

With a noun and a pronoun: Since the pronoun will have the same grammatical function as the noun, you can look at the noun's function to determine the pronoun's:

> **Incorrect:** *Patty* and *him* were wondering if they could do their grammar project with *Mattie* and *I*.

Patty is the subject (*Patty . . . was wondering*): subjective form is *he*.

Mattie is the object of the preposition *with* (. . . *with Mattie*): objective form is *me*.

The other pronouns in the sentence are correct: *they* is the subject of the dependent clause that begins with *if*; *their* is the possessive form, modifying *grammar project* and referring to *Patty and him* (*he*).

> **Correct:** *Patty and he* were wondering if they could do their grammar project with *Mattie and me*.

It might sound more natural to say, *He and Patty . . .* (or, of course, to name the person).

Interrogative Pronoun Forms

For the interrogative pronouns, *who/whom*:

1. If the pronoun is the subject of the sentence that asks a question or the subject complement with a linking verb, use *who*, the subjective form.
2. If it is the object of the verb or object of a preposition in the sentence, use *whom*, the objective form.

Whose is the possessive form of the interrogative pronoun.

> *Who* wants to work with Mattie and me on the grammar project?

The subjective form, *who*, is used because it is subject of the verb, *wants*.

> With *whom* do Mattie and I want to work on the grammar project?

Whom is object of the preposition, *with*. Note: do not repeat the preposition later in the sentence:

> **Incorrect:** With *whom* do Mattie and I want to work ~~with~~ on the grammar project?

When the pronoun is separated from the preposition, it may be harder to see that the objective case should be used.

Hint: You can alter word order so that the preposition precedes the pronoun, or "answer" the question, substituting a personal pronoun for the interrogative one.

If you've written: Who do Mattie and I want to work with on the grammar project?

Answer the question: Mattie and I want to work with *him* (objective case), not *he* (subjective).

Corrected: *Whom* do Mattie and I want to work with on the grammar project?

Relative Pronoun Forms

For the relative pronouns, *who/whom, whoever/whomever*:

1. If the pronoun is the subject of the dependent clause that it introduces or the subject complement with a linking verb in the same clause, use *who/whoever*, the subjective form.
2. If the pronoun is the object of the verb in the dependent clause or the object of a preposition in the clause, use *whom/whomever*, the objective form.

Whose is the possessive form of the relative pronoun.

In the two sentences below, *who* functions as the subject in the clause it begins:

Mattie and I didn't really want to work with Hattie, *who* was known for her bad temper.

Who is subject of the relative (dependent) clause *who was known for her bad temper*.

Hint: One way to test whether *who* or *whom* is correct in a relative clause is to substitute the personal pronoun and, if necessary, rearrange the clause in a natural order.

If you've written: Mattie and I didn't really want to work with Hattie, who Mattie didn't like.

Rearrange clause and substitute personal pronoun: Mattie didn't like *her*. [objective case]

Corrected: Mattie and I didn't really want to work with Hattie, *whom* Mattie didn't like. [objective case]

By changing word order in the clause, it also becomes apparent that the clause has a subject, *Mattie*; therefore, *who* couldn't be the clause's subject.

Note the spelling of the possessive singular pronoun *whose*—without an apostrophe.

The same test can be done when *whoever/whomever* is the relative pronoun introducing a relative clause:

I didn't want to work with whoever Mattie didn't like.

. . . Mattie didn't like *him*

I didn't want to work with *whomever* Mattie didn't like.

EXERCISE 13.3

Fix the sentences below, which all contain one of the kinds of pronoun errors discussed above: pronoun reference, consistency, or case. A sample sentence has been done for you.

> During his career, Jackie Robinson was subjected to racial hatred from many people who he came in contact with.

> During his career, Jackie Robinson was subjected to racial hatred from many people whom he came in contact with. [or . . . *with whom he came in contact*]

1. The new regulations mean that every new driver will have to wait two years until you are eligible for a class-five licence.
2. Some athletes get paid more than doctors or lawyers for something that they once did for free.
3. It is essential to educate Internet users about "Internet ethics." This could greatly reduce the incidence of piracy today.
4. The royal couple, who some Canadians regard as celebrities, recently toured the country.
5. In the article, it states that the right hemisphere of the brain processes visual information.

◎ Modifier Errors

Modifiers, adjectives and adverbs, make sentences more interesting and informative. However, modifiers can sometimes stray from the words they are intended to modify or incorrectly modify a part of speech, thereby confusing a reader.

Misplaced Modifiers

A misplaced modifier modifies a word that it is not intended to modify. Misplaced modifiers can be avoided by placing the adjective or adverb as close as possible to the word it is intended to modify.

Modifiers are usually placed next to the word(s) they modify. Limiting adverbs, such as *almost, even, just, nearly, not, merely,* and *only,* need to be placed before their modifier.

Imprecise: Islamic men are permitted up to four wives, though women are *only permitted* one husband.

Precise: Islamic men are permitted up to four wives, though women are permitted *only one husband.*

Only should modify the adjective *one,* not the verb *permitted.*

Other one-word modifiers should also be placed as close as possible to the word(s) you want them to modify:

Imprecise: She contemplated the article she had been *given thoughtfully.*

Precise: She *thoughtfully contemplated* the article she had been given.

Although it's possible that the adverb *thoughtfully* should really modify the verb *had been given,* context suggests that *thoughtfully* should modify *contemplated.*

Phrases and clauses should also be placed as close as possible to the word they are intended to modify:

Imprecise: Two of my closest *friends* have been in car accidents *with cellphones.*

Precise: Two of my closest *friends with cellphones* have been in car accidents.

In the first sentence, *with cellphones,* an adjectival (prepositional) phrase, seems to modify *car accidents,* but it is the *friends* who have cellphones.

Imprecise: This essay will examine if animals suffer *through empirical evidence.*

Precise: This essay will *examine, through empirical evidence,* if animals suffer.

In the first sentence, *through empirical evidence,* an adverbial (prepositional) phrase, seems to modify the verb *suffer,* but it answers the question *How?* of the verb *examine.*

Alternative: *Through empirical evidence*, this essay will examine if animals suffer.

If the adverbial phrase is placed at the beginning, it is still clear that it modifies *examine*.

Hint: Misplaced modifiers can occur anywhere in the sentence but are particularly common at the end, seeming almost an afterthought. Ask yourself if readers might misread part of the sentence due to the modifier's placement.

If you've written: Moving to Montreal has been a difficult experience because I left my father at home, who is a recent widower.

Possible misreading: at home, who is a recent widower

Corrected: Moving to Montreal has been a difficult experience because I left *my father, who is a recent widower*, at home.

Dangling Modifiers

Dangling modifiers have nothing to do with the position of modifiers but, rather, with the absence of a word to modify. The intended noun/pronoun may be implied, but is not actually in the sentence. Once you identify a dangling modifier, there are usually two ways to fix it:

No word to modify: Looking out the ferry window, several whales were frolicking.

Words added to introductory (participial) phrase: As *I looked out* the ferry window, several whales were frolicking.

Words added to independent clause: Looking out the ferry window, *I saw* several whales were frolicking.

In the first sentence, it appears that the whales are looking out the ferry window.

The middle sentence fixes the problem by changing the participial phrase, *looking out the ferry window*, into a dependent clause with a subject, *I*, and a complete verb form, *looked out*. The last sentence fixes the problem by changing the subject of the independent clause to *I*, giving the phrase an appropriate word to modify; a complete verb form is also needed, *saw*.

Avoid using long phrases and clauses as modifiers if they disrupt the sentence, such as those separating a subject from its verb or a verb from its object:

Modifier separates subject from verb: Solar energy, using photovoltaic panels that are expensive to manufacture, is nonetheless a clean and limitless energy source.

Consider revising so verb directly follows subject: Using photovoltaic panels that are expensive to manufacture, *solar energy is* nonetheless a clean and limitless energy source.

Dangling modifiers do not have a suitable word to modify and usually appear to modify the closest noun. They can be fixed by including the intended information either in the dangling phrase or in the independent clause.

ELLIPTICAL CLAUSES are grammatically incomplete (ellipses = omission) but may be acceptable if the context is clear. If the clause is dangling (appears to modify an unintended word), the context is not clear, and the missing words need to be supplied.

In the following sentence, *though uncommon in the Islamic world*, an elliptical clause, modifies *men*, making it seem that men are uncommon in the Islamic world.

No word to modify: *Though uncommon in the Islamic world*, *men* are permitted up to four wives.

Words added: Though *polygamous marriages are* uncommon in the Islamic world, men are permitted up to four wives.

OR

Though uncommon in the Islamic world, *men in polygamous marriages* are permitted up to four wives.

Hint: Dangling modifiers can occur anywhere in a sentence but are particularly common at the beginning of the sentence before the main idea (independent clause). They are often participial (*-ing*, *-ed*, *-en*) phrases or elliptical clauses without suitable words to modify.

If you've written: As a first-year student, my professors do not accept Wikipedia as a credible source.

Ask who or what is the actor: Who is the first-year student? *My professors??*

Corrected: *As a first-year student, I* am not allowed by my professors to use Wikipedia as a credible source.

OR

As *I am* a first-year student, my professors . . .

EXERCISE 13.4

Fix the problems with modifiers. A sample sentence has been done for you.

Having learned about feminism in college, short stories by women are often appreciated. [who is the actor?—i.e., who learned about feminism in college?]

Having learned about feminism in college, students often appreciate short stories by women.

(continued)

1. Birth defects are common among addicted mothers, such as chronic lung diseases.
2. Watching Disney movies, heroines are usually long-legged, ample breasted beauties.
3. A healthy lifestyle can help reduce stress by simply staying active and allowing time to relax.
4. Many animals only use their vocal organs during breeding season in order to attract a mate.
5. Studying the use of stem cells, the benefits to society appear numerous.

◎ Parallelism

Using parallel structures will make your prose more coherent and accessible. By contrast, a lack of parallelism might make part of a sentence sound "off kilter," or even confusing.

> **PARALLELISM** refers to using similar forms for similar elements in a sentence. Parallelism should be used in both compounds and series.

Making items parallel in a compound (two items) or a series (three or more items) consists of matching grammatical forms or structures. Being conscious of when and how to apply parallelism will enable you to better communicate your meaning.

Stylistically, writers use parallel structures to make their writing memorable or rhetorically effective.

Consider the following list from the essay on p. 181. Can you spot the one item that has been changed so it does not match the others?

> Among [the reasons for keeping pets] are the misfiring of parental instincts, biophilia, social contagion, the middle class often tries to imitate the fashions of wealthy individuals, [and] the need to dominate the natural world . . . (p. 181).

Some of the items are shorter than others, but length does not usually play a role in making elements parallel. You might have noticed that the fourth item is the only one that includes a complete verb form, *tries*. In fact, it is an independent clause with a subject and predicate. The others are just nouns with modifiers or objects. In the original (see par. 2, p. 181), all the items are parallel because they all consist of nouns phrases—none includes a verb.

Parallelism in a Compound (two items)

A compound consists of two of something, whether single words, such as two nouns or two verbs, two phrases, or two clauses. One way to recognize compounds is to look for the word that joins them, often a coordinating conjunction. The coordinating

One way to recognize compounds is to look for the word that joins them, often a coordinating conjunction. Then, match the form of the element that follows the joiner to that which precedes it.

conjunctions (italicized) below join three compounds, including two independent clauses (*so*). The parts of the compounds joined by *and* are underlined.

> She wanted the <u>sunglasses</u> *and* the <u>hat</u>, *so* she <u>placed</u> her bids *and* <u>waited</u> for the results.

In order to create balance by using parallel structures, first isolate the word that connects the two parts. In the first compound above, *and* joins a noun, *sunglasses*, and another noun, *hat*. In the second underlined compound, *and* joins a verb, *placed*, and another verb, *waited*. Finally, *so* (preceded by a comma) grammatically joins two independent clauses. All elements are parallel.

Now, consider an unbalanced structure in which the elements in the compound are not parallel:

> Minor league professionals live a nomadic lifestyle with endless bus journeys and living in cheap hotels.

Although the meaning of the sentence is clear enough, it sounds, and is, off balance due to the identical positions of non-parallel elements, *journeys* and *living*. Gerunds, which end in *-ing*, function as nouns in a sentence but are different in form from other nouns and shouldn't be matched with them to achieve parallelism in formal writing. In the sentence below, the noun *hotels* replaces the gerund, *living*, creating parallelism:

> Minor league professionals live a nomadic lifestyle with endless bus *journeys* and cheap *hotels*.

When correlative conjunctions are used as joiners, parallelism can be achieved by matching the word(s) following each part of the conjunction.

Correlative conjunctions include *either . . . or, neither . . . nor, both . . . and, not . . . but, not only . . . but also*.

Non-matching elements: As many athletes lack a good education, the options are *either accepting* the minor league lifestyle *or to get* a low-paying job.

Strategy

1. Isolate the joiner(s): *either . . . or*
2. Identify the word(s), phrases, or clauses that are being joined: *accepting . . . to get*
3. Match to achieve parallelism: *accepting. . . getting* OR *to accept . . . to get*

Matching (parallel) elements: As many athletes lack a good education, the options are *either accepting* the minor league lifestyle *or getting* a low-paying job.

Comparisons are another kind of compound since they always have two parts: something is *compared to* something else. Always ensure that the second object being compared is completely expressed. What is missing in this sentence—in other words, what exactly are being compared?

> **Non-matching elements:** The salaries of minor league baseball players are still very low compared to professional baseball players today.

Strategy

1. Isolate the joiner: *compared to*
2. Identify the word(s), phrases, or clauses that are being joined: *salaries of minor league baseball players . . . professional baseball players* (it's illogical to compare salaries to baseball players!)
3. Match to achieve parallelism: *salaries of minor league baseball players . . . salaries of professional baseball players* (salaries of one group are now compared to salaries of another)

> **Matching (parallel) elements:** The *salaries of* minor league baseball players are still very low compared to the *salaries of* professional baseball players today.
>
> OR
>
> The *salaries of* minor league baseball players are still very low compared to *those of* professional baseball players today.

Parallelism in a Series (more than two items)

Achieving parallelism with items in a series also involves matching forms. Consider the following sentence:

> **Non-matching elements:** Music can directly affect your thoughts, emotions, and how you feel.

The list is composed of three items: *thoughts*, a noun; *emotions*, a noun; *how you feel*, a dependent clause (note the pronoun subject, *you*, and the verb, *feel*).

> **Matching elements:** Music can directly affect your thoughts, emotions, and feelings.

As sentences get more complex, it may become more difficult to isolate elements that need to be parallel, as in the following sentence:

> Although living off-campus has its disadvantages, it offers better stability in social relationships, greater health benefits, and allows for improved academic performance.

Strategy with a Series

A series consists of three or more items. To check for parallel structure, first determine where the list begins. Then, ensure that the items in the series have the same form—for example, all are nouns, verbs, prepositional phrases, or dependent clauses.

1. Determine where the list begins (you can use a vertical line to show this): *offers | better stability*
2. Identify the first, second, third . . . items: *stability* [noun] . . . *benefits* [noun] . . . *allows for* [verb] . . .
3. Match all items to achieve parallelism: *stability . . . benefits . . . performance.*

> **Matching (parallel) elements:** Although living off-campus has its disadvantages, it offers better stability in social relationships, greater health benefits, and improved academic performance.

When you match for parallel items, you look at single words if the list consists of only those words; however, if the words have modifiers or objects, you do not usually need to consider them in making the items parallel. For example, the three parallel nouns in the sentence above, *stability*, *benefits*, and *performance*, have modifiers, but they do not affect parallelism in the series.

> **Non-matching elements:** If you live on campus you can make more friends, travel to your classes more easily, and you get the benefits of meal plans.

Strategy

1. Determine where the list begins: *campus | you can . . .*
2. Identify the first, second, third . . . items: *you can make more friends* [independent clause] . . . *travel to your classes more easily* [verb + object and modifiers] . . . *you can get the benefits of meal plans* [independent clause] . . .
3. Match all items to achieve parallelism: independent clause, independent clause, independent clause:

> **Matching elements:** If you live on campus you can make more friends, you can travel to your classes more easily, and you get the benefits of meal plans.

A more concise option would be to use three verbs after *can*, which you could make the new starting point for the series. Notice that all items are now composed of verb phrases:

> **Matching elements:** If you live on campus you can | *make* more friends, *travel* to your classes more easily, and *get* the benefits of meal plans.

EXERCISE 13.5

Correct the parallelism errors. A sample sentence has been done for you.

> Television can affect children in a variety of negative ways since children often lack judgment, are naturally curious, and easily influenced.

> Television can affect children in a variety of negative ways since children often *lack* judgment, *are* naturally curious, and *are* easily influenced.

1. To some extent, the media is a major cause of extreme diets, eating disorders, and of plastic surgery.
2. Highway safety programs increase public safety by either enforcing existing laws that limit speed or lower speed limits.
3. Purchasing goods locally leads not only to a healthy environment but also healthier economies and communities.
4. Dove is educating people about negative pressure from the media, eating disorders, and what beauty really is.
5. The writer effectively portrays the nature of social hierarchies and how they relate to economic inequality.

◎ Chapter 13 Review Questions

1. a. What is subject–verb agreement?
   b. What is pronoun–antecedent agreement? In your answer, explain what an "antecedent" is.
2. When does the subject not precede the verb in the sentence? How can it be found in such cases?
3. What is a compound subject? How is agreement determined with a compound subject (give three rules)?

4. Choose the correct answers: Indefinite pronouns like *everyone*, *somebody*, and *anything* are considered (singular/plural); when they are used as subjects, the verb is (singular/plural). If these pronouns are replaced by personal pronouns later in the sentence, these pronouns are (singular/plural).

5. What is a collective noun? How can you decide whether the verb or antecedent that it replaces should be singular or plural?

6. Choose the correct answer: Academic writing is gender-neutral writing, and a student should learn to make (his/her/their / his or her) prose gender-neutral too.

7. What does it mean to say that "the antecedent is ambiguous"? "the antecedent is missing"? How can these two problems be fixed?

8. What does pronoun inconsistency refer to? How can it be avoided in your sentences?

9. The subjective forms of the third-person singular personal pronouns are _____, _____, and *it*. The objective forms of these pronouns are _____, _____, and *it*.

10. How can you determine whether you should use the pronoun *who* or *whom* in a relative clause?

11. Answer true or false:
    a. Misplaced modifiers are often found at the end of a sentence or clause.
    b. Modifiers should be placed within two words of the part of speech they are intended to modify.
    c. A misplaced modifier error could confuse a reader.
    d. A dangling modifier is another name for a misplaced modifier.

12. What are two ways to correct a dangling modifier error?

13. What steps can be used to ensure that both elements in a compound are parallel?

14. Indicate which of the following series contain parallel items:
    a. noun, noun, noun phrase
    b. independent clause, independent clause, dependent clause
    c. verb, verb, gerund
    d. adverb, adverb, noun phrase

15. What steps can be used to ensure that all the elements in a series are parallel?

◎ Key Terms

collective noun (p. 416)

compound subject (p. 412)

delayed subject construction (p. 411)

elliptical clause (p. 428)

indefinite pronoun (p. 413)

parallelism (p. 429)

question construction (p. 411)

◎ Answers to Grammar Preview (p. 367)

1. Obsession over one's weight is a common practice in todays society. [apostrophe error; see p. 405]
2. The desire to be thin and the need to possess the perfect body overshadows everything else. [subject–verb agreement error; see p. 410]
3. Advertisements that feature skinny models help fuel this desire; promoting unhealthy expectations for young women. [semicolon error; see p. 392]
4. Expectations that can't be met by the average woman, who weighs 140 pounds. [sentence fragment; see p. 383]
5. By contrast, the average model weighs less than 120 pounds, and is almost 6 feet tall. [comma error; see p. 392]
6. Body consciousness begins early, it can even be seen in young girls following exposure to Barbie dolls. [comma splice; see p. 386]
7. At age 13 50 per cent of girls exposed to Barbie dolls don't like the way they look. [comma error; see p. 396]
8. Increasing by age 18 to more than 80 per cent. [sentence fragment; see p. 384]
9. If we change our cultural ideals, young girls will begin to see themselves as "normal." [no error]
10. With a positive self-image, young women will be better able to succeed socially, academically, and in their chosen vocation. [parallelism error; see p. 431]

Corrected paragraph: Obsession over one's weight is a common practice in today's society. The desire to be thin and the need to possess the perfect body overshadow everything else. Advertisements that feature skinny models help fuel this desire, promoting unhealthy expectations for young women, expectations that can't be met by the average woman, who weighs 140 pounds. By contrast, the average model weighs less than 120 pounds and is almost 6 feet tall. Body consciousness begins early; it can even be seen in young girls following exposure to Barbie dolls. At age 13, 50 per cent of girls exposed to Barbie dolls don't like the way they look, increasing by age 18 to more than 80 per cent. If we change our cultural ideals, young girls will begin to see themselves as "normal." With a positive self-image, young women will be better able to succeed socially, academically, and professionally.

Glossary

abstract

An abstract is a condensed summary used mostly in empirical studies; it is placed before the study begins and includes its purpose, method, results, and conclusion.

active reading

Active reading refers to an approach to reading in which you take an active, rather than a passive role—first, by considering your purpose for reading.

adjective

Adjectives give information about (modify) nouns or pronouns. They answer questions like *Which (one)?*, *What kind?*, or *How many?* When they are one word, they usually precede nouns, unless they follow linking verbs as predicate adjectives.

adverb

Adverbs give information about (modify) verbs, adjectives, and other adverbs. They answer questions like *How?*, *When?*, *Where?*, *How much?*, or *To what degree?*

adverbial conjunction

Adverbial conjunctions are adverbs used to connect two independent clauses. They are punctuated differently from adverbs that interrupt the sentence flow.

analogy

An analogy is a systematic comparison between one item and another one that is similar in the point being discussed but is otherwise unlike the first one.

analysis

When you analyze, you break something down in order to look more closely at its parts.

anecdotal evidence

Anecdotal evidence is suggestive rather than conclusive; it is often based on reliable observation.

annotated bibliography

An annotated bibliography is an expanded bibliography that includes not only the information of standard bibliographies but also brief summaries of related works.

apostrophe

Apostrophes are used to indicate possession and other relationships between two nouns or an indefinite pronoun and a noun, and to show the omission of one or more letters in contractions.

appositive

An appositive is a word or phrase that names, specifies, or explains the previous noun or noun phrase and is usually set off by commas.

audience

Most texts, whether written, oral, or visual, are directed to an intended audience— for writing, a group of readers. Each writer is keenly aware of his or her audience and uses the most effective methods possible to reach this audience.

brackets

Brackets are used to show a change or addition to a direct quotation or indicate parentheses inside parentheses.

brainstorming

Brainstorming is a pre-writing technique in which you list your associations with a subject in the order they occur to you.

circular conclusion

A circular conclusion is primarily concerned with reinforcing the thesis.

claim

A claim is an assertion that you will attempt to prove through evidence. Claims occur in the thesis statement; many topic sentences also assert a claim about the topic of the paragraph.

climax order

Climax order is the order of points that proceeds from the weakest to the strongest; other orders include inverse climax order and mixed order.

clustering

Clustering is a pre-writing technique that works spatially to generate associations with a subject and connections among them.

coherence

Coherence is the principle of paragraph construction in which ideas are logically laid out with clear connections between them.

collective noun

Collective nouns refer to groups of people, usually acting as a unit.

colloquial language

Colloquial, or conversational, language is a feature of some non-academic writing.

common ground

Establishing common ground is an argumentative strategy in which you show readers that you share many of their values, making you appear open and approachable.

complete subject

A complete subject contains not only the main noun/pronoun but also any modifiers of the subject.

complex sentence

A complex sentence consists of an independent and one or more dependent clauses. A compound-complex sentence contains two independent clauses (the "compound" part) and at least one dependent clause (the "complex" part).

compound sentence

A compound sentence consists of two independent clauses joined by a comma and coordinating conjunction, a semicolon, or a colon.

compound subject

A compound subject is composed of two nouns, two pronouns, or a noun and a pronoun.

concession

Making concessions is an argumentative strategy in which you concede or qualify a point in order to come across as fair and reasonable.

concision

Concision is effective writing in which you use only the words that are essential to express your meaning and do not waste words.

conclusion

The last paragraph usually summarizes the thesis and/or main points in the body of the essay. A circular conclusion reinforces the thesis; a spiral conclusion suggests applications or further research.

conjunction

Conjunctions join words, phrases, or clauses in a sentence. Coordinating conjunctions join equal grammatical units. Subordinating conjunctions join unequal grammatical units. Adverbial conjunctions join independent clauses. Correlative conjunctions join in pairs.

connotation

Connotations are "shades" of meaning or associations (often determined by context).

convention

Conventions are practices that direct the actions and thinking of specific groups. You can consider them a set of instructions that help us communicate with one another.

coordinate adjectives

Coordinate adjectives precede a noun and modify it individually.

coordinating conjunction

Coordinating conjunctions join *equal* grammatical units.

correlative conjunction

Correlative conjunctions are paired conjunctions.

credibility

Credibility is essential for all writing: Appearing credible involves showing knowledge as well as coming across as trustworthy and fair.

critical response

A critical response focuses on your own opinions or observations about an issue raised in a text. Although a response is usually more informal than a rhetorical analysis, it should clearly demonstrate critical thinking.

critical thinking

Critical thinking involves a series of logical mental processes, including evaluating and weighing the evidence, that leads to a conclusion.

cumulative sentence

In cumulative sentences, the writer begins with the main idea and follows with words, phrases, or clauses that extend this idea.

deductive reasoning

Deductive reasoning is based on a generalization, which is applied to a specific example or subset to form a conclusion.

delayed subject construction

In the delayed subject construction, the verb is placed before the subject.

demonstrative pronoun

The demonstrative pronouns *this, that, these, those* point to nouns.

denotation
Denotation is a word's dictionary meaning.

dependent clause
A dependent clause contains a subject and a predicate but does not express a complete thought.

descriptive heading
Descriptive headings summarize section contents.

digital object identifier
A digital object identifier (DOI) is a number-alphabet sequence often found on journal articles and begins with the number 10; it serves as a permanent link for digital material.

Discussion
One of the headings of the IMRAD structure. The Discussion includes a summary of the results and compares them with similar studies; the section ends by suggesting directions for future research and, often, practical applications of the findings.

documentation style
Documentation style refers to guidelines for citing sources put forth in style manuals and handbooks for researchers and other academic writers.

dramatic opening
A dramatic opening is a technique for creating reader interest by beginning with a question, illustration, anecdote, quotation, description, or other attention-grabbing technique.

ellipses
Ellipses indicate that you have left out words in a direct quotation by replacing the omitted word(s) by three or four spaced dots.

elliptical clause
Elliptical clauses are grammatically incomplete (ellipses = omission) but may be acceptable if the context is clear.

emotional and ethical fallacies
Emotional fallacies appeal to the emotions in a manipulative or unfair way; ethical fallacies misuse morality.

essay plan
An essay plan includes the main points or main sections of the essay's development. It may use the first-person voice.

ethos

An argument that uses ethos is founded on morality.

focused reading

In focused reading, you read the text closely line by line and word by word.

formal heading

Formal headings divide an experiment into stages.

freewriting

Freewriting is a pre-writing technique in which you write on a subject without stopping to edit.

general scan

Scanning is a form of selective reading in which you look for features that will tell you more about the text, ignoring most detail. In a general scan, you try to get the essence of the work.

gerund

Gerunds are formed from present participles of verbs; they end in -ing and function as nouns.

gerund (noun) phrase

Gerund phrases are formed from present participles of verbs and function as nouns.

helping (auxiliary) verb

A helping (auxiliary) verb combines with the main verb to express a condition such as time, necessity, probability, and other relationships.

hypothesis

A hypothesis is a prediction or probable outcome of an experiment.

imperative sentence

An imperative sentence issues an order or direction and is a complete sentence even if it consists of only one word, a verb.

IMRAD

IMRAD stands for **i**ntroduction, **m**ethods, **r**esults, and **d**iscussion, the sections that compose an empirical study.

indefinite pronoun

Indefinite pronouns refer to non-specified individuals or groups.

independent clause

A clause is a group of words that contains a subject and a predicate and is equivalent to a complete sentence.

inductive reasoning

Inductive reasoning relies on facts, details, and observations to form a conclusion.

inference

An inference is a conclusion based on what the evidence shows or points to, without the author stating that conclusion. More than one inference might be possible in a given situation, but the most *probable* one is the best inference.

infinitive, infinitive phrase

Infinitives include *to* along with the base verb form and act as nouns, adjectives, or adverbs.

interrogative pronoun

Interrogative pronouns introduce questions.

Introduction

One of the headings of the IMRAD structure. The Introduction announces the topic and includes summaries of previous research; it ends with a hypothesis or research question.

irony

In irony, a second, or "deeper," meaning exists below the literal meaning, which contradicts the literal meaning.

jargon

Jargon is discipline- or subject-specific language used to communicate among members.

journal

A journal is a kind of periodical designed for readers with specialized interests and knowledge containing original research, reviews, editorials—but little, if any, advertising; it may be issued in print and/or online format.

justification

Academic writers usually justify their study in the introduction, either directly stating why it is needed or indirectly stressing its significance. A typical justification is that there is a gap in knowledge, which the researcher will try to fill.

linking verb

A linking verb connects the subject to the predicate.

literature review
Literature review is the term for the section of the introduction that summarizes related studies on the topic. Some essays are devoted entirely to reviewing related studies.

logical fallacy
Logical fallacies are categories of faulty reasoning.

logical opening
A logical opening is a technique for creating reader interest by beginning with a generalization and narrowing to the thesis.

logos
An argument that uses logos is founded on reason.

Method(s)
One of the headings of the IMRAD structure. The Method(s) explains how the experiment was conducted—for example, *who* took part, *how* it was designed, and *what* procedures were used.

mixed order
See climax order.

non-coordinate adjectives
Adjectives that together modify a noun and cannot be separated without changing the meaning.

non-essential (parenthetical) information
Information that does not affect the basic meaning of the sentence or clause is called non-essential, or parenthetical, information. Commas are used to separate this information from the more important information.

noun
Nouns name people, places, things, qualities, or conditions.

object
The object receives the verb's action.

object of a preposition
The object of a preposition is the indirect object of the verb.

outline
An outline is a linear or graphic representation of main points and sub-points, showing an essay's structure.

parallelism

Parallelism refers to using similar forms for similar elements in a sentence. Parallelism should be used in both compounds and series.

paraphrase

When you paraphrase, you put someone else's ideas in your own words, keeping the length of the original.

participle

Participles usually end in *-ing*, *-ed*, *-en*, or *-t* and act as adjectives.

participle (adjective) phrase

Participle phrases are formed from present or past participles of verbs.

passive construction

In a passive construction, the subject of the sentence is the receiver of the action.

pathos

An argument that uses pathos is founded on emotion.

peer-reviewed (refereed)

Peer-reviewed (refereed) articles are those that have been reviewed by experts. These "peers" suggest whether the article meets the exacting standards in their discipline and merits publication.

peer-reviewed journals

In peer-reviewed journals, submissions are reviewed by experts before publication.

periodic sentence

In periodic sentences, the writer builds towards the main idea, which is expressed at the end of the sentence.

periodical

A periodical is a general term for the kind of publication that is issued at regular intervals.

personal pronoun

Personal pronouns refer to people and sometimes animals, things, or places.

phrase

A phrase is a group of two or more words acting as a unit of speech. Thus, a group of words modifying a noun is an adjectival phrase while one modifying a verb is an adverbial phrase.

plagiarism

You plagiarize if you use any material that is not your own—whether you quote directly, summarize, paraphrase, or refer to it in passing in your essay—without acknowledging it. You also plagiarize if you use the exact words of the source and do not put them in quotation marks or if you follow the structure of the original too closely.

policy claim

A policy claim is an assertion about a topic that proposes an action (e.g., to fix a problem or improve a situation).

precedent

A precedent is a specific example that refers to the way a situation was dealt with in the past in order to argue for its similar use in the present.

précis

Précis is a term for a stand-alone summary.

predicate

The predicate is the part of the sentence that contains at least a verb that states something about the subject—for example, what it is doing.

preposition

A preposition, which often refers to place or time, joins the noun/pronoun that follows to the rest of the sentence.

prepositional phrase

A prepositional phrase begins with a preposition and can act adjectivally or adverbially.

primary sources

Primary sources are original, or first-hand, material in a field of study.

prompt

Though it does not contain important information, a prompt can direct you to where important information is found.

pronoun

Most pronouns replace nouns. Personal pronouns refer to people, places, and things. Relative pronouns refer to a previous noun/pronoun. Interrogative pronouns introduce questions. Indefinite pronouns refer to non-specified groups. Other pronouns include demonstrative, intensive, reflexive, and reciprocal.

question construction
In some question constructions, the verb is placed before the subject.

questioning
Questioning is a pre-writing technique in which you list questions about the topic.

reader-based prose
Reader-based prose is clear, accessible writing designed for an intended reader.

rebuttal
Rebuttal is an argumentative strategy of raising opposing points in order to counter them with your own points.

relative clause
A relative clause follows a noun or pronoun and modifies it.

relative pronoun
A relative pronoun relates what follows to a preceding noun or pronoun.

Results
One of the headings of the IMRAD structure, the Results presents the raw data generated by the experiment, often with accompanying tables and figures.

rhetoric
Rhetoric concerns the structure and strategies of argumentation to persuade the members of a specific audience.

rhetorical analysis
In a rhetorical analysis, you break down a text in order to examine its parts and the author's rhetorical strategies, using your critical thinking skills and your knowledge of texts themselves.

rhetorical patterns
Rhetorical patterns are methods for organizing and presenting information in essays and paragraphs.

satire
Satire is a genre that mocks or criticizes institutions or commonly held attitudes.

secondary sources
Secondary sources comment on, interpret, or analyze primary sources.

selective reading
Selective reading is planned, conscious reading in which you choose strategies that best reflect your reading purpose, what you are reading, and similar factors.

sentence

A sentence can be defined grammatically as a group of words that contains a subject and a predicate and that needs nothing else to complete it.

sentence fragment

A sentence fragment lacks a subject and/or predicate or consists only of a dependent clause, which does not express a complete thought.

signal phrase

Signal phrases introduce a reference in a phrase that names the author(s) and usually includes a "signal verb" and, in APA style, year of publication.

simple sentence

A simple sentence is equivalent to an independent clause.

simple subject

A simple subject consists only of the main noun/pronoun.

slanted language

Slanted language is extreme or accusatory language; it reveals an arguer's bias.

spiral conclusion

A spiral conclusion suggests applications or further research.

subject

The subject performs the verb's action.

subject complement

A subject complement completes the subject after a linking verb.

subject index

A subject index is a list of important words in a text, ordered alphabetically and usually placed at the end of the text.

subordinating conjunction

Subordinating conjunctions introduce dependent clauses.

summarize

When you summarize, you include the main idea (or ideas) from a source, expressing it in your own words.

support

Support consists of evidence to help prove a claim.

syllogism

A syllogism is a logical three-part structure that can illustrate how deductive reasoning works.

synthesis

When you synthesize, you put together in order to reach a conclusion.

target scan

Scanning is a form of selective reading in which you look for features that will tell you more about the text, ignoring most detail. A target scan looks for specific content, such as a subject or keyword.

theme

A theme is an overarching meaning or universal aspect, seen through a work's basic elements, such as plot, setting, character, images, language, and figurative techniques.

thesis

A thesis statement sets down a generalization that is applicable to the entire essay (simple thesis) or includes the essay's main points (expanded thesis, or essay plan).

thesis statement

A thesis statement includes the main point(s) of your essay or what you will attempt to prove; it is placed at the end of your introduction.

tone

Tone involves the use of language to convey the writer's attitude toward the subject or the audience.

topic sentence

A topic sentence, usually the first sentence, states the main idea in the paragraph.

unity

Unity is the principle of paragraph construction in which only one idea is developed throughout the paragraph.

value claim

A value claim is an assertion about a topic that appeals to its ethical nature (e.g., good/bad or fair/unfair).

verb

The verb conveys (1) an action or (2) state of being, or (3) combines with a main verb to express conditions like possibility or a complex temporal (time-related) action.

verbal

Incomplete verb forms, or verbals, can be used as nouns, adjectives, and adverbs. They shouldn't be mistaken for complete verb forms.

verb phrase

A verb phrase consists of a main verb and any helping verbs.

warrant

A warrant provides the foundation of a claim, linking the evidence to the claim being made.

Appendix

Answers to Exercises

Answers are given for even-numbered questions. Other options than the one(s) shown may exist.

Exercise 11.2

2. Hockey (N) is (V) certainly (ADV) a (ADJ) very (ADV) aggressive (ADJ) sport (N).
4. Most (ADJ) people (N) in (PRE) North America (N) now (ADV) access (V) their (ADJ) news (N) on (PRE) the (ADJ) Internet (N).

Exercise 11.3

2. Approximately 3,000 inmates currently reside <u>on death row</u>. (adverbial prepositional phrase)
4. <u>Having murderers pay for crimes with their own lives</u> is considered barbaric by many people. (noun phrase subject)

Exercise 11.4

2. <u>The battle against cancer will continue</u> (until) a cure is found).
4. <u>The game "Baggataway,"</u> (which) was played by many Aboriginal tribes), <u>intrigued British colonizers</u>.

Exercise 11.5

2. A novel about a boy who loses his parents to a disaster at sea *has many sad passages.*
   Life of Pi is a novel about a boy who loses his parents to a disaster at sea.
4. Many people today are obsessed with the Internet whether they connect with friends on Facebook or watch videos on YouTube.

Exercise 11.6

2. *The reporter spoke to two* women from Afghanistan who share the Muslim religion.
4. Modern technology has resulted in astonishing benefits for our communities, *though* it has created many new problems as well.

Exercise 12.1

2. The language of music is universal; *indeed,* people everywhere connect with others through some form of music.
   People everywhere connect with others through some form of music *as the* language of music is universal.
4. Global warming and the depletion of our resources are major problems; *however*, they are preventable ones.

Exercise 12.2

2. After the 1976 Olympics, an economic disaster for taxpayers, Canadians looked forward to the 2010 Olympics.
4. Penicillin, an antibiotic crucial in treating bacterial infection, was possible due to the biodiversity of plants.

Exercise 12.3

Selah wanted to be cool and healthy, [1]so she thought she would make a New Year's resolution to go vegan. She knew that beans, tofu, and nuts[2] were high-protein options for vegans. Unfortunately, [3]Selah was allergic to nuts; [4]they made her violently ill. She had tried tofu, which consists of mashed soya beans,[5]and found it had a rubbery, [6]mushy texture. She liked beans well enough, [7]but not every day!

1. Independent clauses (commas)
2. Series
3. Introductions
4. Independent clauses (semicolon)
5. Non-essential elements: relative clauses
6. Coordinate adjectives
7. Non-essential concluding phrase

Exercise 12.4

2. The first video game, *Tennis for Two*, was created in 1958.
4. To relieve stress, explore the world, and have fun, students should take a break after high school.
6. It was predicted that the movie *The King's Speech* would win the Oscar for Best Picture—and it did. (or comma)
8. On July 19, 2005, the same-sex marriage law in Canada was passed, but many Christians remained opposed to this law.
10. Alcohol affects every part of the body and the brain, such as the circulatory, nervous, and gastrointestinal systems.

Exercise 12.5

2. A student's grade point average can affect an employer's hiring decision.
4. Two reasons for pet overpopulation today include society's lack of awareness and pet owners' refusal to have their pets neutered.

Exercise 13.1

2. Small class sizes and a low student population (means/<u>mean</u>) few opportunities to meet new people.
4. One-half of the participants in each group (has/<u>have</u>) been asked to complete a questionnaire.
6. With shipping and oil drilling (<u>comes</u>/come) the risk of oil spills.
8. Overindulging in alcohol and drugs often (<u>leads</u>/lead) to unsafe sex.
10. The regular practice of yoga in addition to a healthy diet (<u>inhibits</u>/inhibit) cell deterioration, according to one study.

Exercise 13.2

2. The ad hoc committee on gender equity will be submitting its interim report on April 30.
4. In laparoscopic surgery, the surgeon operates through small insertions using information he or she receives from a camera inside the patient.

Exercise 13.3

2. Some athletes get paid more than doctors or lawyers for something that the athletes once did for free.
    Some athletes, who once played their sport for free, get paid more than doctors and lawyers do.
4. The royal couple, whom some Canadians regard as celebrities, recently toured the country.

Exercise 13.4

2. Watching Disney movies, we see heroines who are usually long-legged, ample-breasted beauties.
    Or, simply,
    Heroines in Disney movies are usually long-legged, ample-breasted beauties.
4. Many animals use their vocal organs only during breeding season in order to attract a mate.

Exercise 13.5

2. Highway safety programs increase public safety either by enforcing existing laws that limit speed or by lowering speed limits.
4. Dove is educating people about negative pressure from the media, eating disorders, and the essence of beauty.

Index

Credits

Grateful acknowledgment is made for permission to use the following material:

Alang, Navneet, "Big Brother, C'est Moi." This (Sept/Oct., 2011): 42.

Alini, Erica, "Generation Spend." Maclean's (Nov. 15, 2010): 45-46.

Brown, Ian, "I'm Glad I Never Had to Decide Whether My Strange, Lonely Boy Ought to Exist." *Globe and Mail*, August 27, 2011.

Clark, Andrew. 2004. *Natural-born Cyborgs: Minds, Technologies, and the Future of Human Intelligence*. New York: Oxford University Press. pp. 176-77.

Clark, Warren, "Delayed Transitions of Young Adults." Canadian Social Trends (No. 11, 2008): 14.22.

Doctorow, Cory, "You DO Like Reading Off a Computer Screen" Content: Selected Essays on Technology, Creativity, Copyright, and the Future of the Future, Tachyon Publication, 2008, 51-54.

Doyle, Brian, "Joyas Voladoras", American Scholar 73.4 (2005): 25-27.

Edmundson, Mark, "Narcissus Regards a Book." The Chronicle of Higher Education 57.22 (2011): B10-11.

Fox, Nick & Katie Ward, "Health, Ethics and Environment: A Qualitative Study of Vegetarian Motivations." *Appetite* 50 (2008): 422-29.

Gibson, Robert, "Bullshit." This edition of Gibson's column "What's the Big Idea?" is from Alternatives, 37:1 (2011) and has been reprinted with permission. Subscribe at alternativesjournal.ca.

Glavin, Terry, "An Enviro's Case for Seal Hunt", The Tyee 2007.

Gray, Jonathan, "Coming Up Next': Promos in the Future of Television and Television Studies", Journal of Popular Film and Television, 38.2 (2010): 54-57.

Groc, Isabelle, "Orca Encounters", British Columbia Magazine 52.3 (2010): 28-35.

Helding, Lynn, "Creativity in Crisis?" *Journal of Singing*, 67.5 (2011): 597-604.

Herzog, Harold, "The Impact of Pets on Human Health and Psychological Well-Being: Fact, Fiction, or Hypothesis?" Psychological Science 20.4 (2011): 236-239.

Hicks, Bruce M., "The Undiscovered Province." This Magazine 43.4 (Jan/Feb 2012): 14-15.

Horgan, John, "Does Peace Have a Chance?" Slate (Aug. 4, 2009).

Irvine, Andrew, "Is Scientific Progress Inevitable?" In the Agora: The Public Face of Canadian Philosophy (UTP: 2006) 45-49. Reprinted with permission of the publisher.

Mack, Adrian, & Miranda Nelson, "Vancouver Hockey Riot is a Symptom of a Larger Problem." The Georgia Straight (June 16, 2012).

MacQueen, Ken, and Martin Patriquin, "Are We Ready to Subsidize Heroin?", Maclean's 124.40 (Oct. 7, 2011): 18-22.

Manguel, Alberto, "Burning Mistry". Geist (May 2011).

Marche, Stephen, "N(O) Canada!" Walrus (July/August 2010).

Midgley, Mary, "The Selfish Metaphor." New Scientist, Jan. 29, 2011.

Mooney, Chris, "We Can't Handle the Truth: The Science of Why People Don't Believe Science", Mother Jones, 36.3 (May-June 2011).

Pepler, Debra J., et al. (2006). A developmental perspective on bullying. *Aggressive Behavior* 32, 376–384.

Pinto, Andrew D., "Denaturalizing "Natural" Disasters: Haiti's Earthquake and the Humanitarian Impulse." Open Medicine 4.4 (2010): E193-98.

Rosenfield, Daniel, et al., "Canadian Lifestyle Choices: A Public Health Failure." CMAJ 183.13 (2011): 1461.

Rublack, Ulinka, "The Birth of Power Dressing." History Today 61.1 (2011):20-27.

Saunders, Doug, "When a Cellphone Beats a Royal Flush", *Globe and Mail*, March 26, 2011.

Savulescu, J., B. Foddy, & M. Clayton, "Why We Should Allow Performance Enhancing Drugs in Sport." British Journal of Sports Medicine 38 (2004): 666-70.

Sonik, Madeline, "Flush." Afflictions and Departures, Anvil Press (2011): 163-74.

Spiridon, Alethea, "Generation Debt." Briarpatch Magazine (38.5 2009): 29.

Sternberg, Robert J., "Slip-Sliding Away, Down the Ethical Slope." The Chronicle of Higher Education, 57.19 (2011): A23. Used with permission of The Chronicle of Higher Education. All rights reserved

Swift, Richard, "Predators and Scavengers", New Internationalist (July-August, 2010): 34-35.

Vazire, Simine & Erika N. Carlson, "Others Sometimes Know Us Better Than We Know Ourselves." Current Directions in *Psychological Science* 20.2 (2011): 104-108.

Waldau, Paul, "Animal Welfare and Conservation: An Essential Connection" , Minding Nature 4.1 (2011): 12-16, published by the Center for Humans and Nature.

Webb, Chris, "Occupy Canada," Canadian Dimension, Volume 46, issue 1 (Jan/Feb 2012): pp. 40-41.

Wegner, Daniel M., "How to Think, Say, or Do Precisely the Worst Thing for Any Occasion." *Science* 325 (2009): 48-50.

Whitchurch, Erin R., Timothy D. Wilson, & Daniel T. Gilbert, "He Loves Me, He Loves Me Not...': Uncertainty Can Increase Romantic Attraction." *Psychological Science* 22.2 (2011): 172-75.

Woodend, Dorothy, "Generation Velcro." They Tyee, (Nov. 21, 2008).

Screen capture: Subject Guide, University of Victoria, Courtesy University of Victoria Libraries.

Screen capture: Academic Search Complete, all terms; Screen capture: Academic Search Complete, options set; Screen capture: Academic Search Complete, scholarly journals, all Courtesy of EBSCO Publishing.

Spelling List

The following list contains words that many writers—students as well as professionals—frequently misspell. If you are at all weak in spelling, test yourself on these words, adding any others you frequently have trouble with.

a lot	emphasize	plagiarism
absence	environment	pollution
accessible	equipment, equipped	possess, possessed
accommodate	erupt	practice (noun)
acknowledgement	exaggerate	practise (verb)
acquire	exercise	prejudice
affect	existence	primitive
allege	foreign	privilege
analyze	foresee	procedure
arctic	forty, fourth	professor
argument	fulfill	pursue
article	grammar	reality
ascent	guarantee	receive
audience	guard	recognize
beginning	harass	recommend
benefit	height	relevant, relevance
boarder	hypocrisy, hypocrite	repetition
calendar	illegal	roommate
careful	imagery	sacrifice
category	imitate	safety
challenge	immediate, immediately	sentence
changeable	importance	separate
coarse	influence	skilful
coincide	initiative	solely
commit, commitment, committed	innocent	speech
complement	integrate	strategy
conscious	interrupt	subtly
consider	judgment	successful
control, controlled	knowledge, knowledgeable	supersede
convenient	likelihood	suspense
create	marriage	their
criticism, criticize	meant	theory
curiosity	metaphor	threshold
definitely	misspell	tomorrow
dependence, dependent	necessary	tragedy
desperate	ninety	undoubtedly
develop	obsess, obsessed	unmistakable
dilemma	obstacle	until
discipline	occasion	usefulness
efficient	occur, occurred, occurrence	vehicle
eligible	parallel, paralleled	withdrawal
embarrass, embarrassment	persuade	writer, writing, written